Lecture Notes in Computer Science   3188

Commenced Publication in 1973
Founding and Former Series Editors:
Gerhard Goos, Juris Hartmanis, and Jan van Leeuwen

Frank S. de Boer   Marcello M. Bonsangue
Susanne Graf   Willem-Paul de Roever (Eds.)

Formal Methods for Components and Objects

Second International Symposium, FMCO 2003
Leiden, The Netherlands, November 4-7, 2003
Revised Lectures

 Springer

Volume Editors

Frank S. de Boer
Centre for Mathematics and Computer Science, CWI
Kruislaan 413, 1098 SJ Amsterdam, The Netherlands
E-mail: F.S.de.Boer@cwi.nl

Marcello M. Bonsangue
Leiden University, Leiden Institute of Advanced Computer Science
P.O. Box 9512, 2300 RA Leiden, The Netherlands
E-mail: marcello@liacs.nl

Susanne Graf
VERIMAG
2 Avenue de Vignate, Centre Equitation, 38610 Grenoble-Gières, France
E-mail: Susanne.Graf@imag.fr

Willem-Paul de Roever
Christian-Albrechts-University of Kiel
Institute of Computer Science and Applied Mathematics
Hermann-Rodewald-Straße 3, 24118 Kiel, Germany
E-mail: wpr@informatik.uni-kiel.de

Library of Congress Control Number: 2004112623

CR Subject Classification (1998): D.2, D.3, F.3, F.4

ISSN 0302-9743
ISBN 3-540-22942-6 Springer Berlin Heidelberg New York

Springer is a part of Springer Science+Business Media

springeronline.com

© Springer-Verlag Berlin Heidelberg 2004
Printed in Germany

Typesetting: Camera-ready by author, data conversion by Scientific Publishing Services, Chennai, India
Printed on acid-free paper   SPIN: 11315810   06/3142   5 4 3 2 1 0

Preface

Large and complex software systems provide the necessary infrastucture in all industries today. In order to construct such large systems in a systematic manner, the focus in the development methodologies has switched in the last two decades from functional issues to structural issues: both data and functions are encapsulated into software units that are integrated into large systems by means of various techniques supporting reusability and modifiability. This encapsulation principle is essential to both the object-oriented and the more recent component-based software engineering paradigms.

Formal methods have been applied successfully to the verification of medium-sized programs in protocol and hardware design. However, their application to large systems requires a further development of specification and verification techniques supporting the concepts of reusability and modifiability.

In order to bring together researchers and practioners in the areas of software engineering and formal methods, we organized the 2nd International Symposium on Formal Methods for Components and Objects (FMCO) in Leiden, The Netherlands, from November 4 to 7, 2003. The program consisted of invited tutorials and technical presentations given by leading experts in the fields of theoretical computer science and software engineering. The symposium was attended by more than 80 people from all over the world.

This volume contains the contributions of the invited speakers to FMCO 2003. We believe that the presented material provides a unique combination of ideas on software engineering and formal methods which we hope will form an inspiration for those aiming at further bridging the gap between the theory and practice of software engineering.

The very idea to organize FMCO arose out of the NWO/DFG bilateral project Mobi-J. In particular we acknowledge the financial support of the NWO funding of Mobi-J. Additional financial support was provided by the Lorentz Center, the IST project Omega (2001-33522), the Dutch Institute for Programming Research and Algorithmics (IPA), the Royal Netherlands Academy of Arts and Sciences (KNAW), the Centrum voor Wiskunde en Informatica (CWI), and the Leiden Institute of Advanced Computer Science (LIACS).

July 2004

F.S. de Boer
M.M. Bonsangue
S. Graf
W.-P. de Roever

The Mobi-J Project

Mobi-J is a project funded by a bilateral research program of the Dutch Organization for Scientific Research (NWO) and the Central Public Funding Organization for Academic Research in Germany (DFG).

The partners of the Mobi-J projects are:

- Centrum voor Wiskunde en Informatica (F.S. de Boer)
- Leiden Institute of Advanced Computer Science (M.M. Bonsangue)
- Christian-Albrechts-Universität Kiel (W.-P. de Roever)

This project aims at the development of a programming environment which supports component-based design and verification of Java programs annotated with assertions. The overall approach is based on an extension of the Java language called Mobi-J with a notion of component which provides for the encapsulation of its internal processing of date and composition in a network by means of mobile asynchronous channels.

The activities of Mobi-J include the organization of international symposia funded by the NWO and Ph.D. research funded by the DFG. By means of regular meetings the partners discuss intensively Ph.D. research involving Mobi-J related topics. Mobi-J also maintains contacts with other German universities, including the universities of Oldenburg and Munich, and a close collaboration with the European IST project OMEGA.

The Omega Project

The overall aim of the European IST project Omega (2001-33522) is the definition of a development methodology in UML for embedded and real-time systems based on formal verification techniques. The approach is based on a formal semantics of a suitable subset of UML, adapted and extended where needed with a special emphasis on time-related aspects.

The Omega project involves the following partners: VERIMAG (France, Coordinator), Centrum voor Wiskunde en Informatica (The Netherlands), Christian-Albrechts-Universität (Germany), University of Nijmegen (The Netherlands), Weizmann Institute (Israel), OFFIS (Germany), EADS Launch Vehicles (France), France Telecom R&D (France), Israeli Aircraft Industries (Israel), and National Aerospace Laboratory (The Netherlands).

Table of Contents

Causality and Scheduling Constraints in Heterogeneous Reactive
Systems Modeling
  *Albert Benveniste, Benoît Caillaud, Luca P. Carloni, Paul Caspi,
  Alberto L. Sangiovanni-Vincentelli* 1

Machine Function Based Control Code Algebras
  Jan A. Bergstra 17

Exploiting Abstraction for Specification Reuse. The Java/C♯ Case Study
  Egon Börger, Robert F. Stärk 42

On the Verification of Cooperating Traffic Agents
  Werner Damm, Hardi Hungar, Ernst-Rüdiger Olderog 77

How to Cook a Complete Hoare Logic for Your Pet OO Language
  Frank S. de Boer, Cees Pierik 111

Behavioural Specification for Hierarchical Object Composition
  Răzvan Diaconescu 134

Consistency Management Within Model-Based Object-Oriented
Development of Components
  Jochen M. Küster, Gregor Engels 157

CommUnity on the Move: Architectures for Distribution and Mobility
  José Luiz Fiadeiro, Antónia Lopes 177

TulaFale: A Security Tool for Web Services
  *Karthikeyan Bhargavan, Cédric Fournet, Andrew D. Gordon,
  Riccardo Pucella* 197

A Checker for Modal Formulae for Processes with Data
  Jan Friso Groote, Tim A.C. Willemse 223

Semantic Essence of AsmL
  Yuri Gurevich, Benjamin Rossman, Wolfram Schulte 240

An MDA Approach to Tame Component Based Software Development
  Jean-Marc Jézéquel, Olivier Defour, Noël Plouzeau 260

An Application of Stream Calculus to Signal Flow Graphs
  J.J.M.M. Rutten 276

Synchronous Closing and Flow Analysis for Model Checking Timed
Systems
  Natalia Ioustinova, Natalia Sidorova, Martin Steffen 292

Priority Systems
  Gregor Gössler, Joseph Sifakis 314

Preserving Properties Under Change
  Heike Wehrheim 330

Tools for Generating and Analyzing Attack Graphs
  Oleg Sheyner, Jeannette Wing 344

Author Index 373

Causality and Scheduling Constraints in Heterogeneous Reactive Systems Modeling[*]

Albert Benveniste[1], Benoît Caillaud[1], Luca P. Carloni[2], Paul Caspi[3] and Alberto L. Sangiovanni-Vincentelli[2]

[1] Irisa/Inria, Campus de Beaulieu, 35042 Rennes cedex, France
Albert.Benveniste@irisa.fr
http://www.irisa.fr/sigma2/benveniste/
[2] U.C. Berkeley, Berkeley, CA 94720
{lcarloni,alberto}@eecs.berkeley.edu
http://www-cad.eecs.berkeley.edu/HomePages/{lcarloni,alberto}
[3] Verimag, Centre Equation, 2, rue de Vignate, F-38610 Gieres
Paul.Caspi@imag.fr
http://www.imag.fr/VERIMAG/PEOPLE/Paul.Caspi

Abstract. Recently we proposed a mathematical framework offering diverse models of computation and a formal foundation for correct-by-construction deployment of synchronous designs over distributed architecture (such as GALS or LTTA). In this paper, we extend our framework to model explicitly causality relations and scheduling constraints. We show how the formal results on the preservation of semantics hold also for these cases and we discuss the overall contribution in the context of previous work on desynchronization.

1 Introduction

Embedded systems are intrinsically heterogeneous since they are based on processors that see the world digitally and an environment that is analog. In addition, the processing elements are heterogeneous too since they often include micro-controllers and digital signal processors in addition to special purpose computing engines. These parts must communicate and exchange information in a consistent and reliable way over media that are often noisy and unreliable. Some of the tasks that embedded systems must carry out are safety-critical, e.g., in medical and transportation systems (cars, airplanes, trains) and for this reason have hard constraints on timing and reliability. As technology advances, increasingly more computing power becomes available thus offering the opportunity of adding functionality to the system to such an extent that the complexity of the design task is unmanegeable without a rigorous design methodology based on

---

[*] This research was supported in part by the European Commission under the projects COLUMBUS, IST-2002-38314, and ARTIST, IST-2001-34820, by the NSF under the project ITR (CCR-0225610), and by the GSRC.

F.S. de Boer et al. (Eds.): FMCO 2003, LNCS 3188, pp. 1–16, 2004.

sound principles. In particular, the need for fast time-to-market and reasonable development cost imposes design re-use. And design re-use implies the use of software for as many parts of the functionality as possible given size, production cost and power consumption constraints. Consequently, software accounts for most of the design costs today and it is responsible for delays in product delivery because of the lack of a unified design process that can guarantee correct behavior.

Today, designers face a very diversified landscape when it comes to methodologies, supporting tools, and engineering best practices. This would not necessarily be a problem if it were not for the fact that transitioning between tools that are based on different paradigms is increasingly becoming a design productivity bottleneck as it has been underlined by the road map work performed in the framework of the ARTIST network of excellence [3]. A solution to this problem would be to impose a "homogeneous" design policy, such as the fully synchronous approach. However, implementation costs in terms of performance and components require a more diversified view. Heterogeneity will manifest itself at the component level where different models of computation may be used to represent component operation and, more frequently, at different levels of abstraction, where, for example, a synchronous-language specification of the design may be refined into a globally asynchronous locally synchronous (GALS) architecture, thus alleviating some of the cost issues outlined above. Having a mathematical framework for the heterogeneous modeling of reactive systems gives freedom of choice between different synchronization policies at different stages of the design process and provides a solid foundation to handle formally communication and coordination among heterogeneous components. Interesting work along similar lines has been the Ptolemy project [13, 15], the MoBIES project [1], the Model-Integrated Computing (MIC) framework [16], and *Interface Theories* [14].

This paper is an extension of [7] where we proposed *Tagged Systems*, a variation of Lee and Sangiovanni-Vincentelli's (LSV) Tagged-Signal Model [22], as a mathematical model for heterogeneous systems. Originally, we restricted ourselves to Tagged Systems in which parallel composition is by intersection, meaning that unifiable events of each component must have identical variable, data, and tag. While this restriction has allowed us to handle GALS models of design, it does not cover all cases of interest. For example, causality relations and scheduling constraints are not compatible with parallel composition by intersection. Neither are earliest execution times. Yet causality and scheduling constraints are very important to include when implementing an embedded systems. Hence, it is sometimes useful to have a notion of parallel composition that accepts the unification of events having different tags (while the data that they carry must still be equal). In this work, we propose an extension of Tagged Systems where the unification rule for tags is itself parameterized. We show that this model captures important properties such as causality and scheduling constraints. Then, we extend the general theorems of [7] on the preservation of semantics during distributed deployment.

2   Tagged Systems and Heterogeneous Systems

2.1   Tagged Systems and Their Parallel Composition

Throughout this paper, $\mathbf{N} = \{1, 2, \ldots\}$ denotes the set of positive integers; $\mathbf{N}$ is equipped with its usual total order $\leq$. $X \mapsto Y$ denotes the set of all partial functions from X to Y. If $(X, \leq_X)$ and $(Y, \leq_Y)$ are partial orders, $f \in X \mapsto Y$ is called *increasing* if $f(\leq_X) \subseteq \leq_Y$, i.e., $\forall x, x' \in X : x \leq_X x' \Rightarrow f(x) \leq_Y f(x')$.

Tag Structures. A *tag structure* is a triple $(\mathcal{T}, \leq, \sqsubseteq)$, where $\mathcal{T}$ is a set of *tags*, and $\leq$ and $\sqsubseteq$ are two partial orders. Partial order $\leq$ relates tags seen as time stamps. Call a *clock* any increasing function $(\mathbf{N}, \leq) \mapsto (\mathcal{T}, \leq)$. Partial order $\sqsubseteq$, called the *unification order*, defines how to unify tags and is essential to express coordination among events. Write $\tau_1 \bowtie \tau_2$ to mean that there exists $\tau \in \mathcal{T}$ such that $\tau_i \sqsubseteq \tau$. We assume that any pair (τ_1, τ_2) of tags, such that $\tau_1 \bowtie \tau_2$ holds, possesses an upper bound. We denote it by $\tau_1 \sqcup \tau_2$. In other words, $(\mathcal{T}, \sqsubseteq)$ is a sup-semi-lattice. We call $\bowtie$ and $\sqcup$ the *unification relation* and *unification map*, respectively.

We assume that unification is causal with respect to partial order of time stamps: the result of the unification cannot occur prior in time than its constituents. Formally, if $\tau_1 \bowtie \tau_2$ is a unifiable pair then $\tau_i \leq (\tau_1 \sqcup \tau_2)$, for $i = 1, 2$. Equivalently:

$$\forall \tau, \tau' : \quad \tau \sqsubseteq \tau' \Rightarrow \tau \leq \tau'. \tag{1}$$

Condition (1) has the following consequence: if $\tau_1 \leq \tau_1'$, $\tau_2 \leq \tau_2'$, $\tau_1 \bowtie \tau_2$, and $\tau_1' \bowtie \tau_2'$ together hold, then $(\tau_1 \sqcup \tau_2) \leq (\tau_1' \sqcup \tau_2')$ must also hold. This ensures that the system obtained via parallel composition preserves the agreed order of its components.

Tagged Systems. Let $\mathcal{V}$ be an underlying set of variables with domain D. For $V \subset \mathcal{V}$ finite, a *V-behaviour*, or simply behaviour, is an element:

$$\sigma \in V \mapsto \mathbf{N} \mapsto (\mathcal{T} \times D), \tag{2}$$

meaning that, for each $v \in V$, the n-th occurrence of v in behaviour σ has tag $\tau \in \mathcal{T}$ and value $x \in D$. For v a variable, the map $\sigma(v) \in \mathbf{N} \mapsto (\mathcal{T} \times D)$ is called a *signal*. For σ a behaviour, an *event* of σ is a tuple $(v, n, \tau, x) \in V \times \mathbf{N} \times \mathcal{T} \times D$ such that $\sigma(v)(n) = (\tau, x)$. Thus we can regard behaviours as sets of events. We require that, for each $v \in V$, the first projection of the map $\sigma(v)$ (it is a map $\mathbf{N} \mapsto \mathcal{T}$) is increasing. Thus it is a clock and we call it the *clock of v in σ*. A *tagged system* is a triple $P = (V, \mathcal{T}, \Sigma)$, where V is a finite set of variables, $\mathcal{T}$ is a tag structure, and Σ a set of V-behaviours.

Homogeneous Parallel Composition. Consider two tagged systems $P_1 = (V_1, \mathcal{T}_1, \Sigma_1)$ and $P_2 = (V_2, \mathcal{T}_2, \Sigma_2)$ with identical tag structures $\mathcal{T}_1 = \mathcal{T}_2 = \mathcal{T}$. Let $\sqcup$ be the unification function of $\mathcal{T}$. For two events $e = (v, n, \tau, x)$ and $e' = (v', n', \tau', x')$, define

$$e \bowtie e' \quad \text{iff} \quad v = v', n = n', \tau \bowtie \tau', x = x', \quad \text{and}$$

$$e \bowtie e' \Rightarrow e \sqcup e' =_{\text{def}} (v, n, \tau \sqcup \tau', x).$$

The unification map $\sqcup$ and relation $\bowtie$ extend point-wise to behaviours. Then, for σ a V-behaviour and and σ' a V'-behaviour, define, by abuse of notation: $\sigma \bowtie \sigma'$ iff $\sigma_{|V\cap V'} \bowtie \sigma'_{|V\cap V'}$, and then

$$\sigma \sqcup \sigma' =_{def} \left(\sigma_{|V\cap V'} \sqcup \sigma'_{|V\cap V'}\right) \cup \sigma_{|V\setminus V'} \cup \sigma'_{|V'\setminus V}.$$

where $\sigma_{|W}$ denotes the restriction of behaviour σ to the variables of W. Finally, for Σ and Σ' two sets of behaviours, define their *conjunction*

$$\Sigma \wedge \Sigma' =_{def} \{\sigma \sqcup \sigma' \mid \sigma \in \Sigma, \sigma' \in \Sigma' \text{ and } \sigma \bowtie \sigma'\} \tag{3}$$

The *homogeneous parallel composition* of P_1 and P_2 is

$$P_1 \parallel P_2 =_{def} (V_1 \cup V_2, \mathcal{T}, \Sigma_1 \wedge \Sigma_2) \tag{4}$$

2.2   Theme and Variations on the Pair $(\mathcal{T}, \sqcup)$

Parallel Composition by Intersection. This is the usual case, already investigated in [7]. It corresponds to:

- The tag set $\mathcal{T}$ is arbitrary.
- The unification function $\sqcup$ is such that $\tau \bowtie \tau'$ iff $\tau = \tau'$, and $\tau \sqcup \tau' =_{def} \tau$.

Modeling synchronous systems, asynchronous systems, timed systems, with this framework, is extensively discussed in [7]. We summarize here the main points.

To represent *synchronous systems* with our model, take for $\mathcal{T}$ a totally ordered set (e.g., $\mathcal{T} = \mathbf{N}$), and require that all clocks are strictly increasing. The tag index set $\mathcal{T}$ organizes behaviours into successive reactions, as explained next. Call *reaction* a maximal set of events of σ with identical τ. Since clocks are strictly increasing, no two events of the same reaction can have the same variable. Regard a behaviour as a sequence of global reactions: $\sigma = \sigma_1, \sigma_2, \ldots$, with tags $\tau_1, \tau_2, \ldots \in \mathcal{T}$. Thus $\mathcal{T}$ provides a global, logical time basis.

As for *asynchronous systems,* we take a very liberal interpretation for them. If we interpret a tag set as a constraint on the coordination of different signals of a system and the integer $n \in \mathbf{N}$ as the basic constraint of the sequence of events of the behaviour of a variable, then the most "coordination unconstrained" system, the one with most degrees of freedom in terms of choice of coordination mechanism, could be considered an ideal asynchronous system. Then an asynchronous system corresponds to a model where the tag set does not give any information on the absolute or relative ordering of events. In more formal way, take $\mathcal{T} = \{.\}$, the trivial set consisting of a single element. Then, behaviours identify with elements $\sigma \in V \mapsto \mathbf{N} \mapsto D$.

Capturing Causality Relations and Scheduling Specifications. How can we capture causalities relations or scheduling specifications in the above introduced asynchronous tagged systems? The intent is, for example, to state that "the 2nd occurrence of x depends on the 3rd occurrence of b". Define $\mathbf{N}_0 =_{\text{def}} \mathbf{N} \cup \{0\}$. Define a *dependency* to be a map:

$$\delta = \mathcal{V} \mapsto \mathbf{N}_0.$$

We denote by Δ the set of all dependencies, and we take $\mathcal{T} = \Delta$. Thus an event has the form:

$$e = (v, n, \delta, x), \tag{5}$$

with the following interpretation: event e has v as associated variable, it is ranked n among the events with variable v, and it depends on the event of variable w that is ranked $\delta(w)$. The special case $\delta(w) = 0$ is interpreted as the absence of dependency. We take the convention that, for e as in (5), $\delta(v) = n - 1$. Thus, on $\sigma(v)$, the set of dependencies reproduces the ranking. Δ is equipped with the partial order defined by $\delta \leq \delta'$ iff $\forall v : \delta(v) \leq \delta'(v)$. Then we define the unification map $\sqcup$ for this case:

$$\mathbf{dom}\,(\sqcup) = \mathcal{T} \times \mathcal{T} \text{ and } \delta \sqcup \delta' =_{\text{def}} \max(\delta, \delta'). \tag{6}$$

With this definition, behaviours become labelled preorders as explained next. For σ a behaviour, and e, e' two events of σ, write:

$$e' \to_\sigma e \text{ iff } \begin{cases} e = (v, n, \delta, x) \\ e' = (v', n', \delta', x') \\ \delta(v') = n' \end{cases} \tag{7}$$

Note that, since $n' > 0$, the condition $\delta(v') = n'$ makes this dependency effective. Definition (7) makes σ a labeled directed graph. Denote by $\preceq_\sigma$ the transitive reflexive closure of $\to_\sigma$, it is a preorder [1].

Capturing Earliest Execution Times. Here we capture earliest timed executions of concurrent systems. Take $\mathcal{T} = \mathbf{R}_+$, the set of non-negative real numbers. Thus a tag $\tau \in \mathcal{T}$ assigns a date, and we define

$$\tau \sqcup \tau' =_{\text{def}} \max(\tau, \tau').$$

Hence $\sqcup$ is here a total function. Composing two systems has the effect that the two components wait for the latest date of occurrence for each shared variable. For example, assume that variable v is an output of P and an input of Q in $P \,\|\, Q$. Then the earliest possible date of every event of variable v in Q is by convention 0, whereas each event associated to v has a certain date of production in P. In the parallel composition $P \,\|\, Q$, the dates of production by P prevail.

---

[1] We insist: "preorder", not "partial order"—this should not be a surprise, since the superposition of two partial orders generally yields a preorder.

Capturing Timed Systems. Various classes of timed automata models have been proposed since their introduction by Alur and Dill in [2]. In timed automata, dates of events are subject to constraints of the form $C : \tau \in \cup_{i \in I} [\![s_i, t_i]\!]$, where I is some finite set whose cardinality depends on the considered event, and $[\![= [$ or $($, and symmetrically for $]\!]$. The classes of timed automata differ by the type of constraint that can be expressed, and therefore they differ in their decidability properties. Nevertheless, they can all be described by the following kind of Tagged System[2].

Take $\mathcal{T} = Pow(\mathbf{R}_+)$, where *Pow* denotes powerset. Thus, a tag $\tau \in \mathcal{T}$ assigns to each event a constraint on its possible dates of occurrence. Then, several definitions are of interest:

 – $\tau_1 \bowtie \tau_2$ iff $\tau_1 \cap \tau_2 \neq \emptyset$, and $\tau_1 \sqcup \tau_2 = \tau_1 \cap \tau_2$. This is the straightforward definition, it consists in regarding tags as constraints and combining them by taking their conjunction.
 – the unification of tags is a total function, defined as follows: $\tau_1 \sqcup \tau_2 = \{\max(t_1, t_2) | t_1 \in \tau_1, t_2 \in \tau_2\}$. In this case, events are synchronized by waiting for the latest one.

Hybrid Tags. Define the product $(\mathcal{T}, \sqcup) =_{\text{def}} (\mathcal{T}', \sqcup') \times (\mathcal{T}'', \sqcup'')$ in a standard way. This allows us to combine different tags into a compound, heterogeneous, tag. For instance, one can consider synchronous systems that are timed and enhanced with causality relations. Such systems can be "desynchronized", meaning that their reaction tag is erased, but their causality and time tags are kept.

2.3   Running Example

The Base Case: Synchronous Systems. Let P and Q be two synchronous systems involving the same set of variables: b of type boolean, and x of type integer. Each system possesses only a single behaviour, shown on the right hand side of $P : \dots$ and $Q : \dots$, respectively. Each behaviour consists of a sequence of successive reactions, separated by vertical bars. Each reaction consists of an assignment of values to a subset of the variables; a blank indicates the absence of the considered variable in the considered reaction.

$$
P : \begin{array}{c|c|c|c|c|c|c|c}
b : & t & f & t & f & t & f & \dots \\
x : & 1 & & 1 & & 1 & & \dots
\end{array}
$$

$$
Q : \begin{array}{c|c|c|c|c|c|c|c}
b : & t & f & t & f & t & f & \dots \\
x : & & 1 & & 1 & & 1 & \dots
\end{array}
$$

The single behavior of P can be expressed formally in our framework as

$$
\sigma(b)(2n - 1) = (2n - 1, t) \quad , \quad \sigma(b)(2n) = (2n, f)
$$
$$
\sigma(x)(n) \quad = (2n - 1, 1)
$$

(8)

---

[2] Our framework of Tagged Systems handles (infinite) behaviours and is not suited to investigate decidability properties, this explains why we can subsume all variants of timed automata into a unique Tagged Systems model.

where we take $\mathcal{T} = \mathbf{N}$ to index the successive reactions. Note the absence of x at tag $2n$. Similarly, for Q we have the following where x is absent at tag $2n - 1$:

$$\sigma(b)(2n - 1) = (2n - 1, t) \; , \; \sigma(b)(2n) = (2n, f) \qquad\qquad (9)$$
$$\sigma(x)(n) = (2n, 1)$$

Now, the synchronous parallel composition of P and Q, defined by intersection: $P \parallel Q =_{\mathrm{def}} P \cap Q$, is empty. The reason is that P and Q disagree on where to put absences for the variable x. Formally, they disagree on their respective tags.

Desynchronizing the Base Case. The *desynchronization* of a synchronous system like P or Q consists in (i) removing the synchronization barriers separating the successive reactions, and, then, (ii) compressing the sequence of values for each variable, individually. This yields:

$$P_\alpha = Q_\alpha : \frac{b : t\; f\; t\; f\; t\; f \ldots}{x : 1\; 1\; 1 \ldots}$$

where the subscript $_\alpha$ refers to asynchrony. The reader may think that events having identical index for different variables are aligned, but this is not the case. In fact, as the absence of vertical bars in the diagram suggests, there is *no alignment* at all between events associated with different variables.

Formally, we express asynchrony by taking $\mathcal{T} = \{.\}$, the trivial set with a single element. The reason is that we do not need any additional time stamping information. Thus, the single behavior of $P_\alpha = Q_\alpha$ is written as

$$\sigma_\alpha(b)(2n - 1) = t, \sigma_\alpha(b)(2n) = f, \text{ and } \sigma_\alpha(x)(n) = 1. \qquad (10)$$

Regarding desynchronization, the following comments are in order. Note that $P \neq Q$ but $P_\alpha = Q_\alpha$. Next, the synchronous system R defined by $R = P \cup Q$, the nondeterministic choice between P and Q, possesses two behaviours. However, its desynchronization R_α equals P_α, and possesses only one behaviour. Now, since $P_\alpha = Q_\alpha$, then $P_\alpha \parallel Q_\alpha =_{\mathrm{def}} P_\alpha \cap Q_\alpha = P_\alpha = Q_\alpha \neq \emptyset$. Thus, for the pair (P, Q), desynchronization does not preserve the semantics of parallel composition, in any reasonable sense.

Adding Causality Relations. Suppose that some analysis of the considered program allows us to add the following causality relations to P and Q:

For example, in accordance to the above causality relations, the meaning of P could be: if $b = t$ then get x (and similarly for Q). By using the dependency relation defined in (6), we can express formally the behavior of P_c as

$$\sigma(b)(2n-1) = ([2n-1,(x,0)],t) \qquad , \quad \sigma(b)(2n) = ([2n,(x,0)],f)$$
$$\sigma(x)(n) \quad = ([2n-1,(b,2n-1)],1)$$

and the behavior of Q_c as

$$\sigma(b)(2n-1) = ([2n-1,(x,0)],t) \qquad , \quad \sigma(b)(2n) = ([2n,(x,0)],f)$$
$$, \quad \sigma(x)(n) \quad = ([2n,(b,2n)],1)$$

As for the base case and for the same reason, $P_c \parallel Q_c = \emptyset$.

Then, Desynchronizing. Removing the synchronization barriers from P_c and Q_c yields

$$
P_c^\alpha : \quad
\begin{array}{l}
b : t\ f\ t\ f\ t\ f \ldots \\
\quad\ \downarrow\ \ \downarrow\ \ \downarrow\ \quad \ldots \\
x : 1\quad 1\quad 1\quad \ldots
\end{array}
$$

$$
Q_c^\alpha : \quad
\begin{array}{l}
b : t\ f\ t\ f\ t\ f \ldots \\
\quad\quad\ \downarrow\ \ \downarrow\ \ \downarrow \ldots \\
x : \quad 1\quad 1\quad 1 \ldots
\end{array}
$$

We insist that, again, desynchronizing consists in (i) removing the synchronization barriers, and then (ii) compressing the sequence of values for each variable, individually—this last step is not shown on the drawing, just because it is a lot easier to draw vertical arrows. Formally, for P_c^α we have

$$\sigma(b)(2n-1) = ((x,0),t) \qquad , \quad \sigma(b)(2n) = ((x,0),f)$$
$$\sigma(x)(n) \quad = ((b,2n-1),1)$$

and, for Q_c^α we have

$$\sigma(b)(2n-1) = ((x,0),t) \qquad , \quad \sigma(b)(2n) = ((x,0),f)$$
$$, \quad \sigma(x)(n) \quad = ((b,2n),1)$$

These two behaviours are unifiable and yield the dependency $(b,2n)$, by the max rule (6). In fact, the reader can check that $P_c^\alpha \parallel Q_c^\alpha = Q_c^\alpha$. Thus P_c and Q_c did not include enough causality relations for desynchronization to properly preserve the semantics.

Adding More Causality Relations. Suppose that "oblique" causality relations are added, from each previous occurrence of x to the current occurrence of b:

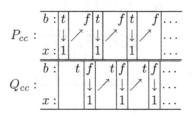

These supplementary causality relations conform to the synchronous model since they agree with the increasing reaction index. Formally, the single behavior of P_{cc} is written

$$\sigma(b)(2n-1) = ([2n-1,(x,0)],t) \quad , \quad \sigma(b)(2n) = ([2n,(x,n)],f)$$
$$\sigma(x)(n) \quad = ([2n-1,(b,2n-1)],1)$$

and the one of Q_{cc} is

$$\sigma(b)(2n-1) = ([2n-1,(x,n-1)],t) \quad , \quad \sigma(b)(2n) = ([2n,(x,0)],f)$$
$$\quad , \quad \sigma(x)(n) \quad = ([2n,(b,2n)],1)$$

Again, $P_{cc} \,\|\, Q_{cc} = \emptyset$.

Then, Again Desynchronizing. Removing the synchronization barriers from P_{cc} and Q_{cc} yields

$$
\begin{array}{l}
P^{\alpha}_{cc} : \quad
\begin{array}{llllll}
\hline
b:t & f\,t & f\,t & f\ldots \\
\downarrow\nearrow & \downarrow\nearrow & \downarrow\nearrow & \ldots \\
x:1 & 1 & 1 & \ldots \\
\hline
\end{array}
\\[2ex]
Q^{\alpha}_{cc} : \quad
\begin{array}{llllll}
\hline
b: & t\,f & t\,f & t\,f\ldots \\
& \downarrow\nearrow & \downarrow\nearrow & \downarrow\ldots \\
x: & 1 & 1 & 1\ldots \\
\hline
\end{array}
\end{array}
$$

In our framework, for P^{α}_{cc} we have

$$\sigma(b)(2n-1) = ((x,0),t) \quad , \quad \sigma(b)(2n) = ((x,n),f)$$
$$\sigma(x)(n) \quad = ((b,2n-1),1)$$

and, for Q^{α}_{cc} we have

$$\sigma(b)(2n-1) = ((x,n-1),t) \quad , \quad \sigma(b)(2n) = ((x,0),f)$$
$$\quad , \quad \sigma(x)(n) \quad = ((b,2n),1)$$

However, now the composed behavior does not coincide with Q^{α}_{cc} but is

$$
P^{\alpha}_{cc} \,\|\, Q^{\alpha}_{cc} = \quad
\begin{array}{llllll}
\hline
b: & t\,f & t\,f & t\,f\ldots \\
& \updownarrow\nearrow & \updownarrow\nearrow & \updownarrow\ldots \\
x: & 1 & 1 & 1\ldots \\
\hline
\end{array}
$$

The reason for the double causality between x and f-occurrences of b is that the n-th x causes the $(2n)$-th b (i.e. the n-th f-occurrence of b) in P_{cc} whereas the $(2n)$-th b causes the n-th x in Q_{cc}. Formally, by the max rule (6), the composed behavior of $P^{\alpha}_{cc} \,\|\, Q^{\alpha}_{cc}$ is written

$$\sigma(b)(2n-1) = ((x,n-1),t) \quad , \quad \sigma(b)(2n) = ((x,n),f)$$
$$\quad , \quad \sigma(x)(n) \quad = ((b,2n),1)$$

In conclusion, $P^{\alpha}_{cc} \,\|\, Q^{\alpha}_{cc}$ possesses causality loops and may be considered pathological and thus "rejected" in accordance with the original semantics $P \,\|\, Q = \emptyset$.

2.4   Heterogeneous Systems

Assume a functional system specification using a synchronous approach, for subsequent deployment over a distributed asynchronous architecture (synchronous and asynchronous are considered in the sense of subsection 2.1). When we deploy the design on a different architecture, we must make sure that the original intent of the designer is maintained. This step is non trivial because the information on what is considered correct behaviour is captured in the synchronous specifications that we want to relax in the first place. We introduce the notion of semantic-preserving transformation to identify precisely what is a correct deployment. We present the idea with our running example:

Running Example, Cont'd. Regarding semantics preserving deployment, the following comments can be stated on our running example. The synchronous parallel composition of P and Q, defined by intersection: $P \parallel Q =_{\text{def}} P \cap Q$, is empty. The reason is that P and Q disagree on where to put absences for the variable x. On the other hand, since $P_\alpha = Q_\alpha$, then $P_\alpha \parallel Q_\alpha =_{\text{def}} P_\alpha \cap Q_\alpha = P_\alpha = Q_\alpha \neq \emptyset$. Thus, for the pair (P, Q), desynchronization does not preserve the semantics of parallel composition, in any reasonable sense. $\diamond$

How to model that semantics is preserved when replacing the ideal synchronous broadcast by the actual asynchronous communication? An elegant solution was proposed by Le Guernic and Talpin for the former GALS case [21]. We cast their approach in the framework of tagged systems and we generalize it.

Tag Morphisms. For T, T' two tag structures, call *morphism* a map $\rho : T \mapsto T'$ which is increasing w.r.t. $\leq$ and $\leq'$, surjective, and such that

$$\rho \circ \sqcup = \sqcup' \circ (\rho, \rho) \tag{11}$$

holds, where $\circ$ denotes the composition of functions. As expected from their name, morphisms compose. For $\rho : T \mapsto T'$ a morphism, and $\sigma \in V \mapsto \mathbf{N} \mapsto (T \times D)$ a behaviour, replacing τ by $\rho(\tau)$ in σ defines a new behaviour having T' as tag set. We denote it by

$$\sigma_\rho, \text{ or by } \sigma \circ \rho. \tag{12}$$

Performing this for every behaviour of a tag system P yields the tag system

$$P_\rho. \tag{13}$$

For $T_1 \xrightarrow{\rho_1} T \xleftarrow{\rho_2} T_2$ two morphisms, define:

$$T_1 \, _{\rho_1}\!\times_{\rho_2} T_2 =_{\text{def}} \{ (\tau_1, \tau_2) \mid \rho_1(\tau_1) = \rho_2(\tau_2) \} . \tag{14}$$

A case of interest is $T_i = T_i' \times T, i = 1, 2$, and the T_i' are different. Then $T_1 \, _{\rho_1}\!\times_{\rho_2} T_2$ identifies with the product $T_1' \times T \times T_2'$. For example, the *desynchronization* of synchronous systems is captured by the morphism $\alpha : T_{\text{synch}} \mapsto \{.\}$, which erases all global timing information (see Equations (8,9), and (10)).

Heterogeneous Parallel Composition. In this subsection we define the composition of two tagged systems $P_i = (V_i, \mathcal{T}_i, \Sigma_i), i = 1, 2$, when $\mathcal{T}_1 \neq \mathcal{T}_2$. Assume two morphisms $\mathcal{T}_1 \xrightarrow{\rho_1} \mathcal{T} \xleftarrow{\rho_2} \mathcal{T}_2$. Write:

$$\sigma_1 \;_{\rho_1}\bowtie_{\rho_2} \sigma_2 \quad \text{iff} \quad \sigma_1 \circ \rho_1 \bowtie \sigma_2 \circ \rho_2. \tag{15}$$

For (σ_1, σ_2) a pair satisfying (15), define

$$\sigma_1 \;_{\rho_1}\sqcup_{\rho_2} \sigma_2 \tag{16}$$

as being the set of events $(v, n, (\tau_1, \tau_2), x)$ such that $\rho_1(\tau_1) = \rho_2(\tau_2) =_{\text{def}} \tau$ and (v, n, τ, x) is an event of $\sigma_1 \circ \rho_1 \sqcup \sigma_2 \circ \rho_2$. We are now ready to define the *heterogeneous conjunction* of Σ_1 and Σ_2 by:

$$\Sigma_1 \;_{\rho_1}\wedge_{\rho_2} \Sigma_2 =_{\text{def}} \left\{ \sigma_1 \;_{\rho_1}\sqcup_{\rho_2} \sigma_2 \mid \sigma_1 \;_{\rho_1}\bowtie_{\rho_2} \sigma_2 \right\}. \tag{17}$$

Finally, the *heterogeneous parallel composition* of P_1 and P_2 is defined by:

$$P_1 \;_{(\rho_1}\|_{\rho_2)} P_2 = \left(V_1 \cup V_2 \,, \mathcal{T}_1 \;_{\rho_1}\times_{\rho_2} \mathcal{T}_2 \,, \Sigma_1 \;_{\rho_1}\wedge_{\rho_2} \Sigma_2 \right). \tag{18}$$

We simply write $_{(\rho_1}\|$ instead of $_{(\rho_1}\|_{\rho_2)}$ when ρ_2 is the identity.

GALS, Hybrid Timed/Untimed Systems, and More. To model the interaction of a synchronous system with its asynchronous environment, take the heterogeneous composition $P_{(\alpha}\| A$, where $P = (V, \mathcal{T}_{\text{synch}}, \Sigma)$ is a synchronous system, $A = (W, \{.\}, \Sigma')$ is an asynchronous model of the environment, and $\alpha : \mathcal{T}_{\text{synch}} \mapsto \{.\}$ is the trivial morphism, mapping synchrony to asynchrony (hence the special notation).

For GALS, take $\mathcal{T}_1 = \mathcal{T}_2 = \mathcal{T}_{\text{synch}}$, where $\mathcal{T}_{\text{synch}}$ is the tag set of synchronous systems. Then, take $\mathcal{T} = \{.\}$ is the tag set of asynchronous ones. Take $\alpha : \mathcal{T}_{\text{synch}} \mapsto \{.\}$, the trivial morphism. And consider $P_1 \;_{(\alpha}\|_{\alpha)} P_2$.

For timed/untimed systems, consider $P \;_{(\rho}\| Q$, where $P = (V, \mathcal{T}_{\text{synch}} \times \mathcal{T}_\varphi, \Sigma)$ is a synchronous timed system, $Q = (W, \mathcal{T}_{\text{synch}}, \Sigma')$ is a synchronous but untimed system, and $\rho : \mathcal{T}_{\text{synch}} \times \mathcal{T}_\varphi \mapsto \mathcal{T}_{\text{synch}}$ is the projection morphism.

This machinery of morphisms provides a framework for the different manipulations of tags that were performed in Section 2.3 on our running example.

3   Application to Correct Deployment

In this section we apply our framework to the formalization of the practically important—but generally informal—requirement of "correct deployment".

3.1   Preserving Semantics: Formalization

We are given a pair $P_i = (V_i, \mathcal{T}_i, \Sigma_i), i = 1, 2$, such that $\mathcal{T}_1 = \mathcal{T}_2$, and a pair $\mathcal{T}_1 \xrightarrow{\rho} \mathcal{T} \xleftarrow{\rho} \mathcal{T}_2$ of identical morphisms. We can consider two semantics:

$$\text{The strong semantics} : P_1 \| P_2$$
$$\text{The weak semantics} : P_1 \;_{(\rho}\|_\rho) P_2.$$

We say that ρ is *semantics preserving* with respect to $P_1 \parallel P_2$ if

$$P_1 {}_{(\rho\|\rho)} P_2 \equiv P_1 \parallel P_2. \tag{19}$$

Running Example, Cont'd. The reader can check the following as an exercise: $P \parallel Q = \emptyset$, and, as we already discussed, $P_\alpha \parallel Q_\alpha = P_\alpha$. Now we compute $P {}_{(\alpha\|\alpha)} Q$. From (16) we get that, using obvious notations, (σ_P, σ_Q) is a pair of behaviours that are unifiable modulo desynchronization, i.e., $\sigma_P {}_\alpha\bowtie_\alpha \sigma_Q$. Then, unifying these yields the behaviour σ such that:

$$\forall n \in \mathbf{N} : \sigma(b)(n) = ((n, n), v_b) \text{ and } \sigma(x)(n) = ((2n - 1, 2n), 1) \tag{20}$$

where $v_b = t$ if n is odd, and $v_b = f$ if n is even. In (20), the expression for $\sigma(b)(n)$ reveals that desynchronizing causes no distortion of logical time for b, since (n, n) attaches the same tag to the two behaviours for unification. On the other hand, the expression for $\sigma(x)(n)$ reveals that desynchronizing actually causes distortion of logical time for x, since $(2n - 1, 2n)$ attaches different tags to the two behaviours for unification. Thus $P \parallel Q = \emptyset$, but $P {}_{(\alpha\|\alpha)} Q$ consists of the single behaviour defined in (20). Hence, $P {}_{(\alpha\|\alpha)} Q \not\equiv P \parallel Q$ in this case: semantics is not preserved. $\diamond$

3.2   A General Result on Correct Deployment

Here we analyse requirement (19). The following theorem holds (see (13) for the notation P_ρ used in this theorem):

Theorem 1. *The pair (P_1, P_2) satisfies condition (19) if it satisfies the following two conditions:*

$$\forall i \in \{1, 2\} : (P_i)_\rho \text{ is in bijection with } P_i \tag{21}$$

$$(P_1 \parallel P_2)_\rho = (P_1)_\rho \parallel (P_2)_\rho \tag{22}$$

Comments. The primary application of this general theorem is when P and Q are synchronous systems, and $\rho = \alpha$ is the desynchronization morphism. This formalizes GALS deployment. Thus, Theorem 1 provides sufficient conditions to ensure correct GALS deployment. Conditions (21) and (22) are not effective because they involve (infinite) behaviours. In [5, 6], for GALS deployment, condition (21) was shown equivalent to some condition called *endochrony*, expressed in terms of the transition relation, not in terms of behaviours. Similarly, condition (22) was shown equivalent to some condition called *isochrony*, expressed in terms of the pair of transition relations, not in terms of pairs of sets of behaviours. Endochrony and isochrony are model checkable and synthesizable, at least for synchronous programs involving only finite data types (see [5, 6] for a precise statement of these conditions).

Proof. Inclusion $\supseteq$ in (19) always hold, meaning that every pair of behaviours unifiable in the right hand side of (19) is also unifiable in the left hand side.

Thus it remains to show that, if the two conditions of Theorem 1 hold, then inclusion $\subseteq$ in (19) does too. Now, assume (21) and (22). Pick a pair (σ_1, σ_2) of behaviours which are unifiable in $P_1 \;_{(\rho\|\rho)}\; P_2$. Then, by definition of $_{(\rho\|\rho)}$, the pair $((\sigma_1)_\rho, (\sigma_2)_\rho)$ is unifiable in $(P_1)_\rho \| (P_2)_\rho$. Next, (22) guarantees that $(\sigma_1)_\rho \sqcup (\sigma_2)_\rho$ is a behaviour of $(P_1 \| P_2)_\rho$. Hence there must exist some pair (σ_1', σ_2') unifiable in $P_1 \| P_2$, such that $(\sigma_1' \sqcup \sigma_2')_\rho = (\sigma_1)_\rho \sqcup (\sigma_2)_\rho$. Using the same argument as before, we derive that $((\sigma_1')_\rho, (\sigma_2')_\rho)$ is also unifiable with respect to its associated (asynchronous) parallel composition, and $(\sigma_1')_\rho \sqcup (\sigma_2')_\rho = (\sigma_1)_\rho \sqcup (\sigma_2)_\rho$. But $(\sigma_1')_\rho$ is the restriction of $(\sigma_1')_\rho \sqcup (\sigma_2')_\rho$ to its events labeled by variables belonging to V_1, and similarly for $(\sigma_2')_\rho$. Thus $(\sigma_i')_\rho = (\sigma_i)_\rho$ for $i = 1, 2$ follows. Finally, using (21), we know that if (σ_1', σ_2') is such that, for $i = 1, 2$: $(\sigma_i')_\rho = (\sigma_i)_\rho$, then: $\sigma_i' = \sigma_i$. Hence (σ_1, σ_2) is unifiable in $P_1 \| P_2$. $\diamond$

Corollary 1. *Let P_1 and P_2 be synchronous systems whose behaviors are equipped with some equivalence relation $\sim$, and assume that P_1 and P_2 are closed with respect to $\sim$. Then, the pair (P_1, P_2) satisfies condition (19) if it satisfies the following two conditions:*

$$\forall i \in \{1, 2\} : (P_i)_\rho \text{ is in bijection with } P_i / \sim \tag{23}$$

$$(P_1 \| P_2)_\rho = (P_1)_\rho \| (P_2)_\rho \tag{24}$$

where $P_i / \sim$ is the quotient of P_i modulo $\sim$.

Proof. Identical to the proof of Theorem 1 until the paragraph starting with "Finally". Finally, using (23), we know that if (σ_1', σ_2') is such that, for $i = 1, 2$: $(\sigma_i')_\rho = (\sigma_i)_\rho$, then: $\sigma_i' \sim \sigma_i$. Hence (σ_1, σ_2) is unifiable in $P_1 \| P_2$, since all synchronous systems we consider are closed under $\sim$. $\diamond$

This result is of particular interest when $\sim$ is the equivalence modulo stuttering, defined in [7].

Running Example, Cont'd. Since P and Q possess a single behaviour, they clearly satisfy condition (21). However, the alternative condition (22) is violated: the left hand side is empty, while the right hand side is not. This explains why semantics is not preserved by desynchronization, for this example. In fact, it can be shown that the pair (P, Q) is not isochronous in the sense of [5, 6].

More Examples and Counter-Examples. Our running example was a counter-example where condition (22) is violated.

For the following counter-example, condition (21) is violated: P emits to Q two signals with names x and y. Signal y is emitted by P if and only if $x > 0$ (assuming, say, x integer). Signals x and y are awaited by Q. Formally:

$$P : \begin{cases} \sigma(x)(n) = (n, -) \\ \sigma(y)(n) = (m(n), -), \text{ where} \\ \quad m(n) = \min\{m \mid m > m(n-1) \wedge \sigma(x)(m) > 0\} \end{cases} \tag{25}$$

$$Q : \begin{cases} \sigma(x)(n) = (k(n), -) \\ \sigma(y)(n) = (l(n), -) \end{cases}$$

In (25), symbol $-$ denotes an arbitrary value in the domain D, and $k(.), l(.)$ are arbitrary strictly increasing maps, from $\mathbf{N}$ to $\mathbf{N}$. As the reader can check, P satisfies (21) but Q does not. The desynchronization α is not semantics preserving for this pair (P, Q).

Now, consider the following modification of (P, Q): P' emits to Q' two signals with names x and y. Signal y is emitted by P' if and only if $x > 0$ (assuming, say, x integer). In addition, P' emits a boolean guard b simultaneously with x, and b takes the value $true$ iff $x > 0$. Signals x and y are awaited by Q'. In addition, Q' awaits the boolean guard b simultaneously with x, and Q' knows that he should receive y simultaneously with the $true$ occurrences of b. Formally:

$$
P' : \begin{cases} \sigma(x)(n) = (n, -) \\ \sigma(b)(n) = \text{if } \sigma(x)(n)(n) > 0 \text{ then } (n, t) \text{ else } (n, f) \\ \sigma(y)(n) = (m(n), -), \text{ where} \\ \quad m(n) = \min\{m \mid m > m(n-1) \wedge \sigma(x)(m) > 0\} \end{cases}
$$

$$(26)$$

$$
Q' : \begin{cases} \sigma(x)(n) = (k(n), -) \\ \sigma(b)(n) = (k(n), -) \\ \sigma(y)(n) = (l(n), -), \text{ where} \\ \quad l(n) = \min\{k(m) \mid k(m) > l(n-1) \wedge \sigma(b)(m) = t\} \end{cases}
$$

The guard b explicitly says when y must be awaited by Q', this guarantees that Q' satisfies (21) (and so does P'). On the other hand, the pair (P', Q') satisfies (22). Thus the modified pair (P', Q') is semantics preserving, for desynchronization. The modification, from (P, Q) to (P', Q'), has been by adding the explicit guard b. This can be made systematic, as outlined in [6].

4   Discussion and Perspectives

In [11] the following result was proved. For P and Q two synchronous systems such that both P, Q, and $P \| Q$ are functional, clock-consistent, and with loop-free combinational part, then $P \| Q$ can be seen as a Kahn network—for our purpose, just interpret Kahn networks as functional asynchronous systems. This result applies to functional systems with inputs and outputs, it gives no help for partial designs or abstractions. Our conditions of endochrony and isochrony allows us to deal even with partial designs, not only with executable programs. Hence, they do represent effective techniques that can be used as part of the formal foundation for a successive-refinement design methodology.

As said before, this paper extends the ideas of [21] on desynchronization. A more naive "token-based" argument to explain GALS deployment is also found in [8], Sect. V.B. This argument is closely related to the use of Marked Graphs in [12] to justify GALS desynchronization in hardware.

Another example can be found in theory of latency-insensitive design [10]: here, if $P \| Q$ is a specification of a synchronous system and P and Q are *stallable* processes, then it is always possible to automatically derive two corresponding *patient* processes P_p and Q_p that seamlessly compose to give a system implementation $P_p \parallel Q_p$ that preserves semantics while being also robust to arbitrary, but discrete, latency variations between P and Q. Again, $P_p \parallel Q_p$ is a correct deterministic executable system made of endochronous sub-systems. In fact, as the notion of stallable system and patient system correspond respectively to the notion of stuttering-invariant system and endochronous system, Corollary 1 subsumes the result presented in [10] on the compositionality of latency-insensitivity among patient processes.

Now, the remaining key challenge is to make the theory of this paper effective. In this respect, Theorem 1 and its corollary are not enough, since they involve (infinite) behaviours. What is needed is sort of a counterpart of "automata" for our Tagged Systems. Synchronous Transition Systems as used in [6] are an example. Order automata are another example, that can be associated to Tagged Systems with causality relations. How to define such machines for general Tagged Systems is our next objective. Then, having this at hand, we will have to properly extend the "endochrony" and "isochrony" results of [6], thus providing effective algorithms to generate adaptors that ensure correct-by-construction deployment for general Tagged Systems.

References

1. R. Alur, T. Dang, J. Esposito, Y. Hur, F. Ivancic, V. Kumar, I. Lee, P. Mishra, G. J. Pappas and O. Sokolsky. Hierarchical Modeling and Analysis of Embedded Systems. *Proc. of the IEEE,* 91(1), 11–28, Jan. 2003.
2. R. Alur and D. L. Dill. A Theory of Timed Automata. *Theor. Comp. Science,* 126(2), 183–235, Apr. 1994.
3. ARTIST Network of Excellence. Roadmap on Hard Real-Time Development Environments. Available in may 2003 from url http://www.systemes-critiques.org/ARTIST/.
4. A. Benveniste. Some synchronization issues when designing embedded systems from components. In *Proc. of 1st Int. Workshop on Embedded Software, EMSOFT'01,* T.A. Henzinger and C.M. Kirsch Eds., LNCS 2211, 32–49, Springer.
5. A. Benveniste, B. Caillaud, and P. Le Guernic. From synchrony to asynchrony. In J.C.M. Baeten and S. Mauw, Eds., *CONCUR'99, Concurrency Theory, 10th Intl. Conference,* LNCS 1664, pages 162–177. Springer, Aug. 1999.
6. A. Benveniste, B. Caillaud, and P. Le Guernic. Compositionality in dataflow synchronous languages: specification & distributed code generation. *Information and Computation,* 163, 125-171 (2000).
7. A. Benveniste, L. P. Carloni, P. Caspi, and A. L. Sangiovanni-Vincentelli. Heterogeneous reactive systems modeling and correct-by-construction deployment. In R. Alur and I. Lee, Eds., *Proc. of the Third Intl. Conf. on Embedded Software, EMSOFT 2003,* LNCS 2855, Springer, 2003.
8. A. Benveniste, P. Caspi, S. Edwards, N. Halbwachs, P. Le Guernic, and R. de Simone. The Synchronous Language Twelve Years Later. *Proc. of the IEEE,* 91(1):64–83, January 2003.
9. G. Berry. The Foundations of Esterel. MIT Press, 2000.

10. L. P. Carloni, K. L. McMillan, and A. L. Sangiovanni-Vincentelli. Theory of Latency-Insensitive Design. *IEEE Transactions on Computer-Aided Design of Integrated Circuits and Systems*, 20(9):1059–1076, September 2001.

11. P. Caspi, "Clocks in Dataflow languages", *Theor. Comp. Science*, 94:125–140, 1992.

12. J. Cortadella, A. Kondratyev, L. Lavagno, and C. Sotiriou. A concurrent model for de-synchronization. In *Proc. Intl. Workshop on Logic Synthesis*, May 2003.

13. J. Eker, J.W. Janneck, E.A. Lee, J. Liu, J. Ludwig, S. Neuendorffer, S. Sachs, and Y. Xiong. Taming heterogeneity—The Ptolemy approach. *Proc. of the IEEE*, 91(1), 127–144, Jan. 2003.

14. L. de Alfaro and T.A. Henzinger. Interface Theories for Component-Based Design. In *Proc. of 1st Int. Workshop on Embedded Software, EMSOFT'01*, T.A. Henzinger and C.M. Kirsch Eds., LNCS 2211, 32–49, Springer, 2001.

15. E.A. Lee and Y. Xiong. System-Level Types for Component-Based Design. In *Proc. of 1st Int. Workshop on Embedded Software, EMSOFT'01*, T.A. Henzinger and C.M. Kirsch Eds., LNCS 2211, 32–49, Springer, 2001.

16. G. Karsai, J. Sztipanovits, A. Ledeczi, and T. Bapty. Model-Integrated Development of Embedded Software. *Proc. of the IEEE*, 91(1), 127–144, Jan. 2003.

17. N. Halbwachs, P. Caspi, P. Raymond, and D. Pilaud. The Synchronous Data Flow Programming Language LUSTRE. *Proc. of the IEEE*, 79(9):1305–1320, Sep. 1991.

18. D. Harel. Statecharts: A visual formalism for complex systems. *Science of Computer Programming*, 8(3):231–274, June 1987.

19. H. Kopetz, Real-Time Systems: Design Principles for Distributed Embedded Applications. Kluwer Academic Publishers. 1997. ISBN 0-7923-9894-7.

20. P. Le Guernic, T. Gautier, M. Le Borgne, and C. Le Maire. Programming real-time applications with SIGNAL. *Proc. of the IEEE*, 79(9):1326–1333, Sep. 1991.

21. P. Le Guernic, J.-P. Talpin, J.-C. Le Lann, Polychrony for system design. *Journal for Circuits, Systems and Computers*. World Scientific, April 2003.

22. E.A. Lee and A. Sangiovanni-Vincentelli. A Framework for Comparing Models of Computation. *IEEE Trans. on Computer-Aided Design of Integrated Circuits and Systems*, 17(12), 1217–1229, Dec. 1998.

23. M. Mokhtari and M. Marie. Engineering Applications of MATLAB 5.3 and SIMULINK 3. Springer, 2000.

Machine Function Based Control Code Algebras

Jan A. Bergstra[1,2]

[1] University of Amsterdam, Programming Research Group
janb@science.uva.nl
[2] Utrecht University, Department of Philosophy, Applied Logic Group
janb@phil.uu.nl

Abstract. Machine functions have been introduced by Earley and Sturgis in [6] in order to provide a mathematical foundation of the use of the T-diagrams proposed by Bratman in [5]. Machine functions describe the operation of a machine at a very abstract level. A theory of hardware and software based on machine functions may be called a machine function theory, or alternatively when focusing on inputs and outputs for machine functions a control code algebra (CCA). In this paper we develop some control code algebras from first principles. Machine function types are designed specifically for various application such as program compilation, assembly, interpretation, managed interpretation and just-in-time compilation. Machine function dependent CCA's are used to formalize the well-known compiler fixed point, the managed execution of JIT compiled text and the concept of a verifying compiler.

1 Introduction

Machine models can be given at a very high level of abstraction by using so-called machine functions, a concept due to [6] as a basis. Machine functions are hypothetical functions, which may be classified by machine function types. Machine function types provide information about the expected inputs and outputs, or more general the behavior of a machine. Machine functions are named elements of machine function types. Machine functions are used as the primitive operators of a control code algebra. Machine functions may be viewed as black box containers of behavior. It is not expected that machine functions are actually either formally specified or algorithmically given in any detail. Important, however is the realization that different machine architectures may use different machine functions as realizations of the same machine function type. A number of issues is can be clarified using machine functions only: the so-called compiler fixed point, the distinction between compilation and interpretation, the role of intermediate code, managed execution and JIT compilation, and finally verifying compilation.

1.1 Motivation

The identification of machine function types and the description of machine models as composed from named but otherwise unspecified machine functions may be helpful for the following reasons:

F.S. de Boer et al. (Eds.): FMCO 2003, LNCS 3188, pp. 17–41, 2004.

- A multitude of different machine models and instantiations thereof can be described in some formal detail while at the same time ignoring the massive complexities of processor architecture and program execution.
- Machine function theory can be used to obtain logically complete machine models. A machine model is logically complete if all of its concepts are explained in internal technical terms in a bottom up fashion, permitting a reader to understand the model and stories about it without the use of subject related external knowledge and without understanding in advance the whole story of modern computer architecture.
- By giving names to machine functions simple calculations are made possible which may produce insights unavailable otherwise. In addition system specifications can be given in terms of combinations of requirements on a family of named machine functions. Machine function theory is a very elementary axiomatic theory of machine behavior, not claiming that the essential properties of machine functions are captured by axioms. The more limited claim, however, is that the role that machine functions play in a larger architectural framework can be analyzed in some useful detail.
- Pseudo-empirical semantics explains the meaning of codes and concepts regarding codes by means of hypothetical experiments with the relevant machine functions. The phrase 'the meaning of a code is given via its compiler' belongs to the dogma's of pseudo-empirical semantics. Pseudo-empirical semantics provides definitions close to what computer users without a background in formal semantics may have in mind when working with machines.

1.2   Control Code Algebras

Each machine function gives rise to an algebra with codes as its domain. Codes are represented as finite sequences of bits. The codes play the role of input data and output data as well as of control codes. As the main focus of the use of machine functions is in analyzing semantic generalities of control codes at a very abstract level these algebras will be referred to as control code algebras (CCA's).[1] Control code algebra (CCA) is the meta theory of the control code algebras. It might just as well be called machine function theory.

1.3   Scope of CCA

The simplest CCA may be viewed as another form of theory of T-diagrams from [5], and implicitly present in [7], which has been further developed in [6]. Similar work appeared in [1]. Clearly the limits of CCA are reached when modeling a phenomenon requires significant information concerning the details of machine code execution at the lowest level of abstraction. An extreme view might be that each insight in computer software processing which is independent of the details

---

[1] The acronym CCA is a mere abbreviation, having well over a million hits on Google and in no way specific. Its expansion 'Control Code Algebra' generates no single hit, however, at the time of this writing.

of code may lie within the scope of CCA. Here are some interesting issues for which that is unclear:

- Can the phenomenon of computer viruses can be modeled at the level of CCA. Many computer users are supposed to use their computers in such a way that infections are prevented, while no plausible argument can be given that these users must understand the details of how a machine works. The question may therefore be rephrased as follows: can an explanation via an appropriate CCA be given of what machine users must do in order to prevent virus infections of their systems. And, moreover can it be formulated what requirements systems must satisfy if these prescriptions for user behavior are to guarantee that systems remain clear of infections.
- Another question that may be answered at the level of an appropriate CCA is what an operating system is. Textbooks on operating systems never introduce the concept of an operating system as a concept that merits a definition in advance. Substantial questions concerning what minimum might be called an OS and whether or not an OS is a computer program or a control code are impossible to answer without proper definitions, however.
- A third question which may or may not lie within the scope of CCA is the question as to what constitutes a software component. By its nature the concept of a software component abstracts from the details of computation. But a first attempt to define software components in the framework of CCA reveals that some non-algorithmic knowledge about software component internals may be essential and outside the scope of CCA at the same time.

2   External Functionality Machine Functions

A way to capture the behavior of a machine is to assume that it has a simple input output behavior, taking an number of bit sequences as its an put and producing similar outputs. Taking multiple inputs into account is a significant notational overhead but it will be indispensable for instance when discussing the notion of an interpreter (for the case of multiple inputs) whereas multiple outputs arise with a compiler that may produce a list of warnings in addition to its compilation result. A list (with length $k > 0$) of bit sequences (codes) is taken as an input and the result takes the form of one or more bit sequences. If f is the name of a machine function and n is a natural number then f_n names the mapping that yields the n-th result. The result of f on an input list $\boldsymbol{y}$ may be undefined (M, for meaningless) or divergent (D). In case of divergence none of the outputs gets computed, in the case of convergence from some index onwards all outputs are M, indicating that it has not been provided. The following axioms are imposed:

$$\forall n, m \ (f_n(\boldsymbol{y}) = D \rightarrow f_m(\boldsymbol{y}) = D)$$

$$\forall n, m \ (f_n(\boldsymbol{y}) = M \ \& \ m > n \rightarrow f_m(\boldsymbol{y}) = M)$$

$$\forall n \ (f_n(\boldsymbol{y}) \neq D \rightarrow \exists m > n \ f_m(\boldsymbol{y}) = M)$$

$$\forall n \, (f_n(\boldsymbol{y} \frown \boldsymbol{z}) = M \rightarrow f_m(\boldsymbol{y}) = M)$$

$$\forall n \, (f_n(\boldsymbol{y}) = D \rightarrow f_m(\boldsymbol{y} \frown \boldsymbol{z}) = D)$$

These rules express that

- The sequence of outputs is computed in a single computation. A divergence implies that no bit sequences can be produced, whereas an error (M) only indicates that a certain output is not produced. Only finitely many outputs bit sequences are produced, and beyond that number an error occurs.
- There is one algorithm doing the computation accessing more arguments when needed. When arguments are lacking an error (M) will occur, rather than D. Providing more inputs ($\boldsymbol{y} \frown \boldsymbol{z}$ instead of $\boldsymbol{y}$) cannot cause an error (M). In other words if a computation on a list of inputs runs into an error than each computation on a shorter list must run into an error as well.
- A divergence taking place on a given sequence of inputs cannot be prevented by supplying more inputs. (This in contrast with an error which may result from a lack of inputs.)

2.1   External Functionality

A machine function produces external functionality if the transformations it achieves are directly contributing to what users intend to do. A typical example may be a formatting/typesetting functionality. Often user commands directly invoke the operation of an external functionality.

External functionality machine functions describe external functionalities. Their operation can (but need not) be exclusively under the control of manually entered user commands. Here is a somewhat artificial example involving a compiler and a cross-assembler producing executable code for another machine. Because the produced code must be moved elsewhere before use, its machine may be regarded external functionality.

Using Bit Sequence Machine Functions, an Example. One may imagine a machine P powered by the, bit sequence machine function Fc, requiring one input and producing three outputs for each input, and the bit sequence machine function Fd also requiring a single input and producing 2 outputs in all cases. The inputs are taken from a stack, the first input from the top and so on, while the outputs are placed on the stack in reversed order, after removing the inputs.

For instance Fc takes a program in and compiles it in the context of a list of programs (encoded in the second argument), producing the output code, a listing with error messages and warnings and an assembled version of the compiled code. Fd applies a disassembler to its first argument producing the result as well as a listing of errors and/or warnings.

A manual operation of the system is assumed with the following instructions: `s.load:`f, pushing file f on the stack and `s.store:`g, placing the top of the stack in file g while subsequently popping the stack. Here `s` stands for the machine command interface able to accept and process manual user commands. `s.Fc` is the command that invokes the operation of the first of the two machine functions and produces three output sequences that are placed on top of the stack. `s.Fd` is the command for the second one, which places two results on the top of the stack consecutively. How such commands are entered is left unspecified in the model at hand.

Consider the command sequence

$$CS = \texttt{s.load:f;s.Fc;s.store:g;s.pop;}$$
$$\texttt{s.pop;s.load:g;s.Fd;s.store:h;s.pop}$$

If the content of `f` before operation is x then after performing CS the content of `h` is $Fd_1(Fc_1(x))$. This output is probably empty if either one of the two commands lead to error messages, whereas if the error message output is empty on may assume that the other outputs are 'correct'. It also follows from this model that the operation of the system is deterministic for command sequences of this kind. Several potentially relevant system properties may now be formulated:

Code is produced unless errors are found $Fc_2(x) = [\,] \rightarrow Fc_1(x) \neq [\,]$
Disassembly succeeds unless errors are found $Fd_2(x) = [\,] \rightarrow F_1(x) \neq [\,]$
Disassembly inverts of assembly $Fc_2(x) = [\,] \rightarrow Fd_1(Fc_3(x)) = Fc_1(x)$

The use of machine functions in the examples mentioned above is in making these requirement descriptions more readable than it would be possible without them. With these few primitives there appears to be no significant reasoning involving calculation, however.

Non-programmable Machines. If a machine is given by means of a finite list of machine functions one may imagine its user to be able to enter inputs, select a function to be applied and to retrieve outputs thereafter. We will not provide syntax or notation for the description of these activities. As it stands a non-programmable machine may be given in terms of finite listing of machine functions. As the number of machine functions of a machine increases it becomes increasingly useful to represent machine functions as codes and to use a single universal machine function from which the other machine functions are derived. In this way a control code dependent machine emerges. This universal machine function is used to bring other codes into expression. Therefore the phrase code expression machine functions will be used rather than the term universal machine function, which is somewhat unclear regarding to the scope of its universality.

3   Code Expression Machine Functions

It is now assumed that the first argument of a machine function consists of a bit sequence which is viewed as control code for a machine. Through the application of the machine function the control code finds its expression. Formally there is no difference with the case of an external functionality machine function. But the idea is that without a useful control code (i.e. a first argument for the machine function) no significant external functionality may be observed. It is a reasonable assumption for a simplest model that a machine which can be controlled via exchangeable data must be controlled that way. At this stage the important question what makes a bit sequence a control code (rather than just its place in the argument listing of a machine function) is left for later discussion.

For code expression machine functions another notation is introduced which separates the first and other arguments. A notation for the n'th result of a code expression function taking k arguments (except the code argument x) is as follows:

$$x \bullet \bullet^n y_1, .., y_k$$

By default the first argument is meant of no superscript is given:

$$x \bullet \bullet y_1, .., y_k = x \bullet \bullet^1 y_1, .., y_k$$

If the name f is given this can be made explicit with $x \bullet \bullet^n_f y_1, .., y_k$. The semantics of a control code x w.r.t. a machine function is the family of all machine functions taking x fixed, denoted $|x|_{\bullet\bullet}$. Thus semantic equivalence for control codes reads

$$x \equiv_{beh} z \leftrightarrow |x|_{\bullet\bullet} = |z|_{\bullet\bullet} \leftrightarrow \forall n, k, y_1, .., y_k (x \bullet \bullet^n y_1, .., y_k = z \bullet \bullet^n y_1, .., y_k).$$

With an explicit name of the machine function this reads:

$$x \equiv_{beh} z \leftrightarrow |x|_{\bullet\bullet_f} = |z|_{\bullet\bullet_f} \leftrightarrow \forall n, k, y_1, .., y_k (x \bullet \bullet^n_f y_1, .., y_k = z \bullet \bullet^n_f y_1, .., y_k).$$

Bit sequence generating machine functions are less useful when it comes to the description of interactive systems. But code expression machine functions are very simple as a concept and they can be used until a lack of expressive power or flexibility forces one to move to a different model.[2]

3.1   Split Control Code Machine Models

A code expression machine function $- \bullet \bullet_f -$ determines all by itself a machine model. For an execution, which takes a single step, a triple of the code and a sequence of inputs and the machine function are needed. This may be formalized as $m_f(x, \boldsymbol{y})$. The code is not integrated in the machine in any way. Thus it is

---

[2] The discussion may be made more general by using a terminology consistent with the possibility that a machine function produces an interactive behavior (i.e. a process). A bit sequence generating machine function is just a very simple example of a behavior. If the behavior of a machine is described in terms of a polarized process its working may be determined through a function that produces a rational polarized behavior over a given collection A of basic actions from the codes that have been placed in the machine as an input or as a control code. The reason to consider a mapping function, say $F_M : BS \times BS \times BS \rightarrow BPPA(A)$, as the description of a machine if a control code dependent machine is to be compared with a programmable machine. BPPA is the algebra of basic polarized process from [2]. As will become clear below polarized processes are well-suited for the specification of programs and programmed machine behavior. In the case such a machine needs to be viewed as a control code dependent machine a polarized process machine function results.

implausible to speak of a stored code. For that reason the model is classified as a split control code machine model. This is in contrast with a stored code machine model for which it is required that code storage is achieved by means of the same mechanisms as any storage during computation. As nothing is known about these mechanisms due to the abstract nature of machine functions, being no more than formal inhabitants of their types, the model cannot be classified as a stored control model.

Having available the notion of a split control code machine, it is possible to characterize when a code is an executable for it: x is an *executable* for $\bullet\bullet_f$ if for some y, $x \bullet \bullet_f y \neq M$. Because this criterion depends on an application of the code in an execution it is a dynamic criterion. In practice that may be useless and entirely undecidable. For that reason a subset (or predicate) E_c of the executables may be put forward as the collection of 'certified' executables. Here it is understood that certification can be checked efficiently. A pair $(\bullet\bullet_f, E_c)$ is a split control machine with certified executables.

It is always more or less taken for granted that modern computer programming is based on the so-called stored program computer model. In the opinion of the author a bottom up development of the concept of a program starts with a split program machine model, however, the register machine constituting a prime example of a split program machine model. Having available a split program machine model one may then carry on to develop stored program machine models. The usual objection against this argument is that a Turing machine ([9]) constitutes a stored program machine model already. That, however, is debatable because it is not clear which part of the tape content or state space of a Turing might be called a program on compelling grounds. Usually some intuition from an implicit split machine model is used to provide the suggestion that a part of the tape contains a program in encoded form. That, however, fails to be a compelling argument for it being a program.

3.2   Two Conceptual Issues on Split Code Machine Models

The split control code machine model aims at providing a very simple account of control code dependent machines while ignoring the aspect of the control code being either a program or being cast in software. There are two philosophical issues that immediately emerge from the introduction of the concept of a split control code machine.

The Control Code Identification Problem. An explanation is needed for why the first code argument is said to contain the control code. It seems to be a rather arbitrary choice to declare the first argument the control code argument rather than for instance the second argument. This is the control code identification problem for an external machine function. The question is about the machine function and irrespective of any of its actual arguments. So the problem is: determine, given a code expression machine function, which of its argument contains the control code if any.

Below in 5.2 we will see that the situation is not symmetric indeed and sound reasons may exist for taking one code argument to play the role of containing the control code rather than another argument.[3]

The Program Recognition Problem. An obvious question raised by the split control code machine model is this: under which circumstances is it appropriate to view an executable control code as a program? This is the program recognition problem. It presumes that the control code identification has successfully led to the classification of an argument position as the (unique) position for control code. This question is important for an appreciation of the distinction between control code an programs. This question can be answered first by means of the hypothetical program explanation principle which has been proposed in [3].

4   Split Program Machine Models

Complementary to split control code machine models there are split program machine models. For the development of CCA it is in fact immaterial how the concept of a program is defined. What matters is that for some code to be called a program some definition of what it is to be a program is needed. Let some theory of programming be given which provides one with a reliable definition of the concept of a program.

A split code machine model (i.e. a code expression machine function) qualifies as a split program machine model if there is for each code a mapping to an acknowledged program notation (which may be hypothetical) for a (hypothetical) machine model such that the machine function describes the behavior of the (hypothetical) machine as programmed by a code (viewed as a program). Thus each code may be read as a program for a machine with a well-understood operational meaning which produces results that happen to coincide with those of the given machine function. In other words the code expression machine function is an abstraction of a split program machine model.

As a notation for a split program machine model with name f we take

$$x \bullet \bullet^n_{\mathrm{spm}-f} y_1, .., y_k$$

The semantics of a program u in a split program machine model is derived in a completely similar style to the split control code case with notation $|u|_{\bullet\bullet_{\mathrm{spm}-f}}$.

A split program machine model will also called an analytical architecture because it focuses on the analysis and explanation of behavior, whereas a split control code machine model may be called a synthetic architecture because it focuses on the components from which the machine is physically synthesized, without any commitment to the explanation of behavior.

---

[3] When investigating stored control code machines or stored program machines this question reappears in the following form: which memory compartment contains control code or program code?

4.1   Hypothetical Architectures and Program Recognition

For this section it will be assumed that a split program machine is like a split control code machine with the additional information that the control code constitutes a program irrespective of the definition of a program that has been used. Further it is assumed that the behavior for a split program machine can be found in such a way that the program helps to understand the code expression machine function (or process machine) function at hand. That is to say, the split program machine is considered more easily understood or explained because its program and the working of that program is known and it is also known how the program is transformed into the produced behavior by means of interaction with other relevant parts of the machine.

A control code is just data without any indication that it has the logical structure of a program.

Having available the concept of a split control code machine model one may then investigate under which conditions a split control code may appropriately be called a control code and even a program. This is the program recognition that was problem mentioned above.

The Program Recognition Problem: An Informal Solution. A code is a program if it can be viewed as the product of some computable transformation translating (machine) programs for some conceivable programmable architecture to code for a split code machine. This state of affairs indicates that the reasons for classifying code as a program lie in the possibility of reverse engineering, or rather disassembling, the code into a program for some programmable machine, which may serve as an explanation for the given code.

The Program Recognition Problem: A Formalized Solution. Given the split control code machine $\bullet\bullet_f$ and a collection R of relevant functionalities for $\bullet\bullet_f$, a control code x is a program if there exists a split program machine model[4] $\bullet\bullet_{\mathrm{spm}-g}$ and a computable code generation mapping[5] ψ_{g2f} from programs for $\bullet\bullet_{\mathrm{spm}-g}$ to codes for $\bullet\bullet_f$ such that

- *Hypothetical program existence:* x is in the range of ψ (e.g. for some z, $x = \psi_{\mathrm{g2f}}(z)$),
- *Hypothetical assembler soundness:* for all programs u (for $\bullet\bullet_{\mathrm{spm}-g}$) $|\psi_{\mathrm{g2f}}(u)|_{\bullet\bullet_{\mathrm{spm}-f}} = |u|_{\bullet\bullet_g}$, and:
- *Functional assembler completeness:* for all control codes x for $\bullet\bullet_f$: if the behavior $|u|_{\bullet\bullet_f}$ belongs to the collection R, which covers the relevant functionalities for which the machine model has been designed, then either
  - u has a disassembled version (z with $\psi_{\mathrm{g2f}}(z) = x$)) (which qualifies as a program for the split program model architecture providing the same functionality), or otherwise,

---

[4] The hypothetical programmed machine architecture.

[5] Also called assembler mapping, the inverse being an assembly projection.

- there is a program z such that $|z|_{\bullet\bullet_{\mathrm{spm}-g}} = |x|_{\bullet\bullet_f}$ and consequently $|\psi_{\mathrm{g2f}}(z)|_{\bullet\bullet_f} = |x|_{\bullet\bullet_f}$.

This last condition guarantees that the split program machine has not been concocted specifically to turn the particular control code x into a program (according to our proposed definition) but instead that this hypothetical machine provides an explanation of the full operational range of $\bullet\bullet_f$ by providing a program for each relevant behavior.

4.2   Control Code Need Not Originate Through Programming

One may wonder whether split control code is in all cases a transformation product of programs. If that were true the conceptual distinction between programs and code is marginal, a matter of phase in the software life-cycle only, and as a consequence the concept of control code is only seemingly independent of that of a program. We give two examples of control code that fails to qualify as a program. The conclusion is drawn that there are (at least) two entirely different strategies for computer software engineering, only one of which involves programming. Machine functions provides an abstraction level that both strategies have in common.

Two Examples of Non-programmed Control Code. A counterexample to the hypothesis that all control code originates as the result of program production may be as follows: one imagines a neural network in hardware form, able to learn while working on a problem thereby defining parameter values for many firing thresholds for artificial neurons. Then the parameter values are downloaded to a file. Such a file can be independently loaded on a machine, depending on the particular problem it needs to address. These problem dependent parameter files can be considered control code by all means. In all likelihood they are not programs in any sense supported by our theory of programming, however. The particular property of neural networks is their ability to acquire control code along another path than human based computer programming.

Another example of control code which may rather not be understood as a program is the geographical information downloaded in a purely hardware made robot together with a target location it is supposed to find. The robot will apply its fixed processing method to these data, but the data determine the behavior of the robot. The loaded data constitute control code (this follows from the absence of other software in the robot). But programming (compliant with the assumed theory of computer programming) has played no role in the construction of this control code.

In both mentioned examples of control code which is not the result of program transformation artificial intelligence plays a role. In the case of the neural network the learning process itself is an example of artificial intelligence, whereas in the case of the robot the processing performed by the robot must involve significant AI applications. In the robot case the preparation of control code is similar to the briefing a human being might get when confronted with the same task.

Two Software Engineering Strategies. Machine learning may altogether be understood as an alternative form of control code production, contrasting with the currently more usual control code development starting with computer programming and followed by compilation and assembly phases.

Examples of non-programming based software engineering outside artificial intelligence seem to be hard to find. Both examples above embody different aspects of artificial intelligence based software engineering: control code construction by means of artificial intelligence and control code construction for an artificially intelligent system play a role in non-programming based software engineering. Therefore software engineering is in terms of software construction techniques covered strictly larger than computer programming, as it also covers these AI based techniques.

A Third Option: Genetic Control Code Evolution. A third option for software engineering that may avoid programming as well as neural network training lies in the application of genetic algorithms. This involves a number of operators for constructing new control codes from (pairs of) known ones. Then by randomly applying these operations on some initial codes and by filtering out codes that are bad solutions for the software engineering problem at hand an evolutionary process may produce adequate solutions.

5   The Code Identification Problem

The essential simplification of split control code in comparison to split programs lies in the decision to view code as binary data without any need to explain why these data play the role of programs or may be best understood as programs. This, however, leaves open the question as to why a certain code is classified as a control code.

5.1   Splitting Control Code from Inputs

Given a split control code machine, one may take its first argument as just one of the arguments, thus obtaining a code expression machine function. Looking at the split control code machine from this level of abstraction, a question similar to the program recognition problem appears: why has the first of the arguments been split of to play the role of the control code. The notion of *overruling* is now proposed to deal with this issue.

Symmetry Prevents Control Code Identification. It is useful to experiment for a while with one simple design for the split control code machine, by assuming that there is just a single input. In particular consider the split control code machine $\bullet\bullet_f$. By forgetting the control code role of the first argument a control code independent machine is found (say S_f) and its behavior is given by $S_f(x, y) = x \bullet \bullet_f y$ The only possible justification for making the first argument play the role of a control code and the second code argument the role of an input code must lie in properties of the code expression machine function S_f.

Indeed suppose, hypothetically that for all x and y, $S_f(x,y) = S_f(y,x)$. Then the symmetry is complete and a justification for putting the first argument of S_f in the role of control code and the other argument in the role of input data cannot be found.

A justification for putting the first argument in the control code role can only be found if the code expression machine function is asymmetric and if, moreover, the first code argument (x) can be said to be 'more in control' than the second one (y) or any other argument. The control code identification problem will now be simplified to the case that the code expression machine function has exactly two inputs. The task is to select the control code input, if that can be done. Here are three informal criteria that may be applied to argue that indeed, the first argument has the role of a control code:

Overruling Argument Positions. For a two place function $F : BS \times BS \to BS \cup \{D, M\}$ the first argument overrules the second if there can be found different sequences e.g. $O_1 = "0"$ and $O_2 = "1"$ and codes x_1 and x_2 such that for all code arguments y, $F(x_1, y) = O_1$ and $F(x_2, y) = O_2$.

If the first argument overrules the second, the second one cannot overrule the first argument at the same time. Indeed suppose that $O_3 \neq O_4$ and that y_3 and y_4 are found such that for all x, $F(x, y_3) = O_3$ and $F(x, y_4) = O_4$. Then it follows that $O_3 = F(x_1, y_3) = O_1 = F(x_1, y_4) = O_4$, which contradicts the assumptions.

5.2   Control Code Overrules Non-control Code

Consider $S_f(x, Y)$, then the first argument is said to be at the control code position (for S_f) if the first argument overrules the second argument. If this condition is met that condition solves the control code identification problem and justifies the notation $x \bullet \bullet_f y = S_f(x, y)$.

The criterion of overruling becomes more interesting if there are more than two code arguments needed to have a successful (not yielding M) computation of the split control code function. Below the concept of a split interpreter control machine model will be outlined. In the case of split interpreter control two argument positions have great influence on machine operation: the control code position where the interpreter control code is located and the position where the code to be interpreted is located. In this setting the first position overrules the second position and the second position overrules the third position. But the dependence of behavior from the second argument is more flexible than for the first argument.

6   Control Code Assembly Notations

In the sequel the assumption is made that for the class of split control code machines of interest all control codes are actually transformed programs in the sense of 4.1. This assumption justifies the jargon used.

6.1   Executables

Given a split control code machine the control codes may as well be called executables. This phrase is often used if control codes are transformed programs. It is common to make a distinction, however, between arbitrary control codes and executable control codes, or simply 'executables' where executables are those control codes really meant for execution on the model. Lacking any intrinsic criterion as to which codes are to be considered executable it is reasonable to assume that some collection E_c of codes comprises the executables. This collection is specific to the code expression machine function of the machine model under consideration.

6.2   Assembly and Executable

One may consider the notion of an assembly notation for a given split control code machine with certified executables E_c. An assembly code should be a useful tool for a human author in the production of control code. It allows the production of readable and meaningful texts which may be automatically transformed into control codes by means of an assembler which is given in the form of another control code. In this discussion the question who wrote the assembler and how this may have been done without the help of an appropriate design code is ignored. The simplest view is that producing the assembler in the absence of a suitable control code design notation has been an enormous amount of work that may be seen as a part of the investment of the development of a split control code machine, which is useless otherwise.

A control code assembly notation (say A) is simply viewed as a subset of the possible codes. An assembler for A is an executable control code $n{:}a2e{:}e$. Here the colon is part of the name, which thereby carries the following information: code reference n including a version number, functionality $a2e$ (from assembly to executable) and code class e (for executable). The assembler must satisfy this criterion: for each code $x{:}a \in A$, $n{:}a2e{:}e \bullet \bullet x{:}a \in E_c$. Thus, a compiler transforms each control code design into an executable.[6]

6.3   Assembling an Assembler in Assembly

An interesting thought experiment now runs as follows. Let an assembler $x1{:}a2e{:}e$ for A be given. Assume that a version of an assembler for a is made available, written in the assembly notation A represented by a itself.[7] The following name will be used for this new version of the compiler: $u{:}a2e{:}a$. The name combines a local name (u), a functionality ($a2e$) and a notation that is used (A). The new assembler cannot be used without preparatory steps. It needs to be assembled

---

[6] It is a common additional requirement that for codes outside A a non-executable output is produced together with a second output which contains a list of so-called errors allowing the control code designer to find out what is wrong.

[7] This is not implausible as the compiler is a complex piece of control code which may profit from advanced design technology.

itself by means of the existing assembler which is available in an executable form already. With that in mind first of all the correctness of this new assembler can be formalized as follows:

(1) It can be assembled successfully by means of the given assembler i.e., $x1 : a2e : e \bullet \bullet u : a2e : a \in E_c$, which permits one to write $x2 : a2e : e$ for $x1{:}a2e{:}e \bullet \bullet u{:}a2e{:}a$.
(2) $x2{:}a2e{:}e$ is a control code that transforms each a code into an executable.
(3) For all control code designs $y{:}a$ the two executable assemblers mentioned in (2) produce equivalent control executables. That is, $|x1{:}a2e{:}e \bullet \bullet y{:}a|_{\bullet\bullet} = |x2{:}a2e{:}e \bullet \bullet y{:}a|_{\bullet\bullet}$.

Assembling an Assembler Once More. Now the following well-known question can be raised: is it useful to use $x2{:}a2e{:}e$ to assemble the code $u{:}a2e{:}a$ once more? Let $x3{:}a2e{:}e = x2{:}a2e{:}e \bullet \bullet u{:}a2e{:}a$. This must be an executable because $x2{:}a2e{:}e$ is an assembler for A. Due to the assumption that $x2{:}a2e{:}e$ is a correct compiler this second new assembler must also be a correct one because it determines a semantics preserving code transformation, i.e $x3{:}a2e{:}e =_{behavior} x2{:}a2e{:}e$, or equivalently: $|x3{:}a2e{:}e|_{\bullet\bullet} = |x2{:}a2e{:}e|_{\bullet\bullet}$.

Why may it be an advantage to make this second step? The second step takes the new executable assembler (obtained after assembling with the old one) to assemble the new non-executable. A useful criterion here is code compactness, measuring the length of control codes. Now suppose that the new assembler produces much shorter code than the old one, then the second step is useful to obtain a more code compact executable for the new assembler. The executable version of the new assembler $x2{:}a2e{:}e$ has already the virtue of producing short codes but its own code may still be 'long' because it was produced by the old assembler.

The Assembler Fixed Point. The obvious next question is whether it is useful to repeat this step once more, i.e. to use $x3{:}a2e{:}e$ once more to assemble the new assembler. It is now easy to prove that this will bring no advantage, because it will produce exactly the code of $x3{:}a2e{:}e$. This is the so-called compiler fixed point phenomenon (but phrased in terms of an assembler). In more detail, let $x4{:}a2e{:}e = x3{:}a2e{:}e \bullet \bullet u{:}a2e{:}a$. Because $|x3{:}a2e{:}e|_{\bullet\bullet} = |x2{:}a2e{:}e|_{\bullet\bullet}$, which has been concluded above, $x3{:}a2e{:}e \bullet \bullet u{:}a2e{:}a = x2{:}a2e{:}e \bullet \bullet u{:}a2e{:}a = x3{:}a2e{:}e$.

This leads to the following conclusion: if a new assembler is brought in for a notation for which a assembler in an executable form is available and if the new code is written in the assembly notation itself then it is necessary to translate the new assembler with the old executable assembler first. Thereafter it may be an advantage to do this once more with the executable assembler just obtained. Repeating this step a second time is never needed. This is a non-trivial folk-lore insight in systems administration/software configuration theory. It exists exactly at the level of abstraction of machine functions.

The Assembler Application Notation. The machine function of an assembler code merits its own notation: $x{:}a \bullet \bullet_a y{:}d = (x1{:}a2e{:}e \bullet \bullet x{:}a) \bullet \bullet y{:}d$.

Using this notation the versions of the executable code that occur in the description of the fixed point are: $x3:a2e:e = u:a2e:a \bullet \bullet_a u:a2e:a$, and $x4{:}a2e{:}e = (u{:}a2e{:}a \bullet \bullet_a u{:}a2e{:}a) \bullet \bullet u{:}a2e{:}a (= x3{:}a2e{:}e \bullet \bullet u{:}a2e{:}a)$. The fixed point fact itself reads: $(u{:}a2e{:}a \bullet \bullet_a u{:}a2e{:}a) \bullet \bullet u{:}a2e{:}a = u{:}a2e{:}a \bullet \bullet_a u{:}a2e{:}a$.

Correct Assembly Code. An assembly code is correct if its image under the assembler is an executable, thus $z \in A_c$ if $x1{:}a2e{:}e \bullet \bullet z \in E_c$.[8] The correct codes depend on the available assembler codes. Improved assemblers may accept (turn into an executable) more codes, however, thereby increasing the extension of 'correct assembly codes'.

7   More Dedicated Codes

It is reasonable to postulate the availability of an executable code which allows to test the certified executability of codes. Let $a1:t4e:e$ be the application code a testing for executability (functionality $t4e$) in executable form. Then $a1{:}t4e{:}e \bullet \bullet u{:}d$ produces an empty file on input $u{:}d$ (data file u which may or may not admit the stronger typing $u{:}e$) if $u{:}d$ is a certified executable (i.e. $\in E_c$), and a non-empty result e.g. containing a listing of warnings or mistakes otherwise.

7.1   Source Level Code

A code notation for source level code S may be modeled as a collection of bit sequences. Its codes are denoted e.g. with $x{:}s$. A special notation for the application of a source level code is useful. The action of source level code on a sequence of inputs $\boldsymbol{y}$ is given by $x{:}s \bullet \bullet_s \boldsymbol{y}$. Given a compiler $u{:}s2a{:}a$ for S this can be defined by: $x{:}s \bullet \bullet_s \boldsymbol{y} = (u{:}s2a{:}a \bullet \bullet_a x{:}s) \bullet \bullet_a \boldsymbol{y}$.

It is assumed that $u{:}s2a{:}a \bullet \bullet_a x{:}s$ never produces D and that the first output is a correct assembler code provided the second result $(u{:}s2a{:}a \bullet \bullet_a^2 x{:}s)$ is the empty sequence. The correct S codes[9] are denoted with S_c.

Compiling a 'New' Compiler. Given a compiler $u1{:}s2a{:}a$ for S a new compiler $u{:}s2a{:}s$ for S written in S may be provided. Then to make this new compiler effective it should itself be compiled first and subsequently be used to compile itself. Then the compiler fixed point is found entirely similar to the case of the assembler fixed point mentioned before. The new compiler may be compiled into assembly: $u2{:}s2a{:}a = u1{:}s2a{:}a \bullet \bullet_a u{:}a2e{:}s$. It is then required that for all $y{:}s \in S_c$, $|u1{:}s2a{:}a \bullet \bullet_a y{:}s|_{\bullet\bullet_a} = |u2{:}s2a{:}a \bullet \bullet_a y{:}s|_{\bullet\bullet_a}$.

The Compiler Fixed Point. The next phases are given using source level application notation: $x{:}s \bullet \bullet_s y{:}d = (u1{:}s2a{:}a \bullet \bullet_a x{:}s) \bullet \bullet_a y{:}d$. Using this notation the versions of the assembler code that occur in the description of the fixed point are: $u3{:}s2a{:}a = u{:}s2a{:}s \bullet \bullet_s u{:}s2a{:}s$, and $x4{:}a2e{:}e = (u{:}a2e{:}a \bullet \bullet_a u{:}a2e{:}a) \bullet \bullet u{:}a2e{:}a$. The fixed point fact itself reads: $(u{:}s2a{:}s \bullet \bullet_s u{:}s2a{:}s) \bullet \bullet u{:}s2a{:}s = u{:}s2a{:}s \bullet \bullet_s u{:}s2a{:}s$.

---

[8] A_c may be called the pseudo-empirical syntax of A.
[9] Compiler based pseudo-empirical syntax of S.

7.2   Interpreted Intermediate Code

Taking three or more inputs and two outputs it becomes possible to view the first input as the control code for an interpreter, the second input as a control code to be interpreted and the third input (and further inputs) as an ordinary argument, while the first output serves as the standard output and the second output serves as error message listing when needed. In actual computer technology compilation and interpretation are not alternatives for the same codes. A plausible setting uses an interpreted intermediate code notation I Correct intermediate codes must be defined via some form of external criterion. Thus I_c may be the collection of certified intermediate codes. The functionality of interpreters for I is denoted $int4i$, an interpreter for I is an executable $u{:}int4i{:}e$. The application of I code is then defined as $x{:}i \bullet \bullet_{int4i} \boldsymbol{y} = u{:}int4i{:}e \bullet \bullet x{:}i \frown \boldsymbol{y}$.

Compiling to Interpreted Code. A compiler from source code notation S to I is an executable $u{:}s2i{:}e$. Having available a compiler to I an alternative definition of the correct codes for S is given by: $x \in S_{c{:}int}$ if and only if $u{:}s2i{:}$ $e \bullet \bullet x \in I_c$.[10]

In the presence of a compiler for S to I as well as to A (which has a definitional status for S by assumption) the following correctness criterion emerges: (i) for all $x{:}s \in S_c \cap S_{c{:}int}$, and for all data files $\boldsymbol{y}$: $x{:}s \bullet \bullet_s \boldsymbol{y} = (u{:}s2i{:}e \bullet \bullet x{:}s) \bullet \bullet_{int4i} \boldsymbol{y}$ and (ii) $S_c \subseteq S_{c{:}int}$.

It is also possible that S is primarily defined in terms of its projection to I. Then the second condition becomes $S_c \supseteq S_{c{:}int}$, thus expressing that the compiler which now lacks a definitional status can support all required processing.

7.3   Managed Execution of Compiled Intermediate Code

The intermediate code is managed (executed in a managed way) if it is both assembled and compiled. Thus an interpreter, vm called a run-time (system) $vm{:}rt4ae{:}e$ acts as an interpreter for a compiled version of the intermediate code. $rt4ae$ is the role of run-time for an almost executable code. This code is also called a virtual machine, which has been reflected in its mnemonic name. The intermediate code is compiled by $c{:}i2ae{:}e$ to a stage between the assembly level and the executable level denoted AE. This leads to the definition $x{:}i \bullet \bullet_{i{:}m} \boldsymbol{y} = vm{:}rt4ae{:}e \bullet \bullet (c{:}i2ae{:}e \bullet \bullet x{:}i) \frown \boldsymbol{y}$.

Managed code execution allows the virtual machine to perform activities like garbage collection in a pragmatic way, not too often and not too late, depending on statistics regarding the actual machine. Other activities may involve various forms of load balancing in a multi-processor system. Also various security checks may be incorporated in managed execution.

JIT Compiled Intermediate Code. At this stage it is possible to indicate in informal terms what is actually supposed to happen in a modern computer system. Source codes are compiled to an intermediate code format. That code

---

[10] Interpreter based pseudo-empirical syntax for S.

format is assumed to be widely known thus permitting execution on a large range of machines. Its execution involves managed execution after compilation. However, compilation is performed in a modular and fashion and the run-time system calls the compiler which then compiles only parts of the intermediate code when needed, throwing the resulting codes away when not immediately needed anymore, and recompiling again when needed again. This is called 'just in time compilation' (or JITting for short). The use of JIT compiler based managed execution has the following advantages:

(i) The accumulation of a machine specific (or rather a machine architecture specific) code base is avoided, in favor of a code base consisting of intermediate code which can be processed on many different machine architectures. Especially if the code is very big and during an execution only a small fraction of it is actually executed integral compilation before execution becomes unfeasible. Therefore mere code size implies that a decision to design an intermediate code for compilation forces one to opt for JIT compilation.

(ii) The advantages of managed execution are as mentioned above. Only managed execution can provide a high quality garbage collection service, because a naive approach where all garbage is removed immediately after its production (i.e. becoming garbage) is impractical and inefficient.

(iii) The advantages of (JIT) compilation in comparison to intermediate code interpretation are classical ones. Compiled code execution may be faster than code interpretation, and, perhaps more importantly, because the intermediate code will be (JIT) compiled, it may be more abstract and therefore shorter, more comprehensible and more amenable to maintenance than it would be were it to be interpreted.

8   Machine Functions for JIT Compilation

The formalization of JIT compilation requires code to consist of parts that can be independently compiled. The syntax of multi-part code below will admit this aspect of formalization. For the various parts of multi-part code to work together intermediate results of a computation need to be maintained. That can be modeled by using machine functions that produce a state from a state rather than a code from one or more codes. State machine functions (also termed state transition functions) will be introduced to enable the formalization of the sequential operation of different program parts. Finally program parts may be executed several times during a computation in such a way that different entry points in the code are used. Natural numbers will be used as code entry points.

8.1   Multi-part Code

Code can be extended to code families in various ways. Here we will consider so-called flat multi-part code. A flat multi-part code is a sequence of codes separated by colons such as for instance 10011:1110:0:0001. The collection of these codes is denoted with MPC (multi-part codes). It will now be assumed that the input of a machine function is a code family. The case dealt with up to now is the special case where multi-part codes have just one part (single part codes: SPC). Access to a part can be given via its rank number in the flat multipart code listing, starting with 1 for the first part. MPCN, (multi-part code notation) admits bit sequences and the associative operator ':'. Brackets are admitted in MPCN but do not constitute elements of the code families, for instance: $(10{:}011){:}00 = 10{:}(011{:}00) = 10{:}011{:}00$. When multi-part codes are used it is practical to modify the type of machine functions in order to admit multi-part inputs.

The n'th part of a multi-part code x is denote $\mathtt{part}_n(x)$. This notation produces empty codes if n is too large.

Non-separate Assembly and Compilation. An assembler or a compiler for multipart code that produces a single executable will be called a non-separate assembler or a non-separate compiler. To use a positive jargon a non-separate assembler or compiler may be called a gluing assembler or compiler. It is assumed that a gluing assembler/compiler detects itself which parts of a code must be used, for instance by looking at a code that contains some marker and using some form of cross referencing between the parts. Let MPA be a multipart assembly code notation. $c{:}mpa2e{:}e$ is an executable which transforms multi-part control codes to single-part executables. A gluing compiler can be used to define the meaning of multi-part control codes as follows:

$$x{:}mpa \bullet \bullet_{mpa} y = (c{:}mpa2e{:}e \bullet \bullet x{:}mpa) \bullet \bullet y.$$

Similarly for a notation s, mps may be its multi-part extension. Then one may define its meaning given a non-separate compiler by

$$x{:}mps \bullet \bullet_{mps} y = (c{:}mps2a{:}e \bullet \bullet x{:}mps) \bullet \bullet_a y.$$

Separate Compilation. Separate compilation holds for code families of some code notation if a compiler ψ distributes over the code part separator : $\psi(x{:}y) = \psi(x){:}\psi(y))$. A compiler with this property is called separation modular. So it may now be assumed that mS (modular S) consists of sequences of S separated by ':' and that $u{:}ms2e{:}e$ is a separation modular compiler for mS i.e., using MPCN, $u{:}ms2e{:}e \bullet \bullet y{:}z = (u{:}ms2e{:}e \bullet \bullet y){:}(u{:}ms2e{:}e \bullet \bullet z)$ for all y and z which may themselves be code families recursively. For the second output component there is a similar equation: $u{:}ms2e{:}e \bullet \bullet^2 y{:}z = (u{:}ms2e{:}e \bullet \bullet^2 y){:}(u{:}ms2e{:}e \bullet \bullet^2 z)$; corresponding equations are assumed for the other output components.

8.2   State Machine Functions

Machine functions, as used above, transform sequences of (possibly multi-part) input files into output files. This is adequate as long as intermediate stages of a computation need not be taken into account. Modeling separate compilation typically calls for taking into account intermediate stages of a computation. In order to do so we will use state machine functions rather than machine functions. State machine functions provide a new state given a control code and a state. At the same time it becomes necessary to deal with code entry points. A code entry point is a natural number used to indicate where in (the bit sequence of) a code execution is supposed to start. Code entry points will arise if code has been produced via imperative programming using a program notation with subroutine calls and subsequent compilation and/or assembly. In addition a state machine function must produce information concerning which part of the multipart code is to be executed next. It is now assumed that ST denotes the collection of states of a machine model. A multipart part code state machine function has the following type:

$$(SPC \times CEP \times ST) \to ((ST \cup \{D, M\}) \times CPN \times CEP)$$

Here CPN is the collection of code part numbers and CEP is the the collection of code entry points. The CEP argument indicates where in the control code execution is supposed to start. These two numbers at the output side indicate the code part that must be executed in the next phase of the execution and the entry point within that code part which will be used to start the computation for the next phase. If the code part number is outside the range of parts of the MPC under execution (in particular if it equals 0), the computation terminates, and if the exit point is outside the range of exit points of a part termination will also result.

Relating Machine Functions with State Machine Functions. The connection with machine functions can be given if input files can be explicitly incorporated in the state (using a function 'in') and output functions can be extracted (by means of 'out'). State machine functions will be denoted with a single bullet. A CEP argument will be represented as superscript, a CPN argument may be given as another superscript, (preceding the CPN superscript), and other information may be given in subscripts. For single part code x one may write:

$$x{:}e \bullet \bullet y = \mathbf{out}(\text{state}(x{:}e \bullet^1 \text{in}(y, s_0))).$$

Here **out** produces a sequence of outputs different from M, unless the computation diverges. This equation provides a definition that works under the assumptions that the computation starts in state s_0 and that at the end of the single part computation the next part result equals 0: i.e. for some s' and p', $x{:}e \bullet^1 (\text{in}(y, s_0))) = (s', 0, p')$. Moreover it must be noticed that in the notation used the separator in the code argument separates name parts for a single part code rather than code parts of a multi-part code.

State Machine Functions for Multi-part Control Code. Assuming that multi-part code execution starts by default with the first code part at its first entry point the following pair of equations (start equation and progress equation) defines the machine function for multi-part executable code (tagged with mpe). Start equation:

$$x{:}mpe \bullet \bullet y = \mathbf{out}(\text{state}(x{:}mpe \bullet^{1,1} (\text{in}(y, s_0))))$$

expressing that execution starts with the first code part at entry point 1, and with the following progress equation:

$$\text{part}_p(x{:}mpe) \bullet^q s = (p', q', s') \to x{:}mpe \bullet^{p,q} s = (s' \lhd p' = 0 \rhd (x{:}mpe \bullet^{q', p'} s'))$$

where the progress equation is valid under the assumption that the only returned code part number outside the code part range of $x{:}mpe$ equals 0.

8.3   Unmanaged JIT

The JIT equation for (almost) unmanaged[11] multi-part intermediate code execution connects the various ingredients to a semantic definition of JIT execution for a multi-part intermediate code $x{:}i$. The start equation reads

$$x{:}mpi \bullet \bullet_{jit} \boldsymbol{y} = \mathbf{out}(\text{state}(x{:}mpi \bullet_{jit}^{1,1} (\text{in}(\boldsymbol{y}, s_0))))$$

with the progress equation:

$$(c{:}i2e{:}e \bullet \bullet \text{part}_p(x{:}mpi)) \bullet^q s = (p', q', s') \rightarrow$$
$$x{:}mpi \bullet_{jit}^{p,q} s = (s' \lhd p' = 0 \rhd (x{:}mpi \bullet_{jit}^{q',p'} s'))$$

For the progress equation it is assumed that a compiler/assembler $c{:}i2e{:}e$ for the intermediate code is available that translates it into executable code.

Limited Buffering of Compiled Parts. A buffer with the most recent compilations (i.e. files of the form $c{:}i2e{:}e \bullet \bullet \text{part}_p(x{:}i)$) of code parts can be maintained during the execution of the multi-part intermediate code. Ass this buffer has a bounded size, some code fragments will probably have to be deleted during a run[12] and may subsequently need to be recompiled. The idea is that a compilation is done only when absolutely needed, which justifies the phrase JIT.

8.4   Managed (and Interpreted) Multi-part Code Execution

Managed code execution involves the interpretation of (JIT) compiled intermediate code. The start equation reads

$$x{:}mpi \bullet \bullet_{manjit} \boldsymbol{y} = \mathbf{out}(\text{state}(x{:}mpi \bullet_{manjit}^{1,1} (\text{in}(\boldsymbol{y}, s_0))))$$

The corresponding progress equation reads

$$vm{:}rt4ae{:}e \bullet^q \text{in}(c{:}i2ae{:}e \bullet \bullet \text{part}_p(x{:}mpi), s) = (p', q', s') \rightarrow$$
$$x{:}mpi \bullet_{manjit}^{p,q} s = (s' \lhd p' = 0 \rhd (x{:}mpi \bullet_{manjit}^{q',p'} s'))$$

The virtual machine $vm{:}rt4ae{:}e$ computes the intermediate state reached after execution has exited from code part p after incorporating the code to be executed in the state. The interpreter takes into account that the code to be interpreted has to be started at entry state q.

---

[11] The only aspect of execution management is taking care of JIT compiling an intermediate code part when needed and starting its execution subsequently.

[12] Code garbage collection.

A Requirement Specification for Managed JITting. Provided a compiler $c{:}mpi2a{:}e$ is known the following identity must hold:

$$x{:}mpi \bullet \bullet_{\text{manjit}} y = (c{:}mpi2a{:}a \bullet \bullet x{:}mpi) \bullet \bullet_a y.$$

This equation may be used alternatively as a correctness criterion for the definitions using managed JIT compiled execution. The compiler based definition will not capture any of the features of execution management but it may be very useful as a semantic characterization of the execution of multi-part intermediate code.

9   Verifying Compilers

Recent work of Hoare (e.g. [4]) has triggered a renewed interest in the idea that program verification may be included in the tasks of a compiler. The notion of a verifying compiler has been advocated before by Floyd in 1967, [8], but it has not yet been made practical, and according to Hoare it might well be considered a unifying objective which may enforce systematic cooperation from many parts of the field. Getting verifying compilers used in practice at a large scale is certainly a hard task and Hoare refers to this objective as a 'grand challenge' in computing. Turning quantum computing into practice, resolving P versus NP, proofchecking major parts of mathematics and the theory of computing in the tradition of de Bruijn's type theory, removing worms and viruses from the internet, and (more pragmatically) the .NET strategy for using the same intermediate program notation for all purposes may be viewed as other grand challenges. In computational science the adequate simulation of protein unfolding stands out as a grand challenge; in system engineering the realization of the computing grid and the design of open source environments of industrial strength for all major application areas, constitute grand challenges as well.

Program verification has been advocated by Dijkstra (e.g. in EWD 303) because testing and debugging cannot provide adequate certainty. Indeed, if human certainty is to be obtained proofs may be unavoidable. For the design of complex systems, however, the need for proofs is harder to establish. The biological evolution of the human mind has produced a complex system, at least from the perspective of current computer technology, through a design process using natural selection (which seems to be a form of testing rather than a form of verification) as its major methodology for the avoidance of design errors. This might suggest a way around program verification as well: rather than verifying program X, one may design a far more complex system C using X and many variations of it which is then tested. A test of X may involve millions of runs of X and its variations. Usability of C, as demonstrated using tests, will provide confidence in components like X, as well as the possibility to use these components in a complex setting. Whether confidence or certainty is what people expect from computing systems is not an obvious issue, however. As a consequence this particular grand challenge has a subjective aspect regarding the value of its objective that the other examples mentioned above seem not to have.

In this section the phenomenon of a verifying compiler will be discussed at the level of (state) machine functions and control code algebra.

9.1   Requirement Codes and Satisfaction Predicates

REQ will represent a collection of predicates on behaviors that will viewed as descriptions of properties of codes under execution. $r \in$ REC may serve a s a requirement on a behavior. A given predicate $\underline{sat}_{req}$ ($B \underline{sat}_{req} r$, for behavior B and requirement $r \in$ REQ) determines the meaning of requirements. Having available the satisfaction predicate at the level of behaviors, it may be gradually lifted to source codes.

If B is the behavior of executable code x on machine m ($B = |x|_{\bullet\bullet^m}$), then $x \underline{sat}_{m:e} r$ if $B \underline{sat}_{req} r$. Further for an assembly code $x{:}a$ one may write $x{:}a \underline{sat}_{m:a} r$ if $(c{:}a2e{:}e \bullet \bullet^m x{:}a) \underline{sat}_{m:e} r$, given an assembler $c{:}a2e{:}e$ for A.

For a high-level and machine independent program notation s we define $x{:}s \underline{sat}_s r$ if $(v{:}s2a{:}e \bullet \bullet^m x{:}s) \underline{sat}_{m:a} r$ for a machine m and a compiler $v{:}s2a{:}e$ on the same machine m. In the sequel the machine superscripts will be omitted, because machine dependence is not taken into account.

9.2   Proofs and Proof Checking

Given r it may be viewed a design task to find a control code $x{:}s$ such that $x{:}s \underline{sat}_s r$. A proof for this fact is a code p in a collection PROOFS of codes such that $p \vdash x{:}s \underline{sat}_s r$, where $\vdash$ is a relation such that $p \vdash x{:}s \underline{sat}_s r$ implies that $x{:}s \underline{sat}_s r$. This implication represents the so-called soundness of the proof method. Validating $\vdash$ requires a proof checking tool $w{:}ch4p4s{:}e$ (check for being a proof for an s code) such that $w{:}ch4p4s{:}e \bullet \bullet p, x{:}s, r$ always terminates, never produces an error, and produces the code "0" exactly if the code p constitutes a proof of $x{:}s \underline{sat}_s r$.

Non-automatic Proof Generation. Proving the correctness of control codes by hand, as a control code production strategy, amounts to the production of a pair (x, p) such that $w{:}ch4p4s{:}e \bullet \bullet p, x, r = $ "0". Here it is taken for granted that if there is to be any chance of obtaining a proof for the control code that code may have to be specifically designed with the objective to deliver the required proof in mind. It seems to be a folk-lore fact in system verification practice that hand made proofs can only be given if the code to be verified is somehow prepared for that purpose, though in theory that need not be the case. A complete proof method guarantees the existence of a proof for each required fact (concerning a code that satisfies a requirement) . But actually finding a proof which theory predicts to exist is by no means an easy matter.

Infeasibility of Proof Search. The task to prove code correctness manually (and have it machine checked thereafter) may be considered an unrealistic burden for the programmer. Therefore control code production methods are needed which can take this task out of the hands of human designers. The most obvious strategy is automated proof search.

Having available a proof method and a proof checker, one may design an automated proof generator as a code $u{:}pg4s{:}e$, such that $u{:}pg4s{:}e \bullet\bullet x{:}s, r$ produces a proof p with $p \vdash x{:}s \underline{sat}_s r$ if such a proof exists with the computation diverging otherwise (or preferably producing a negative answer, i.e. a code outside REQ). Even if a proof checker exists in theory its realization as an executable code with useful performance seems to be elusive. Therefore this strategy to avoid the need for people to design proofs has been considered infeasible and a different strategy is needed.

9.3   Verifying Compilers

Given the high-level control code notation s a version as of it that admits annotations is designed. A code in as is considered an annotated code for s. Using a tool $strip:as2s:e$ the annotations can be removed and a code in s is found which determines the meaning of an annotated s code. In other words: $x{:}as \bullet \bullet_{as} y = (strip{.}as2s{:}e \bullet \bullet x{:}as) \bullet \bullet_s y.$

A requirement r may will be included as a part of the annotation. The requirement can be obtained (extracted) from the annotated code by means of the application of a tool $u{:}as2r{:}e$. The computation $u{:}as2r{:}e \bullet \bullet x{:}as$ either produces a requirement $r \in$ REQ or it produces an error (M for meaningless). If a requirement is produced that implies that as a part of the extraction the computation has succeeded in generating a proof for the asserted program and checking that proof. Thus in this case it is guaranteed that $strip{.}as2s{:}e \bullet \bullet x{:}as \underline{sat}_s (u{:}as2r{:}e \bullet \bullet x{:}as).$

The production of adequately annotated control code may be simpler than the production of proofs as it allows the designer to distribute requirements over the code thus simplifying the proofs that the extraction tool needs to find by itself. In addition it is held by some that for each construction of a source code a 'natural' assertion may be found, which the conscious control code author should have in mind. This allows to provide a canonical annotation for any source code, which can be proved without much trouble. Then follows a stage of logic that helps to derive the 'required' requirement from a requirement that has been automatically synthesized from the canonical annotation. This piece of logic needs careful attention, because by itself it is as unfeasible as $P \neq NP$. The asserted code needs a good deal of guidance cast in the form of annotations for this matter.

Verifying Compilers and Multi-part Code. Large amounts of code will be organized as multi-part codes, admitting JIT compilation strategies. A computation in this setting uses the JIT compiler to transform part after part in an (almost) executable form. It may be assumed that verifying compilers are used to obtain the various code parts in the code base at hand. It is reasonable to assume that these requirements have been stored in a database annex to the code base. In that context it is preferable to refer to the stored requirements as specifications. Indeed, because the JIT compiler using the various parts must rely on the use of valid code it cannot accept the possibility that a code part defeats the extraction of a requirement.

Now complimentary to JIT compilation there is JIT requirements integration, a process that allows the computation to dynamically synthesize a requirement from the requirements known to be satisfied by the various parts it uses. The JIT compiler should combine requirements synthesis and verification. This is a difficult task that by itself leads to different solution architectures.

Trivial Requirement Synthesis JIT Compilation. A straightforward way to obtain the requirements integration functionality is to assume that all specifications for parts used during a computation are identical (which is plausible if these are understood as global system invariants), thereby shifting the engineering burden to the production of the code base. This solution architecture will be called the trivial requirements synthesis JIT architecture (TRS-JIT).

For TRS-JIT it becomes helpful to admit storing a collection of requirements for the various code parts in the annex database. It should be noticed, however, that the previous discussion of verifying compilers provides no technique for finding a multitude of validated requirements for the same (compiled) code. In addition, as the code base contains code parts with different requirements (stored in the annex data base), the JIT compiler now faces the possibility of running into a code part that is not equipped with a suitable requirement. It may be the case that the requirement for the part is logically stronger than needed, but that is impossible to check dynamically. Thus it must be accepted that executions may always stop in an error condition indicating that a part had to be JIT compiled for which the needed requirement was absent. This is a severe drawback because it is useless for real time control applications. If this drawback is unacceptable the JIT compiler must be shown always to ask for a code that exists in the code base and that is equipped with the required specification.

A Verifying JIT Compiler. Guaranteeing that a computation will not halt at an ill-specified of even absent code part is the task of the verifying JIT compiler in the case of the trivial requirements synthesis architecture. This leads to a two-phase strategy that first checks this latter property using a dataflow analysis on the initial code, and thereafter a check that all needed parts are equipped with the required specification. In this stage a limited amount of proof generation may be used to allow parts that have logically stronger specifications to be used if the required specifications can be derived by these limited means.

10   Conclusion

Machine functions have been used to formalize several software processing mechanisms at a high level of abstraction, by means of the formation of code algebras. This abstract formalization has been proposed in particular for compilation, assemblage, interpretation, and for managed and unmanaged, interpreted and just in time compiled multi-part code execution, and for verifying compilers. While the notion of a verifying compiler can be captured to some extent at the abstraction level of CCA, this seems not to be the case for the unavidable concept of a verifying JIT compiler, however.

References

1. A.W.Appel. Axiomatic bootstrapping, a guide for compiler hackers. *ACM TOPLAS*, 16(6):1699–1719, 1994.
2. J.A. Bergstra and M.E. Loots. Program algebra for sequential code. *Journal of Logic and Algebraic Programming*, 51(2):125–156, 2002.
3. J.A. Bergstra and S.F.M. van Vlijmen. *Theoretische Software-Engineering*. ZENO-Institute, Leiden, Utrecht, The Netherlands, 1998. In Dutch.
4. C.A.Hoare. The verifying compiler, a grand challenge for computer research. *JACM*, 50(1):63–69, 2003.
5. H.Bratman. An alternate form of the UNCOL diagram. *CACM*, 4(3):142, 1961.
6. J.Earley and H.Sturgis. A formalism for translator interactions. *CACM*, 13(10):607–617, 1970.
7. M.I.Halpern. Machine independence: Its technology and economics. *CACM*, 8(12):782–785, 1965.
8. R.W.Floyd. Assigning meanings to programs. *Proc. Amer. Soc. Symp. Appl. Math.*, 19:19–31, 1967.
9. A. Turing. On computable numbers, with an application to the entscheidungsproblem. *Proc. London Math. Soc. Ser 2*, 42,43:230–265,544–564, 1936.

Exploiting Abstraction for Specification Reuse. The Java/C♯ Case Study

Egon Börger[1] and Robert F. Stärk[2]

[1] Dipartimento di Informatica, Università di Pisa
boerger@di.unipi.it
[2] Computer Science Department, ETH Zürich
staerk@inf.ethz.ch

Abstract. From the models provided in [14] and [4] for the semantics of Java and C♯ programs we abstract the mathematical structure that underlies the semantics of both languages. The resulting model reveals the kernel of object-oriented programming language constructs and can be used for teaching them without being bound to a particular language. It also allows us to identify precisely some of the major differences between Java and C♯.

1 Introduction

In this work the models developed in [14] and in [4] for a rigorous definition of Java and C♯ and their implementations on the Java Virtual Machine (JVM) resp. in the Common Language Runtime (CLR) of .NET are analyzed to extract their underlying common mathematical structure. The result is a platform-independent interpreter of high-level programming language constructs which can be instantiated to concrete interpreters of specific languages like Java, C♯, C++. It is structured into components for imperative, static, object-oriented, exception handling, concurrency, pointer related, and other special language features (like delegates in C♯) and thus can be used in teaching to introduce step by step the basic concepts of modern programming languages and to explain the differences in their major current implementations.

The task is supported by the fact that the models in [14, 4] have been defined in terms of stepwise refined Abstract State Machines (ASMs), which

- separate the static and the dynamic parts of the semantics,
- capture the dynamics by ASM rules, one rule set for each cluster of language constructs[1], describing their run-time effect on the abstract program state, guided by a walk through the underlying attributed abstract syntax tree.

---

[1] A related modular approach, to define the semantics of a language by a collection of individual language construct descriptions, now named "incremental semantics", appears in [12, 6].

F.S. de Boer et al. (Eds.): FMCO 2003, LNCS 3188, pp. 42–76, 2004.
© Springer-Verlag Berlin Heidelberg 2004

The stepwise refined definitions unfold in particular the following layered modules of orthogonal language features, which are also related to the historical development of programming concepts from say FORTRAN, via PASCAL and MODULA, SMALLTALK and EIFFEL, to JAVA and C♯:

- imperative constructs, related to sequential control by while programs, built from statements and expressions over simple types,
- classes with so-called static class features, namely procedural abstraction with class initialization and global (module) variables,
- object-orientation with class instances, instance creation, instance methods, inheritance,
- exception handling,
- concurrency (threads),
- special features like delegates, events, etc.
- so-called unsafe features like pointers with pointer arithmetic.

This leads us to consider a sequence of sublanguages $L_{\mathcal{I}} \subset L_{\mathcal{C}} \subset L_{\mathcal{O}} \subset L_{\mathcal{E}} \subset L_{\mathcal{T}} \subset L_{\mathcal{D}} \subset L_{\mathcal{U}}$ of a general language L, which can be instantiated to the corresponding sublanguages of Java and C♯ defined in [14, 4]. The interpreter $\text{EXEC}L_{\mathcal{S}}$ of each language $L_{\mathcal{S}}$ in the sequence conservatively (purely incrementally) extends its predecessor. We show how it can be instantiated to an interpreter of Java$_{\mathcal{S}}$ or C♯$_{\mathcal{S}}$ by variations of well-identified state or machine components. The interpreter $\text{EXEC}L$ of the entire language L is the parallel composition of those submachines:

$$
\begin{aligned}
\text{EXEC}L \equiv \\
\quad \text{EXEC}L_I \\
\quad \text{EXEC}L_C \\
\quad \text{EXEC}L_O \\
\quad \text{EXEC}L_E \\
\quad \text{EXEC}L_T \\
\quad \text{EXEC}L_D \\
\quad \text{EXEC}L_U
\end{aligned}
$$

Delegates and unsafe code are peculiar features of C♯ and not included at all into Java, therefore we refer for the two corresponding submachines to [4]. Since the thread models of Java and C♯ have been analyzed and compared extensively in [14, 1, 13], we skip here to reformulate the interpreter $\text{EXEC}L_T$. The static semantics of most programming languages can be captured appropriately by mainly declarative descriptions of the relevant syntactical and compile-time checked language features, e.g., typing rules, control-flow analysis, name resolution, etc.; as a consequence we concentrate our attention here on the more involved language dynamics for whose description the run-time oriented ASM framework turns out to be helpful. So we deal with the static language features in the form of conditions on the attributed abstract syntax tree, resulting from parsing and elaboration and taken as starting point of the language interpreter $\text{EXEC}L$.

This paper does not start from scratch. We tailor the exposition for a reader who has some basic knowledge of (object-oriented) programming. A detailed definition of ASMs and their semantics, as originally published in [11], is skipped here, because ASMs can be correctly understood as pseudo-code operating over abstract (domains of) data. A textbook-style definition is available in Chapter 2 of the AsmBook [5].

2   The Imperative Core L_I

In this section we define the sequential imperative core L_I of our general language L together with a model for its semantics. The model takes the form of an interpreter $EXECL_I$, which defines the basic machinery for the execution of the single language constructs. L_I provides structured while-programs consisting of statements to be executed (appearing in method bodies), which are built from expressions to be evaluated, which in turn are constructed using predefined operators over simple types. The computations of our interpreter are supposed to start with an arbitrary but fixed L-program. As explained above, syntax and compile-time matters are separated from run-time issues by assuming that the program is given as an attributed abstract syntax tree, resulting from parsing and elaboration.

2.1   Static Semantics of L_I

Expressions and statements of the sublanguage L_I are defined as usual by a grammar, say the one given in Fig. 1. We view this figure as defining also the corresponding ASM domains, e.g., the set *Exp* of expressions built from *Lit*erals and variable expressions using the provided operators (unary, binary, conditional) and including besides some possibly language-specific expressions the set *Sexp* of statement expressions, i.e., expressions than can be used on the top-level like an assignment to a variable expression using '=' (or an assignment operator from a set *Aop* or one of the typical prefix/postfix operators '++' or '--'). In this model the set *Vexp* of variable expressions (lvalues) consists of the local variables only and will be refined below. The prefix operators '++' and '--' are syntactically reduced to assignment operators, e.g., ++v is reduced to v += 1.

The auxiliary sets, like *Uop* of unary operators, which one may think of as including also operators to construct type cast expressions of form '(' *Type* ')' *Exp*, vary from language to language. *SpecificExp*(L) may include expressions that are specific for the language L, like 'checked' '(' *Exp* ')' and 'unchecked' '(' *Exp* ')' in the model C$\sharp_I$ in [4, Fig. 1]. In the model Java$_I$ in [14, Fig. 3.1] the set *SpecificExp*(L) is empty. Similarly, the set *JumpStm* of jump statements may vary from language to language; in Java$_I$ it consists of 'break' *Lab* ';' and 'continue' *Lab* ';', in C$\sharp_I$ of 'break' ';' | 'continue' ';' | 'goto' *Lab* ';'. *SpecificStm*(L) may contain statements that are specific to the language L, e.g., 'checked' *Block* | 'unchecked' *Block* for the language C$\sharp_I$. In Java$_I$ it is empty. *Bstm* may also contain block statements for the declaration of constant expres-

$$Exp \quad ::= Lit \mid Vexp \mid Uop\ Exp \mid Exp\ Bop\ Exp \mid Exp\ '?'\ Exp\ ':'\ Exp$$
$$\mid Sexp \mid SpecificExp(L)$$

$$Vexp \quad ::= Loc$$

$$Sexp \quad ::= Vexp\ '='\ Exp \mid Vexp\ Aop\ Exp \mid Vexp\ '++' \mid Vexp\ '--'$$

$$Stm \quad ::= ';' \mid Sexp\ ';' \mid Lab\ ':'\ Stm \mid JumpStm$$
$$\mid\ 'if'\ '('\ Exp\ ')'\ Stm\ 'else'\ Stm \mid 'while'\ '('\ Exp\ ')'\ Stm$$
$$\mid SpecificStm(L) \mid Block$$

$$Block ::= '\{'\ \{Bstm\}\ '\}'$$

$$Bstm \quad ::= Type\ Loc\ ';' \mid Stm$$

Fig. 1. Grammar of expressions and statements in $L_{\mathcal{I}}$

sions whose value is known at compile time, like 'const' $Type\ Loc\ '='\ Cexp\ ';'$ in $C\sharp_{\mathcal{I}}$.

Not to burden the exposition with repetitions of similar arguments, we do not list here statements like do, for, switch, goto case, goto default, etc., which do appear in real-life languages and are treated analogously to the cases we discuss here. When referring to the set of sequences of elements from a set *Item* we write *Items*. We usually write lower case letters e to denote elements of a set E, e.g., *lit* for elements of *Lit*. For expository purposes, in Fig. 1 we also neglect that in $C\sharp$ labeled statements are only allowed as block statements, whereas in Java, every statement (also embedded statements) can have a label.

Different languages usually exhibit not only differences in syntax, but above all different notions of types with their conversion and promotion rules (subtype or compatibility definition), different type constraints on the operand and result values for the predefined operators, different syntactical constraints for expressions and statements like scoping rules, definite assignment and reachability rules, etc. As a consequence, the static analysis differs, e.g., to establish the correctness of the definite assignment conditions or more generally of the type safety of well-typed programs (for Java see the type safety proof in [14, Ch. 8], for $C\sharp$ see the proof of definite assignment correctness in [8]). Since this paper is focused on modeling the dynamic semantics of a language, we omit here any general discussion of standard static semantics issues and come back to them only where needed to explain how the interpreter uses the attributed abstract syntax tree of a well-typed program. E.g., we will use that each expression node exp in the attributed syntax tree is annotated with its compile-time type $type(exp)$, that type casts are inserted in the syntax tree if necessary (reflecting implicit type conversions at compile-time), etc.

2.2 Dynamic Semantics of $L_{\mathcal{I}}$

The dynamic semantics for $L_{\mathcal{I}}$ describes the effect of statement execution and of expression evaluation upon the program execution state, so that the transition rule for the $L_{\mathcal{I}}$ interpreter (the same for its extensions) has the form

$$\text{ExecL}_I \equiv$$
$$\quad \text{ExecLExp}_I$$
$$\quad \text{ExecLStm}_I$$

The first subrule defines one execution step in the evaluation of expressions; the second subrule defines one step in the execution of statements.

Syntax Tree Walk. To facilitate further model refinements by purely incremental extensions, the definition proceeds by walking through the abstract syntax tree, starting at $pos =$ root-position, to compute at each node the effect of the program construct attached to the node. We formalize the walk by a cursor ▶, whose position in the tree – represented by a dynamic function $pos: Pos$ – is updated using static tree functions, leading from a node in the tree down to its *first* child, from there to the *next* brother or *up* to the parent node (if any), as illustrated by the following self-explanatory example. *Pos* is the set of positions in the abstract syntax tree. A function $label: Pos \rightarrow Label$ decorates nodes with the information which identifies the grammar rule associated with the node. For the sake of notational succinctness and in adherence to widespread programming notations, we use some concrete syntax from Java or C♯ to describe the labels, thus hiding the explicit introduction of auxiliary non-terminals[2]. In the example the *label* of the root node is the auxiliary non-terminal *If*, identifying the grammar rule which produces the construct if (exp) stm_1 else stm_2—the 'occurrence' of which here constitutes what we are really interested in when considering the tree. As explained below, this construct determines what we will call the *context* of the root node or of its children nodes.

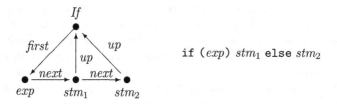

if (exp) stm_1 else stm_2

Local Variable Values. The next question is what are the values computed for expressions and how they are stored as current values of local variables, namely upon executing an assignment statement or as side effect of an expression evaluation. The answer to the second question depends upon whether such values are stored directly, as for example in Java, or indirectly via an addressing mechanism, as for example in C♯. To capture both possibilities we introduce two domains, namely of values and of addresses, and use the following two dynamic functions

$$locals: Loc \rightarrow Adr, \quad mem: Adr \rightarrow SimpleValue \cup \{Undef\}$$

---

[2] In [12] an abstract syntax notation is proposed which avoids Java or C♯ like notation.

which can be used to assign memory addresses to local variables and to store the values there. To simplify the formulation of how to instantiate our interpreter for Java or C♯ and to prepare the way for later refinements, we use a macro WRITEMEM(adr, t, val) to denote writing a value of given type t to a given address. For the sublanguage $L_{\mathcal{I}}$ (as for Java) the macro is only an abbreviation for $mem(adr) := val$, which will be refined in the model for $L_{\mathcal{O}}$.

One possible instance of this scheme, namely for Java, is to identify Loc and Adr so that $locals$ becomes mem. It goes without saying and will not be mentioned any more in the sequel that a similar simplification applies to all other functions, predicates, and macros introduced below in connection with handling the values stored at addresses.

Since the values we consider in $L_{\mathcal{I}}$ are of simple types, in this model the equation

$$Value = Simple\,Value \cup Adr$$

holds, which will be refined for $L_{\mathcal{O}}$ to include references (and structs, which appear in C♯). The fact that local variables have to be uniquely identified can be modeled by stipulating $Loc = Identifier \times Pos$. For the initialization of the interpreter it is natural to require that an address has been assigned to each local variable, but that the value stored there is still undefined.

- $locals(x) \in Adr$ for every variable x
- $mem(i) = Undef$ for every $i \in Adr$

Recording Intermediate Values. During the walk through the tree, also intermediate results of the elaboration of syntactical constructs appear, which have to be recorded somewhere, namely values of evaluated (sub-) expressions, but also possible results of the execution of statements. Statements may terminate normally, but also abruptly due to jumps (in $L_{\mathcal{I}}$) or returns from method calls (in $L_{\mathcal{C}}$) or to the occurrence of exceptions (in $L_{\mathcal{E}}$). There are many ways to keep track of such temporary items, e.g., using a stack (as do many virtual machines, see for example the Java Virtual Machine operand stack opd in [14, pg. 140]), or replacing directly the elaborated syntactical constructs by their intermediate result (as do SOS-based formalisms, see for example the $restbody$ concept in [14, pg. 38]), or via some dynamic functions defined on the static syntax tree. We choose here to use a partial function to record the $values$ computed for the syntactic construct labeled by the node with each node.

$values: Pos \rightarrow Result$

For $L_{\mathcal{I}}$, the range $Result$ of this function contains a) $Undef$, to signal that no value is defined yet, b) simple values, resulting from expression evaluation, c) $Norm$, for normal termination of statement execution, and d) reasons for abruption of statement execution. The set Abr of abruptions derives here from the jump statements (see below) and will be refined in successive models to also contain statement returns and exceptions.

$Result = Value \cup Abr \cup \{Undef, Norm\}$

As intermediate *values* at a position p the cursor is at or is passing to, the computation may yield directly a simple value; at *AddressPos*itions as defined below it may yield an address; but it may also yield a *memValue* which has to be retrieved indirectly via the given address (where for $L_\mathcal{I}$ the memory value of a given type t at a given address adr is defined by $memValue(adr, t) = mem(adr)$; the parameter t will become relevant only in the refinements of *memValue* in $L_\mathcal{O}$ and $L_\mathcal{U}$). This is described by the following two macros:

$\text{Y\textsc{ield}}(val, p) \equiv$
$\quad values(p) := val$
$\quad pos := p$

$\text{Y\textsc{ield}I\textsc{ndirect}}(adr, p) \equiv$
$\quad \textbf{if } AddressPos(p) \textbf{ then } \text{Y\textsc{ield}}(adr, p)$
$\quad \textbf{else } \text{Y\textsc{ield}}(memValue(adr, type(p)), p)$

We will use the macros in the two forms $\text{Y\textsc{ield}}(val) \equiv \text{Y\textsc{ield}}(val, pos)$ and $\text{Y\textsc{ield}U\textsc{p}}(val) \equiv \text{Y\textsc{ield}}(val, up(pos))$, similarly for $\text{Y\textsc{ield}I\textsc{ndirect}}(adr)$ and $\text{Y\textsc{ield}U\textsc{p}I\textsc{ndirect}}(adr)$.

A context where an address and not a value is required characterizes the context of first children of parent nodes labeled with an assignment or prefix/postfix operator. It can thus be defined as follows:

$AddressPos(\alpha) \iff FirstChild(\alpha) \wedge label(up(\alpha)) \in \{\texttt{++}, \texttt{--}\} \cup Aop$
$FirstChild(\alpha) \iff first(up(\alpha)) = \alpha$

Notational Conventions. To reduce any notational overhead not needed by the human reader, in spelling out the ASM rules below we identify positions with the occurrences of the syntactical constructs nodes encode via their labels and those of their children. This explains updates like $pos := exp$ or $pos := stm$, which are used as shorthand for updating pos to the node labeled with the corresponding occurrence of exp respectively stm.[3]

For a succinct formulation of the interpreter rules we use a macro $context(pos)$ to describe the context of the expression or statement currently to be handled in the syntax tree. $context(pos)$ has to be matched against the cases appearing in the ASM rules below, choosing for the next computation step the first possible match following the textual order of the rules. If the elaboration of the subtree at the position pos has not yet started, then $context(pos)$ is the construct encoded by the labels of pos and of its children. Otherwise, if pos carries already its result in *values*, $context(pos)$ is the pseudo-construct encoded by the labels of the parent node of pos and of its children after replacing the already evaluated constructs by their *values* in the corresponding node. This explains notations like $uop \blacktriangleright val$ to describe the *context* of pos, where pos is marked with the cursor

---

[3] An identification of this kind, which is common in mathematics, has clearly to be resolved in an executable version of the model.

($\blacktriangleright$), resulting from the successful evaluation of the argument *exp* of the construct *uop exp* (encoded by *up(pos)* and its child *pos*), just before *uop* is applied to *val* to YIELDUP(*Apply(uop, val)*).

Expression Evaluation Rules. We are now ready to define EXECLEXP$_I$, the machine for expression evaluation. We do this in a compositional way, namely proceeding expression-wise: for each group of structurally similar expressions, defined by an appropriate parameterization described in Fig. 1,[4] there is a set of rules covering each intermediate phase of their evaluation. *SpecificExp*ressions of *L* are separately discussed below. The machine passes control from unevaluated expressions to the appropriate subexpressions until an atom (a literal or a local variable) is reached. It can continue its computation only as long as no operator exception occurs (see below for the definition of *UopException* and *BopException*). When an operator has to be applied, we use a static function *Apply* to determine the value the operator provides for the given arguments. This function can be separately described, as is usually done in the language manual. Similarly for the static function defining the *ValueOfLiteral*s.

$$
\begin{aligned}
&\text{EXECLEXP}_I \equiv \textbf{match } context(pos) \\
&\quad lit \rightarrow \text{YIELD}(ValueOfLiteral(lit)) \\
&\quad loc \rightarrow \text{YIELDINDIRECT}(locals(loc)) \\[4pt]
&\quad uop\ exp\ \ \rightarrow pos := exp \\
&\quad uop \blacktriangleright val \rightarrow \textbf{if } \neg UopException(uop, val) \textbf{ then} \\
&\qquad\qquad\qquad\qquad \text{YIELDUP}(Apply(uop, val)) \\[4pt]
&\quad exp_1\ bop\ exp_2\ \rightarrow pos := exp_1 \\
&\quad \blacktriangleright val\ bop\ exp\ \rightarrow pos := exp \\
&\quad val_1\ bop \blacktriangleright val_2 \rightarrow \textbf{if } \neg BopException(bop, val_1, val_2) \textbf{ then} \\
&\qquad\qquad\qquad\qquad\quad \text{YIELDUP}(Apply(bop, val_1, val_2)) \\[4pt]
&\quad exp_0\ ?\ exp_1\ :\ exp_2 \rightarrow pos := exp_0 \\
&\quad \blacktriangleright val\ ?\ exp_1\ :\ exp_2 \rightarrow \textbf{if } val \textbf{ then } pos := exp_1 \textbf{ else } pos := exp_2 \\
&\quad True\ ?\ \blacktriangleright val\ :\ exp \rightarrow \text{YIELDUP}(val) \\
&\quad False\ ?\ exp\ :\ \blacktriangleright val \rightarrow \text{YIELDUP}(val) \\[4pt]
&\quad loc = exp\ \ \rightarrow pos := exp \\
&\quad loc = \blacktriangleright val \rightarrow \{\text{WRITEMEM}(locals(loc), type(loc), val), \text{YIELDUP}(val)\} \\[4pt]
&\quad vexp\ op{=}\ exp\ \rightarrow pos := vexp \\
&\quad \overset{\blacktriangleright}{} adr\ op{=}\ exp \rightarrow pos := exp \\
&\quad adr\ op{=}\ \blacktriangleright val \rightarrow \textbf{let } t = type(up(pos)) \textbf{ and } v = memValue(adr, t) \textbf{ in} \\
&\qquad\qquad\qquad\quad \textbf{if } \neg BopException(op, v, val) \textbf{ then} \\
&\qquad\qquad\qquad\qquad \textbf{let } w = Apply(op, v, val) \textbf{ in} \\
&\qquad\qquad\qquad\qquad\quad \textbf{let } result = Convert(t, w) \textbf{ in} \\
&\qquad\qquad\qquad\qquad\qquad \text{WRITEMEM}(adr, t, result) \\
&\qquad\qquad\qquad\qquad\qquad \text{YIELDUP}(result)
\end{aligned}
$$

---

[4] The desired specializations can be obtained expression-wise by mere parameter expansion, a form of refinement that is easily proved to be correct.

$vexp\ op\ \rightarrow pos := vexp$ // for postfix operators $op \in \{\text{++}, \text{--}\}$

$\blacktriangleright adr\ op \rightarrow \textbf{let}\ old = memValue(adr, type(pos))\ \textbf{in}$
$\qquad\qquad \textbf{if}\ \neg UopException(op, old)\ \textbf{then}$
$\qquad\qquad\qquad \text{WRITEMEM}(adr, type(up(pos)), Apply(op, old))$
$\qquad\qquad\qquad \text{YIELDUP}(old)$

SPECIFICEXP$_I$

Note that in an assignment operator op= the result of the operation has to be converted back to the type of the variable expression, e.g., if c is a variable of type char, then c += 'A' is evaluated as c = (char)$(c$ + 'A'), since the operands of + are promoted to the type int in Java as well as in C♯.

Language-Specific Expressions. In Java$_\mathcal{I}$ the set of *SpecificExp*ressions and therefore the submachine SPECIFICEXP$_I$ is empty, whereas in the model for C♯$_\mathcal{I}$ the set contains checked and unchecked expressions 'checked' '(' *Exp* ')' and 'unchecked' '(' *Exp* ')'. The notion of *Checked* positions serves to define when an operator exception occurs due to arithmetical *Overflow* (for which case a rule will be added in the model for L$_\mathcal{E}$). The principle is that operators for integral types only throw overflow exceptions in a checked context except for the division by zero; operators for the type decimal always throw overflow exceptions. By default every position is unchecked, unless explicitly declared otherwise. This is formally expressed as follows.

$UopException(uop, val) \iff Checked(pos) \wedge Overflow(uop, val)$

$BopException(bop, val_1, val_2) \iff$
$\quad DivisonByZero(bop, val_2) \vee DecimalOverflow(bop, val_1, val_2) \vee$
$\quad (Checked(pos) \wedge Overflow(bop, val_1, val_2))$

$Checked(\alpha) \iff label(\alpha) = Checked \vee$
$\quad (label(\alpha) \neq Unchecked \wedge up(\alpha) \neq Undef \wedge Checked(up(\alpha)))$

As a consequence of these definitions and of the fact that the extension by rules to handle exceptions is defined in the model extension EXECL$_E$, the following SPECIFICEXP$_I$ rules of EXECC♯$_I$ do not distinguish between checked and unchecked expression evaluation.

match $context(pos)$
$\quad$ checked(exp) $\rightarrow pos := exp$
$\quad$ checked($\blacktriangleright val$) $\rightarrow \text{YIELDUP}(val)$
$\quad$ unchecked(exp) $\rightarrow pos := exp$
$\quad$ unchecked($\blacktriangleright val$) $\rightarrow \text{YIELDUP}(val)$

Statement Execution Rules. The machine EXECLSTM$_I$ is defined statement-wise. It transfers control from structured statements to the appropriate substatements, until the current statement has been computed normally or abrupts the computation. Abruptions trigger the control to propagate through all the enclosing statements up to the target labeled statement. The concept of propagation is defined for $L_\mathcal{I}$ in such a way that in the refined model $L_\mathcal{E}$ the concept of finally blocks can easily be specified. In case of a new execution of the body of a while statement, the previously computed intermediate results have to be cleared.[5] Since we formulate the model for the human reader, we use the ...-notation, for example in the rules for abruption or for sequences of block statements. This avoids having to fuss with an explicit formulation of the context, typically determined by a walk through a list.

$\textsc{ExecLStm}_I \equiv \textbf{match } context(pos)$
  $; \rightarrow \textsc{Yield}(Norm)$

  $exp; \quad \rightarrow pos := exp$
  $\blacktriangleright val; \rightarrow \textsc{YieldUp}(Norm)$

$\textsc{JumpStm}(L)$

  $\texttt{if } (exp)\ stm_1 \texttt{ else } stm_2 \qquad \rightarrow pos := exp$
  $\texttt{if } (\blacktriangleright val)\ stm_1 \texttt{ else } stm_2 \qquad \rightarrow \textbf{if } val \textbf{ then } pos := stm_1 \textbf{ else } pos := stm_2$
  $\texttt{if } (True)\ \blacktriangleright Norm \texttt{ else } stm \rightarrow \textsc{YieldUp}(Norm)$
  $\texttt{if } (False)\ stm \texttt{ else } \blacktriangleright Norm \rightarrow \textsc{YieldUp}(Norm)$

  $\texttt{while } (exp)\ stm \qquad \rightarrow pos := exp$
  $\texttt{while } (\blacktriangleright val)\ stm \qquad \rightarrow \textbf{if } val \textbf{ then } pos := stm$
  $\qquad\qquad\qquad\qquad\qquad\qquad \textbf{else } \textsc{YieldUp}(Norm)$
  $\texttt{while } (True)\ \blacktriangleright Norm \rightarrow \{pos := up(pos),\ \textsc{ClearValues}(up(pos))\}$
$\textsc{PropagateJump}(L)$

  $type\ loc; \rightarrow \textsc{Yield}(Norm)$

  $lab : stm \qquad \rightarrow pos := stm$
  $lab : \blacktriangleright Norm \rightarrow \textsc{YieldUp}(Norm)$

$\textsc{SpecificStm}_I$

  $\ldots \blacktriangleright abr \ldots \rightarrow \textbf{if } up(pos) \neq Undef \wedge PropagatesAbr(up(pos)) \textbf{ then}$
  $\qquad\qquad\qquad \textsc{YieldUp}(abr)$

  $\{\ \} \qquad\qquad\qquad\qquad\qquad \rightarrow \textsc{Yield}(Norm)$
  $\{stm \ \ldots\} \qquad\qquad\qquad\quad\ \rightarrow pos := stm$
  $\{\ldots \blacktriangleright Norm\} \qquad\qquad\quad\ \rightarrow \textsc{YieldUp}(Norm)$
  $\{\ldots \blacktriangleright Norm\ stm \ \ldots\} \quad \rightarrow pos := stm$
$\textsc{JumpOutOfBlockStm}$
  $\{\ldots \blacktriangleright abr \ \ldots\} \qquad\qquad \rightarrow \textsc{YieldUp}(abr)$

In $Java_\mathcal{I}$ the set $JumpStm$ consists of the jump statements $\texttt{break } lab;$ and $\texttt{continue } lab;$, so that the set of abruptions is defined as $Abr = Break(Lab)\ |$

---

[5] CLEARVALUES is needed in the present rule formulation due to our decision to have a static function *label* and a dynamic function to record the intermediate *values* associated to nodes. In a more syntax-oriented SOS-style, as used for the Java model in [14] where a function *restbody* combines the two functions *label* and *values* into one, CLEARVALUES results automatically from re-installing the body of the while statement as new rest program.

Continue(Lab). In C$\sharp_{\mathcal{I}}$ the set *JumpStm* contains the jump statements break; |
continue; | goto *lab*;, so that *Abr = Break | Continue | Goto(Lab)*. The
differences in the scoping rules for break; and continue; statements in the two
languages are reflected by differences in the corresponding interpreter rules.

$\text{JumpStm}(Java) \equiv \textbf{match } context(pos)$
  break *lab*; $\rightarrow \text{Yield}(Break(lab))$
  continue *lab*; $\rightarrow \text{Yield}(Continue(lab))$

$\text{PropagateJump}(Java) \equiv \textbf{match } context(pos)$
  lab: ▸*Break(lab_b)* $\rightarrow \textbf{if } lab = lab_b \textbf{ then } \text{YieldUp}(Norm)$
                          $\textbf{else } \text{YieldUp}(Break(lab_b))$
  lab: ▸*Continue(lab_c)* $\rightarrow \textbf{if } lab = lab_c \textbf{ then}$
                          $\{pos := up(pos), \text{ClearValues}(up(pos))\}$
                          $\textbf{else } \text{YieldUp}(Continue(lab_c))$

$\text{JumpStm}(C\sharp) \equiv \textbf{match } context(pos)$
  break; $\rightarrow \text{Yield}(Break)$
  continue; $\rightarrow \text{Yield}(Continue)$
  goto *lab*; $\rightarrow \text{Yield}(Goto(lab))$

$\text{PropagateJump}(C\sharp) \equiv \textbf{match } context(pos)$
  while (*True*) ▸*Break* $\rightarrow \text{YieldUp}(Norm)$
  while (*True*) ▸*Continue* $\rightarrow \{pos := up(pos), \text{ClearValues}(up(pos))\}$
  while (*True*) ▸*abr* $\rightarrow \text{YieldUp}(abr)$

Due to the differences in using syntactical *lab*els to denote jump statement
scopes, the definitions of how abruptions are propagated upwards differ slightly
for Java$_{\mathcal{I}}$ and for C$\sharp_{\mathcal{I}}$, though the conceptual content is the same, namely to prevent propagation at statements which are relevant for determining the abruption
target. For Java$_{\mathcal{I}}$ we have the simple definition[6]

$PropagatesAbr(\alpha) \iff label(\alpha) \neq LabeledStm$

whereas for C$\sharp_{\mathcal{I}}$ we have the following definition:

$PropagatesAbr(\alpha) \iff label(\alpha) \notin \{Block, While, Do, For, Switch\}$

Since Java has no goto statements, it has an empty JumpOutOfBlockStm
rule, whereas $\text{ExecC}\sharp\text{Stm}_I$ contains the rule

$\text{JumpOutOfBlockStm} \equiv \textbf{match } context(pos)$
  $\{ \ldots$ ▸*Goto(l)* $\ldots \} \rightarrow \textbf{let } \alpha = GotoTarget(first(up(pos)), l)$
                          $\textbf{if } \alpha \neq Undef \textbf{ then}$
                          $\{pos := \alpha, \text{ClearValues}(up(pos))\}$
                          $\textbf{else } \text{YieldUp}(Goto(l))$

---

[6] We disregard here the minor difference in the formulation of *PropagatesAbr* in [14],
where the arguments are not positions, but syntactical constructs or intermediate
values.

where an auxiliary function is needed to compute the target of a label in a list of block statements, recursively defined as follows:

$GotoTarget(\alpha, l) =$
    if $label(\alpha) = Lab(l)$ **then** α
    elseif $next(\alpha) = Undef$ **then** $Undef$
    else $GotoTarget(next(\alpha), l)$

Analogously to $\text{EXECC}\sharp\text{EXP}_I$ also $\text{EXECC}\sharp\text{STM}_I$ has checked contexts and therefore the following submachine (which in EXECJAVASTM_I is empty):

$\text{SPECIFICSTM}_I \equiv$ **match** $context(pos)$
    checked $block$ $\rightarrow pos := block$
    checked $\blacktriangleright Norm$ $\rightarrow \text{YIELDUP}(Norm)$
    unchecked $block$ $\rightarrow pos := block$
    unchecked $\blacktriangleright Norm \rightarrow \text{YIELDUP}(Norm)$

The auxiliary macro $\text{CLEARVALUES}(\alpha)$ to clear all values in the subtree at position α can be defined by recursion as follows, proceeding from top to bottom and from left to right[7]:

$\text{CLEARVALUES}(\alpha) \equiv$
    $values(\alpha) := Undef$
    if $first(\alpha) \neq Undef$ **then** $\text{CLEARVALUESSEQ}(first(\alpha))$

$\text{CLEARVALUESSEQ}(\alpha) \equiv$
    $\text{CLEARVALUES}(\alpha)$
    if $next(\alpha) \neq Undef$ **then** $\text{CLEARVALUESSEQ}(next(\alpha))$

3   Extension $\mathbf{L}_\mathcal{C}$ of $\mathbf{L}_\mathcal{I}$ by Procedures (Static Classes)

In $\text{L}_\mathcal{C}$ the concept of procedures (also called subroutines or functions) is added to the purely imperative instructions of $\text{L}_\mathcal{I}$. We introduce the basic mechanism of procedures first for so-called static methods, which belong to classes playing the role of modules. Different languages have different mechanisms to pass the parameters to a procedure call. In Java parameters are passed by-value, whereas in C♯ also call-by-reference is possible. Classes[8] come with variables which play the role of global module variables, called class or static variables or fields to distinguish them from instance fields provided in $\text{L}_\mathcal{O}$. Usually classes come with some special methods, so-called static initializers or static constructors, which are used to 'initialize' the class. The initialization concepts of different languages usually differ, in particular through different policies of when a class is initialized. In the extension EXECL_C of EXECL_I we illustrate these differences for Java

---

[7] Intuitively it should be clear that the execution of this recursive ASM provides simultaneously – in one step – the set of all updates of all its recursive calls, as is needed here for the clearing purpose; see [3] for a precise definition.

[8] We disregard here the slight variations to be made for interfaces.

and C♯. Normally classes are also put into a hierarchy, which is used to inherit methods among classes to reduce the labor of rewriting similar code fragments. As is to be expected, different languages come with different inheritance mechanisms related to their type concepts. Since the definition of the inheritance mechanism belongs mainly to the static semantics of the language, we mention it only where it directly influences the description of the dynamics.

We present the extension as a conservative (purely incremental) refinement of the ASM EXECL$_I$, which is helpful for proving properties of the extended machine on the basis of properties of the basic machine. Conservative refinement means that we perform the following three tasks (see [2] for a general description of the ASM refinement method).

- Extension of the ASM universes and functions, or introduction of new ones, for example to reflect the grammar extensions for expressions and statements. This goes together with the addition of the appropriate constraints needed for the static analysis of the new items (like type constraints, definite assignment rules, etc.).
- Extension of some of the definitions or macros, here for example the predicate *PropagatesAbr*(α), to make them work also for the newly occurring cases.
- Addition of new ASM rules, in the present case to define the semantics of the new expressions and statements.

3.1   Static Semantics of L$_\mathcal{C}$

In L$_\mathcal{C}$ a program is a set of compilation units, each coming with declarations of names spaces (also called packages), using directives (import declarations), type declarations (classes, interfaces, structs and enumerations), conditions on class extension, accessibility, visibility, etc. Since in this paper the focus is on dynamic semantics, we assume nested namespaces to be realized by the adoption of fully qualified names. We also do not discuss here the rules for class extensions (inheritance), for overriding of methods, for the accessibility of types and members via access modifiers like public, private, etc. This allows us to make use, for example, of a static function *body*(m) which associates to a method its code.

The extension of the grammars for *Vexp*, *Sexp*, *Stm* and thereby of the corresponding ASM domains reflects the introduction of *Classes* with static *Fields* and static *Methods*, which can be called with various arguments and upon returning may pass a computed value to the calling method. The new set *Arg* of arguments appearing here foresees that different parameters may be used. For example, Java provides value parameters (so that *Arg* ::= *Exp*), whereas C♯ allows also ref and out parameters (in which case *Arg* ::= *Exp* | 'ref' *Vexp* | 'out' *Vexp*). We do not discuss here the different static constraints (on types, definite assignment, reachability, etc.) which are imposed on the new expressions and statements in different languages.[9]

---

[9] See for example [8] for a detailed analysis of the extension of the definite assignment rules needed when allowing besides by-value parameter passing (as does Java) also call-by-reference (as does C♯).

$Vexp ::= \ldots \mid Field \mid Class \ `.` \ Field$

$Sexp ::= \ldots \mid Meth \ (\ [Args] \ ) \mid Class \ `.` \ Meth \ (\ [Args] \ )$

$Args ::= Arg \ \{`,` \ Arg\}$

$Stm \ ::= \ldots \mid `\texttt{return}' \ Exp \ `;` \mid `\texttt{return}' \ `;`$

The presence of method calls and of to-be-initialized classes makes it necessary to introduce new universes to denote multiple methods (pairs of type and signature), the initialization status of a type (which may have additional elements in specific languages, e.g., *Unusable* for the description of class initialization errors in Java, see below) and the sequence of still active method calls (so-called frame stack of environments of method executions). One also has to extend the set *Abr* of reasons for abruption by returns from a method, with or without a computed value which has to be passed to the caller.

$Meth = Type \times Msig$
$TypeState = Linked \mid InProgress \mid Initialized$
$Frame = Meth \times Pos \times Locals \times Values$
  where $Values = (Pos \rightarrow Result)$ and $Locals = (Loc \rightarrow Adr)$

A method signature *Msig* consists of the name of a method plus the sequence of types of the arguments of the method. A method is uniquely determined by the type in which it is declared and its signature. The reasons for abruptions are extended by method return:

$Abr = \ldots \mid Return \mid Return(Value)$

3.2 Dynamic Semantics of $\mathbf{L_C}$

To dynamically handle the (addresses of) static fields, the initialization state of types, the current method and the execution stack, we use the following new dynamic functions:

$globals$: $Type \times Field \rightarrow Adr$ $frames$: $List(Frame)$
$typeState$: $Type \rightarrow TypeState$ $meth$: $Meth$

To allow us to reuse without any rewriting the $\textsc{ExecL}_I$ rules as part of the $\textsc{ExecL}_C$ rules, we provide a separate notation $(meth, pos, locals, values)$ for the current frame, instead of having it on top of the frame stack. We extend the stipulations for the initial state as follows:

- $typeState(c) = Linked$ for each class c
- $meth = EntryPoint::\texttt{Main}()$ [*EntryPoint* is the main class]
- $pos = body(meth)$ [The root position of the body]
- $locals = values = \emptyset$ and $frames = []$

The submachine $\textsc{ExecL}_C$ extends the interpreter $\textsc{ExecL}_I$ for $\mathbf{L_I}$ by additional rules for the evaluation of the new expressions and for the execution of return statements. In the same way the further refinements in the sections below consist in the parallel addition of appropriate submachines.

$\text{EXECL}_C \equiv$
  EXECLEXP_C
  EXECLSTM_C

Expression Evaluation Rules. The rules in EXECLEXP_C for class field evaluation are analogous to those for the evaluation of local variables in EXECLEXP_I, except for using *globals* instead of *locals* and for the additional clause for class initialization. The rules for method calls use the macro INVOKESTATIC explained below, which takes care of the class initialization. The submachine ARGEVAL for the evaluation of sequences of arguments depends on the evaluation strategy of L. The definition of the submachine PARAMEXP for the evaluation of special parameter expressions depends on the parameter types provided by the language L. If $Arg = Exp$ as in Java, this machine is empty; for the case of C♯, where $Arg ::= Exp \mid \text{'ref'} \; Vexp \mid \text{'out'} \; Vexp$, we show below its definition.

$\text{EXECLEXP}_C \equiv \textbf{match} \; context(pos)$
  $c.f \rightarrow \textbf{if} \; Initialized(c) \; \textbf{then} \; \text{YIELDINDIRECT}(globals(c::f))$
      $\textbf{else} \; \text{INITIALIZE}(c)$

  $c.f = exp \;\;\rightarrow pos := exp$
  $c.f = {}^{\blacktriangleright}val \rightarrow \textbf{if} \; Initialized(c) \; \textbf{then}$
          $\text{WRITEMEM}(globals(c::f), type(c::f), val)$
          $\text{YIELDUP}(val)$
        $\textbf{else} \; \text{INITIALIZE}(c)$

  $c.m(args) \;\;\rightarrow pos := (args)$
  $c.m^{\blacktriangleright}(vals) \rightarrow \text{INVOKESTATIC}(c::m, vals)$

  ARGEVAL
  PARAMEXP

Once the arguments of a method call are computed, INVOKESTATIC invokes the method if the initialization of its class is not triggered, otherwise it initializes the class. In both Java and C♯, the initialization of a class is not triggered if the class is already initialized.[10] For methods which are not declared external or native, INVOKEMETHOD updates the frame stack and the current frame in the expected way (the same in both Java and C♯), taking care also of the initialization of local variables, which includes passing the call parameters. Consequently the definition of the macro INITLOCALS depends on the parameter passing mechanism of the considered language L, which is different for Java and for C♯. Since we will also have to deal with external (native) methods – whose declaration includes an **extern** (**native**) modifier and which may be implemented using a language other than L – we provide here for their invocation

---

[10] See [9] for other cases where the initialization is not triggered in C♯, in particular the refinement for classes which are marked with the implementation flag **beforefieldinit** to indicate that the reference of the static method does not trigger the class initialization.

a submachine INVOKEEXTERN, to be defined separately depending on the class of external/native (e.g. library) methods. The predicate *StaticCtor* recognizes static class constructors (class initialization methods); their implicit call interrupts the member access at *pos*, to later return to the evaluation of *pos* instead of *up(pos)*.

INVOKESTATIC(c::m, *vals*) ≡
    if *triggerInit*(c) **then** INITIALIZE(c) **else** INVOKEMETHOD(c::m, *vals*)
    where *triggerInit*(c) = ¬*Initialized*(c) ∧ ¬*BeforeFieldInit*(c)

INVOKEMETHOD(c::m, *vals*) ≡
    if extern ∈ *modifiers*(c::m) **then** INVOKEEXTERN(c::m, *vals*)
    else let p = **if** *StaticCtor*(c::m) **then** *pos* **else** *up(pos)* **in**
    frames := *push(frames,* (*meth, p, locals, values*))
    meth   := c::m
    pos   := *body*(c::m)
    values := ∅
    INITLOCALS(c::m, *vals*)

The definition of the macro INITLOCALS for the initialization of local variables depends on the parameter passing mechanism. In Java the macro simply defines *locals* (which assumes the role of *mem* in our general model) to take as first arguments the actual values of the call parameters (the *ValueParams* for call-by-value). In C♯ one has to add a mechanism to pass **reference** parameters, including so-called **out** parameters, which can be treated as **ref** parameters except that they need not be definitely assigned until the function call returns. In the following definition of INITLOCALS for C♯, all (also simultaneous) applications of the external function *new* during the computation of the ASM are supposed to provide pairwise different fresh elements from the underlying domain *Adr*.[11] *paramIndex*(c::m, x) yields the index of the formal parameter x in the signature of c::m.

INITLOCALS(c::m, *vals*)(C♯) ≡
    forall x ∈ *LocalVars*(c::m) **do**   // addresses for local variables
      locals(x) := *new(Adr, type(x))*
    forall x ∈ *ValueParams*(c::m) **do**   // copy value arguments
    let *adr* = *new(Adr, type(x))* **in**
      locals(x) := *adr*
      WRITEMEM(*adr, type(x), vals(paramIndex(c::m, x))*)
    forall x ∈ *RefParams*(c::m) ∪ *OutParams*(c::m) **do**
      locals(x) := *vals(paramIndex(c::m, x))*   // ref and out arguments

The difference between **ref** and **out** parameters at function calls and in function bodies of C♯ is reflected by including as *AddressPositions* all nodes

---

[11] See [10] and [5, 2.4.4] for a justification of this assumption. See also the end of Sect. 4 where we provide an abstract specification of the needed memory allocation.

whose parent node is labeled by `ref` or `out` and by adding corresponding definite assignment constraints (listed in [4]):

$$AddressPos(\alpha) \iff FirstChild(\alpha) \land label(up(\alpha)) \in \{\texttt{ref}, \texttt{out}, \texttt{++}, \texttt{--}\} \cup Aop$$

Therefore the following rules of PARAMEXP for C♯ can ignore `ref` and `out`:

PARAMEXP(C♯) ≡ **match** $context(pos)$
  $\texttt{ref } vexp \;\rightarrow\; pos := vexp$
  $\texttt{ref }^{\blacktriangleright} adr \;\rightarrow\; \text{YIELDUP}(adr)$

  $\texttt{out } vexp \;\rightarrow\; pos := vexp$
  $\texttt{out }^{\blacktriangleright} adr \;\rightarrow\; \text{YIELDUP}(adr)$

For the sake of illustration we provide here a definition for the submachine ARGEVAL with left-to-right evaluation strategy for sequences of arguments. The definition has to be modified in case one wants to specify another evaluation order for expressions, involving the use of the ASM **choose** construct if some non-deterministic choice has to be formulated. For a discussion of such model variations we refer to [15] where an ASM model is developed which can be instantiated to capture the different expression evaluation strategies in Ada95, C, C++, Java, C♯ and Fortran.

ARGEVAL ≡ **match** $context(pos)$
  $()\qquad\qquad\qquad \rightarrow \text{YIELD}([])$
  $(arg, \ldots)\qquad\quad\; \rightarrow pos := arg$
  $(val_1, \ldots, {}^{\blacktriangleright}val_n) \;\rightarrow \text{YIELDUP}([val_1, \ldots, val_n])$
  $(\ldots {}^{\blacktriangleright}val, arg \ldots) \rightarrow pos := arg$

Statement Execution Rules. The semantics of static initialization is language dependent and is further discussed below for Java and C♯. The rules for method return in EXECLSTM$_C$ trigger an abruption upon returning from a method. Via the RETURNPROPAGATION submachine defined below, an abruption $Return$ or $Return(val)$ due to method return is propagated to the beginning of the body of the method one is returning from. There an execution of the submachine EXITMETHOD is triggered, which restores the environment of the caller. This abruption propagation mechanism allows one an elegant refinement for $L_{\mathcal{E}}$, where the method exit is subject to the prior execution of so-called `finally` code which may be present in the method. The rule to YIELDUP($Norm$) does not capture falling off the method body, but yields up the result of the normal execution of the invocation of a method with void return type in an expression statement.

EXECC♯STM$_C$ ≡ **match** $context(pos)$
  STATICINITIALIZER(L)
  $\texttt{return } exp; \;\rightarrow\; pos := exp$
  $\texttt{return }^{\blacktriangleright} val; \rightarrow \text{YIELDUP}(Return(val))$
  $\texttt{return}; \qquad \rightarrow \text{YIELD}(Return)$

RETURNPROPAGATION(L)
▸ *Norm*; → YIELDUP(*Norm*)

The return propagation machine for C♯ is simpler than (in fact part of) that for Java due to static differences (including the different use of labels) in the two languages. As mentioned above, both machines, instead of transferring the control from a return statement directly to the invoker, propagate the return abruption up to the starting point of the current method body, from where the method is exited.

RETURNPROPAGATION(C♯) ≡ **match** *context*(*pos*)
   Return   → **if** *pos* = *body*(*meth*) ∧ ¬*Empty*(*frames*) **then**
                EXITMETHOD(*Norm*)
   Return(*val*) → **if** *pos* = *body*(*meth*) ∧ ¬*Empty*(*frames*) **then**
                EXITMETHOD(*val*)

RETURNPROPAGATION(*Java*) ≡ **match** *context*(*pos*)
  lab : ▸ *Return*   → YIELDUP(*Return*)
  lab : ▸ *Return*(*val*) → YIELDUP(*Return*(*val*))
RETURNPROPAGATION(C♯)

To complete the return propagation in Java one still has to treat the special case of a return from a class initialization method. In [14, Fig. 4.5] this has been formulated as part of the STATICINITIALIZER machine, which also realizes the condition for the semantics of Java that before initializing a class, all its superclasses have to be initialized. To stop the return propagation at the point of return from a class initialization, in the case of Java the predicate *PropagatesAbr* has to be refined as follows:

$$PropagatesAbr(\alpha) \iff label(\alpha) \notin \{LabeledStm, StaticBlock\}$$

In C♯ the initialization of a class does not trigger the initialization of its direct base class, so that STATICINITIALIZER(C♯) is empty.

STATICINITIALIZER(*Java*) ≡ **match** *context*(*pos*)
  `static` *stm* → **let** *c* = *classNm*(*meth*) **in**
                 if *c* = `Object` ∨ *Initialized*(*super*(*c*)) **then** *pos* := *stm*
                 else INITIALIZE(*super*(*c*))
  `static` *Return* → YIELDUP(*Return*)

The machine EXITMETHOD, which is the same for Java and for C♯ (modulo the submachine FREELOCALS), restores the frame of the invoker and passes the result value (if any). Upon normal return from a static constructor it also updates the *typeState* of the relevant class as *Initialized*. We also add a rule FREELOCALS to free the memory used for local variables and value parameters, using an abstract notion FREEMEMORY of how addresses of local variables and value parameters are actually de-allocated.[12]

---

[12] Under the assumption of a potentially infinite supply of addresses, which is often made when describing the semantics of a programming language, one can dispense with FREELOCALS.

ExitMethod(*result*) ≡
  let (*oldMeth, oldPos, oldLocals, oldValues*) = *top*(*frames*) **in**
    meth   := *oldMeth*
    pos   := *oldPos*
    locals := *oldLocals*
    frames := *pop*(*frames*)
    if *StaticCtor*(*meth*) ∧ *result* = *Norm* **then**
       typeState(*type*(*meth*)) := *Initialized*
       values := *oldValues*
    else
       values := *oldValues* ⊕ {*oldPos* ↦ *result*}
    FreeLocals

FreeLocals ≡
  forall *x* ∈ *LocalVars*(*meth*) ∪ *ValueParams*(*meth*) **do**
    FreeMemory(*locals*(*x*), *type*(*x*))

For both Java and C♯, a type *c* is considered as initialized if its static constructor has terminated normally, as is expressed by the update of *typeState*(*c*) to *Initialized* in ExitMethod above. In addition, *c* is considered as initialized already if its static constructor has been invoked, to guarantee that during the execution of the static constructor accesses to the fields of *c* or invocations of methods of *c* do not trigger a new initialization of *c*. This explains the update of *typeState*(*c*) to *InProgress* in the definition of Initialize and the following definition of *Initialized*:

$$Initialized(c) \iff typeState(c) = Initialized \lor typeState(c) = InProgress$$

To initialize a class its static constructor is invoked (denoted `<clinit>` in Java and `.cctor` in C♯). All static fields of the class are initialized with their default value. The typeState of the class is updated to prevent further invocations of Initialize(*c*) during the execution of the static constructor of *c*. The macro will be further refined in $L_{\mathcal{E}}$ to account for exceptions during an initialization.

Initialize(*c*) ≡
  if *typeState*(*c*) = *Linked* **then**
    typeState(*c*) := *InProgress*
    forall *f* ∈ *staticFields*(*c*) **do**
      let *t* = *type*(*c*::*f*) **in** WriteMem(*globals*(*c*::*f*), *t*, *defaultValue*(*t*))
    InvokeMethod(*c*::.`cctor`, [])

With respect to the execution of initializers of static class fields the ECMA standard [7, §17.4.5.1] for C♯ says that the static field initializers of a class correspond to a sequence of assignments that are executed in the textual order in which they appear in the class declaration. If a static constructor exists in the class, execution of the static field initializers occurs immediately prior to executing that static constructor. Otherwise, the static field initializers are executed at an *implementation-dependent* time prior to the first use of a static field of that class.

Our definitions above for C♯ express the decision taken by Microsoft's current C♯ compiler, which in the second case creates a static constructor and adds the `beforefieldinit` flag to the class. If one wants to reflect also the non-determinism suggested by the ECMA formulation, one can formalize the implementation-dependent initialization of `beforefieldinit` types by the following rule:[13]

$\text{EXECC}\sharp_C \equiv$ **choose** $x \in \{0, 1\}$ **do**
  if $x = 0$ **then** $\{\text{EXECC}\sharp\text{EXP}_C, \text{EXECC}\sharp\text{STM}_C\}$
  if $x = 1$ **then**
    choose $c \in Class$ **with** $BeforeFieldInit(c) \land \neg Initialized(c)$ **do**
    $\text{INITIALIZE}(c)$

4   Extension $\mathbf{L_O}$ of $\mathbf{L_C}$ by Object-Oriented Features

In this section we extend L_C to an object-oriented language L_O by adding objects for class instances, formally represented as elements of a new set *Ref* of references. The extension provides new expressions, namely for *instance* fields, instance methods and constructors, and for the dynamic creation of new class instances. The inheritance mechanism we consider supports overriding and overloading of methods, dynamic type checks, and type casts. We skip the (via syntactical differences partly language-specific) treatment of arrays; their description for Java and C♯ can be found in [14, 4]. The interpreter EXECL_O is defined as a refinement of EXECL_C, obtained from the latter by extending its universes, functions, macros and rules to make them work also for the new expressions.

4.1   Static Semantics of $\mathbf{L_O}$

The first extension concerns the sets *Exp*, *Vexp*, *Sexp* where the new reference types appear. 'null' denotes an empty reference, 'this' is interpreted as the current reference. A *RefExp* is an expression of a reference type. We use 'pred' to denote a predecessor class, in Java written 'super' and in C♯ 'base'.

Exp ::= ... | 'null' | 'this' | *Exp* '.' *Field* | '(' *Type* ')' *Exp* | *SpecificExp(L)*

Vexp ::= ... | *Vexp* '.' *Field* | *RefExp* '.' *Field* | 'pred' '.' *Field*

Sexp ::= ... | 'new' *Type* ([*Args*]) | *Exp* '.' *Meth* ([*Args*])
         | 'pred' '.' *Meth* ([*Args*])

---

[13] This is discussed in detail in [9]. The reader finds there also a detection of further class initialization features that are missing in the ECMA specification, related to the definition of when a static class constructor has to be executed and to the initialization of structs.

The specific expressions of $Java_\mathcal{I}$ and $C\sharp_\mathcal{I}$ are extended by specific object-oriented expressions of these languages as follows:

$$SpecificExp(Java) ::= \ldots \mid Exp \text{ 'instanceof' } Type$$
$$SpecificExp(C\sharp) \quad ::= \ldots \mid \text{'typeof' '(' } RetType \text{ ')' } \mid Exp \text{ 'is' } Type$$
$$\mid Exp \text{ 'as' } RefType$$

Type Structure. To be able to explain by variations of our interpreter EXECL the major differences between Java and C$\sharp$, we need to mention here some of the major differences in the type structure underlying the two languages. For efficiency reasons C$\sharp$ distinguishes between value types and reference types. When a compiler encounters the declaration of a variable of value type, it directly allocates the memory to that variable, whereas for declarations of variables of reference type it creates a pointer to an object on the heap. A mediation between the two types is provided, known under the name of boxing, to convert values into references, and of an inverse operation called unboxing. At the level of $L_\mathcal{O}$, besides the new type of *Ref*erences present in both languages, C$\sharp$ also introduces so-called *Struct* types, a value-type restricted version of classes, to circumvent the overhead associated with class instances.

Therefore, to be prepared to instantiate our L-interpreter to an interpreter for both Java and C$\sharp$, the domain of values of $L_\mathcal{I}$ is extended to contain not only *Ref*erences (with a special value $null \in Ref$ to denote a null reference), as would suffice for interpreting $Java_\mathcal{O}$, but also struct values. For the case of C$\sharp$ we assume furthermore references to be different from addresses, i.e., $Ref \cap Adr = \emptyset$.

$$Value = SimpleValue \cup Adr \cup Ref \cup Struct$$

The set *Struct* of struct values can be defined as the set of mappings from *StructType::Field* to *Value*. The value of an instance field of a value of struct type T can then be extracted by applying the map to the field name, i.e., $structField(val, T, f) = val(f)$. We abstract from the implementation-dependent layout of structs and objects and use a function

$$fieldAdr: (Adr \cup Ref) \times Type::Field \rightarrow Adr$$

to record addresses of fields. This function is assumed to satisfy the following properties, where the static function

$$instanceFields: Type \rightarrow Powerset(Type::Field)$$

yields the set of instance fields of any given type t; if t is a class type, it includes the fields declared in all pred(ecessor) classes of t:

- If t is a *struct type*, then $fieldAdr(adr, t::f)$ is the address of field f of a value of type t stored in *mem* at address adr.
- A value of struct type t at address adr occupies the following addresses:

$$\{fieldAdr(adr, f) \mid f \in instanceFields(t)\}$$

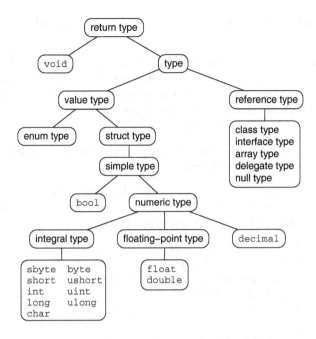

Fig. 2. The classification of types of C♯

- If *runTimeType*(*ref*) is a *class type*, then *fieldAdr*(*ref*, *t*::*f*) is the address of field *t*::*f* of the object referenced by *ref* and the object represented by *ref* occupies the addresses

$$\{ \mathit{fieldAdr}(\mathit{ref}, f) \mid f \in \mathit{instanceFields}(c) \}$$

where $c = \mathit{runTimeType}(\mathit{ref}) = c$.

For our language L we do not specify further types. For the sake of illustration see Fig. 2 with the extended type classification of C♯, where the simple types of $L_{\mathcal{I}}$ became aliases for struct types.

Syntax-Tree Information. According to our assumption that the attributed syntax tree has exact information, for the formulation of our model we assume as result of field and method resolution that each field access has the form T::f, where f is a field declared in the type T. Similarly, each method call has the form T::m(*args*), where m is the signature of a method declared in type T. Moreover, for the access of fields and methods via the current instance or the predecessor class we know the following:

- **pred**.f in class C has been replaced by **this**.B::f, where B is the first predecessor class of C where the field f is declared.
- **pred**.m(*args*) in class C has been replaced by **this**.B::M(*args*), where B::M is the method signature of the method selected by the compiler (the set of applicable methods is constructed starting in the *pred class* of C).

- If f is a field, then f has been replaced by **this**. $T::f$, where f is declared in T.

Instance creation expressions are treated like ordinary method invocations, splitting an instance creation expression into a creation part and an invocation of an instance constructor. To make the splitting correctly reflect the intended meaning of **new** $T::M(args)$, we assume in our model without loss of generality that class instance constructors return the value of **this**.[14]

- Let T be a class type. Then the instance creation expression **new** $T::M(args)$ is replaced by **new** T. $T::M(args)$.

Also for constructors of structs we assume that they return the value of **this**. For instance constructors of structs one has to reflect that in addition they need an address for **this**. Let S be a struct type. Then:

- $vexp$ = **new** $S::M(args)$ has been replaced by $vexp$. $S::M(args)$. This reflects that such a **new** triggers no object creation or memory allocation since structs get their memory allocated at declaration time.
- Other occurrences of **new** $S::M(args)$ have been replaced by x. $S::M(args)$, where x is a new temporary local variable of type S.

For automatic boxing we have:

- $vexp$ = exp is replaced by $vexp$ = $(T)exp$ if $type(exp)$ is a value type, $T = type(vexp)$ and T is a reference type. In this case we must have $type(exp) \preceq T$, where $\preceq$ denotes the here not furthermore specified subtype relation (standard implicit conversion) resulting from the inheritance and the 'implements' relation between classes and interfaces.
- arg is replaced by $(T)arg$ if $type(arg)$ is a value type, the selected method expects an argument of type T and T is a reference type. In this case we must have $type(arg) \preceq T$.

4.2   Dynamic Semantics of L$_\mathcal{O}$

Two new dynamic functions are needed to keep track of the $runTimeType: Ref \to Type$ of references and of the type object $typeObj: RetType \to Ref$ of a given type, where $RetType ::= Type \mid$ '**void**'. The memory function is extended to store also references:

$$mem: Adr \to SimpleValue \cup Ref \cup \{Undef\}$$

For boxing we need a dynamic function $valueAdr: Ref \to Adr$ to record the address of a value in a box. If $runTimeType(ref)$ is a value type, then $valueAdr(ref)$ is the address of the struct value stored in the box.

---

[14] The result of a constructor invocation with **new** is the newly created object, which is stored in the local environment as value for **this**. Therefore one can equivalently refine the macro EXITMETHOD for constructors to pass the value of **this** upon returning from a constructor, see [14, pg. 82].

The this reference is treated as first parameter with index zero. It is passed by value in instance methods of classes. It is passed by reference in struct methods, as an out paramter in constructors and as a ref paramter in instance methods.

For the refinement of the EXECL$_C$ transition rules it suffices to add the new machine EXECLEXP$_O$ for evaluating the new expressions, since L$_O$ introduces no new statements.

EXECL$_O$ ≡
   EXECLEXP$_O$

In EXECLEXP$_O$ the type cast rule contains three clauses concerning value types, which are needed for C♯ but are not present for Java. In fact for Java the first *RefType* subrule suffices, the one where both the declared type and the target type are compatible reference types and the reference is passed through. FIELDEXP$_O$ contains the rules for field access and assignment as needed for C♯, where for Java the additional access rule for value types is not needed (and the macros for getting and setting field values are simplified correspondingly). NEW$_O$ differs for Java and C♯, reflecting the different scheduling for the initialization, as specified below. The rules for instance method invocation are the same for Java and C♯ modulo different definitions for the macro INVOKE and except that for C♯ an additional clause is needed for *StructValueInvocations*. A struct value invocation is a method invocation on a struct value which is not stored in a variable. For such struct values a temporary storage area (called 'home') has to be created which is passed in the invocation as value of this. The submachine SPECIFICEXP$_O$ is specified below for Java and C♯.

EXECLEXP$_O$ ≡ **match** *context*(*pos*)
   null → YIELD(*null*)
   this → YIELDINDIRECT(*locals*(this))
   (*t*) *exp* → *pos* := *exp*
   (*t*)▶ *val* →
     if *type*(*pos*) ∈ *RefType* **then**
       if *t* ∈ *RefType* ∧ (*val* = *null* ∨ *runTimeType*(*val*) ⪯ *t*) **then**
         YIELDUP(*val*) // pass reference through
       if *t* ∈ *ValueType* ∧ *val* ≠ *null* ∧ *t* = *runTimeType*(*val*) **then**
         // un-box a copy of the value
         YIELDUP(*memValue*(*valueAdr*(*val*), *t*))
     if *type*(*pos*) ∈ *ValueType* **then**
       if *t* = *type*(*pos*) **then** YIELDUP(*val*) // compile-time identity
       if *t* ∈ *RefType* **then** YIELDUPBOX(*type*(*pos*), *val*) // box value
   FIELDEXP$_O$
   NEW$_O$
   exp.*T*::*M*(*args*) → *pos* := *exp*
   ▶*val*.*T*::*M*(*args*) →
     pos := (*args*)

if *StructValueInvocation*($up(pos)$) **then**
  let $adr = new(Adr, type(pos))$ **in**   // create home for struct value
    WRITEMEM($adr, type(pos), val$)
    $values(pos) := adr$
$val \, . \, T{::}M^{\blacktriangleright}(vals) \; \rightarrow \;$ INVOKE($val, T{::}M, vals$)

SPECIFICEXP$_O$

The following definition formalizes that a struct value invocation is a method invocation on a struct value which is not stored in a variable.

$StructValueInvocation(exp \, . \, T{::}M\,(args)) \; \Longleftrightarrow \;$
  $type(exp) \in StructType \land exp \notin Vexp$

The rules for instance field access and assignment in FIELDEXP$_O$ are equivalent for Java and C♯ modulo two differences. The first difference comes through the different definitions for the macro SETFIELD explained below. The second difference consists of the fact that C♯ needs the struct type clause formulated below (in the second rule for field access), which is not needed for Java.[15] We use $type(exp \, . \, t{::}f) = type(t{::}f)$.

FIELDEXP$_O$ $\equiv$ **match** *context*(pos)
  $exp \, . \, t{::}f \;\; \rightarrow \; pos := exp$
  $^{\blacktriangleright}val \, . \, t{::}f \; \rightarrow$ **if** $type(pos) \in ValueType \land val \notin Adr$ **then**
        YIELDUP($structField(val, type(pos), t{::}f)$)
      elseif $val \neq null$ **then**
        YIELDUPINDIRECT($fieldAdr(val, t{::}f)$)

  $exp_1 \, . \, t{::}f = exp_2 \; \rightarrow \; pos := exp_1$
  $^{\blacktriangleright}val \, . \, t{::}f = exp \;\; \rightarrow \; pos := exp$
  $val_1 \, . \, t{::}f = \; ^{\blacktriangleright}val_2 \; \rightarrow$ **if** $val_1 \neq null$ **then**
        SETFIELD($val_1, t{::}f, val_2$)
        YIELDUP(val_2)

The different schedules for the initialization of classes in Java and C♯ appear in the different definitions for their submachines NEW$_O$ and INVOKE. When creating a new class instance, Java checks whether the class is initialized. If not, it initializes the class. Otherwise it does what also the machine NEW$_O$(C♯) does, namely it creates a new class instance on the heap, initializing all instance fields with their default values. See below for the detailed definition of HEAPINIT.

---

[15] As in most parts of this paper, we disregard merely notational differences between the two models, here the fact that due to the presence of both memory addresses and values, the C♯$_O$ model uses the machine YIELDUPINDIRECT($fieldAdr(val, t{::}f)$) where the Java$_O$ model has the simpler update YIELDUP($getField(val, t{::}f)$).

$\text{NEW}_O(Java) \equiv \textbf{match } context(pos)$
$\quad \textbf{new } c \rightarrow \textbf{if } Initialized(c) \textbf{ then}$
$\qquad\qquad\quad \textbf{let } ref = new(Ref, c) \textbf{ in}$
$\qquad\qquad\qquad \text{HEAPINIT}(ref, c)$
$\qquad\qquad\qquad \text{YIELD}(ref)$
$\qquad\qquad\quad \textbf{else } \text{INITIALIZE}(c)$

$\text{NEW}_O(\text{C}\sharp) \equiv \textbf{match } context(pos)$
$\quad \textbf{new } c \rightarrow \textbf{let } ref = new(Ref, c) \textbf{ in}$
$\qquad\qquad\quad runTimeType(ref) := c$
$\qquad\qquad\quad \textbf{forall } f \in instanceFields(c) \textbf{ do}$
$\qquad\qquad\qquad \textbf{let } adr = fieldAdr(ref, f) \textbf{ and } t = type(f) \textbf{ in}$
$\qquad\qquad\qquad\quad \text{WRITEMEM}(adr, t, defaultValue(t))$
$\qquad\qquad\quad \text{YIELD}(ref)$

The INVOKE rule for Java is paraphrased from [14, Fig. 5.2]. The compile-time computable static function *lookup* yields the class where the given method specification is defined in the class hierarchy, depending on the run-time type of the given reference.

$\text{INVOKE}(val, T{::}M, vals)(Java) \equiv$
$\quad \textbf{let } S = \textbf{case } callKind(up(pos)) \textbf{ of}$
$\qquad Virtual \rightarrow lookup(runTimeType(val), T{::}M)$
$\qquad Super \rightarrow lookup(super(classNm(meth)), T{::}M)$
$\qquad Special \rightarrow T$
$\quad \text{INVOKEMETHOD}(S{::}M, [val]vals)$

C$\sharp$ performs the initialization test only in the very moment of performing INVOKE, after the evaluation of the constructor arguments. Thus the invocation of an instance constructor of a class may trigger the class initialization (see the detailed analysis in [9]). The split into virtual and non-virtual method calls is reflected in the submachine INVOKEINSTANCE.

$\text{INVOKE}(val, T{::}M, vals)(\text{C}\sharp) \equiv$
$\quad \textbf{if } InstanceCtor(M) \wedge triggerInit(T) \textbf{ then } \text{INITIALIZE}(T)$
$\quad \textbf{elseif } val \neq null \textbf{ then } \text{INVOKEINSTANCE}(T{::}M, val, vals)$

$\text{INVOKEINSTANCE}(T{::}M, val, vals) \equiv$
$\quad \textbf{if } callKind(T{::}M) = Virtual \textbf{ then}$ $\qquad\qquad$ // indirect call, $val \in Ref$
$\qquad \textbf{let } S = lookup(runTimeType(val), T{::}M) \textbf{ in}$
$\qquad \textbf{let } this = \textbf{if } S \in StructType \textbf{ then } valueAdr(val) \textbf{ else } val \textbf{ in}$
$\qquad\quad \text{INVOKEMETHOD}(S{::}M, [this] \cdot vals)$
$\quad \textbf{if } callKind(T{::}M) = NonVirtual \textbf{ then}$ $\qquad$ // direct call, $val \in Adr \cup Ref$
$\qquad \text{INVOKEMETHOD}(T{::}M, [val] \cdot vals)$

The machines SPECIFICEXP$_O$ define the semantics of the language-specific expressions listed above, which are all related to type checking.

$\text{SPECIFICEXP}_O(Java) \equiv \textbf{match } context(pos)$
$\quad exp \texttt{ instanceof } t \;\rightarrow\; pos := exp$
$\quad \blacktriangleright val \texttt{ instanceof } t \rightarrow \text{YIELDUP}(val \neq null \wedge runTimeType(val) \preceq t)$

$\text{SPECIFICEXP}_O(\text{C}\sharp)$ contains $\text{SPECIFICEXP}_O(Java)$ as a submachine (modulo notational differences), namely consisting of the first and the third rule for the is-instruction. In addition we have rules to yield the type of an object and for type conversion between compatible types, which needs a new macro YIELDUPBOX defined below for yielding the reference of a newly created box.

$\text{SPECIFICEXP}_O(\text{C}\sharp) \equiv \textbf{match } context(pos)$
$\quad \texttt{typeof}(t) \rightarrow \text{YIELD}(typeObj(t))$

$\quad exp \texttt{ is } t \;\rightarrow\; pos := exp$
$\quad \blacktriangleright val \texttt{ is } t \rightarrow \textbf{if } type(pos) \in ValueType \textbf{ then}$
$\qquad\qquad\qquad \text{YIELDUP}(type(pos) \preceq t) \quad // \text{ compile-time property}$
$\qquad\qquad \textbf{else}$
$\qquad\qquad\qquad \text{YIELDUP}(val \neq null \wedge runTimeType(val) \preceq t)$

$\quad exp \texttt{ as } t \;\rightarrow\; pos := exp$
$\quad \blacktriangleright val \texttt{ as } t \rightarrow \textbf{if } type(pos) \in ValueType \textbf{ then}$
$\qquad\qquad\qquad \text{YIELDUPBOX}(type(pos), val) \quad // \text{ box a copy of the value}$
$\qquad\qquad \textbf{elseif } (val \neq null \wedge runTimeType(val) \preceq t) \textbf{ then}$
$\qquad\qquad\qquad \text{YIELDUP}(val) \quad // \text{ pass reference through}$
$\qquad\qquad \textbf{else } \text{YIELDUP}(null) \quad // \text{ convert to null reference}$

Memory Refinement. Due to the appearance of reference (and in C$\sharp$ also struct) types an extension of the memory notion is needed. To model the dynamic state of objects, storage is needed for all instance variables and to record to which class an object belongs. The model for Java$_O$ in [14] provides for this reason a dynamic function $heap\colon Ref \rightarrow Heap$ to record every class instance together with the values of its fields. $Heap$ can be considered as an abstract set of elements of form $Object(t, fields)$, where $fields$ is a map associating a value with each field in $instanceFields(t)$. One can then define two simple macros SETFIELD and GETFIELD to manipulate references on this abstract heap as follows (where $\oplus$ denotes adding a new (argument,value)-pair to a function, or overwriting an existing value by a new one):

$\text{GETFIELD}(ref, f)(Java) \equiv \textbf{case } heap(ref) \textbf{ of}$
$\quad \texttt{Object}(t, fields) \rightarrow fields(f)$
$\text{SETFIELD}(ref, f, val)(Java) \equiv \textbf{let } \texttt{Object}(t, fields) = heap(ref) \textbf{ in}$
$\quad heap(ref) := \texttt{Object}(t, fields \;\oplus\; \{(f, val)\})$

For modeling C$\sharp_O$ a further refinement of both reading from and writing to memory is needed, due to the presence of struct types and call-by-reference. The notion of reading from the memory is refined by extending the simple equation $memValue(adr, t) = mem(adr)$ of C$\sharp_I$ to fit also struct types, in addition to reference types. This is done by the following simultaneous recursive definition of $memValue$ and $getField$ along the given struct type.

$memValue(adr, t) =$
  if $t \in SimpleType \cup RefType$ **then** $mem(adr)$
  elseif $t \in StructType$ **then**
    $\{f \mapsto getField(adr, t::f) \mid f \in instanceFields(t)\}$

$getField(adr, t::f) = memValue(fieldAdr(adr, t::f), type(t::f))$

Similarly, writing to memory is refined from

$\textsc{WriteMem}(adr, t, val) \equiv mem(adr) := val$

in C♯$_{\mathcal{I}}$, recursively together with SETFIELD along the given struct type:

$\textsc{WriteMem}(adr, t, val) \equiv$
  if $t \in SimpleType \cup RefType$ **then** $mem(adr) := val$
  elseif $t \in StructType$ **then**
    forall $f \in instanceFields(t)$ **do** $\textsc{SetField}(adr, t::f, val(f))$

$\textsc{SetField}(adr, t::f, val) \equiv \textsc{WriteMem}(fieldAdr(adr, t::f), type(t::f), val)$

The notion of *AddressPos* from C♯$_{\mathcal{C}}$ is refined to include also lvalue nodes of *StructType*, so that address positions are of the following form:

ref $\square$, **out** $\square$, $\square$++, $\square$--, $\square$ *op= exp*, $\square$.*f*, $\square$.*m(args)*

$AddressPos(\alpha) \iff FirstChild(\alpha) \wedge$
  $label(up(\alpha)) \in \{\mathbf{ref}, \mathbf{out}, ++, --\} \cup Aop \vee$
  $(label(up(\alpha)) = '.' \wedge \alpha \in Vexp \wedge type(\alpha) \in StructType)$

YIELDUPBOX creates a box for a given value of a given type and returns its reference. The run-time type of a reference to a boxed value of struct type t is defined to be t. The struct is copied in both cases, when it is boxed and when it is un-boxed.

$\textsc{YieldUpBox}(t, val) \equiv \textbf{let } ref = new(Ref) \textbf{ and } adr = new(Adr, t) \textbf{ in}$
  $runTimeType(ref) := t$
  $valueAdr(ref) := adr$
  $\textsc{WriteMem}(adr, t, val)$
  $\textsc{YieldUp}(ref)$

5 Extension L$_{\mathcal{E}}$ of L$_{\mathcal{O}}$ by Exceptions

L$_{\mathcal{E}}$ extends L$_{\mathcal{O}}$ with exceptions, designed to provide support for recovering from abnormal situations, separating normal program code from exception handling code. When an *L*-program violates certain semantic constraints at run-time, the interpreter signals this as an *exception*. The control is transferred, from the point where the exception occurred, to a point that can be specified by the programmer. An exception is said to be *thrown* from the point where it occurred, and it is said to be *caught* at the point to which control is transferred. The model for L$_{\mathcal{E}}$

makes explicit how jump statements from $L_{\mathcal{I}}$, return statements from $L_{\mathcal{C}}$ and the initialization of classes from $L_{\mathcal{O}}$ interact with catching and handling exceptions.

Technically, exceptions are represented as objects of predefined system exception classes (in Java `java.lang.Throwable` and in C♯ `System.Exception`) or of user-defined application exception classes. Once 'thrown', these objects trigger an abruption of the normal program execution to 'catch' the exception – in case it is compatible with one of the exception classes appearing in the program in an enclosing try-catch-finally statement. Optional finally statements are guaranteed to be executed independently of whether the try statement completes normally or is abrupted. We consider *run-time exceptions*, which correspond to invalid operations violating the semantic constraints of the language (like an attempt to divide by zero or to index an array outside its bounds) and *user-defined exceptions*. We do not treat *errors* which are failures detected by the underlying virtual machine machine (JVM or CLR).

5.1   Static Semantics of $\mathbf{L}_{\mathcal{E}}$

For the refinement of $\textsc{ExecL}_{\mathcal{O}}$ by exceptions, it suffices to extend the static semantics and to add the new rules for exception handling. The set of statements is extended by throw and try-catch-finally statements as defined by he following grammar (where the throw statement without expression and so-called *general catch clauses* of form `catch` *block* are present only in C♯, not in Java):

$$Stm \quad ::= \dots \mid \text{‘throw’} \; Exp \; \text{‘;’} \mid \text{‘throw’} \; \text{‘;’}$$
$$\mid \text{‘try’} \; Block \; \{Catch\} \; [\text{‘catch’} \; Block] \; [\text{‘finally’} \; Block]$$

$$Catch ::= \text{‘catch’} \; \text{‘(’} \; ClassType \; [Loc] \; \text{‘)’} \; Block$$

Various static constraints are imposed on try-catch-finally statements in *L*-programs, like the following ones that we need to explain the correctness of the transition rules below:

- every try-catch-finally statement contains at least one *catch clause, general catch clause*, or *finally block*
- the exception classes in a catch clause appear there in a non-decreasing type order, more precisely for every try-catch statement

     `try` *block* `catch` ($E_1 \; x_1$) *block*$_1$ ... `catch` ($E_n \; x_n$) *block*$_n$

holds: $i < j \implies E_j \not\preceq E_i$

Some static constraints on try-catch-finally statements are language-specific. We only list the following three specific constraints of C♯ which will be needed to justify the correctness of the transition rules below.

- no `return` statements are allowed in finally blocks
- a `break`, `continue`, or `goto` statement is not allowed to jump out of a finally block
- a `throw` statement without expression is only allowed in catch blocks

To simplify the exposition we assume that general catch clauses 'catch *block*' are replaced at compile-time by 'catch (Object x) *block*' with a new variable x and that try-catch-finally statements have been reduced to try-catch and try-finally statements, e.g., as follows:

try *TryBlock*
catch (E_1 x_1) *CatchBlock$_1$*
⋮
catch (E_n x_n) *CatchBlock$_n$*
finally *FinallyBlock*

$\Longrightarrow$

try {
  try *TryBlock*
  catch (E_1 x_1) *CatchBlock$_1$*
  ⋮
  catch (E_n x_n) *CatchBlock$_n$*
} finally *FinallyBlock*

Since throwing an exception completes the computation of an expression or a statement abruptly, we introduce into the model a new type of reasons of abruptions and type states, namely references $Exc(Ref)$ to an exception object. Due to the presence of **throw** statements without expression in C♯, also a stack of references is needed to record exceptions which are to be re-thrown.

$$Abr = \ldots \mid Exc(Ref), \quad TypeState = \ldots \mid Exc(Ref), \quad excStack\colon List(Ref)$$

5.2   Dynamic Semantics of $\mathbf{L_{\mathcal{E}}}$

The transition rules for EXECL$_E$ are defined by adding two submachines to EXECL$_O$. The first one provides the rules for handling the exceptions which may occur during the evaluation of expressions, the second one describes the meaning of the new throw and try-catch-finally statements.

EXECL$_E$ ≡
  EXECLEXP$_E$
  EXECLSTM$_E$

Expression Evaluation Rules. EXECLEXP$_E$ contains rules for each of the forms of run-time exceptions foreseen by L. We give here some characteristic examples and group them for the ease of presentation into parallel submachines by the form of expression they are related to, namely for arithmetical exceptions and for those related to cast and reference expressions. The notion of FAILUP we use is supposed to execute the code **throw new** E() at the parent position, which allocates a new object for the exception and throws the exception (whereby the execution of the corresponding finally code starts, if there is any, together with the search for the appropriate exception handler. Therefore one can define the macro by invoking an internal method Throw$E$ with that effect for each of the exception classes E used as parameter of FAILUP.

In the formulation of the following rules we use the exception class names from C♯, which are often slightly different from those of Java. A binary expression throws an arithmetical exception, if the operator is an integer division or remainder operator and the right operand is 0. The overflow-clause for unary or binary operators is expressed using the above defined *Checked* predicate from C♯.

EXECLEXP$_E$ ≡ **match** *context*(*pos*)
  val$_1$ *bop* ▶ *val*$_2$ → **if** *DivisionByZero*(*bop*, *val*$_2$) **then**
         FAILUP(DivideByZeroException)
      elseif *DecimalOverflow*(*bop*, *val*$_1$, *val*$_2$)∨
         (*Checked*(*pos*) ∧ *Overflow*(*bop*, *val*$_1$, *val*$_2$))
      then FAILUP(OverflowException)
  uop ▶ *val* → **if** *Checked*(*pos*) ∧ *Overflow*(*uop*, *val*) **then**
         FAILUP(OverflowException)
  CASTEXCEPTIONS
  NULLREFEXCEPTIONS

In Java, a reference type *cast expression* throws a `ClassCastException`, if the value of the direct subexpression is neither *null* nor *compatible* with the required type. This is the first clause in the rule below which is formulated for C♯, where additional clauses appear due to value types.

CASTEXCEPTIONS ≡ **match** *context*(*pos*)
  (*t*) ▶ *val* →
    if *type*(*pos*) ∈ *RefType* **then**
      if *t* ∈ *RefType* ∧ *val* ≠ *null* ∧ *runTimeType*(*val*) ⋠ *t* **then**
        FAILUP(InvalidCastException)
      if *t* ∈ *ValueType* **then**   // attempt to unbox
        if *val* = *null* **then** FAILUP(NullReferenceException)
        elseif *t* ≠ *runTimeType*(*val*) **then**
           FAILUP(InvalidCastException)
    if *type*(*pos*) ∈ *SimpleType* ∧ *t* ∈ *SimpleType* ∧
    Checked(*pos*) ∧ *Overflow*(*t*, *val*)
    then FAILUP(OverflowException)

An instance target expression throws a `NullReferenceException`, if the operand is *null* (in Java a `NullPointerException`).

NULLREFEXCEPTIONS ≡ **match** *context*(*pos*)
  ▶ *ref* . *t*::*f*   → **if** *ref* = *null* **then**
                  FAILUP(NullReferenceException)
  ref . *t*::*f* = ▶ *val*   → **if** *ref* = *null* **then**
                  FAILUP(NullReferenceException)
  ref . *T*::*M* (▶ *vals*) → **if** *ref* = *null* **then**
                  FAILUP(NullReferenceException)

Statement Execution Rules. The statement execution submachine splits naturally into submachines for throw, try-catch, try-finally statements and a rule for the propagation of an exception (from the root position of a method body) to the method caller. We formulate the machine below for C♯ and then explain its simplification for the case of Java (essentially obtainable by deleting every exception-stack-related feature).

When the exception value *ref* of a `throw` statement has been computed, and if it turns out to be *null*, a `NullReferenceException` is reported to the enclosing phrase using FAILUP, which allocates a new object for the exception and throws the exception. If the exception value *ref* of a **throw** statement is not *null*, the abruption *Exc(ref)* is passed up to the (position of the) **throw** statement, thereby abrupting the control flow with the computed exception as reason. The semantics of the parameterless **throw;** statement is explained as throwing the top element of the exception stack *excStack*.

Upon normal completion of a **try** statement, the machine passes the control to the parent statement, whereas upon abrupted completion the machine attempts to catch the exception by one of the **catch** clauses. The catching condition is the compatibility of the class of the exception with one of the catcher classes. If the catching fails, the exception is passed to the parent statement, as is every other abruption which was propagated up from within the **try** statement. Otherwise the control is passed to the execution of the relevant **catch** statement, recording the current exception object in the corresponding local variable and pushing it on the exception stack (thus recording the last exception in case it has to be re-thrown). Upon completion of this **catch** statement, the machine passes the control up and pops the current exception object from the exception stack—the result of this statement execution may be normal or abrupted, in the latter case the new exception is passed up to the parent statement. No special rules are needed for general catch clauses '**catch** *block*' in try-catch statements, due to their compile-time transformation mentioned above.

For a **finally** statement, upon normal or abrupted completion of the first direct substatement, the control is passed to the execution of the second direct substatement, the **finally** statement proper. Upon normal completion of this statement, the control is passed up, together with the possible reason of abruption, the one which was present when the execution of **finally** statement proper was started, and which in this case has to be resumed after execution of the **finally** statement proper. However, should the execution of this **finally** statement proper abrupt, then this new abruption is passed to the parent statement and a possible abruption of the try block is discarded. The constraints listed above for C♯ restrict the possibilities for exiting a finally block to normal completion or triggering an exception, whereas in Java also other abruptions may occur here.

In Java there is an additional rule for passing exceptions when they have been propagated to the position directly following a label, namely:

$$lab : \ ^{\blacktriangleright} Exc(ref) \ \rightarrow \ \textsc{YieldUp}(Exc(ref))$$

If the attempt to catch a thrown exception in the current method fails, the exception is propagated to the caller using the submachine explained below.

$$\textsc{ExecC♯Stm}_E \equiv \textbf{match } context(pos)$$
$$\textbf{throw } exp; \ \rightarrow pos := exp$$
$$\textbf{throw } ^{\blacktriangleright} ref ; \ \rightarrow \textbf{if } ref = null \textbf{ then } \textsc{FailUp}(\texttt{NullReferenceException})$$
$$\textbf{else } \textsc{YieldUp}(Exc(ref))$$
$$\textbf{throw; } \rightarrow \textsc{Yield}(Exc(top(excStack)))$$

try *block* `catch` $(E\ x)$ *stm* ... $\rightarrow pos := block$
try $^\blacktriangleright Norm$ `catch` $(E\ x)$ *stm* ... $\rightarrow$ YIELDUP$(Norm)$
try $^\blacktriangleright Exc(ref)$ `catch(`$E_1\ x_1$`)` stm_1 ... `catch(`$E_n\ x_n$`)` $stm_n \rightarrow$
   if $\exists i \in [1 .. n]\ runTimeType(ref) \preceq E_i$ **then**
     let $j = \min\{i \in [1 .. n] \mid runTimeType(ref) \preceq E_i\}$ **in**
     $pos := stm_j$
     $excStack := push(ref, excStack)$
     WRITEMEM$(locals(x_j),$ `object`$, ref)$
   else YIELDUP$(Exc(ref))$
try $^\blacktriangleright abr$ `catch(`$E_1\ x_1$`)` stm_1 ... `catch(`$E_n\ x_n$`)` stm_n $\rightarrow$ YIELDUP(abr)
try $Exc(ref)$ ... `catch(...)` $^\blacktriangleright res$ ... $\rightarrow$
   $\{excStack := pop(excStack),$ YIELDUP(res)

try *tryBlock* `finally` *finallyBlock* $\rightarrow pos := tryBlock$
try $^\blacktriangleright res$ `finally` *finallyBlock* $\rightarrow pos := finallyBlock$
try *res* `finally` $^\blacktriangleright Norm$ $\rightarrow$ YIELDUP(res)
try *res* `finally` $^\blacktriangleright Exc(ref)$ $\rightarrow$ YIELDUP$(Exc(ref))$
PROPAGATETOCALLER$(Exc(ref))$

If the attempt to catch a thrown exception in the current method fails, the exception is passed by PROPAGATETOCALLER(Exc(ref)) to the invoker of this method (if there is some), to continue the search for an exception handler there. In case an exception was thrown in the static constructor of a type, in C♯ its type state is set to that exception to prevent its re-initialization and instead to re-throw the old exception object, performed by an extension of INITIALIZE(c) by the clause **if** $typeState(c) = Exc(ref)$ **then** YIELD$(Exc(ref))$. In Java, the corresponding type becomes *Unusable*, meaning that its initialization is not possible, which is realized by the additional INITIALIZE(c)-clause **if** $typeState(c) = Unusable$ **then** FAIL(`NoClassDefFoundErr`).

PROPAGATETOCALLER$(Exc(ref)) \equiv$ **match** $context(pos)$
  $Exc(ref) \rightarrow$
    if $pos = body(meth) \wedge \neg Empty(frames)$ **then**
     if $StaticCtor(meth)$ **then** $typeState(type(meth)) := Exc(ref)$
    EXITMETHOD$(Exc(ref))$

The model EXECJAVASTM$_E$ in [14, Fig. 6.2] has the following rule for uncaught exceptions in class initializers, which is inserted before the general rule PROPAGATETOCALLER$(Exc(ref))$. Java specifies the following strategy for this case. If during the execution of a static initializer an exception is thrown, and if this is not an `Error` or one of its subclasses, an `ExceptionInInitializerError` is thrown. If the exception is compatible with `Error`, then the exception is rethrown in the directly preceding method on the frame stack.

match $context(pos)$
  `static` $Exc(ref) \rightarrow$
    if $runTimeType(ref) \preceq$ `Error` **then** YIELDUP$(Exc(ref))$
    else FAILUP(`ExceptionInInitializerError`)

An alternative treatment appears in the model $\text{EXECC}\sharp\text{STM}_E$ in [4] where unhandled exceptions in a static constructor are wrapped into an exception of type `TypeInitializationException` by translating the static constructor

```
static T() { BlockStatements }
```

into

```
static T() {
  try { BlockStatements }
  catch (Exception e) {
    throw new TypeInitializationException(T, e);
  }
}
```

The interpreter for $\text{Java}_\mathcal{E}$ needs also a refinement of the definition of propagation of abruptions, to the effect that `try` statements suspend jump and return abruptions for execution of relevant `finally` code. For $C\sharp$ this is not needed due to the constraints cited above for finally code in $C\sharp$. As explained above, after the execution of this `finally` code, that abruption will be resumed (unless during the `finally` code a new abruption did occur which cancels the original one).

$PropagatesAbr(\alpha) \Longleftrightarrow$
$\quad label(\alpha) \notin \{LabeledStm, StaticBlock, TryCatchStm, TryFinallyStm\}$

6   Conclusion

We have defined hierarchically structured components of an interpreter for a general object-oriented programming language. In doing this we have identified a certain number of static and dynamic parameters and have shown that they can be instantiated to obtain an interpreter for Java or $C\sharp$. As a by-product this pinpoints in a precise and explicit way the main differences the two languages have in their dynamic semantics. The work confirms the idea that one can use ASMs to define in an accurate way appropriate abstractions to support the development of *precise patterns for fundamental computational concepts* in the fields of hardware and software, reusable for design-for-change and useful for communicating and teaching design skills.

Acknowledgement. We gratefully acknowledge partial support of this work by a Microsoft grant within the ROTOR project during the years 2002–2003.

References

1. V. Awhad and C. Wallace. A unified formal specification and analysis of the new Java memory models. In E. Börger, A. Gargantini, and E. Riccobene, editors, *Abstract State Machines 2003–Advances in Theory and Applications*, volume 2589 of *Lecture Notes in Computer Science*, pages 166–185. Springer-Verlag, 2003.

2. E. Börger. The ASM refinement method. *Formal Aspects of Computing*, 15:237–257, 2003.

3. E. Börger and T. Bolognesi. Remarks on turbo ASMs for computing functional equations and recursion schemes. In E. Börger, A. Gargantini, and E. Riccobene, editors, *Abstract State Machines 2003 – Advances in Theory and Applications*, volume 2589 of *Lecture Notes in Computer Science*, pages 218–228. Springer-Verlag, 2003.

4. E. Börger, N. G. Fruja, V. Gervasi, and R. Stärk. A high-level modular definition of the semantics of C♯. *Theoretical Computer Science*, 2004.

5. E. Börger and R. F. Stärk. *Abstract State Machines. A Method for High-Level System Design and Analysis*. Springer, 2003.

6. K. G. Doh and P. D. Mosses. Composing programming languages by combining action-semantics modules. *Science of Computer Programming*, 47(1):3–36, 2003.

7. C♯ Language Specification. Standard ECMA–334, 2001. http://www.ecma-international.org/publications/standards/ECMA-334.HTM.

8. N. G. Fruja. The correctness of the definite assignment analysis in C♯. In V. Skala and P. Nienaltowski, editors, *Proc. 2nd International Workshop on .NET Technologies 2004*, pages 81–88, Plzen, Czech Republic, 2004. ISBN 80-903100-4-4.

9. N. G. Fruja. Specification and implementation problems for C♯. In W. Zimmermann and B. Thalheim, editors, *11th International Workshop on Abstract State Machines, ASM 2004, Wittenberg, Germany*, pages 127–143. Springer-Verlag, Lecture Notes in Computer Science 3052, 2004.

10. N. G. Fruja and R. F. Stärk. The hidden computation steps of turbo Abstract State Machines. In E. Börger, A. Gargantini, and E. Riccobene, editors, *Abstract State Machines 2003 – Advances in Theory and Applications*, volume 2589 of *Lecture Notes in Computer Science*, pages 244–262. Springer-Verlag, 2003.

11. Y. Gurevich. Evolving algebras 1993: Lipari Guide. In E. Börger, editor, *Specification and Validation Methods*, pages 9–36. Oxford University Press, 1995.

12. P. Mosses. Definitive semantics. Version 0.2 of Lecture Notes made available at http://www.mimuw.edu.pl/ mosses/DS-03, May 2003.

13. R. F. Stärk and E. Börger. An ASM specification of C♯ threads and the .NET memory model. In W. Zimmermann and B. Thalheim, editors, *11th International Workshop on Abstract State Machines, ASM 2004, Wittenberg, Germany*, pages 38–60. Springer-Verlag, Lecture Notes in Computer Science 3052, 2004.

14. R. F. Stärk, J. Schmid, and E. Börger. *Java and the Java Virtual Machine—Definition, Verification, Validation*. Springer-Verlag, 2001.

15. W. Zimmermann and A. Dold. A framework for modeling the semantics of expression evaluation with Abstract State Machines. In E. Börger, A. Gargantini, and E. Riccobene, editors, *Abstract State Machines 2003–Advances in Theory and Applications*, volume 2589 of *Lecture Notes in Computer Science*, pages 391–406. Springer-Verlag, 2003.

On the Verification of Cooperating Traffic Agents[*]

Werner Damm[1,2], Hardi Hungar[2], and Ernst-Rüdiger Olderog[1]

[1] Carl von Ossietzky University, Oldenburg, Germany
[2] OFFIS, Oldenburg, Germany

Abstract. This paper exploits design patterns employed in coordinating autonomous transport vehicles so as to ease the burden in verifying cooperating hybrid systems. The presented verification methodology is equally applicable for avionics applications (such as TCAS), train applications (such as ETCS), or automotive applications (such as platooning). We present a verification rule explicating the essence of employed design patters, guaranteeing global safety properties of the kind "a collision will never occur", and whose premises can either be established by off-line analysis of the worst-case behavior of the involved traffic agents, or by purely local proofs, involving only a single traffic agent. In a companion paper we will show, how such local proof obligations can be discharged automatically.

1 Introduction

Automatic collision avoidance systems form an integral part of ETCS-compatible train systems, are appearing or about to appear in cars, and – in the somewhat weaker form of only providing recommendations to the pilot – required to be installed on any aircraft with more than 30 passengers. The verification of the correctness of such collision avoidance system has been studied extensively e.g. within the PATH project (see [12]), by Leveson et al. [10], Sastry et al. [17] and Lynch et al. [11] for various versions of the TCAS system, or by Peleska et al. [6] and Damm et al. [4] for train system applications. Shankar et al presents in [12] a general approach of developing such distributed hybrid systems.

Our paper aims at reducing the complexity of the verification of collision avoidance systems. To this end, we explicate typical design approaches for such protocols, and cast this into a proof rule reducing the global safety requirement "a collision will never occur" to simpler proof tasks, which can either be established off line, involve purely local safety- or real-time properties, or pure protocol verification. We illustrate our approach by showing how the correctness

[*] This work was partly supported by the German Research Council (DFG) as part of the Transregional Collaborative Research Center "Automatic Verification and Analysis of Complex Systems" (SFB/TR 14 AVACS). See www.avacs.org for more information.

F.S. de Boer et al. (Eds.): FMCO 2003, LNCS 3188, pp. 77–110, 2004.

of TCAS and a protocol for wireless safe railroad crossings can be established by instantiating the proposed verification rule. While the methodology as such is applicable to any bounded number of agents, we will illustrate our approach considering only collision avoidance for two agents.

The approach centers around the following key design concepts.

Each traffic agent is equipped with a *safety envelope*, which is never to be entered by another agent. The safety envelope of an agent is an open ball around the agent's current three-dimensional position, with an agent-specific diameter. We allow the extent of the diameter to be mode dependent, thus e.g. enforcing different degrees of safety margins during different flight phases, or allowing a train to actually cross a railroad crossing if this is in mode "secured". The global safety property we want to prove is, that safety envelopes of agents are always kept apart.

To enforce separation of safety envelopes, the controllers' coordinating collision avoidance offers a choice of corrective actions, or maneuvers. E.g. TCAS distinguishes "steep descent", "descent", "maintain level", "climb", "steep climb", thus restricting the maneuvers to adjustment of the height of the involved aircrafts (with future versions expected to also offer lateral avoidance maneuvers). In the train-system application, the maneuvers of the crossing are simple (flash light and lower barriers), and the train will be brought to a complete stop, trying first the service brake, and resorting to an emergency brake as backup option. From the point of view of our methodology, we will assume a set of explicitly designated states for such collision avoidance maneuvers, henceforth called *corrective modes*. It is the task of the collision-avoidance protocol to select matching pairs of corrective modes: the joint effect of the strategies invoked by the chosen states ensures, that the agents will pass each other without intruding safety envelopes – a condition, which we refer to as *adequacy*. E.g. TCAS will never ask both aircrafts to climb – the decision of which aircraft should climb, and which descend, is taken based on the relative position and the identity of the aircraft (to break symmetry, identities are assumed to be totally ordered).

A key design aspect of collision avoidance protocols is the proper determination of invocation times for corrective maneuvers. Due to the safety criticality of the application, such triggering points must be determined taking into account the most adversary behavior of traffic agents, within the overall limits stipulated by traffic regulation authorities. As an example, triggering a mode switch to enforce safe braking of the train must be done in time to allow the train to come to a complete stop even when driving the maximal allowed speed for the current track segment, as well as the maximally allowed slope for track segments. This in fact *simplifies* the analysis, because it both requires as well as allows to perform the analysis using an *over-approximation* of the agents' behavior. Conformance to such upper bounds on velocity must be established separately – note, that this is a verification task local to the agent. We can then use off-line analysis based on the over-approximated behavior of the plant and knowledge of the corrective maneuvers to determine the need for a mode switch to one of the corrective modes.

We will show that we can determine off line, which combinations of corrective states will satisfy the adequacy condition (we call these *matching* corrective states), by exploiting guarantees about invocation time for corrective actions, and analyzing the possible evolutions from the plant regions characterized by the predicates inducing mode switching, thus reducing the global verification of adequacy to the verification, that only matching corrective states are selected.

This paper is structured as follows. The next section explicates our mathematical model of cooperating traffic agents, enriching the well known model of cooperating hybrid automata with sufficient structure to perform our analysis. The ingredients of our verification methodology are elaborated in Section 3. We discuss to which extent the analysis from [11] differs from our decomposition approach in Section 4, and perform likewise for the railroad crossing in Section 5. We will discuss possible extensions of the methodology in the conclusion.

2   Model of Cooperating Traffic Agents

This section introduces our mathematical model of cooperating traffic agents, using a variant of communicating hybrid automata from Tomlin et al [16] allowing general ordinary differential equations as specifications of continuous evolutions.

An agent's controller is typically organized hierarchically. A *cooperation layer* is responsible for the protocol with other agents, allowing each agent to acquire approximate knowledge about the state of other agents, and exchanging information on the chosen strategies for collision avoidance. At the lowest level, which we will refer to as the *reflex layer*, basic control laws are provided for all normal modes of operations, such as maintaining the speed of the train at a given set point. We abstract from the concrete representation of the control laws, assuming that they can be cast into a set of differential equations, expressing how actuators change over time. The state space of the controller is spanned from a finite set of discrete modes M and a set of (real-valued) state variables V, subsuming sensors and actuators of the controlled plant. We assume a special variable id to store the identity of an agent. We explicitly designate a set of modes as *corrective modes*, implementing the control laws for collision avoidance maneuvers. E.g. in the TCAS context, this would include the control laws for the various degrees of strength for climb, respectively descent maneuvers, or in the train system context, the selection of either activating the service brake, or the emergency brake. A *coordination layer* is responsible for mode switching in general, and in particular for the selection of the collision avoidance maneuvers, by entering the control mode activating the control law associated with the chosen maneuver. Mode switching can be triggered by communication events, by timeouts, and by conditions on the plant state becoming true. We allow to capture typical assumptions on discrete and continuous variables to be expressed as global invariances or mode invariances. Typical usages of invariants for discrete modes will relate to the cooperation protocol, as well as the stipulation, that corrective maneuvers will be maintained until potentially critical situations have been resolved.[1] Typical usages of invariances for continuous variables will be the enforcement of regulatory stipulations such as regarding maximal allowed speed, or tolerated degrees of acceleration resp. deceleration.

As to the model of the traffic agent's plant, we assume, that the set of plant variables subsumes the traffic agents space coordinates x, y, z, its velocity in each dimension v_x, v_y, v_z, as well as its acceleration a_x, a_y, a_z in each dimension, a set of actuator variables A, as well as a set of disturbances D. A subset S of the system variables, the sensor variables, are observable by the plant's controller, which in turn can influence the plant by the setting of actuators. We assume that space coordinates, velocity, and acceleration are directly observable by the controller. For the current version, we consider simple plant models without discrete state components.[2] The dynamics of the system is specified by giving for each non-input system variable an ordinary differential equation, whose right hand side may contain all variables of the plant. This includes the standard dependencies between acceleration, velocity, and space coordinates. Plant invariances allow to place bounds on disturbances. In particular, we will assume for each disturbance upper and lower bounds under which the agent is expected to operate.

A *traffic-agent model* combines an agent controller with its plant model, using standard parallel composition of hybrid automata. Communication between these automata is based solely on the actuator and sensor variables shared between these. We thus abstract in this paper from noise in sensor readings and inaccuracy of actuators when observing resp. controlling its own plant. Note, that the parallel composition used is just a standard parallel composition of automata, hence we can view a traffic agent model again as a hybrid automaton.

A *distributed traffic system* consists of the parallel composition of N traffic agents. We abstract in this paper from modeling communication channels, and assume, that all communication between traffic agents is based on variables shared between their controllers, of mode "output" on the one side and of mode "input" on the other. As noted before, mode-switches can be initiated by communication events, which in this setting is expressed by allowing as trigger to test for a condition involving communication variables to become true. We make the simplifying assumption, that the variables shared between traffic-agent controllers include the sensor variables for its coordinates and its speed, as well as the identity of the controllers. It is straightforward to extend our approach to message-passing based information and accordingly delayed knowledge about the other agent's whereabouts, by interpolating from the last known readings, using worst-case bounds dictated by regulations to safely over-approximate the actual readings.

---

[1] The TCAS protocol actually allows to withdraw a given recommendation in restricted situations, complicating the analysis, see [11]. The above assumption indeed eases the off-line analysis required in our approach, but is not inherent. We leave it to a later paper to consider more flexible strategies.

[2] In the formal development, we view a plant as a hybrid automaton with a single state and no discrete transitions.

Since a distributed traffic system is again just built by parallel composition of hybrid automata, we can safely identify it with the well-defined hybrid automaton resulting from the parallel composition of its agents. We can thus focus the remainder of this chapter on defining a sufficiently rich class of hybrid automata offering all constructs elaborated above for the agents controller and its plant, and closed under parallel composition.

Definition 1 (Hybrid Automaton). *A hybrid automaton is a tuple*

$$HA = (M, V, R^d, R^c, m_0, \Theta)$$

where

- *M is a finite set of* modes,
- *V is a real-valued set of* variables, *partitioned into* input, local *and* output variables, *respectively:*

$$V = V^i \,\dot{\cup}\, V^\ell \,\dot{\cup}\, V^o,$$

- *m_0 is the* initial mode,
- *Θ associates with each mode m a* local invariant $\Theta(m)$ *(a quantifier free boolean formula over V),*
- *R^d is the* discrete transition relation *with transitions $(m, \uparrow \varphi, \mathcal{A}, m')$, also written as $m \xrightarrow{\uparrow \varphi / \mathcal{A}} m'$, where*
  - *$m, m' \in M$,*
  - *$\mathcal{A}$ is a (possibly empty) set of (disjoint) assignments of the form $v := e_v$ with $v \in V^\ell \cup V^o$ and e_v an expression over V,*
  - *the trigger $\uparrow \varphi$ is the event that a quantifier-free boolean formula φ over V becomes true.*
- *R^c is the* continuous transition relation *associating with each mode m and each non-input variable v an expression $R^c(m)(v)$ over V. Intuitively, R^c thus defines for mode m and each v the differential equation*

$$\dot{v} = R^c(m)(v)$$

governing the evolution of v while HA is in mode m. □

Additionally we require of the discrete transition relation, that the execution of one transition does not immediately enable a further transition.

Definition 2 (Transition Separation). *Let $\sigma : V \to \mathbb{R}$ be a valuation of the variables V. Then $\mathcal{A}(\sigma)$ denotes the update of σ according to the assignments in $\mathcal{A}$, i.e.*

$$\forall\; v \in V : \quad (\exists\; e_v : v := e_v \in \mathcal{A}) \Rightarrow \mathcal{A}(\sigma)(v) = \sigma(e_v)$$
$$\wedge \; \neg(\exists\; e_v : v := e_v \in \mathcal{A}) \Rightarrow \mathcal{A}(\sigma)(v) = \sigma(v).$$

The discrete transitions in a hybrid automaton are separated, *if for any two transitions $(m_1, \uparrow \varphi_1, \mathcal{A}_1, m_1')$ and $(m_2, \uparrow \varphi_2, \mathcal{A}_2, m_2')$ with $m_1' = m_2$ it holds that*

$$\forall\; \sigma : V \to \mathbb{R} : (\sigma \models \varphi_1 \;\Rightarrow\; \mathcal{A}_1(\sigma) \not\models \varphi_2).$$

Separation implies that at any given point in time during a run, at most one discrete transition fires. I.e., our models have dense time, not *superdense* time, where a sequence of discrete transitions is permitted to fire at one instant in time.

Discrete variables may be included into hybrid automata according to our definition via an embedding of their value domain into the reals, and associating a derivation of constantly zero to them (locals and outputs). Timeouts are easily coded via explicit local timer variables with a derivative in $\{-1, 0, 1\}$, as required respectively.

Note, that indeed this general model subsumes both controller and plant models, by choosing the set of variables appropriately and enforcing certain modeling restrictions. For our plant models, we require the absence of discrete transitions. This entails in particular, that plant variables only evolve continuously, and cannot be changed by discrete jumps. This is convenient for the formulation of our approach but not essential.

We will in the definition of *runs* of a hybrid automaton interpret all transitions as urgent, i.e. a mode will be left as soon as the triggering event occurs. This can either be the expiration of a time-out, or a condition on e.g. the plant sensors becoming true. Valid runs also avoid Zeno behavior and time-blocks, i.e. each run provides a valuation for each positive point in time. We did not take provisions to ensure the existence of such a run, nor the property that each initial behavior segment can be extended to a full run. Such might be added via adequate modeling guidelines (e.g. by including the negation of an invariant as trigger condition on some transition leaving the mode). As these properties are not essential to the purpose of this paper we left them out.

We now give the formal definition of runs of a hybrid automaton HA. To this end we consider continuous time and let $Time = \mathbb{R}_{\geq 0}$. Further on, we use the notation

$$previous(\hat{v}, t) = \lim_{u \to t}(\hat{v}(u))$$

for some $\hat{v} : Time \to \mathbb{R}$ and $0 < t \in Time$. Satisfaction of a condition containing *previous* entails that the respective limes does exist.[3]

Definition 3 (Runs of a Hybrid Automaton). *A tuple of trajectories*

$$\pi = (\hat{m}, (\hat{v})_{v \in V}), \ \ with$$
$$\hat{m} : Time \to M$$
$$\hat{v} : Time \to \mathbb{R}, \ v \in V$$

capturing the evolution of modes and valuations of continuous variables is called a run of HA *iff*

$$\exists \, (\tau_i)_{i \in \omega} \in Time^\omega : \ \tau_0 = 0 \ \land \ \forall \ i : \tau_i < \tau_{i+1},$$

a strictly increasing sequence of discrete switching times s.t.

---

[3] In fact, our definition of a run implies that these limits do exist for all local and output variables in any run.

1. non-Zeno

$$\forall \; t \in \textit{Time} \; \exists \; i : t \leq \tau_i$$

2. mode switching times

$$\forall \; i \; \forall \; t \in [\tau_i, \tau_{i+1}) : \hat{m}(t) = \hat{m}(\tau_i).$$

3. continuous evolution

$$\forall \; i \; \forall \; t \in [\tau_i, \tau_{i+1}) \; \forall \; v \in V :$$
$$\frac{d \, \hat{v}(t)}{dt} = R^c(\hat{m}(\tau_i))[\hat{w}(t)/w \mid w \in V]$$

4. invariants

$$\forall \; t \in \textit{Time} : (\lambda \; v. \; \hat{v}(t)) \models \Theta(\hat{m}(t)),$$

5. urgency

$$\forall \; i \; \forall \; t \in [\tau_i, \tau_{i+1}) \; \forall \; (m, \uparrow\varphi, \mathcal{A}, m') \in R^d :$$
$$\hat{m}(t) = m \; \Rightarrow \; (\lambda \; v. \; \hat{v}(t)) \not\models \varphi$$

6. discrete transition firing

$$\forall \; i : \; \hat{m}(\tau_{i+1}) = \hat{m}(\tau_i) \; \wedge \; (\forall \; v \in V^\ell \cup V^o : \hat{v}(\tau_{i+1}) = previous(\hat{v}(\tau_{i+1}))$$
$$\vee$$
$$\exists \; (m, \uparrow\varphi, \mathcal{A}, m') \in R^d :$$
$$\hat{m}(\tau_i) = m \; \wedge \; \hat{m}(\tau_{i+1}) = m'$$
$$\wedge \; \exists \; \sigma \in V \rightarrow \mathbb{R} :$$
$$(\forall \; v \in V^\ell \cup V^o : \; \sigma(v) = previous(\hat{v}, \tau_{i+1})$$
$$\wedge \; \sigma \models \varphi$$
$$\wedge \; \forall \; v \in V^i : \hat{v}(\tau_{i+1}) = \sigma(v)$$
$$\wedge \; \forall \; v \in V^\ell \cup V^o : \hat{v}(\tau_{i+1}) = \mathcal{A}(\sigma)(v)$$

The time sequence $(\tau_i)_{i \in \omega}$ identifies the points in time, at which mode-switches may occur, which is expressed in Clause (2). Only at those points discrete transitions (having a noticeable effect on the state) may be taken. On the other hand, it is not required that any transition fires at some point τ_i, which permits to cover behaviors with a finite number of discrete switches within the framework above. Our simple plant models with only one mode provide examples. As usual, we exclude non-zeno behavior (in Clause (1)). As a consequence of the requirement of transition separation, after each discrete transition some time must elapse before the next one can fire. Clause (4) requires, for each mode, the valuation of continuous variables to meet the local invariant while staying in this mode. Clause (3) forces all local and output variables (whose dynamics is constrained by the set of differential equations associated with this mode) to actually obey their respective equation. Clause (5) forces a discrete transition to fire when its trigger condition becomes true. The effect of a discrete transition is described by Clause (6). Whenever a discrete transition is taken, local and output variables may be assigned new values, obtained by evaluating the right-hand side of the respective assignment using the previous value of locals and outputs and the current values of the input. If there is no such assignment, the variable maintains its previous value, which is determined by taking the limit of the trajectory of the variable as t converges to the switching time τ_{i+1}. Values of inputs may change arbitrarily. They are not restricted by the clauses, other that they obey mode invariants and contribute to the satisfaction of discrete transitions when those fire.

The parallel composition of two such hybrid automata HA_1 and HA_2 pre-supposes the typical disjointness criteria for modes, local variables, and output variables. Output variables of HA_1 which are at the same time input variables of HA_2, and vice versa, establish communication channels with instantaneous communication. Those variables establishing communication channels become local variables of $HA_1 \parallel HA_2$ (in addition to the local variables of HA_1 and HA_2), for other variable sets we simply take the union of those not involved in communication. Modes of $HA_1 \parallel HA_2$ are the pairs of modes of the component automata. One may define the set of runs of HA as those tuples of trajectories which project to runs of HA_1 and HA_2, respectively. It is not always possible to give a hybrid automaton for $HA_1 \parallel HA_2$, because of problems with cycles of instantaneous communications. Therefore, we impose the following additional condition on the composability of hybrid automata.

Definition 4 (Composable Hybrid Automata). *Let two hybrid automata HA_i, $i = 1, 2$, with discrete transition relations R_i^d, $i = 1, 2$, be given. For a pair of transitions $s_i = (m_i, \uparrow \varphi_i, \mathcal{A}_i, m_i') \in R_i^d$, $i = 1, 2$, the transition s_1 is unaffected by s_2, if each variable for which there is an assignment in $\mathcal{A}_2$ appears neither in φ_1 nor in $\mathcal{A}_1$ (on any of the right-hand sides).*

The two transition relations are composable, *if for each pair of transitions $s_i \in R_i^d$, $i = 1, 2$, either s_1 is unaffected by s_2 or vice versa.*

Composability establishes essentially a direction on instantaneous communications – communications may have an immediate effect on the output and thus the partner automaton, but they must not immediately influence the originator of the information. Assuming composability, the rest of the construction of the parallel composition automaton is rather standard.

For a mode (m_1, m_2), the associated invariant condition is the conjunction of the invariance conditions associated with m_1 and m_2. Similarly, the set of differential equations governing the continuous evolution while in mode (m_1, m_2) is obtained by simply conjoining the set of differential equations attached to m_1 and m_2, respectively – note that the disjointness conditions on variables assure, that this yields a consistent set of differential equations. Finally, the discrete transition relation consists of the following transitions:

1. $((m_1, m_2), \varphi_1 \wedge \mathcal{A}_1(\varphi_2), \mathcal{A}_1 \cup \mathcal{A}_1(\mathcal{A}_2), (m'_1, m'_2))$
   for each pair of transitions $s_i = (m_i, \uparrow \varphi_i, \mathcal{A}_i, m'_i) \in R_i^d$, $i = 1, 2$ where s_1 is unaffected by s_2,
2. $((m_1, m_2), \varphi_1 \wedge \{\neg \mathcal{A}_1(\varphi_2) \mid \varphi_2 \text{ trigger in } R_2^d\}, \mathcal{A}_1, (m'_1, m_2))$
   for each $(m_1, \uparrow \varphi_1, \mathcal{A}_1, m'_1) \in R_1^d$, and
3. transitions of the forms (1) and (2) with the role of HA_1 and HA_2 interchanged,

where

1. $\mathcal{A}(\varphi)$ denotes the substitution into φ of e_v for v for each assignment $v := e_v \in \mathcal{A}$, and
2. $\mathcal{A}_1(\mathcal{A}_2)$ denotes the substitution of the assignments of $\mathcal{A}_1$ into the right-hand terms of $\mathcal{A}_2$.

Composability ensures that the simultaneous transitions of Clause (1) indeed capture the combined effect of both transitions. The separation of transitions in the resulting automaton is inherited from separation in the component automata by the way single-automata transitions (Clause (2)) are embedded.

In the sequel, we will analyse two-agent systems

$$(C_1 \parallel P_1) \parallel (C_2 \parallel P_2),$$

consisting of a controller and a plant automaton each. We will establish a proof rule allowing to reduce the global requirement of collision freedom between these two traffic agents to safety requirements of a single agent $C_i \parallel P_i$. A follow-up paper will show, how by a combination of first-order model checking and Lyapunov's approach of establishing stability for the individual modes such local verification tasks can be fully automated.

3   A Proof Rule for Cooperating Traffic Agents

This section develops a generic proof-rule to establish collision freedom between cooperating traffic agents. In doing so, we contribute to the verification of this class of properties in two ways. First, by extracting a generic pattern, we identify the key ingredients involved in such classes of cooperation protocols. We are guided in this process by the in-depth knowledge of a spectrum of applications, notably from the train system and the avionics domain, and will use examples of each of these domains, which demonstrate, how the generic approach we develop can be specialized to both concrete protocol instances, though they differ in a significant number of design decisions. Jointly, the two example show, that we can cover with one generic scheme the design space ranging from completely symmetric solutions without fail-safe states, to asymmetric solutions involving heterogeneous traffic agents with fail safe states. Secondly, the proof rule demonstrates, how the verification problem for collision freedom, which involves a hybrid system composed of two traffic agents – each a pair $(C_j \parallel P_j)$ of the agent's controller and its plant-model – can be reduced to simpler verification tasks, of the following classes:

(A) Off-line analysis of the dynamics of the plant assuming worst-cases dynamics
(B) Mode invariants for $C_1 \parallel C_2$
(C) Real-time properties for C_j
(D) Local safety properties, i.e. hybrid verification tasks for $C_j \parallel P_j$

Type (A) verification tasks capture, how we can capitalize on rigorous design principles for safety-critical systems, where a high degree of robustness must be guaranteed in cooperation procedures for collision avoidance. This entails, that potentials for collision must be analysed assuming only a minimum of well-behavedness about the other agent's behavior, as expressed in invariance properties guaranteed by the controller (these will lead to proof obligations of type (D)). As a concrete example, when analyzing a two-aircraft system, given their current position and speed, we will bound changes in speed, height and direction when analyzing their worst case behavior in detecting potentials for collision. These invariances reflect typical requirements for flight phases – the aircraft must stay within safety margins of its current flight corridor, and maintain a separation with aircrafts traveling in the same flight corridor ahead and behind the considered aircraft. Type (A) verification tasks are simple, because they do not involve reasoning about hybrid systems. They consider the evolvement of all possible trajectories from a subregion of $P_1 \parallel P_2$ and asks about reachability of forbidden plant regions. In this analysis trajectories are evolving according to the differential equations of $P_1 \parallel P_2$,[4] with input changes restricted by constants (such as maximal allowed setting of actuators) or invariances guaranteed by the controller (such as "velocity is within the interval $[v_{min}, v_{max}]$"), or invariances bounding disturbances specified as operating conditions (such as "the maximal slope for a track for high-speed trains is $5 \, ^0/_{00}$"), which must be stated as plant invariances in order to enter the analysis.

Type (B) verification tasks ensure, that both agents take decisions which co-operate in avoiding potential collision situations. To this end, we assume that each controller has a designated set of modes called *correcting* modes, which define the agents capabilities for performing collision avoidance maneuvers. Examples of maneuvers are the resolution advisories issued by TCAS, such as "climb", "descend", ... Clearly, the combined system of two aircrafts will only avoid collisions, it the advisories of the two controllers *match*. E.g. in most situations, asking both aircrafts to climb, might actually increase the likelihood of a collision. It is the task of the designer of the cooperation protocol, to designate *matching* pairs of modes, and to characterize the plant states of $P_1 \parallel P_2$ under which invoking a matching pair of maneuvers is guaranteed to resolve a

---

[4] Recall that plant-models are assumed to only have a single discrete state. Note that we can still model so-called switched dynamical systems, where the dynamics of the system depends on the setting of switch variables, typically occurring as input to the plant-model. Worst-case analysis is then performed for all valuations of switch variables conforming to invariant properties. Here it will sufficient to work with over-approximations (such as the flow pipe approximation technique developed in [5]).

potential collision situation. Demonstrating, that two matching maneuvers avoid collision when the maneuvers are invoked in a state meeting the characterizing predicate is a type (A) verification task. Demonstrating, that only matching correcting modes are selected by the protocol leads to simple invariance properties for $C_1 \parallel C_2$.

Finally, type (C) verification conditions stem from the need to enforce timeliness properties for correcting maneuvers. At protocol design time, upper bounds on the time interval between detecting a potentially hazardous plant state and the actual invocation of correcting maneuvers must be determined. Establishing these timeliness properties allows to place further bounds on the state-space exploration in type (A) verification tasks.

We start the formal development of our proof rule by formalizing our notion of collision freedom as maintaining disjointness of the safety envelopes associated with each traffic agent. A safety envelope of an agent is a vicinity of its position which must not overlap the other agent's safety envelope for otherwise a collision might not be safely excluded. This vicinity may depend on the agent's state. For instance, a railroad crossing might be passed by trains if the barriers are closed and the crossing is considered safe. Then, its safety envelope is empty, otherwise it covers the width of the crossing. The safety envelope of the train encloses all of the train.

In our second example, that of the TCAS system, we have a more symmetrical situation. Both aircrafts have a nonempty safety envelope when in flight, which must be sufficient to exclude any dangerous interferences (direct collisions or turbulances due to near passage) between planes.

In the formal definition, safety envelopes are convex subspaces of $\mathbb{R}^3$ surrounding the current position, whose extent can be both dependent on the mode as well as the current valuation of other plant variables, including in particular the current velocity.

Definition 5. *The* safety envelope *of an agent is a function*

$$\text{SE} : M \times \mathbb{R}^V \to \mathcal{P}(\mathbb{R}^3),$$

which in our applications is a convex subset of $\mathbb{R}^3$ *including the current position, i.e. if* $\text{SE}(m, \sigma) = \mathcal{S}$ *then* $(\sigma(x), \sigma(y), \sigma(z)) \in \mathcal{S}$. *Given a run* π, *and a point in time* t, *the* current safety envelope *is given by* $\text{SE}(\pi(t))$.

Collision freedom of traffic agents is satisfied, if in all trajectories of the composed traffic system $(C_1 \parallel P_1) \parallel (C_2 \parallel P_2)$ the safety envelopes associated with $(C_1 \parallel P_1)$ and $(C_2 \parallel P_2)$ have an empty intersection (assuming that trajectories start in plant states providing "sufficient" distance between the agents, a predicate to be made precise below).

Definition 6. *Two runs* π_1 *and* π_2 *are* collision free *if*

$$\forall t \in \text{Time} : \ \text{SE}_1(\pi_1(t)) \cap \text{SE}_2(\pi_2(t)) = \varnothing.$$

Two sets of runs are collision free *if each pair of runs of the respective sets are collision free.*

We will now introduce a set of verification conditions, which jointly allow to infer collision freedom, and start by outlining the "essence" of collision avoidance protocols, as depicted in the phase-transition diagram of Fig. 1

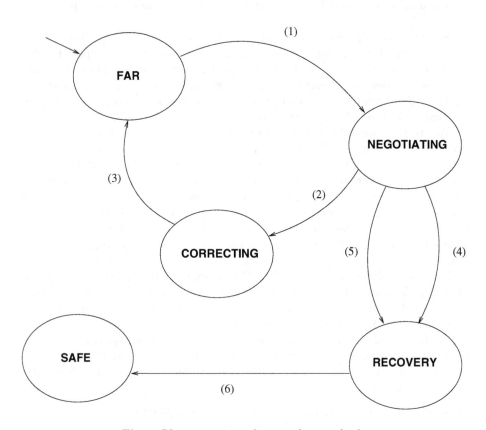

Fig. 1. Phase transition diagram for proof rule

Fig. 1 distinguishes the following *phases* of such protocols. Phase *FAR* subsumes all controller modes, which are not pertinent to collision avoidance. The protocol may only be in phase FAR if it is known to the controller, that the two agents are "far apart" – the agents' capabilities for executing maneuvers are such, that maintaining collision freedom can be guaranteed by not yet invoking correcting actions. Determining conditions for entering and leaving phase FAR is thus safety critical. The *NEGOTIATION* phase is initiated, as soon as the two agent system might evolve into a potentially hazardous situation. The derivation of the predicate φ_N guarding transition (1) is non-trivial and discussed below. Within the negotiation phase, the two agents determine the set of maneuvers to be performed. The *CORRECTING* phase is entered via transition (2), when matching correcting modes have been identified and no abnormal conditions – discussed below – have occurred. During the correcting phase, control laws associated with the correcting modes will cause the distance between traffic agents to increase, eventually allowing to (re-)enter the FAR-phase via transition (3).

The cycle of transitions numbered (1) to (3) described above characterizes successful collision avoidance maneuvers. Other phases and transitions shown in Fig. 1 increase the robustness of the protocol, by providing recovery actions in case of protocol failures in the negotiation phase (e.g. because of disturbed communication channels). A key concept here is that of *fail-safe* states: we say that a traffic agent offers a fail-safe state, if there is a stable state of $C_j \parallel P_j$, i.e. a valuation of the plant variables and actuators, such that their derivative is zero, and in particular the traffic agent maintains its current position, such as e.g. for train-system applications. For such traffic agents, any failure encountered during the negotiation or correcting phase will lead to the activation of recovery modes, whose control law will be guaranteed to drive the agent into a fail-safe state, as long as it is entered within a predicate characterizing its application condition. For simplicity, we assume only a single designated recovery mode for such traffic agents. Correcting collision avoidance even in case of failures can only be guaranteed, if *both* agents offer fail-safe states, and the recovery modes driving the system to a fail-safe state are entered while the plant is (still) in a state meeting the application condition for both recovery modes. Transitions (4) and (5) are guarded by conditions catering for

- an inconsistent selection of correcting modes,
- a timely invocation of recovery actions so as to allow the system to reach the fail-safe state.

As mentioned above, we assume the existence of an upper bound on the time to conclude the negotiation phase, and exploit this in analyzing, that correcting maneuvers are initiated in time for the maneuver to be performed successfully. To guarantee success of recovery actions, we similarly exploit the fact, that either the negotiation phase is concluded within the above bound, or a failure is detected and recovery mechanisms are initiated. Transition (5) provides an additional safeguard, in that the transition to the recovery mode will be taken as soon as its application condition applies. The activation of such recovery mechanisms should only be performed, if in addition the duration allowed for a successful conclusion of the negotiation phase has expired. Once the recovery mode is entered, the system will then eventually be driven to a fail-safe state via transition (6), causing it to remain in phase *SAFE*.

For systems not offering fail-safe states, no formal analysis can be performed as to the effects of initiating a recovery strategy. Recovery modes for such systems reflect the "never-give-up" design strategy for safety-critical systems, where "best guesses" as to the possible state of the other agent are made in the determination of control-laws associated with such recovery modes.

The phase-transition diagram defines a set of type (C) verification tasks appearing as premises of our proof rule for establishing collision freedom. To instantiate the proof rule for a concrete conflict-resolution protocol, the phases discussed above must be defined as (derived) observables of the concrete protocol. Often, phases can be characterized by being in a set of modes of the concrete protocol. In general, we assume that phases are definable by first-order quantifier-free formula in terms of the variables and mode of the concrete system. We denote by Φ_{obs} the set of equivalences defining phases and transition guards in terms of the entities of the concrete protocol. It is then straightforward to generate verification conditions enforcing compliance of the concrete protocol to the phase-transition system of Fig. 1, such as by using the subclass of so called "implementables" of the Duration Calculus (c.f. [15]), or some variant of real-time temporal logic. Such verification conditions take the general form "when in phase p then remain in phase p unless trigger condition occurs", and "when in phase p then switch to phase p' if trigger condition is met".[5] We denote the set of temporal logic formula jointly characterizing the phase-transition diagram of Fig. 1 assuming Φ_{obs} by Φ_{phase}.

This leads to the first set of verification conditions for establishing collision freedom. Here and in the remainder of this section we assume a fixed system $(C_1 \parallel P_1) \parallel (C_2 \parallel P_2)$ as given.

(VC 1) Controllers observe phase-transition diagram

$$C_i \models \Phi_{phase} \text{ (for } i = 1, 2)$$

Prior to deriving trigger conditions for phase-transitions, let us first elaborate on three verification conditions to be established by what we refer to as "off-line analysis". These verification conditions serve to establish at design time, that the invocation of matching maneuvers will guarantee collision freedom, as long as these are initiated while the global plant state satisfies a predicate characterizing the application condition of the pair of maneuvers. A similar off-line analysis must be carried out for recovery mechanism, where it must be verified, that any plant state meeting the application condition for such recovery states will drive both agents into their fail-safe state prior to reaching a collision situation.

As discussed in Section 2, we assume as given a subset of correcting modes CM_j of the Modes M_j of C_j. If C_j has fail-safe states, we denote by $m_{rec2fss,C_j}$ the unique mode of C_j defining the control strategy for reaching fail-safe states.

We assume a binary relation MATCH $\subseteq CM_1 \times CM_2$ to be given, which captures the designer's understanding, of which maneuvers are compatible and hence expected to resolve potential collision situations. To this end, she will also determine application conditions $\Phi_{(m_1, m_2)}$, where $(m_1, m_2) \in$ MATCH, under which these maneuvers are expected to be successful. Typically, these application conditions will involve the relative position of the traffic agents, as well as their velocity. Maneuvers are typically executed under assumptions on some of the system variables (e.g. bounding speed or lateral movement), which must be established separately. Similarly, let $\Phi_{rec2fss}$ denote the application condition for recovery to fail-safe states (see the following sections for examples).

---

[5] We assume in this paper that the successor phase is uniquely determined by the trigger condition. Time-bounds on taking the transition when the trigger is enabled are discussed below.

The first verification condition requires a proof, that indeed matching maneuvers avoid collision. It states that all trajectories obeying the set of differential equations governing the maneuvers and the plants will be free of collisions, as long as they are initiated in a state satisfying the application conditions of matching modes. The runs to be considered are assumed to meet the plant invariants on boundary conditions for the plants' variables. Moreover, any local invariances associated with the correcting modes may be assumed during off-line analysis – separate verification conditions cater for these.

(VC 2) Adequacy of matching modes

$$\forall \, (m_1, m_2) \in \mathrm{MATCH} :$$
$$(R_{C_1}^c(m_1) \, \| \, R_{P_1}^c()) \, \| (R_{P_2}^c() \, \| (R_{C_2}^c(m_2)))$$
$$\models \Box(\Theta(m_1) \wedge \Theta(m_2) \wedge \Theta(P_1) \wedge \Theta(P_2) \wedge \Phi_{(m_1, m_2)})$$
$$\Rightarrow \Box(\text{collision-free})$$

A key point to note is, that the above verification condition does not involve state-based reasoning. By abuse of notation, we have replaced hybrid automata by differential equations in the parallel composition above. To establish the verification condition, we must analyze the possible evolution of trajectories of the plant variables in subspaces characterized by the application condition. We can do so by over-approximation, using boundary conditions on plant variables (such as maximal speed, maximal acceleration, maximal disturbance) and actuators (as determined by the control laws associated with the correcting modes), and invariance conditions associated with correcting modes. See the next section for a concrete example, demonstrating in particular the ease in establishing such verification conditions. For more involved maneuvers, we can resort to classical methods from control-theory such as using Lyapunov functions (c.f. [9]) for establishing collision freedom, since no state-based behaviour must be analyzed. A follow-up paper will solve the constraint system induced by (VC 2) generically, establishing constraints on the involved design parameters under which (VC 2) is guaranteed to hold.

A similar verification condition must be established for recovery modes driving the system to fail-safe states. It requires each traffic agent to reach a fail-safe state without colliding with the other agent, as long as the recovery maneuver is initiated in a plant state meeting its applicability condition.

(VC 3) Adequacy of recovery maneuvers

$$(R_{C_1}^c(m_{\text{rec2fss},1}) \, \| \, R_{P_1}^c()) \, \| (R_{P_2}^c() \, \| \, R_{C_2}^c(m_{\text{rec2fss},2}))$$
$$\models \Box(\Theta(m_{\text{rec2fss},1}) \wedge \Theta(m_{\text{rec2fss},2}) \wedge \Theta(P_1) \wedge \Theta(P_2) \wedge \Phi_{\text{rec2fss}})$$
$$\Rightarrow \Diamond\text{fail-safe} \wedge \Box\text{collision-free}$$

So far we have only discussed the adequacy of the maneuvers for avoiding collision avoidance. This must be complemented by a proof of *completeness* of the proposed methods. More specifically, for any trajectory of the unconstrained plants (respecting only global invariances on maximal disturbances, maximal rate of acceleration, etc) leading to a collision situation, there must be at least be one pair of matching maneuvers, whose application condition is reached during the trajectory.

(VC 4) Completeness of maneuvers

$$\forall\, \pi \in [\![P_1 \parallel P_2]\!]\,:\; \pi \models \Theta(P_1) \wedge \Theta(P_2) \Rightarrow$$
$$(\;\forall\; t:\; \pi(t) \models \text{collision} \wedge \pi[0, t) \models \text{collision-free}$$
$$\Rightarrow \exists\; t' < t\; \exists (m, m`) \in \text{MATCH}:\; \pi(t') \models \Phi_{(m,m')}\;)$$

We will now derive a sufficient condition for the predicate Φ_N guarding the transition to the negotiation phase. This must ensure, that in any potentially hazardous situation, the negotiation phase is allowed in time to ensure, that correcting maneuvers can still be executed successfully. To derive this condition, we perform the following simple Gedankenexperiment. Assume, that the negotiation phase can be performed in zero time. Then, by completeness of maneuvers, it would be sufficient to trigger the transition into the negotiation phase, if at least one activation condition of the set of possible maneuvers is met. Indeed, by completeness, any potentially hazardous "legal" trajectory would have to pass at least one of the activation conditions of the set of maneuvers, hence by selecting one of these, the maneuver will ensure, that the potentially hazardous situation is resolved (by the adequacy of matching correcting modes).

To complete the Gedankenexperiment, we now drop the assumption, that negotiation is performed in zero time. Instead, we assume that at protocol design time, a time window Δ_N is determined, in which the negotiation phase will be left, either successfully, by entering phase CORRECTING, or otherwise by invoking a recovery mode. To determine the trigger condition Φ_N, we must derive the set of states which can evolve during this time window Δ_N into a potentially hazardous situation, i.e. into a state meeting at least one of the activation conditions of matching maneuvers. When performing this pre-image computation, we must take into account the dynamics of both traffic agents. In this paper, we assume a cooperative approach: the pre-image computation is performed, assuming that the speed of the traffic agent is not increased while performing the negotiation phase – an assumption, which must then be established separately as verification condition.

Let pre $=$ pre$_{P_1 \parallel P_2}(\Delta, [v_{1,l}, v_{1,u}], [v_{2,l}, v_{2,u}], \Phi)$ be a predicate which over-approximates the set of plant states which in Δ time units can evolve into a state satisfying Φ, assuming that the speed v of agent i is bound by $[v_{i,l}, v_{i,u}]$ (a vector of bounds for all three dimensions, if applicable), and restricted by $\Theta(P_i)$. (VC 5) below expresses the restriction on the condition Φ_N triggering the transition to phase NEGOTIATING, given the time bound Δ_N for the NEGOTIATION to complete.

(VC 5) Negotiation is initiated in time

$$\models \Phi_N \Leftarrow \text{pre}_{P_1 \parallel P_2}(\Delta_N, [v_{1,l}, v_{1,u}], [v_{2,l}, v_{2,u}], \bigvee_{(m_1,m_2) \in \text{MATCH}} \Phi_{(m_1,m_2)})$$

That Δ_N is met by the agents' negotiation is to be verified separately. We assume that the necessary communication can be performed by the controllers on their own.

(VC 6) Negotiation completes in time

$$C_1 \parallel C_2 \models \Box(\text{NEGOTIATING}(C_1) \vee \text{NEGOTIATING}(C_2)$$
$$\Rightarrow \Diamond_{\leq \Delta_N}(\neg\text{NEGOTIATING}(C_1) \wedge \neg\text{NEGOTIATING}(C_2)))$$

To cover the assumptions made in preconditions, we require the control laws active during the negotiation phase to maintain the speed of traffic agents within the bounds used in (VC 5) in pre-image computation.

(VC 7) Speed stays bounded during negotiation

$$C_i \parallel P_i \models \Box(\text{NEGOTIATING}(C_i) \Rightarrow v_i \in [v_{i,l}, v_{i,u}]) \text{ (for } i = 1, 2)$$

For traffic systems allowing recovery to fail-safe states, we would like to ensure additionally, that the negotiation is initiated in system states allowing to invoke recovery actions if negotiation fails.

(VC 8) Recovery actions will be possible

$$\models \Phi_N \Rightarrow \text{pre}_{P_1 \parallel P_2}(\Delta_N, [v_{1,l}, v_{1,u}], [v_{2,l}, v_{2,u}], \Phi_{\text{rec2fss}})$$

Jointly, (VC 5), (VC 6) and (VC 7) guarantee, that the activation conditions of maneuvers remain true during negotiation, hence are still valid when actually invoking the maneuvers, and (VC 7) in conjunction with (VC 6) and (VC 8) guarantees, that the activation condition for recovery to fail-safe states is met, if the negotiation phase fails.

That the negotiation results in matching modes being selected is stated in the following condition.

(VC 9) Only matching modes with satisfied activation condition are selected

$$C_1 \parallel C_2 \models \Box(\uparrow (\text{CORRECTING}(C_1) \wedge \text{CORRECTING}(C_2))$$
$$\Rightarrow (\text{Mode}(C_1), \text{Mode}(C_2)) \in \text{MATCH} \wedge \Phi_{(\text{Mode}(C_1), \text{Mode}(C_2))})$$

We must finally ensure, that a selected maneuver is not abandoned until the hazardous situation has been resolved, i.e., until phase FAR can be reentered. Hence, while in mode CORRECTING, the maneuver may not be changed.

(VC 10) Correcting modes are not changed

$$C_1 \parallel C_2 \models \forall (m_1, m_2) \in \text{MATCH}:$$
$$\Box(\bigwedge_{i=1,2} \text{CORRECTING}(C_i) \wedge \text{Mode}(C_i) = m_i$$
$$\Rightarrow \bigwedge_{i=1,2} (\text{Mode}(C_i) = m_i \textbf{ while } \text{CORRECTING}(C_i)))$$

The condition Φ_F guarding the transition to phase FAR is easily derived: by completeness of the set of maneuvers, the plant state is no longer potentially hazardous, if all activation conditions of maneuvers are false. In this case, the controllers are permitted to leave the correcting mode.

(VC 11) Termination of Maneuver

$$\models \Phi_F \Rightarrow \bigwedge_{(m_1,m_2)\in\mathrm{MATCH}} \neg\Phi_{(m_1,m_2)}$$

Jointly, these verification conditions are sufficient to establish collision freedom. A later version of this paper will prove this formally, by performing the required off-line analysis and pre-image computation symbolically on parameterized models. In the following, we give two examples of proofs of collision freedom and discuss how they can be rephrased in terms of our proof rule.

4   Decomposition in the Verification of Safety of the TCAS System

4.1   A Short Description of the TCAS System

The *Traffic Alert and Collision Avoidance System* (TCAS) serves to detect and avoid the danger of aircraft collisions. It is realized by electronic units on board of the aircraft. Its task is to detect potential threats, to alert the pilot and to give advice in maneuvers which resolve the conflicts. To achieve this, the system gathers information from nearby aircraft to predict the vertical separation at the point of closest horizontal approach. If the vertical separation is deemed insufficient, it issues "Resolution Advisories" (RAs) to the pilot ("climb", "descend", . . .) which, assuming unchanged horizontal course, shall avoid that the aircraft come dangerously close. The TCAS units of different aircraft communicate, to alert the other of its classification as a threat, to ensure consistency of RAs, and to avoid unnecessary alarms by taking intended course changes into account. Each TCAS system resorts to deciding on its own if communication cannot be established. Fig. 2 from [11] gives an overview of the components involved in conflict avoidance in the case of two aircraft.

There have been several versions of the system. We will discuss the TCAS II-7. This version is in widespread use, and has undergone quite some analysis, both internally during its development and externally in e.g. [1]. The precise analysis from [11] comes closest to our approach, and we will point out similarities and differences, to highlight to which extent the formulated goal of establishing safety has been proven to be achieved by the TCAS system.

4.2   The Analysis of TCAS by Livadas, Lygeros and Lynch

The general approach of [11] is to use hybrid automata to model all components involved in conflict avoidance for a two-aircraft instance, and to analyse the runs

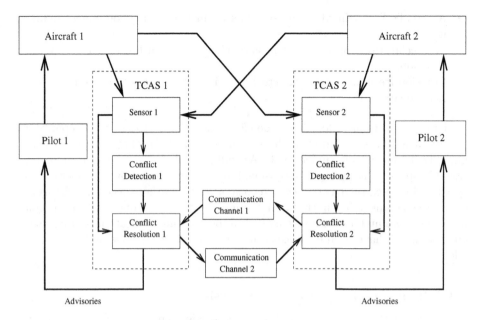

Fig. 2. TCAS-System for two aircraft

of the combined automata to check for the absence of collisions. The real system would then have to shown to be a refinement of the respective components (or have to be assumed to act as it were a refinement – the model includes components for pilots, which would hardly be provable refinements of an automaton). Though the automaton format differs (hybrid I/O automata with superdense time are used), this is very much in line with our approach.

Several assumptions are stated under which the analysis is performed. Some of them serve to reduce the computational complexity of trajectory analysis, which may limit the practical relevance but is conceptually reasonable. Some are even indispensable, as the one restricting pilot behavior to not oppose traffic advisories. Others limit the relevance of the derived safety result if compared to our stated goal. Our discussion will center around these latter issues.

Disregarding simplifying assumptions, the safety theorem of [11] can be stated as follows:

> All assumption-compliant runs where a conflict is detected will either evolve to retraction of the conflict declaration before passage, or to a passage where sufficient vertical separation is kept at the point of closest approach.

This can be rephrased as saying that the proof establishes that the interplay between discrete and continuous components will ensure that TCAS' operational goals are met. An "operational" goal is formulated via the system's own definitions:

- A "conflict" is defined as the system's conflict-detection component defines it.
- "Undeclaration" of a conflict is similarly taken from the respective system criterion.
- Collision-freedom of two trajectories is given if passages have sufficient vertical separation.

This theorem tells a lot about the effects of TCAS – the vertical separation will be achieved as required in the system specification. However, it does not imply that two aircraft guided by TCAS will not collide. The latter is an extensional property, the former is intensional and presupposes that the operational specification is consistent (which is, considering the rather successful history of guaranteeing safety in air traffic, not unreasonable). But our verification goal would be more ambitious. So let us have a look at the verification conditions of our rule which have been established in [11], and those which would have to be added.

4.3   Items for Completing the Analysis

The extensional goal is formulated in terms of safety envelopes. Such notions do exist in air traffic regulations – there is for instance a safety distance between landing aircraft which depends on the weight class of the leading aircraft. Similar separation requirements can be derived for mid-air traffic. So we may assume adequate definitions of safety envelopes as given.

Our approach presupposes a compliance of the resolution procedure to the state diagram Fig. 1. In the case of TCAS, there are no fail-safe states, which reduces the picture to the three states FAR, NEGOTIATING and CORRECTING. On the other hand, as TCAS follows the "never give up" strategy, there are further situations not taken care of in the general picture. We will have to extend our approach to cater for these. In the meantime, we resort to excluding further behavior from our analysis by adequate assumptions. Then, one may indeed view TCAS II-7 as adhering to the three-state cycle, if attention is restricted to the two-aircraft case. Adherence to the behavior pattern is implicitly shown in [11], we may conclude that (VC 1) does not pose a problem.

As there are no fail-safe states, the verification conditions (VC 3) and (VC 8) do not apply here. We will go through the list of remaining verification conditions in the following.

A central part of the adequacy of matching modes (VC 2) is indeed established by the essence of the proof from [11]: Trajectories resulting from selected correcting strategies will result in sufficient separation. To complete the proof of (VC 2), we have to add that the intensional (TCAS-internal) criterion of "vertical separation at closest approach" implies disjointness of safety envelopes. This will (likely) be a consequence of the bounds on climb and descend speeds of aircraft following TCAS resolution advisories. Of course, also a precise definition of the conditions $\Phi_{(m_1,m_2)}$ on matching modes will be required to formally complete the proof.

The completeness of maneuvers, (VC 4), is also addressed partly: After a conflict has been detected, there will be a pair of maneuvers selected. To be added is the important argument that each conflict is detected, and detected in time for some maneuver to be successful. This is again the (missing) part distinguishing intensional and extensional arguments.

The conditions regarding timing (VC 5), and (VC 6) have been left out of consideration by adding appropriate assumptions. The speed bound (VC 7) is rendered trivial by assumption. Adding proofs (and weakened assumptions) for these three verification conditions would be rather easy.

The selection of matching modes with satisfied verification conditions (VC 9) is addressed implicitly by the proof, since for all cases of selections it is shown that the corrections will be successful. Our proof rule requires a separation of the proof via the introduction of MATCH and $\Phi_{(m_1,m_2)}$. A case split according to the matching mode pair is actually performed in [11], and can be extended to the additional proof obligations.

Adherence to a selection of correction modes (VC 10) is a condition simplifying our proof rule and restricting the solution space. TCAS II-7 matches this restriction, if the definition of correction is made adequately, and "never give up" is left out of consideration. The reversal of correcting actions in one aircraft – one of the new features in the version II-7 – seems to violate this requirement. But it fits into the picture as it reverses a correcting maneuver which has started before the end of negotiations. The reversal caters (among others) for the not unlikely situation that one aircraft pilot ignores resolution advisories.

Termination of maneuvers (VC 11) is of course also not addressed extensionally in [11]. We think that it will follow easily from the definition of the application conditions $\Phi_{(m_1,m_2)}$.

5   Decomposition in the Verification of Safety of a Railroad Crossing

Railroad crossings are often taken as case studies for real-time systems [3, 7]. Here we consider a railroad crossing as a hybrid system taking the continuous dynamics of train and gate into account. Our formal model extends that in [14] by some aspects of the radio controlled railroad crossing, a case study of the priority research program "Integration of specification techniques with applications in engineering"[6] of the German Research Council (DFG) [8].

We start from domains $Position = \mathbb{R}_{\geq 0}$ with typical element p for the position of the train on the track and $Speed = \mathbb{R}_{\geq 0}$ with typical element v for the speed of the train. Let v_{max} denotes the maximal speed of the train. As part of the *track atlas* we find the positions of all crossings along the track. In particular, the function

$next : Position \rightarrow Position$

---

[6] http://tfs.cs.tu-berlin.de/projekte/indspec/SPP/index.html

yields for each position of the train the start position of the *next crossing* ahead such that $\forall\, p \in Position : p < next(p)$ holds. Further on,

$$inCr : Position \to \mathbb{B}$$

is a predicate describing all positions *in the crossing* and

$$afterCr : Position \to \mathbb{B}$$

is a predicate describing the positions in a section immediately *after the crossing*. For simplicity we shall not be explicit about the extension of the train and the crossing. We use *inCr* to describe all positions where the train (or its safety envelope) overlaps with the crossing.

There is a section *near the crossing* in which the train has to request permission from the gate to enter the next crossing. The extension of this section depends of the train's speed. The predicate

$$nearCr : Speed \to (Position \to \mathbb{B})$$

describes for a given speed all positions and that are in such a section. The positions satisfying these predicates are illustrated in Fig. 3. The predicate

$$farCr : Speed \to (Position \to \mathbb{B})$$

describes for a given speed v all positions that are far away from the next crossing, i.e. the complement of all positions satisfying $nearCr(v)$ or $inCr$ or $afterCr$. Note that we expect the following implications to hold:

$$\forall\, v_1 \le v_2 \in Speed : \ (nearCr(v_1) \Rightarrow nearCr(v_2)) \wedge (farCr(v_2) \Rightarrow farCr(v_1))$$

We assume that subsequent crossings on the track are far apart so that even for the maximal speed v_{max} of the train there is a nonempty section $farCr(v_{max})$ between each section *afterCr* and the section *inCr* of the *next* crossing. We model the gate by its angle α ranging from 0 to 90 degrees.

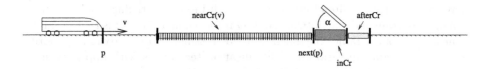

Fig. 3. Parameters of the railroad crossing

The railroad crossing will now be modelled by four components: a train plant and controller interacting with a gate plant and controller. Fig. 4 shows how these plants are represented by continuous variables *pos(ition)*, *speed* and α, and which variables the four components share for communication with each other. For simplicity we shall ignore the communication times in the subsequent analysis.

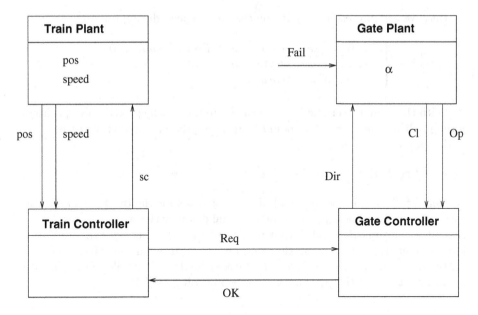

Fig. 4. Communication in the train gate system

Train Plant

We assume that the train has knowledge of its position on the track and controls its speed depending on requests from the train controller. It will react to speed control commands from the train controller. Thus we consider the variables below. We do not distinguish between the (syntactic) variables of the automaton and the corresponding trajectories in runs. So we take for the type of a variable the type of its time-dependent trajectory, and we permit variables with discrete ranges without explicitly coding them in reals.

Variables:		
input	$sc : Time \rightarrow \{Normal, Keep, Brake\}$	(speed control)
output	$pos : Time \rightarrow Position$	(position of the train)
	$speed : Time \rightarrow Speed$	(speed of the train)

Dynamics. Let $-a_{reg}$ be the deceleration of the train when braking (in regular operational mode, not in emergency mode which is not modeled). Thus we assume that the following invariants hold:

$$pos^\bullet = speed$$
$$-a_{reg} \leq speed^\bullet$$
$$speed \leq v_{max}$$

Here we are interested only in the change of speed during braking:

$$speed^\bullet = \begin{cases} 0 & \text{if } sc = Keep \lor (sc = Brake \land speed = 0) \\ -a_{reg} & \text{if } sc = Brake \land speed > 0 \\ \dots & \text{if } sc = Normal \end{cases}$$

With these characteristics we can calculate for which speeds v and positions p the predicate $nearCr(v)(p)$ should hold taking the maximal closing time ε_{max} of the gate into account:

$$nearCr(v)(p) \Leftarrow (next(p) - v^2/2 \cdot a_{reg} - \varepsilon_{max} \cdot v) \leq p$$

Here $v^2/2 \cdot a_{reg}$ is the maximal distance it takes for the train with an initial speed of v to stop, and $\varepsilon_{max} \cdot v$ is the maximal distance the train can travel while the gate is closing. Remember that we do not take the time for communication into account here. We assume that initially the train is far away from the next crossing, i.e. the predicate $farCr(speed)(pos)$ holds for a while. This, and the definition of $nearCr(v)(p)$ is needed for establishing (VC 4).

Train Controller

The train controller monitors the position and speed of the train, sends requests to enter the next crossing, and waits for an OK signalling permission by the crossing to enter. If this OK signal does not occur within some time bound measured by a clock x, the train controller will request the train to enforce braking in order to stop before entering the crossing. Thus the train controller has the following time dependent variables.

Variables:		
input	$pos : Time \rightarrow Position$	(position of the train)
	$speed : Time \rightarrow Speed$	(speed of the train)
	$OK : Time \rightarrow \mathbb{B}$	(permission to enter crossing)
local	$x : Time \rightarrow Time$	(clock)
output	$Req : Time \rightarrow \mathbb{B}$	(request to enter crossing)
	$sc : Time \rightarrow \{Normal,$	
	$\qquad\qquad Keep, Brake\}$	(speed control)
Modes:	**Far, Appr, SafeAppr, FailSafe**	

Dynamics. The dynamics of the train controller is described by the hybrid automaton in Fig. 5. Initially, the controller is in the mode **Far**. When for the current values of *pos* and *speed* the predicate $near(speed)(pos)$ becomes true, the controller switches to the mode **Appr** setting *Req* to true and starting the clock x. When things proceed as expected the crossing should respond with an *OK* signal within ε_{max} time, the maximal time the gate needs to close. On occurrence of *OK* the controller switches to the mode **SafeAppr** indicating that the train can safely approach the crossing. However, if the *OK* signal does not arrive within ε_{max} time, the controller enters the mode **FailSafe** where the train is forced to brake until it stops. Only if later an *OK* signal arrives it may resume its safe approach to the crossing.

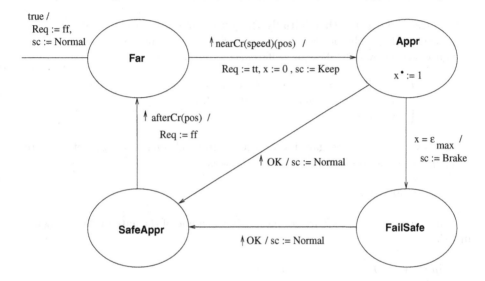

Fig. 5. Train controller

The controller states correspond nicely to the phases from Fig. 1: **Far** is FAR, **Appr** is NEGOTIATING, **FailSafe** is RECOVERY, and **SafeAppr** is CORRECTING. The only action the train does in correcting is keeping the *Req* signal up.[7]

Gate Plant

The gate controls its angle α depending on the direction requested by the variable *Dir* of the gate controller. If *Dir* is *Up* the gate should open, and if it is *Down* the gate should close. The gate outputs whether it is completely open by a signal *Op* or completely closed by a signal *Cl*. We take into account that the gate may fail to open or close when requested. This it is modelled by the following time dependent variables.

---

[7] Thus, one might also view the mode **Appr** as already CORRECTING.

Variables:

input	$Dir : Time \rightarrow \{Up, Down\}$	(direction of the gate)
	$Fail : Time \rightarrow \mathbb{B}$	(gate failure)
local	$\alpha : Time \rightarrow [0, 90]$	(angle of the gate)
output	$Op : Time \rightarrow \mathbb{B}$	(gate is open)
	$Cl : Time \rightarrow \mathbb{B}$	(gate is closed)

Dynamics. We assume that initially the gate is open. i.e. $\alpha(0) = 90$, that c is the speed with which the gate can change its angle α, and that the gate plant is characterised by the following differential equation:

$$\alpha^\bullet = \begin{cases} c & \text{if } Dir = Up \wedge \alpha < 90 \wedge \neg Fail \\ -c & \text{if } Dir = Down \wedge \alpha > 0 \wedge \neg Fail \\ 0 & \text{otherwise} \end{cases}$$

Thus when there is no gate failure the maximal closing time ε_{max} of the gate (plus one extra second) is calculated as follows:

$$\varepsilon_{max} = 90/c + 1$$

The outputs Op and Cl are coupled with the angle of the gate by the following invariants:

$$Op \Leftrightarrow \alpha = 90 \quad \text{and} \quad Cl \Leftrightarrow \alpha = 0$$

Gate Controller

The gate controller reacts to the presence or absence of requests by the train (controller) to enter the crossing by issuing *GoUp* and *GoDown* signals to the gate plant. Depending on the messages Op and Cl of the gate plant it can signal an *OK* to the train controller as a permission to enter the crossing. This motivates the following time dependent variables.

Variables:

input	$Op : Time \rightarrow \mathbb{B}$	(gate open)
	$Cl : Time \rightarrow \mathbb{B}$	(gate closed)
	$Req : Time \rightarrow \mathbb{B}$	(request to enter crossing)
output	$Dir : Time \rightarrow \{Up, Down\}$	(direction of the gate)
	$OK : Time \rightarrow \mathbb{B}$	(permission to enter crossing)

Modes: **CrUnsafe, CrSafe, CloseGate, OpenGate**

Dynamics. The dynamics of the gate controller is described by the automaton in Fig. 6. Initially, the controller is in the mode **CrUnsafe** where it does not grant any permission to enter the crossing. When it senses a request by the train to enter it orders the gate to go down and switches to the mode **CloseGate**. It stays there until the gate signals that it it completely closed. Only then the controller gives permission to the train to enter the crossing by issuing an *OK* signal and switches to the mode **CrSafe**. It stays there until the request to enter the crossing is withdrawn. Then the controller switches to the mode **OpenGate**, withdraws the permission to enter the crossing and orders the gate to go up. When the gate is completely open, the controller switches back to its initial mode.

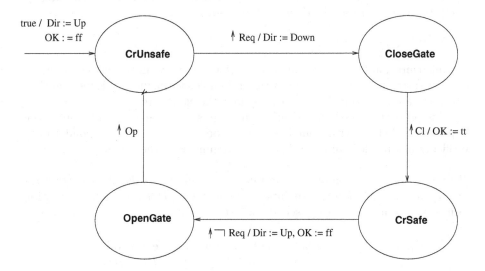

Fig. 6. Gate controller

The mode **CrUnsafe** belongs to the gate's phase FAR, **CloseGate** and **CrSafe** form the phase CORRECTING, and **OpenGate** is again FAR. The phase NEGOTIATING has no corresponding mode in this model: The gate does not negotiate, and one may view the transition from **CrUnsafe** to **CloseGate** as passing NEGOTIATING in an instant.

Correctness Proof

Desired Safety Property. We wish to show that whenever the train is in the critical section the gate is closed. This might be formulated in terms of safety envelopes as follows. For $SE_{Train}(pos)$ we choose an extension around the current position *pos* which encompasses the extension of the train, independent of mode and speed. The crossing's safety envelope is

$$SE_{Cr}(m) = \begin{cases} \varnothing & \text{if } m = \textbf{CrSafe} \\ Q & \text{otherwise} \end{cases}$$

for some adequate set of positions Q. This choice of $\varnothing$ as the extension of the safety envelope in mode **CrSafe** permits the train to pass the crossing when the bars are closed without safety violation. We assume that $inCr(pos)$ includes all train positions which could, if the crossing is not safe, violate safety, i.e.

$$SE_{Train}(pos) \cap Q \neq \varnothing \Rightarrow inCr(pos).$$

To perform the proof, we use the State Transition Calculus [18], an extension of the Duration Calculus [19, 15] to deal with instantaneous transitions. The Duration Calculus itself is a temporal logic and calculus for expressing and proving real-time interval properties of trajectories or observables of the form $obs : Time \rightarrow Data$. As a consequence of our assumption above, the desired safety property can then be expressed as follows:

$$\Box(\lceil inCr(pos) \rceil \Rightarrow \lceil Cl \rceil)$$

This Duration Calculus formula states that for every time intervals whenever the state assertion $inCr(pos)$ about the train holds throughout this interval then also the state assertion Cl holds throughout the same interval.

This property is established in a complete, self-contained proof. This proof is presented below, with added comments on which parts correspond to the verification conditions of our rule and the argument of the rule itself.

Notation. Duration formulas are evaluated in time intervals whereas state assertions are evaluated in time points. In the following D, D_1, D_2 denote duration formulas, S denotes a state assertion, and $t \in Time$.

$D_1; D_2$ (chop operator)	holds in a given time interval if first D_1 and then D_2 holds
$\Diamond D \Leftrightarrow true;\ D;\ true$	holds in a given time interval if on some subinterval D holds
$\Box D \Leftrightarrow \neg \Diamond \neg D$	holds in a given time interval if for all subintervals D holds
$\lceil \rceil \Leftrightarrow \ell = 0$	holds in a given time interval if this is a point interval (i.e. has length 0)
$\lceil S \rceil \Leftrightarrow \ell > 0 \wedge \int S = \ell$	holds for a non-point interval in which S holds throughout
$\lceil S \rceil^t \Leftrightarrow \ell = t \wedge \int S = \ell$	holds for an interval of length t and S holds throughout
$D \longrightarrow_0 \lceil S \rceil \Leftrightarrow \neg(D;\ \lceil \neg S \rceil)$	holds in an interval starting at 0 if D is followed by $\lceil S \rceil$
$D \longrightarrow \lceil S \rceil \Leftrightarrow \Box \neg(D;\ \lceil \neg S \rceil)$	holds in a given time interval if always D is followed by $\lceil S \rceil$

$D \xrightarrow{t} \lceil S \rceil \Leftrightarrow (D \land \ell = t) \longrightarrow \lceil S \rceil$ holds in a given time interval
if whenever D is true for t time
it is followed by $\lceil S \rceil$

$\uparrow S$ (start transition)   holds for a point interval where S
switches from false to true

$\downarrow S$ (end transition)   holds for a point interval where S
switches from true to false

To avoid unnecessary brackets, we assume that the chop operator ; binds stronger than the binary Boolean connectives $\land, \lor, \Rightarrow, \Leftrightarrow$ and the derived binary operators $\longrightarrow_0, \longrightarrow, \xrightarrow{t}, \xrightarrow{\leq t}$. In state assertions, equations $obs = d$ are abbreviated to d if it is clear to which observable obs the data value d belongs. For instance, $\lceil Keep \rceil$ abbreviates $\lceil sc = Keep \rceil$. For Boolean observables obs we abbreviate $obs = true$ to obs. For instance, $\lceil Cl \rceil$ abbreviates $\lceil Cl = true \rceil$.

Train Plant. The properties of the train plant are expressed in the State Transition Calculus as follows:

Invariants:
$$\Box \lceil pos^\bullet = speed \rceil$$
$$\Box \lceil speed \leq v_{max} \rceil$$

Initial state of the train on the track:
$$\lceil\rceil \lor \lceil farCr(speed)(pos) \rceil; \; true$$

The assumption about the initial state is needed for (VC 4).
Assertions about the train movements:
$$\lceil farCr(speed)(pos) \rceil \longrightarrow \lceil farCr(speed)(pos) \lor nearCr(speed)(pos) \rceil$$
$$\lceil nearCr(speed)(pos) \rceil \longrightarrow \lceil nearCr(speed)(pos) \lor inCr(pos) \rceil$$
$$\lceil inCr(pos) \rceil \longrightarrow \lceil inCr(pos) \lor afterCr(pos) \rceil$$
$$\lceil afterCr(pos) \rceil \longrightarrow \lceil afterCr(pos) \lor farCr(speed)(pos) \rceil$$

These assertion establish the necessary properties for reasoning about trajectories for (VC 2) and (VC 3) on the abstract level with the predicates $farCr$, $nearCr$, $inCr$ and $afterCr$.

The *speed* is stable under $sc = Keep$:
$$\forall v \in Speed : \lceil speed \leq v \land sc = Keep \rceil \longrightarrow \lceil speed \leq v \rceil$$

Stability of speed directly establishes (VC 7).
Braking:
$$\forall v \in Speed : \lceil speed \leq v \rceil; \lceil sc = Brake \rceil^{v/a_{reg}} \longrightarrow \lceil speed = 0 \rceil$$
$$\lceil speed = 0 \land Brake \rceil \longrightarrow \lceil speed = 0 \rceil$$
$$\forall v \in Speed : \uparrow nearCr(v)(pos); \lceil speed \leq v \rceil^{\varepsilon_{max}} \longrightarrow \lceil nearCr(v)(pos) \rceil$$
$$\forall v \in Speed : (\uparrow nearCr(v)(pos);$$
$$\lceil speed \leq v \rceil^{\varepsilon_{max}}; \lceil (speed^\bullet = -a_{reg}) \lor speed = 0 \rceil^{v/a_{reg}})$$
$$\longrightarrow \lceil nearCr(v)(pos) \rceil$$

The behavior while braking is needed for the adequacy and feasibility of recovery actions (VC 3) and (VC 8), while further properties of the abstract logical level, insofar as the interaction with the train's movement is concerned.

The train does not move at $speed = 0$:
$$\forall\, p \in Position : \lceil speed = 0 \rceil \wedge \lceil pos = p \rceil;\ true \Rightarrow \square\lceil pos = p \rceil$$

Train Controller. The following characterization of the train controller of Fig. 5 in terms of Duration Calculus formulas is not related to the decomposition proof rule. It only serves to lift reasoning about the automaton to the level of the Duration Calculus.

Initial mode:
$$\lceil\ \rceil \vee \lceil Far \rceil;\ true$$

Mode sequencing:
$$\lceil Far \rceil \longrightarrow \lceil Far \vee Appr \rceil$$
$$\lceil Appr \rceil \longrightarrow \lceil Appr \vee SafeAppr \vee FailSafe \rceil$$
$$\lceil SafeAppr \rceil \longrightarrow \lceil SafeAppr \vee Far \rceil$$
$$\lceil FailSafe \rceil \longrightarrow \lceil FailSafe \vee SafeAppr \rceil$$

Stabilities:
$$\lceil Far \rceil;\ \lceil farCr(speed)(pos) \rceil \Rightarrow \lceil Far \rceil$$
$$\lceil Appr \rceil;\ (\lceil \neg OK \rceil \wedge \ell < \varepsilon_{max}) \Rightarrow \lceil Appr \rceil$$
$$\lceil SafeAppr \rceil;\ \lceil \neg afterCr(pos) \rceil \Rightarrow \lceil SafeAppr \rceil$$
$$\lceil FailSafe \rceil;\ \lceil \neg OK \rceil \Rightarrow \lceil FailSafe \rceil$$

Transitions upon input events:
$$\lceil Far \rceil;\ \uparrow nearCr(speed)(pos) \longrightarrow \lceil Appr \rceil$$
$$\lceil Appr \rceil;\ \uparrow OK \longrightarrow \lceil SafeAppr \rceil$$
$$\lceil SafeAppr \rceil;\ \uparrow afterCr(pos) \longrightarrow \lceil Far \rceil$$
$$\lceil FailSafe \rceil;\ \uparrow OK \longrightarrow \lceil SafeAppr \rceil$$

Timeout transition:
$$\uparrow Appr;\ \lceil Appr \rceil \overset{\varepsilon_{max}}{\longrightarrow} \lceil FailSafe \rceil$$

The output variables *Req* and *sc* depend on the mode only:
$$\square\lceil Far \Leftrightarrow \neg Req \rceil$$
$$\square\lceil (Far \vee SafeAppr) \Leftrightarrow sc = Normal \rceil$$
$$\square\lceil Appr \Leftrightarrow sc = Keep \rceil$$
$$\square\lceil FailSafe \Leftrightarrow sc = Brake \rceil$$

Gate Plant. The following assumptions serve to characterize the trajectories resulting from the hybrid automaton in terms of the Duration Calculus formulas, similar to the characterization of the train plant above.

Initial state of the gate:
$$\lceil\ \rceil \vee \lceil \alpha = 90 \rceil;\ true$$

Assertions on the dynamics of the gate:
$$\lceil \alpha = 90 \wedge Dir = Up \rceil \longrightarrow \lceil \alpha = 90 \rceil$$
$$\lceil Dir = Up \wedge \neg Fail \rceil \xrightarrow{\varepsilon_{max}} \lceil \alpha = 90 \rceil$$
$$\lceil \alpha = 0 \wedge Dir = Down \rceil \longrightarrow \lceil \alpha = 0 \rceil$$
$$\lceil Dir = Down \wedge \neg Fail \rceil \xrightarrow{\varepsilon_{max}} \lceil \alpha = 0 \rceil$$

The output variables Op and Cl depend on the state of the gate only:
$$\square \lceil Op \Leftrightarrow \alpha = 90 \rceil$$
$$\square \lceil Cl \Leftrightarrow \alpha = 0 \rceil$$

Gate Controller. We formalise the properties of the automaton in Fig. 6.

Initial mode:
$$\lceil \rceil \vee \lceil CrUnsafe \rceil; \text{ true}$$

Mode sequencing:
$$\lceil CrUnsafe \rceil \longrightarrow \lceil CrUnsafe \vee CloseGate \rceil$$
$$\lceil CloseGate \rceil \longrightarrow \lceil CloseGate \vee CrSafe \rceil$$
$$\lceil CrSafe \rceil \longrightarrow \lceil CrSafe \vee OpenGate \rceil$$
$$\lceil OpenGate \rceil \longrightarrow \lceil OpenGate \vee CrUnsafe \rceil$$

Stabilities:
$$\lceil CrUnsafe \rceil; \lceil \neg Req \rceil \Rightarrow \lceil CrUnsafe \rceil$$
$$\lceil CloseGate \rceil; \lceil \neg Cl \rceil \Rightarrow \lceil CloseGate \rceil$$
$$\lceil CrSafe \rceil; \lceil Req \rceil \Rightarrow \lceil CrSafe \rceil$$
$$\lceil OpenGate \rceil; \lceil \neg Op \rceil \Rightarrow \lceil OpenGate \rceil$$

Transitions upon input events:
$$\lceil CrUnsafe \rceil; \uparrow Req \longrightarrow \lceil CloseGate \rceil$$
$$\lceil CloseGate \rceil; \uparrow Cl \longrightarrow \lceil CrSafe \rceil$$
$$\lceil CrSafe \rceil; \uparrow \neg Req \longrightarrow \lceil OpenGate \rceil$$
$$\lceil OpenGate \rceil; \uparrow Op \longrightarrow \lceil CrUnsafe \rceil$$

The output variables Dir and OK depend on the mode only:
$$\square \lceil (CrUnsafe \vee OpenGate) \Leftrightarrow Dir = Up \rceil$$
$$\square \lceil (CloseGate \vee CrSafe) \Leftrightarrow Dir = Down \rceil$$
$$\square \lceil CrSafe \Leftrightarrow OK \rceil$$

Proof of the Safety Property

The proof of the safety property is sketched by the following timing diagrams showing interpretations of the time dependent variables that satisfy the above formulas of the State Transition Calculus.

Fig. 7 shows the normal case where for the interval when pos takes the value $inCr$ we have $\lceil Cl \rceil$ as desired. For the adequacy (VC 2) and completeness (VC 4) arguments, we need that the Req signal is sent in time to close the gate. As NEGOTIATING is rather trivial here, and MATCH consists of just one pair of modes, (VC 9) and (VC 10) are rather trivial. Maneuvers are terminated on

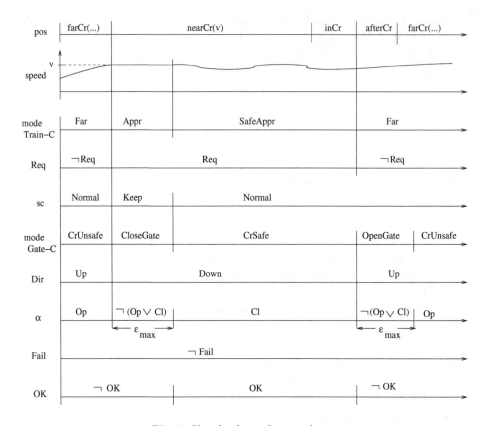

Fig. 7. Sketch of proof: normal case

reaching the noncritical **Far** again, which, due to the assumption on separation of crossings, dissatisfies the application condition of correcting maneuvers. The timing diagram in Fig. 7 sketches the combined behavior of controllers and plants, and thus subsumes (one part of) the discrete phase-transitions addressed in (VC 1) and the dynamic trajectories from (VC 3).

Fig. 8 shows the failure case where upon the train's request to enter the crossing the gate continues to show $\neg Cl$ for more than ε_{max} time and thus the train is prevented from entering the crossing. Here, the condition on the definition of $nearCr(v)(p)$ becomes essential in all its parts. It directly translates into a condition $\Phi_{rec2fss}$ for the train, with resulting proof obligations (VC 3), (VC 7) and (VC 8), which sum up into a maximal delay in the timing diagram from sending Req to coming to a full stop when the gate does not close.

We may note that, if there were more matching modes, each would require a corresponding timing diagram, enforcing the use of a global diagram fixing the relations between the cases. This argumentation pattern would, by and large, have to follow our proof rule, only that the rule further decomposes the (somewhat

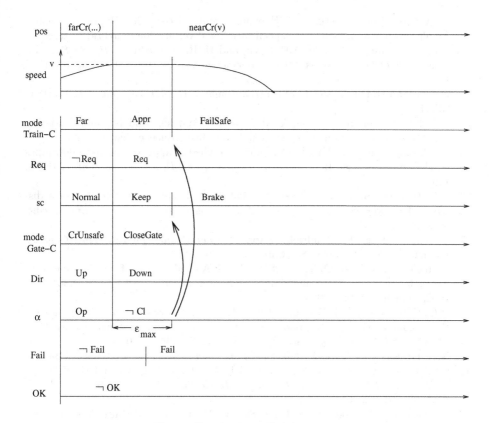

Fig. 8. Sketch of proof: failure case

informal) timing diagrams into completely formalized peaces, with well-defined interrelations.

6   Conclusion

We have presented an approach to the verification of cooperating traffic agents and shown its applicability to two radically different examples. Future work will complement this paper by formally proving the soundness of the proposed verification rule, formally instantiating this to the examples of this paper, and by demonstrating how the derived verification conditions can be discharged by automatic verification methods.

References

1. B. Abdul-Baki, J. Baldwin, and M.-P. Rudel. Independent validation and verification of the TCAS II collision avoidance subsystem. *Aerospace and Electronic Systems Mag.*, 15(8):3–21, 2000.

2. R. Alur, C. Courcoubetis, T.A. Henzinger, and Pei-Hsin Ho. Hybrid automata: An algorithmic approach to the specification and verification of hybrid systems. In R.L. Grossman, A. Nerode, A.P. Ravn, and H. Rischel, editors, *Hybrid Systems*, volume 736 of *Lecture Notes in Computer Science*, pages 209–229. Springer-Verlag, 1992.

3. R. Alur and D. Dill. A theory of timed automata. *Theoret. Comput. Sci.*, 126:183–235, 1994.

4. J. Bohn, W. Damm, J. Klose, A. Moik, and H. Wittke. Modeling and validating train system applications using statemate and live sequence charts. 2002.

5. A. Chutinam and B.H. Krogh. Computing polyhedral approximations in flow pipes for dynamic systems. In *37th IEEE Conference on Decision and Control*. IEEE, 1998.

6. A.E. Haxthausen and J. Peleska. Formal development and verification of a distributed railway control system. *IEEE Transactions on Software Engineering*, 26(8):687–701, 2000.

7. C. Heitmeyer and D. Mandrioli, editors. *Formal Methods for Real-Time Computing*, number 5 in Trends in Software. Wiley, 1996.

8. J. Hoenicke and E.-R. Olderog. CSP-OZ-DC: A combination of specification techniques for processes, data and time. *Nordic Journal of Computing*, 9(4):301–334, 2002. appeared March 2003.

9. R.E. Kalman and J.E. Bertram. Control system analysis and system design via the "second method" of lyapunov – Part I: Continuous time systems. *Transactions of the ASME, Journal of Basic Engineering*, 82:371–393, 1960.

10. N.G. Leveson. *Safeware: System Safety and Computers*. Addison Wesley, 1995.

11. C. Livadas, J. Lygeros, and N.A. Lynch. High-level modeling and analysis of TCAS. *Proceedings of IEEE — Special Issue on Hybrid Systems: Theory & Applications*, 88(7):926–947, 2000.

12. J. Lygeros, D.N. Godbole, and S.S. Sastry. Verified hybrid controllers for automated vehicles. *IEEE Transactions on Automatic Control*, 43(4):522–539, 1998.

13. N.A. Lynch, R. Segala, and F. Vaandrager. Hybrid I/O automata. *Information and Computation*, 185(1):105–157, 2003.

14. E.-R. Olderog, A. P. Ravn, and J. U. Skakkebæk. Refining system requirements to program specifications. In C. Heitmeyer and D. Mandrioli, editors, *Formal Methods for Real-Time Computing*, pages 107–134. Wiley, 1996.

15. A.P. Ravn. Design of embedded real-time computing systems. Technical Report ID-TR: 1995-170, Tech. Univ. Denmark, 1995. Thesis for Doctor of Technics.

16. C. Tomlin, J. Lygeros, and S.S. Sastry. A game theoretic approach to controller design for hybrid systems. *Proc. of the IEEE*, 88(7):949–970, 2000.

17. C. Tomlin, G. Pappas, and S.S. Sastry. Conflict resolution for air traffic management: A case study in multi-agent hybrid systems. *IEEE Transactions on Automatic Control*, 43(4), April 1998.

18. C. Zhou and M.R. Hansen. *Duration Calculus: A Formal Approach to Real-Time Systems*. Springer, 2004.

19. C. Zhou, C.A.R. Hoare, and A.P. Ravn. A calculus of durations. *Information Processing Letters*, 40(5):269–276, 1991.

How to Cook a Complete Hoare Logic for Your Pet OO Language

Frank S. de Boer[1,2,3] and Cees Pierik[3]

[1] Centre of Mathematics and Computer Science, The Netherlands
[2] Leiden Institute of Advanced Computer Science, The Netherlands
[3] Utrecht University, The Netherlands
F.S.de.Boer@cwi.nl cees@cs.uu.nl

Abstract. This paper introduces a general methodology for obtaining complete Hoare logics for object-oriented languages. The methodology is based on a new completeness result of a Hoare logic for a procedural language with dynamically allocated variables. This new result involves a generalization of Gorelick's seminal completeness result of the standard Hoare logic for recursive procedures with simple variables. We show how this completeness result can be generalized to existing Hoare logics for typical object-oriented concepts like method calls, sub-typing and inheritance, and dynamic binding, by transforming an encoding of these concepts into this procedural language with dynamically allocated variables.

1 Introduction

Information technology industry is still in need for more reliable techniques that guarantee the quality of software. This need is recognized by C.A.R. Hoare as a Grand Challenge for Computing Research in his proposal of the Verifying Compiler [14].

A verifying compiler resembles a type checker in the sense that it *statically* checks properties of a program. The properties that should be checked have to be stated by the programmer in terms of assertions in the code. The first sketch of such a tool is given by Floyd [10]. In recent years, several programming languages (e.g., EIFFEL [16], Java [9]) have been extended to support the inclusion of assertions in the code. These assertions can be used for testing but they can also be used as a basis for a proof outline of a program. Hoare logic [13] can be seen as a systematic way of generating the verification conditions which ensure that an annotated program indeed constitutes a proof outline. A verifying compiler then consists of a front-end tool to a theorem prover which checks the automatically generated verification conditions (see for example [7]).

Obviously, to be useful in practice Hoare logics should, first of all, be *sound*, i.e., only correct programs should be provably correct. Conversely, *completeness* means that all correct programs are provably correct. Its practical relevance, apart from providing a firm formal justification, is that in case we cannot prove

F.S. de Boer et al. (Eds.): FMCO 2003, LNCS 3188, pp. 111–133, 2004.
© Springer-Verlag Berlin Heidelberg 2004

our program correct, we know that this is due to incorrectness of our program (which in practice is most frequently the case). An incomplete proof method does not allow this simple inference.

Furthermore, to be useful in practice Hoare logics should allow the specification and verification of a program at the same level of abstraction as the programming language itself. This requirement has some important consequences for the specification of programs which involve dynamically allocated variables (e.g., 'pointers' or 'objects'). Firstly, this means that, in general, there is no explicit reference in the assertion language to the heap which stores the dynamically allocated variables at run-time. Moreover, it is only possible to refer to variables in the heap that do exist. Variables that do not (yet) exist never play a role.

The main contribution of this paper is a recipe for complete Hoare logics for reasoning about *closed* object-oriented programs at an abstraction level which coincides with that of object-oriented languages in general. This recipe is based on the transformational approach as introduced and applied in [18]: we first present a new completeness result of a Hoare logic for what is basically a procedural language with dynamically allocated variables. This result itself involves a non-trivial generalization of Gorelick's basic completeness result of the standard Hoare logic for recursive procedures with simple variables only ([11]). Then we show how this completeness result can be further generalized to existing Hoare logics for typical object-oriented concepts like method calls, sub-typing and inheritance by transforming an encoding of these concepts into this procedural language with dynamically allocated variables.

Proving Completeness

Below we summarize Gorelick's seminal completeness proof for recursive procedures with simple variables to clarify the context of the crucial steps in the enhanced proof.

Consider a simple sequential programming language with (mutually) recursive (parameterless) procedures. Let

$$p_1 \Leftarrow S_1, \ldots, p_n \Leftarrow S_n$$

be a set of mutually recursive procedure definitions, where $p \Leftarrow S$ indicates that the statement S is the body of procedure p. Central to the completeness proof is the Most General (correctness) Formula (MGF) of a statement S, which is a formula of the form

$$\{\bar{x} = \bar{z}\} S \{\mathrm{SP}(S, \bar{x} = \bar{z})\}.$$

Here, $\bar{z} = z_1, \ldots, z_n$ is a sequence of logical variables (not occurring in statements) that correspond with the program variables $\bar{x} = x_1, \ldots, x_n$ of S. The precondition $\bar{x} = \bar{z}$, which abbreviates the conjunction of the equalities $x_i = z_i$, for $i = 1, \ldots, n$, states that the (initial) values of the program variables are stored in the corresponding logical variables. For this reason, these logical variables are called 'freeze' variables. The postcondition $\mathrm{SP}(S, \bar{x} = \bar{z})$ describes the *strongest* postcondition of the statement S with respect to the precondition $\bar{x} = \bar{z}$.

The completeness proof in [11] shows that every valid correctness formula $\{P\}S\{Q\}$ can be derived if we first prove the most general correctness formula $\{\bar{x} = \bar{z}\}p_i\{SP(p_i, \bar{x} = \bar{z})\}$ of every procedure p_i. In the sequel, we denote this formula by Φ_i (for $i = 1, \ldots, n$). The above claim is proved by induction on the complexity of S. The most interesting case where S equals p_i, for some $i = 1, \ldots, n$, requires an application of the *invariance* axiom:

$$\{P[\bar{z}/\bar{x}]\}p_i\{P[\bar{z}/\bar{x}]\}.$$

Here $P[\bar{z}/\bar{x}]$ denotes the result of replacing the program variables by their corresponding logical variables. By the conjunction rule this is combined with Φ_i to obtain

$$\{P[\bar{z}/\bar{x}] \wedge \bar{x} = \bar{z}\}p_i\{P[\bar{z}/\bar{x}] \wedge SP(p_i, \bar{x} = \bar{z})\}.$$

From the validity of the given correctness formula $\{P\}p_i\{Q\}$ and the definition of the strongest postcondition one then proves the validity of the assertion

$$P[\bar{z}/\bar{x}] \wedge SP(p_i, \bar{x} = \bar{z}) \to Q.$$

This formula and the consequence rule allows us to replace the postcondition by Q. By applying a substitution rule and the rule of consequence we finally change the precondition to P and obtain $\{P\}p_i\{Q\}$.

The final step in the proof consists of deriving the MGF of every procedure call p_i (that is, Φ_i) in the logic by means of the recursion rule

$$\frac{F_1, \ldots, F_n \vdash \{P_1\}S_1\{Q_1\}, \ldots, \{P_n\}S_n\{Q_n\}}{F_1}.$$

Here, F_i denotes $\{P_i\}p_i\{Q_i\}$, for $i = 1, \ldots, n$. Since

$$\{\bar{x} = \bar{z}\}S_i\{SP(p_i, \bar{x} = \bar{z})\}$$

(with S_i the body of p_i) is by definition a valid correctness formula, we have as a particular case of the above, its derivability from $\Phi_1, \ldots, \Phi_n$. The above rule then allows us to conclude Φ_i, for $i = 1, \ldots, n$, thus finishing the completeness proof.

Our generalization of the above requires an intricate analysis of some general characteristics of correctness proofs for a procedural language with dynamically allocated variables. First, we have to formulate an assertion corresponding to $\bar{x} = \bar{z}$ which 'freezes' an initial state. In our setting, a state describes the heap which cannot captured statically by a finite number of variables. Next, we observe that the above invariance axiom as such is also not valid because the creation of new variables (or objects in object-oriented jargon) affects the scope of quantified logical variables. Therefore, creation of new variables in general will affect the validity of an assertion even if it does not refer to program variables at all. Summarizing, dynamically allocated variables basically require a proof-theoretical reconsideration of the concepts of initialization and invariance.

Below, the operator op is an element of Op, the language-specific set of operators, and m is an arbitrary identifier.

Table 1. The syntax of the programming language

$$
\begin{aligned}
e \in \text{Expr} \ &::= \ y \mid \text{op}(e_1, \ldots, e_n) \\
y \in \text{Var} \ &::= \ u \mid e.x \\
s \in \text{SExpr} \ &::= \ \text{new } C() \mid m(e_1, \ldots, e_n) \\
S \in \text{Stat} \ &::= \ y = e \ ; \mid y = s \ ; \mid \text{while } (e) \ \{ \ S \ \} \\
&\quad \mid \ S \ S \mid \text{if } (e) \ \{ \ S \ \} \ \text{else} \ \{ \ S \ \} \\
meth \in \text{Meth} \ &::= \ m(u_1, \ldots, u_n) \ \{ \ S \ \text{return } e \ ; \ \} \\
\pi \in \text{Prog} \ &::= \ class^*
\end{aligned}
$$

The results of the transformational approach then justifies our conclusion that Hoare logic for object-oriented programs basically boils down to a formalization of dynamically allocated variables.

Plan of the Paper
This paper is organized in the following way. Section 2 and 3 introduce a procedural programming language with dynamically allocated variables and the assertion language. In Section 4 we outline the corresponding Hoare logic. Section 5 contains the completeness proof. In Section 6 we introduce the transformational approach and sketch briefly some of its applications to typical object-oriented concepts. In the last section we draw some conclusions.

2 A Procedural Language with Dynamically Allocated Variables

The syntax of the basic strongly typed programming language considered in this paper is described in Table 1. We only consider the built-in types boolean and int. We assume given a set C of *class names*, with typical element C. The set of (basic) types T is the union of the set $\{\text{int}, \text{boolean}\}$ and C. In the sequel, t will be a typical element of T.

We assume given a set TVar of typed temporary (or local) variables and a set IVar of typed instance variables. Instance variables belong to a specific instance of a class and store its internal state. Temporary variables belong to a method and last as long as this method is active. A method's formal parameters are also temporary variables. We use u and x as typical elements of the set of temporary variables and the set of instance variables, respectively. We denote by $[\![u]\!]$ and $[\![x]\!]$ the (static) type of the temporary variable u and instance variable x, respectively. A *variable* y is either a temporary variable or a navigation expression $e.x$. A navigation expression $e.x$, with C the static type of e, refers to the value of the variable x of the instance e of the class C.

A program is a finite set of classes. A class defines a finite set of procedures (or methods in object-oriented jargon). A method m consists of its formal parameters $u_1, \ldots, u_n$, a statement S, and an expression e without side effects which denotes the return value. We have the usual assignments $y = e$ without side effect and $y = s$ with side effect. A variable y of type C, for some class C, can be dynamically allocated by means of an assignment $y = $ **new** $C()$ which involves the creation of an instance of class C. An assignment $y = m(e_1, \ldots, e_n)$ involves a call of method m with actual parameters $e_1, \ldots, e_n$.

Observe that our language does not support constructor methods. Therefore, an expression like **new** $C()$ will call the default constructor method, which will assign to all instance variables their default value.

2.1   Semantics

In this section, we will only describe the overall functionality of the semantics of the presented language because this suffices to understand the completeness proof.

Each instance of a class (or object in object-oriented jargon) has its own identity. For each class $C \in \mathcal{C}$ we introduce therefore an infinite set $\text{dom}(C)$ of identities of instances of class C, with typical element o. For different classes these sets of object identities are assumed to be disjoint. By O we denote the union of the sets $\text{dom}(C)$. For $t = \text{int}, \text{boolean}$, $\text{dom}(t)$ denotes the set of boolean and integer values, respectively.

A configuration σ (also called the *heap*) is a partial function that maps each *existing* object to its internal state (a function that assigns values to the instance variables of the object). Formally, σ is an element of the set

$$\Sigma = O \rightharpoonup \prod_{x \in \text{IVar}} \text{dom}(\llbracket x \rrbracket).$$

Here $\prod_{i \in I}$ denotes a generalized cartesian product over an index set I. In this way, $\sigma(o)$, if defined, denotes the internal state of an object, i.e., $\sigma(o)(x)$ denotes the value of the instance variable x of the object o. It is not defined for objects that do not exist in a particular configuration σ. Thus the domain of σ specifies the set of existing objects. We will only consider configurations that are *consistent*. We say that a configuration is consistent if no instance variable of an existing object refers to a non-existing object.

On the other hand, a temporary context γ specifies the values of the temporary variables of the executed method: γ is a typical element of the set

$$\Gamma = \prod_{u \in \text{TVar}} \text{dom}(\llbracket u \rrbracket).$$

The value of a temporary variable u is denoted by $\gamma(u)$.

A state is a pair (σ, γ), where the temporary context γ is required to be consistent with the configuration σ, which means that all temporary variables refer to objects that exist in σ.

Given a set of class definitions the semantics of statements is given by the (strict) function:

$$\mathcal{S} : \text{Stat} \rightarrow (\Sigma \times T)_\perp \rightarrow (\Sigma \times T)_\perp,$$

such that $\mathcal{S}(S)(\sigma, \gamma) = (\sigma', \gamma')$ indicates that the execution of S in the configuration (σ, γ) terminates in the configuration (σ', γ'). Divergence is denoted by $\perp$. A compositional characterization of $\mathcal{S}$ - which is fairly standard - can be given following [5].

In this paper we only need the following semantic definition of a method call $y = m(e_1, \ldots, e_n)$, with method body S. We have that

$$\mathcal{S}(y = m(e_1, \ldots, e_n))(\sigma, \gamma) = (\sigma', \gamma')$$

if

$$\mathcal{S}(S)(\sigma, \gamma_0) = (\sigma'', \gamma'')$$

where

- γ_0 results from γ by assigning to the formal parameters of m the values of the actual parameters $e_1, \ldots, e_n$ in (σ, γ);
- (σ', γ') results from (σ'', γ) by assigning the value of the result expression e in (σ'', γ'') to the variable y (which either will affect γ, in case of a local variable, or σ'', in case of a navigation expression).

3   The Assertion Language

In this section we present an assertion language for the specification of properties of dynamically evolving object structures. We want to reason about these structures on an abstraction level that is *at least as high as that of the programming language*. In more detail, this means the following:

- The only operations on "pointers" (references to objects) are
  - testing for equality
  - dereferencing (looking at the value of an instance variable of the referenced object)
- In a given state of the system, it is only possible to mention the objects that exist in that state. Objects that do not (yet) exist never play a role.

The above restrictions have quite severe consequences for the proof system. The limited set of operations on pointers implies that first-order logic is too weak to express some interesting properties of pointer structures like *reachability*. Therefore we have to extend our assertion language to make it more expressive. We will do so by allowing the assertion language to reason about *finite sequences* of objects.

The set of logical expressions in the assertion language is obtained by simply extending the set of programming language expressions without side effect (Expr) with *logical variables*. Logical variables are used for quantification and for reasoning about the constancy of program expressions. In the sequel, z will be a typical element of the set of logical variables LVar. Logical variables can also have a sequence type t^*, for some $t \in \mathcal{T}$. In such a case, its value is a finite sequence of elements of type t.

The syntax of the assertion language is summarized as follows.

$$l \in \text{LExpr} ::= u \mid z \mid l.x \mid \text{if } l_0 \text{ then } l_1 \text{ else } l_2 \text{ fi} \mid \text{op}(l_1, \ldots, l_n)$$
$$P, Q \in \text{Ass} ::= l_1 = l_2 \mid \neg P \mid P \wedge Q \mid \exists z : t(P)$$

(we omit typing information: e.g., the expression l in $l.x$ should refer to an object of some class and only boolean expressions can be used as assertions).

The conditional expression is introduced in order to reason about aliases, i.e., variables which refer to the same object. To reason about sequences we assume the presence of notations to express the length of a sequence (denoted by $|l|$) and the selection of an element of a sequence (denoted by $l[n]$, where n is an integer expression). More precisely, we assume in this paper that the elements of a sequence are indexed by $1, \ldots, n$, for some integer value $n \geq 0$ (the sequence is of zero length, i.e., empty, if $n = 0$). Accessing a sequence with an index which is out of its bounds results in the value $\bot$.

Only equations are allowed as basic assertions. This allows us to remain within the realm of a two-valued boolean logic, as explained in more detail below.

As stated above, quantification over finite sequences allows us to specify interesting properties of the heap. For example, that two objects hd and tl are connected in a linked list. This is asserted by the formula

$$\exists\, z : C^* \,(z[1] = \text{hd} \,\wedge z[|z|] = \text{tl} \,\wedge$$
$$\forall\, i : \text{int}(1 \leq i \wedge i < |z| \rightarrow z[i].\text{next} = z[i+1])).$$

Here z is a logical variable ranging over finite sequences of objects in class C and next is an instance variable of class C.

Logical expressions are evaluated in a configuration σ, a temporary context γ, and a logical environment ω, which assigns values to the logical variables. The logical environment should also be consistent with the configuration σ in the sense that no logical variable should refer to a non-existing object. The resulting value is denoted by $\mathcal{L}(l)(\sigma, \gamma, \omega)$. By $\mathcal{L}(l)(\sigma, \gamma, \omega) = \bot$ we indicate that the value of the expression is undefined (e.g., dereferencing the null-pointer, division by zero, etc.). The definition of $\mathcal{L}$ is rather standard and therefore omitted.

The resulting boolean value of the evaluation of an assertion P is denoted by $\mathcal{A}(P)(\sigma, \gamma, \omega)$. We define

$$\mathcal{A}(l_1 = l_2)(\sigma, \gamma, \omega) = \begin{cases} \text{true if } \mathcal{A}(l_1)(\sigma, \gamma, \omega) = \mathcal{A}(l_2)(\sigma, \gamma, \omega) \\ \text{false otherwise} \end{cases}$$

Assuming the constant nil for denoting the value $\bot$, we can can assert that the value of an expression e is undefined simply by the equation $e = \text{nil}$.

As already explained above, a formula $\exists z : C(P)$ states that P holds for an *existing* instance of class C. Thus the quantification domain of a variable depends not only on the (static) type of the variable but also dynamically on the configuration. Similarly, a formula $\exists z : C^*(P)$ states the existence of a sequence of existing objects (in class C).

The notation $\sigma, \gamma, \omega \models P$ means that $\mathcal{A}(P)(\sigma, \gamma, \omega) = \text{true}$. An assertion P is valid, denoted by $\models P$, if $\sigma, \gamma, \omega \models P$ for every state (σ, γ), and logical environment ω which are consistent w.r.t. the existing objects of σ, i.e., instance variables of existing objects, temporary variables and logical variables refer only to existing objects.

It is worthwhile to observe that quantification over finite sequences implies that the logic is not compact [8] (and as such transcends the realm of first-order logic) because we can express that there exists a finite number of objects (in a given class C): The assertion

$$\exists z : C^* \forall v : C \exists n : \text{int}(v = z[n])$$

states that there exists a finite sequence that stores all (existing) objects in class C.

Furthermore, we observe that the domain of discourse of our assertion language consists only of the built-in data types of the integers and booleans, and the program variables, i.e., it excludes the methods. This allows for a clear separation of concerns between *what* a program is supposed to do as expressed by the assertion language and *how* this is implemented as described by its methods.

4   The Proof System

Given a set of class definitions, correctness formulas are written in the usual form $\{P\}S\{Q\}$, where P and Q are assertions and S is a statement. We say that a correctness formula $\{P\}S\{Q\}$ is true w.r.t. a state (σ, γ) and a logical environment ω, written as $\sigma, \gamma, \omega \models \{P\}S\{Q\}$, if $\sigma, \gamma, \omega \models P$ and $\mathcal{S}(S)(\sigma, \gamma) = (\sigma, \gamma')$ implies $\sigma', \gamma', \omega \models Q$. This corresponds with the standard *partial* correctness interpretation of correctness formulas. By $\models \{P\}S\{Q\}$, i.e., the correctness formula $\{P\}S\{Q\}$ is valid, we denote that $\sigma, \gamma, \omega \models \{P\}S\{Q\}$, for every state (σ, γ) and logical environment ω which are consistent. Finally, $\vdash \{P\}S\{Q\}$ denotes derivability of $\{P\}S\{Q\}$ in the logic.

We only discuss the rules for method invocations in detail. The axioms for the other statements of our basic language are already introduced in, for example, [7]. Here, we will only give a brief description of these axioms. They all involve substitution operations that compute the weakest precondition of a statement. By a standard argument this implies that we can derive all valid specifications of such statements. For this reason, we focus on reasoning about methods invocations in this paper.

For an assignment to temporary variables, we have the usual axiom

$$\{P[e/u]\}\, u = e\, \{P\},$$

where $P[e/u]$ denotes the result of replacing every occurrence of the temporary variable u in P by the expression e. Soundness of this axiom is stated by the following theorem.

Theorem 1. *We have*

$$\sigma, \gamma, \omega \models P[e/u] \text{ if and only if } \sigma, \gamma', \omega \models P,$$

where γ' results from γ by assigning $\mathcal{L}(e)(\sigma, \gamma, \omega)$ to u.

Proof. Standard induction on the complexity of P.

We have a similar theorem for the substitution of logical variables.

Theorem 2. *We have*

$$\sigma, \gamma, \omega \models P[e/z] \text{ if and only if } \sigma, \gamma, \omega' \models P,$$

where ω' results from ω by assigning $\mathcal{L}(e)(\sigma, \gamma, \omega)$ to z.

In the axiom
$$\{P[e'/e.x]\} \; e.x = e' \; \{P\}$$
for assignments to instance variables the substitution operation $[e'/e.x]$ differs from the standard notion of structural substitution. An explicit treatment of possible aliases is required for this type of assignments. Possible aliases of the variable $e.x$ are expressions of the form $l.x$: After the assignment it is possible that l refers to the object denoted by e, so that $l.x$ is the same variable as $e.x$ and should be substituted by e'. It is also possible that, after the assignment, l does not refer to the object denoted by e, and in this case no substitution should take place. Since we can not decide between these possibilities by the form of the expression only, a conditional expression is constructed which decides "dynamically". Let l' denote the expression $l[e'/e.x]$. If $[\![l]\!] = [\![e]\!]$, i.e., the expressions l and e refer to objects of the same class, we define $(l.x)[e'/e.x]$ inductively by

$$\texttt{if } l' = e \texttt{ then } e' \texttt{ else } l'.x \texttt{ fi}$$

In case the types of the expressions l and e do not coincide, i.e., they do not refer to objects of the same class, aliasing does not occur, and we can simply define $(l.x)[e'/e.x]$ inductively by $l'.x$.

Soundness of the above axiom for assignments to instance variables is stated by the following theorem.

Theorem 3. *We have that*

$$\sigma, \gamma, \omega \models P[e'/e.x] \text{ if and only if } \sigma', \gamma, \omega \models P,$$

where $\sigma'(o)(x) = \mathcal{L}(e')(\sigma, \gamma, \omega)$, for $o = \mathcal{L}(e)(\sigma, \gamma, \omega)$, and in all other cases σ agrees with σ'.

Proof. Induction on the complexity of P (for details see [21]).

In [7] we also discuss the substitution operation [new C/u], which computes the weakest precondition of an assignment $u = $ new $C()$ involving a temporary variable u. The definition of this substitution operation is complicated by the fact that the newly created object does not exists in the state just before its creation, so that in this state we can not refer to it! We however are able to carry out the substitution due to the fact that this variable u can essentially occur only in a context where either one of its instances variables is referenced, or it is compared for equality with another expression. In both of these cases we can predict the outcome without having to refer to the new object. Another complication dealt with by this substitution operation is the changing scope of a bound occurrence of a variable z ranging over objects in class C which is induced by the creation of a new object (in class C). For example, we define $\exists z : C(P)[\text{new } C/u]$ by

$$\exists z : C(P[\text{new } C/u]) \vee (P[u/z][\text{new } C/u]).$$

The first disjunct $\exists z : C(P[\text{new } C/u])$ represents the case that P holds for an 'old' object (i.e. which exists already before the creation of the new object) whereas the second disjunct $P[u/z][\text{new}/u]$ represents the case that the new object itself satisfies P. Since a logical variable does not have aliases, the substitution $[u/z]$ consists of simply replacing every occurrence of z by u.

Given this substitution we have the following axiom for object creation involving a temporary variable:

$$\{P[\text{new } C/u]\} \; u = \text{new } C() \; \{P\}.$$

Soundness of this axiom is stated by the following theorem.

Theorem 4. *We have*

$$\sigma, \gamma, \omega \models P[\text{new}/u] \text{ if and only if } \sigma', \gamma', \omega \models P,$$

where σ' is obtained from σ by extending the domain of σ with a new object o and initializing its instance variables. Furthermore the resulting local context γ' is obtained from γ by assigning o to the variable u.

Proof. The proof proceeds by induction on the complexity of P (for the details we refer to [21]).

Observe that an assignment $e.x = $ new $C()$ can be simulated by the sequence of assignments $u = $ new $C(); e.x = u$. Therefore we have the axiom

$$\{P[u/e.x][\text{new } C/u]\} \; e.x = \text{new } C() \; \{P\},$$

where u is a fresh temporary variable which does not occur in P and e. Note that the substitution $[u/e.x]$ makes explicit all possible aliases of $e.x$. Soundness of this axiom follows from the above.

It is worthwhile to observe that aliasing and object creation are phenomena characteristic of dynamically allocated variables. Furthermore, the above substitutions provide a formal account of aliasing and object creation at an abstraction level which coincides with that of the programming language, e.g., without any explicit reference to the heap.

We now turn to method invocations. Suppose we have in class C a method $m(u_1, \ldots, u_n)$ $\{$ S **return** e $\}$. The following rule for method invocation (MI) allows to derive a correctness specification of a call $y = m(e_1, \ldots, e_n)$ from a correctness specification of the body S of m.

$$\frac{\{P\}S\{Q[e/\mathbf{return}]\} \quad Q[\bar{f}/\bar{z}] \rightarrow R[\mathbf{return}/y]}{\{P[\bar{e}/\bar{u}][\bar{f}/\bar{z}]\}\, y = m(e_1, \ldots, e_n)\, \{R\}} \tag{MI}$$

Here we do not allow temporary variables in Q. Except for the formal parameters $u_1, \ldots, u_n$, no other temporary variables are allowed in P.

The simultaneous substitution $[\bar{e}/\bar{u}]$ models the assignment of the actual parameters $\bar{e} = e_1, \ldots, e_n$ to the formal parameters $\bar{u} = u_1, \ldots, u_n$.

The substitution $[e/\mathbf{return}]$ applied to the postcondition Q of S in the first premise models a (virtual) assignment of the result value to the logical variable **return**, which must not occur in the assertion R. The substitution $[\mathbf{return}/y]$ applied to the postcondition R of the call models the actual assignment of the return value to y. It corresponds to the usual notion of substitution if y is a temporary variable. Otherwise, it corresponds to the substitution operation $[e'/e.x]$ for reasoning about aliases.

It is worthwhile to observe that the use of the additional **return** variable allows to resolve possible clashes between the temporary variables of the postcondition R of the call and those possibly occurring in the return expression e. As a typical example, consider the object-oriented keyword **this**, which denotes the current active object, as an additional parameter of each method. We observe that, in case a method returns the identity of the callee, in the postcondition $R[\mathbf{this}/y]$ of the caller, **this**, however, would refer to the caller.

Next, we observe that a temporary expression f of the caller generated by the following abstract syntax

$$f ::= u \mid \mathbf{op}(f_1, \ldots, f_n)$$

is not affected by the execution of S by the receiver. A sequence of such expressions $\bar{f}$ can be substituted by a corresponding sequence of logical variables $\bar{z}$ of exactly the same type in the specification of the body S. Thus the rule reflects the fact that the values of such expressions do not change by the execution of the call. Without these substitutions one cannot prove anything about the temporary state of the caller after the method invocation.

The generalization of the rule for non-recursive method invocations to one for (mutually) recursive method invocations follows the standard pattern. The idea is to assume correctness of the specification of the method call while proving the correctness formula of the body. In case of mutually recursive methods, we may assume correctness of the specification of several method calls. But this also forces us to prove the corresponding specifications of the bodies of all these calls.

The rule schema for mutually recursive method invocations (MRMI) is as follows.

$$\frac{I_1,\ldots,I_k \qquad A_1,\ldots,A_k \vdash F_1,\ldots,F_k}{F_1} \qquad \text{(MRMI)}$$

where

- A_i is a specification of a call, i.e., for $i = 1,\ldots,k$, A_i denotes a correctness formula

$$\{P_i[\bar{e}_i/\bar{u}_i][\bar{f}_i/\bar{z}_i]\}\, y_i = m_i(\bar{e}_i)\, \{R_i\}$$

  with $\bar{u}_i$ the formal parameters of method m_i and $\bar{e}_i$ a corresponding sequence of actual parameters and;
- F_i is a correctness formula

$$\{P_i\}\, S_i\, \{Q_i[e_i/\texttt{return}_i]\}$$

  with S_i the body of method $m_i i$ and e_i its return expression;
- I_i denotes the implication

$$Q_i[\bar{f}_i/\bar{z}_i] \rightarrow R_i[\texttt{return}_i/y_i]$$

which relates he postconditions of the call and the body.

The syntactical restrictions of rule (MI) also apply to all assertions in this rule.

5   Completeness

In this section, we will prove (relative) completeness of the logic [4] (soundness follows from a standard inductive argument). That is, given a finite set of class definitions, we prove that $\models \{P\}S\{Q\}$ implies $\vdash \{P\}S\{Q\}$, assuming as additional axioms all valid assertions. We do so following the structure of the proof that is given in the introduction. In the following sections we give solutions for each of the issues that were mentioned in the introduction.

First we show how to formulate an assertion that freezes the initial state. Subsequently, we give an enhanced version of the invariance axiom. As a counterpart of the substitution $[\bar{z}/\bar{x}]$ in the invariance axiom, we define a substitution that modifies an assertion in such a way, that its validity is not affected by execution of any object-oriented program. In particular, it is immune to object-creation. Next, we show that the our technique for freezing the initial state leads to Most General Formulas about method calls that enable us to derive any valid correctness formula. Finally, we show how to derive these MGFs for method calls.

Definition 1. *Our completeness proof is based on the following standard semantic definition of the strongest postcondition* $\mathrm{SP}(S, P)$ *as the set of triples* (σ, γ, ω) *such that for some initial state* (σ', γ') *we have* $\mathcal{S}(S)(\sigma', \gamma') = (\sigma, \gamma)$ *and* $\sigma', \gamma', \omega \models P$.

It can be shown in a straightforward although rather tedious manner that $SP(S, P)$ is expressible in the assertion language (see [6, 23]). The main idea followed in [6] is based on a logical encoding of states as described in the next section which heavily relies on the presence of quantification over finite sequences.

At several points in the completeness proof, we have to refer to the set $M(S)$ of method calls that might be executed as a result of executing S. This set $M(S)$ is defined as the smallest set which satisfies:

- $y = m(e_1, \ldots, e_n) \in M(S)$ if $y = m(e_1, \ldots, e_n)$ occurs in S
- $M(S') \subseteq M(S)$ if if $y = m(e_1, \ldots, e_n) \in M(S)$, where S' is the body of method m.

5.1   Freezing the Initial State

The first problem is to freeze the initial state which consists of the internal states of the existing objects and the values of the temporary variables. The set of existing objects is not statically given. Therefore we store the existing objects of a class C 'dynamically' in a logical variable seq_C of type C^*. For storing the values of instance variables, we introduce for each class C and instance variable $x \in \text{IVar}$ a corresponding logical variable $\Theta(C, x)$ of type $[\![x]\!]^*$ such that the value of the instance variable x of an existing object of class C is stored in the sequence denoted by $\Theta(C, x)$ at the position of the object in seq_C. Storing the initial values of the temporary variables of the active object in logical variables is straightforward. We simply introduce a logical variable $\Theta(u)$ of type $[\![u]\!]$, for each temporary variable u. Figure 1 pictures the relation between the heap and its representation in the logical state (here C represents the sequence of existing objects in class C and X a sequence storing all the values of the instance variable x).

The above encoding of a configuration can be captured logically by a finite (we assume given a finite set of class definitions) conjunction of the following assertions:

- $\forall z : C(\exists i(z = \text{seq}_C[i]))$
  which states that the sequence seq_C stores all existing objects of class C.
- $\forall i(\text{seq}_C[i].x = \Theta(C, x)[i])$
  which states that for each position in seq_C the value of the instance variable x of the object at that position is stored in the sequence $\Theta(C, x)$ at the same position.
- $u = \Theta(u)$
  which simply states that the value of u is stored in $\Theta(u)$.

The resulting conjunction we denote by init.

In the remainder of this section, we will work towards a new invariance axiom that replaces the old axiom

$$\{P[\bar{z}/\bar{x}]\}S\{P[\bar{z}/\bar{x}]\}.$$

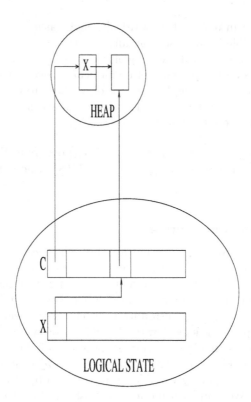

Fig. 1. Freezing the Initial State

We start by introducing a counterpart of the substitution $[\bar{z}/\bar{x}]$. Note that this substitution replaces program variables by their logical counterparts as introduced above. We therefore want to extend the mapping Θ to assertions such that it replaces all references to program variables by their logical counterparts. Since in general we cannot statically determine the position of an object of class C in the sequence seq_C we 'skolemize' the assertion $\forall z : C(\exists i(z = \text{seq}_C[i]))$ by introducing for every class C a function $\text{pos}_C(l)$ which satisfies the assertion

$$\forall z : C(z = \text{seq}_C[\text{pos}_C(z)]).$$

Note that in practice assertion languages should allow the introduction of user-defined functions and predicates.

We have the following main case of the transformation Θ on logical expressions l (using postfix notation).

$$(l.x)\Theta \equiv \Theta(C, x)[\text{pos}_C(l\Theta)]$$

where $C = [\![l]\!]$. As a simple example we have that $(u.x)\Theta$ yields the expression $\Theta(C, x)[\text{pos}_C(\Theta(u))]$, where C is the static type of the temporary variable u.

Quantification requires additional care when extending Θ to assertions because the scope of the quantifiers in general will be affected by object creation.

This can be solved by restricting quantification to the objects that exist in the initial state. That is, by restricting quantification to objects in seq_C. Therefore we introduce the following *bounded* form of quantification:

$$(\exists z : C(P))\Theta \equiv \exists z : C(z \in \text{seq}_C \wedge P\Theta)$$
$$(\exists z : C^*(P))\Theta \equiv \exists z : C^*(z \sqsubseteq \text{seq}_C \wedge P\Theta)$$

The assertions $z \in \text{seq}_C$ and $z \sqsubseteq \text{seq}_C$ stand for $\exists i(z = \text{seq}_C[i])$ and $\forall i \exists j(z[i] = \text{seq}_C[j])$. Note that the assertion $\exists i(z = \text{seq}_C[i])$ states that the object denoted by z appears in the sequence denoted by seq_C. The assertion $\forall i \exists j(z[i] = \text{seq}_C[j])$ states that all objects stored in the sequence denoted by z are stored in the sequence denoted by seq_C. We thus restrict quantification to the sequences seq_C. (For quantification over basic types or sequences of basic types we simply have $(\exists z P)\Theta = \exists z(P\Theta)$.)

The transformation Θ is truth-preserving in the following manner.

Theorem 5. *For every assertion P, and any state (σ, γ) and logical environment ω which are consistent, we have that $\sigma, \gamma, \omega \models \text{init}$ implies $\sigma, \gamma, \omega \models P$ iff $\sigma, \gamma, \omega \models P\Theta$.*

Proof. By structural induction on P. □

The following theorem states that we can prove that $P\Theta$ is an invariant for every statement S and assertion P. Thus this theorem can replace the invariance axiom.

Theorem 6. *For any statement S and assertion P we have $\vdash \{P\Theta\} S \{P\Theta\}$.*

Proof. The main idea behind the proof is that $P\Theta$ is immutable to all substitutions in the proof rules since the transformation Θ replaces all program variables by logical variables. Let P' denote $P\Theta$.

Since P' does not contain any program variables, clearly we have that $P'[e/u]$ and $P'[e'/e.x]$ both equal (syntactically) P', for any substitutions $[e/u]$ and $[e'/e.x]$.

Moreover, since all quantification in P' is bounded we have that $P'[\text{new } C/u]$ is logically equivalent to P': By the soundness of the axiom for object creation (as stated in Theorem 4) we have that $\sigma, \gamma, \omega \models P'[\text{new } C/u]$ if and only if $\sigma', \gamma', \omega \models P'$, where σ' results from adding to the domain of σ a new instance of class C and γ' results from assigning the identity of this newly created instance to the temporary variable u. Since u does not appear in P', it follows that $\sigma', \gamma', \omega \models P'$ if and only if $\sigma', \gamma, \omega \models P'$. Finally, since the newly created object in class C does not appear in $\omega(\text{seq}_C)$ (note that by definition $\omega(\text{seq}_C)$ may refer only to objects existing in σ) and all quantification in P' involving this newly created object is restricted to $\omega(\text{seq}_C)$ it follows that $\sigma', \gamma, \omega \models P'$ if and only if $\sigma, \gamma, \omega \models P'$.

5.2   Most General Correctness Formula

In the previous section, we described a way to freeze the initial state of an object-oriented program. The information about the initial state was captured by the formula init. With this formula we can define the most general correctness formula (MGF) of an object-oriented statement. It is the formula

$$\{\text{init}\}S\{\text{SP}(S, \text{init})\}.$$

In this section, we will show that assuming that the MGF holds for every method invocation in the program suffices to derive every valid correctness formula, as stated by the following theorem.

Theorem 7. *If* $\models \{P\}S\{Q\}$ *we have*

$$A_1, \ldots, A_k \vdash \{P\}S\{Q\},$$

where $A_i = \{\text{init}\}S_i\{\text{SP}(S_i, \text{init})\}$, *for* $i = 1, \ldots, k$, *and* $M(S) = \{S_1, \ldots, S_k\}$.

The proof proceeds by structural induction on S. The theorem holds for assignments $y = e$ and $y = \mathbf{new}\ (C)$ because the soundness of their axioms in fact show that the corresponding substitutions compute the weakest precondition. Complex control structures are treated in a standard manner ([3]). The following lemma describes the most interesting case of a method call.

Lemma 1. *For every call* $S \equiv y = m(e_1, \ldots, e_n)$ *we have*

$$\models \{P\}S\{Q\}\ \text{implies}\ \{\text{init}\}S\{\text{SP}(S, \text{init})\} \vdash \{P\}S\{Q\}$$

Proof. For technical convenience only we assume that P and Q do not contain free occurrences of the logical variables $\Theta(u)$ and $\Theta(C, x)$ (otherwise we first have to rename them). By Theorem 6 we have $\vdash \{P\Theta\}S\{P\Theta\}$. An application of the conjunction rule gives us the correctness formula

$$\vdash \{P\Theta \wedge \text{init}\}S\{P\Theta \wedge \text{SP}(S, \text{init})\}.$$

Our next step is to prove

$$\models P\Theta \wedge \text{SP}(S, \text{init}) \rightarrow Q.$$

Let $\sigma, \gamma, \omega \models P\Theta \wedge \text{SP}(S, \text{init})$. By the definition of SP there exists an initial configuration (σ_0, γ_0) such that both $\sigma_0, \gamma_0, \omega \models \text{init}$ and $\mathcal{S}(S)(\sigma_0, \gamma_0) = (\sigma, \gamma)$ hold.

Next, we show that $\sigma_0, \gamma_0, \omega \not\models P\Theta$ leads to a contradiction in order to obtain $\sigma_0, \gamma_0, \omega \models P\Theta$. So let $\sigma_0, \gamma_0, \omega \not\models P\Theta$. By Theorem 6 we have $\vdash \{\neg P\Theta\}S\{\neg P\Theta\}$. Soundness of the proof system ensures that we also have $\models \{\neg P\Theta\}S\{\neg P\Theta\}$. This implies that $\sigma, \gamma, \omega \not\models P$, which contradicts an earlier assumption.

By $\sigma_0, \gamma_0, \omega \models P\Theta$ and Theorem 5 we arrive at $\sigma_0, \gamma_0, \omega \models P$. Since $\models \{P\}S\{Q\}$ we conclude that $\sigma, \gamma, \omega \models Q$. So we can proceed by an application of the consequence rule to obtain

$$\vdash \{P\Theta \wedge \text{init}\}S\{Q\}.$$

Next, we can apply the standard rules which allow one to replace in the precondition every logical variable $\Theta(u)$ by the temporary variable u and existentially quantifying all the logical variables $\Theta(C, x)$ (x an arbitrary instance variable in an arbitrary class C). Finally, we existentially quantify the variables seq_C, for every C. It is not difficult to prove that the assertion P logically implies the resulting precondition. Therefore an application of the consequence rule finishes the proof.

The final step in the completeness proof is to show that we can derive the correctness formula

$$\{\text{init}\}S\{\text{SP}(S, \text{init})\}$$

for any assignment $S \equiv y = m(e_1, \ldots, e_n)$ that involves a method call.

Theorem 8. *For any assignment $S \equiv y = m(e_1, \ldots, e_n)$ we have*

$$\vdash \{\text{init}\}S\{\text{SP}(S, \text{init})\}.$$

Proof. We use the following notational conventions in this proof. Let

$$M(S) = \{S_1, \ldots, S_k\},$$

with $S_i \equiv y_i = m_i(e_1^i, \ldots, e_{n_i}^i)$, for $i = 1, \ldots, k$. Let S_0 denote $y = m(e_1, \ldots, e_n)$. Let A_i, for $i = 0, \ldots, n$, denote the correctness formula

$$\{\text{init}\}S_i\{\text{SP}(S_i, \text{init})\}.$$

Let S_i', for $i = 0, \ldots, n$, denote the body of m_i and let e_i be its return expression. The expression $\bar{e}_i$ abbreviates the sequence $e_1^i, \ldots, e_{n_i}^i$. We denote the formal parameters $u_1^i, \ldots, u_{n_i}^i$ of method m_i by $\bar{u}_i$.

We must prove $\vdash \{\text{init}\}S\{\text{SP}(S, \text{init})\}$. By the rule (MRMI) and Theorem 7 it suffices to find, for $i = 1, \ldots, k$, *valid* correctness formulas

$$\{P_i\} \, S_i' \, \{Q_i[e_i/\text{return}_i]\}, \tag{1}$$

such that

$$\models \text{init} \rightarrow P_i[\bar{e}_i/\bar{u}_i][\bar{f}_i/\bar{z}_i], \tag{2}$$

and

$$\models Q_i[\bar{f}_i/\bar{z}_i] \rightarrow \text{SP}(S_i, \text{init})[\text{return}_i/y_i], \tag{3}$$

for some substitutions $[\bar{f}_i/\bar{z}_i]$. Observe that Theorem 7 requires us to prove *validity*, not derivability. The substitutions $[\bar{f}_i/\bar{z}_i]$ involve temporary expressions $\bar{f}_i$ and corresponding logical variables satisfying the conditions of rule (MRMI).

Obvious candidates for the assertions P_i and Q_i are the formulas init and $\text{SP}(S_i, \text{init})[\text{return}_i/y_i]$, respectively. However, for (2) and (3) to be valid we introduce a renaming function Φ which transforms any temporary variable u into a (new) logical variable $\Phi(u)$ of the same type. Note that applying Φ to any assertion effectively neutralizes the passing of the actual parameters. That is,

$$(P\Phi)\theta \equiv P\Phi$$

for every assertion P and substitution θ which only transforms temporary variables. So candidates for P_i and Q_i are $\text{init}\Phi$ and $\text{SP}(S_i, \text{init})[\texttt{return}_i/y_i]\Phi$, respectively. Using the inverse Φ^{-1} of Φ for $[\bar{f}_i/\bar{z}_i]$, we trivially obtain (2) and (3).

However, to prove the validity of the correctness formulas in (1) we have to strengthen $\text{init}\Phi$ with additional information about the actual parameters specified by the call S_i. After the invocation of the method the formal parameters should have the values of the actual parameters. This information is given by the conjunction of the equations $u_j^i = (e_j^i\Phi)$, for $j = 1, \ldots, n_i$. Observe that (2) still holds because

$$(u_j^i = (e_j^i\Phi))[\bar{e}_i/\bar{u}_i]\Phi^{-1} \text{ yields } e_j^i = e_j^i.$$

Summarizing, for the assertion P_i defined by

$$\text{init}\Phi \wedge \bigwedge_{j=1}^{n_i} u_j^i = (e_j^i\Phi)$$

we can now prove the validity of the correctness formula

$$\{P_i\}\, S_i'\, \{Q_i[e_i/\texttt{return}_i]\}.$$

The proof proceeds as follows: let $\sigma, \gamma, \omega \models P_i$ and $\mathcal{S}(S_i')(\sigma, \gamma) = (\sigma', \gamma')$. We extend this computation of the method body S_i' to one of the call S_i: we define the initial local context γ_0 of the call S_i by assigning $\omega(\Phi(u))$ to every temporary variable u, i.e., $\gamma_0(u) = \omega(\Phi(u))$. From $\sigma, \gamma, \omega \models \text{init}\Phi$ we derive $\sigma, \gamma_0, \omega \models \text{init}i$ (formally this follows from Theorem 2). Furthermore, from $\sigma, \gamma, \omega \models u_j^i = (e_j^i\Phi)$ it follows that the value of the actual parameter e_j^i, with $j = 1, \ldots, n_i$, in the configuration (σ, γ_0) of the call equals the value of the corresponding formal parameter u_j^i in the configuration (σ, γ) of the method body (formally this follows from Theorem 1).

The final state of the call (σ'', γ_0') can be obtained by assigning the value of the result expression e_i to the variable y_i. We must consider two options, because y_i can be either a navigation expression or a temporary variable. If y_i is a navigation expression of the form $e.x$, we have $\gamma_0' = \gamma_0$, i.e., the initial local context of the call is not affected by the return, and σ'' is obtained from σ' by assigning the value of the return expression e_i in the state (σ', γ') to the instance variable x of the object denoted by e. If y_i is a temporary variable u, we define $\sigma'' = \sigma'$, i.e., the return does not affect the *heap*, and γ_0' is obtained from γ_0 by assigning the value of the return expression e_i to the temporary variable u.

From the semantics of method calls is described in Section 2.1it follows that

$$\mathcal{S}(S_i)(\sigma, \gamma_0) = (\sigma'', \gamma_0').$$

Since $\sigma, \gamma_0, \omega \models \text{init}$, we have by Definition 1 that $\sigma'', \gamma_0', \omega \models \text{SP}(S_i, \text{init})$. Next, let ω' be obtained from ω by assigning the result value, i.e., the value of $y_i$in the configuration (σ'', γ_0') of the call, to the logical variable $\texttt{return}_i$. It follows that $\sigma'', \gamma_0', \omega' \models \text{SP}(S_i, \text{init})[\text{return}_i/y_i]$. Observe that the truth of the assertion $\text{SP}(S_i, \text{init})[\text{return}_i/y_i]\Phi$ does not depend on the local context or the variable y_i due to the substitutions $[\text{return}_i/y_i]\Phi$. So we have

$$\sigma', \gamma', \omega' \models \text{SP}(S_i, \text{init})[\text{return}_i/y_i]\Phi.$$

Finally, because of the definition of ω' (note that $\omega(\text{return}_i)$ equals the value of the return expression e_i in state (σ', γ')) we conclude

$$\sigma', \gamma', \omega \models \text{SP}(S_i, \text{init})[\text{return}_i/y_i]\Phi[e_i/\text{return}_i].$$

6   The Transformational Approach

In this section we introduce a general methodology for generalizing our completeness result to more advanced object-oriented concepts. Our methodology is based on the transformational approach introduced in [18]. Given an object-oriented extension $\mathcal{L}^+$ of our very simple object-oriented language $\mathcal{L}$, this transformational approach consists of the definition of a translation

$$T : \mathcal{L}^+ \to \mathcal{L}$$

such that for every statement S in $\mathcal{L}^+$ we have

$$\{P\}S\{Q\} \text{ iff } \{P\}T(S)\{Q\},$$

for every precondition P and postcondition Q. A complete Hoare logic for $\mathcal{L}^+$ thus can be derived by transforming the translation T into corresponding proof rules.

Let us apply this approach first to the proof rule MI for method calls. Consider the translation of statements in our language $\mathcal{L}$ which transforms every object-oriented method call

$$e_0.m(e_1, \ldots, e_n)$$

into the procedural call

$$m(e_0, e_1, \ldots, e_n),$$

where the typical object-oriented concept of this is simply viewed as an additional formal parameter of the method m. We thus obtain the following new rule for typical object-oriented method invocations $y = e_0.m(e_1, \ldots, e_n)$.

$$\frac{\{P\}S\{Q[e/\text{return}]\} \quad Q[\bar{f}/\bar{z}] \to R[\text{return}/y]}{\{P[\bar{e}/\bar{u}][\bar{f}/\bar{z}]\} \, y = e_0 m(e_1, \ldots, e_n) \, \{R\}} \tag{MI'}$$

where $[\bar{e}/\bar{u}]$ abbreviates the substitution $[e_0, e_1, \ldots, e_n/\text{this}, u_1, \ldots, u_n]$. The syntactic restrictions of rule MI also apply to this rule MI'.

Next we apply the transformational approach to dynamic binding (in the context of inheritance and sub-typing as defined in Java [12]). In general, dynamic binding destroys the static connection between a method call and the implementation that is bound to the call. This implies that every implementation that might possibly be bound to a call must satisfy the specification of the call. That is the most significant change that has to be made to the rule for reasoning about methods calls. In order to obtain such a rule we first add to each class its inherited methods. Moreover, in order to avoid name clashes, we rename every method of a class C by $C.m$. We extend the assertion language with for every class C a monadic predicate $C(e)$, which holds if and only if the run-time type of the object denoted by e is C.

In the context of dynamic binding of method we then translate every call $e_0.m(e_1, \ldots, e_n)$ into the (nested) conditional statement:

```
if C₁(e₀)
then e₀.C₁.m(e₁,...,eₙ)
else if C₂(e₀)
     then e₀.C₂.m(e₁,...,eₙ)
          ⋮
             if Cₖ(e₀)
             then e₀.Cₖ.m(e₁,...,eₙ)
             fi
          ⋮
     fi
fi
```

where $\{C_1, \ldots, C_n\}$ are all the subclasses of C_1 and C_1 the (static) type of the expression e_0. This translation forms the basis of the existing logical formalizations of dynamic binding as described, for example, in [1] and [22]. We refer to [20] for the details of a transformation of this translation into a corresponding proof rule for the given method call $e_0.m(e_1, \ldots, e_n)$.

Of particular interest is an application of the transformational approach to Hoare logics for various object-oriented concurrency models. We are already working on a completeness proof of a Hoare logic for a simple extension with shared-variable concurrency of our object-oriented language: We assume that each class contains a so-called start-method denoted by start. The body of the start method is executed by a new thread and the calling thread continues its own execution. Like in Java we assume that the start method can be called upon an object only once (consequently the number of threads is less than or equal to the number of existing objects). A thread is formally defined as a stack of temporary configurations of the form $\langle S, \gamma \rangle$, where S denotes the statement to be executed and γ specifies the values of the temporary variables in S and the identity of the active object (denoted by this).

The assertions in an annotated program describe the top configurations of the existing threads. The verification conditions underlying the Hoare logic presented in Section 4 describe the sequential flow of control of a thread.

In order to characterize the interference between different threads we assume that each method has a formal parameter thread which is used to identify the executing thread. Every method invocation not involving the start method is assumed to be of the form

$$e_0.m(\text{thread}, e_1, \ldots, e_n).$$

That is, we pass the identity of the thread to which the caller belongs to the callee. On the other hand, the invocation of a start method is assumed to be of the form

$$e_0.\text{start}(e_0, e_1, \ldots, e_n),$$

because this invocation starts a new thread originating from the callee denoted by e_0.

We can now generalize the interference freedom test introduced in [19] to threads as follows. Let P be the precondition of an assignment $y := e$ and P' be the precondition of a statement S. We define P' to be invariant over the execution of the assignment $y := e$ by a *different* thread if the following verification condition holds:

$$(P \wedge P'' \wedge \text{thread} \neq \text{thread}') \rightarrow P''[e/y],$$

where P'' is obtained from P' by replacing every temporary variable u by a fresh u' and this by this$'$, in order to avoid name clashes between the temporary variables and the keyword this in P and P'. Note that thread is assumed to be a temporary variable too and is therefore also renamed by thread$'$.

This simple extension of our Hoare logic for shared variable concurrency will form the basis of an application of the transformational approach to the concurrency model of Java involving threads and coordination via reentrant synchronization monitors (as described in [2]).

7   Conclusions

In recent years, many formal analysis techniques for object-oriented programming languages have been proposed. The large amount of interest can be explained by the wide-spread use of object-oriented languages. However, the formal justification of many existing Hoare logics for object-oriented programming languages is still under investigation. Notably the problem of completeness until now defied clear solutions. For example, the logic of object-oriented programs as given by Abadi and Leino was not complete [1]. They suspect that their use of a "global store" model is the source of the incompleteness.

Von Oheimb showed that his logic for reasoning about a substantial subset of Java is (relatively) complete [24]. However, he uses the logic of Isabelle/HOL (higher order logic) as specification language. This trivializes the matter of expressiveness of the intermediate assertions. Therefore their result does not automatically carry over to assertion languages that are closer to the programming language. This point is further discussed in [17].

Future work concerns first of all the further development of the transformational approach to Hoare logics of object-oriented programming. Of particular interest is an application of the transformational approach to Hoare logics for various object-oriented concurrency models.

Another interesting line of research concerns the systematic development of *compositional* Hoare logics for object-oriented programs. Note that the Hoare logic presented in this paper is compositional only with respect to the flow of control structures. However, it is not compositional in the sense of *class-based*. Also our Hoare logic does not provide any formalization of the basic concept of an object as an unit of data-encapsulation. We think that such a logic requires a formalization of the external observable behavior of an object in terms of its traces of events which indicate the sending and reception of messages (as described for example in [15]). It is worthwhile to observe that such a notion of external observable behavior (which abstracts from the internal state space of an object) in fact involves a concurrency view even if the object-oriented programming language is purely sequential.

Finally, we remark that most existing logics for object-oriented programs deal with closed programs. Currently we are also investigating trace semantics as a possible semantic basis of Hoare logics for *open* object-oriented programs.

References

1. M. Abadi and R. Leino. A logic of object-oriented programs. In M. Bidoit and M. Dauchet, editors, *TAPSOFT '97: Theory and Practice of Software Development, 7th International Joint Conference CAAP/FASE, Lille, France*, volume 1214, pages 682–696. Springer-Verlag, 1997.
2. E. Abraham-Mumm, F. de Boer, W. de Roever, and M. Steffen. Verification for Java's reentrant multithreading concept. In *Proc. of FoSSaCS 2002*, volume 2303 of *LNCS*, pages 5–20, 2002.
3. K. R. Apt. Ten Years of Hoare's Logic: A Survey - Part I. *ACM Transactions on Programming Languages and Systems*, 3(4):431–483, October 1981.
4. S. A. Cook. Soundness and completeness of an axiom system for program verification. *Siam Journal of Computing*, 7(1):70–90, February 1978.
5. J. de Bakker. *Mathematical theory of program correctness*. Prentice-Hall, 1980.
6. F. de Boer. *Reasoning about dynamically evolving process structures*. PhD thesis, Vrije Universiteit, 1991.
7. F. de Boer and C. Pierik. Computer-aided specification and verification of annotated object-oriented programs. In B. Jacobs and A. Rensink, editors, *FMOODS V*, pages 163–177. Kluwer Academic Publishers, 2002.
8. H.-D. Ebbinghaus and J. Flum. *Finite Model Theory*. Springer-Verlag, 1995.
9. C. Flanagan, K. R. M. Leino, M. Lillibridge, G. Nelson, J. B. Saxe, and R. Stata. Extended static checking for Java. In *Proceedings of the ACM SIGPLAN 2002 Conference on Programming Language Design and Implementation (PLDI)*, pages 234–245, 2002.
10. R. W. Floyd. Assigning meaning to programs. In *Proc. Symposium on Applied Mathematics*, volume 19, pages 19–32. American Mathematical Society, 1967.

11. G. Gorelick. A complete axiomatic system for proving assertions about recursive and non-recursive programs. Technical Report 75, Dep. Computer Science, Univ. Toronto, 1975.
12. J. Gosling, B. Joy, and G. Steele. *The Java Language Specification.* Addison-Wesley, 1996.
13. C. A. R. Hoare. An axiomatic basis for computer programming. *Communications of the ACM*, 12(10):576–580, 1969.
14. T. Hoare. Assertions. In M. Broy and M. Pizka, editors, *Models, Algebras and Logic of Engineering Software*, volume 191 of *NATO Science Series*, pages 291–316. IOS Press, 2003.
15. A. Jeffrey and J. Rathke. A fully abstract may testing semantics for concurrent objects. In *Proceedings of Logics in Computer Science*, pages 101–112, 2002.
16. B. Meyer. *Eiffel: The Language.* Prentice-Hall, 1992.
17. T. Nipkow. Hoare logics for recursive procedures and unbounded nondeterminism. In J. Bradfield, editor, *Computer Science Logic (CSL 2002)*, volume 2471 of *LNCS*, pages 103–119. Springer, 2002.
18. E.-R. Olderog and K. R. Apt. Fairness in parallel programs: The transformational approach. *TOPLAS*, 10(3):420–455, 1988.
19. S. Owicki and D. Gries. An axiomatic proof technique for parallel programs I. *Acta Informatica*, 6:319–340, 1976.
20. C. Pierik and F. S. de Boer. A syntax-directed Hoare logic for object-oriented programming concepts. In E. Najm, U. Nestmann, and P. Stevens, editors, *Formal Methods for Open Object-Based Distributed Systems (FMOODS) VI*, volume 2884 of *LNCS*, pages 64–78, 2003.
21. C. Pierik and F. S. de Boer. A syntax-directed Hoare logic for object-oriented programming concepts. Technical Report UU-CS-2003-010, Institute of Information and Computing Sciences, Utrecht University, The Netherlands, March 2003. Available from http://www.cs.uu.nl/research/techreps/UU-CS-2003-010.html.
22. A. Poetzsch-Heffter and P. Müller. A programming logic for sequential Java. In S. D. Swierstra, editor, *ESOP '99*, volume 1576 of *LNCS*, pages 162–176, 1999.
23. J. Tucker and J. Zucker. *Program correctness over abstract data types with error-state semantics.* North-Holland, 1988.
24. D. von Oheimb. Hoare logic for Java in Isabelle/HOL. *Concurrency and Computation: Practice and Experience*, 13(13):1173–1214, 2001.

Behavioural Specification for Hierarchical Object Composition

Răzvan Diaconescu

Institute of Mathematics "Simion Stoilow", PO-Box 1-764,
Bucharest 014700, Romania
Razvan.Diaconescu@imar.ro

Abstract. Behavioural specification based on hidden (sorted) algebra constitutes one of the most promising recently developed formal specification and verification paradigms for system development.

Here we formally introduce a novel concept of *behavioural object* within the hidden algebra framework. We formally define several object composition operators on behavioural objects corresponding to the hierarchical object composition methodology introduced by CafeOBJ. We study their basic semantical properties and show that our most general form of behavioural object composition with synchronisation has final semantics and a composability property of behavioural equivalence supporting a high reusability of verifications. We also show the commutativity and the associativity of parallel compositions without synchronisation.

1 Introduction

The current Internet/Intranet technologies have led to an explosive increase in demand for the construction of reliable distributed systems. Among the new technologies proposed for meeting this new technological challenge, component-based software engineering is one of the most promising. If we have an adequate set of components and a good design pattern, a system development process may become easier and the quality of the product may be greatly improved. However such development process raises some serious problems. How can we get an adequate set of components or how can we know the components we get are adequate for our systems?

A good solution seems to be given by formal specifications supporting the following characteristics:

- can specify the interface of components,
- can specify the behaviour of components,
- supports a precise semantics of composition, and
- be executable or have tools supporting testing and verification.

Here we adopt the behavioural algebraic specification framework [1, 2, 3, 4]. Due to its simple logical foundations and to its efficient specification and verifi-

F.S. de Boer et al. (Eds.): FMCO 2003, LNCS 3188, pp. 134–156, 2004.

cation methodologies, behavioural algebraic specification provides a good framework for such formal specifications. Informally, behavioural algebraic specification describe both data types and states of abstract machines by axioms based on strict equality, in the case of the data types, and *behavioural* equality (i.e. equality under 'observations' to data), in the case of the states of abstract machines. Implementations of behavioural specifications are formalised as (many sorted) 'hidden' algebras interpreting two kinds of sorts as sets, one kind for the data types, another kind for the states of the abstract machines, and interpreting operations as functions. The operations which determine the behavioural equivalence between states are specified as special 'behavioural' operations. Such a 'hidden' algebra is a model of a specification when all sentences (axioms) of the specification are valid for that algebra.

The work around the CafeOBJ algebraic specification language [5, 6] has proposed a hierarchical object composition methodology (see [5, 7, 8]) based on behavioural specification. The behavioural specification paradigm is reflected rather directly in the definition of CafeOBJ, this being maybe the most distinctive feature of this language among other modern algebraic specification languages such as CASL [9] or Maude [10].

Here we formally define the novel concept of behavioural object within the hidden algebra framework, which is the logic of CafeOBJ behavioural specification. Informally, a behavioural object is just a special kind of behavioural specification which emphasises a special 'hidden' sort for the space of the states of the object and special operations for modelling method invocations and attributes. One of the most important novel related concepts introduced is that of *equivalence* between behavioural objects, which plays an important role in the study of the semantical properties of hierarchical object composition.

This concept is the basis for a precise definition of several types of composition operators on behavioural objects, such as parallel composition (without synchronisation), dynamic composition (in which component objects gets created and deleted dynamically), and composition with synchronisation generalising both the former operators. Informally, these composition operators are based on specifications of projections from the state space of the compound object to the state spaces of the components. Our definitions give mathematical foundations for the corresponding methodological definitions of object composition in [5, 11, 8]. Our composition operators support hierarchical composition processes in the sense that the result of a composition is still a behavioural object which can be therefore used in another composition.

Our framework permits a clear formulation of semantical properties of the composition operators, such as associativity and commutativity, and final semantics (i.e. the existence of final composition models). We show that the basic parallel composition operator is commutative and associative (modulo object equivalence). For the general composition with synchronisation operator we prove a compositionality result for the behavioural equivalence relation, result which constitute the foundation for automation of the verification process at the level of a compound object (see [5, 11, 8]), and the existence of final semantics.

The paper is structured as follows. The first section recalls briefly the basic mathematical notions necessary for this work. We present first general algebra notions, and then we give a very brief overview of hidden algebra. At the end of this section we define the concept of behavioural object. The next section introduces briefly the CafeOBJ notation for behavioural objects, which will be used for the examples, and which is illustrated with two simple examples. The main section of the paper is dedicated to the composition operators and contains their mathematical definitions together with their main semantic properties. All composition operators are illustrated with examples. The final section develops an example showing how the compositionality of behavioural equivalence result for compositions with synchronisation can be applied for reusing verifications within the framework of the CafeOBJ system.

Here we only give the statements of the mathematical results and omit their proofs. These will appear in an extended full version of the paper.

Acknowledgement

The author is grateful to all people who contributed to the development of the CafeOBJ object composition methodology based on projection operations, especially to Shusaku Iida and Kokichi Futatsugi.

2   The Logic of Behavioural Specification

The semantics of behavioural specification is based on hidden algebra [2, 4, 3] which is a refinement of general many-sorted algebra. Although the hidden algebra formalism accommodates well (and even gets more power from) the order-sorted approach (see [12]), for reasons of simplicity of presentation, we develop all formal definition and results in a many-sorted framework.

2.1   General Algebra

We review here the basic general algebra concepts, notations, and terminology, which constitute now the folklore of algebraic specification.

Given a *sort set* S, an *S-indexed* (or *sorted*) *set* A is a family $\{A_s\}_{s \in S}$ of sets indexed by the elements of S. In this context, $a \in A$ means that $a \in A_s$ for some $s \in S$. Similarly, $A \subseteq B$ means that $A_s \subseteq B_s$ for each $s \in S$, and an *S-indexed* (or *sorted*) *function* $f \colon A \to B$ is a family $\{f_s \colon A_s \to B_s\}_{s \in S}$. Also, we let S^* denote the set of all finite sequences of elements from S, with $[]$ the empty sequence. Given an S-indexed set A and $w = s_1...s_n \in S^*$, we let $A_w = A_{s_1} \times \cdots \times A_{s_n}$; in particular, we let $A_{[]} = \{\star\}$, some one point set. Also, for an S-sorted function $f \colon A \to B$, we let $f_w \colon A_w \to B_w$ denote the function product mapping a tuple of elements $(a_1, \ldots, a_n)$ to the tuple $(f_{s_1}(a_1), \ldots, f_{s_n}(a_n))$.

A (n *S-sorted*) *signature* (S, F) is an $S^* \times S$-indexed set $F = \{F_{w \to s} \mid w \in S^*, \ s \in S\}$ of *operation symbols*. Note that this definition permits *overload-*

ing, in that the sets $F_{w \to s}$ need *not* be disjoint. Call $\sigma \in F_{[] \to s}$ (sometimes denoted simply $F_{\to s}$) a *constant symbol* of sort s. A *signature morphism* φ from a signature (S, F) to a signature (S', F') is a pair $(\varphi^{\text{sort}}, \varphi^{\text{op}})$ consisting of a map $\varphi^{\text{sort}} \colon S \to S'$ of sorts and of a map $\varphi^{\text{op}} \colon F \to F'$ on operation symbols such that $\varphi^{\text{op}}_{w \to s}(F_{w \to s}) \subseteq F'_{(\varphi^{\text{sort}})^*(w) \to \varphi^{\text{sort}}(s)}$, where $(\varphi^{\text{sort}})^* \colon S^* \to S'^*$ is the extension of φ^{sort} to strings.

A (S, F)-*algebra* A consists of an S-indexed set A and a function $A_\sigma \colon A_w \to A_s$ for each $\sigma \in F_{w \to s}$; the set A_s is called the *carrier* of A of sort s. If $\sigma \in F_{\to s}$ then A_σ determines a point in A_s which may also be denoted A_σ. An (S, F)-*homomorphism* from one (S, F)-algebra A to another B is an S-indexed function $h \colon A \to B$ such that $h_s(A_\sigma(a)) = B_\sigma(h_w(a))$ for each $\sigma \in F_{w \to s}$ and $a \in A_w$. A (S, F)-homomorphism $h \colon A \to B$ is a (S, F)-*isomorphism* if and only if each function $h_s \colon A_s \to B_s$ is bijective (i.e., one-to-one and onto, in an older terminology). The category (class) of algebras of a signature (S, F) is denoted $\mathbb{A}lg(S, F)$.

A F-*congruence* on a (S, F)-algebra A is an S-sorted family of relations, $\equiv_s$ on A_s, each of which is an equivalence relation, and which also satisfy the *congruence property*, that given any $\sigma \in F_{w \to s}$ and any $a \in A_w$, then $A_\sigma(a) \equiv_s A_\sigma(a')$ whenever $a \equiv_w a'$.[1]

Given a signature morphism $\varphi \colon (S, F) \to (S', F')$ and a (S', F')-algebra A', we can define the *reduct* of A' to (S, F), denoted $A' \upharpoonright_\varphi$, or simply $A' \upharpoonright_{(S,F)}$ when φ is an inclusion of signatures, to have carriers $A'_{\varphi(s)}$ for $s \in S$, and to have operations $(A' \upharpoonright_\varphi)_\sigma = A'_{\varphi(\sigma)}$ for $\sigma \in F$. Then A' is called an *expansion* of A along φ. Reducts can also be easily extended to algebra homomorphisms.

For any signature (S, F) and (S, F)-algebra A, let (S, F_A) be the *elementary extension* of (S, F) *via* A which adds the elements of A as new constants, i.e. $(F_A)_{\to s} = F_{\to s} \cup A_s$ and $(F_A)_{w \to s} = F_{w \to s}$ when w is not empty. Let A_A denote the expansion of A to (S, F_A) interpreting each element of A by itself, i.e. $(A_A)_a = a$ for each $a \in A$.

Any F-*term* $t = \sigma(t_1 \ldots t_n)$, where $\sigma \in F_{w \to s}$ is an operation symbol and $t_1, \ldots, t_n$ are F-(sub)terms corresponding to the arity w, gets *interpreted as an element* $A_t \in A_s$ in a (S, F)-algebra A by $A_t = A_\sigma(A_{t_1} \ldots A_{t_n})$. When each element a of A can be denoted as $a = A_t$ for some term t, then we call A a *reachable* algebra.

For any set X of new constants, called *variables*, the $(F \cup X)$-terms can be regarded as F-*derived operations* by defining the arity $ar(t)$ by the following procedure:

- consider the set $var(t) \subseteq X$ of all variables occurring within t,
- transform $var(t)$ into a string by fixing an arbitrary order on this set, and
- finally, replace the variables in the string previously obtained by their sorts.

Any F-derived operation t with arity w and sort s determines a function $A_t \colon A_w \to A_s$ such that for each string a of elements corresponding to $ar(t)$,

---

[1] Meaning $a_i \equiv_{s_i} a'_i$ for $i = 1, ..., n$, where $w = s_1 \ldots s_n$ and $a = (a_1, \ldots, a_n)$.

$A_t(a)$ is the evaluation of t in the expansion of A to $F \cup X$ which interprets the variables of X be the corresponding elements of a.

A *F-context* $c[z]$ is any F-term c with a marked variable z occurring only once in c.

Given a signature (S, F), the set of (S, F)-*sentences* is the least set of sentences containing the (quantifier-free) equations and which is closed under logical connectives and quantification. An *equation* is an equality $t = t'$ between F-terms t and t'. For ρ_1 and ρ_2 any (S, F)-sentences, let $\rho_1 \wedge \rho_2$ be their conjunction which is also a (S, F)-sentence. Other logical connectives are the disjunction, implication, negation, etc. For any set X of variables for a signature (S, F), then $(\forall X)\rho$ is a (S, F)-sentence for each $(S, F \cup X)$-sentence ρ. Similar definition can be applied to the existential quantification.

Given an algebraic signature morphism $\varphi \colon (S, F) \to (S', F')$, each (S, F)-sentence ρ can be translated to a (S', F')-sentence ρ', denoted $\varphi(\rho)$, by replacing any symbol of (S, F) fro ρ by its corresponding symbol from (S', F') given by φ.[2]

The *satisfaction* between algebras and sentences is the Tarskian satisfaction defined inductively on the structure of sentences. Given a fixed arbitrary signature (S, F) and an (S, F)-algebra A,

- $A \models t = t'$ if $A_t = A_{t'}$ for equations,
- $A \models \rho_1 \wedge \rho_2$ if $A \models \rho_1$ and $A \models \rho_2$ and similarly for the other logical connectives, and
- for each $(S, F \cup X)$-sentence $A \models (\forall X)\rho$ if $A' \models \rho$ for each expansion A' of A along the signature inclusion $(S, F) \hookrightarrow (S, F \cup X)$.

2.2 Hidden Algebra

Hidden algebra (abbreviated *HA*) is the logical formalism underlying behavioural specification. It extends ordinary general algebra with sorts representing 'states' of objects, or abstract machines, rather than data elements and also introduces a new satisfaction between algebras and sentences, called 'behavioural satisfaction'. In the literature there are several versions of hidden algebra, with only slight technical differences between them [2, 3, 4]. In the following we review the basic concepts of hidden algebra.

A *hidden algebraic signature* (H, V, F, F^b) consists of a set H of *hidden sorts*, a set V of ordinary *visible sorts*, a set F of $(H \cup V)$-sorted operation symbols, and a distinguished subset $F^b \subseteq F$ of *behavioural operations*. Behavioural operations are required to have at least one hidden sort in their arity. An operation symbol which has visible arity and sort is called *data operation*.

From an object-oriented methodological perspective, the hidden sorts denote sets of 'states of objects', the visible sorts denote data types, and the operations $\sigma \in F^b_{w \to s}$ can be thought as 'methods' whenever w has exactly one hidden sort

---

[2] In the particular case of quantifications, notice that this changes the sorts of the variables.

and s is hidden also, and as 'attributes' whenever w has exactly one hidden sort and s is visible. This object-oriented interpretation of behavioural logic will be formally clarified in the section below by the introduction of the concept of 'behavioural object'.

A (H, V, F, F^b)-*algebra* is just an $(H \cup V, F)$-algebra. A *homomorphism of hidden algebras* $h \colon A \to B$ for a signature (H, V, F, F^b) is just a $(H \cup V, F)$-algebra homomorphism preserving the behavioural equivalence, i.e. such that $h(\sim_A) \subseteq \sim_B$.

Given a (H, V, F, F^b)-algebra A, a *hidden* congruence $\sim$ on A is just an F^b-congruence which is identity on the visible sorts. The largest hidden F-congruence $\sim_A$ on A is called *behavioural equivalence*. The following is probably the most fundamental result in hidden algebra, providing the foundations for the so-called 'coinduction' proof method.

Theorem 1. *Behavioural equivalence always exists.*

Hence in order to prove by *coinduction* that two elements are behaviourally equivalent it is enough to prove that they are congruent[3] for some arbitrarily but conveniently chosen hidden congruence.

An operation symbol σ is *coherent* for an algebra A when it preserves the behavioural equivalence, i.e. $A_\sigma(a) \sim_A A_\sigma(a')$ whenever $a \sim_a a'$ (possibly component-wise).

A *hidden algebra signature morphism* $\varphi \colon (H, V, F, F^b) \to (H', V', F', F'^b)$ is a signature morphism $(H \cup V, F) \to (H' \cup V', F')$ such that

- $\varphi(V) \subseteq V'$ and $\varphi(H) \subseteq H'$,
- $\varphi(F^b) = F'^b$ and $\varphi^{-1}(F'^b) \subseteq F^b$,

These conditions say that hidden sorted signature morphisms preserve visibility and invisibility for both sorts and operations, and the object-oriented intuition behind the inclusion $F'^b \subseteq \varphi(F^b)$ is the encapsulation of classes (in the sense that no new 'methods' or 'attributes' can be defined on an imported class)[4]. However, this last inclusion condition applies only to the case when signature morphisms are used as module imports (the so-called *horizontal* signature morphisms); when they model specification refinement this condition might be dropped (this case is called *vertical* signature morphism).

Algebra reducts along hidden algebra signature morphisms are instances of the ordinary general algebra reducts along algebraic signature morphisms.

Given a hidden algebraic signature (H, V, F, F^b), a *behavioural equation* $t \sim t'$ consists of a pair of F-terms of the same sort. An (H, V, F, F^b)-algebra A satisfies it, i.e. $A \models t \sim t'$, when $A_t \sim_A A_{t'}$.

Full first order behavioural sentences are constructed from strict and behavioural equations by iteration of logical connectives and first order quantification in a way similar to the case of ordinary general algebra.

---

[3] In a hidden congruence relation.

[4] For the model theoretic relevance of this condition see [1].

A *behavioural presentation* (Σ, E) consists of a hidden algebraic signature Σ and a set E of Σ-sentences. A *presentation morphism* $\varphi \colon (\Sigma, E) \to (\Sigma', E')$ is just a signature morphism $\varphi \colon \Sigma \to \Sigma'$ such that $E' \models \varphi(E)$.[5]

An operation symbol σ is *coherent* with respect to a presentation (Σ, E) when it is coherent in each algebra of the presentation.

2.3   Behavioural Objects

The definition below introduces the novel concept of 'behavioural object' as a stylised way of structuring a hidden algebra based behavioural specification, so that it models the behaviour of objects from object-oriented programming. Notice that our hidden algebra approach to object semantics is more general than corresponding co-algebraic approaches (such as [13], for example) because of the much greater specification power of hidden algebras, which is due to the smooth integration between state and data types, and to the possibility of operations with multiple hidden sorts in the arity.

Definition 1. *A behavioural object B is pair consisting of a behavioural presentation $((H_B, V_B, F_B^{\mathrm{b}}, F_B), E_B)$ and a hidden sort $h_B \in H_B$ such that each behavioural operation in F_B^{b} is monadic, i.e. it has only one hidden sort in its arity.*

The hidden sort h_B denotes the states of B. The visible sorted behavioural operations on h_B are called B-observations and the h_B-sorted behavioural operations on h_B are called B-actions. The h_B-sorted operations with visible sorted arity are called constant states.[6]

For the sake of simplifying notation, without loss of generality, we may assume that the arity of any behavioural operation of an object is of the form hw with h hidden sort.

A derived behavioural operation is any derived operation of the form $\sigma(\tau, t)$ such that σ is a behavioural operation or coherent with respect to the behavioural object and τ is a variable or a derived behavioural operation. Notice that ordinary behavioural operations can be regarded as special cases of derived behavioural operations.

The following expresses the fact that any object is essentially defined by its state space, its actions, and the behavioural equivalence between the states.

Definition 2. *For any behavioural object B, a B-algebra is just an algebra for the signature of B satisfying the sentences E_B of the presentation of the object B. The category of B-algebras is denoted by $\mathbb{A}lg(B)$.*

Two B-algebras A and A' are equivalent, *denoted $A \equiv A'$, when*

- $A_{h_B} = A'_{h_B}$ *and* $\sim_A = \sim_{A'}$ *(on the sort h_B), and*
- $A_\sigma = A'_\sigma$ *for each B-action σ*

Definition 3. *Two behavioural objects B and B' are* equivalent, *denoted $B \equiv B'$, when there exists a pair of functors $\Phi \colon \mathbb{A}lg(B) \to \mathbb{A}lg(B')$ and $\Psi \colon \mathbb{A}lg(B') \to$*

---

[5] Any hidden algebra satisfying E' satisfies $\varphi(E)$ too.

[6] They should be considered as parameterised by the data arguments of the arity.

$\mathbb{A}lg(B)$ such that $A \equiv \Psi(\Phi(A))$ for each B-algebra A and $A' \equiv \Phi(\Psi(A'))$ for each B'-algebra A'.

Therefore behavioural objects are equivalent when they admit the same 'implementations'. Notice that this defines indeed an equivalence relation and that isomorphic objects are equivalent.

We may also extend the concept of reduct of algebras from behavioural presentation morphisms to behavioural object morphisms.

3   The CafeOBJ Notation

CafeOBJ (whose definition is given by [5] and logical foundations in [6]) is a modern successor of the OBJ [14] language incorporating several new major developments in algebraic specification theory and practice. CafeOBJ is aimed both to researchers and (industry) practitioners.

Behavioural specification might be the most distinctive feature of CafeOBJ within the broad family of algebraic specification languages. This is incorporated into the design of the language in a rather direct way.

CafeOBJ methodologies introduce a graphical notation extending the classical ADJ-diagram notation for data types to behavioural objects in which

G1. *Sorts are represented by ellipsoidal disks with visible (data) sorts represented in white and hidden (state) sorts represented in grey, and*
G2. *Operations are represented by multi-source arrows with the monadic part from the hidden sort thickened in case of actions and observations.*

As example let us consider the signature of a bank account behavioural object ACCOUNT which uses a pre-defined data type of natural numbers (represented in this figure by the sort Nat and in the equations below by the operation _ + _):

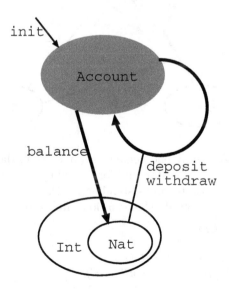

and with the following universally quantified equations

    eq *balance(init-account) = 0* .
    eq *balance(deposit(A, N)) = balance(A) + N* .
    ceq *balance(withdraw(A, N)) = balance(A) - N*   if *N <= balance(A)* .
    ceq *balance(withdraw(A, N)) = balance(A)*   if *N > balance(A)* .

Notice that the last two equations are *conditional*, i.e. they are universally quantified implications between a condition and an equation. In this example the conditions are just binary relations, however they can be regarded as equations between Boolean-valued terms. More generally, a condition of a conditional equation can be thought as quantifier-free formula formed from equations by iterative applications of conjunction, disjunction, and negation.

We can also easily prove that in any ACCOUNT-algebra A,

$$a \sim_A a' \text{ if and only if } A_{\text{balance}}(a) = A_{\text{balance}}(a')$$

A more sophisticated example is provided by a behavioural object of sets BSET in which the sets of elements appear as states of this object. The signature of BSET is given by the diagram below and which uses a sort Elt for elements of sets and a pre-defined Boolean type (represented in the figure by the sort Bool and in the equations below by several standard Boolean operations):

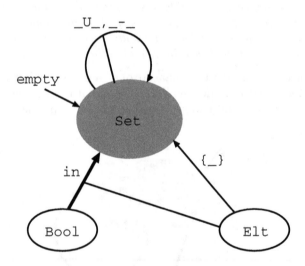

Notice that there is only one behavioural operation, the membership observation in, the operations {_} standing for regarding elements as singleton sets, U standing for union of sets, and - standing for the difference between sets not being specified as behavioural. The equations are as follows:

    eq *E in empty = false* .
    eq *E in { E' } = (E == E')* .
    eq *E in (S U S') = (E in S) or (E in S')* .
    eq *E in (S - S') = (E in S) and not(E in S')* .

Notice that the behavioural equivalence is given by the element membership observation only and that in all algebras the interpretation of the other operations preserve the behavioural equivalence, hence these operations are coherent with respect to this specification.

The reader is invited to compare the level of complexity of the behavioural specification of sets with that of the classical data type specification based on initial semantics. This gap in favour the behavioural style is even bigger in the case of proofs, such as distributivity of the set difference $\_\text{-}\_$ over the set union $\_\text{U}\_$.

4   Hierarchical Object Composition

4.1   General Considerations

Our methodology for behavioural object composition has been defined informally within the framework of the CafeOBJ language [5, 7]. Here by formally defining composition operations on behavioural objects (see Definition 1), we can export the CafeOBJ behavioural object composition methodology to any specification and verification language implementing a form of behavioural logic close to our hidden algebra formalism.

Our behavioural object composition methodology is *hierarchical* in the sense that the composition of behavioural objects yields another behavioural object in the sense of Definition 1, which can also be used for another composition. Hierarchical behavioural object composition can be represented in UML notation as follows:

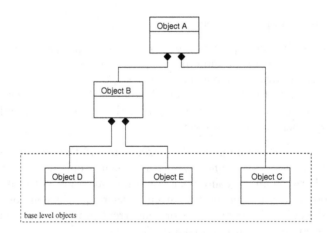

In the above UML figure, B is composed of D and E, A of B and C, and non-compound objects (i.e., objects with no components) are called *base level objects*. A composition is represented in UML by lines tipped by diamonds, and if necessary, qualified by the numbers of components (1 for one and * for many).

Projection operations from the hidden sort of the states of the compound object to the hidden sorts of the states of the component objects constitute the main technical concept underlying the CafeOBJ composition method; projection operations are related to the lines of UML figures. Projection operations are subject to several mathematical conditions which will be formally clarified later. These are in essence as follows:

1. all actions of the compound object are related via projection operations to actions in each of the components,
2. each observation of the compound object is related via the projection operations to an observation of some component, and
3. each constant state of the compound object is projected to a constant state on each component.

In the compound objects we only define communication between the components; this means that the only equations at the level of the specification of the compound objects are the ones relating the actions and observations of the compound objects to those of the components as described above. All the equations for the projection operations are strict rather than behavioural, however we may also define them behaviourally without affecting our semantics and methodology.

The components of a compound object are connected in *parallel* if there is no synchronisation between them. In order to define the concept of synchronisation, we have to introduce the following concept.

Definition 4. *Two actions of a compound object are in the same action group when they change the state of the same component object via a projection operation.*

Synchronisation appears when:

- there exists an overlapping between some action groups, in the sense that some action of the compound object is projected to at least two components affecting their state changing simultaneously, or
- the projected state of the compound object (via a projection operation) depends on the state of a different (from the object corresponding to the projection operation) component.

The first case is sometimes called *broadcasting* and the second case is sometimes called *client-server computing*. In the unsynchronised case, we have full concurrency between all the components, which means that all the actions of the compound object can be applied concurrently, therefore the components can be implemented as distributed processes or concurrent processes with multi-thread which are based on asynchronous communications.

In the case of synchronised compositions, the equations for the projection operations are conditional rather than unconditional. Informally, their conditions are subject to the following conditions:

- each condition is a quantifier-free formula formed from equations by iteration of negation, conjunction, and disjunction, the terms in the equations being compositions between a projection and a composition chain of actions/observations (at the level of the component) or terms in the data signature, and

– the disjunction of all the conditions corresponding to a given left hand side (of equations regarded as a rewrite rule) is true.

4.2   Parallel Composition

Parallel composition (i.e. without synchronisation) is the most fundamental form of behavioural object composition. As example we consider a very simple bank account system which consists of a fixed numbers of individual accounts, lets actually consider the case of just two accounts. The specification of an account can be obtained just by renaming the specification ACCOUNT of a counter object with integers. In CafeOBJ notation this is achieved as follows

```
mod* ACCOUNT1 { protecting(ACCOUNT *{ hsort Account -> Account1,
                                      op init-account -> init-account1 })}
mod* ACCOUNT2 { protecting(ACCOUNT *{ hsort Account -> Account2,
                                      op init-account -> init-account2 })}
```

We then compose these two account objects as in the following double figure containing both the UML and the CafeOBJ graphical[7] representation of this composition, where *deposit1* and *withdraw1* are the actions for the first account, *balance1* is the observation for the first account, *account1* is the projection operation for the first account, and *deposit2, withdraw2, balance2*, and *account2* are the corresponding actions, observation, and projection operation for the second account:

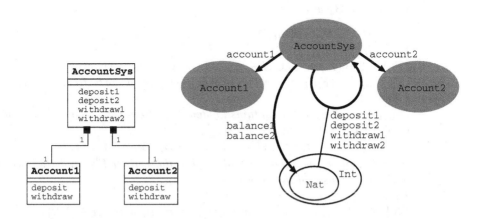

---

[7] The CafeOBJ graphical representation corresponds to the module defining this object composition rather than to the "flattened" specification, hence the operations of the components are not included in the figure.

The equations for this parallel composition are as follows:

```
eq balance1(AS) = balance(account1(AS)) .
eq balance2(AS) = balance(account2(AS)) .
eq account1(deposit1(AS, N)) = deposit(account1(AS), N) .
eq account1(deposit2(AS, N)) = account1(AS) .
eq account1(withdraw1(AS, N)) = withdraw(account1(AS), N) .
eq account1(withdraw2(AS, N)) = account1(AS) .
eq account2(init-account-sys) = init-account2 .
eq account2(deposit1(AS, N)) = account2(AS) .
eq account2(deposit2(AS, N)) = deposit(account2(AS), N) .
eq account2(withdraw1(AS, N)) = account2(AS) .
eq account2(withdraw2(AS, N)) = withdraw(account2(AS), N) .
```

Notice that besides the first two equations relating the observations on the compound object to those on the components, the other equations relate the actions of the account system to the actions of the components. Remark that the actions corresponding to one component do not change the state of the second component (via the projection operation), hence this composition is unsynchronised. In fact these equations expressing the concurrency of composition need not be specified by the user, in their absence they may be generated internally by the system, thus reducing the specification of the composition to the essential information which should be provided by the user.

The following provides a formal definition for parallel composition of behavioural objects. Another parallel composition concept as operators on specifications has been defined in [1] within a more restricted hidden algebra framework.

Definition 5. *A behavioural object B is a* parallel composition *of behavioural objects B_1 and B_2 when*

- $H_B = H_{B_1} \uplus H_{B_2} \uplus \{h_B\}$,[8]
- $V_B = V_{B_1} \cup V_{B_2}$,
- $(F_B)_{w \to s} = (F_{B_1})_{w \to s} \cup (F_{B_2})_{w \to s}$ *when all sorts in ws are visible,*
- $(F_B)_{w \to s} = (F_{B_i})_{w \to s}$ *when ws contains hidden sorts from H_i only, for $i \in \{1, 2\}$,*
- $(F_B)_{w \to s} = \emptyset$ *when ws contains hidden sorts from both H_1 and H_2 only,*
- $(F_B)_{h_B \to h_{B_i}} = \{\pi_i\}$ *for $i \in \{1, 2\}$,*
- $(F_B)_{h_B w \to h_B} = \{\sigma_i \mid \sigma \in (F_{B_i})_{h_{B_i} w \to h_{B_i}} \ B_i\text{-action}, \ i \in \{1, 2\}\}$
- *the behavioural operations F_B^b of F_B are those from $F_{B_1}^b$ and $F_{B_2}^b$, π_1, π_2, and the actions and the observations on h_B,*
- $E_B = E_{B_1} \cup E_{B_2} \cup$
  $\{(\forall \{x\} \cup W)\pi_i(\sigma_i(x, W)) = \sigma(\pi_i(x), W) \mid \sigma \ B_i\text{-action}, i \in \{1, 2\}\}$
  $\cup \{(\forall \{x\} \cup W)\pi_j(\sigma_i(x, W)) = \pi_j(x) \mid \sigma \ B_i\text{-action} \ \{i, j\} = \{1, 2\}\}$
  $\cup \{e(\sigma) \mid \sigma \ B\text{-observation}\} \cup \bigcup_c B\text{-state constant} \ E(c)$

---

[8] By $\uplus$ we denote the disjoint union.

where $e(\sigma)$ is a derived observational definition of σ and $E(c)$ is a derived constant set of definitions for c.

For each B-observation σ we say that an equation $(\forall\{x\} \cup W)\sigma(x, W) = \tau_\sigma(\pi_i(x), W)$ is a derived observational definition of σ when $i \in \{1, 2\}$ and where τ_σ is a (possibly derived) B_i-observation.

For each B-state constant c we say that $E(c) = \{\pi_i(c) = c_i \mid i \in \{1, 2\}\}$ for some c_i is a B_i-state constant is a derived constant set of definitions for c.

Let us denote by $B_1 \| B_2$ the class of behavioural objects B which are parallel compositions of behavioural objects B_1 and B_2.

This definition can be easily extended to any finite number of objects.

The following shows that in the case of parallel composition without synchronisation the behavioural equivalence on the compound object is compositional with respect to the behavioural equivalences of its components.

Proposition 1. *For any behavioural objects B_1 and B_2, for each parallel composition $B \in B_1 \| B_2$, we have that*

$$a \sim_A a' \text{ if and only if } A_{\pi_1}(a) \sim_{A_1} A_{\pi_1}(a') \text{ and } A_{\pi_2}(a) \sim_{A_2} A_{\pi_2}(a')$$

for each B-algebra A, elements $a, a' \in A_{h_B}$, and where $A_i = A{\restriction}_{B_i}$ for each $i \in \{1, 2\}$.

The following shows that parallel composition is unique up to object equivalence.

Proposition 2. *Let B_1 and B_2 be behavioural objects. Then all $B, B' \in B_1 \| B_2$ have isomorphic classes of algebras.*

Corollary 1. *For all behavioural objects B_1 and B_2, all $B, B' \in B_1 \| B_2$ are equivalent objects, i.e. $B \equiv B'$.*

Notice that we cannot expect two parallel compositions to be isomorphic (as presentations) because observations on the compound objects can be defined differently, hence their signatures need not be isomorphic. However, modulo the definition of the observations on the compound objects, parallel composition without synchronisation is uniquely determined. This permits a high degree of automation of the specification of parallel composition.

Definition 6. *Let $B \in B_1 \| B_2$ and let A_i be algebras of B_i for $i \in \{1, 2\}$ such that they are consistent on the common data part.[9] A B-algebra A expands A_1*

---

[9] $B_1{\restriction}_{(V, F_V)} = B_2{\restriction}_{(V, F_V)}$ where $V = V_{B_1} \cap V_{B_2}$ and F_V is the set of all data operation symbols in $F_{B_1} \cap F_{B_2}$.

and A_2 when $A\restriction_{B_i} = A_i$ for each $i \in \{1,2\}$. A B-algebra homomorphism $f : A \to A'$ expands A_1 and A_2 when $f\restriction_{B_i} = 1_{A_i}$ for each $i \in \{1,2\}$.

The following shows that parallel composition admits final semantics:

Theorem 2. *Let $B \in B_1\|B_2$ and let A_i be algebras of B_i for $i \in \{1,2\}$ such that they are consistent on the common data part. Then there exists a B-algebra A expanding A_1 and A_2 such that for any other B-algebra A' expanding A_1 and A_2 there exists an unique B-algebra homomorphism $A' \to A$ expanding A_1 and A_2.*

Parallel composition has several expected semantic properties such as associativity and commutativity.

Theorem 3. *For all behavioural objects B_1 and B_2 and B_3*

1. $B_1\|B_2 = B_2\|B_1$, *and*
2. $B_{(12)3} \equiv B_{1(23)}$ *for all $B_{(12)3} \in B_{12}\|B_3$ and all $B_{1(23)} \in B_1\|B_{23}$, where B_{ij} is any composition in $B_i\|B_j$.*

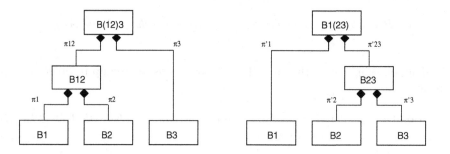

4.3   Dynamic Composition

Let us extend the previous bank account system example to support an arbitrary number of accounts as a 'dynamic' object ACCOUNT-SYS. The accounts are created or deleted dynamically, so we call such architecture pattern *dynamic composition* and we call the objects composed dynamically as *dynamic objects*.

The actions *add-account* and *del-account* maintain the user accounts. *add-account* creates accounts while *del-account* deletes the accounts; both of them are parameterised by the user identifiers UID (represented by the sort Uid). Each of *deposit* and *withdraw* are also parameterised by the user identifiers. Most notably, the projection operation for ACCOUNT is also parameterised by UID. The structure of the new bank account system can be represented in UML and CafeOBJ graphical notation as follows:

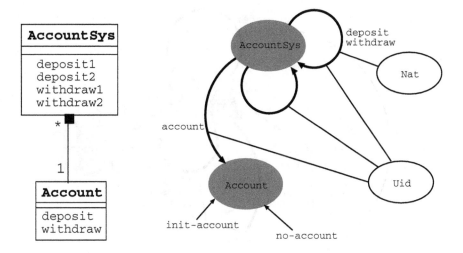

Finally, the equations relate the actions of ACCOUNT-SYS to those of AC-COUNT via the projection operation only when they correspond to the specified user account. Here is the essential part of the CafeOBJ equations for the dynamic system of accounts specification:

ceq *account(add-account(AS, U'), U) = init-account* if $U == U'$.
ceq *account(add-account(AS, U'), U) = account(AS, U)*   if $U =/= U'$.
ceq *account(del-account(AS, U'), U) = no-account*   if $U == U'$.
ceq *account(del-account(AS, U'), U) = account(AS, U)*   if $U =/= U'$.
ceq *account(deposit(AS, U', N), U) = deposit(account(AS, U), N)*   if $U == U'$.
ceq *account(deposit(AS, U', N), U) = account(AS, U)*   if $U =/= U'$.
ceq *account(withdraw(AS, U', N), U) = withdraw(account(AS, U), N)*   if $U == U'$.
ceq *account(withdraw(AS, U', N), U) = account(AS, U)*   if $U =/= U'$.

Notice that dynamic object compositions generalise the ordinary projections to projections which are parameterised by the data types (*Uld*) and also that dynamic compound objects might add new actions (*add-account* and *del-account*) which do not correspond to actions of the components.

4.4   Synchronised Parallel Composition

In this section we define the most general form of object composition of our approach. This supports dynamic compositions and synchronisation both in the broadcasting and client-server computing forms.

As example let us add to the parallel system of two accounts specified above a transfer action *transfer* from the first account to the second one. This is of course parameterised by the amount of money to be transfered. The signature of this composition looks now as follows:

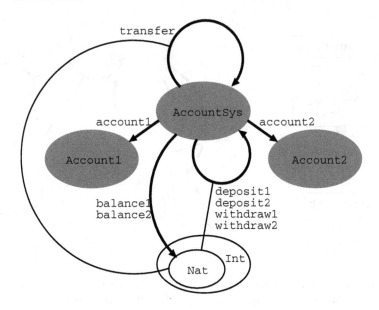

and the equations for the transfer are as follows:

eq *account1(transfer(AS, N))* = *withdraw(account1(AS), N)* .
ceq *account2(transfer(AS, N))* = *account2(AS)*   if $N >$ *balance1(AS)* .
ceq *account2(transfer(AS, N))* = *deposit(account2(AS), N)*   if $N <=$ *balance1(AS)*

This example of *transfer* between accounts, although very simple, contains both the broadcasting and the client-server computing cases. Broadcasting appears because the *transfer* changes the states of both account components. Client-server computing appears because *transfer* is related to *deposit* of ACCOUNT2 and using information of ACCOUNT1.

The following is the formal definition of composition with synchronisation generalising the Definition 5 of parallel composition without synchronisation.

Definition 7. *A behavioural object B is a synchronised composition of behavioural objects B_1 and B_2 when*

- $H_B = H_{B_1} \uplus H_{B_2} \uplus \{h_B\}$,
- $V_B \supseteq V_{B_1} \cup V_{B_2}$,
- $(F_B)_{w \to s} \supseteq (F_{B_1})_{w \to s} \cup (F_{B_2})_{w \to s}$ *when all sorts in ws are visible,*
- $(F_B)_{w \to s} = (F_{B_i})_{w \to s}$ *when ws contains hidden sorts from H_{B_i} only, for $i \in \{1, 2\}$,*
- $(F_B)_{w \to s} = \emptyset$ *when ws contains hidden sorts from both H_{B_1} and H_{B_2} only,*
- *for each $i \in \{1, 2\}$, there exists an unique w_i string of visible sorts, such that $(F_B)_{h_B w_i \to h_{B_i}}$ is not empty, and it contains only one operation symbol π_i,*
- $(F_B)_{h_B w \to h_B} \supseteq \{\sigma_i \mid \sigma \in (F_{B_i})_{h_{B_i} w \to h_{B_i}} \ B_i\text{-action}, \ i \in \{1, 2\}\}$
- *the behavioural operations F_B^b of F_B are those from $F_{B_1}^b$ and $F_{B_2}^b$, π_1, π_2, and the actions and the observations on h_B,*
- $E_B = E_{B_1} \cup E_{B_2} \cup \bigcup_{\sigma \ B\text{-action}} E_\sigma \cup \{e(\sigma) \mid \sigma \ B\text{-observation}\}$
  $\cup \bigcup_c \ B\text{-state constant} \ E(c)$

where E_σ is a complete set of derived action definitions for σ, $e(\sigma)$ is a derived observational definition for σ, and $E(c)$ is a derived constant set of definitions for c.

For any B-action σ,

$$\{(\forall\{x\} \cup W \cup W_i)\, \pi_i(\sigma(x,W), W_i) \;=\; \tau^i_{\sigma,k}[x,W,W_i] \;\; \textbf{if} \;\; C^i_{\sigma,k}[x,W,W_i] \mid$$

$\tau^i_{\sigma,k}$ *term*, $i \in \{1,2\}, k \in \{1,\dots,n_i\}\}$ *is a complete set of derived action definitions for σ when*

1. *each $\tau^i_{\sigma,k}[x,W,W_i]$ is a h_{B_i}-sorted term of behavioural or coherent B_i-operations applied either to $\pi_i(x,W_i)$ or to a B_i-state constant, and*
2. *each $C^i_{\sigma,k}[x,W,W_i]$ is a quantifier-free formula formed by iterations of negations, conjunctions, and disjunctions, from equations formed by terms which are either data signature terms or visible sorted terms of the form $c[\pi_j(x,W_j)]$ for c some derived behavioural B_j-operation with $W_j \subseteq W \cup W_j$ and such that*
   (2.1) *the disjunction $(\forall\{x\} \cup W \cup W_i) \vee \{C^i_{\sigma,k} \mid k \in \{1,\dots,n_i\}\}$ is true for each $i \in \{1,2\}$,*
   (2.2) *for a given i, the conditions $C^i_{\sigma,k}$ are disjoint, i.e. $(\forall\{x\} \cup W \cup W_i)$ $C^i_{\sigma,k} \wedge C^i_{\sigma,k'}$ is false whenever $k \neq k'$,*

The meaning of condition (2.1) is that of completeness in the sense that all cases are covered, while the meaning of (2.2) is that of non-ambiguity in the sense that each case falls exactly within the scope of only one conditional equation.

Let us denote by $B_1 \otimes B_2$ the class of behavioural objects B which are synchronised compositions of behavioural objects B_1 and B_2.

The above definition for composition with synchronisation can be extended easily to the case of any finite number of objects.

Notice that the example of dynamic account system presented above is a special case of Definition 7.

The following result showing that the behavioural equivalence on the compound object is compositional with respect to the behavioural equivalences of its components extends Proposition 1.

Theorem 4. *For any behavioural objects B_1 and B_2, for each composition with synchronisation $B \in B_1 \otimes B_2$, we have that*

$$a \sim_A a' \;\; \text{if and only if} \;\; (\forall W_i)A_{\pi_i}(a,W_i) \sim_{A_i} A_{\pi_i}(a',W_i) \;\; \text{for} \;\; i \in \{1,2\}$$

for each B-algebra A, elements $a,a' \in A_{h_B}$, and where $A_i = A{\restriction}_{B_i}$ for each $i \in \{1,2\}$.

Our object composition with synchronisation has final semantics shown by the result below generalising Theorem 2:

Theorem 5. *Let $B \in B_1 \otimes B_2$ and let A_i be algebras of B_i for $i \in \{1,2\}$ such that they are consistent on the common data part. Then there exists a B-algebra A expanding A_1 and A_2 such that for any other B-algebra A' expanding A_1 and A_2 there exists an unique B-algebra homomorphism $A' \to A$ expanding A_1 and A_2.*

5   Compositionality of Verifications

In object-oriented programming, reusability of the source code is important, but in object-oriented specification, reusability of the proofs is also very important because of the complexity of the verification process. We call this *compositionality of verifications* of components. Our approach supports compositionality of verifications via Theorem 4.

Let us specify a dynamic bank account system having a user management mechanism given by a user database (USER-DB) which enables querying whether an user already has an account in the bank account system. The users data base is obtained just by reusing (renaming) the behavioural sets object BSET.

mod* USER-DB { protecting(BSET *{ hsort BSet -> UserDB, hsort Elt -> UId})}

The following is the UML and CafeOBJ graphical representation of this dynamic bank account system specification:

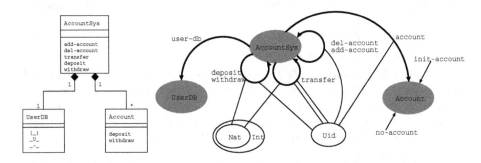

and here are the CafeOBJ equations for the projection operation for UserDB:

eq *user-db(add-account(AS, U)) = { U } U user-db(AS))* .
eq *user-db(del-account(AS, U)) = user-db(AS) - { U }* .
eq *user-db(transfer(AS, U, U', N)) = user-db(AS)* .
eq *user-db(deposit(AS, U, N)) = user-db(AS)* .
eq *user-db(withdraw(AS, U, N)) = user-db(AS)* .

The following is the CafeOBJ code for the equations for the projection operation for Account:

ceq *account(add-account(AS, U'), U) = init-account*
        if *(U == U') and not(U in user-db(AS))* .
ceq *account(add-account(AS, U'), U) = account(AS, U)*
        if *(U =/= U') or (U in user-db(AS))* .
ceq *account(del-account(AS, U'), U) = no-account*
        if *(U == U')* .
ceq *account(del-account(AS, U'), U) = account(AS, U)*
        if *(U =/= U')* .
ceq *account(transfer(AS, U', U'', N), U) = account(AS, U)*
        if *(U' == U'')* .

ceq *account(transfer(AS, U', U", N), U)* = *account(AS, U)*
      if *(U' =/= U") and (U' =/= U) and (U" =/= U)* .
ceq *account(transfer(AS, U', U", N), U)* = *withdraw(account(AS, U), N)*
      if *(U' =/= U") and (U' == U)*
ceq *account(transfer(AS, U', U", N), U)* = *account(AS, U)*
      if *(U' =/= U") and (U" == U) and (balance(account(AS, U'))) < N)* .
ceq *account(transfer(AS, U', U", N), U)* = *deposit(account(AS, U), N)*
      if *(U' =/= U") and (U" == U) and (N <= balance(account(AS, U')))* .
ceq *account(deposit(AS, U', N), U)* = *deposit(account(AS, U), N)*
      if *(U == U')* .
ceq *account(deposit(AS, U', N), U)* = *account(AS, U)*
      if *(U =/= U')* .
ceq *account(withdraw(AS, U', N), U)* = *withdraw(account(AS, U), N)*
      if *(U == U')* .
ceq *account(withdraw(AS, U', N), U)* = *account(AS, U)*
      if *(U =/= U')* .

By iterative application of Theorem 4, in the case of a hierarchic object composition, the behavioural equivalence for the whole system is just the conjunction of the behavioural equivalences of the base level objects, which are generally rather simple.

For example, the behavioural equivalence for the bank account system is a conjunction of the behavioural equivalence Account (indexed by the user identifiers) and UserDB, and these two are checked automatically by the CafeOBJ system. This means that behavioural proofs for the bank account system are almost automatic, without having to go through the usual coinduction process. Therefore, the behavioural equivalence _R[_]_ of AccountSys can be defined by the following CafeOBJ code:

```
mod BEQ-ACCOUNT-SYSTEM {   protecting(ACCOUNT-SYSTEM)
op _R[_]_ : AccountSys Uid AccountSys -> Bool
vars AS1 AS2 : AccountSys
var U : Uid
eq AS1 R[U] AS2 = account(AS1, U) =b= account(AS2, U) and
                  user-db(AS1) =b= user-db(AS2) . }
```

Notice the use of the parameterized relation for handling the conjunction indexed by the user identifiers, and we use =b= to denote the behavioural equivalence on the components. We may recall that the definition of =b= for ACCOUNT is just equality under the observation *balance* and that of =b= for USER-DB is just equality under arbitrary membership, thus both of them are coded very easily.

Now, we will prove the true concurrency of deposit operations of two (possibly but not necessarily different) users, which can be considered as a safety property for this system of bank accounts and which is formulated as the following behavioural commutativity property:

$$deposit(deposit(as, u2, n2), u1, n1) \sim deposit(deposit(as, u1, n1), u2, n2)$$

The following CafeOBJ code builds the proof tree containing all possible cases formed by orthogonal combinations of atomic cases for the users with respect to their membership to the user accounts data base. The basic proof term is *TERM*. The automatic generation of the proof tree (*RESULT*) is done by a meta-level encoding in CafeOBJ by using its rewrite engine for one-directional construction of the proof tree (this process uses the rewriting logic feature of CafeOBJ, hence the use of transitions (trans) rather than equations).

```
mod PROOF-TREE { protecting(BEQ-ACCOUNT-SYSTEM)
  ops n1 n2 : -> Nat  -- arbitrary amounts for deposit
  ops u u1 u1' u2 u2' : -> Uld  -- arbitrary user identifiers
  op as : -> AccountSys  -- arbitrary state of the account system
  eq u1 in user-db(as) = true .  -- first user is in the data base
  eq u2 in user-db(as) = true .  -- second user is in the data base
  eq u1' in user-db(as) = false .  -- first user is not in the data base
  eq u2' in user-db(as) = false .  -- second user is not in the data base
  vars U U1 U2 : Uld
  op TERM : Uld Uld Uld -> Bool  -- basic proof term
  trans TERM(U, U1, U2) => deposit(U1, n1, deposit(U2, n2, as)) R[U]
                              deposit(U2, n2, deposit(U1, n1, as)) .
  op TERM1 : Uld Uld -> Bool
  trans TERM1(U, U1) => TERM(U, U1, u2) and TERM(U, U1, u2') .
  op TERM2 : Uld -> Bool
  trans TERM2(U) => TERM1(U, u1) and TERM1(U, u1') .
  op RESULT : -> Bool  -- final proof term
  trans RESULT => TERM2(u1) and TERM2(u1') and TERM2(u) . }
```

The execution of the proof term *RESULT* gives true.

The same problem for withdrawals rather than deposits is a bit more subtle. If we run the system for the behavioural commutativity property

$$withdraw(withdraw(as, u2, n2), u1, n1) \sim withdraw(withdraw(as, u1, n1), u2, n2)$$

in the same manner as for the deposit case, we do not get true because for the case when the users are not different, two withdrawals are not necessarily commutative. This is due to the relation between the amount required for withdrawals and the actual balance of the account. However we still get useful information consisting of the list of cases which cannot be reduced to true. This shows the debugging power of this verification methodology.

As further exercise the reader is invited to check other behavioural properties of the dynamic bank account system with user data base, such as

$$transfer(transfer(as, u1, u2, n), u2, u3, n) \sim transfer(as, u1, u3, n)$$

6   Conclusions and Future Research

Based on a novel formalisation of the concept of behavioural object in hidden algebra, we have formally defined several composition operators underlying the object composition methodology of CafeOBJ, including parallel composition (without synchronisation), dynamic composition, and a most general form of composition with synchronisation. We have showed the associativity and commutativity of parallel composition (without synchronisation), the existence of final semantics and a compositionality result for the behavioural equivalence in the most general case of composition with synchronisation. This latter result is the basis for making the verification process almost automatic and also leads to easy debugging.

Within this framework we plan to investigate sufficient conditions on synchronisation allowing final associativity and/or commutativity of the composition operator.

The concepts introduced in this paper can also be used for the definition of an object-oriented algebraic specification language supporting hierarchical object composition on top of existing algebraic specification languages. For example, any specification in such object-oriented extension of CafeOBJ could be compiled into a CafeOBJ specification.

References

1. Goguen, J., Diaconescu, R.: Towards an algebraic semantics for the object paradigm. In Ehrig, H., Orejas, F., eds.: Recent Trends in Data Type Specification. Volume 785 of Lecture Notes in Computer Science., Springer (1994) 1–34
2. Diaconescu, R., Futatsugi, K.: Behavioural coherence in object-oriented algebraic specification. Universal Computer Science **6** (2000) 74–96 First version appeared as JAIST Technical Report IS-RR-98-0017F, June 1998.
3. Hennicker, R., Bidoit, M.: Observational logic. In Haeberer, A.M., ed.: Algebraic Methodology and Software Technology. Number 1584 in LNCS, Springer (1999) 263–277 Proc. AMAST'99.
4. Goguen, J., Roşu, G.: Hiding more of hidden algebra. In Wing, J.M., Woodcock, J., Davies, J., eds.: FM'99 – Formal Methods. Volume 1709 of Lecture Notes in Computer Science., Springer (1999) 1704–1719
5. Diaconescu, R., Futatsugi, K.: CafeOBJ Report: The Language, Proof Techniques, and Methodologies for Object-Oriented Algebraic Specification. Volume 6 of AMAST Series in Computing. World Scientific (1998)
6. Diaconescu, R., Futatsugi, K.: Logical foundations of CafeOBJ. Theoretical Computer Science **285** (2002) 289–318
7. Iida, S., Futatsugi, K., Diaconescu, R.: Component-based algebraic specification: - behavioural specification for component-based software engineering -. In: Behavioral specifications of businesses and systems. Kluwer (1999) 103–119
8. Diaconescu, R., Futatsugi, K., Iida, S.: Component-based algebraic specification and verification in CafeOBJ. In Wing, J.M., Woodcock, J., Davies, J., eds.: FM'99 – Formal Methods. Volume 1709 of Lecture Notes in Computer Science., Springer (1999) 1644–1663
9. Astesiano, E., Bidoit, M., Kirchner, H., Krieg-Brückner, B., Mosses, P., Sannella, D., Tarlecki, A.: CASL: The common algebraic specification language. Theoretical Computer Science **286** (2002) 153–196
10. Meseguer, J.: A logical theory of concurrent objects and its realization in the Maude language. In Agha, G., Wegner, P., Yonezawa, A., eds.: Research Directions in Concurrent Object-Oriented Programming. The MIT Press (1993)

11. Iida, S., Futatsugi, K., Diaconescu, R.: Component-based algebraic specifications: - behavioural specification for component based software engineering -. In: 7th OOPSLA Workshop on Behavioral Semantics of OO Business and System Specification. (1998) 167–182 Also in the technical report of Technical University of Munich TUM-I9820.
12. Burstall, R., Diaconescu, R.: Hiding and behaviour: an institutional approach. In Roscoe, A.W., ed.: A Classical Mind: Essays in Honour of C.A.R. Hoare. Prentice-Hall (1994) 75–92 Also in Technical Report ECS-LFCS-8892-253, Laboratory for Foundations of Computer Science, University of Edinburgh, 1992.
13. Reichel, H.: An approach to object semantics based on terminal co-algebras. Mathematical Structures in Computer Science 5 (1995) 129–152
14. Goguen, J., Winkler, T., Meseguer, J., Futatsugi, K., Jouannaud, J.P.: Introducing OBJ. In Goguen, J., Malcolm, G., eds.: Software Engineering with OBJ: algebraic specification in action. Kluwer (2000)

Consistency Management Within Model-Based Object-Oriented Development of Components

Jochen M. Küster and Gregor Engels

Faculty of Computer Science, Electrical Engineering and Mathematics,
University of Paderborn, Germany
{jkuester,engels}@upb.de

Abstract. The Unified Modeling Language (UML) favors the construction of models composed of several submodels, modeling the system components under development at different levels of abstraction and from different viewpoints. Currently, consistency of object-oriented models expressed in the UML is not defined in the UML language specification. This allows the construction of inconsistent UML models. Defining consistency of UML models is complicated by the fact that UML models are applied differently, depending on the application domain and development process. As a consequence, a form of consistency management is required that allows the software engineer to define, establish and manage consistency, tailored specifically to the development context. In recent years, we have developed a general methodology and tool support to overcome this problem. The methodology is based on a thorough study of the notion of consistency and has led to a generic definition of the notion of consistency. Our methodology itself aims at a step-wise systematic construction of a consistency management process, by providing a number of activities to be performed by the software engineer. It is complemented by a tool called *Consistency Workbench* which supports the software engineer in performing the methodology. In this paper, we provide an overview and summary of our approach.

1 Introduction

A model-based approach to the development of component-based systems favors the construction of models prior to the coding of components. Benefits of such an approach are the ability to study properties of the system early in the development process on the model level and the idea that components can be deployed more easily to different target platforms.

Currently, the Unified Modeling Language [27] is the de-facto industrial standard for object-oriented modeling of components. In the UML a model is composed of several submodels for modeling the system at different levels of abstraction and from different viewpoints. As the UML language specification does not sufficiently define consistency of UML models, inconsistent UML models can be constructed. This may lead to a situation where no common implementation conforming to all submodels exists. Further, with the UML being applied in diverse

F.S. de Boer et al. (Eds.): FMCO 2003, LNCS 3188, pp. 157–176, 2004.

contexts, the ability of defining and checking consistency conditions depending on the application domain, development process, and platform is of increasing importance.

Besides well-formedness rules in OCL as part of user-defined UML profiles, little support is available for customized specification and checking of consistency conditions. This applies both for the definition as well as check of consistency conditions. In particular, no support is provided to the developer to specify behavioral consistency conditions, like specific notions of compatibility between statecharts and sequence diagrams. The general problem of defining and establishing consistency in UML is complicated by a missing formal semantics.

In [12, 8] we have developed a general methodology for consistency management in UML-based development. Our approach to defining consistency concepts is by means of partial translations of models into a formal language (called semantic domain) that provides a language and tool support to formulate and verify consistency conditions. For a given consistency concept, within a consistency check one or more submodels are translated into a semantic domain and the specified consistency conditions are verified. The result may then be translated back into a UML notation or simply expressed in a message to the modeller.

Given a development process and application domain, our approach systematically constructs a consistency management process in several activities. First, consistency problem types are identified and then formalized in consistency concepts. The formalization includes the choice of a suitable semantic domain, the specification of partial translations and consistency conditions. For each consistency concept, consistency checks are defined and integrated into the development process. Primary ideas of our approach are to define consistency concepts based on the development context, i. e. depending on application domain, development process and platform, and further to abstract from unnecessary details of the model not relevant to the consistency condition.

In order to make our approach applicable in practice, tool support is required both for the definition of translations and consistency checks and for their automated execution. This has led to the development of the *Consistency Workbench*, a research prototype for demonstrating the feasibility of our approach.

In this paper, we give an overview and summary of our approach. We first discuss the issue of consistency of models made up of different submodels, introducing a generic definition of consistency and the notion of consistency management. We then present a general methodology for consistency management. Based on this methodology, we summarize the tool support we have developed. We finally sketch the application of the methodology to an example consistency problem. This paper summarizes contributions previously published: The concepts of the methodology have first been presented in [12] and then been elaborated in [10] and [11]. The concepts of the consistency management tool have been published in [9]. In [22], the methodology is described in detail, together with an application to a simplified development process.

2   Concepts of Consistency and Consistency Management

In this section, we first introduce the main notions of our definition of consistency. We then explain the idea of consistency management and briefly discuss related approaches.

2.1   Consistency

The use of models consisting of different submodels within software development has numerous advantages. Different persons may work on different submodels simultaneously driving forward the development of the system. Different types of submodels allow the separation of different aspects of the system to be built such as structural aspects or dynamic behavior of system components.

However, making use of different submodels also involves drawbacks. In a traditional approach, there exists only one model of the system. This model can then be transformed during coding into a running software product. In the case of a collection of submodels, this is not as easy anymore because one needs to describe which submodel is transformed into which part of the code. This gives rise to the problem of different parts of the code not working together as one wishes leading to a system not functioning. In order not to run into such problems, it has to be ensured that different submodels are compatible with each other or consistent on the model level.

Different submodels of a model are usually called consistent if they can be integrated into a single model with a well-defined semantics. The required form of integration is dependent on the type of models, the modeling process and the application domain. One important aspect of consistency is to ensure the existence of an implementation conforming to all submodels. If consistency of a model is ensured, an implementation of submodels is obtained by implementing the integrated model. Otherwise, such an integrated model and implementation might not exist.

Technically, consistency of a model is defined by establishing a set of *consistency conditions*. A consistency condition is a predicate that defines whether or not a model is consistent with respect to this consistency condition. We can distinguish between consistency conditions defined on the syntax and on the semantics of models, leading to *syntactic* and *semantic consistency conditions*. In case of defining consistency conditions on the semantics of models, typically also a semantic mapping is required. This can be the semantic mapping of the modeling language definition but can also involve an abstraction of this semantics.

Different related consistency conditions can be grouped to form a *consistency concept*. Such a consistency concept consists of a set of syntactic and semantic consistency conditions and a semantic mapping of each submodel type into a common semantic domain if applicable. The definition of a consistency concept is illustrated in Figure 1. Mappings of submodel types are called m_i in the figure, consistency conditions are called c_i. As a consistency concept consists of a semantic mapping into a common semantic domain and conditions specified

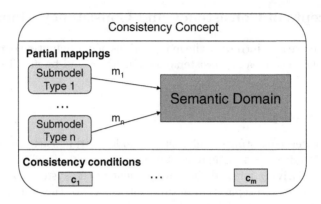

Fig. 1. Visualization of consistency concept

on the syntax and within the semantic domain, a consistency concept can be viewed as a sort of integration of submodels.

Within our approach, we can define different consistency concepts for a modeling language. As a consequence, a model can be consistent with respect to one consistency concept but inconsistent with respect to another consistency concept. This is motivated by different application domains, development processes and platforms a modeling language can be applied to and in contrast to the idea that a modeling language comes with pre-defined consistency concepts in the language specification.

The motivation that gives rise to defining a consistency concept is called a *consistency property*. Such a consistency property is a model-independent description of a property that a model should have. A consistency property can be informally characterized by stating what it ensures i. e. what characteristics a model must have that conforms to the consistency property. Examples for consistency properties include syntactic correctness, trace consistency or timing consistency.

On the basis of consistency properties and consistency concepts, we can define consistency checks. A consistency check is a description how, given a model and a consistency condition, to decide whether or not the model fulfills the consistency condition. As a consequence, consistency checks can be thought of definining the fulfillment relation between a model and a consistency condition. Consistency checks can be performed using theorem proving, model checking [5] or by executing specialized algorithms [6].

Given a consistency condition and a concrete model, we can identify those submodel types of the larger model that lead to the inconsistency. This allows the distinction between consistency problem types and consistency problem instances: A *consistency problem type* is a configuration of submodel types that may give rise to the violation of a consistency condition. On the contrary, a *consistency problem instance* is a configuration of submodels such that each submodel corresponds to a submodel type of a given consistency problem type violating the consistency condition. This distinction between consistency prob-

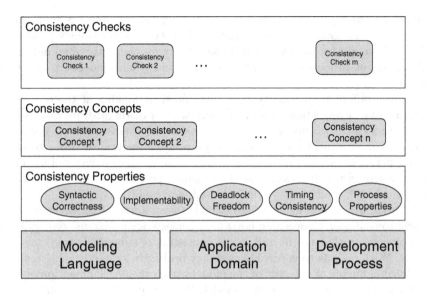

Fig. 2. Layers of consistency

lem type and instance is similar to the type-instance notions commonly known from object-orientation. Note that a consistency concept can also be thought of as one solution of a consistency problem type.

In this section, we have introduced a generic definition of consistency. The terms in our definition of consistency lead to a layered approach to consistency, illustrated in Figure 2. Given a modeling language, in the property layer, different properties exist that drive the definition of the consistency concept. A consistency concept comprises a number of consistency conditions and a semantic domain (not shown in the figure but cf. Figure 1). Once the conditions are determined, consistency checks are defined which verify or validate a consistency condition.

2.2 Characteristics of Consistency Problems

Consistency problems can be characterized on the one hand according to the situation they occur and on the other hand depending on the consistency conditions.

One problem of consistency arises in cases where a model consists of different submodels because a system is modeled from different viewpoints [2, 13]. This allows the concentration on different aspects in different submodels. However, different viewpoint specifications must be consistent and not contradictory, because the implementation of such an inconsistent model would otherwise be infeasible. This type of consistency problem we will call *horizontal consistency*.

Another quite different problem of consistency arises when a model is transformed into another model by replacing one or more submodels. It is then desirable that the replaced submodel is a refinement of the previous submodel, in order to keep the overall model consistent. This type of consistency problem we will call *vertical consistency*. Vertical consistency problems are often induced by a development process which prescribes how and when models are iteratively refined.

A quite different characterization is obtained by looking at the consistency conditions for a consistency problem. Here we can distinguish between *syntactic consistency conditions* and *semantic consistency conditions*. In general, consistency can be considered a semantic property. However, in order to ensure consistency, a number of inconsistent models can already be detected by regarding their syntax which means that the semantic property of consistency can be established by formulating syntactic consistency conditions.

Additionally, we can make a distinction between *syntactic consistency* and *semantic consistency*. Concerning horizontal consistency problems, syntactic consistency ensures that the overall model consisting of submodels is syntactically correct. With regards to vertical consistency problems, syntactic consistency ensures that changing of one part of the model within the development process still results into a syntactically correct model. With respect to a horizontal consistency problem, semantic consistency requires models of different viewpoints to be semantically compatible with regards to the aspects of the system which are described in the submodels. For vertical consistency problems, semantic consistency requires that a refined model is semantically consistent with the model it refines.

In this section, we have introduced a characterization of consistency problems, using our notion of consistency. We have clarified the notions of syntactic and semantic consistency and horizontal and vertical consistency. Such characterizations will prove helpful when identifying consistency problem types in a given development process. In the next section, we will introduce the idea of an explicit consistency management on the basis of consistency properties and consistency concepts.

2.3   The Notion of Consistency Management

Given a set of models and a development process, it arises the question how to ensure consistency of such models within the development process. Obviously, this requires specific activities taken including the definition of consistency conditions, the specification when consistency conditions are checked and what to do in the case of inconsistencies in order to resolve these. We thus need a sort of management of consistency and introduce the term *consistency management*. The importance of consistency management has been apparent in other disciplines of computer science such as databases and programming languages (see e. g. Tarr et al. [28]). In general, *a consistency management process* is a process in the larger software engineering process. The goal of a consistency management process is to define and ensure a certain form of consistency of models.

In order to generally ensure the consistency of models, the foundation of any consistency management is the ability to decide whether a model composed of

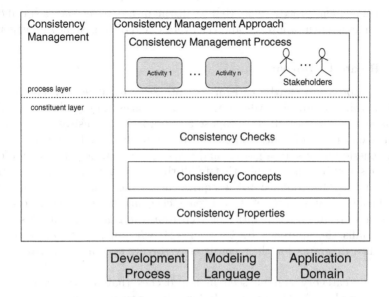

Fig. 3. Layers of Consistency Management

submodels is consistent or not. As a consequence, consistency management relies on a so-called *constituent layer* consisting of consistency properties, consistency concepts and consistency checks. In addition to these basic constituents, there might also be further specialized constituents.

Consistency management also involves dealing with consistency within a development process. This leads to a so-called *process layer* of consistency management. Here it must be determined how to organize the constituents within a consistency management process i. e. how to make use of the constituents to form a consistency management process. For example, it must be prescribed which consistency checks should be performed when and in which order. This includes the description when to, given a concrete model consisting of submodels, look for potential inconsistencies. If an inconsistency occurs, then it must be prescribed within the process when to handle and resolve it, if possible.

A consistency management process is described by activities and stakeholders performing the activities. Activities include when to locate potential inconsistencies within models and when to perform a consistency check associated to a consistency condition. In addition to these general activities, consistency management may also involve the description of how to avoid rechecking of consistency conditions and how to organize consistency checks in order to achieve consistency with respect to all consistency conditions.

In Figure 3 consistency management is illustrated. In the lower part, the development process, modeling language and application domain are visualized. On top of them, a consistency management approach is shown being composed of consistency properties, consistency concepts, consistency checks and the consistency management process. Note that we distinguish between such a specific consistency management approach and the overall field of consistency management.

2.4   Related Approaches

Existing approaches can be categorized into several categories. The first category contains approaches where a particular consistency problem is tackled. For instance, Fradet et al. [15] propose an approach to consistency checking of diagrams consisting of nodes and edges with multiplicities. They distinguish between generic and instance graphs and define the semantics of a generic graph to be the set of instance graphs that fulfill the constraints of the generic graph. Consistency is then defined to be equivalent to the semantics of the generic graph being not an empty set. Consistency checking is then performed by solving a system of linear inequalities derived from the generic graph. Also in this category falls the approach by Li et al. [24] who analyze timing constraints of sequence diagrams for their consistency solving systems of linear inequalities.

Another category can be seen in approaches that achieve consistency of object-oriented models by completely formalizing them, thereby integrating all models into one semantic domain. Moreira and Clark [25] translate object-oriented analysis models to LOTOS in order to detect inconsistencies. Cheng et al. [4] formalize OMT models in terms of LOTOS specifications. Using these specifications, they perform consistency analysis using tools for state exploration and concurrency analysis. Grosse-Rhode [18] integrates all models by translating them into transformation systems. The problem involved with completely formalizing models is that the application is then restricted to certain consistency problems mirrored by the choice of semantic domain. For example, a formalization in terms of LOTOS is not capable of dealing with consistency problems involving the aspect of time because LOTOS does not support this aspect. For a general-purpose modeling language such as UML, different application domains may give rise to quite different consistency problems which are difficult to treat within one formalization, not to speak of the numerous problems of formalizing UML itself. As an example, for some applications modeled with UML, consistency problems involving the aspect of time might be of no relevance at all whereas in other applications (e. g. real-time applications), timing consistency is of high importance. As a consequence, approaches involving a complete formalization are currently not capable of dealing with all the consistency problems arising within the development with UML in various application domains involving quite different sets of consistency problems.

A third category can be seen in approaches that deal with consistency of models that are not object-oriented. Zave et al. [31] define consistency based on a translation into logics and define a set of partial specifications to be consistent if and only if its composition is satisfiable. Their approach therefore requires that models are given a semantics in form of logics. Boiten et al. [3] define consistency on the basis of development relations and define a set of partial specifications to be consistent if and only if a common development relation exists. This approach requires the existence of a formal semantics for models and the concept of development relations defined for models used within the development process.

Another, quite different, category of related work can be seen in approaches that deal with inconsistency management [26] [17]. Rather then trying to achieve complete consistency, these approaches tackle the problem of managing inconsistencies. This management is based on the location of inconsistencies and the appropriate handling (resolving of inconsistency or tolerating it). Concentrating on the process of consistency management, they assume that the foundation of consistency management in terms of consistency conditions is already in place.

From our discussion of related work we can see that our generic definition of consistency is applicable: In the first category, we are dealing with quite different semantic domains such as systems of linear inequalities or the set of instance graphs. In the second category, semantic domains used are LOTOS or transformation systems and in the third category first-order logic is used as semantic domain. On the contrary to existing approaches, we concentrate on the technical mechanisms that are used to define consistency in different scenarios. This will enable us to describe a general methodology how to deal with consistency in a situation as currently encountered by the UML: consistency is not defined as part of the standard and further, quite different consistency concepts are needed depending on the development context. Before we move on to our methodology, we will first discuss characteristics of consistency problems.

In the following section, we present an approach to consistency management based on the idea of partially formalizing the model for enabling consistency checks. As a consequence, our approach can be regarded as a combination of the approaches in the first and the second category. As our approach also comprises the idea of consistency management within a development process, it is also related to the fourth category although the idea of tolerating inconsistencies is not in focus.

3   A General Methodology for Consistency Management

Due to the unclear semantics and different employments of UML within the development process, a general concept of consistency management for UML models is missing [7]. Concerning syntactic consistency, this type of consistency is partially achieved by defining well-formedness rules on the metamodel. Due to the absence of a generally-accepted formal semantics, semantic consistency is currently not well-supported. Nevertheless, semantic consistency is of great importance and must be dealt with. In our opinion, waiting for a complete formalization of UML models is not feasible as we need consistency management now and the existence of a complete formalization of UML models applicable to all usages of UML models is doubtful. Another problem is the informal development process followed which leads to the need of flexible notions of consistency.

Our approach to consistency management is based on the following observation: The fundamental question to answer when given a model consisting of

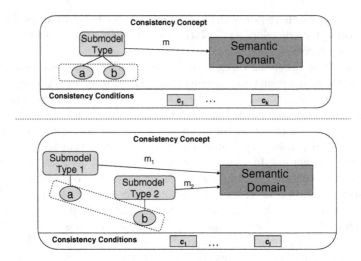

Fig. 4. Concept of our approach

submodels and a consistency property is whether there exists an integration of the submodels fulfilling the consistency property. Although a formally defined semantics does not exist, it is still possible to restrict oneself to certain aspects of models and then determine whether an integration fulfilling the consistency property exists. The concept of our approach is illustrated in Figure 4. Submodels used within development overlap in a number of aspects. For ensuring consistency, submodels are integrated into a common semantic domain, that supports these overlapping aspects. Note that our approach also applies to a submodel type with overlapping aspects, to deal with consistency problem types within a submodel type. If a concrete model cannot be integrated, then it is inconsistent.

Our idea of partially formalizing models for the purpose of consistency management yields a better degree of consistency than without any formalization and overcomes the problems associated with complete formalizations. It allows to conduct suitable consistency checks for consistency problems within quite different application domains by using different semantic domains. Our approach of partially formalizing models therefore uses the strength of completely formalizing approaches because it allows precisely stated consistency conditions. On the other hand, it also overcomes the disadvantage of restricted applicability by the idea of partial formalization within a suitable semantic domain. Furthermore, partial formalizations are often easier to handle than one large complex complete formalization trying to capture all possible aspects.

Given the goal of achieving consistency by constructing suitable partial formalizations, each providing a consistency concept, we are faced with the problem of how to come up with suitable consistency concepts, consistency conditions, consistency checks and how to integrate all these into a consistency management process.

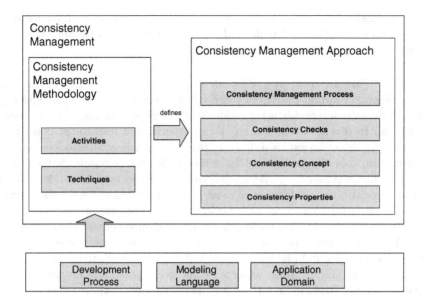

Fig. 5. The consistency management methodology

Our approach to consistency management is to describe a *methodology* for consistency management. By a methodology, we understand a set of methods and techniques [16] that are used for consistency management. A method contains a set of activities and general guidelines how to execute the activities. Insofar, our methodology contains activities and techniques that yield a particular consistency management process, taking into account different application domains and development processes. The methodology can be applied to different problem situations and therefore constitutes a set of methods rather than one particular method.

In Figure 5, the idea of defining a methodology is illustrated, building on the explanation of consistency management in the previous chapter. On the right, the ingredients of a consistency management approach are shown which are consistency properties, consistency concepts, consistency checks and a consistency management process. On the left, we introduce the methodology, which takes as input the development process, the modeling language and the application domain and then produces the consistency management approach. In the following, we describe the activities of our methodology.

Activity 1: Identification of Consistency Problem Types. The goal of this activity is the identification of all relevant consistency problem types. The basis for the identification of consistency problem types is obtained by discovering which submodel types model the same aspects of the system and which aspects consistency properties affect. Due to the common description of aspects in different submodel types or the aspectual overlap of a submodel type and a consistency property, consistency problems may occur. These consistency problems are identified, categorized to consistency problem types and informally defined, including an informal description of the desired consistency condition to hold. Each consistency problem type must be documented.

Activity 2: Formalization of a Consistency Problem Type. This activity aims at establishing a formal consistency concept for each consistency problem type. For each consistency problem type identified, we choose an appropriate semantic domain. In this semantic domain, those aspects that lead to the consistency problem type must be expressible (i. e. the aspects where submodels overlap). Furthermore, tool support should be available for the semantic domain in order to facilitate consistency checks. All aspects of the model that lead to the identified consistency problem type must be mapped into the semantic domain. Formal consistency conditions must be formulated that correspond to the informal description of consistency conditions. The definition of the partial mapping is crucial for the correctness of later defined consistency conditions and no aspects of the model should be left out that influence the consistency of the model. On the other hand, only those aspects of the model should be mapped into the semantic domain that are important for the consistency because otherwise analysis may get too complex.

Activity 3: Operational Specification of Model Transformations. Each formal consistency concept must be transformed such that models can be mapped into the semantic domain in an automated way. For that purpose, model transformations for the mappings of the consistency concept will be introduced. Further, it must be taken care of that consistency conditions can also be generated automatically.

Activity 4: Specification of Consistency Checks. For each consistency problem type, a consistency check is defined that validates the formal consistency conditions. For each consistency problem type, it must also be determined what to do in case of an inconsistency. The handling of such an inconsistency involves either the resolution or tolerance of the inconsistency.

Activity 5: Embedding of Consistency Management into Development Process. For each consistency problem type, it must be specified when to deal with it in an existing development process. The order of consistency checks to be performed by grouping the consistency conditions must be determined and fixed within the development process. The existing development process must be adapted in so far that concrete activities must be introduced that define when to perform which consistency check. These activities include the location of inconsistencies in a concrete model and the handling of inconsistencies.

The final result of having performed all these meta-level activities is a development process that contains a concrete consistency management process. It is in so far concrete that it defines consistency management for a given development process, application domain and modeling language. The concrete consistency management process, together with a concrete development problem, is simultaneously the starting situation for the activities performed on the concrete level which are the location and handling of inconsistencies.

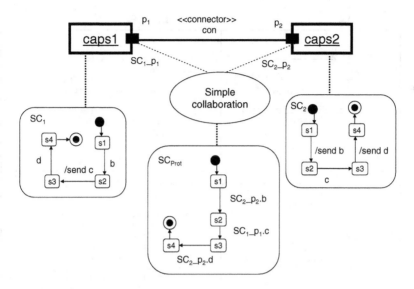

Fig. 6. Consistency problem example

In the following section, we sketch the application of the activities to an example consistency problem type. Then, we discuss how the methodology can be supported in order to be performable by the software engineer.

4   Application

In this section, we sketch the application of our methodology to a sample consistency problem type.

In Figure 6, two structured objects caps1 and caps2 are shown, joined by a connector via two ports p_1 and p_2. Attached to this connector is a collaboration with its behavior modeled in the protocol statechart SC_{Prot}. The behavior of the structured objects is specified in two statecharts, named SC_1 and SC_2. Intuitively, the interaction arising from executing the statecharts of the structured objects should conform to the protocol specified in the protocol statechart. Activity 1 of the methodology will yield as outcome that there exists a consistency problem type in this case (called *protocol consistency*), together with the informal consistency condition formulated above.

Activity 2 aims at constructing a formal consistency concept. In this case, we will choose CSP [21] as a semantic domain. The formal method CSP is supported by the model checker FDR [14] for evaluating consistency conditions formulated in CSP. We then have to define partial mappings of the statecharts and the protocol statechart into the semantic domain of CSP. In other words, the consistency concept consists of the submodel types protocol statechart, the statechart of structured objects and the collaboration, mappings of these submodel types

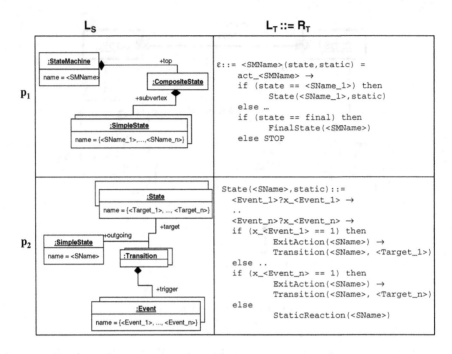

Fig. 7. Two rules for statechart translation

into CSP and a set of consistency conditions formalizing the informally noted form of consistency.

For the consistency problem of protocol consistency, we can define two different consistency conditions: For *weak protocol consistency* we require that all traces of the interaction of the structured object statecharts must be contained in the set of traces of the protocol statechart. For *strong protocol consistency* we additionally assume that all the traces of the protocol statechart must occur in the system. Extending the statechart SC_1 by introducing another transition sending another event will violate the condition of *weak protocol consistency*. Removing the last transition of SC_2 will violate the condition of *strong protocol consistency*. In previous work (e.g. [22]), we have reported on the details of such a consistency concept which are beyond the scope of this work.

Activity 3 aims at making the consistency concept operational. In our case, the partial translations of the submodel types must be defined in such a way that they are executable automatically. We have recently explored a graph transformation approach [19] [8] [23] which allows the translation to be specified by a set of compound graph transformation rules. In our case, such a compound graph transformation rule consists of two parts, a source production rule specified by a UML metamodel extract and a target production rule in the semantic formalism, here CSP. As we do not want to change the source model, the source production is the identical production, with equal left and right side. In Figure 7, two compound graph transformation rules are shown for translating statecharts to CSP, inspired by existing work of Hiemer [20].

Graph transformation rules of this form can then be used to specify a model transformation from a given source UML model to a target CSP model. The semantics of rule applications is briefly described as follows: Given a concrete UML model, a match for the UML metamodel extract is searched for in the concrete UML model. Once such a match is found, a match of the left side of the target production is searched for in the CSP model. Once the two matches have been found, the match of the CSP model is replaced by the right side of the target production. Note that using these kind of graph transformation rules, no additional specification language for describing the transformation is needed: Each rule is basically expressed in terms of the source and target language, in our case in UML and CSP, enriched with mechanisms for c3ommon variables and placeholders. A detailed explanation of this model transformation approach can be found in [19] and [8]. The problem of ensuring termination and confluence of such rule-based transformations is treated in [23]. For this activity, also related model transformation approaches such as the one by Whittle [30] or Varro et al. [29] could be used.

In Activity 4, the consistency check must be defined, on the basis of the previously developed transformation units. Typically, such a consistency check can be specified by using activity diagram for modeling the overall workflow. Such an activity diagram will define for example that given a situation like in Figure 6, first the statecharts of the structured objects are translated to CSP and then the protocol statechart. The overall result will then be fed into a model checker and the result will be interpreted.

On the basis of such consistency checks, an overall development process can be modified, by introducing consistency checks. For that, the order of consistency checks must be determined and also how inconsistency handling influences the overall consistency of a model. The details of these tasks are defined in Activity 5. In our sample application we have not described a development process but concentrated on one consistency problem. For a more detailed example of this activity, the reader is referred to [22].

5   The Consistency Workbench

In this section, we provide an overview of the consistency workbench, a research prototype that has been developed for consistency management. In principle, the software engineer needs support for all activities of the methodology. Nevertheless, one quickly realizes that adequate tool support for all activities is difficult to provide. For example, the formalization process in Activity 2 cannot be supported by tools. In the following, we describe the main functionalities of the consistency workbench:

1. *Definition of Consistency Problem Catalogue.* Using a template that contains a name, classification, and informal description of the problem, a pattern of the

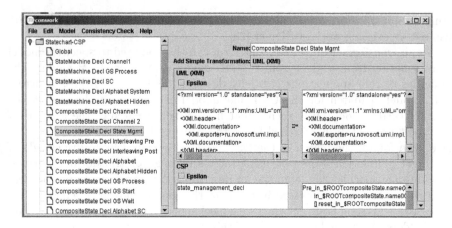

Fig. 8. Defining a Transformation Unit

meta model to localize potential occurrences, and an example, the Consistency Workbench allows the software engineer to define a catalogue of problem types that may be reused in different development processes.

2. Definition of Transformations. By a set of graph transformation rules, controlled by a simple control flow language based on regular expressions, the software engineer can define translations of models into a semantic domain. Each such transformation rule consists of two parts, a source and a target transformation rule (see Figure 8), coupled by the use of common variables. The source transformation rule is specified by providing a UML metamodel extract, represented by an XMI description which is an existing exchange format for UML models. Note that other than the concept explained in Figure 7, the tool also supports full source productions which also enables changes of the UML model (not implemented at the moment). Rather than writing an XMI description by hand, we currently use existing UML CASE tools for designing the UML metamodel extract. The generated XMI description can then be used after slight modifications. The target transformation rule is defined by providing a transformation rule in a context-free grammar notation for textual languages such as CSP [21]. Here, additional iteration constructs are provided for looping over multi-objects matched at the UML side.

3. Definition of Consistency Checks. Based on previously defined transformation units, the software engineer can define consistency checks for a problem type in the catalogue. Such a consistency check is modeled as a workflow consisting of several activities, like the localization of potential problems based on the pattern defined in 1., the translation defined in 2., the generation of a consistency condition in the target language defined by a transformation in 2., and its ver-

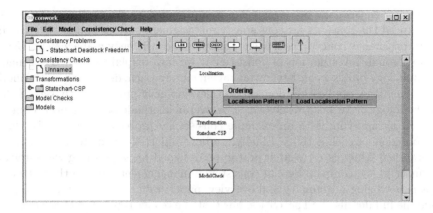

Fig. 9. Defining a Consistency Check

ification by an external tool (e.g., a model checker). In Figure 9, the definition of a consistency check is illustrated.

4. Execution of Consistency Checks. Consistency checks can then be executed on a concrete UML model following the workflows defined. For that purpose, UML models constructed with UML CASE tools such as Poseidon [1] can be loaded into the consistency workbench. Currently, such models can be visualized but not edited. For a given model, a consistency check can be manually triggered. Intermediate results of the consistency check such as models constructed during execution of the model transformations can be accessed in the consistency workbench. The result of a consistency check is currently displayed in the consistency workbench by showing the result of the model checker, together with a predefined explanation.

Being a research prototype, the consistency workbench has currently several limitations: The capability of illustrating an inconsistency by means of a counterexample expressed in an additional UML sequence diagram has not yet been implemented. Further, complex transformation units have been developed for translating statecharts to CSP but, apart from that, no other semantic domain has been used in the consistency workbench so far. Nevertheless, the main idea of our approach can be considered feasible: by systematically developing partial translations of UML models into suitable semantic domains, the consistency workbench could evolve into a technical support tool for the software engineer.

6   Conclusion

In this paper, we have presented our approach to consistency management of object-oriented models. Motivated by the situation that currently a general approach for consistency management is not provided by the UML, we have first introduced the concepts for consistency management such as consistency condition, consistency concept, consistency check and consistency management. Using this thorough investigation of consistency, we have explained how our general methodology builds a consistency management approach, depending on the modeling language, application domain and development process. Activities of this methodology have been discussed. The overall methodology has been demonstrated by applying it to an example consistency problem type and sketching the outcome of each activity. Finally, we have reported on the tool *Consistency Workbench* which is a research prototype designed for supporting the software engineer in the complex task of consistency management. Due to the nature of this paper being a summary and overview paper, we have not been able to provide the full details of all activities. For that the reader is referred to the existing publications.

Future work can be performed into several directions: With regards to our general methodology, by applying it to real-world development processes, it can be validated and refined. Furthermore, more consistency problems occuring in UML-based development will be discovered and treated which will lead to a number of predefined model transformations. Further, also suitable abstraction mechanisms must be developed. In the context of our work, it has turned out that this issue is vital for being able to perform consistency checking on larger, real-world models. This is due to the underlying approach of model checking which suffers from the well-known state explosion problem. With regards to tool support, we envisage that our consistency workbench could be integrated into an existing CASE tool.

References

1. M. Boger, T. Sturm, E. Schildhauer, and E. Graham. *Poseidon for UML Users Guide*. Gentleware AG, 2003. Available under http://www.gentleware.com.
2. E. Boiten, H. Bowman, J. Derrick, P. Linington, and M. Steen. Viewpoint Consistency in ODP. *Computer Networks*, 34(3):503–537, August 2000.
3. E. Boiten, H. Bowman, J. Derrick, and M. Steen. Viewpoint consistency in Z and LOTOS: A case study. In J. Fitzgerald, C. B. Jones, and P. Lucas, editors, *FME'97: Industrial Applications and Strengthened Foundations of Formal Methods (Proc. 4th Intl. Symposium of Formal Methods Europe, Graz, Austria, September 1997)*, volume 1313 of *Lecture Notes in Computer Science*, pages 644–664. Springer-Verlag, Heidelberg, September 1997.
4. B. Cheng, L. Campbell, and E. Wang. Enabling Automated Analysis Through the Formalization of Object-Oriented Modeling Diagrams. In *Proceedings of IEEE International Conference on Dependable Systems and Networks*, pages 433–442. IEEE Computer Society, 2000.
5. E. M. Clarke, O. Grumberg, and D. A. Peled. *Model Checking*. The MIT Press, Cambridge, MA, 1999.
6. A. Egyed. *Heterogenous View Integration and its Automation*. Dissertation, University of Southern California, 2000.

7. G. Engels and L. Groenewegen. Object-Oriented Modeling: A Roadmap. In Anthony Finkelstein, editor, *Future Of Software Engineering 2000*, pages 105–116. ACM, June 2000.

8. G. Engels, R. Heckel, and J. M. Küster. Rule-Based Specification of Behavioral Consistency Based on the UML Meta-model. In M. Gogolla and C. Kobryn, editors, *UML 2001 - The Unified Modeling Language. Modeling Languages, Concepts, and Tools., 4th International Conference, Toronto, Canada, October 1-5, 2001, Proceedings*, volume 2185 of *LNCS*, pages 272–287. Springer-Verlag, 2001.

9. G. Engels, R. Heckel, and J. M. Küster. The Consistency Workbench - A Tool for Consistency Management in UML-based Development. In P. Stevens, J. Whittle, and G. Booch, editors, *UML 2003 - The Unified Modeling Language. Modeling Languages and Applications. 6th International Conference, San Francisco, October 20-24, USA, Proceedings*, volume 2863 of *LNCS*, pages 356–359. Springer-Verlag, 2003.

10. G. Engels, J. M. Küster, and L. Groenewegen. Consistent Interaction of Software Components. In *Proceedings of Sixth International Conference on Integrated Design and Process Technology (IDPT 2002)*, 2002.

11. G. Engels, J. M. Küster, and L. Groenewegen. Consistent Interaction of Software Components. *Transactions of the SDPS: Journal of Integrated Design and Process Science*, 6(4):2–22, December 2002.

12. G. Engels, J. M. Küster, L. Groenewegen, and R. Heckel. A Methodology for Specifying and Analyzing Consistency of Object-Oriented Behavioral Models. In V. Gruhn, editor, *Proceedings of the 8th European Software Engineering Conference (ESEC)*, pages 186–195. ACM Press, 2001.

13. A. Finkelstein, D. Gabbay, A. Hunter, J. Kramer, and B. Nuseibeh. Inconsistency Handling in Multi-Perspective Specifications. In Ian Sommerville and Manfred Paul, editors, *Proceedings of the Fourth European Software Engineering Conference*, pages 84–99. Springer-Verlag, 1993.

14. Formal Systems Europe (Ltd). *Failures-Divergence-Refinement: FDR2 User Manual*, 1997.

15. P. Fradet, D. Le Métayer, and M. Périn. Consistency Checking for Multiple View Software Architectures. In O. Nierstrasz and M. Lemoine, editors, *ESEC/FSE '99*, volume 1687 of *Lecture Notes in Computer Science*, pages 410–428. Springer-Verlag/ ACM Press, 1999.

16. C. Ghezzi, M. Jazayeri, and D. Mandrioli. *Fundamentals of Software Engineering*. Prentice-Hall, 1991.

17. C. Ghezzi and B. A. Nuseibeh. Special Issue on Managing Inconsistency in Software Development (2). *IEEE Transactions on Software Engineering*, 25(11), November 1999.

18. M. Grosse-Rhode. Integrating Semantics for Object-Oriented System Models. In F. Orejas, P. G. Spirakis, and J. van Leeuwen, editors, *Proceedings of ICALP'01*, LNCS 2076, pages 40–60. Springer-Verlag, 2001.

19. R. Heckel, J. M. Küster, and G. Taentzer. Towards Automatic Translation of UML Models into Semantic Domains. In H.-J. Kreowski and P. Knirsch, editors, *Proceedings of the Appligraph Workshop on Applied Graph Transformation*, pages 11–22, March 2002.

20. J.-J. Hiemer. *Statecharts in CSP: Ein Prozessmodell in CSP zur Analyse von STATEMATE-Statecharts*. DrKovac Verlag, Hamburg, 1999.

21. C. A. R. Hoare. *Communicating Sequential Processes*. Prentice Hall, 1985.

22. J. M. Küster. *Consistency Management of Object-Oriented Behavioral Models*. PhD thesis, University of Paderborn, March 2004.

23. J. M. Küster, R. Heckel, and G. Engels. Defining and Validating Transformations of UML Models. In J. Hosking and P. Cox, editors, *IEEE Symposium on Human Centric Computing Languages and Environments (HCC 2003) - Auckland, October 28 - October 31 2003, Auckland, New Zealand, Proceedings*, pages 145–152. IEEE Computer Society, 2003.
24. X. Li and J. Lilius. Timing Analysis of UML Sequence Diagrams. In Robert France and Bernhard Rumpe, editors, *UML'99 - The Unified Modeling Language. Beyond the Standard. Second International Conference, Fort Collins, CO, USA, October 28-30. 1999, Proceedings*, volume 1723 of *LNCS*, pages 661–674. Springer-Verlag, 1999.
25. A. Moreira and R. Clark. Combining Object-Oriented Modeling and Formal Description Techniques. In M. Tokoro and R. Pareschi, editors, *Proceedings of the 8th European Conference on Object-Oriented Programming (ECOOP'94)*, pages 344 – 364. LNCS 821, Springer-Verlag, 1994.
26. B. Nuseibeh, S. Easterbrook, and A. Russo. Making Inconsistency Respectable in Software Development. *Journal of Systems and Software*, 58(2):171–180, September 2001.
27. Object Management Group (OMG). *OMG Unified Modeling Language Specification, Version 1.5. OMG document formal/03-03-01*, March 2003.
28. P. Tarr and L. A. Clarke. Consistency Management for Complex Applications. Technical report, Technical Report 97-46, Computer Science Department, University of Massachusetts at Amherst, 1997.
29. D. Varró, G. Varró, and A. Pataricza. Designing the Automatic Transformation of Visual Languages. *Science of Computer Programming*, 44(2):205–227, August 2002.
30. J. Whittle. Transformations and Software Modeling Languages: Automating Transformations in UML. In J.-M. Jezequel, H. Hussmann, and S. Cook, editors, *UML 2002 - The Unified Modeling Language. 5th International Conference, Dresden, Germany, September 30 - October 4, 2002, Proceedings*, volume 2460 of *LNCS*, pages 227–242. Springer-Verlag, 2002.
31. P. Zave and M. Jackson. Conjunction as Composition. *ACM Transactions on Software Engineering and Methodology*, 2(4):379–411, October 1993.

CommUnity on the Move:
Architectures for Distribution and Mobility

José Luiz Fiadeiro[1] and Antónia Lopes[2]

[1] Department of Computer Science, University of Leicester
University Road, Leicester LE1 7RH, UK
jose@fiadeiro.org
[2] Department of Informatics, Faculty of Sciences, University of Lisbon
Campo Grande, 1749-016 Lisboa, PORTUGAL
mal@di.fc.ul.pt

Abstract. Mobility has become a new factor of complexity in the construction and evolution of software systems. In this paper, we report on the extensions that we have made to CommUnity, a prototype language for architectural description, with modelling techniques that support the incremental and compositional construction of location-aware systems. We illustrate, around an example, how the proposed extensions lead to a true separation of concerns between computation, coordination and distribution in architectural models.

1   Introduction

The evolution of the internet and wireless communication is inducing an unprecedented and unpredictable variety and complexity on the roles that software can play. Now that software development methods and techniques were finally starting to cope with the building of distributed applications over static configurations, mobility is introducing an additional factor of complexity due to the need to account for the changes that can occur, at run time, at the level of the topology over which components perform computations and interact with one another.

Architectural modelling techniques [16] have helped to tame the complexity of building distributed applications over static networks by enforcing a strict separation of concerns. On the one hand, we have what in systems can account for the operational aspects (what we call "computations" in general) that are responsible for the behaviour that individual components ensure locally, e.g. the functionality of the services that they offer. On the other hand, we have the mechanisms that control the behaviour of individual components and coordinate the interconnections among groups of components, so that global properties of systems emerge.

This separation between "Computation" and "Coordination" [11] supports the externalisation, and definition as first-class citizens, of the rules according to which the joint behaviour of given components of a system needs to be controlled. As a consequence, one can build complex systems from simpler components by superposing the architectural connectors that coordinate their interactions. This gross modularisation

F.S. de Boer et al. (Eds.): FMCO 2003, LNCS 3188, pp. 177–196, 2004.

of systems can also be progressively refined, in a compositional way, by adding detail to the way computations execute in chosen platforms and the communication protocols that support coordination. Compositionality means that refinements over one of the dimensions can be performed without interfering with the options made already on the other one.

The levels of compositionality that architectural approaches can bring to software development also apply to evolution [2]. On the one hand, connectors can be changed or replaced without interfering with the code that components execute locally to perform the computations required by system services. On the other hand, the code running in the core components of the system can itself be evolved, e.g. optimised, without interfering with the connectors, for instance with the communication protocols being used for interconnecting components.

The major challenge that we face, and that justifies this paper, is to take this separation of concerns one step further and address distribution/mobility aspects as a first-class architectural dimension. On the one hand, it seems clear that, when we (re)configure a system, we need to take into account the support that locations provide for the operational/computational aspects of the individual components, and the ability for the interconnections to be effective over the communication network. For instance, it is essential that a system as a whole may self-adapt to changes occurring in the network topology, either to maintain agreed levels of quality of service, or to take advantage of new services that may become available. On the other hand, we need to be able to understand and refine global properties of a system separately in each of the three dimensions.

In this paper, we report on work that we are pursuing within the IST-2001-32747 project *AGILE – Architectures for Mobility –* with the aim of extending the level of separation and compositionality that has been obtained for computation and coordination to distribution/mobility. By focusing on an example – an airport luggage handling system – that, in past papers, we handled both in a location-transparent way [19] and in a preliminary experiment of the new primitives [3], we show how we can support the construction and evolution of location-aware architectural models by superposing explicit connectors that handle the mobility aspects. In this sense, this paper can be used as a companion to [13], which is where we have formalised the new architectural modelling techniques that we shall be discussing.

2   Designing Location-Aware Components in CommUnity

Location-transparency is usually considered to be an important abstraction principle for the design of distributed systems. It assumes that the infrastructure masks the physical and logical distribution of the system, and provides location-transparent communication and access to resources: components do not need to know where the components to which they are interconnected reside and execute their computations, nor how they themselves move across the distribution network.

Traditionally, architectural approaches to software design also adhere to this principle; essentially, they all share the view that system architectures are structured in terms of components and architectural connectors. Components are computation loci while connectors, superposed on certain components or groups of components, explicitly define the way these components interact. In this section, we focus on the way individual components are designed in CommUnity with a special emphasis on the primitives that capture distribution and mobility aspects.

2.1   Location-Unaware Components

CommUnity is a parallel program design language that is similar to Unity [6] and IP [10] in its computational model but adopts a different coordination model. More concretely, whereas, in Unity, the interaction between a program and its environment relies on the sharing of memory, CommUnity relies on the sharing (synchronisation) of actions and exchange of data through input and output channels.

To illustrate the way components can be designed in CommUnity, and provide a fair idea of the range of situations that our approach can address, we use a variation of a problem that we previously developed in [3,19] – a typical airport luggage delivery system in which carts move along a track and stop at designated stations for handling luggage.

In order to illustrate how incremental development is supported in CommUnity, we start with a very high-level design of a cart:

```
design Cart is
prv    busy:bool
do     move[]: ¬busy, false → true
 ▯     dock[busy]: ¬busy, false → busy'
 ▯     undock[busy]: busy, false → ¬busy'
```

This design caters for the very basic description that we gave of a cart's behaviour: the fact that it can move and stop at stations to handle luggage. In CommUnity, components are designed having in mind the interactions that they can establish with other components in terms of exchanging data through communication channels and synchronising to perform joint actions. The design above does not mention any public channels because, at this stage, we have not identified any need for the cart to exchange data with its environment. However, the cart needs to keep some internal data to know when it is parked at a station; this is modelled by the private channel *busy*. We call it channel because it can be used to exchange information between different components inside the cart, but we make it private to hide it from the environment.

The actions that a component can perform are declared under "do" and their specification takes the general form:

$$g[D(g)]: L(g), U(g) \rightarrow R(g)$$

where

- $D(g)$ consists of the local channels into which executions of the action can place values. This is normally called the *write frame* of g. We omit this set when it can be inferred from the assignments in $R(g)$. Given a private or output channel v, we will also denote by $D(v)$ the set of actions g such that $v \in D(g)$. Hence, above, *move* has an empty write frame and *busy* is in the write frames of *dock* and *un-dock*.

- $L(g)$ and $U(g)$ are two conditions that establish the interval in which the enabling condition of any guarded command that implements g must lie: the *lower bound* $L(g)$ is implied by the enabling condition, and the *upper bound* $U(g)$ implies the enabling condition. Hence, the enabling condition of g is fully determined only if $L(g)$ and $U(g)$ are equivalent, in which case we write only one condition. From a specification point of view, $U(g)$ allows us to place requirements on the states in which the action should be enabled *(progress)* and $L(g)$ allows us to restrict the occurrence of the action to given sets of states *(safety)*. By setting U to *false*, as in the examples above, we are not making any requirements as to when we want the actions to be enabled; this is useful for being able to add requirements in an incremental way as illustrate below. For instance, restrictions on how a cart can move will certainly arise when taking into consideration other aspects of the system. On the other hand, each of the three actions was given a safety guard, basically ensuring that carts do not move while docked at a station for handling luggage.

- $R(g)$ is a condition that uses primed channels to account for references to the values that the channels take after the execution of the action. This is usually a conjunction of implications of the form *pre* $\supset$ *pos* where *pre* does not involve primed channels. Each such implication corresponds to a pre/post-condition specification in the sense of Hoare. When $R(g)$ is such that the primed channels are fully determined, we obtain a conditional multiple assignment, in which case we can use the notation that is normally found in programming languages $(\parallel_{v \in D(g)} v := F(g,v))$. Hence, we could have used *busy:=true* for $R(dock)$ and *busy:=false* for $R(undock)$. When the write frame $D(g)$ is empty, $R(g)$ is tautological. This is the case of *move*.

A CommUnity design is called a program when, for every $g \in \Gamma$, $L(g)$ and $U(g)$ coincide, and the relation $R(g)$ defines a conditional multiple assignment. The behaviour of a program is as follows. At each execution step, any of the actions whose enabling condition holds can be executed if requested, in which case its assignments are performed atomically.

Actions can also be declared to be private, a situation not illustrated above, meaning that they cannot be shared with the environment of the component. Private actions that are infinitely often enabled are guaranteed to be selected for execution infinitely often. A model-theoretic semantics of CommUnity can be found in [15].

2.2 Location-Aware Components

The design that we gave above does not take into account the fact that the cart can only dock when it reaches the station to which it has been sent, nor does it model the way a cart comes to know about its destination. The design below refines the previous one with this kind of information:

```
design Located Cart is
inloc  pos
in     next:Loc
prv    busy@pos:bool, dest@pos:Loc
do     move[]@pos: ¬busy∧pos≠dest, false → true
[]     dock[busy]@pos: ¬busy∧pos=dest, false → busy:=true
[]     undock[busy,dest]@pos:
           busy∧pos=dest, false → busy:=false ‖ dest:=next
```

This design uses new primitives, some of which relate to the way we handle the notions of location, distribution and mobility. In CommUnity, the underlying "space of mobility" is constituted by the set of possible values of a special data type with a designated sort *Loc* and whatever operations are necessary to characterise locations, for instance hierarchies or taxonomies. The only requirement that we make is for a special position $-\perp-$ to be distinguished; its role will be discussed further below.

By not adopting a fixed notion of location, CommUnity can remain independent of any specific notion of space and, hence, be used for designing systems with different kinds of mobility. For instance, for physical mobility, the space is, typically, the surface of the earth, represented through a set of GPS coordinates, but it may also be a portion of a train track represented through an interval of integers. In other kinds of logical mobility, space is formed by IP addresses. Other notions of space can be modelled, namely multidimensional spaces, allowing us to accommodate richer perspectives on mobility. For instance, in order to combine logical mobility with security concerns, it is useful to consider locations that incorporate information about administrative domains.

CommUnity designs are made location-aware by associating their "constituents" — code and data — with "containers" that can move to different positions. Designs are not located: they can address components that are distributed across different locations. Hence, the unit of mobility, i.e., the smallest constituent of a system that is allowed to move, is fine-grained and different from the unit of execution.

More precisely, location-awareness comes about in CommUnity designs as follows:

- *Location variables,* or locations for short, can be declared as "containers" that can be moved to different positions. Locations can be *input* or *output*. Inputlocations, declared under *inloc*, are controlled by the environment and cannot be modified by the component. Hence, the movement of any constituent located at an input location is operated by the environment. Outputlocations, declared under *outloc*, can only be modified locally through assignments performed within actions and, hence, the movement of any constituent located at an output location is under the control of the component. In the case above, we declared only one location – *pos* – because the cart is not a distributed component. This location is declared as input because we want other components to be able to control the movement of the cart.

- Each local channel *x* is associated with a location variable *l*. We make this assignment explicit by simply writing *x@l* in the declaration of *x*. The intuition is that the value of *l* indicates the current position of the space where the values of *x* are made available. A modification in the value of *l* entails the movement of *x* as well as of the other channels and actions located at *l*. Because the cart is not distributed, *busy* has no choice but to be located at *pos*.

- Every action *g* is associated with a set of location variables $\Lambda(g)$ meaning that the execution of action *g* is distributed over those locations. In other words, the execution of *g* consists of the synchronous execution of a guarded command in each of these locations: given $l \in \Lambda(g)$, $g @ l$ is the guarded command that *g* executes at *l*. Again, because carts are not distributed, all the actions are located at *pos*.

Notice that guarded commands may now include assignments involving the reading or writing of location variables. This is the case of the actions of the cart: they were refined in order to make use of locations. More precisely, we have now restricted the enabling of *move* to the situation in which the cart has not reached its destination, and *dock* and *undock* to when the cart is at its destination.

The destination of the cart is kept in a private channel *dest* and updated before leaving the station by reading it from an input channel *next*. Input channels are used for reading data from the environment; the component has no control on the values that are made available in such channels. Notice that reading a value at a channel does not consume it: the value will remain available until it is changed by the environment.

Input channels are assigned a distinguished output location – λ – usually omitted in designs. This location has the special value $\bot$ that is used whenever one wants to make no commitment as to the location of a channel or action. For instance, input channels are always located at λ because the values that they carry are provided by the environment in a way that is location-transparent; their location is determined at configuration time when they are connected to output channels of other components.

Actions uniquely located at λ model activities for which no commitments with respect to location-awareness have been mad. The reference to λ in these cases is usually omitted. This is what happened with our first design: all its constituents were assumed to be located at λ. In later stages of the development process, the execution of such actions can be distributed over several locations, i.e. the guarded command associated with $g @ \lambda$ can be split in several guarded commands associated with located actions of the form $g @ l$, where *l* is a proper location. Whenever the command associated with $g @ \lambda$ has been fully distributed over a given set of locations in the sense that all its guards and effects have been accounted for, the reference to $g @ \lambda$ is usually omitted. In the second design, we made location-awareness more explicit and introduced references to specific location variables. However, distribution was not illustrated. This will be done below.

2.3 Distributed Components

In order to illustrate how CommUnity can handle distribution, consider the situation in which a cart can move in two different modes: slow and fast. More specifically, by default, a cart will move in fast mode. However, control points may be placed dynamically along the track to slow down the cart: when the cart comes in the proximity

of a control point, it changes to slow mode and, before it leaves the restricted area, it
goes back to fast mode.

```
design Controlled Located Cart is
outloc pos:Loc
inloc  cpoint:Loc
in     next:Loc
prv    busy@pos, in@cpoint:bool, dest@pos:Loc, mode@pos:[slow,fast]
do     move[pos]@pos:
           ¬busy∧pos≠dest, false → pos:=controlled(mode,pos)
 ▯ prv enter[mode,in]
           @pos: true → mode:=slow
           @cpoint: ¬in → in:=true
 ▯ prv leave[mode,in]
           @pos: true → mode:=fast
           @cpoint: in → in:=false
 ▯     dock[busy]@pos: ¬busy∧pos=dest, false → busy:=true
 ▯     undock[busy,dest]@pos:
           busy∧pos=dest, false → busy:=false ∥ dest:=next
```

This design introduces a new location *cpoint* accounting for a control point; this
location is declared to be *input* because we are leaving to the environment to
(re)distribute the control points along the track. However, the position *pos* of the cart
has now become output because it became under the control of the extended component (subsystem).

A private channel *in* is located at the control point to indicate when a cart enters its
proximity, which is controlled by the action *enter*. This action is distributed between
the control point, where it updates *in*, and the cart, where it changes the mode to *slow*.
The action *leave* operates the other way around. Both actions are declared to be private and their components are designed with a fully determined enabling condition
because their execution is completely under the control of the component.

The execution of a distributed action requires that the locations involved be "in-
touch" so that one can ensure that they are executed as a single transaction. For instance, the physical links that support communication between the positions of the
space of mobility (e.g. wired networks, or wireless communications through infrared
or radio links) may be subject to failures or interruptions, making communication
temporarily impossible. Formally, we rely on a set *bt(l)* for every location *l* that, at
any given moment of time, consists of the locations that are "in touch" with *l*. Hence,
for any action *g* and any locations l_1, l_2 to which it is distributed, *g* can only be executed if $l_1 \in bt(l_2)$ and $l_2 \in bt(l_1)$. In the case of the cart, this means that *enter* and
leave actions can only take place when the cart is in the proximity of the control point.

Notice that the action *move* is now making explicit that the next position is calculated from the current one taking the mode into account. The function *controlled* that
is being used will need to be defined, at specification time, on the representation chosen for the tracks. However, because *move* implies calculating a new position, an
important condition applies: it can only be executed if the new position can be
reached from the current one.

Typically, the space of mobility has some structure, which can be given by walls
and doors, barriers erected in communication networks by system administrators, or
the simple fact that not every position of the space has a host where code can be exe-

cuted. This structure can change over time. Hence, it is not realistic to imagine that entities can migrate from any point to any point at any time without restrictions.

Formally, we rely, for every location *l*, on a set *reach(l)* consisting, at any given instant of time, of the locations that can be reached from *l*. Hence, for any located action $g@l$, if a location l_1 can be affected by the execution of $g@l$, then the new value of l_1 must be a position reachable from *l*. In the case of the cart, this means that *move* can only be executed if *controlled* returns a position that is reachable from the current one – e.g. no other cart is in between.

Simpler modes of the movement of the cart could be envisioned, for instance

```
design Step Located Cart is
outloc pos:Loc
in      next:Loc
prv     busy@pos:bool, dest@pos:Loc
do      move[pos]@pos: ¬busy∧pos≠dest, false → pos:=inc(pos)
▯       dock[busy]@pos: ¬busy∧pos=dest, false → busy:=true
▯       undock[busy,dest]@pos:
            busy∧pos=dest, false → busy:=false ∥ dest:=next
```

In this case, we are relying on a simpler *increment* function on locations that leads the cart step by step through a path of a pre-established graph. The function itself can define the graph. For instance, by defining *Loc* as nat_5, two different alternative graphs are:

 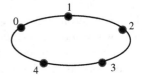

2.4   Formal Semantics

In this section, we provide a summary of the mathematical semantics of CommUnity designs. More details can be found in [9,13].

We start by mentioning that designs in CommUnity are defined over a collection of data types that are used for structuring the data that the channels transmit and define the operations that perform the computations that are required. Hence, the choice of data types determines, essentially, the nature of the elementary computations that can be performed locally by the components, which are abstracted as operations on data elements. For simplicity, we assume a fixed collection of data types, i.e. we shall not discuss the process of data refinement that needs to be involved when mapping designs and their interconnections to the platforms that support computations and coordination. In order to remain independent of any specific language for the definition of these data types, we take them in the form of a first-order algebraic specification. That is to say, we assume a data signature $\Sigma=<S,\Omega>$, where S is a set (of sorts) and Ω is a $S^*\times S$-indexed family of sets (of operations), to be given together with a collection Φ of first-order sentences specifying the functionality of the operations. We refer to this data type specification by Θ.

A CommUnity design is a pair $<\theta,\Delta>$ where:

— *θ, the signature of the design, is a tuple $<L,X,\Gamma,tv,ta,D,\Lambda>$ where*

- *L is a finite pointed set, we use λ to designate its point;*
- *X is an S-indexed family of mutually disjoint finite sets;*
- *Γ is a finite set;*
- *$tv: X\cup L\rightarrow\{out,in,prv\}$ is a total function s.t. $tv(\lambda)=out$; for $A\subseteq X\cup L$, we shall use $out(A)$ to denote the set $\{a\in A:tv(a)=out\}$ (and similarly for $in(A)$ and $prv(A)$) and $local(A)$ to denote $out(A)\cup prv(A)$;*
- *$ta: \Gamma\rightarrow\{sh,prv\}$ is a total function,*
- *$\Lambda: X\cup\Gamma\rightarrow2^{L}$ is a total function s.t. $\lambda\in\Lambda(g)$, for every $g\in X\cup\Gamma$ and $\Lambda(i)=\{\lambda\}$, for every $i\in in(X)$;*
- *$D: \Gamma\rightarrow2^{local(X\cup L)}$ is a total function.*

— *Δ, the body of the design, is a tuple $<R,L,U>$ where:*

- *R assigns to every action $g\in\Gamma$ and $l\in\Lambda(g)$, a proposition over $X\cup L\cup D(g)'$ s.t. $\vdash R(g@\lambda)\supset\Lambda_{l\in\Lambda(g)}R(g@l)$;*
- *L and U assign a proposition over $X\cup L$ to every action $g\in\Gamma$ and $l\in\Lambda(g)$ s.t. $\vdash L(g@\lambda)\supset\Lambda_{l\in\Lambda(g)}L(g@l)$ and $\vdash U(g@\lambda)\supset\Lambda_{l\in\Lambda(g)}U(g@l)$.*

It is important to notice that the conditions on the guarded commands associated with located actions of the form $g@\lambda$ justify why, as mentioned before, the reference to $g@\lambda$ can be omitted in some situations. When the command associated with g has been fully distributed over a given set of locations (i.e., $R(g@\lambda)\Leftrightarrow\Lambda_{l\in\Lambda(g)}R(g@l)$, $L(g@\lambda)\Leftrightarrow\Lambda_{l\in\Lambda(g)}L(g@l)$ and $U(g@\lambda)\Leftrightarrow\Lambda_{l\in\Lambda(g)}U(g@l))$, the guard of $g@\lambda$ and its effects have been accounted for and, hence, $g@\lambda$ can be omitted because it does not provide any additional information.

In order to define the behaviour of a program P, we have to fix, first of all, an algebra $\mathcal{U}$ for the data types in Σ. The sets $\mathcal{U}_s$ define the possible values of the each data sort s in Σ. In particular, the set $\mathcal{U}_{Loc}$ defines the positions of the space of mobility for the situation at hand. In addition, we also have to fix a function $rs:\Omega\rightarrow N$. This function establishes the level of resources required for the computation of each operation in Ω. In order to define the behaviour of P, we also need a model of the "world" where P is placed to run which should capture that this world may be continuously changing. In fact, we only need to know the properties and behaviour of the part of the environment that may affect the program execution – its context.

In CommUnity, the context that a component perceives is determined by its current position. A context is defined by a set Cxt of pairs $obs:type$, where obs is simply an identifier and $type$ is a data sort. Cxt models the notion of context that is considered to be suitable for the situation at hand. Each obs represents an observable that can be used for designing the system, and $type$ defines the type of its values. As a consequence, obs can be used in CommUnity designs as any other term of sort $type$. The only requirement that we make is for three special observables – $rssv:nat\times2^{\Sigma}$, $bt:2^{Loc}$ and $reach:2^{Loc}$ – to be distinguished.

The purpose of $rssv:nat\times2^{\Sigma}$ is to represent the *resources* and *services* that are available for computation. The first component of $rssv$ quantifies the resources available. It may be defined as a function of more specific observables in Cxt, for instance, the remaining lifetime of a battery or the amount of memory available. In this way, it is possible to model the fact that the same resources may affect different applications in different ways. The second component of *rssv* represents the services available and it is taken as a part of the data signature Σ. This is because, as we have seen in the previous sections, the services that perform the computations are abstracted as operations on data elements. In this paper, we will not illustrate this particular aspect of CommUnity; see [13] instead.

The intuition behind $bt:2^{Loc}$ and $reach:2^{Loc}$ is even simpler: both represent the set of locations that are accessible. The former represents the locations that can be reached through communication while the latter concerns reachability through movement. We have already motivated the use of these relations in section 2.3.

We consider that such models are *Cxt*-indexed sets $\{M_{obs:type}\}_{obs:type \in Cxt}$ of infinite sequences of functions over U_{Loc}. Each $M_{obs:type}$ is an infinite sequence of functions that provide the value of the observable *obs* at every position of the space, at a particular instant of time. For the special observables $rssv:nat \times 2^{\Sigma}$, $bt:2^{Loc}$ and $reach:2^{Loc}$, these functions are constrained as follows.

Every function in M_{bt} and M_{reach} maps a position m into a set of positions that must include m. Intuitively, this means that we require that "be in touch" and "reachability" are reflexive relations. Furthermore, for the observable *bt*, only the sets of positions that include the special position $\perp_U$ are admissible values. This condition establishes part of the special role played by $\perp_U$: at every position of the space, the position $\perp_U$ is always "in touch". In addition, we require that every function in M_{bt} maps $\perp_U$ to *Loc*. In this way, any entity located at $\perp_U$ can communicate with any other entity in a location-transparent manner and vice-versa.

The position $\perp_U$ is also special because it supports context-transparent computation, i.e. a computation that takes place at $\perp_U$ is not subject to any kind of restriction. This is achieved by requiring that every function in M_{rssv} assigns the value $(+\infty, \Sigma)$ to the position $\perp_U$. In other words, the computational resources available at $\perp_U$ are unlimited and all the services are available.

The behaviour of a program running in the context of $\{M_{obs:type}\}_{obs:type \in Cxt}$ is as follows. The conditions under which a distributed action g can be executed at time i are the following:

1. *For every* $l_1, l_2 \in \Lambda(g)$, $[l_2]^i \in M_{bt}{}^i([l_1]^i)$ *and* $[l_1]^i \in M_{bt}{}^i([l_2]^i))$: the execution of g involves the synchronisation of its local actions and, hence, their positions have to be mutually in touch.

2. *For every* $l \in \Lambda(g)$, *g@l can be executed, i.e.,*
   i. *If* $M_{rssv}([l]^i) = (n, \Sigma)$ *then, for every operation symbol f used in the guarded command associated to g@l, f is an operation in* Σ *and* $rs(f) \leq n$: in order to perform the computations that are required, the services and the level of resources needed for these computations have to be available.
   ii. *For every local channel x used in the guarded command associated to g@l, if x is located at* l, $(x@l)$, *then* $[l]^i \in M_{bt}{}^i([l]^i)$: the execution of the guarded command associated with *g@l* requires that every channel in its frame can be accessed from its current position and, hence, *l* has to be in touch with the locations of each of these channels.

iii. *For every location* $l_i \in D(g)$, $[F(g@l,l_i)]^i \in \mathcal{M}_{reach}{}^i([l_i]^i)$: if a location l_i can be effected by the execution of $g@l$, then the new value of l_i must be a position reachable from the current one.

iv. *The local guard* $L(g@l)(=U(g@l))$ *evaluates to true.*

By $[e]^i$ we denote the value of the expression e at time i. It is important to notice that, because observables can be used in programs as terms, the evaluation of an expression e at time i may also depend on the model of *Cxt*.

Given this, the execution of the action consists of the transactional execution of its guarded commands at their locations, which requires the atomic execution of the multiple assignments. Private actions are subject to a fairness requirement: if infinitely often enabled, they are guaranteed to be selected infinitely often.

3 Architectural Concerns in CommUnity

Section 2 illustrated several of the primitives provided in CommUnity for the design of distributed and mobile components. It did so through an incremental process of addition of detail to an initial, abstract account of the behaviour of a cart. CommmUnity does not prescribe any specific method of incremental development. Instead, it provides the ability for different concerns to be modelled independently and superposed dynamically over the configuration of a system to account for new design decisions.

For instance, if we consider the addition of the distribution/mobility aspects in section 2.3, it is clear that the behaviour of the cart at the stations is not concerned. Moreover, it should be possible to capture these aspects as an architectural element (connector) that is being plugged to control the movement of cart. Changing from the fast/slow control to the step-by-step mode should be just a matter of unplugging a connector and plugging a new one; it should not require the cart to be re-designed or re-implemented.

Another example can be given as follows. Consider that we now need to monitor the number of times a cart docks at a station. It seems clear that we should be able to:

- Address this issue independently of the way the movement of the cart is being controlled, i.e. regardless of whether we are monitoring a step or a controlled located cart.
- Separate the "logic" of monitoring from the location in which the data that is required is provided, i.e. address interaction separately from the location aspects.

In this section, we address these issues in two steps. First, we illustrate how connectors can be externalised from components. Then, we address the separate modelling of coordination and distribution.

3.1   Externalising the Connector

Consider again the controlled located cart and the way it was obtained from the located cart. The following design attempts at externalising the extension that was performed.

```
design Mode controller is
inloc  mine:Loc
outloc theirs:Loc
prv    in@mine:bool, mode@theirs:[slow,fast]
do     control[theirs]@theirs: true → theirs:=controlled(mode,theirs)
□ prv  enter[mode,in]
          @theirs: true → mode:=slow
          @mine: ¬in → in:=true
□ prv  leave[mode,in]
          @theirs: true → mode:=fast
          @mine: in → in:=false
```

This design contains more than just what was added to the located cart; it repeats the elements that are necessary for this extension to be autonomous as a design. This is why it includes both the location of the cart and the action of the cart that is being controlled. Notice, however, that the action *control* is always enabled; the idea, as detailed below, is that restrictions on its occurrence are left to the component being controlled.

We deliberately changed the names of some of the design elements to highlight the fact that we want this mode controller to exist, as a design, independently of the located cart. However, this renaming is not necessary because it is automatically enforced in Category Theory [8], which is the mathematical framework in which we give semantics to our interconnection mechanisms. As far as we are concerned, this mode controller could even pre-exist the located cart as part of a library of connectors that a software architect uses for designing a system. What we need to say is how it can be applied to a component like a located car.

CommUnity supports the design of interactions through configurations; these are diagrams that exhibit interconnections between designs. For instance, a located cart under the control of a mode controller is specified by the following configuration:

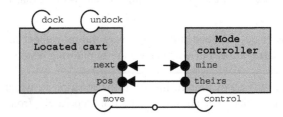

In configuration diagrams, components only depict their public elements. The lines connect locations, channels and actions. In contrast with what happens with most architectural description languages, "boxes and lines" in CommUnity have a mathematical semantics. As explained in section 3.2, configuration diagrams are diagrams in a category of CommUnity designs whose morphisms capture notions of superposition that are typical in parallel program design [6,10,12]. The semantics of such a diagram is given by its colimit [8], which can be informally explained as the design of the system viewed as a single, distributed component:

- Connected locations are amalgamated; input locations can be connected with input connections, in which case their amalgamation is an input location, our with output locations, in which case their amalgamation is an output location; output locations cannot be connected with output locations.
- The same rule applies to channels; only channels carrying the same type of data can be connected.
- Connected actions give rise to joint distributed actions; every set $\{g_1,...,g_n\}$ of actions that are synchronised is represented by a single action $g_1\|...\|g_n$ whose occurrence captures the joint execution of the actions in the set. The transformations performed by the joint action are distributed over the locations of the synchronised actions. Each located action $g_1\|...\|g_n@l$ is specified by the conjunction of the specifications of the local effects of each of the synchronised actions g_i that is distributed over l, and the guards of joint actions are also obtained through the conjunction of the guards specified by the components.

We must call attention to the fact that elements (locations, channels and actions) that have the same name in different designs but are not connected need to be renamed. This is because there can be no implicit interconnection between designs resulting from accidental naming of locations, channels or actions. Any name binding needs to be made explicit through a line as illustrated.

The design that we have just described is itself obtained only up to renaming; the actual choice of names for locations, channels, and actions does not really matter as long as all the interconnections are respected and no additional interconnections are introduced. Hence, in the case of the cart, what we obtain from the configuration above is a specification of the controlled located cart as given in section 2.3. Notice in particular that the result of synchronising the action

```
move[pos]@pos: ¬busy∧pos≠dest, false → true
```

of located cart, and the action

```
control[theirs]@theirs: true → theirs:=controlled(mode,theirs)
```

of mode controller is, after the amalgamation of the locations,

```
move[pos]@pos: ¬busy∧pos≠dest, false → pos:=controlled(mode,pos)
```

This is because the semantics of the composition is given by the conjunction of the guards and of the effects of the component actions.

Summarising, we have expressed the behaviour of the controlled located cart as resulting from a configuration in which the located cart is connected to a component that controls its movement. The advantage of this representation is that, in order to change to a step-by-step control, we just need to replace the mode controller by another connector, namely

```
design Step controller is
outloc theirs:Loc
do      control[theirs]@theirs: true → theirs:=inc(theirs)
```

In this case, the required configuration is

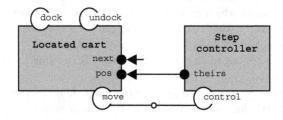

3.2   Semantics of Interconnection

As already mentioned, the semantics of interconnection and configuration in CommUnity is based on Category Theory [8]. In this section, we will only provide the basic ingredients of this semantics. More details are available in [9,13].

We call a morphism $\sigma: P_1 \rightarrow P_2$ of CommUnity designs a triple consisting of a total function $\sigma_{ch}: X_1 \rightarrow X_2$, a partial mapping $\sigma_{ac}: \Gamma_2 \rightarrow \Gamma_1$ and a total function $\sigma_{lc}: L_1 \rightarrow L_2$ that maps the designated location of P_1 to that of P_2, satisfying:

1. *for every $x \in X_1$:*
   (a) $sort_2(\sigma_{ch}(x))=sort_1(x)$;
   (b) if $x \in out(X_1)$ then $\sigma_{ch}(x) \in out(X_2)$;
   (c) if $x \in prv(X_1)$ then $\sigma_{ch}(x) \in prv(X_2)$;
   (d) if $x \in in(X_1)$ then $\sigma_{ch}(x) \in out(X_2) \cup in(X_2)$.
2. *for every $g \in \Gamma_2$ s.t. $\sigma_{ac}(g)$ is defined:*
   (a) if $g \in sh(\Gamma_2)$ then $\sigma_{ac}(g) \in sh(\Gamma_1)$;
   (b) if $g \in prv(\Gamma_2)$ then $\sigma_{ac}(g) \in prv(\Gamma_1)$.
3. *for every $x \in X_1$ and $l \in L_1$*
   (e) $\sigma_{lc}^{-1}(\lambda_2)=\{\lambda_1\}$
   (f) if $l \in out(L_1)$ then $\sigma_{lc}(l) \in out(L_2)$;
   (g) $\sigma_{lc}(\Lambda_1(x)) \subseteq \Lambda_2(\sigma_{ch}(x))$.
4. *for every $g \in \Gamma_2$ s.t. $\sigma_{ac}(g)$ is defined:*
   (c) $\sigma_{lc}(\Lambda_1(\sigma_{ac}(g))) \subseteq \Lambda_2(g)$.
5. *for every $x \in local(X_1 \cup L_1)$, σ_{ac} is total on $D_2(\sigma_{ch}(x))$ and*
   $\sigma_{ac}(D_2(\sigma_{ch}(x))) \subseteq D_1(x)$.
6. *for every $g \in \Gamma_2$ s.t. $\sigma_{ac}(g)$ is defined and $l \in \Lambda_1(\sigma_{ac}(g))$:*
   (a) $\sigma(D_1(\sigma_{ac}(g)) \subseteq D_2(g)$;
   (b) $\Phi \vdash R_2(g@\sigma_{lc}(l)) \supset \underline{\sigma}(R_1(\sigma_{ac}(g)@l))$;
   (c) $\Phi \vdash L_2(g@\sigma_{lc}(l)) \supset \underline{\sigma}(L_1(\sigma_{ac}(g)@l))$;
   (d) $\Phi \vdash U_2(g@\sigma_{lc}(l)) \supset \underline{\sigma}(U_1(\sigma_{ac}(g)@l))$.

By $\vdash$ we mean validity in the first-order sense taken over the axiomatisation Φ of the underlying data types. These morphisms define a category **MDSG**.

Configuration diagrams define diagrams in this category, i.e. graphs whose nodes are labelled with CommUnity designs as defined in section 2.4, and arrows are labelled with morphisms as defined above. Colimits of such diagrams define the semantics of configurations.

3.3   Separating Coordination and Distribution

Consider now the situation described at the beginning of this section: assume that we want to monitor how many times a cart has docked at a station. Intuitively, we should be able to start by putting in place just the mechanisms that coordinate the interaction between the cart and the monitor, which should not depend on the location and mobility aspects of the cart.

The interaction aspects of the monitor can be resumed to a counting function and designed as follows:

```
design Counter is
out    count:nat
do     inc[count]: true → count:=count+1
[]     reset[count]: true → count:=0
```

The counter can be connected to the original design of the cart because their interaction does not involve mobility explicitly:

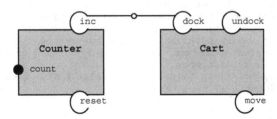

The semantics of the configuration is given by the following design:

```
design Monitored cart is
prv    busy:bool
out    count:nat
do     move[]: ¬busy, false → true
[]     dock[busy,count]: ¬busy, false → busy:=true || count:=count+1
[]     undock[busy]: busy, false → busy:=false
[]     reset[count]: true → count:=0
[]     move&reset[count]: ¬busy, false → count:=0
[]     undock&reset[busy,count]: busy, false → busy:=false || count:=0
```

Notice that the synchronisations of *reset* with *move* and *undock* are automatically added! This is because there is no reason to prevent the counter from being reset while the cart is moving or undocking. Should such synchronisations be undesirable, one would have to configure the system in a way that prevents them; the default semantics is of maximum parallelism. It is important to stress that this complex design is just providing the semantics of the configuration; it is the configuration that one should use to develop and evolve the system, not its semantics! In order to simplify the presentation, we shall omit these synchronisations in the examples below and replace them by '...'.

This interconnection can be extended to the located cart because the designs Cart and Located Cart are related by a morphism as defined in 3.2. Indeed, because morphisms preserve locations, channels and actions, the interconnection propagates from the source to the target of the morphism:

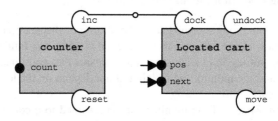

Once again, details on the semantics of this propagation of interconnections can be found in [13]. This semantics is based on the fact that, as explained in section 2.4, every design involves the implicit location λ.

```
design Monitored Located cart is
outloc pos:Loc
in      next:Loc
out     count@λ:nat
prv     busy@pos:bool, dest@pos:Loc
do      move[pos]@pos: ¬busy∧pos≠dest, false → true
▯       dock[busy,count]
            @pos: ¬busy∧pos=dest, false → busy:=true
            @λ: ¬busy∧pos=dest, false → busy:=true ‖ count:=count+1
▯       undock[busy,dest]@pos:
            busy∧pos=dest, false → busy:=false ‖ dest:=next
▯       reset[count]@λ: true → count:=0
...
```

Decisions on the location of the counter can now be made independently of those made for the cart. A "minimal" decision is to consider that the location and mobility of the counter is left to the environment:

```
design Counter' is
inloc  where:Loc
out     count@where:nat
do      inc[count]@where: true → count:=count+1
▯       reset[count]@where: true → count:=0
```

If one wants to place the counter in the cart, then the following configuration should be used:

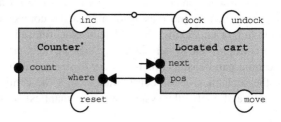

```
design Monitored co-Located cart is
inloc  pos:Loc
in     next:Loc
out    count@pos:nat
prv    busy@pos:bool, dest@pos:Loc
do     move[pos]@pos: ¬busy∧pos≠dest, false → true
▯      dock[busy,count]@pos:
           ¬busy∧pos=dest, false → busy:=true ‖ count:=count+1
▯      undock[busy.dest]@pos:
           busy∧pos=dest, false → busy:=false ‖ dest:=next
▯      reset[count]@pos: true → count:=0
...
```

Notice that the *dock* action is no longer distributed and combines the actions of the cart and the counter.

If one wants to place the counter at some fixed location, the following connector can be used:

```
design Fixed is
outloc stay:Loc
```

Notice that, because no actions are provided for changing the location of Fixed, it cannot be moved!

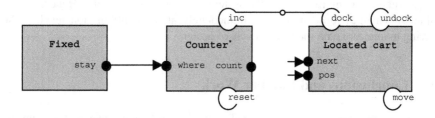

```
design Fixed Monitored Located cart is
outloc stay:Loc
inloc  pos:Loc
in     next:Loc
out    count@stay:nat
prv    busy@pos:bool, dest@pos:Loc
do     move[pos]@pos: ¬busy∧pos≠dest, false → true
▯      dock[busy,count]
           @pos: ¬busy∧pos=dest, false → busy:=true
           @stay: true → count:=count+1
▯      undock[busy,dest]@pos:
           busy∧pos=dest, false → busy:=false ‖ dest:=next
▯      reset[count]@stay: true → count:=0
...
```

We can now put together our system by combining these different connectors, for instance a cart monitored by a fixed counter and step controller:

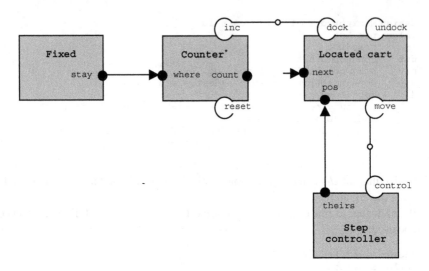

The ability to externalise connectors and address coordination and distribution in a separate way is what supports a true compositional approach to development and evolution: we can plug-in and plug-out the connectors that address the different concerns without having to redesign the system at the level of its code. Hence, it is possible for changes to be performed immediately at the configuration level, without having to interfere with the lower levels of design.

4   Conclusions and Further Work

This paper presented, around a typical example – a luggage handling system, how CommUnity is being extended with primitives that support the modelling of distribution and mobility aspects at an architectural level. This extension is being pursued within the IST-2001-32747 Project *AGILE – Architectures for Mobility* with two main goals in mind:

- To provide support for the description of the mobility aspects of systems in a way that is completely separated from the computational and coordination concerns.
- To be based on proper abstractions for modelling the part of the run-time environment that may affect their behaviour, what is often referred as *context*.

This paper focused essentially on the first goal. We showed how a new class of architectural connectors can be defined that externalise patterns and policies related to the locations in which components perform computations and the network topology that supports coordination.   Such connectors can be superposed over location-transparent models of components and connectors as a means of addressing the mobility-based aspects that reflect the properties of the operational and communication infrastructure without having to redesign the other dimensions.

In this respect, our work goes one step beyond what can be found in the literature that addresses the formalisation of software architectures, e.g. [1].   In all the approaches that we know, including those around Mobile Unity [17,18], the mobility dimension is not taken as a separate and first-class aspect.

Further work is in progress in several directions.

On the one hand, we are using these results on CommUnity to make available this level of architectural support in modelling languages like the UML. The aim is to extend the set of coordination-based semantic primitives that we developed in the past [2] with similar ones for distribution and mobility [4]. At the same time, we are relating architectural design in CommUnity with extensions of process languages like KLAIM [5] that can handle distribution and mobility at a lower level of abstraction.

On the other hand, and towards the second goal mentioned above, we are further exploring the notion of context that we only briefly mentioned in section 2.4. Contexts usually model these different types of resources as well as other kinds of external factors, from the screen size of a device to the power left on a battery. Given that different kinds of applications typically require different notions of context, it is important that formalisms for designing mobile systems consider contexts as first-class design entities and support their explicit modelling. If a specific notion of context is assumed as, for instance, in Ambients [7], the encoding of a different notion of context can be cumbersome and entangled with other aspects, if at all possible. By extending CommUnity with the explicit modelling of a notion of context, we hope to make it possible for such aspects to be progressively refined through the addition of detail, without interfering with the parts of the system already designed.

Acknowledgements

This work was partially supported through the IST-2001-32747 Project *AGILE – Architectures for Mobility*. We wish to thank our partners for much useful feedback.

References

1. R.Allen and D.Garlan, "A Formal Basis for Architectural Connectors", *ACM TOSEM* 6(3), 213-249, 1997.
2. L.F.Andrade and J.L.Fiadeiro, "Architecture Based Evolution of Software Systems", in M.Bernardo and P.Inverardi (eds), *Formal Methods for Software Architectures*, LNCS 2804, 148-181, Springer Verlag 2003.
3. L.F.Andrade, J.L.Fiadeiro, A.Lopes and M.Wermelinger, "Architectural Techniques for Evolving Control Systems", in G.Tarnai and E.Schnieder (eds), *Formal Methods for Railway Operation and Control Systems,* 61-70, L'Harmattan Press 2003
4. N.Aoumeur, J.L.Fiadeiro and C.Oliveira, "Towards an Architectural Approach to Location-Aware Business Processes", in *Proc. 13th IEEE International Workshops on Enabling Technologies: Infrastructures for Collaborative Enterprises (WETICE-2004)*, IEEE Computer Society Press 2004.
5. L. Bettini, M. Loreti, and R. Pugliese "An Infrastructure Language for Open Nets", in *Proceedings of the 2002 ACM Symposium on Applied Computing*, 373-377, ACM 2002
6. K.Chandy and J.Misra, *Parallel Program Design - A Foundation*, Addison-Wesley 1988.

7. L.Cardelli and A.Gordon, "Mobile Ambients", in Nivat (ed), *FOSSACS'98*, LNCS 1378, 140-155, Springer-Verlag 1998.

8. J.L.Fiadeiro, *Categories for Software Engineering*, Springer-Verlag 2004.

9. J.L.Fiadeiro, A.Lopes and M.Wermelinger, "A Mathematical Semantics for Architectural Connectors", in R.Backhouse and J.Gibbons (eds), *Generic Programming*, LNCS 2793, 190-234, Springer-Verlag 2003.

10. N.Francez and I.Forman, *Interacting Processes*, Addison-Wesley 1996.

11. D.Gelernter and N.Carriero, "Coordination Languages and their Significance", *Communications ACM* 35(2), 97-107, 1992.

12. S.Katz, "A Superimposition Control Construct for Distributed Systems", *ACM TOPLAS* 15(2), 337-356, 1993.

13. A.Lopes and J.L.Fiadeiro, "Adding Mobility to Software Architectures", in A.Brogi and J.-M.Jacquet (eds), *FOCLASA 2003 – Foundations of Coordination Languages and Software Architecture*, Electronic Notes in Theoretical Computer Science. Elsevier Science, in print.

14. A.Lopes, J.L.Fiadeiro and M.Wermelinger, "Architectural Primitives for Distribution and Mobility", in *Proc. SIGSOFT 2002/FSE-10*, 41-50, ACM Press 2002.

15. A.Lopes and J. L. Fiadeiro, "Using Explicit State to Describe Architectures", in E.Astesiano (ed), *FASE'99*, LNCS 1577, 144–160, Springer-Verlag 1999.

16. D.Perry and A.Wolf, "Foundations for the Study of Software Architectures", *ACM SIGSOFT Software Engineering Notes* 17(4), 40-52, 1992.

17. G.Picco, G.-C.Roman and P.McCann, "Expressing Code Mobility in Mobile Unity", in M.Jazayeri and H.Schauer (eds), *Proc. 6th ESEC*, LNCS 1301, 500-518, Springer-Verlag 1998.

18. G.-C.Roman, A.L.Murphy and G.P.Picco, "Coordination and Mobility", in A.Omicini et al (eds), *Coordination of Internet Designs: Models, Techniques, and Applications*, 253-273, Springer-Verlag 2001.

19. M.Wermelinger and J.Fiadeiro, "Connectors for Mobile Programs", *IEEE Transactions on Software Engineering* 24(5), 331-341, 1998.

TulaFale: A Security Tool for Web Services

Karthikeyan Bhargavan, Cédric Fournet,
Andrew D. Gordon, and Riccardo Pucella

Microsoft Research

Abstract. Web services security specifications are typically expressed as a mixture of XML schemas, example messages, and narrative explanations. We propose a new specification language for writing complementary machine-checkable descriptions of SOAP-based security protocols and their properties. Our TulaFale language is based on the pi calculus (for writing collections of SOAP processors running in parallel), plus XML syntax (to express SOAP messaging), logical predicates (to construct and filter SOAP messages), and correspondence assertions (to specify authentication goals of protocols). Our implementation compiles TulaFale into the applied pi calculus, and then runs Blanchet's resolution-based protocol verifier. Hence, we can automatically verify authentication properties of SOAP protocols.

1 Verifying Web Services Security

Web services are a wide-area distributed systems technology, based on asynchronous exchanges of XML messages conforming to the SOAP message format [BEK+00, W3C03]. The WS-Security standard [NKHBM04] describes how to sign and encrypt portions of SOAP messages, so as to achieve end-to-end security. This paper introduces TulaFale, a new language for defining and automatically verifying models of SOAP-based cryptographic protocols, and illustrates its usage for a typical request/response protocol: we sketch the protocol, describe potential attacks, and then give a detailed description of how to define and check the request and response messages in TulaFale.

1.1 Web Services

A basic motivation for web services is to support programmatic access to web data. The HTML returned by a typical website is a mixture of data and presentational markup, well suited for human browsing, but the presence of markup makes HTML a messy and brittle format for data processing. In contrast, the XML returned by a web service is just the data, with some clearly distinguished metadata, well suited for programmatic access. For example, search engines export web services for programmatic web search, and e-commerce sites export web services to allow affiliated websites direct access to their databases.

Generally, a broad range of applications for web services is emerging, from the well-established use of SOAP as a platform and vendor neutral middleware

F.S. de Boer et al. (Eds.): FMCO 2003, LNCS 3188, pp. 197–222, 2004.

within a single organisation, to the proposed use of SOAP for device-to-device interaction [S+04].

In the beginning, "SOAP" stood for "Simple Object Access Protocol", and was intended to implement "RPC using XML over HTTP" [Win98, Win99, Box01]. HTTP facilitates interoperability between geographically distant machines and between those in protection domains separated by corporate firewalls that block many other transports. XML facilitates interoperability between different suppliers' implementations, unlike various binary formats of previous RPC technologies. Still, web services technology should not be misconstrued as HTTP-specific RPC for distributed objects [Vog03]. HTTP is certainly at present the most common transport protocol, but the SOAP format is independent of HTTP, and some web services use other transports such as TCP or SMTP [SMWC03]. The design goals of SOAP/1.1 [BEK+00] explicitly preclude object-oriented features such as object activation and distributed garbage collection; by version 1.2 [W3C03], "SOAP" is a pure name, not an acronym. The primitive message pattern in SOAP is a single one-way message that may be processed by zero or more intermediaries between two end-points; RPC is a derived message pattern built from a request and a response. In brief, SOAP is not tied to objects, and web services are not tied to the web. Still, our running example is an RPC over HTTP, which still appears to be the common case.

1.2   Securing Web Services with Cryptographic Protocols

Web services specifications support SOAP-level security via a syntax for embedding cryptographic materials in SOAP messages. To meet their security goals, web services and their clients can construct and check *security headers* in messages, according to the WS-Security format [IM02, NKHBM04]. WS-Security can provide message confidentiality and authentication independently of the underlying transport, using, for instance, secure hash functions, shared-key encryption, or public-key cryptography. WS-Security has several advantages compared to using a secure transport such as SSL, including scalability, flexibility, transparency to intermediaries such as firewalls, and support for non-repudiation. Significantly, though, WS-Security does not itself prescribe a particular security protocol: each application must determine its security goals, and process security headers accordingly.

Web services may be vulnerable to many of the well-documented classes of attack on ordinary websites [SS02, HL03]. Moreover, unlike typical websites, web services relying on SOAP-based cryptographic protocols may additionally be vulnerable to a new class of *XML rewriting attacks*: a range of attacks in which an attacker may record, modify, replay, and redirect SOAP messages, but without breaking the underlying cryptographic algorithms. Flexibility comes at a price in terms of security, and it is surprisingly easy to misinterpret the guarantees actually obtained from processing security headers. XML is hence a new setting for an old problem going back to Needham and Schroeder's pioneering work on authentication protocols; SOAP security protocols should be judged safe, or not, with respect to an attacker who is able to "interpose a computer on all communication paths, and thus can alter or copy parts of messages, replay messages, or emit false material" [NS78]. XML rewriting attacks are included in the WS–I threat model [DHK⁺04]. We have found a variety of replay and impersonation attacks in practice.

1.3   Formalisms and Tools for Cryptographic Protocols

The use of formal methods to analyze cryptographic protocols and their vulnerabilities begin with work by Dolev and Yao [DY83]. In the past few years there has been intense research on the Dolev-Yao model, leading to the development of numerous formalisms and tools.

TulaFale builds on the line of research using the pi calculus. The pi calculus [Mil99] is a general theory of interaction between concurrent processes. Several variants of the pi calculus, including spi [AG99], and a generalization, applied pi [AF01], have been used to formalize and prove properties of cryptographic protocols. A range of compositional reasoning techniques is available for proving protocol properties, but proofs typically require human skill and determination. Recently, however, Blanchet [Bla01, Bla02] has proposed a range of automatic techniques, embodied in his theorem prover ProVerif, for checking certain secrecy and authentication properties of the applied pi calculus. ProVerif works by compiling the pi calculus to Horn clauses and then running resolution-based algorithms.

1.4   TulaFale: A Security Tool for Web Services

TulaFale is a new scripting language for specifying SOAP security protocols, and verifying the absence of XML rewriting attacks:

TulaFale = processes + XML + predicates + assertions

The pi calculus is the core of TulaFale, and allows us to describe SOAP processors, such as clients and servers, as communicating processes. We extend the pi calculus with a syntax for XML plus symbolic cryptographic operations; hence, we can directly express SOAP messaging with WS-Security headers. We declaratively specify the construction and checking of SOAP messages using Prolog-style predicates; hence, we can describe the operational details of SOAP processing. Independently, we specify security goals using various assertions, such as correspondences for message authentication and correlation.

It is important that TulaFale can express the detailed structure of XML signatures and encryption so as to catch low-level attacks on this structure, such as copying part of an XML signature into another; more abstract representations of message formats, typical in the study of the Dolev-Yao model and used for instance in previous work on SOAP authentication protocols [GP03], are insensitive to such attacks.

Our methodology when developing TulaFale has been to study particular web services implementations, and to develop TulaFale scripts modelling their security aspects. Our experiments have been based on the WSE development

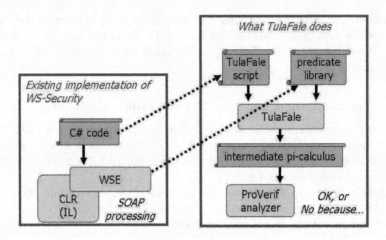

Fig. 1. Modelling WS-Security protocols with TulaFale

kit [Mic02], a particular implementation of WS-Security and related specifications. We have implemented the running example protocol of this paper using WSE, and checked that the SOAP messages specified in our script faithfully reflect the SOAP messages observed in this implementation. For a discussion of the implementation of related protocols, including logs of SOAP messages, see the technical report version of an earlier paper [BFG04a].

Fig. 1 illustrates our methodology. On the left, we have the user-supplied code for implementing a web services protocol, such as the one of this paper, on top of the WSE library. On the right, we have the TulaFale script modelling the user-supplied code, together with some library predicates modelling operations performed by WSE. Also on the right, we have the TulaFale tool, which compiles its input scripts into the pure applied pi calculus to be analyzed via ProVerif.

TulaFale is a direct implementation of the pi calculus described in a previous formal semantics of web services authentication [BFG04a]. The original contribution of this paper is to present a concrete language design, to report an implementation of automatic verification of assertions in TulaFale scripts using Blanchet's ProVerif, and to develop a substantial example.

Section 2 informally introduces a simple request/response protocol and its security goals: authentication and correlation of the two messages. Section 3 presents TulaFale syntax for XML with symbolic cryptography and for predicates, and as a source of examples, explains a library of TulaFale predicates for constructing and checking SOAP messages. Section 4 describes predicates specific to the messages of our request/response protocol. Section 5 introduces processes and security assertions in TulaFale, and outlines their implementation via ProVerif. Section 6 describes processes and predicates specific to our protocol, and shows how to verify its security goals. Finally, Section 7 concludes.

2   A Simple Request/Response Protocol

We consider a simple SOAP-based request/response protocol, of the kind easily implemented using WSE to make an RPC to a web service. Our security goals are simply message authentication and correlation. To achieve these goals, the request includes a *username token* identifying a particular user and a *signature token* signed by a key derived from user's password; conversely, the response includes a signature token signed by the server's public key. Moreover, to preserve the confidentiality of the user's password from dictionary attacks, the username token in the request message is encrypted with the server's public key. (For simplicity, we are not concerned here with any secrecy properties, such as confidentiality of the actual message bodies, and we do not model any authorization policies.)

In the remainder of this section, we present a detailed but informal specification of our intended protocol, and consider some variations subject to XML rewriting attacks. Our protocol involves the following principals:

- A single certification authority (CA) issuing X.509 public-key certificates for services, signed with the CA's private key.
- Two servers, each equipped with a public key certified by the CA and exporting an arbitrary number of web services.
- Multiple clients, acting on behalf of human users.

Trust between principals is modelled as a database associating passwords to authorized user names, accessible from clients and servers. Our threat model features an active attacker in control of the network, in possession of all public keys and user names, but not in possession of any of the following:

(1) The private key of the CA.
(2) The private key of any public key certified by the CA.
(3) The password of any user in the database.

The second and third points essentially rule out "insider attacks"; we are assuming that the clients, servers, and CA belong to a single close-knit institution. It is easy to extend our model to study the impact of insider attacks, and indeed to allow more than two servers, but we omit the details in this expository example.

Fig. 2 shows an intended run of the protocol between a client and server.

- The principal Client(kr,U) acts on behalf of a user identified by U (an XML encoding of the username and password). The parameter kr is the public key of the CA, needed by the client to check the validity of public key certificates.
- The principal Server(sx,cert,S) implements a service identified by S (an XML encoding of a URL address, a SOAP action, and the subject name appearing on the service's certificate). The parameter sx is the server's private signing key, while cert is its public certificate.
- The client sends a request message satisfying isMsg1($-$,U,S,id1,t1,b1), which we define later to mean the message has body b1, timestamp t1, and message

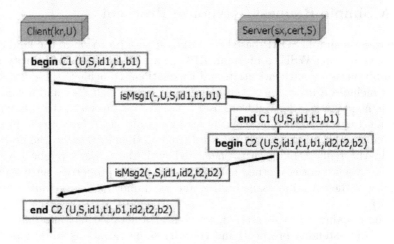

Fig. 2. An intended run of a client and server

identifier id1, is addressed to a web service S, and has a `<Security>` header
containing a token identifying U and encrypted with S's public key, and a
signature of S, id1, t1, and b1 by U.
- The server sends a response message satisfying isMsg2($-$,S,id1,id2,t2,b2),
  which we define later to mean the message has body b2, timestamp t2,
  and message identifier id2, is sent from S, and has a `<Security>` header
  containing S's certificate cert and a signature of id1, id2, t2, and b2 by S.
- The client and server enact begin- and end-events labelled C1(U,S,id1,t1,b1)
  to record the data agreed after receipt of the first message. Similarly, the
  begin- and end-events labelled C2(U,S,id1,t1,b1,id2,t2,b2) record the data
  agreed after both messages are received. Each begin-event marks an intention
  to send data. Each end-event marks apparently successful agreement on data.

The begin- and end-events define our authentication and correlation goals: for
every end-event with a particular label, there is a preceding begin-event with the
same label in any run of the system, even in the presence of an active attacker.
Such goals are known as one-to-many correspondences [WL93] or non-injective
agreements [Low97]. The C1 events specify authentication of the request, while
the C2 events specify authentication of the response. By including data from the
request, C2 events also specify correlation of the request and response.

Like most message sequence notations, Fig. 2 simply illustrates a typical
protocol run, and is not in itself an adequate specification. In Sections 4 and 6 we
present a formal specification in TulaFale: we define the principals Client(kr,U)
and Server(sx,cert,S) as parametric processes, and we define the checks isMsg1
and isMsg2 as predicates on our model of XML with symbolic cryptography. The
formal model clarifies the following points, which are left implicit in the figure:

Suppose a client does not sign the timestamp t1...

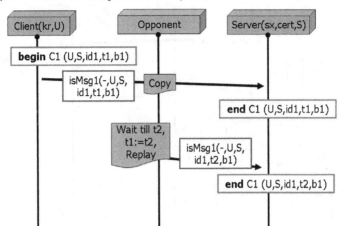

Fig. 3. A replay attack

- The client can arbitrarily choose which service S to call, and which data
  t1 and b1 to send. (In the formal model, we typically make such arbitrary
  choices by inputting the data from the opponent.) Conversely, the client
  must generate a fresh identifier id1 for each request, or else it is impossible to
  correlate the responses from two simultaneous requests to the same service.
- Similarly, the server can arbitrarily choose the response data id2, t2, and b2.

On the other hand, our formal model does not directly address replay protection. To rule out direct replays of correctly signed messages, we would need
to specify that for each end-event there is a unique preceding begin-event with
the same label. This is known as a one-to-one correspondence or injective agreement. In practice, we can protect against direct replays using a cache of recently
received message identifiers and timestamps to ensure that no two messages are
accepted with the same identifier and timestamp. Hence, if we can prove that
the protocol establishes non-injective agreement on data including the identifiers
and timestamps, then, given such replay protection, the protocol implementation
also establishes injective agreement.

We end this section by discussing some flawed variations of the protocol,
corresponding to actual flaws we have encountered in user code for web services.

- Suppose that the check isMsg1(−,U,S,id1,t1,b1) only requires that S, id1, and
  b1, are signed by U, but not the timestamp t1. Replay protection based on
  the timestamp is now ineffective: the opponent can record a message with
  timestamp t1, wait until some time t2 when the timestamp has expired,
  and the message identifier id1 is no longer being cached, rewrite the original

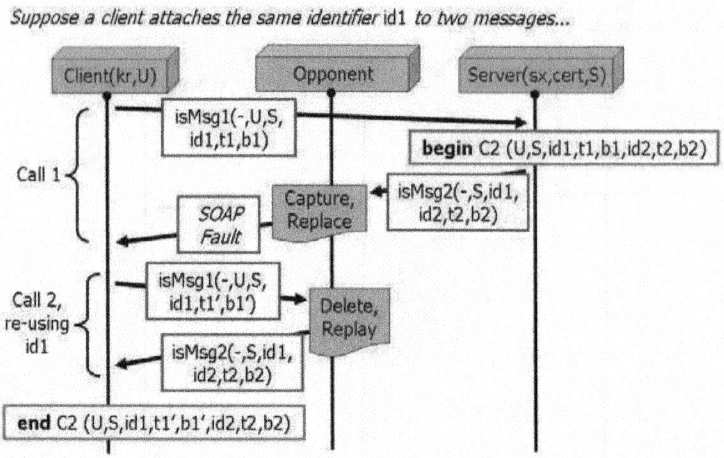

Suppose a client attaches the same identifier id1 to two messages...

Fig. 4. A failure of message correlation

message with timestamp t2, and then replay the message. The resulting message satisfies isMsg1($-$,U,S,id1,t2,b1), since t2 does not need to be signed, and hence is accepted by the server. Fig. 3 shows the attack, and the resulting failure of correspondence C1.

– Suppose that a client re-uses the same message identifier in two different calls to a web service; the opponent can manipulate messages so that the client treats the response to the first call as if it were the response to the second call. Fig. 4 shows the attack. The client sends a first request with body b1 and identifier id1. The opponent intercepts the response with body b2, and sends a SOAP fault back to the client. Subsequently, the client sends a second request with the same identifier id1 as the first, and body b1'. The opponent can delete this request to prevent it reaching the service, and then replay the original response. The client now considers that b2 is the response to b1', when in fact it is the response to b1, perhaps completely different. Formally, this is a failure of correspondence C2.

– Suppose that the server does not include the request identifier id1 in the signature on the response message. Then the opponent can mount a similar correlation attack, breaking C2—we omit the details.

We can easily adapt our TulaFale script to model these variations in the protocol. Our tool automatically and swiftly detects the errors, and returns descriptions of the messages sent during the attacks. These flaws in web services code are typical of errors in cryptographic protocols historically. The practical impact of these flaws is hard to assess, as they were found in preliminary code, before deployment. Still, it is prudent to eliminate these vulnerabilities, and tools such as TulaFale can systematically rule them out.

3   XML, Principals, and Cryptography in TulaFale

This section introduces the term and predicate language of TulaFale, via a series of basic constructions needed for the example protocol of Section 2. Throughout the paper, for the sake of exposition, we elide some details of SOAP envelopes, such as certain headers and attributes, that are unconnected to security.

3.1   XML Elements, Attributes, and Strings

Here is a TulaFale term for a SOAP request, illustrating the format of the first message in our example protocol:

```
<Envelope>
  <Header>
    <To>uri</>
    <Action>ac</>
    <MessageId>id</>
    <Security>
      <Timestamp><Created>"2004-03-19T09:46:32Z"</></>
      utok
      sig
    </>
  </>
  <Body Id="1">request</>
</>
```

Every SOAP message consists of an XML `<Envelope>` element, with two children: an optional `<Header>` and a mandatory `<Body>`. In this example, the header has four children, and the body has an Id-attribute, the literal string "1".

We base TulaFale on a sorted (or typed) term algebra, built up from a set of function symbols and variables. The basic sorts for XML data include **string** (for string literals), **att** (for named attributes), and **item** (either an element or a string). Every element or attribute tag (such as Envelope or Id, for example) corresponds to a sorted function symbol in the underlying algebra.

Although TulaFale syntax is close to the XML wire format, it is not identical. We suppress all namespace information. As previously mentioned, we omit closing element tags; for example, we write `</>` instead of `</Envelope>`. Literal strings are always quoted, as in `<Created>"2004-03-19T09:46:32Z"</>`. In the standard wire format, the double quotes would be omitted when a string is an element body. We use quotation to distinguish strings from term variables, such as the variables uri, ac, id, utok, sig, and request in the example above.

3.2   Symbolic Cryptography

In TulaFale, we represent cryptographic algorithms symbolically, as function symbols that act on a sort **bytes** of byte arrays. Each function is either a data constructor, with no accompanying rewrite rule, or it is a destructor, equipped with a rewrite rule for testing or extracting data from an application of a constructor.

For example, encryption functions are constructors, and decryption functions are destructors. This approach, the basis of the Dolev-Yao model [DY83], assumes that the underlying cryptography is *perfect*, and can be faithfully reflected by abstract equational properties of the functions. It also abstracts some details, such as the lengths of strings and byte arrays. The TulaFale syntax for introducing constructors and destructors is based on the syntax used by ProVerif.

For instance, we declare function symbols for RSA key generation, public-key encryption, and private-key decryption using the following TulaFale declarations:

constructor pk(**bytes**):**bytes**.
constructor rsa(**bytes**,**bytes**):**bytes**.
destructor decrsa(**bytes**,**bytes**):**bytes with**
  decrsa(s,rsa(pk(s),b)) = b.

The constructor pk represents the relationship between private and public keys (both byte arrays, of sort **bytes**); it takes a private key and returns the corresponding public key. There is no inverse or destructor, as we intend to represent a one-way function: given only pk(s) it is impossible to extract s.

The constructor rsa(k,x) encrypts the data x:**bytes** under the public key k, producing an encrypted byte array. The destructor decrsa(s,e) uses the corresponding private key s to decrypt a byte array generated by rsa(pk(s),x). The destructor definition expresses the decryption operation as a rewrite rule: when an application of decrsa in a term matches the left-hand side of the rule, it may be replaced by the corresponding right-hand side.

To declare RSA public-key signatures, we introduce another constructor rsasha1(s,x) that produces a RSA signature of a cryptographic hash of data x under the private key s:

constructor rsasha1(**bytes**,**bytes**):**bytes**.
destructor checkrsasha1(**bytes**,**bytes**,**bytes**):**bytes with**
  checkrsasha1(pk(s),x,rsasha1(s,x))=pk(s).

To check the validity of a signature sig on x using a public key k, one can form the term checkrsasha1(k,x,sig) and compare it to k. If k is a public key of the form pk(s) and sig is the result of signing x under the corresponding private key s, then this term rewrites to k.

For the purposes of this paper, an X.509 certificate binds a key to a subject name by embedding a digital signature generated from the private key of some certifying authority (CA). We declare X.509 certificates as follows:

constructor x509(**bytes**,**string**,**string**,**bytes**):**bytes**.
destructor x509key(**bytes**):**bytes with**
  x509key(x509(s,u,a,k))=k.
destructor x509user(**bytes**):**string with**
  x509user(x509(s,u,a,k))=u.
destructor x509alg(**bytes**):**string with**
  x509alg(x509(s,u,a,k))=a.
destructor checkx509(**bytes**,**bytes**):**bytes with**
  checkx509(x509(sr,u,a,k),pk(sr))=pk(sr).

The term x509(sr,u,a,k) represents a certificate that binds the subject name u to the public key k, for use with the signature algorithm a (typically rsasha1). This certificate is signed by the CA with private key sr. Given such a certificate, the destructors x509key, x509user, and x509alg extract the three public fields of the certificate. Much like checkrsasha1 for ordinary digital signatures, an additional destructor checkx509 can be used to check the authenticity of the embedded signature.

3.3   XML Encryption and Decryption

Next, we write logical predicates to construct and parse XML encrypted under some known RSA public key. A predicate is written using a Prolog-like syntax; it takes a tuple of terms and checks logical properties, such as whether two terms are equal or whether a term has a specific format. It is useful to think of some of the terms given to the predicate as inputs and the others as outputs. Under this interpretation, the predicate computes output terms that satisfy the logical properties by pattern-matching.

The predicate mkEncryptedData takes a plaintext plain:**item** and an RSA public encryption key ek:**bytes**, and it generates an XML element encrypted containing the XML encoding of plain encrypted under ek.

```
predicate mkEncryptedData (encrypted:item,plain:item,ek:bytes) :−
    cipher = rsa(ek,c14n(plain)),
    encrypted = <EncryptedData>
                    <CipherData>
                    <CipherValue>base64(cipher)</></></>.
```

The first binding in the predicate definition computes the encrypted byte array, cipher, using the rsa encryption function applied to the key ek and the plaintext plain. Since rsa is only defined over byte arrays, plain:**item** is first converted to **bytes** using the (reversible) c14n constructor. The second binding generates an XML element (`<EncryptedData>`) containing the encrypted bytes. Since only strings or elements can be embedded into XML elements, the encrypted byte array, cipher, is first converted to a string using the (reversible) base64 constructor.

In this paper, we use three transformation functions between sorts: c14n (with inverse ic14n) transforms an **item** to a **bytes**, base64 (with inverse ibase64) transforms a **bytes** to a **string**, and utf8 (with inverse iutf8) transforms a **string** to a **bytes**. All three functions have specific meanings in the context of XML transformations, but we treat them simply as coercion functions between sorts.

To process a given element, `<Foo>` say, we sometimes write distinct predicates on the sending side and on the receiving side of the protocol, respectively. By convention, to construct a `<Foo>` element, we write a predicate named mkFoo whose first parameter is the element being constructed; to parse and check it, we write a predicate named isFoo.

For `<EncryptedData>`, for instance, the logical predicate isEncryptedData parses elements constructed by mkEncryptedData; it takes an element encrypted and a decryption key dk:**bytes** and, if encrypted is an `<EncryptedData>` element with some plaintext encrypted under the corresponding encryption key pk(dk), it returns the plaintext as plain.

predicate isEncryptedData (encrypted:**item**,plain:**item**,dk:**bytes**) :−
    encrypted = `<EncryptedData>`
                `<CipherData>`
                    `<CipherValue>`base64(cipher)`</></></>`,
    c14n(plain) = decrsa(dk,cipher).

Abstractly, this predicate reverses the computations performed by mkEncryptedData. One difference, of course, is that while mkEncryptedData is passed the public encryption key ek, the isEncryptedData predicate is instead passed the private key, dk. The first line matches encrypted against a pattern representing the `<EncryptedData>` element, extracting the encrypted byte array, cipher. Relying on pattern-matching, the constructor base64 is implicitly inverted using its destructor ibase64. The second line decrypts cipher using the decryption key dk, and implicitly inverts c14n using its destructor ic14n to compute plain.

3.4   Services and X509 Security Tokens

We now implement processing for the service identifiers used in Section 2. We identify each web service by a structure consisting of a `<Service>` element containing `<To>`, `<Action>`, and `<Subject>` elements. For message routing, the web service is identified by the HTTP URL uri where it is located and the name of the action ac to be invoked at the URL. (In SOAP, there may be several different actions available at the same uri.) The web service is then willing to accept any SOAP message with a `<To>` header containing uri and an `<Action>` header containing ac. Each service has a public key with which parts of requests may be encrypted, and parts of responses signed. The `<Subject>` element contains the subject name bound to the server's public key by the X.509 certificate issued by the CA. For generality, we do not assume any relationship between the URL and subject name of a service, although in practice the subject name might contain the domain part of the URL.

The logical predicate isService parses a service element to extract the `<To>` field as uri, the `<Action>` field as ac, and the `<Subject>` field as subj:

predicate isService(S:**item**,uri:**item**,ac:**item**,subj:**string**) :−
    S = `<Service><To>`uri`</>` `<Action>`ac`</>` `<Subject>`subj`</></>`.

We also define predicates to parse X.509 certificates and to embed them in SOAP headers:

predicate isX509Cert (xcert:**bytes**,kr:**bytes**,u:**string**,a:**string**,k:**bytes**) :−
    checkx509(xcert,kr) = kr,
    u = x509user(xcert),
    k = x509key(xcert),
    a = x509alg(xcert).

predicate isX509Token (tok:**item**,kr:**bytes**,u:**string**,a:**string**,k:**bytes**) :−
  tok = <BinarySecurityToken ValueType="X509v3">base64(xcert)</>,
  isX509Cert (xcert,kr,u,a,k).

The predicate isX509Cert takes a byte array xcert containing an X.509 certificate, checks that it has been issued by a certifying authority with public key kr, and extracts the user name u, its user public key k, and its signing algorithm a. In SOAP messages, certificates are carried in XML elements called security tokens. The predicate isX509Token checks that an XML token element contains a valid X.509 certificate and extracts the relevant fields.

3.5   Users and Username Security Tokens

In our system descriptions, we identify each user by a <User> element that contains their username and password. The predicate isUser takes such an element, U, and extracts its embedded username u and password pwd.

  U = <User><Username>u</><Password>pwd</></>.

In SOAP messages, the username is represented by a UsernameToken that contains the <Username> u, a freshly generated nonce n, and a timestamp t. The predicate isUserTokenKey takes such a token tok and extracts u, n, t, and then uses a user U for u to compute a key from pwd, n, and t.

predicate isUserTokenKey (tok:**item**,U:**item**,n:**bytes**,t:**string**,k:**bytes**) :−
  isUser(U,u,pwd),
  tok = <UsernameToken @ _>
          <Username>u</>
          <Nonce>base64(n)</>
          <Created>t</></>,
  k = psha1(pwd,concat(n,utf8(t))).

The first line parses U to extract the username u and password pwd. The second line parses tok to extract n and t, implicitly checking that the username u is the same. In TulaFale, lists of terms are written as $tm_1 \ldots tm_m @ \, tm$ with $m \geq 0$, where the terms tm_1, ..., tm_m are the first m members of the list, and the optional term tm is the rest of the list. Here, the wildcard @ _ of the <UsernameToken> element matches the entire list of attributes. The last line computes the key k by applying the cryptographic hash function psha1 to pwd, n, and t (converted to **bytes**). (This formula for k is a slight simplification of the actual key derivation algorithm used by WSE.) The concat function returns the concatenation of two byte arrays.

3.6   Polyadic Signatures

An XML digital signature consists of a list of references to the elements being signed, together with a *signature value* that binds hashes of these elements using some signing secret. The signature value can be computed using several different cryptographic algorithms; in our example protocol, we rely on hmacsha1 for user signatures and on rsasha1 for service signatures.

The following predicates describe how to construct (mkSigVal) and check (isSigVal) the signature value sv of an XML element si, signed using the algorithm a with a key k. Each of these predicates is defined by a couple of clauses, representing symmetric and asymmetric signature algorithms. When a predicate is defined by multiple clauses, they are interpreted as a disjunction; that is, the predicate is satisfied if any one of its clauses is satisfied.

predicate mkSigVal (sv:**bytes**,si:**item**,k:**bytes**,a:**string**) :−
  a = "hmacsha1", sv = hmacsha1(k,c14n(si)).

predicate isSigVal (sv:**bytes**,si:**item**,k:**bytes**,a:**string**) :−
  a = "hmacsha1", sv = hmacsha1(k,c14n(si)).

predicate mkSigVal (sv:**bytes**,si:**item**,k:**bytes**,a:**string**) :−
  a = "rsasha1", sv = rsasha1(k, c14n(si)).

predicate isSigVal (sv:**bytes**,si:**item**,p:**bytes**,a:**string**) :−
  a = "rsasha1", p = checkrsasha1(p,c14n(si),sv).

The first clause of mkSigVal takes an item si to be signed and a key k for the symmetric signing algorithm hmacsha1, and generates the signature value sv. The first clause of isSigVal reverses this computation, taking sv, si, k, and a = "hmacsha1" as input and checking that sv is a valid signature value of si under k. Since the algorithm is symmetric, the two clauses are identical. The second clause of mkSigVal computes the signature value using the asymmetric rsasha1 algorithm, and the corresponding clause of isSigVal checks this signature value. In contrast to the symmetric case, the two clauses rely on different computations.

A complete XML signature for a SOAP message contains both the signature value sv, as detailed above, and an explicit description of the message parts are used to generate si. Each signed item is represented by a <Reference> element.

The predicate mkRef takes an item t and generates a <Reference> element r by embedding a sha1 hash of t, with appropriate sort conversions. Conversely, the predicate isRef checks that r is a <Reference> for t.

predicate mkRef(t:**item**,r:**item**) :−
  r = <Reference>
        <Other></> <Other></>
        <DigestValue> base64(sha1(c14n(t))) </> </>.

predicate isRef(t:**item**,r:**item**) :−
  r = <Reference>
        − −
        <DigestValue> base64(sha1(c14n(t))) </> </>.

(The XML constructed by mkRef abstracts some of the detail that is included in actual signatures, but that tends not to vary in practice; in particular, we include `<Other>` elements instead of the standard `<Transforms>` and `<DigestMethod>` elements. On the other hand, the `<DigestValue>` element is the part that depends on the subject of the signature, and that is crucial for security, and we model this element in detail.)

More generally, the predicate mkRefs(ts,rs) constructs a list ts and from a list rs, such that their members are pairwise related by mkRef. Similarly, the predicate mkRefs(ts,rs) checks that two given lists are pairwise related by mkRef. We omit their definitions.

A `<SignedInfo>` element is constructed from `<Reference>` elements for every signed element. A `<Signature>` element consists of a `<SignedInfo>` element si and a `<SignatureValue>` element containing sv. Finally, the following predicates define how signatures are constructed and checked.

predicate mkSigInfo (si:**item**,a:**string**,ts:**item**) :−
  mkRefs(ts,rs),
  rs = `<list>`@ refs`</>`,
  si = `<SignedInfo>`
      `<Other></>` `<SignatureMethod Algorithm=a> </>`
      @ refs `</>`.

predicate isSigInfo (si:**item**,a:**string**,ts:**item**) :−
  si = `<SignedInfo>`
    _ `<SignatureMethod Algorithm=a> </>`
    @ refs`</>`,
  rs = `<list>`@ refs`</>`,
  isRefs(ts,rs).

predicate mkSignature (sig:**item**,a:**string**,k:**bytes**,ts:**item**) :−
  mkSigInfo(si,a,ts),
  mkSigVal(sv,si,k,a),
  sig = `<Signature>` si `<SignatureValue>` base64(sv) `</>` `</>`.

predicate isSignature (sig:**item**,a:**string**,k:**bytes**,ts:**item**) :−
  sig = `<Signature>` si `<SignatureValue>` base64(sv) `</>`@ _`</>`,
  isSigInfo(si,a,ts),
  isSigVal(sv,si,k,a).

The predicate mkSigInfo takes a list of items to be signed, embedded in a `<list>` element ts, and generates a list of references refs for them, embedded in a `<list>` element rs, which are then embedded into si. The predicate isSigInfo checks si has been correctly constructed from ts.

The predicate mkSignature constructs si using mkSigInfo, generates the signature value sv using mkSigVal, and puts them together in a `<Signature>` element called sig; isSignature checks that a signature sig has been correctly generated from a, k, and ts.

4   Modelling SOAP Envelopes for our Protocol

Relying on the predicate definitions of Section 3, which reflect (parts of) the
SOAP and WS-Security specifications but do not depend on the protocol, we
now define custom "top-level" predicates to build and check Messages 1 and 2
of our example protocol.

4.1   Building and Checking Message 1

Our goal C1 is to reach agreement on the data

  $(U,S,id1,t1,b1)$

where

```
U=<User><Username>u</><Password>pwd</></>
S=<Service><To>uri</><Action>ac</><Subject>subj</></>
```

after receiving and successfully checking Message 1. To achieve this, the message
includes a username token for U, encrypted with the public key of S (that is, one
whose certificate has the subject name subj), and also includes a signature token,
signing (elements containing) uri, ac, id1, t1, b1, and the encrypted username
token, signed with the key derived from the username token.

We begin with a predicate setting the structure of the first envelope:

predicate env1(msg1:**item**,uri:**item**,ac:**item**,id1:**string**,t1:**string**,
                eutok:**item**,sig1:**item**,b1:**item**) :−

```
msg1 =
  <Envelope>
    <Header>
      <To>uri</>
      <Action>ac</>
      <MessageId>id1</>
      <Security>
        <Timestamp><Created>t1</></>
        eutok
        sig1</></>
      <Body>b1</></>.
```

On the client side, we use a predicate mkMsg1 to construct msg1 as an output,
given its other parameters as inputs:

predicate mkMsg1(msg1:**item**,U:**item**,S:**item**,kr:**bytes**,cert:**bytes**,
                n:**bytes**,id1:**string**,t1:**string**,b1:**item**) :−

```
isService(S,uri,ac,subj),
isX509Cert(cert,kr,subj,"rsasha1",ek),
isUserTokenKey(utok,U,n,t1,sk),
mkEncryptedData(eutok,utok,ek),
mkSignature(sig1,"hmacsha1",sk,
  <list>
```

```
    <Body>b1</>
    <To>uri</>
    <Action>ac</>
    <MessageId>id1</>
    <Created>t1</>
    eutok</>),
 env1(msg1,uri,ac,id1,t1,eutok,sig1,b1).
```

On the server side, with server certificate cert, associated private key sx, and expected user U, we use a predicate isMsg1 to check the input msg1 and produce S, id1, t1, and b1 as outputs:

predicate isMsg1(msg1:**item**,U:**item**,sx:**bytes**,cert:**bytes**,S:**item**,
                  id1:**string**,t1:**string**,b1:**item**) :−
    env1(msg1,uri,ac,id1,t1,eutok,sig1,b1),
    isService(S,uri,ac,subj),
    isEncryptedData(eutok,utok,sx),
    isUserTokenKey(utok,U,n,t1,sk),
    isSignature(sig1,"hmacsha1",sk,
```
      <list>
      <Body>b1</>
      <To>uri</>
      <Action>ac</>
      <MessageId>id1</>
      <Created>t1</>
      eutok</>).
```

4.2   Building and Checking Message 2

Our goal C2 is to reach agreement on the data

    (U,S,id1,t1,b1,id2,t2,b2)

where

    U=<User><Username>u</><Password>pwd</></>
    S=<Service><To>uri</><Action>ac</><Subject>subj</></>

after successful receipt of Message 2, having already agreed on

    (U,S,id1,t1,b1)

after receipt of Message 1.

A simple implementation is to make sure that the client's choice of id1 in Message 1 is fresh and unpredictable, to include `<relatesTo>id1</>` in Message 2, and to embed this element in the signature to achieve correlation with the data sent in Message 1. In more detail, Message 2 includes a certificate for S (that is, one with subject name subj) and a signature token, signing (elements containing) id1, id2, t2, and b2 and signed using the private key associated with S's certificate. The structure of the second envelope is defined as follows:

predicate env2(msg2:**item**,uri:**item**,id1:**string**,id2:**string**,
          t2:**string**,cert:**bytes**,sig2:**item**,b2:**item**) :−
  msg2 =
    <Envelope>
     <Header>
      <From>uri</>
      <RelatesTo>id1</>
      <MessageId>id2</>
      <Security>
        <Timestamp><Created>t2</></>
        <BinarySecurityToken>base64(cert)</>
        sig2</></>
     <Body>b2</></>.

A server uses the predicate mkMsg2 to construct msg2 as an output, given its other parameters as inputs (including the signing key):

predicate mkMsg2(msg2:**item**,sx:**bytes**,cert:**bytes**,S:**item**,
          id1:**string**,id2:**string**,t2:**string**,b2:**item**):−
  isService(S,uri,ac,subj),
  mkSignature(sig2,"rsasha1",sx,
    <list>
     <Body>b2</>
     <RelatesTo>id1</>
     <MessageId>id2</>
     <Created>t2</></>),
  env2(msg2,uri,id1,id2,t2,cert,sig2,b2).

A client, given the CA's public key kr, and awaiting a response from S to a message with unique identifier id1, uses the predicate isMsg2 to check its input msg2, and produce data id2, t2, and b2 as outputs.

predicate isMsg2(msg2:**item**,S:**item**,kr:**bytes**,
          id1:**string**,id2:**string**,t2:**string**,b2:**item**) :−
  env2(msg2,uri,id1,id2,t2,cert,sig2,b2),
  isService(S,uri,ac,subj),
  isX509Cert(cert,kr,subj,"rsasha1",k),
  isSignature(sig2,"rsasha1",k,
    <list>
     <Body>b2</>
     <RelatesTo>id1</>
     <MessageId>id2</>
     <Created>t2</></>).

5   Processes and Assertions in TulaFale

A TulaFale script defines a system to be a collection of concurrent processes that may compute internally, using terms and predicates, and may also communicate by exchanging terms on named channels. The top-level process defined by a TulaFale script represents the behaviour of the principals making up the system—some clients and servers in our example. The attacker is modelled as an arbitrary process running alongside the system defined by the script, interacting with it via the public channels. The style of modelling cryptographic protocols, with an explicit given process representing the system and an implicit arbitrary process representing the attacker, originates with the spi calculus [AG99]. We refer to the principals coded explicitly as processes in the script as being *compliant*, in the sense they are constrained to follow the protocol being modelled, as opposed to the non-compliant principals represented implicitly by the attacker process, who are not so constrained.

A TulaFale script consists of a sequence of declarations. We have seen already in Sections 3 and 4 many examples of Prolog-style declarations of clauses defining named predicates. This section describe three further kinds of declaration—for channels, correspondence assertions, and processes. Section 6 illustrate their usage in a script that models the system of Section 2.

We describe TulaFale syntax in terms of several metavariables or nonterminals: *sort*, *term*, and *form* range over the sorts, algebraic terms, and logical formulas, respectively, as introduced in Section 3; and *ide* ranges over alphanumeric identifiers, used to name variables, predicates, channels, processes, and correspondence assertions.

A declaration **channel** $ide(sort_1, \ldots, sort_n)$ introduces a channel, named *ide*, for exchanging n-tuples of terms with sorts $sort_1, \ldots, sort_n$. As in the asynchronous pi calculus, channels are named, unordered queues of messages. By default, each channel is public, that is, the attacker may input or output messages on the channel. The declaration may be preceded by the **private** keyword to prevent the attacker accessing the channel. Typically, SOAP channels are public, but channels used to represent shared secrets, such as passwords, are private.

In TulaFale, as in some forms of the spi calculus, we embed correspondence assertions in our process language in order to state certain security properties enjoyed by compliant principals.

A declaration **correspondence** $ide(sort_1, \ldots, sort_n)$ introduces a label, *ide*, for events represented by n-tuples of terms with sorts $sort_1, \ldots, sort_n$. Each event is either a begin-event or an end-event; typically, a begin-event records an initiation of a session, and an end-event records the satisfactory completion of a session, from the compliant principals' viewpoint. The process language includes constructs for logging begin- and end-events. The attacker cannot observe or generate events. We use correspondences to formalize the properties (C1) and (C2) of Section 2. The declaration of a correspondence on *ide* specifies a security assertion: that in any run of the explicit system composed with an arbitrary implicit attacker, every end-event labelled *ide* logged by the system corresponds to a previous begin-event logged by the system, also labelled *ide*, and with the same tuple of data. We name this property *robust safety*, following Gordon and Jeffrey [GJ03]. The implication of robust safety is that two compliant processes have reached agreement on the data, which typically include the contents of a sequence of one or more messages.

A declaration **process** $ide(ide_1{:}sort_1, \ldots, ide_n{:}sort_n) = proc$ defines a parametric process, with body the process *proc*, named *ide*, whose parameters ide_1, $\ldots$, ide_n have sorts $sort_1, \ldots, sort_n$, respectively.

Next, we describe the various kinds of TulaFale process.

- A process **out** $ide(tm_1, \ldots, tm_n)$; *proc* sends the tuple $(tm_1, \ldots, tm_n)$ on the *ide* channel, then runs *proc*.
- A process **in** $ide(ide_1, \ldots, ide_n)$; *proc* blocks awaiting a tuple $(tm_1, \ldots, tm_n)$ on the *ide* channel; if one arrives, the process behaves as *proc*, with its parameters $ide_1, \ldots, ide_n$ bound to $tm_1, \ldots, tm_n$, respectively.
- A process **new** *ide*:**bytes**; *proc* binds the variable *ide* to a fresh byte array, to model cryptographic key or nonce generation, for instance, then runs *proc*. Similarly, a process **new** *ide*:**string**; *proc* binds the variable *ide* to a fresh string, to model password generation, for instance, then runs as *proc*.
- A process $proc_1|proc_2$ is a parallel composition of subprocesses $proc_1$ and $proc_2$; they run in parallel, and may communicate on shared channels.
- A process $!proc$ is a parallel composition of an unbounded array of replicas of the process *proc*.
- The process 0 does nothing.
- A process **let** $ide = tm$; *proc* binds the term *tm* to the variable *ide*, then runs *proc*.
- A process **filter** $form \rightarrow ide_1, \ldots, ide_n$; *proc* binds terms $tm_1, \ldots, tm_n$ to the variables $ide_1, \ldots, ide_n$ such that the formula *form* holds, then runs *proc*. (The terms $tm_1, \ldots, tm_n$ are computed by pattern-matching, as described in a previous paper [BFG04a].)
- A process $ide(tm_1, \ldots, tm_n)$, where *ide* corresponds to a declaration **process** $ide(ide_1{:}sort_1, \ldots, ide_n{:}sort_n) = proc$ binds the terms $tm_1, \ldots, tm_n$ to the variables $ide_1, \ldots, ide_n$, then runs *proc*.
- A process **begin** $ide(tm_1, \ldots, tm_n)$; *proc* logs a begin-event labelled with *ide* and the tuple $(tm_1, \ldots, tm_n)$, then runs *proc*.
- A process **end** $ide(tm_1, \ldots, tm_n)$; *proc* logs an end-event labelled with *ide* and the tuple $(tm_1, \ldots, tm_n)$, then runs *proc*.
- Finally, the process **done** logs a done-event. (We typically mark the successful completion of the whole protocol with **done**. Checking for the reachability of the done-event is then a basic check of the functionality of the protocol, that it may run to completion.)

The main goal of the TulaFale tool is to prove or refute robust safety for all the correspondences declared in a script. Robust safety may be proved by a range of techniques; the first paper on TulaFale [BFG04a] uses manually developed proofs of behavioural equivalence. Instead, our TulaFale tool translates scripts into the applied pi calculus, and then runs Blanchet's resolution-based protocol verifier;

the translation is essentially the same as originally described [BFG04a]. ProVerif (hence TulaFale) can also check secrecy assertions, but we omit the details here. In addition, TulaFale includes a sort-checker and a simulator, both of which help catch basic errors during the development of scripts. For example, partly relying on the translation, TulaFale can show the reachability of **done** processes, which is useful for verifying that protocols may actually run to completion.

6   Modelling and Verifying Our Protocol

Relying on the predicates given in Section 4, we now define the processes modelling our sample system.

6.1   Modelling the System with TulaFale Processes

In our example, a public channel publish gives the attacker access to the certificates and public keys of the CA and two servers, named "BobsPetShop" and "ChasMarket". Another channel soap is for exchanging all SOAP messages; it is public to allow the attacker to read and write any SOAP message.

channel publish(**item**).
channel soap(**item**).

The following is the top-level process, representing the behaviour of all compliant principals.

new sr:**bytes**; **let** kr = pk(sr);
new sx1:**bytes**; **let** cert1 = x509(sr,"BobsPetShop","rsasha1",pk(sx1));
new sx2:**bytes**; **let** cert2 = x509(sr,"ChasMarket","rsasha1",pk(sx2));
out publish(base64(kr));
out publish(base64(cert1));
out publish(base64(cert2));
(!MkUser(kr) |!MkService(sx1,cert1) |!MkService(sx2,cert2) |
  (!**in** anyUser(U); Client(kr,U)) |
  (!**in** anyService(sx,cert,S); Server(sx,cert,S)))

The process begins by generating the private and public keys, sr and kr, of the CA. It generates the private keys, sx1 and sx2, of the two servers, plus their certificates, cert1 and cert2. Then it outputs the public data kr, cert1, cert2 to the attacker. After this initialization, the system behaves as the following parallel composition of five processes.

!MkUser(kr) |!MkService(sx1,cert1) |!MkService(sx2,cert2) |
(!**in** anyUser(U); Client(kr,U)) |
(!**in** anyService(sx,cert,S); Server(sx,cert,S)

As explained earlier, the ! symbol represents unbounded replication; each of these processes may execute arbitrarily many times. The first process allows the opponent to generate fresh username/password combinations that are shared between all clients and servers. The second and third allow the opponent to generate fresh services with subject names "BobsPetShop" and "ChasMarket", respectively. The fourth acts as an arbitrary client U, and the fifth acts as an arbitrary service S.

The process MkUser inputs the name of a user from the environment on channel genUser, then creates a new password and records the username/password combination U as a message on private channel anyUser, representing the database of authorized users.

```
channel genUser(string).
private channel anyUser(item).
process MkUser(kr:bytes) =
  in genUser(u);
  new pwd:string;
  let U = <User><Username>u</><Password>pwd</></>;
  !out anyUser (U).
```

The process MkService allows the attacker to create services with the subject name of the certificate cert.

```
predicate isServiceData(S:item,sx:bytes,cert:bytes) :−
  isService(S,uri,ac,x509user(cert)),
  pk(sx) = x509key(cert).


channel genService(item).
private channel anyService(bytes,bytes,item).
process MkService(sx:bytes,cert:bytes) =
  in genService(S);
  filter isServiceData(S,sx,cert) → ;
  !out anyService(sx,cert,S).
```

Finally, we present the processes representing clients and servers. Our desired authentication and correlation properties are correspondence assertions embedded within these processes. We declare the sorts of data to be agreed by the clients and servers as follows.

```
correspondence C1(item,item,string,string,item).
correspondence C2(item,item,string,string,item,string,string,item).
```

The process Client(kr:bytes,U:item) acts as a client for the user U, assuming that kr is the CA's public key.

```
channel init(item,bytes,bytes,string,item).
process Client(kr:bytes,U:item) =
  in init (S,certA,n,t1,b1);
  new id1:string;
  begin C1 (U,S,id1,t1,b1);
  filter mkMsg1(msg1,U,S,kr,certA,n,id1,t1,b1) → msg1;
```

```
out soap(msg1);
in soap(msg2);
filter isMsg2(msg2,S,kr,id1,id2,t2,b2) → id2,t2,b2;
end C2 (U,S,id1,t1,b1,id2,t2,b2);
done.
```

The process generates a globally fresh, unpredictable identifier id1 for Message 1, to allow correlation of Message 2 as discussed above. It then allows the attacker to control the rest of the data to be sent by receiving it off the public init channel. Next, the TulaFale **filter** operator evaluates the predicate mkMsg1 to bind variable msg1 to Message 1. At this point, the client marks its intention to communicate data to the server by logging an end-event, labelled C1, and then outputs the message msg1. The process then awaits a reply, msg2, checks the reply with the predicate isMsg2, and if this check succeeds, ends the C2 correspondence. Finally, to mark the end of a run of the protocol, it becomes the **done** process—an inactive process, that does nothing, but whose reachability can be checked, as a basic test of the protocol description.

The process Server(sx:**bytes**,cert:**bytes**,S:**item**) represents a service S, with private key sx, and certificate cert.

```
channel accept(string,string,item).
process Server(sx:bytes,cert:bytes,S:item) =
    in soap(msg1);
    in anyUser(U);
    filter isMsg1(msg1,U,sx,cert,S,id1,t1,b1) → id1,t1,b1;
    end C1 (U,S,id1,t1,b1);

    in accept (id2,t2,b2);
    filter mkMsg2(msg2,sx,cert,S,id1,id2,t2,b2) → msg2;
    begin C2 (U,S,id1,t1,b1,id2,t2,b2);
    out soap(msg2).
```

The process begins by selecting a SOAP message msg1 and a user U off the public soap and the private anyUser channels, respectively. It filters this data with the isMsg1 predicate, which checks that msg1 is from U, and binds the variables S, id1, t1, and b1. At this point, it asserts an end-event, labelled C1, to signify apparent agreement on this data with a client. Next, the process inputs data from the opponent on channel accept, to determine the response message. The server process completes by using the predicate mkMsg2 to construct the response msg2, asserting a begin-event for the C2 correspondence, and finally sending the message.

6.2   Analysis

The TulaFale script for this example protocol consists of 200 lines specific to the protocol, and 200 lines of library predicates. (We have embedded essentially the whole script in this paper.) Given the applied pi calculus translation of this script, ProVerif shows that our two correspondences C1 and C2 are robustly safe. Failure of robust safety for C1 or C2 would reveal that the server or the client has failed to authenticate Message 1, or to authenticate Message 2 and correlate it with Message 1, respectively. Processing is swift enough—around 25s on a 2.4GHz 1GB P4—to support easy experimentation with variations in the protocol, specification, and threat model.

7   Conclusions

TulaFale is a high-level language based on XML with symbolic cryptography, clausally-defined predicates, pi calculus processes, and correspondence assertions. Previous work [BFG04a] introduces a preliminary version of TulaFale, defines its semantics via translation into the applied pi calculus [AF01], illustrates TulaFale via several single-message protocols, and describes hand-crafted correctness proofs.

The original reasons for choosing to model WS-Security protocols using the the pi calculus, rather than some other formal method, include the generality of the threat model (the attacker is an unbounded, arbitrary process), the ease of simulating executable specifications written in the pi calculus, and the existence of a sophisticated range of techniques for reasoning about cryptographic protocols.

Blanchet's ProVerif [Bla01, Bla02] turns out to be a further reason for using the pi calculus to study SOAP security. Our TulaFale tool directly implements the translation into the applied pi calculus and then invokes Blanchet's verifier, to obtain fully automatic checking of SOAP security protocols. This checking shows no attacker expressible as a formal process can violate particular SOAP-level authentication or secrecy properties. Hence, we expect TulaFale will be useful for describing and checking security aspects of web services specifications. We have several times been surprised by vulnerabilities discovered by the TulaFale tool and the underlying verifier. Of course, every validation method, formal or informal, abstracts some details of the underlying implementation, so checking with TulaFale only partially rules out attacks on actual implementations. Still, ongoing work is exploring how to detect vulnerabilities in web services deployments, by extracting TulaFale scripts from XML-based configuration data [BFG04b].

The request/response protocol presented here is comparable to the abstract RPC protocols proposed in earlier work on securing web services [GP03], but here we accurately model the SOAP and WS-Security syntax used on the wire. Compared with the SOAP-based protocols in the article introducing the TulaFale semantics [BFG04a], the novelties are the need for the client to correlate the request with the reply, and the use of encryption to protect weak user passwords from dictionary attacks. In future work, we intend to analyse more complex SOAP protocols, such as WS-SecureConversation [KN+04], for securing client-server sessions.

Although some other process calculi manipulate XML [BS03, GM03], they are not intended for security applications. We are beginning to see formal methods applied to web services specifications, such as the TLA+ specification [JLLV04] of the Web Services Atomic Transaction protocol, checked with the TLC model checker. Still, we are aware of no other security tool for web services able to analyze protocol descriptions for vulnerabilities to XML rewriting attacks.

Acknowledgement. We thank Bruno Blanchet for making ProVerif available, and for implementing extensions to support some features of TulaFale. Vittorio Bertocci, Ricardo Corin, Amit Midha, and the anonymous reviewers made useful comments on a draft of this paper.

References

[AF01]   M. Abadi and C. Fournet. Mobile values, new names, and secure communication. In *28th ACM Symposium on Principles of Programming Languages (POPL'01)*, pages 104–115, 2001.

[AG99]   M. Abadi and A. D. Gordon. A calculus for cryptographic protocols: The spi calculus. *Information and Computation*, 148:1–70, 1999.

[BEK+00]   D. Box, D. Ehnebuske, G. Kakivaya, A. Layman, N. Mendelsohn, H. Nielsen, S. Thatte, and D. Winer. *Simple Object Access Protocol (SOAP) 1.1*, 2000. W3C Note, at http://www.w3.org/TR/2000/NOTE-SOAP-20000508/.

[BFG04a]   K. Bhargavan, C. Fournet, and A. D. Gordon. A semantics for web services authentication. In *31st ACM Symposium on Principles of Programming Languages (POPL'04)*, pages 198–209, 2004.

[BFG04b]   K. Bhargavan, C. Fournet, and A. D. Gordon. Verifying policy-based security for web services. Submitted for publicaton, 2004.

[Bla01]   B. Blanchet. An Efficient Cryptographic Protocol Verifier Based on Prolog Rules. In *14th IEEE Computer Security Foundations Workshop (CSFW-14)*, pages 82–96. IEEE Computer Society, 2001.

[Bla02]   B. Blanchet. From Secrecy to Authenticity in Security Protocols. In *9th International Static Analysis Symposium (SAS'02)*, volume 2477 of *Lecture Notes on Computer Science*, pages 342–359. Springer, 2002.

[Box01]   D. Box. A brief history of SOAP. At http://webservices.xml.com/pub/a/ws/2001/04/04/soap.html, 2001.

[BS03]   G. Bierman and P. Sewell. Iota: a concurrent XML scripting language with application to Home Area Networks. Technical Report 557, University of Cambridge Computer Laboratory, 2003.

[DHK+04]   M. Davis, B. Hartman, C. Kaler, A. Nadalin, and J. Schwarz. *WS-I Security Scenarios*, February 2004. Working Group Draft Version 0.15, at http://www.ws-i.org/Profiles/BasicSecurity/2004-02/SecurityScenarios-0.15-WGD.pdf.

[DY83]   D. Dolev and A.C. Yao. On the security of public key protocols. *IEEE Transactions on Information Theory*, IT–29(2):198–208, 1983.

[GJ03]   A. D. Gordon and A. Jeffrey. Authenticity by typing for security protocols. *Journal of Computer Security*, 11(4):451–521, 2003.

[GM03]   P. Gardner and S. Maffeis. Modeling dynamic web data. In *DBPL'03*, LNCS. Springer, 2003.

[GP03]   A. D. Gordon and R. Pucella. Validating a web service security abstraction by typing. In *ACM Workshop on XML Security 2002*, pages 18–29, 2003.

[HL03]   M. Howard and D. LeBlanc. *Writing secure code*. Microsoft Press, second edition, 2003.

[IM02]   IBM Corporation and Microsoft Corporation. Security in a web services world: A proposed architecture and roadmap. At http://msdn.microsoft.com/library/en-us/dnwssecur/html/ securitywhitepaper.asp, April 2002.

[JLLV04]   J. E. Johnson, D. E. Langworthy, L. Lamport, and F. H. Vogt. Formal specification of a web services protocol. In *1st International Workshop on Web Services and Formal Methods (WS-FM 2004)*, 2004. University of Pisa.

[KN⁺04]   C. Kaler, A. Nadalin, et al. *Web Services Secure Conversation Language (WS-SecureConversation)*, May 2004. Version 1.1. At http: //msdn.microsoft.com/ws/2004/04/ws-secure-conversation/.

[Low97]   G. Lowe. A hierarchy of authentication specifications. In *Proceedings of 10th IEEE Computer Security Foundations Workshop, 1997*, pages 31–44. IEEE Computer Society Press, 1997.

[Mic02]   Microsoft Corporation. *Web Services Enhancements for Microsoft .NET*, December 2002. At http://msdn.microsoft.com/webservices/ building/wse/default.aspx.

[Mil99]   R. Milner. *Communicating and Mobile Systems: the π-Calculus*. Cambridge University Press, 1999.

[NKHBM04]   A. Nadalin, C. Kaler, P. Hallam-Baker, and R. Monzillo. *OASIS Web Services Security: SOAP Message Security 1.0 (WS-Security 2004)*, March 2004. At http://www.oasis-open.org/committees/download. php/5941/oasis-200401-wss-soap-message-security-1.0.pdf.

[NS78]   R.M. Needham and M.D. Schroeder. Using encryption for authentication in large networks of computers. *Communications of the ACM*, 21(12):993–999, 1978.

[S⁺04]   J. Schlimmer et al. *A Proposal for UPnP 2.0 Device Architecture*, May 2004. At http://msdn.microsoft.com/library/en-us/dnglobspec/ html/devprof.asp.

[SMWC03]   J. Shewchuk, S. Millet, H. Wilson, and D. Cole. Expanding the communications capabilities of web services with WS-Addressing. At http://msdn.microsoft.com/library/default.asp? url=/library/en-us/dnwse/html/soapmail.asp, 2003.

[SS02]   J. Scambay and M. Shema. *Hacking Web Applications Exposed*. McGraw-Hill/Osborne, 2002.

[Vog03]   W. Vogels. Web services are not distributed objects. *IEEE Internet Computing*, 7(6):59–66, 2003.

[W3C03]   W3C. *SOAP Version 1.2*, 2003. W3C Recommendation, at http:// www.w3.org/TR/soap12.

[Win98]   D. Winer. RPC over HTTP via XML. At http://davenet.scripting. com/1998/02/27/rpcOverHttpViaXml, 1998.

[Win99]   D. Winer. Dave's history of SOAP. At http://www.xmlrpc.com/ discuss/msgReader$555, 1999.

[WL93]   T.Y.C. Woo and S.S. Lam. A semantic model for authentication protocols. In *IEEE Computer Society Symposium on Research in Security and Privacy*, pages 178–194, 1993.

A Checker for Modal Formulae
for Processes with Data

Jan Friso Groote and Tim A.C. Willemse

Department of Mathematics and Computer Science,
Eindhoven University of Technology, P.O. Box 513,
5600 MB Eindhoven, The Netherlands
{J.F.Groote, T.A.C.Willemse}@tue.nl

Abstract. We present a new technique for the automatic verification of
first order modal μ-calculus formulae on infinite state, data-dependent
processes. The use of *boolean equation systems* for solving the model-
checking problem in the finite case is well-studied. We extend this
technique to infinite state and data-dependent processes. We describe a
transformation of the model checking problem to the problem of solving
equation systems, and present a semi-decision procedure to solve these
equation systems and discuss the capabilities of a prototype implementing our procedure. This prototype has been successfully applied to many
systems. We report on its functioning for the Bakery Protocol.

Keywords: Model Checking, μCRL, First Order Modal μ-Calculus,
First Order Boolean Equation Systems, Data-Dependent Systems, Infinite State Systems

1   Introduction

Model checking has come about as one of the major advances in automated verification of systems in the last decade. It has earned its medals in many application areas (e.g. communications protocols, timed systems and hybrid systems),
originating from both academic and industrial environments.

However, the class of systems to which model checking techniques are applicable, is restricted to systems in which dependencies on infinite datatypes
are absent, or can be abstracted from. The models for such systems therefore
do not always represent these systems best. In particular, for some systems the
most vital properties are sensitive to data. There, the model checking technique
breaks down. This clearly calls for an extension of model checking techniques for
systems that are data-dependent.

In this paper, we explore a possibility for extending model checking techniques
to deal with processes which can depend on data. We describe a procedure, for
which we have also implemented a prototype, that verifies a given property
on a given data-dependent process. The problem in general is easily shown to
be undecidable, so, while we can guarantee soundness of our procedure, we
cannot guarantee its termination. However, as several examples suggest, many
interesting systems with infinite state spaces can be verified using our procedure.

F.S. de Boer et al. (Eds.): FMCO 2003, LNCS 3188, pp. 223–239, 2004.

Naturally, our technique also applies to systems with finite (but extremely large) state-spaces.

The framework we use for describing the behaviour of a system is process algebraic. We use the process algebraic language μCRL [10, 11], which is an extension of ACP [2]; this language includes a formal treatment of data, as well as an operational and axiomatic semantics of process terms. Compared to CCS or ACP, the language μCRL is more expressive [17]. For our model checking procedure, we assume that the processes are written in a special format, the *Linear Process Equation* (LPE) format, which is discussed in e.g. [23]. Note that this does not pose a restriction on the set of processes that can be modelled using μCRL, as all sensible process descriptions can be transformed to this format [23]. When dealing with datatypes, an explicit representation of the entire state space is often not possible, since it can very well be infinite. Using the LPE format has the advantage of working with a finite representation of the (possibly infinite) state space.

The language we use to denote our properties in is an extension of the modal μ-calculus [16]. In particular, we allow first order logic predicates and parameterised fixpoint variables in our properties. These extensions, which are also described in e.g. [9], are needed to express properties about data.

The approach we follow is very much inspired by the work of e.g. Mader [18], and uses (in our case, first order) boolean equation systems as an intermediate formalism. We present a translation of first order modal μ-calculus expressions to first order boolean equation systems in the presence of a fixed Linear Process Equation. The procedure for solving the first order boolean equation systems is based on the Gauß elimination algorithm described in, e.g. [18].

This paper is structured as follows: Section 2 briefly introduces the language μCRL and the Linear Process Equations format that is used in all subsequent sections. In Section 3, we describe the first order modal μ-calculus. Section 4 discusses first order boolean equation systems and describes the translation of first order modal μ-calculus formulae, given a Linear Process Equation, to a sequence of first order boolean equations. A procedure for solving the first order boolean equations is then described in Section 5; its implementation is discussed in Section 6, and a sample verification is described in Section 7. Section 8 is reserved for concluding remarks.

2   Preliminaries

Our main focus in this paper is on processes with data. As a framework, we use the process algebra μCRL [10]. Its basic constructs are along the lines of ACP [2] and CCS [20], though its syntax is influenced mainly by ACP. In the process algebra μCRL, data is an integral part of the language. For the exhibition of the remainder of the theory, we assume we work in the context of a data algebra without explicitly mentioning its constituent components. As a convention, we assume the data algebra contains all the required data types; in particular, we always have the domain $\mathbb{B}$ of booleans with functions $\top:\to\mathbb{B}$ and $\bot:\to\mathbb{B}$, representing *true* and *false* at our disposal.

The language μCRL has only a small number of carefully chosen operators and primitives. Processes are the main objects in the language. A set of parameterised actions *Act* is assumed. Actions represent atomic events; for an action $a{\in}Act$, taking a number of data arguments $\overline{d}$, $a(\overline{d})$ is a process. The process representing no behaviour, i.e. the process that cannot perform any actions is denoted δ. This constant is often referred to as *deadlock* or *inaction*. All actions a terminate successfully immediately after execution; δ cannot be executed.

Processes are constructed using several operators. The main operators are alternative composition ($p + q$ for some processes p and q) and sequential composition ($p \cdot q$ for some processes p and q). Conditional behaviour is denoted using a ternary operator (we write $p \lhd b \rhd q$ when we mean process p if b holds and else process q). The process $[b]:\to p$ serves as a shorthand for the process $p\lhd b\rhd\delta$, which represents the process p under the premise that b holds. Recursive behaviour is specified using equations. Process variables are typed; they should be considered as functions from a data domain to processes.

Example 1. The behaviour, denoted by process $X(n)$ is the increasing and decreasing of an internal counter n or showing its current value.

$$X(n{:}\mathbb{N}) = up \cdot X(n{+}1) + show(n) \cdot X(n) + [n > 0]:\to down \cdot X(n{-}1)$$

For the formal exposition, it can be more convenient to assume that actions and processes have a single parameter. This assumption is easily justified, as we can assume the existence of an appropriate data domain, together with adequate pairing and projection functions.

A more complex notion of process composition consists of the parallel composition of processes (we write $p\|q$ to denote the process p parallel to the process q). Synchronisation is achieved using a separate partial communication function γ, prescribing the result of a communication of two actions (e.g. $\gamma(a,b) = c$ denotes the communication between actions a and b, resulting in action c). Two parameterised actions $a(n)$ and $b(n')$ can communicate to action $c(n'')$ only if the communication between actions a and b results in action c (i.e. $\gamma(a,b) = c$) and $n'' = n' = n$.

The communication function is used to specify *when* communication is possible; this, however, does not mean communication is enforced. To this end, we must encapsulate the individual occurrences of the actions that participate in the communication. This is achieved using the encapsulation operator (we write $\partial_H(p)$ to specify that all actions in the set of actions H are to be encapsulated in process p).

The last operator considered here is data-dependent alternative quantification (we write $\sum_{d:D} p$ to denote the alternatives of process p, dependent on some arbitrary datum d selected from the (possibly infinite) data domain D). The $\sum$-operator is best compared to e.g. input prefixing, but is more expressive (see e.g. [17]).

Example 2. The behaviour, denoted by process $V(n)$ is the setting of an internal variable to an arbitrary value, which can be read at will.

$$V(n{:}\mathbb{N}) = read(n) \cdot V(n) + \sum_{n'{:}\mathbb{N}} set(n') \cdot V(n')$$

For the purpose of verification or analysis, it is often most convenient to eliminate parallelism in favour of sequential composition and (quantified) alternative composition. A behaviour of a process can then be denoted as a state-vector of typed variables, accompanied by a set of condition-action-effect rules. Processes denoted in this fashion are called *Linear Process Equations*.

Definition 1. *A Linear Process Equation (LPE) is a parameterised equation taking the form*

$$X(d{:}D) = \sum_{i \in I} \sum_{e_i{:}D_i} [c_i(d, e_i)] :\to a_i(f_i(d, e_i)) \cdot X(g_i(d, e_i))$$

where I is a finite index set; D and D_i are data domains; d and e_i are data variables; $a_i \in Act$ are actions with parameters of sort D_{a_i}; $f_i{:}D \times D_i \to D_{a_i}$, $g_i{:}D \times D_i \to D$ and $c_i{:}D \times D_i \to \mathbb{B}$ are functions. The function f_i yields, on the basis of the current state d and the bound variable e_i, the parameter for action a_i; the "next-state" is encoded in the function g_i. The function c_i describes when action a_i can be executed.

In this paper, we restrict ourselves to the use of non-terminating processes, i.e. we do not consider processes that, apart from executing an infinite number of actions, also have the possibility to perform a finite number of actions and then terminate successfully. Including termination into our theory does not pose any theoretical challenges, but is omitted in our exposition for brevity.

Several techniques and tools exist to translate a guarded μCRL process to linear form (see e.g. [3, 23]) and to further analyse these processes using symbolic manipulation. In the remainder of this paper, we use the LPE-notation as a vehicle for our exposition of the theory and practice.

The operational semantics for μCRL can be found in e.g. [10, 11]. Since we restrict our discussions to process expressions in LPE-form, we here only provide a definition of the labelled transition system that is induced by a process in LPE-form.

Definition 2. *The labelled transition system of a Linear Process Equation X as defined in Def. 1 is a quadruple $M = \langle S, \Sigma, \to, s_0 \rangle$, where*

- *$S = \{X(d) \mid d \in D\}$ is the (possibly infinite) set of states;*
- *$\Sigma = \{a_i(d_{a_i}) \mid i \in I \wedge a_i \in Act \wedge d_{a_i} \in D_{a_i}\}$ is the (possibly infinite) set of labels;*
- *$\to = \{(X(d), a_i(d'_a), X(d')) \mid i \in I \wedge a_i \in Act \wedge \exists_{e_i \in D_i} c_i(d, e_i) \wedge d'_a = f_i(d, e_i) \wedge d' = g_i(d, e_i)\}$ is the transition relation. We write $X(d) \xrightarrow{a(e)} X(d')$ rather than $(X(d), a(e), X(d')) \in \to$;*
- *$s_0 = X(d_0) \in S$, for a given $d_0 \in D$, is the initial state.*

3   First Order Modal μ-Calculus

The logic we consider is based on the modal μ-calculus [16], extended with data variables, quantifiers and parameterisation (see [9]). This logic allows us to express data dependent properties. We refer to this logic as the *first order modal μ-calculus*. Its syntax and semantics are defined below.

Definition 3. *An* action formula *is defined by the following grammar*

$$\alpha ::= a(e) \mid \top \mid \neg\alpha_1 \mid \alpha_1 \wedge \alpha_2 \mid \forall d{:}D.\alpha_1$$

Here, a is a parameterised action of set Act and e of datatype D, is some data expression, possibly containing data variables d of a set $\mathcal{D}$. We use the standard abbreviations $\bot \overset{def}{=} \neg\top$, $(\alpha_1 \vee \alpha_2) \overset{def}{=} \neg(\neg\alpha_1 \wedge \neg\alpha_2)$ and $(\exists d{:}D.\alpha_1) \overset{def}{=} (\neg\forall d{:}D.\neg\alpha_1)$.

The action formulae are interpreted over a labelled transition system M, which is induced by an LPE (see Def. 2).

Remark 1. We use *environments* for registering the (current) values of variables in formulae. Hence, an environment is a (partial) mapping of a set of variables to elements of a given type. We use the following notational convention: for an arbitrary environment θ, a variable x and a value v, we write $\theta[v/x]$ for the environment θ', defined as $\theta'(x') = \theta(x')$ for all variables x' different from x and $\theta'(x) = v$. In effect, $\theta[v/x]$ stands for the environment θ where the variable x has value v. The interpretation of a variable x in an environment θ is written as $\theta(x)$.

Definition 4. *The interpretation of an action formula α in the context of a data environment $\varepsilon{:}\mathcal{D}{\rightarrow}D$, denoted by $[\![\alpha]\!]\varepsilon$, is defined inductively as:*

$$
\begin{aligned}
[\![\top]\!]\varepsilon &= \Sigma \\
[\![a(e)]\!]\varepsilon &= \{a(\varepsilon(e))\} \\
[\![\neg\alpha]\!]\varepsilon &= \Sigma \setminus [\![\alpha]\!]\varepsilon \\
[\![\alpha_1 \wedge \alpha_2]\!]\varepsilon &= [\![\alpha_1]\!]\varepsilon \cap [\![\alpha_2]\!]\varepsilon \\
[\![\forall d{:}D.\alpha]\!]\varepsilon &= \textstyle\bigcap v{\in}D \; [\![\alpha]\!]\varepsilon[v/d]
\end{aligned}
$$

Hence, we can use $\top$ to denote an arbitrary (parameterised) action. This is useful for expressing e.g. progress conditions. We subsequently define the set of *state formulae*.

Definition 5. *A* State Formula *is given by the following grammar.*

$$\varphi ::= b \mid Z(e) \mid \neg\varphi \mid \varphi_1 \wedge \varphi_2 \mid [\alpha]\varphi_1 \mid \forall d{:}D.\varphi \mid (\nu Z(d{:}D).\varphi)(e)$$

where b is an expression of the domain $\mathbb{B}$, possibly containing data variables d of the set $\mathcal{D}$, e of datatype D, is some data expression possibly containing data variables d of the set $\mathcal{D}$, α is an action formula; Z is a propositional variable from a set $\mathcal{P}$, and $(\nu Z(d{:}D).\varphi)(e)$ is subject to the restriction that any free occurrence of Z in φ must be within the scope of an even number of negation symbols.

We use the abbreviations as usual: $(\varphi_1 \vee \varphi_2) \overset{def}{=} \neg(\neg\varphi_1 \wedge \neg\varphi_2)$, $\langle\alpha\rangle\varphi \overset{def}{=} \neg[\alpha]\neg\varphi$, $(\exists d{:}D.\varphi) = (\neg\forall d{:}D.\neg\varphi)$ *and* $(\mu Z(d{:}D).\varphi)(e) \overset{def}{=} (\neg\nu Z(d{:}D).\neg\varphi[\neg Z/Z])(e)$. *We write σ for an arbitrary fixpoint, i.e. $\sigma \in \{\nu, \mu\}$.*

We only consider state formulae in which all variables are bound exactly once by a fixpoint operator or quantifier. State formulae are interpreted over a labelled transition system M, induced by an LPE, according to Def. 2.

Definition 6. *The interpretation of a state formula φ in the context of data environment $\varepsilon{:}D{\to}D$ and propositional environment $\rho{:}\mathcal{P}{\to}(D{\to}2^S)$, denoted by $[\![\varphi]\!]\rho\varepsilon$, is defined inductively as:*

$$
\begin{aligned}
[\![b]\!]\rho\varepsilon &= \begin{cases} S \text{ if } [\![b]\!]\varepsilon \\ \emptyset \text{ otherwise} \end{cases} \\
[\![Z(e)]\!]\rho\varepsilon &= \rho(Z)(\varepsilon(e)) \\
[\![\neg\varphi]\!]\rho\varepsilon &= S \setminus [\![\varphi]\!]\rho\varepsilon \\
[\![\varphi_1 \wedge \varphi_2]\!]\rho\varepsilon &= [\![\varphi_1]\!]\rho\varepsilon \cap [\![\varphi_2]\!]\rho\varepsilon \\
[\![[\alpha]\varphi]\!]\rho\varepsilon &= \{X(v){\in}S \mid \forall v'{\in}D\ \forall a{\in}Act\ \forall v_a{\in}D_a \\
&\qquad (X(v) \overset{a(v_a)}{\longrightarrow} X(v') \wedge a(v_a){\in}[\![\alpha]\!]\varepsilon) \Rightarrow X(v'){\in}[\![\varphi]\!]\rho\varepsilon\} \\
[\![\forall d{:}D.\varphi]\!]\rho\varepsilon &= \bigcap_{v'{\in}D} [\![\varphi]\!]\rho(\varepsilon[v'/d]) \\
[\![(\nu Z(d{:}D).\varphi)(e)]\!]\rho\varepsilon &= (\nu\Phi_{\rho\varepsilon})(\varepsilon(e))
\end{aligned}
$$

where we have $\Phi_{\rho\varepsilon} \overset{def}{=} \lambda F{:}D \to 2^S.\lambda v{:}D.[\![\varphi]\!](\rho[F/Z])(\varepsilon[v/d])$. For states $X(d) \in S$ of the transition system induced by an LPE X, and a formula φ, we write $d \models_X \varphi$ for $X(d) \in [\![\varphi]\!]\rho\varepsilon$.

Remark 2. In the remainder of this paper, we restrict ourselves to state formulae given in *Positive Normal Form* (PNF). This means that negation only occurs on the level of atomic propositions and, in addition, all bound variables are distinct.

We denote the set of functions $D{\to}2^S$ by $[D{\to}2^S]$. Define the ordering $\dot\subseteq$ on the set $[D{\to}2^S]$ as $X \dot\subseteq Y$ iff for all $d{:}D$ we have $X(d) \subseteq Y(d)$. Then, the fixpoint operators are monotonic over the complete lattice $([D{\to}2^S], \dot\subseteq)$ (see [14, 24]). From this, the existence and uniqueness of fixpoints in state formulae immediately follows.

Example 3. Standard (first order) modal μ-calculus formulae often consist of the constructs $\nu Z.([\top]Z \wedge \varphi)$ and $\mu Z.(\varphi \vee ([\top]Z \wedge \langle\top\rangle\top))$. These formulae represent "always φ" and "eventually φ" resp. The greatest fixpoint can be interpreted as "infinitely often", whereas the least fixpoint can be interpreted as "finitely many times".

Example 4. Consider a process with at least the states s_0, s_1 and s_2, the labels $a(\top)$ and $a(\bot)$ and the state formula φ. We write $s \models \varphi$ to denote that φ is satisfied in state s, and, likewise, we write $s \not\models \varphi$ to denote that φ is not satisfied in state s.

1. The state formula $\exists b{:}\mathbb{B}.\ [a(b)]\varphi$ holds in state s_0, since there is a b (viz. $b = \top$), such that whenever we execute $a(b)$, we end up in a state satisfying φ.

2. The state formula $[\exists b{:}\mathbb{B}.a(b)]\varphi$ does not hold in state s_0, since by executing $a(\bot)$ we end up in a state not satisfying φ. An alternative phrasing of the same property is $\forall b{:}\mathbb{B}.[a(b)]\varphi$.

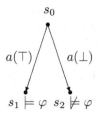

Note that data-quantification in action formulae can be used for abstracting from the actual values for parameterised actions. One may be led to believe that the quantifiers inside modalities can all be replaced by quantifiers in state formulae. This, however, is not true, as we can only derive the following properties.

Property 1. Let φ be a state formula, such that d does not occur in φ, and let α be an action formula. Then, we have the following identities:

1. $\langle \exists d{:}D.\alpha \rangle \varphi \Leftrightarrow \exists d{:}D.\langle \alpha \rangle \varphi$, and $[\exists d{:}D.\alpha]\varphi \Leftrightarrow \forall d{:}D.[\alpha]\varphi$,
2. $\exists d{:}D.[\alpha]\varphi \Rightarrow [\forall d{:}D.\alpha]\varphi$, and $\langle \forall d{:}D.\alpha \rangle \varphi \Rightarrow \forall d{:}D.\langle \alpha \rangle \varphi$

Note: here we use implication as an abbreviation for $\subseteq$ and bi-implication as an abbreviation for $=$ on the interpretations of the state formulae.

These properties state a weak relation between quantifiers in state formulae and quantifiers in action formulae. Note that the converse of the second item does not hold, see e.g. [14, 24] for a counterexample. Thus, compared to the fragment of the first order modal μ-calculus that disallows quantifiers inside action formulae, the quantifiers inside action formulae indeed increase the expressive power of the whole first order modal μ-calculus.

Remark 3. Note that negation in combination with universal quantifiers in action formulae can yield more exciting sets than the empty set.

4   Equation Systems

Following [9], we use an extension of the formalism of *boolean equation systems* (see e.g. [18]) as an intermediate formalism that allows us to combine an LPE with a first order modal μ-calculus expression.

Definition 7. *A first order boolean expression is a formula φ in positive form, defined by the following grammar:*

$$\varphi ::= b \mid \varphi_1 \wedge \varphi_2 \mid \varphi_1 \vee \varphi_2 \mid Z(e) \mid \forall d{:}D.\varphi \mid \exists d{:}D.\varphi$$

where b is an expression of datatype $\mathbb{B}$, possibly containing data variables d of a set D, Z is a variable of a set P of propositional variables and e is a term of datatype D, possibly containing data variables d of a set D.

We denote the set of functions of type $D{\to}\mathbb{B}$ by $[D{\to}\mathbb{B}]$. The set of first order boolean expressions $([D{\to}\mathbb{B}], \Rightarrow)$, where $\varphi{\Rightarrow}\psi$ iff for all $d{:}D$ $\varphi(d){\Rightarrow}\psi(d)$, forms a complete lattice and is isomorphic to $(2^D, \subseteq)$. The propositional variables $Z{\in}\mathcal{P}$, occurring as free variables in first order boolean expressions are bound in *first order boolean equation systems* (also known as *parameterised boolean equation systems* [15] or *equation systems* for short), used in the sequel.

Definition 8. *The* interpretation *of a first order boolean expression φ in the context of propositional environment $\theta{:}\mathcal{P}{\to}(D{\to}\mathbb{B})$ and data environment $\eta{:}D{\to}D$, written as $[\![\varphi]\!]\theta\eta$ is either true or false, determined by the following induction:*

$$
\begin{aligned}
[\![b]\!]\theta\eta &= [\![b]\!]\eta \\
[\![\varphi_1 \wedge \varphi_2]\!]\theta\eta &= [\![\varphi_1]\!]\theta\eta \wedge [\![\varphi_2]\!]\theta\eta \\
[\![\varphi_1 \vee \varphi_2]\!]\theta\eta &= [\![\varphi_1]\!]\theta\eta \vee [\![\varphi_2]\!]\theta\eta \\
[\![Z(e)]\!]\theta\eta &= \theta(Z)([\![e]\!]\eta) \\
[\![\forall d{:}D.\varphi]\!]\theta\eta &= \text{true, if for all } v{:}D \text{ it holds that } [\![\varphi]\!]\theta(\eta[v/d]) \text{ else false} \\
[\![\exists d{:}D.\varphi]\!]\theta\eta &= \text{true, if there exists a } v{:}D \text{ such that } [\![\varphi]\!]\theta(\eta[v/d]) \text{ else false}
\end{aligned}
$$

Lemma 1. *First order boolean expressions are monotone over $([D{\to}\mathbb{B}], \Rightarrow)$, see [14, 24].*

Definition 9. *An equation system $\mathcal{E}$ is a finite sequence of equations of the form $\sigma Z(d{:}D) = \varphi$, where σ is ν or μ and $\varphi{:}D{\to}\mathbb{B}$ is a first order boolean expression. We require that all data variables are bound exactly once and all bound propositional variables are unique; ϵ represents the empty equation system.*

The equation system $\mathcal{E}'$ that is obtained by applying an environment θ to an equation system $\mathcal{E}$ is the equation system in which every propositional variable Z is assigned the value $\theta(Z)$.

Definition 10. *The solution $[\mathcal{E}]\theta$ to the equation system $\mathcal{E}$ (containing only bound data variables), in the context of propositional environment $\theta{:}\mathcal{P}{\to}(D{\to}\mathbb{B})$, is an environment that is defined as follows (see also e.g. [18], Definition 3.3).*

   1) $[\epsilon]\theta = \theta$, *and*   2) $[(\sigma Z(d{:}D) = \varphi)\mathcal{E}]\theta = [\mathcal{E}](\theta[\sigma Z.\varphi([\mathcal{E}]\theta)/Z])$, *where*

$$
\begin{aligned}
\mu Z.\varphi([\mathcal{E}]\theta) &= \bigwedge\{\psi{:}D \to \mathbb{B} \mid \lambda d{:}D.[\![\varphi]\!]([\mathcal{E}]\theta[\psi/Z]){\Rightarrow}\psi\} \\
\nu Z.\varphi([\mathcal{E}]\theta) &= \bigvee\{\psi{:}D \to \mathbb{B} \mid \psi{\Rightarrow}\lambda d{:}D.[\![\varphi]\!]([\mathcal{E}]\theta[\psi/Z])\}
\end{aligned}
$$

where $\bigwedge$ and $\bigvee$ denote the infimum *and the* supremum *from $([D{\to}\mathbb{B}], \Rightarrow)$.*

We denote the set of all environments by $[\mathcal{P}{\to}(D{\to}\mathbb{B})]$. The set $([\mathcal{P}{\to}(D{\to}\mathbb{B})], \leq)$ is a complete lattice, where the ordering $\leq$ is defined as $\theta_1 \leq \theta_2$ iff for all $Z \in \mathcal{P}$, we have $\theta_1(Z){\Rightarrow}\theta_2(Z)$.

Lemma 2. *Equation systems are monotone over $([\mathcal{P}{\to}(D{\to}\mathbb{B})], \leq)$, see [14, 24].*

We subsequently transform the model-checking problem for processes with data to the problem of finding the solution to an equation system. We define a translation, transforming an LPE and a first order modal μ-calculus formula to an equation system.

Definition 11. Let $\varphi = (\sigma Z(d_f{:}D).\Phi)(e)$ be a first order modal μ-calculus formula φ. Let $X(d_p{:}D)$ be an LPE (see Def. 1). The equation system $\mathcal{E}$ that corresponds to the expression φ for LPE X is given by $\mathbf{E}(\varphi)$. The translation function $\mathbf{E}$ is defined by structural induction in Table 1.

Theorem 1. Let X be an LPE with initial state $X(d_0)$ and parameter space D. For each environment $\rho{:}\mathcal{P}{\to}(D'{\to}2^S)$ the environment $\theta_\rho{:}\mathcal{P}{\to}(D{\times}D'{\to}\mathbb{B})$ is defined as $\theta_\rho(\tilde{Z}) \stackrel{def}{=} \lambda(d,d'){:}D{\times}D'.(X(d){\in}\rho(Z)(d'))$. Let $\varphi = (\sigma Z(d{:}D').\Phi)(e)$. Then, we have

$$d_0 \models_X \varphi \ \textit{iff} \ ([\mathbf{E}(\varphi)]\theta_\rho)(\tilde{Z}(e,d_0))$$

Proof. See [9].

The translation function $\mathbf{E}$ splits nested fixpoint expressions into equations for which the right-hand side is determined by the function $\mathbf{RHS}$. This latter function takes care of the logical connectives, such as $\wedge$ and $\vee$, and the modalities $[\alpha]\varphi$ and $\langle\alpha\rangle\varphi$.

Example 5. Consider a coffee-vending machine that produces either cappuccino or espresso on the insertion of a special coin. It accepts coins as long as there is at least one type of coffee that can still be dispensed. If the machine has run out of a type of coffee, it can be filled again with C fillings of cappuccino or E fillings of espresso.

$$
\begin{aligned}
\mathbf{proc}\ X(b{:}\mathbb{B}, c, e{:}\mathbb{N}) = &[b \wedge c > 0]{:}{\to}\ cappuccino \cdot X(\neg b, c-1, e)\\
+ &[b \wedge e > 0]{:}{\to}\ espresso \cdot X(\neg b, c, e-1)\\
+ &[\neg b \wedge c + e > 0]{:}{\to}\ coin \cdot X(\neg b, c, e)\\
+ &[\neg b \wedge c = 0]{:}{\to}\ refill_{cappuccino} \cdot X(b, C, e)\\
+ &[\neg b \wedge e = 0]{:}{\to}\ refill_{espresso} \cdot X(b, c, E)
\end{aligned}
$$

Boolean b indicates whether a coin has been inserted or not and parameters c and e register the number of servings of cappuccino, resp. espresso that are left in the coffee-vending machine. Consider the (first order) modal μ-calculus expression $\mu Z.(\langle coin \vee cappuccino \rangle Z \vee \langle refill_{cappuccino} \rangle \top)$, expressing that there exists a path where cappuccino can be refilled when it is the only thing that has been ordered. We briefly illustrate how we can obtain an equation system by combining process X and the above modal formula using Def. 11:

$$
\begin{aligned}
&\mathbf{E}(\mu Z.(\langle coin \vee cappuccino \rangle Z \vee \langle refill_{cappuccino} \rangle \top))\\
=\ &(\mu\tilde{Z}(b{:}\mathbb{B}, c, e{:}\mathbb{N}) = \mathbf{RHS}((\langle coin \vee cappuccino \rangle Z \vee \langle refill_{cappuccino} \rangle \top))\\
=\ &(\mu\tilde{Z}(b{:}\mathbb{B}, c, e{:}\mathbb{N}) = \mathbf{RHS}(\langle coin \vee cappuccino \rangle Z) \vee \mathbf{RHS}(\langle refill_{cappuccino} \rangle \top))\\
=\ &(\mu\tilde{Z}(b{:}\mathbb{B}, c, e{:}\mathbb{N}) = (\neg b \wedge c + e > 0 \wedge \mathbf{RHS}(Z)[(\neg b, c, e)/(b, c, e)])\\
&\qquad \vee (b \wedge c > 0 \wedge \mathbf{RHS}(Z)[(\neg b, c-1, e)/(b, c, e)])\\
&\qquad \vee (\neg b \wedge c = 0 \wedge \mathbf{RHS}(\top)[(b, C, e)/(b, c, e)]))\\
=\ &(\mu\tilde{Z}(b{:}\mathbb{B}, c, e{:}\mathbb{N}) = (\neg b \wedge (c = 0 \vee (c + e > 0 \wedge \tilde{Z}(\neg b, c, e))))\\
&\qquad \vee (b \wedge c > 0 \wedge \tilde{Z}(\neg b, c-1, e))
\end{aligned}
$$

Notice that this equation carries the parameters of the LPE, even though the first order modal μ-calculus expression was not parameterised.

Table 1. Translation of first order μ-calculus formula φ and LPE $X(d_p{:}D)$ to an equation system $\mathbf{E}(\varphi)$. Note that $\tilde{Z}$ is a fresh propositional variable, associated to the propositional variable Z. Function $\mathbf{E}$ determines the number and order of equations for $\mathbf{E}(\varphi)$, whereas function $\mathbf{RHS}$ breaks down φ to obtain first order boolean expressions that form the right-hand side of each equation in $\mathbf{E}(\varphi)$. The satisfaction relation $\models$ and the function $\mathbf{Par}$ are listed in Table 2. The function $\mathbf{Par}_X(\varphi)$ yields a list of parameters with types that must be bound by the parameterised propositional variable X. Here, we have abused the notation $\mathbf{Par}_X(\varphi)$ to also denote the list of parameters without typing information. Note that $\mathbf{Par}_X(\varphi)$ is always calculated for the entire formula φ, and not for subformulae

$$\mathbf{E}(b) \stackrel{\text{def}}{=} \epsilon$$

$$\mathbf{E}(Z(d_f)) \stackrel{\text{def}}{=} \epsilon$$

$$\mathbf{E}(\Phi_1 \wedge \Phi_2) \stackrel{\text{def}}{=} \mathbf{E}(\Phi_1)\mathbf{E}(\Phi_2)$$

$$\mathbf{E}(\Phi_1 \vee \Phi_2) \stackrel{\text{def}}{=} \mathbf{E}(\Phi_1)\mathbf{E}(\Phi_2)$$

$$\mathbf{E}([\alpha]\Phi) \stackrel{\text{def}}{=} \mathbf{E}(\Phi)$$

$$\mathbf{E}(\langle\alpha\rangle\Phi) \stackrel{\text{def}}{=} \mathbf{E}(\Phi)$$

$$\mathbf{E}(\forall d{:}D.\Phi) \stackrel{\text{def}}{=} \mathbf{E}(\Phi)$$

$$\mathbf{E}(\exists d{:}D.\Phi) \stackrel{\text{def}}{=} \mathbf{E}(\Phi)$$

$$\mathbf{E}((\sigma Z(d_f{:}D_f).\Phi)(e)) \stackrel{\text{def}}{=} (\sigma \tilde{Z}(d_f{:}D_f, d_p{:}D_p, \mathbf{Par}_Z(\varphi)) = \mathbf{RHS}(\Phi))\ \mathbf{E}(\Phi)$$

$$\mathbf{RHS}(b) \stackrel{\text{def}}{=} b$$

$$\mathbf{RHS}(Z(e)) \stackrel{\text{def}}{=} \tilde{Z}(e, d_p, \mathbf{Par}_Z(\varphi))$$

$$\mathbf{RHS}(\Phi_1 \wedge \Phi_2) \stackrel{\text{def}}{=} \mathbf{RHS}(\Phi_1) \wedge \mathbf{RHS}(\Phi_2)$$

$$\mathbf{RHS}(\Phi_1 \vee \Phi_2) \stackrel{\text{def}}{=} \mathbf{RHS}(\Phi_1) \vee \mathbf{RHS}(\Phi_2)$$

$$\mathbf{RHS}([\alpha]\Phi) \stackrel{\text{def}}{=} \bigwedge_{i:I} \forall_{e_i:D_i}(a_i(f_i(d_p, e_i)) \models \alpha \wedge c_i(d_p, e_i)) \Rightarrow \mathbf{RHS}(\Phi)[g_i(d_p, e_i)/d_p]$$

$$\mathbf{RHS}(\langle\alpha\rangle\Phi) \stackrel{\text{def}}{=} \bigvee_{i:I} \exists_{e_i:D_i}(a_i(f_i(d_p, e_i)) \models \alpha \wedge c_i(d_p, e_i) \wedge \mathbf{RHS}(\Phi)[g_i(d_p, e_i)/d_p])$$

$$\mathbf{RHS}(\forall d{:}D.\Phi) \stackrel{\text{def}}{=} \forall d{:}D.\mathbf{RHS}(\Phi)$$

$$\mathbf{RHS}(\exists d{:}D.\Phi) \stackrel{\text{def}}{=} \exists d{:}D.\mathbf{RHS}(\Phi)$$

$$\mathbf{RHS}((\sigma Z(d_f{:}D_f).\Phi)(e)) \stackrel{\text{def}}{=} \tilde{Z}(e, d_p, \mathbf{Par}_Z(\varphi))$$

5   Model-Checking

Mader [18] describes an algorithm for solving boolean equation systems. The method she uses resembles the well-known Gauß elimination algorithm for solving linear equation systems, and is therefore also referred to as Gauß elimination. The semi-decision procedure we use (see Fig. 1) is an extension of the Gauß elimination algorithm of [18]. Basically, all lines (except for line 3) are part of the algorithm of [18]. The essential difference is in the addition of line 3, where an

Table 2. Auxiliary functions used in the translation of Table 1. Here, $+\!\!\!+$ denotes list concatenation. The satisfaction relation $\models$ checks whether a symbolic action $a(d)$ is part of an action formula α. The function $\mathbf{Par}_X(\varphi)$ yields a list of parameters together with their types that have to be bound by the equation for X

$a(d) \models a'(d')$	$\overset{\text{def}}{=}$	$a = a' \wedge d = d'$
$a(d) \models \top$	$\overset{\text{def}}{=}$	true
$a(d) \models \neg\alpha$	$\overset{\text{def}}{=}$	$\neg(a(d) \models \alpha)$
$a(d) \models \alpha_1 \wedge \alpha_2$	$\overset{\text{def}}{=}$	$(a(d) \models \alpha_1) \wedge (a(d) \models \alpha_2)$
$a(d) \models \alpha_1 \vee \alpha_2$	$\overset{\text{def}}{=}$	$(a(d) \models \alpha_1) \vee (a(d) \models \alpha_2)$
$a(d) \models \exists d'{:}D.\alpha$	$\overset{\text{def}}{=}$	$\exists d'{:}D.(a(d) \models \alpha)$
$a(d) \models \forall d'{:}D.\alpha$	$\overset{\text{def}}{=}$	$\forall d'{:}D.(a(d) \models \alpha)$

$\mathbf{Par}_X(b)$	$\overset{\text{def}}{=}$	$[]$
$\mathbf{Par}_X(Z(d_f))$	$\overset{\text{def}}{=}$	$[]$ for all $Z \in \mathcal{P}$
$\mathbf{Par}_X(\Phi_1 \wedge \Phi_2)$	$\overset{\text{def}}{=}$	$\mathbf{Par}_X(\Phi_1) +\!\!\!+ \mathbf{Par}_X(\Phi_2)$
$\mathbf{Par}_X(\Phi_1 \vee \Phi_2)$	$\overset{\text{def}}{=}$	$\mathbf{Par}_X(\Phi_1) +\!\!\!+ \mathbf{Par}_X(\Phi_2)$
$\mathbf{Par}_X([\alpha]\Phi)$	$\overset{\text{def}}{=}$	$\mathbf{Par}_X(\Phi)$
$\mathbf{Par}_X(\langle\alpha\rangle\Phi)$	$\overset{\text{def}}{=}$	$\mathbf{Par}_X(\Phi)$
$\mathbf{Par}_X(\forall d{:}D.\Phi)$	$\overset{\text{def}}{=}$	$[d{:}D] +\!\!\!+ \mathbf{Par}_X(\Phi)$
$\mathbf{Par}_X(\exists d{:}D.\Phi)$	$\overset{\text{def}}{=}$	$[d{:}D] +\!\!\!+ \mathbf{Par}_X(\Phi)$
$\mathbf{Par}_X((\sigma Z(d_f{:}D_f).\Phi)(e))$	$\overset{\text{def}}{=}$	$\mathbf{Par}_X(\Phi)$ for all $Z \in \mathcal{P}$ such that $Z \neq X$
$\mathbf{Par}_X((\sigma X(d_f{:}D_f).\Phi)(e))$	$\overset{\text{def}}{=}$	$[]$

extra loop for calculating a stable point in the (transfinite) approximation for each equation is given.

The reduction of an equation system proceeds in two separate steps. First, a stabilisation step is issued, in which an equation $\sigma_i X_i(d{:}D) = \varphi_i$ is reduced to a stable equation $\sigma_i X_i(d{:}D) = \varphi_i'$, where φ_i' is an expression containing no occurrences of X_i. Second, we substitute each occurrence of X_i by φ_i' in the rest of the equations of the first order boolean equation system. This does not change the solution of the equation system (see [14, 24, 15]). Since there are no more occurrences of X_i in the right-hand side of the equations, it suffices to reduce a smaller equation system. The semi-decision procedure terminates iff the stabilisation step terminates for each equation.

Theorem 2. *On termination of the semi-decision procedure in Fig. 1, the solution of the given equation system has been computed [14, 24].*

Remark 4. Given the undecidability of the model-checking problem in the setting of (arbitrary) infinite state systems, the stabilisation step in our procedure (which is based on transfinite approximations of fixpoints) cannot be made to

---

Input: $(\sigma_1 X_1(d_1{:}D_1) = \varphi_1) \ldots (\sigma_n X_n(d_n{:}D_n) = \varphi_n).$

1. for $i = n$ **downto** 1 **do**
2. $j := 0; \psi_0 := ($ **if** $\sigma_{b_i} = \nu$ **then** $\top$ **else** $\bot);$
3.   **repeat** $\psi_{j+1} := \varphi_i[X_i := \psi_j]; j := j+1$ **until** $(\psi_j \equiv \psi_{j-1})$
4.   **for** $k = 1$ **to** i **do** $\varphi_k := \varphi_k[X_i := \psi_j]$ **od** ;
5. od

Fig. 1. Semi-decision procedure for computing the solution of an equation system

terminate. However, there are a number of cases for which termination is guaranteed, e.g. if all considered datatypes are finite.

Example 6. Consider the infinite-state system $C(0)$ that counts from zero to infinity, and reports its current state via an action *current*. Even though this process is not very complex, it cannot be represented by a finite labelled transition system, which is why most current tools cannot handle such processes.

proc $C(n{:}\mathbb{N}) = current(n) \cdot C(n{+}1)$

Verifying absence of deadlock, i.e. $\nu Z.(\langle\top\rangle\top \wedge [\top]Z)$ on process C requires solving the associated equation system $\nu \tilde{Z}(n{:}\mathbb{N}) = (\tilde{Z}(n{+}1) \wedge \top)$. Substituting $\top$ for $\tilde{Z}(n{+}1)$ immediately leads to the stable solution $\top$.

Example 7. Consider a process C representing a counter that counts down from a randomly chosen natural number to zero and then randomly selects a new natural number.

proc $C(n{:}\mathbb{N}) = \sum_{m:\mathbb{N}} [n = 0]{:}\to reset \cdot C(m) + [n > 0]{:}\to dec \cdot C(n{-}1)$

Verifying whether it is possible to eventually execute a *reset* action, expressed by the formula $\mu Z.([\top]Z \wedge \langle\top\rangle\top) \vee \langle reset\rangle\top$, requires solving the equation system $\mu \tilde{Z}(n{:}\mathbb{N}) = (n = 0 \vee (\tilde{Z}(n{-}1) \wedge (n = 0 \vee n > 0)))$. Here, the approximation of $\tilde{Z}$ does not stabilise in a finite time, as we end up with approximations ψ_k, where $\psi_k = n \leq k$. Thus, we cannot find a ψ_j, such that $\psi_j = \psi_{j+1}$. However, it is straightforward to see that the minimal solution for this equation should be $\mu Z(n{:}\mathbb{N}) = \top$. In [15], we set out to investigate techniques and theorems that allow one to solve (by hand) a substantially larger class of equation systems than the class that can be solved using our semi-decision procedure of Figure 1. This class includes equation system of the type of this example.

6   Implementation

Based on our semi-decision procedure, described in the previous section, we have implemented a prototype of a tool[1]. The prototype implementation of our algorithm employs *Equational Binary Decision Diagrams* (EQ-BDDs) [13] for representing first order boolean expressions. These EQ-BDDs extend on standard BDDs [6] by explicitly allowing equality on nodes. We first define the grammar for EQ-BDDs.

Definition 12. *Assume a set P of propositions and a set V of variables, then EQ-BDDs are formulae, determined by the following grammar.*

$$\Phi ::= 0 \mid 1 \mid ITE(V = V, \Phi, \Phi) \mid ITE(P, \Phi, \Phi)$$

The constants **0** and **1** represent *false* and *true*. An expression of the form $ITE(\varphi, \psi, \xi)$ must be read as an *if-then-else* construct, i.e. $(\varphi \wedge \psi) \vee (\neg\varphi \wedge \xi)$, or, alternatively, $(\varphi \Rightarrow \psi) \wedge (\neg\varphi \Rightarrow \xi)$. For data variables d and e, and φ of the form $d = e$, the extension to EQ-BDDs is used, i.e. we explicitly use $ITE(d = e, \psi, \xi)$ in such cases. Using the standard BDD and EQ-BDD encodings [6, 13], we can then represent all quantifier-free first order boolean expressions.

Representing expressions that contain quantifiers over finite domains is done in a straightforward manner, i.e. we construct explicit encodings for each distinct element in the domain. Expressions containing quantifiers over infinite domains are in general problematic, when it comes to representation and calculation. The following theorem, however, identifies a number of cases in which we can deal with these.

Theorem 3. *Quantification over datatypes can be eliminated in the following cases:*

$$\exists d{:}D.ITE(d = e_1, \varphi_1, ITE(d = e_2, \varphi_2, \dots, ITE(d = e_n, \varphi_n, \psi)\dots))$$
$$= \bigvee_{1 \le i \le n}((\bigwedge_{1 \le j < i} e_j \ne e_i) \wedge \varphi_i[e_i/d]) \vee \psi$$

$$\forall d{:}D.ITE(d = e_1, \varphi_1, ITE(d = e_2, \varphi_2, \dots, ITE(d = e_n, \varphi_n, \psi)\dots))$$
$$= \bigwedge_{1 \le i \le n}((\bigvee_{1 \le j < i} e_j = e_i) \vee \varphi_i[e_i/d]) \wedge \psi$$

provided D contains at least one element not in $\{e_i | 1 \le i \le n\}$. By abuse of notation we write e_i instead of its value.

Proof. See [24].

Even though Theorem 3 applies to a restricted class of first order boolean expressions, we find that in practice, it adds considerably to the verification power of the prototype implementation.

---

[1] The tool, called *MuCheck*, is distributed as part of the μCRL tool-suite [3].

7   Example Verification

We have successfully used the prototype on several applications, including many communications protocols, such as the IEEE-1394 firewire, sliding window protocols, the bounded retransmission protocol, etc. As an example of its capabilities, we here report on our findings for Lamport's Bakery Protocol [21]. A μCRL specification of the Bakery Protocol is given in Fig. 2. The bakery protocol we

---

comm $get, send = c$
init $\partial_{\{get, \, send\}}(P(\top)\|P(\bot))$

proc $P(b{:}\mathbb{B}) = request(b) \cdot P_0(b, 0) + send(b, 0) \cdot P(b)$
proc $P_0(b{:}\mathbb{B}, n{:}\mathbb{N}) = \sum_{m:\mathbb{N}} get(\neg b, m) \cdot P_1(b, m+1) + send(b, n) \cdot P_0(b, n)$
proc $P_1(b{:}\mathbb{B}, n{:}\mathbb{N}) =$
$send(b, n) \cdot P_1(b, n) + \sum_{m:\mathbb{N}} get(\neg b, m) \cdot (C_1(b, n) \lhd n < m \vee m = 0 \rhd P_1(b, n))$
proc $C_1(b{:}\mathbb{B}, n{:}\mathbb{N}) = enter(b) \cdot C_2(b, n) + send(b, n) \cdot C_1(b, n)$
proc $C_2(b{:}\mathbb{B}, n{:}\mathbb{N}) = leave(b) \cdot P(b) + send(b, n) \cdot C_2(b, n)$

Fig. 2. Lamport's Bakery Protocol

consider is restricted to two processes. Each process, waiting to enter its critical section, can choose a number, larger than any other number already chosen. Then, the process with the lower number is allowed to enter the critical section before the process with the larger number. Due to the unbounded growth of the numbers that can be chosen, the protocol has an infinite state-space. However, our techniques are immediately applicable. Below, we list a number of key properties we verify for the bakery protocol.

1. No deadlocks, i.e.
   $\nu Z.([\top]Z \wedge \langle \top \rangle \top)$,
2. Two processes can never be in the critical section at the same time, i.e.
   $\nu Z.([\top]Z \wedge \forall b{:}\mathbb{B}.([enter(b)]\nu Z'.([enter(\neg b)]F \wedge [\neg leave(b)]Z')))$,
3. All processes requesting a number eventually enter the critical section, i.e.
   $\nu Z.([\top]Z \wedge \forall b{:}\mathbb{B}.([request(b)]\mu Z'.(([\top]Z' \wedge \langle \top \rangle \top) \vee \langle enter(b) \rangle \top)))$

The first two properties are satisfied. Using our prototype we were able to produce these results in 1 and 2 seconds[2] resp. The third property was proved not to hold in 1 second.

8   Closing Remarks

Related Work. In a setting without data, the use of boolean equation systems for the verification of modal μ-calculus formulae on finite and infinite state systems

---

[2] These results were obtained using a 1.47Ghz AMD Athlon XP1700+ machine with 256Mb main memory, running Linux kernel 2.2.

was studied by Mader [18]. As observed by Mader, the use of boolean equation systems is closely related to the tableau methods of Bradfield and Stirling [5], but avoids certain redundancy of tableaux. It is therefore likely that in the case with data our approach performs better than tableau methods if these would be extended to deal with data.

Closely related to our work is the tool EVALUATOR 3.0 [19], which is an on-the-fly model checker for the regular alternation-free μ-calculus. The machinery of this tool is based on *boolean equation systems*. Although the alternation-free μ-calculus allows for the specification of temporal logic properties involving data, the current version of the tool does not support the data-based version of this language. It is well imaginable that this tool can be extended with our techniques.

A different approach altogether is undertaken by e.g. Bryant *et al.* [7]. Their *Counter arithmetic with Lambda expressions and Uninterpreted function* (CLU) can be used to model both data and control, and is shown to be decidable. For this, CLU sacrifices expressiveness, as it is restricted to the quantifier-free fragment of first order logic. Moreover, their tool (UCLID) is restricted to dealing with safety properties only. We allow for safety, liveness and fairness properties to be verified automatically. Nevertheless, CLU is interesting as it provides evidence that there may be a fragment in our logic or in our specification language that is decidable, even for infinite state systems.

Much work on symbolic reachability analysis of infinite state systems has been undertaken, but most of it concentrates on safety properties only. Bouaj-jani *et al.* (see e.g. [4]) describe how *first-order arithmetical formulae*, expressing safety and liveness conditions, can be verified over Parametric Extended Automaton models, by specifying extra fairness conditions on the transitions of the models. The main difference with our approach is that we do not require fairness conditions on transitions of our models and that the first order modal μ-calculus is in fact capable of specifying fairness properties.

The technique by Bultan *et al.* [8] seems to be able to produce results that are comparable to ours. Their techniques, however, are entirely different from ours. In fact, their approach is similar to the approach used by Alur *et al.* [1] for hybrid systems. It uses affine constraints on integer variables, logical connectives and quantifiers to symbolically encode transition relations and sets of states. The logic, used to specify the properties is a CTL-style logic. In order to guarantee termination, they introduce conservative approximation techniques that may yield "false negatives", which always converges. It is interesting to investigate whether the same conservative approximation techniques can be adapted to our techniques.

Summary. We discussed a pragmatic approach to verifying data-dependent systems. The techniques and procedure we used, are based upon the techniques and algorithms, described by e.g. Mader [18]. A prototype tool implementation is described and a sample verification is discussed. Apart from the example from Section 7, the prototype was successfully applied to other systems, among others the Alternating Bit Protocol, see the discussion in [24].

Summarising, we find that the verifications conducted with our prototype take in many cases an acceptable run-time, even though for systems with finite state spaces, our prototype is often outperformed by most well-established tool-suites. However, we expect some improvements can still be made on the prototype. More importantly, we have been able to successfully use our prototype on systems with a finite (but extremely large) state-space, for which the standard μCRL tool-suite (which is competitive with tool-suites that use explicit state-space representations) failed to calculate the exact state-space (see [24]). Since this is where current state-of-the-art technologies break down, our technique is clearly a welcome addition.

Still, several other issues remain to be investigated. For instance, we think our technique may eventually be used to generalise specialised techniques, such as developed by Bryant et al. [7, 22]. Furthermore, in [15], we identify several results and techniques for solving equations and equation systems. In some cases, these would allow one to skip or speed up the approximation step in our procedure. A promising step is to implement those techniques and results and integrate them with the approach that is outlined in this paper.

The prototype implementation also revealed a number of issues to be resolved. For instance, using our prototype, we were not able to prove absence of deadlock in the Bounded Retransmision Protocol [12], when the bound on the number of retransmissions is unknown. Finding effective work-arounds such problems is necessary to improve the overall efficacy of our technique. Here, the techniques and results of [15] may turn out to be of particular importance.

References

1. R. Alur, C. Courcoubetis, N. Halbwachs, T.A. Henzinger, P.-H. Ho, X. Nicollin, A. Olivero, J. Sifakis, and S. Yovine. The algorithmic analysis of hybrid systems. *Theoretical Computer Science*, 138:3–34, 1995.

2. J.C.M. Baeten and W.P. Weijland. *Process Algebra*. Cambridge Tracts in Theoretical Computer Science. Cambridge University Press, 1990.

3. S.C.C. Blom, W.J. Fokkink, J.F. Groote, I. Van Langevelde, B.Lisser, and J.C. van de Pol. μCRL: A toolset for analysing algebraic specification. In *CAV'01*, volume 2102 of *LNCS*, pages 250–254. Springer-Verlag, 2001.

4. A. Bouajjani, A. Collomb-Annichini, Y. Lacknech, and M. Sighireanu. Analysis of fair extended automata. In P. Cousot, editor, *Proceedings of SAS'01*, volume 2126 of *LNCS*, pages 335–355. Springer-Verlag, 2001.

5. J.C. Bradfield and C. Stirling. Local model checking for infinite state spaces. *Theoretical Computer Science*, 96(1):157–174, 1992.

6. R.E. Bryant. Graph-based algorithms for Boolean function manipulation. *IEEE Transactions on Computers*, C-35(8):677–691, 1986.

7. R.E. Bryant, S.K. Lahiri, and S.A. Seshia. Modeling and verifying systems using a logic of counter arithmetic with lambda expressions and uninterpreted functions. In *CAV 2002*, volume 2404 of *Lecture Notes in Computer Science*, pages 78–92. Springer-Verlag, 2002.

8. T. Bultan, R. Gerber, and W. Pugh. Symbolic model checking of infinite state systems using Presburger arithmetic. In O. Grumberg, editor, *CAV'97*, volume 1254 of *LNCS*, pages 400–411. Springer-Verlag, 1997.

9. J.F. Groote and R. Mateescu. Verification of temporal properties of processes in a setting with data. In A.M. Haeberer, editor, *AMAST'98*, volume 1548 of *LNCS*, pages 74–90. Springer-Verlag, 1999.

10. J.F. Groote and A. Ponse. The syntax and semantics of μCRL. In A. Ponse, C. Verhoef, and S.F.M. van Vlijmen, editors, *Algebra of Communicating Processes '94*, Workshops in Computing Series, pages 26–62. Springer Verlag, 1995.

11. J.F. Groote and M.A. Reniers. Algebraic process verification. In J.A. Bergstra, A. Ponse, and S.A. Smolka, editors, *Handbook of Process Algebra*, chapter 17, pages 1151–1208. Elsevier (North-Holland), 2001.

12. J.F. Groote and J.C. van de Pol. A bounded retransmission protocol for large data packets. a case study in computer checked verification. In M. Wirsing and M. Nivat, editors, *AMAST'96*, volume 110 of *LNCS*, pages 536–550. Springer-Verlag, 1996.

13. J.F. Groote and J.C. van der Pol. Equational binary decision diagrams. In M. Parigot and A. Voronkov, editors, *LPAR2000*, volume 1955 of *LNAI*, pages 161–178. Springer-Verlag, 2000.

14. J.F. Groote and T.A.C. Willemse. A checker for modal formulas for processes with data. Technical Report CSR 02-16, Eindhoven University of Technology, Department of Mathematics and Computer Science, 2002.

15. J.F. Groote and T.A.C. Willemse. Parameterised Boolean Equation Systems. Technical Report CSR 04-09, Eindhoven University of Technology, Department of Mathematics and Computer Science, 2004. An extended abstract is to appear in *CONCUR'04*, *LNCS*, Springer-Verlag, 2004.

16. D. Kozen. Results on the propositional mu-calculus. *Theoretical Computer Science*, 27:333–354, 1983.

17. S.P. Luttik. *Choice quantification in process algebra*. PhD thesis, University of Amsterdam, April 2002.

18. A. Mader. *Verification of Modal Properties Using Boolean Equation Systems*. PhD thesis, Technical University of Munich, 1997.

19. R. Mateescu and M. Sighireanu. Efficient on-the-fly model-checking for regular alternation-free mu-calculus. In S. Gnesi, I. Schieferdecker, and A. Rennoch, editors, *FMICS'2000*, pages 65–86, 2000.

20. R. Milner. *Communication and Concurrency*. Prentice Hall International, 1989.

21. M. Raynal. *Algorithms for Mutual Exclusion*. North Oxford Academic, 1986.

22. O. Strichman, S.A. Seshia, and R.E. Bryant. Deciding separation formulas with SAT. In *CAV 2002*, volume 2404 of *LNCS*, pages 209–222. Springer-Verlag, 2002.

23. Y.S. Usenko. *Linearization in μCRL*. PhD thesis, Eindhoven University of Technology, December 2002.

24. T.A.C. Willemse. *Semantics and Verification in Process Algebras with Data and Timing*. PhD thesis, Eindhoven University of Technology, February 2003.

Semantic Essence of AsmL: Extended Abstract

Yuri Gurevich, Benjamin Rossman, and Wolfram Schulte

Microsoft Research
One Microsoft Way, Redmond, WA 98052, USA

Abstract. The Abstract State Machine Language, AsmL, is a novel executable specification language based on the theory of Abstract State Machines. AsmL is object-oriented, provides high-level mathematical data-structures, and is built around the notion of synchronous updates and finite choice. AsmL is fully integrated into the .NET framework and Microsoft development tools. In this paper, we explain the design rationale of AsmL and sketch semantics for a kernel of the language. The details will appear in the full version of the paper.

1 Introduction

For years, formal method advocates have criticized specification and documentation practices of the software industry. They point out that neither more rigorous English nor semi-formal notation like UML protect us from unintended ambiguity or missing important information. The more practical among them require specifications to be linked to an executable code. Without such a linkage one cannot debug the specification or impose it. Non-linked specifications tend quickly to become obsolete.

We agree with the critique. We need specifications that are precise, readable and executable. The group of Foundations of Software Engineering at Microsoft Research [4] was not satisfied with existing solutions of the specification problem (we address related work in the full paper [8]) and has worked out a new solution based on the theory of abstract state machines [5, 6, 3, 9]. We think of specifications as executable models that exhibit the desired behavior on the appropriate level of abstraction. Abstract State Machine Language, AsmL, is a language for writing such models [1].

The FSE group has designed AsmL, implemented it and integrated it with the Microsoft runtime and tool environment. Furthermore, the group has built various tools on top of AsmL.

1.1 Language Features

The language features of AsmL were chosen to give the user a familiar programming paradigm. For instance, AsmL supports classes and interfaces in the same way as C# or Java do. In fact all .NET structuring mechanisms are supported: enumerations, delegates, methods, events, properties and exceptions. Nevertheless, AsmL is primarily a specification language. Users familiar with the specification language literature will find familiar data structures and features, like sets, sequences, maps, pattern matching, bounded quantification, and set comprehension.

But the crucial features of AsmL, intrinsic to ASMs, are massive synchronous parallelism and finite choice. These features give rise to a cleaner programming style than is possible with standard imperative programming languages. Synchronous parallelism means that AsmL has transactional semantics. (A single step of AsmL can be viewed as a transaction. This transaction may involve massive parallelism.) This provides for a clean separation between the generation of new values and the committal of those values into the persistent state. For instance, when an exception is thrown, the state is automatically rolled back rather than being left in an unknown and possibly inconsistent state. Finite choice allows the specification of a range of behaviors permissible for an (eventual) implementation.

1.2   AsmL-S, a Core of AsmL

AsmL is rich. It incorporates features needed for .NET integration and features needed to support the tools built on top of AsmL. AsmL-S represents the stable core of AsmL; the S alludes to "simple". In this semantical study we allow ourselves to compactify the syntax and ignore some features that do not add semantical complexity. In particular, maps, sequences and sets are first-class citizens of the full AsmL. In AsmL-S only maps are first-class citizens. Sets of type t can be represented as maps from t to a unit type.

Acknowledgments. Without the support from the FSE group this work would not be possible; particular thanks go to Wolfgang Grieskamp and Nikolai Tillmann for developing the runtime mechanism of AsmL. Thanks to Robert Stärk for his comments on the draft of this extended abstract.

2   AsmL-S Through Examples

One can see AsmL as a fusion of the ASM paradigm and the .NET type system, influenced to an extent by other specification languages like VDM [2] or Z [15]. This makes it a powerful modeling tool. On the other hand, we also aimed for simplicity. That is why AsmL is designed in such a way that its core, AsmL-S, is small. AsmL-S is expression and object oriented. It supports synchronous parallelism, finite choice, sequential composition and exception handling. The rest of this section presents examples of AsmL-S programs and expressions. For the abstract syntax of AsmL-S, see Fig. 1 in Section 3.

Remark 1. The definitions in this section are provisional, having been simplified for the purpose of explaining examples. The notions introduced here (*stores*, *effects*, *evaluation*, etc.) are, of course, defined formally in the full paper.

2.1   Expressions

In AsmL-S, expressions are the only syntactic means for writing executable specifications. Binding and function application are call-by-value. (The necessity of
.NET integration is a good reason all by itself not to use lazy evaluation.)

Literal is the set of literals, like 1, *true*, *null* or *void*. We write the value
denoted by a literal as the literal itself. Literals are typed; for instance, 1 is of
type *Int* and *true* is of type *Bool*. AsmL-S has various operations on *Literal*, like
addition over integers or conjunction, i.e. *and*, over *Bool*.

Exception is an infinite set of exceptions, that is disjoint from *Literal*. For
now, think of exceptions as values representing different kinds of errors. We will
discuss exceptions further in Section 2.8.

If e is a closed expression, i.e. an expression without free variables, and v is a
literal or an exception, then $e \xrightarrow{\text{v}} v$ means that e evaluates to v. The "v" above
the arrow alludes to "value".

Examples 1–5 show how to evaluate simple AsmL-S expressions.

Evaluation of Simple Expressions

$$1 + 2 \xrightarrow{\text{v}} 3 \tag{1}$$

$$1/0 \xrightarrow{\text{v}} argX \tag{2}$$

$$\textbf{let } x = 1 \textbf{ do } x + x \xrightarrow{\text{v}} 2 \tag{3}$$

$$\textbf{let } x = 1/0 \textbf{ do } 2 \xrightarrow{\text{v}} argX \tag{4}$$

$$\textbf{if } true \textbf{ then } 0 \textbf{ else } 3 \xrightarrow{\text{v}} 0 \tag{5}$$

For instance, Example 4 shows that let-expressions expose call-by-value semantics: if the evaluation of the binding fails (in this case, resulting in the argument exception), then the complete let-expression fails, irrespective of whether
the body is used the binding.

2.2   Object Orientation

AsmL-S encapsulates state and behavior in classes. As in C# or Java, classes
form a hierarchy according to single inheritance. We use only the single dispatch
of methods. Objects are dynamically allocated. Each object has a unique identity.
Objects can be created, compared and passed around.

ObjectId is an infinite set of potential object identifiers, that is disjoint from
Literal and *Exception*. *Normal values* are either object identifiers in *ObjectId* or
literals. *Values* are either normal values or exceptions.

$$Nvalue = ObjectId \cup Literal$$
$$Value = Nvalue \cup Exception$$

A *type map* is a partial function from *ObjectId* to *Type*. It sends allocated
objects to their runtime types. A *location* is an object identifier together with a

field name drawn from a set *FieldId*. A *content map* is a partial function from *Location* to *Nvalue*. It records the initial bindings for all locations.

$$TypeMap = ObjectId \rightarrow Type$$
$$Location = ObjectId \times FieldId$$
$$ContentMap = Location \rightarrow Nvalue$$

If e is a closed expression, then $e \xrightarrow{\theta,\omega,v} \theta, \omega, v$ means that the evaluation of e produces the type map θ, the content map ω and the value v. Examples 6–14 demonstrate the object oriented features of AsmL-S.

$$\textbf{class } A \ \{\} : \textbf{new } A() \xrightarrow{\theta,\omega,v} \{o \mapsto A\}, \emptyset, o \tag{6}$$

The execution of a nullary constructor returns a fresh object identifier o and extends the type map. The fresh object identifier o is mapped to the dynamic type of the object.

$$\textbf{class } A \ \{i \textbf{ as } Int\}, \ \textbf{class } B \textbf{ extends } A \ \{b \textbf{ as } Bool\} : \tag{7}$$
$$\textbf{new } B(1, true) \xrightarrow{\theta,\omega,v} \{o \mapsto B\}, \ \{(o, i) \mapsto 1, (o, b) \mapsto true\}, o$$

The default constructor in AsmL-S takes one parameter for each field in the order of their declaration. The constructor extends the type map, extends the field map using the corresponding arguments, and returns a fresh object identifier.

$$\textbf{class } A \ \{i \textbf{ as } Int\} : \textbf{new } A(1).i \xrightarrow{v} 1 \tag{8}$$

Instance fields can immediately be accessed.

$$\textbf{class } A \ \big\{Fact(i \textbf{ as } Int) \textbf{ as } Int \textbf{ do } \big(\textbf{if } i = 0 \textbf{ then } 1 \textbf{ else } i * me.Fact(n - 1)\big)\big\} :$$
$$\textbf{new } A().Fact(3) \xrightarrow{\theta,\omega,v} \{o \mapsto A\}, \emptyset, 6 \tag{9}$$

Method calls have call-by-value semantics. Methods can be recursive. Within methods the receiver object is denoted by *me*.

$$\textbf{class } A \ \{One() \textbf{ as } Int \textbf{ do } 1,$$
$$Two() \textbf{ as } Int \textbf{ do } me.One() + me.One()\}, \tag{10}$$
$$\textbf{class } B \textbf{ extends } A \ \{One() \textbf{ as } Int \textbf{ do } -1\} : \textbf{new } B().Two() \xrightarrow{v} -2$$

As in C# or Java method, dispatch is dynamic. Accordingly, in this example, it is the redefined method that is used for evaluation.

$$\textbf{class } A \ \{i \textbf{ as } Int\} : \tag{11}$$
$$\textbf{let } x = \big(\textbf{if } 3 < 4 \textbf{ then } null \textbf{ else new } A(1)\big) \textbf{ do } x.i \xrightarrow{v} nullX$$

If the receiver of a field or method selection is *null*, evaluation fails and throws a null pointer exception.

$$\textbf{class } A \ \{\}, \ \textbf{class } B \ \textbf{extends } A \ \{\} : \textbf{new } B() \ \textbf{is } A \ \xrightarrow{\text{v}} \ true \qquad (12)$$

The operator **is** tests the dynamic type of the expression.

$$\textbf{class } A \ \{\}, \ \textbf{class } B \ \textbf{extends } A \ \{\} : \textbf{new } B() \ \textbf{as } A \ \xrightarrow{\theta,\omega,\text{v}} \ \{o \mapsto B\}, \emptyset, o \quad (13)$$

Casting checks that an instance is a subtype of the given type, and if so then yields the instance without changing the dynamic type of the instance.

$$\textbf{class } A \ \{\}, \ \textbf{class } B \ \textbf{extends } A \ \{\} : \textbf{new } A() \ \textbf{as } B \ \xrightarrow{\text{v}} \ castX \qquad (14)$$

If casting fails, evaluation throws a cast exception.

2.3   Maps

Maps are finite partial functions. A *map display* is essentially the graph of the partial function. For example, a map display $m = \{1 \mapsto 2, 3 \mapsto 4\}$ represents the partial function that maps 1 to 2 and 3 to 4. The map m consists of two *maplets* $1 \mapsto 2$ and $3 \mapsto 4$ mapping *keys* (or *indices*) $1, 3$ to values $2, 4$ respectively.

Remark 2. In AsmL, maps can be also described by means of comprehension expressions. For example, $\{x \mapsto 2 * x \mid x \in \{1, 2, 3\}\}$ denotes $\{1 \mapsto 2, 2 \mapsto 4, 3 \mapsto 6\}$. In AsmL-S map comprehension should be programmed.

The maps of AsmL-S are similar to associative arrays of AWK or Perl. Maps have identities and each key gives rise to a location. Arbitrary normal values can serve as keys. We extend the notion of a location accordingly.

$$Location = ObjectId \times (FieldId \cup Nvalue)$$

Maps may be modified (see Section 2.4). Maps are often used in forall and choose expressions (see Sections 2.5 and 2.7). Examples 15–19 exhibit the use of maps in AsmL-S.

$$\textbf{new } Int \rightarrow Bool \ \{1 \mapsto true, 5 \mapsto false\} \qquad (15)$$

$$\xrightarrow{\theta,\omega,\text{v}} \ \{o \mapsto (Int \rightarrow Bool)\}, \{(o, 1) \mapsto true, (o, 5) \mapsto false\}, o$$

A map constructor takes the map type and the initial map as arguments.

$$\textbf{new } Int \rightarrow Bool \ \{1 \mapsto true, 1 \mapsto false\} \ \xrightarrow{\text{v}} \ argconsistencyX \qquad (16)$$

If a map constructor is inconsistent (i.e. includes at least two maplets with identical keys but different values), then the evaluation throws an inconsistency exception.

$$(\textbf{new } Int \rightarrow Bool \ \{1 \mapsto true\}) \ [1] \ \xrightarrow{\text{v}} \ true \qquad (17)$$

The value of a key can be extracted by means of an index expression.

$$\left(\textbf{if } true \textbf{ then } null \textbf{ else new } Int \to Int \{1 \mapsto 7\}\right) [1] \xrightarrow{\text{v}} nullX \tag{18}$$

$$\left(\textbf{new } Int \to Int \{1 \mapsto 7\}\right) [2] \xrightarrow{\text{v}} mapkeyX \tag{19}$$

However, if the receiver of the index expression is *null* or if the index is not in the domain of the map, then the evaluation throws a null exception or a map-key exception, respectively.

Remark 3. AsmL-S treats maps differently than the full AsmL. The full AsmL is more sophisticated; it treats maps as values which requires partial updates [7]. In AsmL-S, maps are objects. An example illustrating this difference is given in Section 2.10.

2.4   Assignments

One of AsmL's unique features is its handling of state. In sequential languages, like C# or Java, assignments trigger immediate state changes. In ASMs, and therefore also in AsmL, an assignment creates an *update*. An update is a pair: the first component describes the location to update, the second the value to which it should be updated. An update set is a set of updates. A triple that consists of a type map, a content map and an update set will be called a *store*.

$$Update = Location \times (Value \cup \{DEL\})$$
$$UpdateSet = SetOf(Update)$$
$$Store = TypeMap \times ContentMap \times UpdateSet$$

Note that we extended *Value* with a special symbol *DEL* which is used only with locations given by map keys and which marks keys to be removed from the map.

If e is a closed expression, then $e \xrightarrow{\text{s,v}} s, v$ means that evaluation of e produces the store s and the value v. Examples 20–23 show the three ways to create updates. Note that in AsmL-S, but not in AsmL, all fields and keys can be updated. AsmL distinguishes between constants and variables and allows updates only to the latter.

$$\textbf{class } A \{i \textbf{ as } Int\} : \tag{20}$$

$$\textbf{new } A(1).i := 2 \xrightarrow{\text{s,v}} (\{o \mapsto A\}, \{(o,i) \mapsto 1\}, \{((o,i),2)\}), void$$

A field assignment is expressed as usual. However, it does not change the state. Instead, it returns the proposed update.

$$\left(\textbf{new } Int \to Bool \{1 \mapsto true\}\right) [2] := false \tag{21}$$

$$\xrightarrow{\text{s,v}} (\{o \mapsto Int \to Bool\}, \{(o,1) \mapsto true\}, \{((o,2), false)\}), void$$

A map-value assignment behaves similarly. Note that the update set is created irrespective of whether the location exists or not.

$$\textbf{remove} \left(\textbf{new } Int \rightarrow Bool \{1 \mapsto true\}\right)[1] \tag{22}$$

$$\xrightarrow{\text{s,v}} \left(\{o \mapsto Int \rightarrow Bool\}, \{((o,1) \mapsto true\}, \{(o,1), DEL)\}\right), \ void$$

The remove instruction deletes an entry from the map by generating an update that contains the placeholder DEL in the location to delete.

$$\textbf{class } A \ \{F(map \textbf{ as } Int \rightarrow A, \ val \textbf{ as } A) \textbf{ as } Void \textbf{ do } map[0] := val\},$$

$$\textbf{class } B \textbf{ extends } A \ \{\} \ : \tag{23}$$

$$\textbf{let } a = \textbf{new } A() \textbf{ do } a.F(\textbf{new } Int \rightarrow B \ \{\}, a) \xrightarrow{\text{v}} mapvalueX$$

Since $Int \rightarrow B$ is a subtype of $Int \rightarrow A$, it is reasonable that this piece of code type-checks successfully at compile time. However, the assignment fails at runtime and throws a map-assignment exception. Thus, map assignments must be type-checked at runtime. (The same reason forces runtime type-checks of array assignments in C# or Java.)

2.5   Parallel Composition

Hand in hand with the deferred update of the state goes the notion of synchronous parallelism. It allows the simultaneous generation of finitely many updates. Examples 24–27 show two ways to construct synchronous parallel updates in AsmL-S.

$$\textbf{let } x = \textbf{new } Int \rightarrow Int \ \{\} \textbf{ do } \left(x[2] := 4 \ \| \ x[3] := 9\right) \tag{24}$$

$$\xrightarrow{\text{s,v}} \left(\{o \mapsto Int \rightarrow Int\}, \emptyset, \{((o,2),4),((o,3),9)\}\right), \ void$$

Parallel expressions may create multiple updates. Update sets can be inconsistent. A consistency check is performed when a sequential composition of expressions is evaluated and at the end of the program.

$$\textbf{let } x = \textbf{new } Int \rightarrow Int \ \{\} \textbf{ do}$$

$$\textbf{let } y = \textbf{new } Int \rightarrow Void \ \{2 \mapsto void, 3 \mapsto void\} \textbf{ do}$$

$$\textbf{forall } i \textbf{ in } y \textbf{ do } x[i] := 2 * i \tag{25}$$

$$\xrightarrow{\text{s,v}} \left(\{o_1 \mapsto Int \rightarrow Int, o_2 \mapsto Int \rightarrow Void\},\right.$$

$$\left.\{(o_2,2) \mapsto void, (o_2,3) \mapsto void\}, \{((o_1,2),4),((o_1,3),9)\}\right), \ void$$

Parallel assignments can also be performed using forall expressions. In a forall expression $\textbf{forall } x \textbf{ in } e_1 \textbf{ do } e_2$, the subexpression e_1 must evaluate to a map. The subexpression e_2 is then executed with all possible bindings of the introduced variable to the elements in the domain of the map.

$$\textbf{let } x = \textbf{new } Int \rightarrow Int \ \{\} \textbf{ do } \left(\textbf{forall } i \textbf{ in } x \textbf{ do } x[i] := 1/i\right) \tag{26}$$

$$\xrightarrow{\text{s,v}} (\emptyset, \emptyset, \emptyset), \ void$$

If the range of a forall expression is empty, it simply returns the literal *void*.

$$\textbf{let } x = \textbf{new } \mathit{Int} \to \mathit{Int} \ \{2 \mapsto 4\} \ \textbf{do let } y = x[2] \ \textbf{do} \ \big((x[2] := 8) \parallel y\big) \qquad (27)$$
$$\xrightarrow{\text{s,v}} \ \big(\{o \mapsto \mathit{Int} \to \mathit{Int}\}, \{(o,2) \mapsto 4\}, \{((o,2),8)\}\big), \ 4$$

Parallel expressions can return values. In full AsmL, the return value is distinguished syntactically by writing **return**. In AsmL-S, the value of the second expression is returned, whereas forall-expressions return *void*.

2.6   Sequential Composition

AsmL-S also supports sequential composition. Not only does AsmL-S *commit updates on the state*, as in conventional imperative languages, but it also *accumulates updates*, so that the result of a sequential composition can be used in the context of a parallel update as well. Examples 28–31 demonstrate this important feature of AsmL-S.

$$\textbf{let } x = \textbf{new } \mathit{Int} \to \mathit{Int} \ \{2 \mapsto 4\} \ \textbf{do} \ \big((x[2] := 8) \ ; \ (x[2] := x[2] * x[2])\big) \qquad (28)$$
$$\xrightarrow{\text{s,v}} \ \big(\{o \mapsto \mathit{Int} \to \mathit{Int}\}, \{(o,2) \mapsto 4)\}, \{((o,2),64)\}\big), \ \mathit{void}$$

The evaluation of a sequential composition of $e_1 ; e_2$ at a state S proceeds as follows. First e_1 is evaluated at S. If no exception is thrown and the resulting update set is consistent, then the update set is fired (or executed) at S. This creates an auxiliary state S'. Then e_2 is evaluated at S', after which S' is forgotten. The current state is still S. The accumulated update set consists of the updates generated by e_2 at S' and the updates of e_1 that have not been overridden by updates of e_2.

$$\textbf{let } x = \textbf{new } \mathit{Int} \to \mathit{Int} \ \{2 \mapsto 4\} \ \textbf{do} \qquad\qquad\qquad\qquad (29)$$
$$\big(x[2] := 8 \parallel x[2] := 6\big) \ ; \ x[2] := x[2] * x[2] \ \xrightarrow{\text{v}} \ \mathit{updateX}$$

If the update set of the first expression is inconsistent, then execution fails and throws an inconsistency exception.

$$\textbf{let } x = \textbf{new } \mathit{Int} \to \mathit{Int} \ \{1 \mapsto 2\} \ \textbf{do}$$
$$\big(x[2] := 4 \parallel x[3] := 6\big) \ ; \ x[3] := x[3] + 1 \qquad\qquad\qquad (30)$$
$$\xrightarrow{\text{s,v}} \ \big(\{o \mapsto \mathit{Int} \to \mathit{Int}\}, \{(o,1) \mapsto 2)\}, \{((o,2),4), ((o,3),7)\}\big), \ \mathit{void}$$

In this example, the update $((o,3),6)$ from the first expression of the sequential pair is overridden by the update $((o,3),7)$ from the second expression, which is evaluated in the state with content map $\{(o,1) \mapsto 2, (o,2) \mapsto 4, (o,3) \mapsto 6\}$.

$$\textbf{let } x = \textbf{new } \mathit{Int} \to \mathit{Int} \ \{1 \mapsto 3\} \ \textbf{do} \ \big(\textbf{while } x[1] > 0 \ \textbf{do } x[1] := x[1] - 1\big) \quad (31)$$
$$\xrightarrow{\text{s,v}} \ \big(\{o \mapsto \mathit{Int} \to \mathit{Int}\}, \{(o,1) \mapsto 3)\}, \{((o,1),0)\}\big), \ \mathit{void}$$

While loops behave as in usual sequential languages, except that a while loop may be executed in parallel with other expressions and the final update set is reported rather than executed.

2.7   Finite Choice

AsmL-S supports choice between a pair of alternatives or among values in the domain of a map. The actual job of choosing a value from a given set X of alternatives is delegated to the environment. On the abstraction level of AsmL-S, an external function $\mathsf{oneof}(X)$ does the job. This is similar to delegating to the environment the duty of producing fresh object identifiers, by mean of an external function $\mathsf{freshid}()$.

Evaluation of a program, when convergent, returns one effect and one value. Depending on the environment, different evaluations of the same program may return different effects and values. Examples 32–36 demonstrate finite choice in AsmL-S.

$$1 \parallel 2 \xrightarrow{\text{v}} \mathsf{oneof}\{1,2\} \tag{32}$$

An expression $e_1 \parallel e_2$ chooses between the given pair of alternatives.

$$\textbf{choose } i \textbf{ in } \big(\textbf{new } Int \to Void \ \{1 \mapsto void, 2 \mapsto void\}\big) \textbf{ do } i$$
$$\xrightarrow{\text{s,v}} \mathsf{oneof}\big\{ \big((\{o \mapsto Int \to Void\}, \{(o,1) \mapsto void, (o,2) \mapsto void\}, \emptyset), 1\big) \tag{33}$$
$$\big((\{o \mapsto Int \to Void\}, \{(o,1) \mapsto void, (o,2) \mapsto void\}, \emptyset), 2\big)\big\}$$

Choice-expressions choose from among values in the domain of a map.

$$\textbf{choose } i \textbf{ in } \big(\textbf{new } Int \to Int \ \{\}\big) \textbf{ do } i \xrightarrow{\text{v}} choiceX \tag{34}$$

If the choice domain is empty, a choice exception is thrown. (The full AsmL distinguishes between choose-expressions and choose-statements. The choose-expression throws an exception if the choice domain is empty, but the choose-statement with the empty choice domain is equivalent to *void*.)

$$\textbf{class } Math\{Double(x \textbf{ as } Int) \textbf{ as } Int \textbf{ do } 2*x\} \ : \tag{35}$$
$$\textbf{new } Math().Double(1 \parallel 2) \qquad\qquad \xrightarrow{\text{v}} \mathsf{oneof}\{2,4\}$$

$$\textbf{class } Math\{Double(x \textbf{ as } Int) \textbf{ as } Int \textbf{ do } 2*x\} \ : \tag{36}$$
$$\textbf{new } Math().Double(1) \parallel \textbf{new } Math().Double(2) \xrightarrow{\text{v}} \mathsf{oneof}\{2,4\}$$

Finite choice distributes over function calls.

2.8   Exception Handling

Exception handling is mandatory for a modern specification language. In any case, it is necessary for AsmL because of the integration with .NET. The parallel execution of AsmL-S means that several exceptions can be thrown at once. Exception handling behaves as a finite choice for the specified caught exceptions. If an exception is caught, the store (including updates) computed by the try-expression is rolled back.

In AsmL-S, exceptions are special values similar to literals. For technical reasons, it is convenient to distinguish between literals and exceptions. Even though exceptions are values, an exception cannot serve as the content of a field, for example. (In the full AsmL, exceptions are instances of special exceptional classes.) There are several built-in exceptions: $argX$, $updateX$, $choiceX$, etc. In addition, one may use additional exception names e.g. $fooX$.

$$\textbf{class } A \ \big\{ Fact(n \textbf{ as } Int) \textbf{ as } Int \textbf{ do } \big(\textbf{if } n \geq 0 \textbf{ then}$$
$$\big(\textbf{if } n = 0 \textbf{ then } 1 \textbf{ else } Fact(n-1) \big) \textbf{ else throw } factorialX \big) \big\} : \quad (37)$$
$$\textbf{new } A.Fact(-5) \ \xrightarrow{\ v\ } \ factorialX$$

Custom exceptions may be generated by means of a throw-expression. Built-in exceptions may also be thrown. Here, for instance, **throw** $argX$ could appropriately replace **throw** $factorialX$.

Examples 38–40 explain exception handling.

$$\textbf{let } x = \textbf{new } Int \to Int \ \{\} \textbf{ do } \big(\textbf{try } \big(x[1] := 2 \ ; \ x[3] := 4/0 \big) \textbf{ catch } argX : 5 \big)$$
$$\xrightarrow{\ s,v\ } \ \big(\{o \mapsto Int \to Int\}, \emptyset, \emptyset \big), 5 \quad\quad\quad (38)$$

The argument exception triggered by $4/0$ in the try-expression is caught, at which point the update $((x,1),2)$ is abandoned and evaluation proceeds with the contingency expression 5. In general, the catch clause can involve a sequence of exceptions: a "catch" occurs if the try expression evaluates to any one of the enumerated exceptions. Since there are only finitely many built-in exceptions and finitely many custom exceptions used in a program, a catch clause can enumerate *all* exceptions. (This is common enough in practice to warrant its own syntactic shortcut, though we do not provide one in the present paper.)

$$\textbf{try } \big(\textbf{throw } fooX \big) \textbf{ catch } barX, bazX \ : \ 1 \ \xrightarrow{\ v\ } \ fooX \quad\quad (39)$$

Uncaught exceptions propagate up.

$$\textbf{throw } fooX \ \| \ \textbf{throw } barX \ \xrightarrow{\ v\ } \ \mathsf{oneof}\{fooX, barX\} \quad\quad (40)$$

If multiple exceptions are thrown in parallel, one of them is returned nondeterministically.

$$\textbf{throw } fooX \ [\!] \ 1 \ \xrightarrow{\ v\ } \ \mathsf{oneof}\{fooX, 1\} \quad\quad (41)$$

Finite choice is "demonic". This means that if one of the alternatives of a choice expression throws an exception and the other one converges normally the result might be either that the exception is propagated or that the value of the normally terminating alternative is returned.

2.9 Expressions with Free Variables

Examples 1-41 illustrate operational semantics for closed expressions (containing no free variables). In general, an expression e contains free variables. In this case, operational semantics of e is defined with respect to an *evaluation context* (b, r) consisting of a binding b for the free variables of e and a store $r = (\theta, \omega, u)$ where for each free variable x, $b(x)$ is either a literal or a object identifier in $\mathrm{dom}(\theta)$. We write $e \xrightarrow{\mathrm{v}}_{b,r} v$ if computation of e in evaluation context (b, r) produces value v.

$$x + y \xrightarrow{\mathrm{v}}_{\{x \mapsto 7, y \mapsto 11\}, \, (\emptyset, \emptyset, \emptyset)} 18 \tag{42}$$

$$\ell[2] \xrightarrow{\mathrm{v}}_{\{\ell \mapsto o\}, \, (\{o \mapsto Int \to Bool\}, \{(o, 2) \mapsto false\}, \emptyset)} false \tag{43}$$

A more general notation $e \xrightarrow{\mathrm{s,v}}_{b,r} s, v$ means that a computation of e in evaluation context (b, r) produces new store s and value v.

2.10   Maps as Objects

This subsection expands Remark 3. It was prompted by a question of Robert Stärk who raised the following example.

> **class** A $\{f$ **as** $Int \to Bool$, g **as** $Int \to Bool\}$:
>
>   **let** $a = $ **new** $A($**new** $Int \to Bool \, \{1 \mapsto true, \, 2 \mapsto true\}$,
>
> $$\text{**new** } Int \to Bool \, \{\}) \text{ **do**} \tag{44}$$
>
> $a.g := a.f$; $a.x(2) := false$
>
> $\xrightarrow{\mathrm{s,v}}$ $(\{o_1 \mapsto A, \, o_2 \mapsto Int \to Bool, \, o_3 \mapsto Int \to Bool\}$,
>
> $\{(o_1, f) \mapsto o_2, (o_1, g) \mapsto o_3\}, \, \{((o_1, g), o_2), (o_2, 2), false)\}$), *void*

In this example, the first assignment $a.g := a.f$ is responsible for the update $((o_1, g), o_2)$; the second assignment gives rise to the update $((o_2, 2), false)$. Thus, $a.g[2]$ has value *false* after all updates are executed.

This same program has a different semantics in the full AsmL, where maps are treated as values rather than objects. In AsmL, the assignment $a.g := a.f$ has the effect of updating $a.g$ to the value of $a.f$, i.e., the map $\{1 \mapsto true, \, 2 \mapsto false\}$. The second assignment, $a.f[2] := false$, has no bearing on $a.g$. Thus, $a.g[2]$ has value *true* after all updates are executed.

In treating maps as objects in AsmL-S, we avoid having to introduce the machinery of partial updates [7], which is necessary for the treatment of maps as values in AsmL. This causes a discrepancy between the semantics of AsmL-S and of AsmL. Fortunately, there is an easy AsmL-S expression that updates the value of a map m_1 to the value of another map m_2 (without assigning m_2 to m_1):

> **forall** i **in** m_1 **do remove** $m_1[i]$; **forall** i **in** m_2 **do** $m_1[i] := m_2[i]$

The first forall expression erases m_1; the second forall expression copies m_2 to m_1 at all keys i in the domain of m_2.

3   Syntax and Semantics

The syntax of AsmL-S is similar to but different from that of the full AsmL. In this semantics paper, an attractive and user-friendly syntax is not a priority but brevity is. In particular, AsmL-S does not support the offside rule of the full AsmL that expresses scoping via indentation. Instead, AsmL-S uses parentheses and scope separators like ':'.

3.1   Abstract Syntax

We take some easy-to-understand liberties with vector notation. A vector $\bar{x}$ is typically a list $x_1 \ldots x_n$ of items possibly separated by commas. A sequence $x_1 \alpha y_1, \ldots, x_n \alpha y_n$ can be abbreviated to $\bar{x} \alpha \bar{y}$, where α represents a binary operator. This allows us, for instance, to describe an argument sequence ℓ_1 **as** t_1, ..., ℓ_n **as** t_n more succinctly as $\bar{\ell}$ **as** $\bar{t}$. The empty vector is denoted by ϵ.

Figure 1 describes the abstract syntax of AsmL-S. The meta-variables c, f, m, ℓ, *prim*, *op*, *lit*, and *exc*, in Fig. 1 range over disjoint infinite sets of class names (including *Object*), field names, method names, local variable names (including *me*), primitive type symbols, operation symbols, literals, and exception names (including several built-in exceptions: *argX*, *updateX*, ...). Sequences of class names, field names, method names and parameter declarations are assumed to have no duplicates.

An AsmL-S program is a list of class declarations, with distinct class names different from *Object*, followed by an expression, the body of the program. Each class declaration gives a super-class, a sequence of field declarations with distinct field names, and a sequence of method declarations with distinct method names.

AsmL-S has three categories of types — primitive types, classes and map types — plus two auxiliary types, *Null* and *Thrown*. (*Thrown* is used in the static semantics, although it is absent from the syntax.) Among the primitive types, there are *Bool*, *Int* and *Void*. (Ironically, the type *Void* isn't void but contains a single literal *void*. That is how *Void* is in the C programming language and its relatives. We decided to stick to this tradition.) There could be additional primitive types; this makes no difference in the sequel.

Objects come in two varieties: class instances and maps. Objects are created with the **new** operator only; more sophisticated object constructors have to be programmed in AsmL-S. A new-class-instance expression takes one argument for each field of the class, thereby initializing all fields with the given arguments. A new-map expression takes a (possibly empty) sequence of key-values pairs, called *maplets*, defining the initial map. Maps are always finite. A map can be overridden, extended or reduced (by removing some of its maplets). AsmL-S supports the usual object-oriented expressions for type testing and type casting.

The common sequential programming languages have only one way to compose expressions, namely the sequential composition $e_1 \; ; \; e_2$. To evaluate $e_1 \; ; \; e_2$, first evaluate e_1 and then evaluate e_2. AsmL-S provides two additional compositions: the parallel composition $e_1 \parallel e_2$ and the nondeterministic composition $e_1 \, [] \, e_2$. To evaluate $e_1 \parallel e_2$, evaluate e_1 and e_2 in parallel. To evaluate $e_1 \, [] \, e_2$ eval-

$$
\begin{aligned}
pgm \ &= \ \overline{cls} \ : \ e &&\text{programs} \\
cls \ &= \ \textbf{class} \ c \ \textbf{extends} \ c \ \{\overline{fld} \ \overline{mth}\} &&\text{classes} \\
fld \ &= \ f \ \textbf{as} \ t &&\text{fields} \\
mth \ &= \ m(\overline{\ell} \ \textbf{as} \ \overline{t}) \ \textbf{as} \ t \ \textbf{do} \ e &&\text{methods} \\
lit \ &= \ null \ | \ void \ | \ true \ | \ 0 \ | \ \dots &&\text{literals} \\
op \ &= \ + \ | - \ | \ / \ | = \ | < \ | \ and \ | \ \dots &&\text{primitive operations} \\
prim \ &= \ Bool \ | \ Int \ | \ Void \ | \ \dots &&\text{primitive types} \\
t \ &= \ prim \ | \ Null \ | \ c \ | \ t \to t &&\text{normal types} \\
exc \ &= \ argX \ | \ updateX \ | \ choiceX \ | \ \dots &&\text{exceptions} \\
e \ &= &&\text{expressions}
\end{aligned}
$$

$\quad lit \quad | \quad \ell$	literals/local variables
$| \quad op(\overline{e})$	built-in operations
$| \quad \textbf{let} \ \ell = e \ \textbf{do} \ e$	local binding
$| \quad \textbf{if} \ e \ \textbf{then} \ e \ \textbf{else} \ e$	case distinction
$| \quad \textbf{new} \ c\,(\overline{e})$	creation of class instances
$| \quad \textbf{new} \ t \to t \ \{\overline{e} \mapsto \overline{e}\}$	creation of maps
$| \quad e.f \quad | \quad e\,[e] \quad | \quad e.m(\overline{e})$	field/index/method access
$| \quad e.f := e$	field update
$| \quad e[e] := e \quad | \quad \textbf{remove} \ e[e]$	index update
$| \quad e \ \textbf{is} \ t$	type test
$| \quad e \ \textbf{as} \ t$	type cast
$| \quad e \parallel e \quad | \quad \textbf{forall} \ \ell \ \textbf{in} \ e \ \textbf{do} \ e$	parallel composition
$| \quad e \parallel e \quad | \quad \textbf{choose} \ \ell \ \textbf{in} \ e \ \textbf{do} \ e$	nondeterministic composition
$| \quad e\,;e \quad | \quad \textbf{while} \ e \ \textbf{do} \ e$	sequential composition
$| \quad \textbf{try} \ e \ \textbf{catch} \ \overline{exc} : e$	exception handling
$| \quad \textbf{throw} \ exc$	explicit exception generation

Fig. 1. Abstract Syntax of AsmL-S

uate either e_1 or e_2. The related semantical issues will be addressed later. The **while, forall** and **choose** expressions generalize the two-component sequential, parallel and nondeterministic compositions, respectively.

AsmL-S supports exception handling. In full AsmL, exceptions are instances of special exception classes. In AsmL-S, exceptions are atomic values of type *Thrown*. (Alternatively, we could have introduced a whole hierarchy of exception types.) There are a handful of built-in exceptions, like *argX*; all of them end with "X". A user may use additional exception names. There is no need to declare new exception names; just use them. Instead of prescribing a particular syntactic form to new exception names, we just presume that they are taken from a special infinite pool of potential exception names that is disjoint from other semantical domains of relevance.

3.2   Class Table and Subtypes

It is convenient to view a program as a class table together with the expression to be evaluated [10]. The class table maps class names different from *Object* to the corresponding class definitions. The class table has the structure of a tree with edge relation $c \lhd c'$ meaning that **extends** c' is in the declaration of c; we say c' is the *parent* of c. *Object* is of course the root of class tree.

Remark 4. Whenever the "**extends** c" clause is omitted in examples 1-43, there is an implicit **extends** *Object*.

The subtype relation $\leq$ corresponding to a given class table is generated recursively by the rules in Fig. 2, for arbitrary types t, t', t'', τ, τ' and classes c, c':

- $t \leq t$, $\dfrac{t \leq t'\quad t' \leq t''}{t \leq t''}$ $\leq$ *is a reflexive partial order*

- $\dfrac{c \lhd c'}{c \leq c'}$ $\leq$ *extends the parent relation over classes*

- $t \to t' \leq Object$ *maps are objects*

- $\dfrac{t \leq \tau\quad t' \leq \tau'}{(t \to t') \leq (\tau \to \tau')}$ *maps types are covariant in argument and result types*

- $\dfrac{t \leq Object}{Null \leq t}$ *Null lies beneath all object types*

- $Thrown \leq t$ *Thrown lies beneath all other types*

Fig. 2. Inductive Definition of the Subtype Relation

Call two types *comparable* if one of them is a subtype of the other; otherwise call them *incomparable*. Primitive types compare the least. If t is a primitive type, then $t \leq t$ and $Thrown \leq t$ are the only subtype relations involving t.

The following proposition is easy to check.

Proposition 1. *Every two types t_1, t_2 have a greatest lower bound $t_1 \sqcap t_2$. Every two subtypes of Object have a least upper bound $t_1 \sqcup t_2$.*   □

Remark 5. One may argue that map types should be contravariant in the argument, like function types [13]. In the full paper, we discuss pros and cons of such a decision.

If c is a class different from *Object*, then $addf(c)$ is the sequence of distinct field names given by the declaration of c. These are the new fields of c, acquired in addition to those of $parent(c)$. The sequence of all fields of a class is defined by induction using the concatenation operation.

$$fldseq(Object) = \epsilon$$
$$fldseq(c) = addf(c) \cdot fldseq(parent(c))$$

We assume that $addf(c)$ is disjoint from $fldseq(parent(c))$ for all classes c. If f is a field of c of type t, then $fldtype(f, c) = t$. If $fldseq(c) = (f_1, \ldots, f_n)$ and $fldtype(f_i, c) = t_i$, then

$$fldinfo(c) = \bar{f} \text{ as } \bar{t} = (f_1 \text{ as } t_1, \ldots, f_n \text{ as } t_n).$$

The situation is slightly more complicated with methods because, unlike fields, methods can be overridden. Let $addm(c)$ be the set of method names included in the declaration of c. We define inductively the set of all method names of a class.

$$mthset(Object) = \emptyset$$
$$mthset(c) = addm(c) \cup mthset(parent(c))$$

For each $m \in mthset(c)$, $dclr(m, c)$ is the declaration

$$m(\ell_1 \text{ as } \tau_1, \ldots, \ell_n \text{ as } \tau_n) \text{ as } t \text{ do } e$$

of m employed by c. We assume, as a syntactic constraint, that the variables ℓ_i are all distinct and different from me. The declaration $dclr(m, c)$ is the declaration of m in the class $home(m, c)$ defined as follows:

$$\frac{m \in addm(c)}{home(m, c) = c} \qquad \frac{m \in mthset(c) - addm(c)}{home(m, c) = home(parent(c))}$$

In the sequel, we restrict attention to an arbitrary but fixed class table.

3.3   Static Semantics

We assume that every literal lit has a built-in type $littype(lit)$. For instance, $littype(2) = Int$, $littype(true) = Bool$ and $littype(null) = Null$. We also assume that a type function $optype(op)$ defines the argument and result types for every built-in operation op. For example, $optype(and) = (Bool, Bool) \rightarrow Bool$.

Suppose e is an expression, possibly involving free variables. A *type context* for e is a total function T from the free variables of e to types.

$\mathfrak{T}_T(e)$ is a partial function from expressions and type contexts to types. If $\mathfrak{T}_T(e)$ is defined, then e is said to be *well-typed* with respect to T, and $\mathfrak{T}_T(e)$ is called its *static type*.

The definition of $\mathfrak{T}_T(e)$ is inductive, given by rules in Fig. 3. See the full paper for a more thorough exposition.

- $\mathfrak{T}_T(lit) = littype(lit)$

- $\dfrac{optype(op) = \bar{\tau} \to t \qquad \mathfrak{T}_T(\bar{e}) \leq \bar{\tau}}{\mathfrak{T}_T(op(\bar{e})) = t}$

- $\dfrac{\mathfrak{T}_T(e_1) = t}{\mathfrak{T}_T(\mathbf{let}\ \ell = e_1\ \mathbf{do}\ e_2) = \mathfrak{T}_{T\otimes\{\ell \mapsto t\}}(e_2)}$

- $\dfrac{\mathfrak{T}_T(e_1) = Bool}{\mathfrak{T}_T(\mathbf{if}\ e_1\ \mathbf{then}\ e_2\ \mathbf{else}\ e_3) = \mathfrak{T}_T(e_2) \sqcup \mathfrak{T}_T(e_3)}$

- $\dfrac{fldinfo(c) = \bar{f}\ \mathbf{as}\ \bar{t} \qquad \mathfrak{T}_T(\bar{e}) \leq \bar{t}}{\mathfrak{T}_T(\mathbf{new}\ c(\bar{e})) = c}$

- $\dfrac{\mathfrak{T}_T(e) = c}{\mathfrak{T}_T(e.f) = fldtype(f,c)}$

- $\dfrac{\mathfrak{T}_T(e_1) = c \qquad \mathfrak{T}_T(\overline{e_2}) \leq \bar{\tau}}{\dfrac{dclr(m,c) = m(\bar{\ell}\ \mathbf{as}\ \bar{\tau})\ \mathbf{as}\ t\ \mathbf{do}\ e_3}{\mathfrak{T}_T(e_1.m(\overline{e_2})) = t}}$

- $\dfrac{\mathfrak{T}_T(e_2) \leq \mathfrak{T}_T(e_1.f)}{\mathfrak{T}_T(e_1.f := e_2) = Void}$

- $\dfrac{\mathfrak{T}_T(\overline{e_1}) \leq t_1 \qquad \mathfrak{T}_T(\overline{e_2}) \leq t_2}{\mathfrak{T}_T(\mathbf{new}\ t_1 \to t_2\ \{\overline{e_1} \mapsto \overline{e_2}\}) = t_1 \to t_2}$

- $\dfrac{\mathfrak{T}_T(e_1) = \tau \to t \qquad \mathfrak{T}_T(e_2) \leq \tau}{\mathfrak{T}_T(e_1[e_2]) = t}$

- $\dfrac{\mathfrak{T}_T(e_1) = \tau \to t \qquad \mathfrak{T}_T(e_2) \leq \tau \qquad \mathfrak{T}_T(e_3) \leq t}{\mathfrak{T}_T(e_1[e_2] := e_3) = Void}$

- $\dfrac{\mathfrak{T}_T(e_1) = \tau \to t \qquad \mathfrak{T}_T(e_2) \leq \tau}{\mathfrak{T}_T(\mathbf{remove}\ e_1[e_2]) = Void}$

- $\mathfrak{T}_T(\ell) = T(\ell)$

- $\dfrac{t < \mathfrak{T}_T(e)}{\mathfrak{T}_T(e\ \mathbf{is}\ t) = Bool}$

- $\dfrac{t < \mathfrak{T}_T(e)}{\mathfrak{T}_T(e\ \mathbf{as}\ t) = t}$

- $\dfrac{\mathfrak{T}_T(e_1)\ \text{is defined}}{\mathfrak{T}_T(e_1\ \|\ e_2) = \mathfrak{T}_T(e_2)}$

- $\dfrac{\mathfrak{T}_T(e_1) = \tau \to t}{\dfrac{\mathfrak{T}_{T\otimes\{\ell \mapsto \tau\}}(e_2)\ \text{is defined}}{\mathfrak{T}_T(\mathbf{forall}\ \ell\ \mathbf{in}\ e_1\ \mathbf{do}\ e_2) = Void}}$

- $\mathfrak{T}_T(e_1\ \|\ e_2) = \mathfrak{T}_T(e_1) \sqcup \mathfrak{T}_T(e_2)$

- $\dfrac{\mathfrak{T}_T(e_1) = \tau \to t}{\mathfrak{T}_T(\mathbf{choose}\ \ell\ \mathbf{in}\ e_1\ \mathbf{do}\ e_2) = \mathfrak{T}_{T\otimes\{\ell \mapsto \tau\}}(e_2)}$

- $\dfrac{\mathfrak{T}_T(e_1)\ \text{is defined}}{\mathfrak{T}_T(e_1\ ;\ e_2) = \mathfrak{T}_T(e_2)}$

- $\dfrac{\mathfrak{T}_T(e_1) = Bool \qquad \mathfrak{T}_T(e_2)\ \text{is defined}}{\mathfrak{T}_T(\mathbf{while}\ e_1\ \mathbf{do}\ e_2) = Void}$

- $\mathfrak{T}_T(\mathbf{throw}\ exc) = Thrown$

- $\mathfrak{T}_T(\mathbf{try}\ e_1\ \mathbf{catch}\ \overline{exc} : e_2) = \mathfrak{T}_T(e_1) \sqcup \mathfrak{T}_T(e_2)$

Fig. 3. Static Types of Expressions in AsmL-S

3.4   Well-Formedness

We now make an additional assumption about the underlying class table: *for each class c and each method* $m \in mthset(c)$, *m is well-formed relative to c* (symbolically: *m ok in c*).

The definition of *m ok in c* is inductive. Suppose $dclr(m,c) = m(\ell_1\ \mathbf{as}\ \tau_1,$ $\ldots,\ \ell_n\ \mathbf{as}\ \tau_n)\ \mathbf{as}\ t\ \mathbf{do}\ e$ and $c \lhd c'$. Let T denote the type context $\{me \mapsto c\} \cup \{\ell_1 \mapsto \tau_1, \ldots, \ell_n \mapsto \tau_n\}$.

- $\dfrac{m \in addm(c) - mthset(c') \qquad \mathfrak{T}_T(e) \leq t}{m\ \text{ok in}\ c}$

- $\dfrac{m \in mthset(c) - addm(c) \qquad m\ \text{ok in}\ c'}{m\ \text{ok in}\ c}$

$$\bullet \quad \frac{m \in addm(c) \cap mthset(c') \qquad \mathfrak{T}_T(e) \leq t \qquad m \text{ ok in } c'}{m \text{ ok in } c}$$

The statement $\bar{\tau} \to t \leq \bar{\tau}' \to t'$, in the final premise, abbreviates the inequalities $\tau_1 \leq \tau_1', \ldots, \tau_n \leq \tau_n'$ and $t \leq t'$.

3.5   Operational Semantics

Suppose (b, r) is an evaluation context (Section 2.9) for an expression e, where $r = (\theta, \omega, u)$. Then (b, r) gives rise to a type context $[b, r]$ defined by

$$[b, r](\ell) = \begin{cases} \theta_r(b(\ell)) & \text{if } b(\ell) \in dom(\theta_r) \\ littype(b(\ell)) & \text{if } b(\ell) \in Literal. \end{cases}$$

We say e is (b, r)-*typed* if it is well-typed with respect to the type context $[b, r]$, that is, if $\mathfrak{T}_{[b,r]}(e)$ is defined.

In the full paper we define an operator $\mathfrak{E}_{b,r}$ over (b, r)-typed expressions. The computation of $\mathfrak{E}_{b,r}$ is in general nondeterministic (as it relies on external functions freshid and oneof) and it may diverge (as it is recursive but not necessarily well-founded). If it converges, it produces an *effect* $\mathfrak{E}_{b,r}(e) = (s, v)$ where s is a store and v is a value, that is, $e \xrightarrow{s,v}_{b,r} s, v$ in the notation of Section 2.9.

After seeing the examples in Section 2, the reader should have a fairly good idea how the effect operator works. Figure 4 gives a few of the rules that comprise the definition of $\mathfrak{E}_{b,r}(e)$; each rule covers a different kind of expression e. See the full paper for a complete set of rules defining the effect operator.

4   Analysis

The effect operator is monotone with respect to stores: if $\mathfrak{E}_{b,r}(e) = (s, v)$ then r is a substore of s. Furthermore, if v is an exception then $r = s$, meaning that the store is rolled back whenever an exception occurs.

In addition to these properties, the static-type and effect operators satisfy the usual notions of type soundness and semantic refinement. See the full paper for precise statements and proofs of the theorems mentioned in this section.

The type of an effect (s, v), where $s = (\theta, \omega, u)$, is defined as follows:

$$type(s, v) = \begin{cases} \theta(v) & \text{if } v \in dom(\theta) \\ littype(v) & \text{if } v \in Literal \\ Thrown & \text{if } v \in Exception. \end{cases}$$

Theorem 2 (Type Soundness). *For every evaluation context* (b, r) *and every* (b, r)-*typed expression* e, *we have*

$$type(\mathfrak{E}_{b,r}(e)) \leq \mathfrak{T}_{[b,r]}(e)$$

for any converging computation of $\mathfrak{E}_{b,r}(e)$.

- $\mathfrak{E}_{b,r}(lit) = \langle r, lit \rangle$

- $\dfrac{\mathfrak{E}_{b,r}(\bar{e}) = \langle \bar{s}, \bar{v} \rangle \qquad op(\bar{v}) \text{ is defined}}{\mathfrak{E}_{b,r}(op(\bar{e})) = \langle \bigcup \bar{s}, op(\bar{v}) \rangle}$

- $\dfrac{\mathfrak{E}_{b,r}(e_1) = \langle s, v \rangle}{\mathfrak{E}_{b,r}(\textbf{let } \ell = e_1 \textbf{ do } e_2) = \mathfrak{E}_{b \otimes \{\ell \mapsto v\},\, s}(e_2)}$

- $\dfrac{\mathfrak{E}_{b,r}(\bar{e}) = \langle \bar{s}, \bar{v} \rangle \qquad freshid() = o}{\mathfrak{E}_{b,r}(\textbf{new } c(\bar{e})) = \langle r \cup \bigcup \bar{s} \cup (\{o \mapsto c\}, \{o \mapsto \{\bar{f} \mapsto \bar{v}\}\}, \emptyset),\, o \rangle}$

- $\dfrac{\left(\begin{array}{ccc} \mathfrak{E}_{b,r}(e_1) = \langle s_1, v_1 \rangle & \mathfrak{E}_{b,r}(\overline{e_2}) = \langle \overline{s_2}, \overline{v_2} \rangle & type(\langle s_1, v_1 \rangle) = c \\ \multicolumn{3}{c}{dclr(m,c) = m(\bar{\ell} \textbf{ as } \bar{\tau}) \textbf{ as } t \textbf{ do } e_3} \end{array} \right)}{\mathfrak{E}_{b,r}(e_1.m(\overline{e_2})) = \mathfrak{E}_{\{me \mapsto v_1,\, \bar{\ell} \mapsto \overline{v_2}\},\, s_1 \cup \overline{s_2}}(e_3)}$

- $\dfrac{\mathfrak{E}_{b,r}(e_1) = \langle s_1, v_1 \rangle \qquad \mathfrak{E}_{b,r}(e_2) = \langle s_2, v_2 \rangle \qquad v_1 \neq null}{\mathfrak{E}_{b,r}(e_1.f := e_2) = \langle s_1 \cup s_2 \cup (\emptyset, \emptyset, \{((v_1, f), v_2)\}),\, void \rangle}$

- $\dfrac{\left(\begin{array}{cc} \mathfrak{E}_{b,r}(\overline{e_1}) = \langle \overline{s_1}, \overline{v_1} \rangle & \mathfrak{E}_{b,r}(\overline{e_2}) = \langle \overline{s_2}, \overline{v_2} \rangle \\ consistent(\overline{v_1}, \overline{v_2}) & freshid() = o \end{array} \right)}{\begin{array}{l} \mathfrak{E}_{b,r}(\textbf{new } \tau \rightarrow t\ \{\overline{e_1} \mapsto \overline{e_2}\}) \\ \quad = \langle r \cup \bigcup \overline{s_1} \cup \bigcup \overline{s_2} \cup (\{o \mapsto \tau \rightarrow t\}, \{o \mapsto \{\overline{v_1} \mapsto \overline{v_2}\}\}, \emptyset),\, o \rangle \end{array}}$

  where $consistent(a_1, ..., a_n, b_1, ..., b_n) = \bigwedge_{1 \leq i,j \leq n} (a_i = a_j) \leftrightarrow (b_i = b_j)$

- $\dfrac{\mathfrak{E}_{b,r}(\overline{e_1}) = \langle \overline{s_1}, \overline{v_1} \rangle \qquad \mathfrak{E}_{b,r}(\overline{e_2}) = \langle \overline{s_2}, \overline{v_2} \rangle \qquad \neg consistent(\overline{v_1}, \overline{v_2})}{\mathfrak{E}_{b,r}(\textbf{new } \tau \rightarrow t\ \{\overline{e_1} \mapsto \overline{e_2}\}) = \langle r, argconsistencyX \rangle}$

- $\dfrac{\left(\begin{array}{c} \mathfrak{E}_{b,r}(e_1) = \langle s', v' \rangle \\ \mathfrak{E}_{b \otimes \{\ell \mapsto \rho\},\, s'}(e_2) = \langle s_\rho, v_\rho \rangle \text{ for each } \rho \in dom(\omega_{s'}(v')) \end{array} \right)}{\mathfrak{E}_{b,r}(\textbf{forall } \ell \textbf{ in } e_1 \textbf{ do } e_2) = \langle s' \cup \bigcup_{\rho \in dom(\omega_{s'}(v'))} s_\rho,\, void \rangle}$

- $\dfrac{\left(\begin{array}{cc} \mathfrak{E}_{b,r}(e_1) = \langle s', v' \rangle & v' \notin Exception \\ \multicolumn{2}{c}{\mathfrak{E}_{b \otimes \{\ell \mapsto \rho\},\, s'}(e_2) = \langle s_\rho, v_\rho \rangle \text{ for each } \rho \in dom(\omega_{s'}(v'))} \\ \multicolumn{2}{c}{\{v_\rho : \rho \in dom(\omega_{s'}(v'))\} \cap Exception \neq \emptyset} \end{array} \right)}{\begin{array}{l} \mathfrak{E}_{b,r}(\textbf{forall } \ell \textbf{ in } e_1 \textbf{ do } e_2) = \\ \quad \langle r,\, oneof(\{v_\rho : \rho \in dom(\omega_{s'}(v'))\} \cap Exception) \rangle \end{array}}$

And on the right column:

- $\mathfrak{E}_{b,r}(\ell) = \langle r, b(\ell) \rangle$

- $\dfrac{\mathfrak{E}_{b,r}(\bar{e}) = \langle \bar{s}, \bar{v} \rangle \qquad op(\bar{v}) \text{ is undefined}}{\mathfrak{E}_{b,r}(op(\bar{e})) = \langle r, argX \rangle}$

- $\dfrac{\mathfrak{E}_{b,r}(e_1) = \langle s, true \rangle}{\mathfrak{E}_{b,r}(\textbf{if } e_1 \textbf{ then } e_2 \textbf{ else } e_3) = \mathfrak{E}_{b,s}(e_2)}$

Fig. 4. Examples of rules from the definition of $\mathfrak{E}_{b,r}(e)$

In the full paper we define a relation $\lesssim$ of *semantic refinement* among expressions. (More accurately, a relation $\lesssim_T$ is defined for each type context T.) The essential meaning of $e_1 \lesssim e_2$ is that, for all evaluation contexts (b, r),

- computation of $\mathfrak{E}_{b,r}(e_1)$ potentially diverges only if computation of $\mathfrak{E}_{b,r}(e_2)$ potentially diverges, and
- the set of "core" effects of convergent computations of $\mathfrak{E}_{b,r}(e_1)$ is included in the set of "core" effects of convergent computations of $\mathfrak{E}_{b,r}(e_2)$.

Roughly speaking, the "core" of an effect (s, v) is the subeffect (s', v') that remains after a process of garbage-collection relative to the binding b: we remove all but the objects reachable from values in $rng(b)$.

The refinement relation $\lesssim$ has the following property.

Theorem 3 (Refinement). *Suppose e_0', e_0, e_1 are expressions where e_0 is a subexpression of e_1 and e_0' refines e_0. Let e_1' be the expression obtained from e_1 by substituting e_0' in place of a particular occurrence of e_0. Then e_1' refines e_1.*

Here is a general example for refining binary choice expressions:

$$e_0 \lesssim (true \parallel false) \implies (\textbf{if } e_0 \textbf{ then } e_1 \textbf{ else } e_2) \lesssim e_1 \parallel e_2$$

To give a similar general example involving the choose construct, we need a relation $\lesssim^{c.d.}$ of *choice-domain refinement* defined in the full paper.

Proposition 4

$$e_1' \lesssim^{c.d.} e_1 \implies (\textbf{choose } \ell \textbf{ in } e_1 \textbf{ do } e_2) \lesssim (\textbf{choose } \ell \textbf{ in } e_1' \textbf{ do } e_2)$$

References

1. The AsmL webpage, `http://research.microsoft.com/foundations/AsmL/`.
2. Dines Bjoerner and Cliff B. Jones (Editors), "Formal Specification and Software Development", Prentice-Hall International, 1982.
3. Egon Boerger and Robert Staerk, "Abstract State Machines: A Method for High-Level System Design and Analysis", Springer, Berlin Heidelberg 2003.
4. Foundations of Software Engineering group, Microsoft Research, http://research.microsoft.com/fse/
5. Yuri Gurevich, "Evolving Algebra 1993: Lipari Guide", in "Specification and Validation Methods", Ed. E. Boerger, Oxford University Press, 1995, 9–36.
6. Yuri Gurevich, "For every Sequential Algorithm there is an Equivalent Sequential Abstract State Machine", ACM Transactions on Computational Logic 1:1 (2000), pages 77–111.
7. Yuri Gurevich and Nikolai Tillmann, "Partial Updates: Exploration", Springer J. of Universal Computer Science, vol. 7, no. 11 (2001), pages 918-952.
8. Yuri Gurevich, Benjamin Rossman and Wolfram Schulte, "Semantic Essence of AsmL", submitted for publication. A preliminary version appeared as Microsoft Research Technical Report MSR-TR-2004-27, March 2004.
9. James K. Huggins, ASM Michigan web page, `http://www.eecs.umich.edu/gasm`.
10. Atsushi Igarashi, Benjamin C. Pierce and Philip Wadler, "Featherweight Java: a minimal core calculus for Java and GJ", ACM Transactions on Programming Languages and Systems (TOPLAS) 23:3 (May 2001), 396–450.
11. Gilles Kahn, "Natural semantics", In Proc. of the Symposium on Theoretical Aspects of Computer Science, Lecture Notes in Computer Science 247 (1987), 22–39.
12. Robin Milner, Mads Tofte, Robert Harper, and David MacQueen, "The Definition of Standard ML (Revised)", MIT Press, 1997.
13. Benjamin C. Pierce, "Types and Programming Languages", MIT Press, Cambridge, Massachusetts, 2002

14. Gordon D. Plotkin, "Structural approach to operational semantics", Technical report DAIMI FN-19, Computer Science Department, Aarhus University, Denmark, September 1981
15. J. M. Spivey, "The Z Notation: A Reference Manual", Prentice-Hall, New York, Second Edition, 1992.

An MDA Approach to Tame Component Based Software Development

Jean-Marc Jézéquel, Olivier Defour, and Noël Plouzeau

IRISA - Université de Rennes 1
Campus universitaire de Beaulieu, Avenue du général Leclerc
35042 Rennes Cedex, France
{jean-marc.jezequel, olivier.defour, noel.plouzeau}@irisa.fr
http://www.irisa.fr/triskell

Abstract. The aim of this paper is to show how the Model Driven Architecture (MDA) can be used in relation with component based software engineering. A software component only exhibits its provided or required interfaces, hence defining basic *contracts* between components allowing one to properly wire them. These contractually specified interfaces should go well beyond mere syntactic aspects: they should also involve functional, synchronization and Quality of Service (QoS) aspects. In large, mission-critical component based systems, it is also particularly important to be able to explicitly relate the QoS contracts attached to provided interfaces with the QoS contracts obtained from required interfaces. We thus introduce a QoS contract model (called QoSCL for QoS Constraint Language), allowing QoS contracts and their dependencies to be modeled in a UML2.0 modeling environment. Building on Model Driven Engineering techniques, we then show how the very same QoSCL contracts can be exploited for (1) validation of individual components, by automatically weaving contract monitoring code into the components; and (2) validation of a component assembly, including getting end-to-end QoS information inferred from individual component contracts, by automatic translation to a Constraint Logic Programming language. We illustrate our approach with the example of a GPS (Global Positioning System) software component, from its functional and contractual specifications to its implementation in a .Net framework.

1 Introduction

Szyperski [22] remarked that while objects were good units for modular composition at development time, they were not so good for deployment time composition, and he formulated the now widely accepted definition of a software component: "*a software component is a unit of composition with contractually specified interfaces and explicit context dependencies only. A software component can be deployed independently and is subject to composition by third-party*". In this vision, any composite application is viewed as a particular configuration of components, selected at build-time and configured or re-configured at run-time, as in CORBA [15], or .NET [20].

A software component only exhibits its provided or required interfaces, hence defining basic *contracts* between components allowing one to properly wire them.

F.S. de Boer et al. (Eds.): FMCO 2003, LNCS 3188, pp. 260–275, 2004.

These contractually specified interfaces should go well beyond mere syntactic aspects: they should also involve functional, synchronization and Quality of Service (QoS) aspects. In large, mission-critical component based systems, it is also particularly important to be able to explicitly relate the QoS contracts attached to provided interfaces with the QoS contracts obtained from required interfaces.

It is then natural that people resorted to modelling to try to master this complexity. According to Jeff Rothenberg, "*Modeling, in the broadest sense, is the cost-effective use of something in place of something else for some cognitive purpose. It allows us to use something that is simpler, safer or cheaper than reality instead of reality for some purpose. A model represents reality for the given purpose; the model is an abstraction of reality in the sense that it cannot represent all aspects of reality. This allows us to deal with the world in a simplified manner, avoiding the complexity, danger and irreversibility of reality.*" Usually in science, a model has a different nature that the thing it models. Only in software and in linguistics a model has the same nature as the thing it models. In software at least, this opens the possibility to automatically derive software from its model. This property is well known from any compiler writer (and others), but it was recently be made quite popular with an OMG initiative called the Model Driven Architecture (MDA).

The aim of this paper is to show how MDA can be used in relation with component based software engineering. We introduce a QoS contract model (called QoSCL for QoS Constraint Language), allowing QoS contracts and their dependencies to be modeled in a UML2.0 [13] modeling environment. Building on Model Driven Engineering techniques, we then show how the very same QoSCL contracts can be exploited for (1) validation of individual components, by automatically weaving contract monitoring code into the components; and (2) validation of a component assembly, including getting end-to-end QoS information inferred from individual component contracts, by automatic translation to a Constraint Logic Programming.

The rest of the paper is organized as follows. Using the example of a GPS (Global Positioning System) software component, Section 2 introduces the interest of modelling components, their contracts and their dependencies, and describes the QoS Constraint Language (QoSCL). Section 3 discusses the problem of validating individual components against their contracts, and proposes a solution based on automatically weaving reusable contract monitoring code into the components. Section 4 discusses the problem of validating a component assembly, including getting end-to-end QoS information inferred from individual component contracts by automatic translation to a Constraint Logic Programming. This is applied to the GPS system example, and experimental results are presented. Finally, Section 5 presents related works.

2   The QoS Contracts Language

2.1   Modeling Component-Based Systems

In modelling techniques such as UML2.0 for example, a component is a behavioural abstraction of a concrete physical piece of code, called artifacts. A component has required and provided ports, which are typed by interfaces. These interfaces represent the required and provided services implemented by the modelled artifact. The relationship between the required and provided services within one component must be explicitly stated. The knowledge of this relationship is of utmost importance to the component-based application designer. In the rest of this section, we address this relationship using the example of a GPS device.

A GPS device computes its current location from satellite signals. Each signal contains data which specifies the identity of the emiting satellite, the time of its emission, the orbital position of the satellite and so on. In the illustrating example, each satellite emits a new data stream every fifteen seconds.

In order to compute its current location, the GPS device needs at least three signals from three different satellites. The number of received signals is unknown *a priori*, because obstacles might block the signal propagation.

Our GPS device is modeled as a component which provides a *getLocation()* service, and requires a *getSignal()* service from Satellites components. The GPS component is made up of four components:

- the decoder which contains twelve satellite receivers (only three are shown on Fig. 1). This element receives the satellite streams and demutiplexes it in order to extract the data for each satellite. The number of effective data obtained via the *getData()* service depends not only on the number of powered receivers, but also on the number of received signals. Indeed, this number may change at any time.
- The computer which computes the current location (*getLocation()*) from the data (*getData()*) and the current time (*getTime()*).
- The battery which provides the power (*getPower()*) to the computer and the decoder.
- The clock component which provides the current time (*getTime()*).

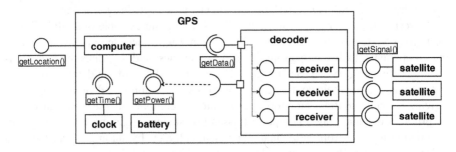

Fig. 1. The GPS component-based model

2.2 Contract Aware Components

In component-based models, the services are usually specified at a syntactic level. This level of specification is not precise enough. Indeed, a service can be unavailable according to the state of the environment and, reciprocally, the environment can be modified by the execution of a service.

Following [2] component contracts can be classified into four levels. The first level is the type compatibility. The second level adds pre/post-conditions: the operation's behavior is specified by using Boolean assertions for each service offered, called pre and post-conditions, as well as class invariants [14]. The third level adds synchronization constraints and the fourth level provides extra-functional constraints. To be more precise, we can build on the well-known idea of design-by-contract [12] negotiable contracts for components. These contracts ensure that a service will perform correctly.

In the previous section 2.1, we have said that a dependency relationship always exists inside one component between its provided and required services. A component provides its services inasmuch as its environment provides the services that it requires. All components always support this implicit contract. The extra-functional properties, which are intrinsic features of services, inherit this dependency relationship. The quality of a provided service depends on the quality of required services that it depends on. This fact is illustrated in our example.

The GPS application contains several time out constraints. For instance, the provided *getLocation()* service must ensure that it is completed in a delay less than 30s, whereas the *getData()* service must be completed in less than 25 s for example.

However, it is obvious that the time spent to acquire data from the decoder, denoted *TethaD*, has a direct impact on the global cost in time of the *getLocation()* service, denoted *ThetaC*. Not only *ThetaC* depends on *ThetaD*, but also on the number of active receivers, denoted *Nbr*, because of the interpolation algorithm implemented by the Computer component. *ThetaD* and *Nbr* are two extra-functional properties associated to the *getData()* service provided by the Decoder component. The relation that binds these three quantities is:

$$ThetaC = ThetaD + Nbr * \log (Nbr) . \qquad (1)$$

Each receiver demultiplexes a signal, in order to extract the data. This operation has a fixed time cost: nearly 2 seconds. In addition, the demultiplexed signals must be transformed into a single data vector. This operation takes 3 s. If *ThetaR* (resp. *ThetaS*) denotes the time spent by the receiver to complete the *getDatal()* service (resp. the satellite to complete its *getSignal()* service), then we have the two following formulae:

$$ThetaR = ThetaS + 2 , \qquad (2)$$
$$ThetaD = \max (ThetaR) + 3 . \qquad (3)$$

There exist many QoS contracts languages which allow the designer to specify the extra-functional properties and their constraints on the provided interfaces only (see section 5). However, none of them allow specifying dependency relationships between the provided and required services of a component. To overcome this limitation we introduce the QoS Constraint Language (QoSCL). This language includes the fundamental QoS concepts defined in the well-known precursor QML [5]. It is the cornerstone to implement in a second time a QoS prediction tool.

2.3 Extra-Functional Dependencies with QoSCL

Our own contract model for extra-functional contracts extends the UML2.0 components metamodel. We designed the QoSCL notation with the following objectives in mind.

1. Since the extra-functional contracts are constraints on continuous values within multidimensional spaces, we wanted to keep the QML definitions of dimensions and contract spaces.
2. Since our extra-functional contracts would be used on software components with explicit dependency specification, we needed means to express a provided contract in terms of required contracts.
3. Since we targeted platform independent designs, we wanted to use the UML notation and its extension facilities.

We thus designed our extra-functional contract notation as an extension of the component part of the UML2.0 metamodel:

– *Dimension*: is a QoS property. This metaclass inherits the operation metaclass. According to our point of view, a QoS property is a valuable quantity and has to be concretely measured. Therefore we have chosen to specify a means of measurement rather than an abstract concept. Its parameters are used to specified the (optional) others dimensions on which it depends. The type of a Dimension is a totally ordered set, and it denotes its unit. The pre and post-conditions are used to specify constraints on the dimension itself, or its parameters.
– *ContractType*: specializes Interface. It is a set of dimensions defining the contract supported by an operation. Like an interface, a ContractType is just a specification without implementation of its dimensions.
– *Contract*: is a concrete implementation of a ContractType. The dimensions specified in the ContractType are implemented inside the component using the aspect weaving techniques (see section 3). An *isValid()* operation checks if the contract is realized or not.
– *QoSComponent* extends Component, and it has the same meaning. However, its ports provides not only required and provided interfaces which exhibit its functional behaviour, but also ContractTypes dedicated to its contractual behaviour.

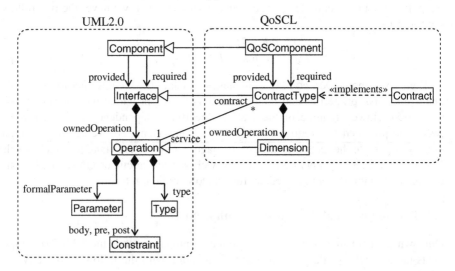

Fig. 2. The QoSCL metamodel

With the QoSCL metamodel, it is possible to specify contracts, such as the Time-Out contract useful for our GPS, as an Interface in any UML case tool:

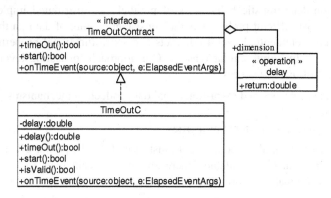

Fig. 3. The TimeOut contract with QoSCL

The QoSCL metamodel handles three specific aspects of contracts: dependency, composition, and adaptative behaviour. The dependency is the core of this work, and our main contribution to enhance existing extra-functional contracts specification languages, such as QML. QoSCL makes it also possible to model a composite contract via generalization association. At last, like any abstract functional model, it is possible to implement different behaviors for the same Operation, such as a Dimension. Thus, the renegotiation of a contract can be implemented according to its environment. This behavior can be specified thanks the UML2.0 sequence diagrams, activity diagrams or state machine for instance.

3 Implementing Contract-Aware Components

QoSCL allows the expression of functional and extra-functional properties in a software component. The declared properties are useful to the software designer because this gives predictability to a component's behaviour. However, this predictability is valid only if the component implementation really has the behaviour declared by the component. This implementation validity is classical software validation problem, whatever the kind of contracts used [11].

These problems are usually addressed by two families of techniques. A first family is based on testing: the system under test is run in an environment that behaves as described in a test case. An oracle observes the behaviour of the system under test and then decides whether the behaviour is allowed by the specification. A second family of techniques relies on formal proof and reasoning on the composition of elementary operations.

Standard software validation techniques deal with pre/post-condition contract types [12]. Protocol validation extends this to the synchronization contract types [8]. The rest of this section discusses issues of testing extra-functional property conformance.

3.1   Testing Extra Functional Behaviour

Level 3 contracts (*i.e.* contracts that include protocols) are more difficult to test because of non-deterministic behaviours of parallel and distributed implementations. One of the most difficult problems is the consistent capture of data on the behaviour of the system's elements. Level 4 contracts (*i.e.* extra-functional properties) are also difficult to test for quite similar reasons. Our approach for testing level 4 contracts relies on the following features:

– existence of probes and extra-functional data collection mechanisms (monitors);
– test cases;
– oracles on extra-functional properties.

In order to be testable, a component must provide probe points where basic extra-functional data must be available. There are several techniques to implement such probe points and make performance data available to the test environment.

1. The component runtime may include facilities to record performance data on various kinds of resources or events (e.g. disk operations, RPC calls, etc). Modern operating systems and component frameworks now provide performance counters that can be "tuned" to monitor runtime activity and therefore deduce performance data on the component's service.
2. The implementation of the component may perform extra computation to monitor its own performance. This kind of "self monitoring" is often found in components that are designed as level 4 component from scratch (*e.g.* components providing multimedia services).
3. A component can be augmented with monitoring facilities by weaving a specific monitor piece of model or of code. Aspect-oriented design (AOD) or aspect-oriented programming can help in automating this extension.

We have chosen this latter approach as our main technique for designing monitors. This choice was motivated mainly by the existence of "legacy" components from industrial partners [17]. From a software design process point of view, we consider that designing monitors is a specialist's task. Monitors rely on low level mechanisms and/or on mechanisms that are highly platform dependant. By using aspect-oriented design (AOD), we separate the component implementation model into two main models: the service part that provides the component's functional services under extra-functional contracts, and the monitor part that supervises performance issues. A designer in charge of the "service design model" does not need to master monitor design. A specific tool[1] (a model transformer) [24] is used to merge the monitor part of the component with its service part.

More precisely, a contract monitor designer provides component designers with a reusable implementation of a monitor. This implementation contains two items: a monitor design model and a script for the model transformer tool (a weaver). The goal of this aspect weaver is to modify a platform specific component model by integrating new QoSCL classes and modifying existing class and their relationships.

---

[1] The Kase tool is developed by TU-Berlin with the support of the European Project "Quality Control of Component-based Software" (QCCS) [17].

3.2 A Practical Example of Weaving

As we have said in the last paragraph of section 2, QoSCL allows us to model the structural, behavioral and contractual components features. These three aspects can be specified using the dedicated UML2.0 diagrams. The QoS aspect weaver is a mechanism integrated into Kase, which:

- modifies the UML diagram (add new classes and associations)
- modifies the behavior of the targeted service

Thanks to QoSCL, it is possible to specify into Kase the contract types and their implementation such as TimeOut and TimeOutC (Fig. 4). According to our vision, detailed in the QoSCL section (§2.3), the TimeOut contract is an interface, which has a special operation denoting the "delay" dimension. The TimeOutC is a .Net class that implements the TimeOut interface. The value of the "delay" dimension is implemented like a private attribute (-delay:double) and its related access/evaluation method (delay():double).

A QoS aspect not only specifies how the structural diagram will be modified, but also how the monitored part and the monitor cooperate: when does the timer start, when does it stop, who handles timeout, etc… This part of the aspect is specified using the Hierarchical Message Sequence Charts (HMSC) notation in the UML 2.0. Fig. 5 shows the behavior of a contractual service, called op(), as a HMSC diagram. The op() operation is the service which must verify a TimeOut contract. The op_c() operation is a new operation, which realizes the op() service and evaluates the TimeOut contract below (Fig. 5). This service has two possible behaviors, depending on whether the op() service finishes before or after the timer.

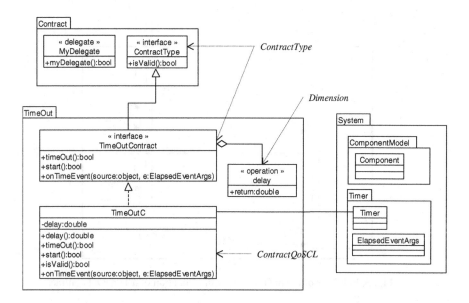

Fig. 4. TheTimeOut contract model for .Net

In addition of its structural (Fig. 4) and behavioral (Fig. 5) parts, a contractual QoS aspect has pre-conditions that must be met at weaving time. For example, a :<u>Cl</u> class abides a TimeOut contract under the condition that it implements the op() service of course. In our tool, the aspect is concretely weaved in the UML diagram by a Python script, which:

- checks the aspect pre-conditions;
- weaves the aspect if these preconditions are satisfied, and this weaving adds new classes, modifies constructors and operations, etc).

The QoS aspect weaver implemented in the Käse tool allows us to:

- specify a QoS aspect;
- implement an evaluation of this aspect for a targeted service.

According to the QoSCL point of view, contracts can be specified at design time as specialized interfaces. Therefore, connecting two components at binding time is easy, using their respectively compliant required and provided interfaces. The QoS aspect weaver implemented in Käse allows to implement in C# any contract type.

In case of failure, an extra-functional contract can be renegotiated. For instance, a time out contract that fails too often obviously needs to be adjusted (alternatively the service bound to that contract has to be shut down).

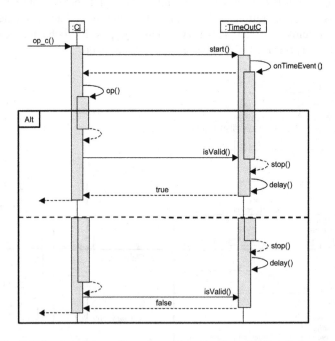

Fig. 5. Behavior of the op() service with evaluation of a TimeOut contract

3.3 Limitations of Extra-Functional Property Testing

The QoSCL notation and the monitor integration technique help the component designer to define and check extra-functional properties. However, application designers rely on component assemblies to build applications. These designers need to estimate at design time the overall extra-functional properties of a given assembly. Using the techniques presented above, they can perform a kind of integration testing. The tests aim at validating the extra-functional behavior of the assembly with respect to the global specification of the application. However, the application designers often have trouble to select and configure the components, make the assembly and match the global application behavior. Conversely, some applications are built with preconfigured components and the application designer needs to build a reasonable specification of the overall extra-functional behavior of the application.

4 Predicting Extra-Functional Properties of an Assembly

4.1 Modeling a QoS-Aware Component with QoSCL

QoSCL is a metamodel extension dedicated to specify contracts whose extra-functional properties have explicit dependencies. Models can be used by aspect weavers in order to integrate the contractual evaluation and renegotiation into the components. However, at design time, it is possible to predict the global quality of the composite software.

Predicting a behaviour is difficult. In the best cases, the behaviour can be proved but this. Otherwise, the behaviour is predicted with uncertainty. Since we want to predict the quality of a composite, i.e. la value of a set of extra-functional properties, this uncertainty will be translated into a numerical interval or an enumerated set of values, called validity domains.

The dependencies defined in QoSCL, which bind the properties, are generally expressed either as formulae or as rules. The quality of a service is defined as the extra-functional property's membership of a specific validity domain. Predicting the global quality of a composite is equivalent to the propagation of the extra-functional validity domains through the dependencies.

For instance, we have defined in section §2.2 a set of extra-functional properties that qualifies different services in our GPS component-based model. In addition, we have specified the dependencies between the extra-functional properties as formulae. This knowledge can be specified in QoSCL. The Fig. 6 below represents the computer component (Fig. 1) refined with contractual properties and their dependencies:

The rules that govern the connection between two (functional) ports are also valid for ports with required or provided ContractTypes. Thus, a port that requires a service with its specific QoS properties can only be connected to another Port that provides this service with the same quality attributes.

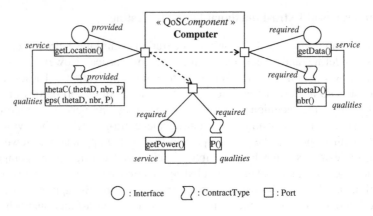

Fig. 6. Quality attributes and dependencies specification of a component

Specifying the QoS properties of required and provided services of a component is not enough to predict the quality of an assembly at design time. Additional information must be supplied:

- constraints on the value of the QoS properties are needed to get the parties to negotiate and to agree; they explain the level of quality required or provided for a service by a component;
- the dependency between these values is an important kind of relationship; it can be described either as with a function (for instance: *ThetaC* = *ThetaD* + *Nbr* * log(*Nbr*) (**1**)) or with a rule (if *Nbr* = 3 and *Eps* = medium then *ThetaC* ≤ 25).

In other words, these constraints can be stated as OCL [14] pre and post-conditions on the Dimensions. For instance:

```
context Computer::thetaC( thetaD : real, nbr : int,
P : real) : real
    pre: thetaD >= 0 and P >= 0
    post: result = thetaD + nbr * log( nbr ) and P =
    3*nbr
```

At design time, the global set of pre and post-conditions of all specified Dimensions of a component builds a system of non-linear constraints that must be satisfied. The Constraint Logic Programming is the general framework to solve such systems. Dedicated solvers will determine if a system is satisfied, and in this case the admissible interval of values for each dimension stressed.

4.2 Prediction of the GPS Quality of Service

In this section we present the set of constraints for the GPS component-based model (Fig. 1). A first subset of constraints defines possible or impossible values for a QoS property. These admissible value sets come on the one hand from implementation or technological constraints and on the other hand from designers' and users' requirements about a service. The fact that the *Nbr* value is 3, 5 or 12 (**2**), or *ThetaC* and *ThetaD* values must be real positive values (**3-4**) belongs to the first category of constraints. Conversely, the facts that *Eps* is at least medium (**5**) and *P* is less or equal than 15mW (**6**) are designers or users requirements.

$$\text{Nbr} \in \{3, 5, 12\}, \tag{2}$$
$$\text{ThetaC} \geq 0, \tag{3}$$
$$\text{ThetaD} \geq 0, \tag{4}$$
$$\text{Eps} \in \{\text{medium, high}\}, \tag{5}$$
$$P \leq 15. \tag{6}$$

Secondly, constraints can also explain the dependency relationships that bind the QoS properties of a component. For instance, the active power level *P* is linearly dependent on the *Nbr* number of receivers according to the formula:

$$P = 3 * \text{Nbr}. \tag{7}$$

Moreover, the time spent by the getLocation() service (*ThetaC*) depends on the time spend by the *getData()* service (*ThetaD*) and the number of data received (*Nbr*), according the equation (**1**). Lastly, a rule binds the precision *Eps*, the time spent to compute the current position *ThetaC* and the number of received data (*Nbr*). The following diagram (Fig. 7) presents this rule:

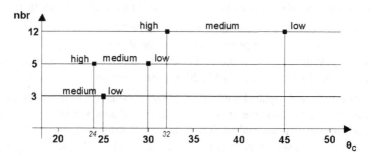

Fig. 7. The rule that binds the Eps, Nbr and ThetaC dimensions

All these constraints, expressed in OCL syntax, can be translated into a specific CLP-compliant language, using a Model Transfomation [24]. For instance, we present below the result of a such transformation applied to the computer QoSComponent (Fig. 6) and its OCL conditions (using the Eclipse™ syntax):

```
01- computer( [ ThetaC, Eps, P, ThetaD, Nbr ] ) :-
02-        ThetaC $>= 0, Eps = high, P $>= 0,
03-        ThetaD $>= 0, member( Nbr, [3,5,12]),
04-        ThetaC $>= 0, ThetaD $>= 0,
05-        ThetaC $= ThetaD + Nbr * log(Nbr),
06-        P $= Nbr * 3,
07-        rule( Eps, ThetaC, Nbr).
08-
09- rule( medium, ThetaC, 3) :- ThetaC  $=< 25.
10-        rule( low, ThetaC, 3) :- ThetaC  $> 25.
11- rule( high, ThetaC, 5) :- ThetaC  $=< 24.
12- rule( medium, ThetaC, 5) :- ThetaC $>24,
```

```
13-           ThetaC $=< 30.
14- rule( low, ThetaC, 5) :- ThetaC  $> 30.
15- rule( high, ThetaC, 12) :- ThetaC  $=< 32.
16- rule( medium, ThetaC, 12) :- ThetaC  $> 32,
17-           ThetaC $=<45.
18- rule( low, ThetaC, 12) :- ThetaC  $> 45.
```

The first line (01) indicates the QoS properties bound by the component. The two following lines (02, 03) are the constraints on the admissible values for these QoS properties, and lines 05 to 07 are the dependency relationships (1-7 and Fig. 7) that bind them.

For each component, it is necessary to check its system of constraints, in order to compute its availability. The result of such request is the whole of admissible values for the QoS properties of the component. Thus, for the computer component, the solutions for the admissible QoS properties values are enumerated below:

ThetaC	ThetaD	Eps	P	Nbr
[3.49 .. 24.0]	[0.0 .. 20.51]	high	15	5
[12.95 .. 32.0]	[0.0 .. 19.05]	high	36	12

The requirement about the estimated position (*Eps* = high) implies that:

− the number of data channels must be either 5 or 12,
− consequently, the active power is either 15 or 36mW,
− and the response times of the *getLocation*() ands *getData*() services are respectively in the [3.49; 32.0] and [0.0; 20.51] real intervals.

At this time, the designer knows the qualitative behavior of all of its components. It is also possible to know the qualitative behavior of an assembly, by conjunction of the constraints systems and unification of their QoS properties.

The following constraint program shows the example of the GPS component:

```
19- satellite( [ ThetaS ] ) :-
20-         ThetaS $>= 15, ThetaS $=< 30.
21-
22- battery( [ P ] ) :-
23-         P $>= 0,
24-         P $=< 15.
25-
26- receiver( [ ThetaR, ThetaS ] ) :-
27-         ThetaR $>= 0, ThetaS $>= 0,
28-         ThetaR $= ThetaS + 2.
29-
30- decoder( [ ThetaD, ThetaS, Nbr ] ) :-
31-         ThetaD $>= 0, ThetaS $>= 0,
32-         member( Nbr, [3,5,12]),
33-         receiver( [ ThetaR, ThetaS ] ),
34-         ThetaD $= ThetaR + 3.
35-
36- gps( [ ThetaC, Eps, ThetaS ] ) :-
37-         ThetaC $>= 0, Eps = high, ThetaS $>= 0,
```

```
38-        computer( [ ThetaC, Eps, P, ThetaD, Nbr ] ),
39-        decoder( [ ThetaD, ThetaS, Nbr ] ),
40-        battery( [ P ] ).
```

Similarly, the propagation of numerical constraints over the admissible sets of values implies the following qualitative prediction behavior of the GPS assembly:

ThetaC	ThetaS	Eps
[23.49 .. 24.0]	[15.0 .. 15.50]	high

The strong requirement on the precision of the computed location implies that the satellite signals have to be received by the GPS component with a delay less than 15.5 s. In this case, the location will be computed in less than 24 s.

5 Related Work

In the Component-Based Software Engineering community, the concept of predictability is getting more and more attention, and is now underlined as a real need [4]. Thus, the Software Engineering Institute (SEI) promotes its Predictable Assembly from Certifiable Components (PACC) initiative: how component technology can be extended to achieve predictable assembly, enabling runtime behavior to be predicted from the properties of components. The ongoing work concentrates in a Prediction-Enabled Component Technology (PECT) as a method to integrate state-of-the-art techniques for reasoning about software quality attributes [23].

In the introduction of the SEI's second workshop on predictable assembly [21], the authors note that component interfaces are not sufficiently descriptive. A syntax for defining and specifying quality of service attributes, called QML, is defined by Frolund and Koistinen in [5], directly followed by Aagedal [1]. The Object Management Group (OMG) has developed its own UML profile for schedulability, performance and time specification [16]. These works emphasize the contractual use of QoS properties, and constitute the fundamental core of QoS specifications.

In the previous approaches, a QoS property is specified as a constant: they do not allow the specification of QoS properties dependency relationships. In contrast, Reussner proposes its parameterized contracts [18]: the set of available services provided by a component depends on its required services that the context can provide. This concept is a generalization of the design-by-contract [11]. The same author has published in 2003 a recent extension of its work dedicated to the QoS [19]. He models the QoS dependency with Markov chains where:

- the states are services, with their QoS values;
- the transitions represent the connections (calls) between components, i.e. the architecture of an assembly;
- the usage profile of the assembly is modeled by probabilities for calls to a provided service. Usage profiles are commonly modeled by Markov chains since Cheung [3] or Whittaker and Thomason [25].

From an assembly model and its usage profile, it seems possible to generate the associated Markov chain and to predict the QoS level of provided services. Conversely, it is not possible to invert the prediction process, in order to propagate a particular QoS requirement applied on a provided service on the QoS properties of required services that it depends. Moreover, via the Chapman-Kolmogorov equation, the Markov processes handle only probabilities, and they are not able to reason about formal un-valued variables. For instance, it is impossible to compare the n^2 and $n*\log(n)$ complexity of two sort algorithms.

Constraints solvers over real intervals and finite domains have already been used in the context of the software engineering. For instance, logic programming techniques can generate test cases for functional properties. More precisely, this technique allows a more realistic treatment of bound values [10]. About the software functional aspect, many authors have successfully used the constraints logic programming, based on translations from the source code to test or its formal specification into constraints: the GATEL system [9] translates LUSTRE [7] expressions, and A. Gotlieb defines directly its transformation from C [6]. The works mentioned above focus on the functional aspects of software only, while our approach encompasses extra-functional properties.

6   Conclusion and Future Work

In mission-critical component based systems, it is particularly important to be able to explicitly relate the QoS contracts attached to provided interfaces of components with the QoS contracts obtained from their required interfaces. In this paper we have introduced a notation called QoSCL (defined as an add-on to the UML2.0 component model) to let the designer explicitly describe and manipulate these higher level contracts and their dependencies. We have shown how the very same QoSCL contracts can then be exploited for:

1   validation of individual components, by automatically weaving contract monitoring code into the components;
2   validation of a component assembly, including getting end-to-end QoS information inferred from individual component contracts, by automatic translation to a Constraint Logic Programming language.

Both validation activities build on the model transformation framework developed at INRIA (cf. http://modelware.inria.fr). Preliminary implementations of these ideas have been prototyped in the context of the QCCS project (cf. http://www.qccs.org) for the weaving of contract monitoring code into components part, and on the Artist project (http://www.systemes-critiques.org/ARTIST) for the validation of a component assembly part. Both parts still need to be better integrated with UML2.0 modelling environments, which is work in progress.

References

1. Aagedal J.O.: *"Quality of service support in development of distributed systems"*. Ph.D thesis report, University of Oslo, Dept. Informatics, March 2001.

2. Beugnard A., Jézéquel J.M., Plouzeau N. and Watkins D.: *"Making components contract aware"* in Computer, pp. 38–45, IEEE Computer Society, July 1999.

3. Cheung R.C.: *"A user-oriented software reliability model"* in IEEE Transactions on Software Engineering vol. 6 (2), pp. 118–125, 1980.

4. de Roever W.P.: *"The need for compositional proof systems: a survey"* in Proceedings of the Int. Symp. COMPOS'97, Bad Malente, Germany, Sept. 8–12, 1997.

5. Frolund S. and Koistinen J.: *"QoS specification in distributed object systems"* in Distributed Systems Engineering, vol. 5, July 1998, The British Computer Society.

6. Gotlieb A., Botella B. and Rueher M.: *"Automatic test data generation using constraint solving techniques"* in ACM Int. Symp. on Software Testing and Analysis (ISSTA'98), also in Software Engineering Notes, 23(2):53–62, 1998.

7. Halbwachs N., Caspi P., Raymond P. and Pillaud D.: *"The synchronous data flow programming language LUSTRE"* in Proc. of IEEE, vol. 79, pp.1305–1320, Sept. 1991.

8. McHale C.: *"Synchronization in concurrent object-oriented languages: expressive power, genericity and inheritance"*. Doctoral dissertation, Trinity College, Dept. of computer science, Dublin, 1994.

9. Marre B. and Arnould A.: *"Test sequences generation from luster descriptions: Gatel"* in 15th IEEE Int. Conf. On Automated Software Engineering (ASE), pp. 229–237, Sept. 2000, Grenoble, France.

10. Meudec C.: *"Automatic generation of software test cases from formal specifications"*. PhD thesis, Queen's University of Belfast, 1998.

11. Meyer B.: *"Object oriented software construction"*, 2nd ed., Prentice Hall, 1997.

12. Meyer B.: *"Applying design by contract"* in IEEE Computer vol. 25 (10), pp. 40–51, 1992.

13. Object Management Group: *"UML Superstructure 2.0"*, OMG, August 2003.

14. Object Management Group: *"UML2.0 Object Constraint Language RfP"*, OMG, July 2003.

15. Object Management Group: *"CORBA Components, v3.0"*, adopted specification of the OMG, June 2002.

16. Object Management Group: *"UML profile for schedulability, performance and time specification"*. OMG adopted specification no ptc/02-03-02, March 2002.

17. http://www.qccs.org, Quality Control of Component-based Software (QCCS) European project home page.

18. Reussner R.H.: *"The use of parameterized contracts for architecting systems with software components"* in Proc. of the 6th Int. Workshop on Component-Oriented Programming (WCOP'01), June 2001.

19. Reusnerr R.H., Schmidt H.W. and Poernomo I.H.: *"Reliability prediction for component-based software architecture"* in the Journal of Systems and Software, vol. 66, pp. 241–252, 2003.

20. Richter, J.: *"Applied Microsoft .Net framework programming"*. Microsoft Press, January 23, 2002.

21. Stafford J. and Scott H.: *"The Software Engineering Institute's Second Workshop on Predictable Assembly: Landscape of compositional predictability"*. SEI report no CMU/SEI-2003-TN-029, 2003

22. Szyperski, C.: *"Component software, beyond object-oriented programming"*, 2nd ed., Addison-Wesley, 2002

23. Wallnau K.: *"Volume III: A technology for predictable assembly from certifiable components"*. SEI report no CMU/SEI-2003-TR-009.

24. Weis T. and al.: *"Model metamorphosis"* in IEEE Software, September 2003, p. 46–51.

25. Whittaker J.A. and Thomason M.G.: *"A Markov chain model for statistical software testing"* in IEEE Transactions on Software Engineering vol.20 (10), pp.812–824, 1994.

An Application of Stream Calculus to Signal Flow Graphs

J.J.M.M. Rutten

CWI and VUA, P.O. Box 94079, 1090 GB Amsterdam, The Netherlands

1 Summary

The present paper can be seen as an exercise in the author's stream calculus [Rut01] and gives a new proof for an existing result about stream circuits. Such circuits are also known under the name of signal flow graphs, and are built from (scalar) multipliers, copiers (fan-out), adders (element-wise sum), and registers (here: one-element memory cells, aka delays). Because of the presence of memory, the input-output behaviour of these circuits is best described in terms of functions from streams to streams (of real numbers). The main statement of this paper (Theorem 6), gives a characterization of the input-output behaviour of finite stream circuits in terms of so-called rational streams. It is well-known in the world of signal processing, where it is formulated and proved in terms of the Z-transform (a discrete version of the Laplace transform) and transfer functions (see for instance [Lah98, p.694]). These transforms are used as *representations* of streams of (real or complex) numbers. As a consequence, one has to deal with two different worlds, and some care is required when moving from the one to the other. In contrast, we use stream calculus to formulate and obtain essentially the same result. What is somewhat different and new here is that we use only streams and nothing else. In particular, expressions for streams such as $\frac{1}{(1-X)^2} = (1, 2, 3, \ldots)$, are not mere representations but should be read as formal identities. Technically, the formalism of stream calculus is simple, because it uses the *constant* stream $X = (0, 1, 0, 0, 0, \ldots)$ as were it a formal variable (cf. work on formal power series such as [BR88]).

We find it worthwhile to present this elementary treatment of signal flow graphs for a number of reasons:

- It explains in very basic terms two fundamental phenomena in the theory of computation: memory (in the form of register or delay elements) and infinite behaviour (in the form of feedback).
- Although Theorem 6 is well-known to electrical engineers, computer scientists do not seem to know it. Also, the result as such is not so easy to isolate in the relevant literature on (discrete-time, linear) system theory.
- Although not worked out here, there is a very close connection between Theorem 6, and a well-known result from theoretical computer science: Kleene's theorem on rational (regular) languages and deterministic finite state automata.

F.S. de Boer et al. (Eds.): FMCO 2003, LNCS 3188, pp. 276–291, 2004.
© Springer-Verlag Berlin Heidelberg 2004

– The present methodology is relevant for the area of component-based software engineering: it has recently been generalised to model software composition by means of so-called component connectors, in terms of relations on the streams of ingoing and outgoing messages (or data elements) at the various communication ports [AR03]. A similar remark applies to our ongoing work on stream-based models of sequential digital circuits.

Stream calculus has been mainly developed as a playground for the use of coinduction definition and proof principles (see [Rut01]). In particular, streams and stream functions can be elegantly defined by so-called stream differential equations. For the elemenary operations on streams that are used in this paper (sum, convolution product and its inverse), the more traditional definitions of the necessary operations on streams suffice and therefore, coinduction is not discussed here.

Acknowledgements. Thanks are due to the referees for their critical yet constructive remarks.

2   Basic Stream Calculus

In this section, we study the set $\mathbb{R}^{\omega} = \{ \sigma \mid \sigma : \{0, 1, 2, \ldots\} \to \mathbb{R} \}$ of streams of real numbers. We shall introduce a number of constants and shall define the operations of sum, product, and inverse of streams. These constants and operations make of $\mathbb{R}^{\omega}$ a calculus with many pleasant properties. In particular, it will be possible to compute solutions of linear systems of equations.

We denote streams $\sigma \in \mathbb{R}^{\omega}$ by $\sigma = (\sigma_0, \sigma_1, \sigma_2, \ldots)$. We define the *sum* $\sigma + \tau$ of $\sigma, \tau \in \mathbb{R}^{\omega}$ by

$$\sigma + \tau = (\sigma_0 + \tau_0,\ \sigma_1 + \tau_1,\ \sigma_2 + \tau_2,\ \ldots)$$

(Note that we use the same symbol $+$ for both the sum of two streams and the sum of two real numbers.) We define the *convolution product* $\sigma \times \tau$ by

$$\sigma \times \tau = (\sigma_0 \cdot \tau_0,\ (\sigma_0 \cdot \tau_1) + (\sigma_1 \cdot \tau_0),\ (\sigma_0 \cdot \tau_2) + (\sigma_1 \cdot \tau_1) + (\sigma_2 \cdot \tau_0),\ \ldots)$$

That is, for any $n \geq 0$,

$$(\sigma \times \tau)_n = \sum_{k=0}^{n} \sigma_k \cdot \tau_{n-k}$$

In general, we shall simply say 'product' rather than 'convolution product'. Note that we use the symbol $\times$ for the multiplication of streams and the symbol $\cdot$ for the multiplication of real numbers. Similar to the notation for the multiplication of real numbers (and functions), we shall write $\sigma^0 \equiv 1$ and $\sigma^{n+1} \equiv \sigma \times \sigma^n$. It will be convenient to define the operations of sum and product also for the combination of a real number r and a stream σ. This will allow us, for instance, to write $3 \times \sigma$ for $\sigma + \sigma + \sigma$. In order to define this formally, it will be convenient to view real numbers as streams in the following manner. We define for every $r \in \mathbb{R}$ a stream $[r] \in \mathbb{R}^\omega$ by

$$[r] = (r, 0, 0, 0, \ldots)$$

Note that this defines in fact a function

$$[\ ] : \mathbb{R} \to \mathbb{R}^\omega, \quad r \mapsto [r]$$

which embeds the set of real numbers into the set of streams. This definition allows us to add and multiply real numbers r with streams σ, yielding:

$$\begin{aligned}
[r] + \sigma &= (r, 0, 0, 0, \ldots) + \sigma \\
&= (r + \sigma_0, \sigma_1, \sigma_2, \sigma_3 \ldots) \\
[r] \times \sigma &= (r, 0, 0, 0, \ldots) \times \sigma \\
&= (r \cdot \sigma_0, \ r \cdot \sigma_1, \ r \cdot \sigma_2, \ \ldots)
\end{aligned}$$

For notational convenience, we shall usually write simply $r + \sigma$ for $[r] + \sigma$, and similarly $r \times \sigma$ for $[r] \times \sigma$. The context will always make clear whether the notation r has to be interpreted as the real number r of as the stream $[r]$. For multiplication, this difference is moreover made explicit by the use of two different symbols: $r \times \sigma$ always denotes the multiplication of streams (and hence r should be read as the stream $[r]$) and $r \cdot s$ always denotes the multiplication of real numbers. We shall also use the following convention:

$$\begin{aligned}
-\sigma &\equiv [-1] \times \sigma \\
&= (-\sigma_0, -\sigma_1, -\sigma_2, \ldots)
\end{aligned}$$

Here are a few basic properties of our operators.

Proposition 1. *For all* $r, s \in \mathbb{R}$ *and* $\sigma, \tau, \rho \in \mathbb{R}^\omega$,

$$\begin{aligned}
[r] + [s] &= [r + s] \\
\sigma + 0 &= \sigma \\
\sigma + \tau &= \tau + \sigma \\
\sigma + (\tau + \rho) &= (\sigma + \tau) + \rho \\
[r] \times [s] &= [r \cdot s] \\
0 \times \sigma &= 0 \\
1 \times \sigma &= \sigma \\
\sigma \times \tau &= \tau \times \sigma \\
\sigma \times (\tau + \rho) &= (\sigma \times \tau) + (\sigma \times \rho) \\
\sigma \times (\tau \times \rho) &= (\sigma \times \tau) \times \rho
\end{aligned}$$

Particularly simple are those streams that from a certain point onwards are constant zero:

$$\sigma = (r_0, r_1, r_2, \ldots, r_n, 0, 0, 0, \ldots)$$

for $n \geq 0$ and $r_0, \ldots, r_n \in \mathbb{R}$. Using the following constant, we shall see that there is a very convenient way of denoting such streams: we define

$$X = (0, 1, 0, 0, 0, \ldots)$$

It satisfies, for all $r \in \mathbb{R}$, $\sigma \in \mathbb{R}^\omega$, and $n \geq 0$:

$$r \times X = (0, r, 0, 0, 0, \ldots)$$
$$X \times \sigma = (0, \sigma_0, \sigma_1, \sigma_2, \ldots)$$
$$X^n = (\underbrace{0, \ldots, 0}_{n \text{ times}}, 1, 0, 0, 0, \ldots)$$

For instance, $2 + 3X - 8X^3 = (2, 3, 0, -8, 0, 0, 0, \ldots)$. More generally, we have, for all $n \geq 0$ and all $r_0, \ldots, r_n \in \mathbb{R}$:

$$r_0 + r_1 X + r_2 X^2 + \cdots + r_n X^n = (r_0, r_1, r_2, \ldots, r_n, 0, 0, 0, \ldots)$$

Such streams are called *polynomial streams*. Note that although a polynomial stream such as $2 + 3X - 8X^3$ looks like a (polynomial) *function* $f(x) = 2 + 3x - 8x^3$, for which x is a variable, it really is a *stream*, built from constant streams $(2, 3, 8, \text{ and } X)$, and the operations of sum and product. At the same time, it is true that we can calculate with polynomial streams in precisely the same way as we are used to compute with (polynomial) functions, as is illustrated by the following example (here we use the basic properties of sum and product listed in Proposition 1): $(2 - X) + (1 + 3X) = 3 + 2X$ and $(2 - X) \times (1 + 3X) = 2 + 5X - 3X^2$.

We shall need to solve linear equations in one unknown τ, such as

$$\tau = 1 + (X \times \tau) \tag{1}$$

(where, recall, $1 = (1, 0, 0, 0, \ldots)$). Ideally, we would like to solve (1) by reasoning as follows:

$$\tau = 1 + (X \times \tau)$$
$$\Rightarrow \tau - (X \times \tau) = 1$$
$$\Rightarrow (1 - X) \times \tau = 1$$
$$\Rightarrow \tau = \frac{1}{1 - X}$$

Recall that we are not dealing with functions but with streams. Therefore it is not immediately obvious what we mean by the 'inverse' of a stream $1 - X = (1, -1, 0, 0, 0, \ldots)$. There is however the following fact: for any stream σ such that $\sigma_0 \neq 0$, there exists a unique stream τ such that $\sigma \times \tau = 1$. A proof of this fact can be given in various ways:

(a) Using the definition of convolution product, one can easily derive the following recurrence relation

$$\tau_n = \frac{1}{\sigma_0} \cdot \sum_{k=0}^{n-1} \sigma_{n-k} \cdot \tau_k$$

by which the elements of τ can be constructed one by one.

(b) Alternatively and equivalently, one can use the algorithm of long division to obtain τ out of σ.

(c) Our personal favourite is a method described in [Rut01], where we have introduced the operation of inverse by means of so-called stream differential equations, formulated in terms of the notions of *stream derivative* $\sigma' = (\sigma_1, \sigma_2, \sigma_3, \ldots)$ and *initial value* σ_0 for $\sigma \in \mathbb{R}^\omega$. (In fact, all the operations on $\mathbb{R}^\omega$ are there introduced by means of such equations.)

Now we can simply define the *inverse* $\frac{1}{\sigma}$ of a stream σ with $\sigma_0 \neq 0$ as the unique stream τ such that $\sigma \times \tau = 1$. Here are a few examples that can be easily computed using any of the methods (a)-(c) above:

$$\frac{1}{1-X} = (1,1,1,\ldots)$$

$$\frac{1}{1-X^2} = (1,0,1,0,1,0,\ldots)$$

$$\frac{1}{(1-X)^2} = (1,2,3,\ldots)$$

As with sum and product, we can calculate with the operation of inverse in the same way as we compute with functions: For all $\sigma, \tau \in \mathbb{R}^\omega$ with $\sigma_0 \neq 0 \neq \tau_0$,

$$\sigma \times \frac{1}{\sigma} = 1$$

$$\frac{1}{\sigma} \times \frac{1}{\tau} = \frac{1}{\sigma \times \tau}$$

$$\frac{1}{\frac{1}{\sigma}} = \sigma$$

Using the various properties of our operators, it is straightforward to see that in the calculus of streams, we can solve linear equations as usual. Consider for instance the following system of equations:

$$\sigma = 1 + (X \times \tau)$$

$$\tau = X \times \sigma$$

In order to find σ and τ, we compute as follows: $\sigma = 1 + (X \times \tau) = 1 + (X \times X \times \sigma) = 1 + (X^2 \times \sigma)$. This implies $\sigma - (X^2 \times \sigma) = 1$ and $(1 - X^2) \times \sigma = 1$. Thus $\sigma = \frac{1}{1-X^2}$ and $\tau = \frac{X}{1-X^2}$.

We conclude this section with the following definition, which is of central importance for the formulation of the main result of this paper.

Definition 2. *The product of a polynomial stream and the inverse of a polynomial stream is called a* rational *stream. Equivalently, a stream σ is rational if there exist $n, m \geq 0$ and coefficients $r_0, \ldots, r_n, s_0, \ldots, s_m \in \mathbb{R}$ with $s_0 \neq 0$, such that*

$$\sigma = \frac{r_0 + r_1 X + r_2 X^2 + \cdots + r_n X^n}{s_0 + s_1 X + s_2 X^2 + \cdots + s_m X^m}$$

$\square$

3   Stream Circuits

Certain functions from $\mathbb{R}^\omega$ to $\mathbb{R}^\omega$ can be represented by means of graphical networks that are built from a small number of basic ingredients. Such networks can be viewed as implementations of stream functions. We call them stream circuits; in the literature, they are also referred to as (signal) flow graphs. Using the basic stream calculus from Section 2, we shall give a formal but simple answer to the question precisely which stream functions can be implemented by such stream circuits.

3.1   Basic Circuits

The circuits that we are about to describe, will generally have a number of *input ends* and a number of *output ends*. Here is an example of a simple circuit, consisting of one input and one output end:

The input end is denoted by the arrow shaft $\vdash\!\!\!-\!\!\!-$ and the output end is denoted by the arrow head $-\!\!\!\longrightarrow$. For streams $\sigma, \tau \in \mathbb{R}^\omega$, we shall write

$$\sigma \longmapsto\!\!\!\!\!\longrightarrow \tau$$

and say that the circuit *inputs* the stream σ and *outputs* the stream τ. Writing the elements of these streams explicitly, this notation is equivalent to

$$(\sigma_0, \sigma_1, \sigma_2, \ldots) \longmapsto\!\!\!\!\!\longrightarrow (\tau_0, \tau_1, \tau_2, \ldots)$$

which better expresses the intended operational behaviour of the circuit: It consists of an infinite sequence of actions, at time moments $0, 1, 2, \ldots$. At each moment $n \geq 0$, the circuit simultaneously inputs the value $\sigma_n \in \mathbb{R}$ at its input end and outputs the value $\tau_n \in \mathbb{R}$ at its output end. In general, this value τ_n depends both on the value σ_n and on the values σ_i that have been taken as inputs at earlier time moments $i < n$. Note that this implies that circuits have memory.

Next we present the four basic types of circuits, out of which all other circuits in this section will be constructed.

(a) For every $a \in \mathbb{R}$, we define a circuit with one input and one output end, called an *a-multiplier*, for all $\sigma, \tau \in \mathbb{R}^\omega$, by

$$\sigma \vdash\!\!-\!\!a\!\!\longrightarrow \tau \iff \tau_n = a \cdot \sigma_n, \text{ all } n \geq 0$$
$$\iff \tau = a \times \sigma$$

This circuit takes, at any moment $n \geq 0$, a value σ_n at its input end, multiplies it with the constant a, and outputs the result $\tau_n = a \cdot \sigma_n$ at its output end. It defines, in other words, a function that assigns to an input stream σ the output stream $\tau = a \times \sigma$.

Occasionally, it will be more convenient to write the multiplying factor a as a super- or subscript of the arrow:

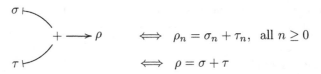

(b) The *adder* circuit has two input and one output ends, and is defined, for all $\sigma, \tau, \rho \in \mathbb{R}^\omega$ by

$$\rho_n = \sigma_n + \tau_n, \text{ all } n \geq 0$$

$$\rho = \sigma + \tau$$

At moment $n \geq 0$, the adder simultaneously inputs the values σ_n and τ_n at its input ends, and outputs their sum $\rho_n = \sigma_n + \tau_n$ at its output end.

(c) The *copier* circuit has one input and two output ends and is defined, for all $\sigma, \tau, \rho \in \mathbb{R}^\omega$, by

$$\tau_n = \sigma_n = \rho_n, \text{ all } n \geq 0$$

$$\tau = \sigma = \rho$$

At any moment $n \geq 0$, the copier inputs the value σ_n at its input end, and outputs two identical copies τ_n and ρ_n at its output ends.

(d) A *register* circuit has one input and one output end and is defined, for all $\sigma, \tau \in \mathbb{R}^\omega$, by

$$\sigma \longmapsto\!\!-R\!\!\rightarrow \tau \iff \tau_0 = 0 \text{ and } \tau_n = \sigma_{n-1}, \text{ all } n \geq 1$$

$$\iff \tau = (0, \sigma_0, \sigma_1, \sigma_2, \ldots)$$

The register circuit can be viewed as consisting of a one-place memory cell that initially contains the value 0. The register starts its activity, at time moment 0, by outputting its value $\tau_0 = 0$ at its output end, while it simultaneously inputs the value σ_0 at its input end, which is stored in the memory cell. At any future time moment $n \geq 1$, the value $\tau_n = \sigma_{n-1}$ is output and the value σ_n is input and stored. (For obvious resaons, the register circuit is sometimes also called a *unit delay*.) Recalling that for the constant stream $X = (0, 1, 0, 0, 0, \ldots)$, we have $X \times \sigma = (0, \sigma_0, \sigma_1, \sigma_2, \ldots)$, it follows that for all $\sigma, \tau \in \mathbb{R}^\omega$,

$$\sigma \longmapsto\!\!-R\!\!\rightarrow \tau \iff \tau = X \times \sigma$$

3.2   Circuit Composition

We can construct a larger circuit out of two smaller ones by connecting output ends of the first to input ends of the second. For instance, for the composition of a 2-multiplier and a 3-multiplier, we shall write

$$\longmapsto\!\!-2\!\!\rightarrow \circ \longmapsto\!\!-3\!\!\rightarrow$$

We call the connection point ∘ an (internal) *node* of the composed circuit. A computation step of this circuit, at any moment in time, consists of the simultaneous occurrence of the following actions: a value is input at the input end of the 2-register; it is multiplied by 2 and output at the output end of the 2-register; the result is input at the input end of the 3-register, is multiplied by 3 and is output at the output end of the 3-multiplier. More formally, and fortunately also more succinctly, we define the behaviour of the composed circuit, for all $\sigma, \tau \in \mathbb{R}^\omega$, by

$$\sigma \longmapsto\!\!-2\!\!\longrightarrow \circ \longmapsto\!\!-3\!\!\longrightarrow \tau$$
$$\Longleftrightarrow \quad \sigma \longmapsto\!\!-2\!\!\longrightarrow \exists\rho \longmapsto\!\!-3\!\!\longrightarrow \tau$$
$$\Longleftrightarrow \quad \exists \rho \in \mathbb{R}^\omega : \quad \sigma \longmapsto\!\!-2\!\!\longrightarrow \rho \quad \text{and} \quad \rho \longmapsto\!\!-3\!\!\longrightarrow \tau$$

We shall consider all three of the above notations as equivalent. Combining the definitions of a 2- and 3-multiplier, we can in the above example easily compute how the output stream τ depends on the input stream σ:

$$\sigma \longmapsto\!\!-2\!\!\longrightarrow \circ \longmapsto\!\!-3\!\!\longrightarrow \tau$$
$$\Longleftrightarrow \quad \exists \rho \in \mathbb{R}^\omega : \quad \sigma \longmapsto\!\!-2\!\!\longrightarrow \rho \quad \text{and} \quad \rho \longmapsto\!\!-3\!\!\longrightarrow \tau$$
$$\Longleftrightarrow \quad \exists \rho \in \mathbb{R}^\omega : \quad \rho = 2 \times \sigma \quad \text{and} \quad \tau = 3 \times \rho$$
$$\Longleftrightarrow \quad \tau = 6 \times \sigma$$

Note that the stream ρ is uniquely determined by the stream σ. The motivation for our notation "$\exists\rho$" is not so much to suggest that there might be more possible candidate streams for ρ, but rather to emphasise the fact that in order to express the output stream τ in terms of σ, we have to compute the value of the stream ρ in the middle.

We can compose circuits, more generally, with several output ends with circuits having a corresponding number of input ends, as in the following example:

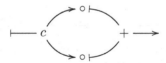

In this example, the behaviour of the resulting circuit is defined, for all $\sigma, \tau \in \mathbb{R}^\omega$, by

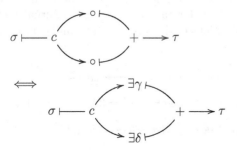

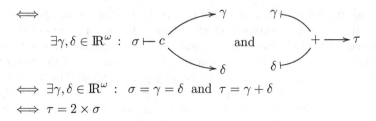

$$\Longleftrightarrow \exists \gamma, \delta \in \mathbb{R}^\omega : \sigma = \gamma = \delta \text{ and } \tau = \gamma + \delta$$
$$\Longleftrightarrow \tau = 2 \times \sigma$$

It will be convenient to have adders with more than two inputs and, similarly, copiers with more than two outputs. We define a ternary adder as the composition of two binary adders as follows:

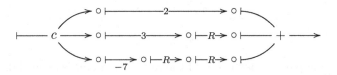

For input streams $\sigma, \tau, \rho \in \mathbb{R}^\omega$, it produces the output stream $\sigma + \tau + \rho$. We define a ternary copier by the following composition:

It takes one input stream and produces three identical copies as output streams. Adders and copiers with four or more inputs and outputs can be constructed in a similar fashion.

The following circuit combines (various instances of) all four basic circuit types:

In order to express the output stream τ for a given input stream σ, we have to compute one intermediate stream for each of the (nine) internal nodes $\circ$ in the circuit above. Using the definitions of the basic circuits, and computing from left to right, we find:

(To save space, we have omitted the symbol × for multiplication.) We can now express the output stream τ in terms of the input stream σ as follows:

$$\tau = (2 \times \sigma) + (3X \times \sigma) + (-7X^2 \times \sigma)$$
$$= (2 + 3X - 7X^2) \times \sigma$$

The circuit above computes — we shall also say *implements* — the following function on streams:

$$f : \mathbb{R}^\omega \to \mathbb{R}^\omega, \quad f(\sigma) = (2 + 3X - 7X^2) \times \sigma$$

If we supply the circuit with the input stream $\sigma = 1 \ (= (1, 0, 0, 0, \ldots))$ then the output stream is $\tau = f(1) = 2 + 3X - 7X^2$. We call this the stream *generated* by the circuit.

Convention 3. *In order to reduce the size of the diagrams with which we depict stream circuits, it will often be convenient to leave the operations of copying and addition implicit. In this manner, we can, for instance, draw the circuit above as follows:*

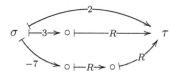

The (respective elements of the) stream σ gets copied along each of the three outgoing arrows. Similarly, the stream τ will be equal to the sum of the output streams of the three incoming arrows. This convention saves a lot of writing. Moreover, if we want to express τ in terms of σ, we now have only three internal streams to compute. If a node has both incoming and outgoing arrows, such as

then first the values of the output streams of the incoming arrows have to be added; then the resulting sum is copied and given as an input stream to each of the outgoing arrows. Consider for instance the circuit below. It has input streams σ and τ, an intermediate stream γ, and output streams δ and ϵ in $\mathbb{R}^\omega$:

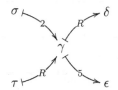

satisfying

$$\gamma = 2\sigma + (X \times \tau)$$
$$\delta = X \times \gamma$$
$$= (2X \times \sigma) + (X^2 \times \tau)$$
$$\epsilon = 5\gamma$$
$$= 10\sigma + (5X \times \tau)$$

□

As an example, we compute the stream function implemented by the following circuit, with input stream σ, output stream τ, and intermediate streams γ and δ:

We have:

$$\gamma = X \times \sigma$$
$$\delta = (3 \times \sigma) + (X^2 \times \sigma)$$
$$\tau = (5 \times \gamma) + (X \times \delta)$$
$$= (8X + X^3) \times \sigma$$

Thus the stream function implemented by this circuit is $f : \mathbb{R}^\omega \to \mathbb{R}^\omega$ with $f(\sigma) = (8X + X^3) \times \sigma$, for all $\sigma \in \mathbb{R}^\omega$. An equivalent circuit, implementing the same stream stream function, is given by:

The following proposition, of which we have omitted the easy proof, characterizes which stream functions can be implemented by the type of circuits that we have been considering so far.

Proposition 4. *For all $n \geq 0$ and $r_0, \ldots, r_n \in \mathbb{R}$, each of the following two circuits:*

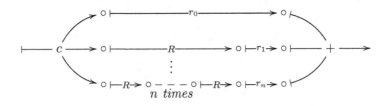

and

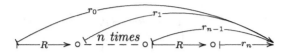

implements the stream function $f : \mathbb{R}^\omega \to \mathbb{R}^\omega$ given, for all $\sigma \in \mathbb{R}^\omega$, by

$$f(\sigma) = \rho \times \sigma$$

where the stream ρ (generated by these circuits) is the polynomial

$$\rho = r_0 + r_1 X + r_2 X^2 + \cdots + r_{n-1} X^{n-1} + r_n X^n$$

$\square$

3.3   Circuits with Feedback Loops

The use of feedback loops in stream circuits increases their expressive power substantially. We shall start with a elementary example and then give a simple and precise characterization of all stream functions that can be implemented by circuits with feedback loops. Consider the following circuit:

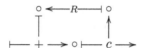

In spite of its simplicity, this circuit is already quite interesting. Before we give a formal computation of the stream function that this circuit implements, we give an informal description of its behaviour first. Assuming that we have an input stream $\sigma = (\sigma_0, \sigma_1, \sigma_2, \ldots)$, we compute the respective elements of the output stream $\tau = (\tau_0, \tau_1, \tau_2, \ldots)$. Recall that a register can be viewed as a one-place memory cell with initial value 0. At moment 0, our circuit begins its activity by inputting the first value σ_0 at its input end. The present value of the register, 0, is added to this and the result $\tau_0 = \sigma_0 + 0 = \sigma_0$ is the first value to be output. At the same time, this value σ_0 is copied and stored as the new value of the register. The next step consists of inputting the value σ_1, adding the present value of the register, σ_0, to it, and outputting the resulting value $\tau_1 = \sigma_0 + \sigma_1$. At the same time, this value $\sigma_0 + \sigma_1$ is copied and stored as the new value of the register. The next step will input σ_2 and output the value $\tau_2 = \sigma_0 + \sigma_1 + \sigma_2$. And so on. We find:

$$\tau = (\sigma_0, \sigma_0 + \sigma_1, \sigma_0 + \sigma_1 + \sigma_2, \ldots)$$

Next we show how the same answer can be obtained, more formally and more systematically, by applying a bit of basic stream calculus. As before, we try to express the output stream τ in terms of the input stream σ by computing the values of intermediate streams $\rho_1, \rho_2, \rho_3 \in \mathbb{R}^\omega$, corresponding to the three internal nodes of the circuit, such that

$$
\begin{array}{ccc}
\rho_1 & \xleftarrow{\quad R \quad} & \rho_2 \\
\big\uparrow & & \big\uparrow \\
\sigma \vdash + \longrightarrow \rho_3 \vdash & c \longrightarrow & \tau
\end{array}
$$

Note that the values of ρ_1, ρ_2, ρ_3 are mutually dependent because of the presence of the feedback loop: ρ_3 depends on ρ_1 which depends on ρ_2 which depends on ρ_3. The stream calculus developed in Section 2 is precisely fit to deal with this type of circularity. Unfolding the definitions of the basic circuits of which the above circuit is composed (one adder, one register, and one copier), we find the following system of equations:

$$
\begin{aligned}
\rho_1 &= X \times \rho_2 \\
\rho_3 &= \sigma + \rho_1 \\
\rho_2 &= \rho_3 \\
\tau &= \rho_3
\end{aligned}
$$

We have seen in the previous section how to solve such systems of equations. The right way to start, which will work in general, is to compute first the output stream of the register:

$$
\begin{aligned}
\rho_1 &= X \times \rho_2 \\
&= X \times \rho_3 \\
&= X \times (\sigma + \rho_1) \\
&= (X \times \sigma) + (X \times \rho_1)
\end{aligned}
$$

This implies $\rho_1 - (X \times \rho_1) = X \times \sigma$, which is equivalent to $\rho_1 = \frac{X}{1-X} \times \sigma$. As a consequence, $\tau = \rho_3 = \rho_2 = \sigma + \rho_1 = \sigma + (\frac{X}{1-X} \times \sigma) = \frac{1}{1-X} \times \sigma$. Thus the stream function $f : \mathbb{R}^\omega \to \mathbb{R}^\omega$ that is implemented by the feedback circuit is given, for all $\sigma \in \mathbb{R}^\omega$, by

$$
f(\sigma) = \frac{1}{1-X} \times \sigma
$$

We see that this function consists again of the convolution product of the argument σ and a constant stream $\frac{1}{1-X}$. The main difference with the examples in the previous subsections is that now this constant stream is no longer polynomial but rational.

We still have to check that the first informal and the second formal computation of the function implemented by the feedback circuit coincide. But this follows from the fact that, for all $\sigma \in \mathbb{R}^\omega$,

$$
\frac{1}{1-X} \times \sigma = (\sigma_0, \sigma_0 + \sigma_1, \sigma_0 + \sigma_1 + \sigma_2, \ldots)
$$

which is an immediate consequence of the definition of the convolution product and the fact that $\frac{1}{1-X} = (1, 1, 1, \ldots)$.

Not every feedback loop gives rise to a circuit with a well-defined behaviour. Consider for instance the following circuit, with input stream σ, output stream τ, and internal streams ρ_1, ρ_2, ρ_3:

In this circuit, we have replaced the register feedback loop of the example above by a 1-multiplier. If we try to compute the stream function of this circuit as before, we find the following system of equations:

$$\rho_1 = 1 \times \rho_2$$
$$\rho_3 = \sigma + \rho_1$$
$$\rho_2 = \rho_3$$
$$\tau = \rho_3$$

This leads to $\rho_3 = \sigma + \rho_3$, which implies $\sigma = 0$. But σ is supposed to be an arbitrary input stream, so this does not make sense.

Problems like this can be avoided by assuming that circuits have the following property.

Assumption 5. *From now on, we shall consider only circuits in which every feedback loop passes through at least one register.*   □

Note that this condition is equivalent to requiring that the circuit has no infinite paths passing through only multipliers, adders, and copiers.

Next we present the main result of the present paper. It is a characterization of which stream functions can be implemented by finite stream circuits. We formulate it for finite circuits that have one input and one output end, but it can be easily generalised to circuits with many inputs and outputs.

Theorem 6. *(a) Let C be any finite stream circuit, possibly containing feedback loops (that always pass through at least one register). The stream function $f : \mathbb{R}^\omega \to \mathbb{R}^\omega$ implemented by C is always of the form:*

$$f(\sigma) = \rho \times \sigma$$

for all $\sigma \in \mathbb{R}^\omega$ and for some fixed rational stream

$$\rho = \frac{r_0 + r_1 X + r_2 X^2 + \cdots + r_n X^n}{s_0 + s_1 X + s_2 X^2 + \cdots + s_m X^m}$$

with $n, m \geq 0$, $r_0, \ldots, r_n, s_0, \ldots, s_m \in \mathbb{R}$, and $s_0 \neq 0$.

(b) Let $f : \mathbb{R}^\omega \to \mathbb{R}^\omega$ be a stream function of the form, for all $\sigma \in \mathbb{R}^\omega$:

$$f(\sigma) = \rho \times \sigma$$

for some fixed rational stream ρ. Then there exists a finite stream circuit C that implements f.

Proof. (a) Consider a finite circuit C containing $k \geq 1$ registers. We associate with the input end of C a stream σ and with the output end of C a stream τ. With the output end of each register R_i, we associate a stream α_i. For the input end of each register R_i, we look at all incoming paths that: (i) start in either an output end of any of the registers or the input end of C, (ii) lead via adders, copiers, and multipliers, (iii) to the input end of R_i. Because of Assumption 5, there are only finitely many of such paths. This leads to an equation of the form

$$\alpha_i = (a_i^1 \times X \times \alpha^1) + \cdots + (a_i^k \times X \times \alpha^k) + (a_i \times X \times \sigma)$$

for some $a_i, a_i^j \in \mathbb{R}$. We have one such equation for each $1 \leq i \leq k$. Solving this system of k equations in stream calculus as before, yields for each register an expression $\alpha_i = \rho_i \times \sigma$, for some rational stream ρ_i. Finally, we play the same game for τ, at the output end of C, as we did for each of the registers. This will yield the following type of expression for τ:

$$\tau = (b_1 \times \alpha_1) + \cdots + (b_k \times \alpha_k) + (b \times \sigma)$$
$$= ((b_1 \times \rho_1) + \cdots + (b_k \times \rho_k) + b) \times \sigma$$

for some $b, b_i \in \mathbb{R}$, which proves (a). For (b), we treat only the special case that

$$\rho = \frac{r_0 + r_1 X + r_2 X^2 + r_3 X^3}{1 + s_1 X + s_2 X^2 + s_3 X^3}$$

where we have taken $n = m = 3$ and $s_0 = 1$. The general case is not more difficult, just more writing. We claim that the following circuit implements the function $f(\sigma) = \rho \times \sigma$ (all $\sigma \in \mathbb{R}^\omega$):

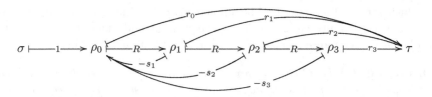

where we have denoted input and output streams by σ and τ, and intermediate streams by $\rho_0, \rho_1, \rho_2, \rho_3$. They satisfy the following equations:

$$\rho_0 = \sigma - (s_1 \times \rho_1) - (s_2 \times \rho_2) - (s_3 \times \rho_3)$$
$$\rho_1 = X \times \rho_0$$
$$\rho_2 = X \times \rho_1$$
$$\rho_3 = X \times \rho_2$$
$$\tau = (r_0 \times \rho_0) + (r_1 \times \rho_1) + (r_2 \times \rho_2) + (r_3 \times \rho_3)$$

It follows that

$$\rho_0 = \sigma - (s_1 X \times \rho_0) - (s_2 X^2 \times \rho_0) - (s_3 X^3 \times \rho_0)$$

As a consequence, we have, for $i = 0, 1, 2, 3$, that

$$\rho_i = \frac{X^i}{1 + s_1 X + s_2 X^2 + s_3 X^3} \times \sigma$$

This implies

$$\tau = \frac{r_0 + r_1 X + r_2 X^2 + r_3 X^3}{1 + s_1 X + s_2 X^2 + s_3 X^3} \times \sigma$$

whereby the claim above is proved. $\square$

Taking $\sigma = 1$ in Theorem 6 gives the following corollary.

Corollary 7. *A stream $\rho \in \mathbb{R}^\omega$ is rational if and only if it is generated by a (finite) stream circuit.* $\square$

References

[AR03]   F. Arbab and J.J.M.M. Rutten. A coinductive calculus of component connectors. In M. Wirsing, D. Pattinson, and R. Hennicker, editors, *Proceedings of WADT 2002*, volume 2755 of *LNCS*, pages 35–56. Springer, 2003.

[BR88]   J. Berstel and C. Reutenauer. *Rational series and their languages*, volume 12 of *EATCS Monographs on Theoretical Computer Science*. Springer-Verlag, 1988.

[Lah98] B.P. Lahti. *Signal Processing & Linear Systems*. Oxford University Press, 1998.

[Rut01] J.J.M.M. Rutten. Elements of stream calculus (an extensive exercise in coinduction). In S. Brooks and M. Mislove, editors, *Proceedings of MFPS 2001*, volume 45 of *ENTCS*, pages 1–66. Elsevier Science Publishers, 2001. To appear in MSCS.

Synchronous Closing and Flow Analysis for Model Checking Timed Systems

Natalia Ioustinova[1], Natalia Sidorova[2], and Martin Steffen[3]

[1] Department of Software Engineering, CWI
P.O. Box 94079, 1090 GB Amsterdam, The Netherlands
Natalia.Ioustinova@cwi.nl
[2] Department of Mathematics and Computer Science
Eindhoven University of Technology
Den Dolech 2, P.O. Box 513,
5612 MB Eindhoven, The Netherlands
n.sidorova@tue.nl
[3] Institute of Computer Science and Applied Mathematics
Christian-Albrechts-Universität
Hermann-Rodewaldstr. 3, 24118 Kiel, Germany
ms@informatik.uni-kiel.de

Abstract. Formal methods, in particular model checking, are increasingly accepted as integral part of system development. With large software systems beyond the range of fully automatic verification, however, a combination of decomposition and abstraction techniques is needed. To model check components of a system, a standard approach is to close the component with an abstraction of its environment, as standard model checkers often do not handle open reactive systems directly. To make it useful in practice, the closing of the component should be automatic, both for data and for control abstraction. Specifically for model checking asynchronous open systems, external input queues should be removed, as they are a potential source of a combinatorial state explosion.

In this paper we investigate a class of environmental processes for which the *asynchronous* communication scheme can safely be replaced by a *synchronous* one. Such a replacement is possible only if the environment is constructed under rather a severe restriction on the behavior, which can be partially softened via the use of a discrete-time semantics. We employ *data-flow analysis* to detect instances of variables and timers influenced by the data passing between the system and the environment.

Keywords: formal methods, software model checking, abstraction, flow analysis, asynchronous communication, open components, program transformation

1 Introduction

Model checking [8] is well-accepted for the verification of reactive systems. To alleviate the notorious state-space explosion problem, a host of techniques has been invented, including partial-order reduction [12, 32] and abstraction [23, 8, 10].

F.S. de Boer et al. (Eds.): FMCO 2003, LNCS 3188, pp. 292–313, 2004.
© Springer-Verlag Berlin Heidelberg 2004

As standard model checkers, e.g., Spin [16], cannot handle open systems, one has to construct a closed model, and a problem of practical importance is how to *close* open systems. This is commonly done by adding an environment process that must exhibit at least all the behavior of the real environment. In the framework of the assume-guarantee paradigm, the environment should model the behavior corresponding to the verified properties of the components forming the environment. However, the way of closing should be well-considered to counter the state-space explosion problem. This is especially true in the context of model checking programs with an *asynchronous* message-passing communication model — sending arbitrary message streams to the unbounded input queues would immediately lead to an infinite state space, unless some assumptions restricting the environment behavior are incorporated in the closing process. Even so, adding an environment process may result in a combinatorial explosion caused by all combinations of messages in the input queues.

A desirable solution would be to construct an environment that communicates to the system *synchronously*. In [29] such an approach is considered for the simplest safe abstraction of the environment, the *chaotically* behaving environment: the outside chaos is *embedded* into the system's processes, which corresponds to the synchronous communication scheme. Though useful at a first verification phase, the chaotic environment may be too general. Here, we investigate for what kind of processes, apart from the chaotic one, the asynchronous communication can be safely replaced with the synchronous one. To make such a replacement possible, the system should be not reactive — it should either only send or only receive messages. However, when we restrict our attention to systems with the discrete-time semantics like the ones of [15, 3], this requirement can be softened in that the restrictions are imposed on time slices instead of whole runs: In every time slice, the environmental process can either only receive messages, or it can both send and receive messages under condition that inputs do not change the state of the environment process.

Another problem the closing must address is that the *data* carried with the messages are usually drawn from some infinite data domains. For *data abstraction,* we combine the approaches from [29] and [17]. The main idea is to condense data exchanged with the environment into a single abstract value $\top$ to deal with the infinity of environmental data. We employ *data-flow analysis* to detect instances of chaotically influenced variables and timers and remove them. Based on the result of the data flow analysis, the system S is transformed into a *closed* system $S^\sharp$ which shows more behavior in terms of traces than the original one. For formulas of next-free LTL [26, 22], we thus get the desired property preservation: if $S^\sharp \models \varphi$ then $S \models \varphi$.

The main target application are protocols specified in SDL (*Specification and Description Language*) [28]. As verification tool, we use the well-known SPIN model checker. Our method is implemented as transformations of PROMELA-programs, SPIN's input language. With this tool we show experiments on a real-life protocol to estimate the effect of removing queues on the state space.

The rest of the paper is organized as follows. In Section 2 we fix syntax and semantics of the language. In Section 3 we describe under which condition the asynchronous communication with the environment can be replaced by synchronous one. In Section 4 we abstract from the data exchanged with the environment and give a data-flow algorithm to optimize the system for model checking. In Section 5 we show some experimental results and in Section 6 we discuss related and future work.

2   Semantics

In this section we fix syntax and operational semantics we work with. Our model is based on asynchronously communicating state machines with top-level concurrency. The communication is done via *channels* and we assume a fixed set *Chan* of channel names for each program, with $c, c', \ldots$ as typical elements. The set of channel names is partitioned into input channels $Chan_i$ and output channels $Chan_o$, and we write $c_i, c'_o, \ldots$ to denote membership of a channel to one of these classes. A program *Prog* is given as the parallel composition $\Pi_{i=1}^{n} P_i$ of a finite number of processes.

A process P is described by a tuple $(in, out, Var, Loc, Edg, \sigma_{init})$, where *in* and *out* are finite sets of *input* resp. *output* channel names of the process, *Var* denotes a finite set of variables, *Loc* denotes a finite set of *locations* or control states, and σ_{init} is the initial state. We assume the sets of variables Var_i of processes P_i in a program $Prog = \Pi_{i=1}^{n} P_i$ to be disjoint. An *edge* of the state machine describes a change of state by performing an *action* from a set *Act*; the set $Edg \subseteq Loc \times Act \times Loc$ denotes the set of edges. For an edge $(l, \alpha, \hat{l}) \in Edg$ of P, we write more suggestively $l \longrightarrow_\alpha \hat{l}$.

A mapping from variables to values is called a valuation; we denote the set of valuations by $Val = Var \to D$. We assume standard data domains such as $\mathbb{N}$, *Bool*, etc., where we write D when leaving the data domain unspecified, and we silently assume all expressions to be well-typed. A location together with a valuation of process variables define a *state* of a process. The set of process states is defined as $\Sigma = Loc \times Val$, and each process has one designated initial state $\sigma_{init} = (l_{init}, \eta_{init})$.

Processes communicate by exchanging *signals* (carrying values) over channels. Signals coming from the environment form the set of external signals Sig_{ext}. Signals that participate in the communication within the system belong to the set Sig_{int} of internal signals. Note that both signal sets are not necessarily disjoint.

As untimed actions, we distinguish (1) *input* over a channel c of a signal s containing a value to be assigned to a local variable, (2) *sending* over a channel c a signal s together with a value described by an expression, and (3) *assignments*. We assume the inputs to be unguarded, while output and assignment are *guarded* by a boolean expression g, its guard. The three classes of actions are written as $c?s(x)$, $g \triangleright c!s(e)$, and $g \triangleright x := e$, respectively, and we use $\alpha, \alpha' \ldots$ when leaving an action unspecified.

Table 1. Step semantics for one process

$$\frac{l \longrightarrow_{c?s(x)} \hat{l} \in Edg}{(l,\eta) \to_{c_i?(s,v)} (\hat{l}, \eta[x \mapsto v])} \ \text{INPUT} \qquad \frac{l \longrightarrow_{c?s(x)} \hat{l} \in Edg \Rightarrow s' \neq s}{(l,\eta) \to_{c_i?(s',v)} (l,\eta)} \ \text{DISCARD}$$

$$\frac{l \longrightarrow_{g \triangleright c!(s,e)} \hat{l} \in Edg \qquad [\![g]\!]_\eta = true \qquad [\![e]\!]_\eta = v}{(l,\eta) \to_{c_o!(s,v)} (\hat{l}, \eta)} \ \text{OUTPUT}$$

$$\frac{l \longrightarrow_{g \triangleright x:=e} \hat{l} \in Edg \qquad [\![g]\!]_\eta = true \qquad [\![e]\!]_\eta = v}{(l,\eta) \to_\tau (\hat{l}, \eta[x \mapsto v])} \ \text{ASSIGN}$$

$$\frac{l \longrightarrow_{g \triangleright set\ t:=e} \hat{l} \in Edg \qquad [\![g]\!]_\eta = true \qquad [\![e]\!]_\eta = v}{(l,\eta) \to_\tau (\hat{l}, \eta[t \mapsto on(v)])} \ \text{SET}$$

$$\frac{l \longrightarrow_{g \triangleright reset\ t} \hat{l} \in Edg \qquad [\![g]\!]_\eta = true}{(l,\eta) \to_\tau (\hat{l}, \eta[t \mapsto off])} \ \text{RESET} \qquad \frac{blocked(\sigma)}{\sigma \to_{tick} \sigma[t \mapsto (t-1)]} \ \text{TICK}_P$$

$$\frac{l \longrightarrow_{g_t \triangleright reset\ t} \hat{l} \in Edg \qquad [\![t]\!]_\eta = on(0)}{(l,\eta) \to_\tau (\hat{l}, \eta[t \mapsto off])} \ \text{TIMEOUT}$$

$$\frac{(l \longrightarrow_\alpha \hat{l} \in Edg \Rightarrow \alpha \neq g_t \triangleright reset\ t) \qquad [\![t]\!]_\eta = on(0)}{(l,\eta) \to_\tau (l, \eta[t \mapsto off])} \ \text{TDISCARD}$$

Time aspects of a system behavior are specified by actions dealing with *timers*. Each process has a finite set of timer variables (with typical elements $t, t'_1, \ldots$). A timer can be either *set* to a value, i.e., activated to run for the designated period, or *reset*, i.e., deactivated, which corresponds to timer values $on(n)$, *off*, respectively. Setting and resetting are expressed by guarded actions of the form $g \triangleright set\ t := e$ and $g \triangleright reset\ t$. If a timer expires, i.e., the value of a timer becomes zero, it can cause a *timeout*, upon which the timer is reset. The timeout action is denoted by $g_t \triangleright reset\ t$, where the timer guard g_t expresses the fact that the action can only be taken upon expiration.

The behavior of a single process is then given by sequences of states $\sigma_{init} = \sigma_0 \to_\lambda \sigma_1 \to_\lambda \ldots$ starting from the initial one. The step semantics is given as a labelled transition relation $\to_\lambda \subseteq \Sigma \times Lab \times \Sigma$ between states. The set of labels *Lab* is formed by τ-labels for internal steps, *tick*-labels for time progression and communication labels. Communication label, either input or output are of the form $c?(s,v)$ resp. $c!(s,v)$. Depending on the location, the valuation, and the potential next actions, the possible successor states are given by the rules of Table 1.

Inputting a signal with a value via a channel means reading a value belonging to a matching signal from the channel and updating the local valuation accordingly (cf. rule INPUT), where $\eta[x \mapsto v]$ stands for the valuation equaling η for all $y \in Var$ except for $x \in Var$, where $\eta[x \mapsto v](x) = v$ holds instead. A specific feature commonly used for communicating finite state machines (e.g. in SDL-

92 [27]) is captured by rule DISCARD: If the input value cannot be reacted upon at the current control state, i.e., if there is no input action originating from the location treating this signal, then the message is just discarded, leaving control state and valuation unchanged. The automaton is therefore input-enabled: it cannot refuse to accept a message; it may throw it away, though.

Unlike inputs, outputs are guarded, so sending a message involves evaluating the guard and the expression according to the current valuation (cf. rule OUTPUT). Assignment in ASSIGN works analogously, except that the step is internal. We assume for the non-timer guards, that at least one of them evaluates to true in each state. At the SDL source language, this assumption corresponds to the natural requirement that each conditional construct must cover all cases, for instance by having at least a default branch. The system should not block because of a non-covered alternative in a decision-construct [25].

Concerning the temporal behavior, timers are treated in valuations as variables, distinguishing active and deactivated timer. We use *off* to represent inactive timers. The value of an active timer shows the delay left until timer expiration. The *set*-command activates a timer, setting its value to the specified period until timer expiration, and *reset* deactivates the timer. Both actions are guarded (cf. rules SET and RESET). A timeout may occur, if an active timer has expired, i.e., reached zero (cf. rule TIMEOUT).

Time elapses by counting down active timers till zero, which happens in case no untimed actions are possible. In rule TICK_P, this is expressed by the predicate *blocked* on states: $blocked(\sigma)$ holds if no move is possible except either a *tick*-step or a reception of a message, i.e., if $\sigma \rightarrow_\lambda$ for some label λ, then $\lambda = tick$ or $\lambda = c?(s, v)$. In other words, the time-elapsing steps are those with *least priority*. The counting down of the timers is written $\eta_{[t \mapsto (t-1)]}$, by which we mean, all currently active timers are decreased by one, i.e., $on(n + 1) - 1 = on(n)$, non-active timers are not affected. Note that the operation is undefined for $on(0)$, which is justified later by Lemma 1.

In SDL, timeouts are often considered as specific timeout *messages* kept in a queue like any other message, and timer-expiration consequently is seen as adding a timeout-message to the queue. We use an equivalent presentation of this semantics, where timeouts are not put into the input queue, but are modelled more directly by guards. The equivalence of timeouts-by-guards and timeouts-as-messages in the presence of SDL's asynchronous communication model is argued for in [3]. The time semantics for SDL chosen here is not the only one conceivable (see e.g. [6] for a broader discussion of the use of timers in SDL). The semantics we use is the one described in [15, 3], and is also implemented in DTSPIN [2, 11], a discrete time extension of the SPIN model checker.

In the asynchronous communication model, a process receives messages via channels modelled as queues. We write ϵ for the empty queue; $(s, v) :: q$ denotes a queue with message (s, v) at the head of the queue, i.e., (s, v) is the message to be input next; likewise the queue $q :: (s, v)$ contains (s, v) most recently entered; Q denotes the set of possible queues. We model the queues implementing asynchronous channels explicitly as separate entities of the form (c, q), consisting of the channel name together with its queue content. We sometimes refer to the channel process (c, q) just by its name c. We require for the input and the output channel names of channel c to be $in(c) = c_o$ and $out(c) = c_i$ resp. The operational rules for queues are shown in Table 2.

In analogy to the *tick*-steps for processes, a queue can perform a *tick*-step iff the only steps possible are input or tick-steps, as captured again by the *blocked*-predicate (cf. rule TICK). Note that a queue is blocked and can therefore tick only if it is empty, and that a queue does not contain any timers. Hence, the counting down operation $[t \mapsto (t-1)]$ has no effect and is therefore omitted in the rule TICK_Q of Table 2.

Table 2. Step semantics for a channel c

$$\frac{}{(c, q) \to_{c_o?(s,v)} (c, q :: (s, v))} \text{ IN} \qquad \frac{blocked(c, q)}{(c, q) \to_{tick} (c, q)} \text{ TICK}_Q$$

$$\frac{}{(c, (s, v) :: q) \to_{c_i!(s,v)} (c, q)} \text{ OUT}$$

A global semantics of a system S is given by a parallel composition of labelled transition systems modelling processes and channels of the specification. The semantics of the parallel composition $S = S_1 \parallel \ldots \parallel S_n$ is given by the rules of Table 3, where $ext(S)$ is used to denote the set of external channel names. Since we assumed the variable sets of the components to be disjoint, the combined state is defined as the product. We write $[\![x]\!]_\sigma$ for the value $[\![x]\!]_{\sigma_i}$ of x, for one

Table 3. Parallel composition

$$\frac{\sigma_i \to_{c!(s,v)} \hat{\sigma}_i \qquad \sigma_j \to_{c?(s,v)} \hat{\sigma}_j \qquad i \neq j}{(\ldots, \sigma_i, \ldots, \sigma_j, \ldots) \to_\tau (\ldots, \hat{\sigma}_i, \ldots, \hat{\sigma}_j, \ldots)} \text{ COMM}$$

$$\frac{\sigma_1 \to_{tick} \hat{\sigma}'_1 \ldots \sigma_n \to_{tick} \hat{\sigma}'_n}{(\sigma_1, \ldots, \sigma_n) \to_{tick} (\hat{\sigma}_1, \ldots, \hat{\sigma}_n)} \text{ TICK}$$

$$\frac{\sigma_i \to_{c?(s,v)} \hat{\sigma}_i \qquad c \in ext(S)}{(\ldots, \sigma_i, \ldots) \to_{c?(s,v)} (\ldots, \hat{\sigma}_i, \ldots)} \text{ INTERLEAVE}_{in}$$

$$\frac{\sigma_i \to_{c!(s,v)} \hat{\sigma}_i \qquad c \in ext(S)}{(\ldots, \sigma_i, \ldots) \to_{c!(s,v)} (\ldots, \hat{\sigma}_i, \ldots)} \text{ INTERLEAVE}_{out}$$

$$\frac{\sigma_i \to_\tau \hat{\sigma}_i}{(\ldots, \sigma_i, \ldots) \to_\tau (\ldots, \hat{\sigma}_i, \ldots)} \text{ INTERLEAVE}_\tau$$

state σ_i being part of σ; analogously, we use the notation $[\![e]\!]_\sigma$ for the value of e in σ. The *initial* state of a parallel composition is given by the array of initial process states together with (c, ϵ) for channels in *Chan*. We call a sequence $\sigma_{init} = \sigma_0 \to_\lambda \sigma_1 \to_\lambda \dots$ starting from an initial state a *run*.

Communication between two processes is done by exchanging a common signal and a value over a channel. According to the syntactic restriction on the use of communication labels, only synchronisation between a process and a channel may happen. Sending of a signal over the channel means synchronising an output step of the process with an input step of the queue, i.e. a $c_o!(s, v)$ step of the process is synchronised with a $c_o?(s, v)$ step of the channel c. Receiving is accomplished by synchronising an output step, which removes first element from the channel queue, with an input step of the process. As defined by the rule COMM of Table 3, systems perform common steps synchronously. The result of communication is relabelled to τ.

Communication steps of two partners may synchronize, if they use the same channel name. Communication steps may be interleaved as in rules INTERLEAVE$_{in}$ and INTERLEAVE$_{out}$ provided the channel name belongs to the set of external channel names $ext(S)$ of the system. As far as τ steps are concerned, each system can act on its own according to rule INTERLEAVE$_\tau$.

Lemma 1. *Let S be a system and $\sigma \in \Sigma$ one of its states.*

1. *If $\sigma \to_{tick} \sigma'$, then $[\![t]\!]_\sigma \neq on(0)$, for all timers t.*
2. *If $\sigma \to_{tick} \sigma'$, then for all channel states (c, q), $q = \epsilon$.*

Proof. For part (1), if $[\![t]\!]_\eta = on(0)$ for a timer t in a process P, then a τ-step is allowed due to either TIMEOUT or TDISCARD of Table 1. Hence, the system is not *blocked* and therefore cannot do a *tick*-step.

Part (2) follows from the fact that a channel can only perform a *tick*-step exactly when it is empty. □

The following lemma expresses that the blocked predicate is compositional in the sense that the parallel composition of processes is blocked iff each process is blocked (cf. rule TICK of Table 3).

Lemma 2. *For a state $\sigma = (\sigma_1, \dots, \sigma_n)$ of a system S, blocked(σ) iff blocked(σ_i) for all σ_i.*

Proof. If σ is not blocked, it can perform a τ-step or an output-step. The output step must originate from a process, which thus is not blocked. The τ-step is either caused by a single process or by a synchronizing action of a sender and a receiver; in both cases at least one process is not blocked. For the reverse direction, a τ-step of a single process being thus not blocked, entails that σ is not blocked. An output step of a single process causes σ either to do the same output step or, in case of internal communication, to do a τ-step. In both cases, σ is not blocked. □

3   Replacing Asynchronous with Synchronous Communication

In a system with asynchronous communication, introducing an environment process can lead to a combinatorial explosion caused by all combinations of messages in the queues modelling channels. An ideal solution from the perspective of the state space would be to construct an environment process that communicates with the system synchronously. In this section, we specify under which conditions we can safely replace the asynchronous communication with an outside environment process, say E, by *synchronous* communication.

A general condition an asynchronously communicating process satisfies is that the process is always willing to accept messages, since the queues are unbounded. Hence, the environment process must be at least *input enabled:* it must always be able to receive messages, lest the synchronous composition will lead to more blockings. Thanks to the DISCARD-rule of Table 1, SDL-processes are input enabled, i.e., at least *input-discard* steps are possible, which throw away the message and do not change the state of the process. Another effect of an input queue is that the queue introduces an arbitrary delay between the reception of a message and the future reaction of the receiving process to this message. For an output, the effect is converse. This means, that in order not to miss any potential behavior, the asynchronous process can be replaced by the analogous synchronous process as long as there are either only input actions or else only output actions, so the process is not reactive.[1] This is related to the so-called *Brock-Ackerman anomaly*, characterizing the difference between buffered and unbuffered communication [7].

Disallowing reactive behavior is clearly a severe restriction and only moderately generalizes completely chaotic behavior. One feature of the timed semantics, though, allows to loosen this restriction. Time progresses by *tick*-steps when the system is blocked. This especially means that when a *tick* happens, all queues of a system are empty (cf. Lemma 1). This implies that the restrictions need to apply only *per time slice*, i.e., to the steps between two ticks,[2] and not to the overall process behavior. Additionally we require that there are no infinite sequences of steps without a *tick*, i.e., there are no runs with *zero-time cycles*. This leads to the following definition.

Definition 3. *A sequence of steps is* tick-separated *iff it contains no zero-time cycle, and for every time slice of the sequence one of the following two conditions holds:*

---

[1] A more general definition would require that the process actions satisfy a *confluence* condition as far as the input and output actions are concerned, i.e., doing an input action does not invalidate the possibility of an output action, and vice versa. Also in this case, the process is not reactive, since there is no feed-back from input to output actions.

[2] A time slice of a run is a maximal subsequence of the run without *tick*-steps.

Table 4. Synchronous communication over rendezvous channel c

$$\frac{\gamma_1 \to_{c_i?(s,v)} \hat{\gamma}_1 \qquad \gamma_2 \to_{c_o!(s,v)} \hat{\gamma}_2}{(\gamma_1, \gamma_2) \to_\tau (\hat{\gamma}_1, \hat{\gamma}_2)} \text{ COMM}_{sync}$$

1. *the time slice contains no output action;*
2. *the time slice contains no output over two different channels, and all locations in the time slice are input-discarding wrt. all inputs of that time slice.*

We call a process tick-separated *if all its runs are* tick-separated.

Further we consider a synchronous version P_s and an asynchronous version P_a of a process P, where P_s is the process P together with a set of rendezvous channels, and P_a is formed by the process P together with a set of channels with the same names as for P_s but which are queues. Synchronous communication over a rendezvous channel c is defined by rule COMM$_{sync}$ of Table 4.

In the following, we call a *configuration* the combined state of a process together with the state of its channels. So given P_s and P_a and two corresponding states $\gamma_s = \sigma_s$ and $\gamma_a = (\sigma_a, (c_i, q_i), (c_o^1, q_1), \ldots, (c_o^k, q_k))$, we define $\unrhd$ as $\gamma_a \unrhd \gamma_s$, if $\sigma_s = \sigma_a$. Comparing the observable behavior of an asynchronous and a synchronous process, we must take into account that the asynchronous one performs more internal steps when exchanging messages with its queues. Hence the comparison is based on a *weak* notion of equivalence, ignoring the τ-steps: so we define a weak step $\Rightarrow_\lambda$ as $\to_\tau^* \to_\lambda \to_\tau^*$ when $\lambda \neq \tau$, and as $\to_\tau^*$ else. Correspondingly, $\Rightarrow_{\vec{\lambda}}$ denotes a sequence of weak steps with labels from a sequence $\vec{\lambda}$.

Lemma 4. *Assume a synchronous and an asynchronous version P_s and P_a of a process P and corresponding states γ_s and γ_a with $\gamma_a \unrhd \gamma_s$, where the queues of γ_a are all empty. If $\gamma_a \Rightarrow_{\vec{\lambda}} \gamma_a'$ by a tick-separated sequence, where $\vec{\lambda}$ does not contain a tick-label, and where the queues of γ_a' are empty, then there exists a sequence $\gamma_s \Rightarrow_{\vec{\lambda}} \gamma_s'$ with $\gamma_a' \unrhd \gamma_s'$.*

Proof. We are given a sequence $\gamma_a = \gamma_0^a \to_{\lambda_0} \gamma_1^a \cdots \to_{\lambda_{n-1}} \gamma_n^a = \gamma_a'$, with the queues of γ_0^a and γ_n^a empty. According to the definition of *tick*-separation, we distinguish the following two cases:

Case 1: $\lambda_i \notin \{tick, c!(s,v)\}$, for all $1 \leq i \leq n-1$

To get a matching reduction sequence of the synchronous system starting at γ_0^s, we apply the following renaming scheme. Input actions $\gamma_a \to_{c?(s,v)} \gamma_a'$ into the queue are just omitted (which means, they are postponed for the synchronous process). τ-steps $\gamma_a \to_\tau \gamma_a'$, inputting a value from the queue into the process, i.e., τ-steps justified by rule COMM where the process does a step $\sigma \to_{c?(s,v)} \sigma'$ by rule INPUT and the queue the corresponding output step by rule OUT, are replaced by a direct input steps $\gamma_s \to_{c?(s,v)} \gamma_s'$. Process internal τ-steps of the asynchronous system are identically taken by the synchronous system, as well. τ-steps caused by output actions from the process into a queue need not be dealt with, since the sequence from γ_0^a to γ_n^a does not contain external output from the queues, and the queues are empty at the beginning and the end of the sequence.

It is straightforward to see that the sequence of steps obtained by this transformation is indeed a legal sequence of the synchronous system. Moreover, the last configurations have the same state component and, due to the non-lossiness and the Fifo-behavior of the input queue, both sequences coincide modulo τ-steps.

Case 2: no output over two different channels, input discarding locations (and no *tick*-steps)

Similar to the previous case, the synchronous system can mimic the behavior of the asynchronous one adhering to the following scheme: τ-steps $\gamma_a \rightarrow_\tau \gamma_a'$, feeding a value from the process into the queue, i.e., τ-steps justified by rule OUTPUT where the process does a step $\sigma \rightarrow_{c!(s,v)} \sigma'$ and the queue the corresponding input step by rule IN, are replaced by a direct output step $\gamma_s \rightarrow_{c!(s,v)} \gamma_s'$. Input actions $\gamma_a \rightarrow_{c?(s,v)} \gamma_a'$ into the queue are mimicked by a discard-step. Output steps from the queue of the asynchronous system are omitted, and so are τ-steps caused by internal communication from the input-queue to the process. All other internal steps are identically taken in both systems. The rest of the argument is analogous to the previous case. □

Note that $\gamma_a' \trianglerighteq \gamma_s'$ means that γ_s' is blocked whenever γ_a' is blocked.

We write $[\![P]\!]_{wtrace}$ to denote the set of all weak traces of process P. To prove that for *tick*-separated processes $[\![P_s]\!]_{wtrace} = [\![P_a]\!]_{wtrace}$, we introduce a notion of *tick*-simulation that captures the ability to simulate any *sequence* of steps up to a *tick* step, i.e. the chosen granularity level are time slices and only the states immediately before and after *tick* are of importance there. (Remember that we assume the absence of zero-time cycles.)

Definition 5. *A binary relation $\mathcal{R} \subseteq \Gamma_1 \times \Gamma_2$ on two sets of states is called a* tick*-simulation, when the following conditions hold:*

1. *If $\gamma_1 \mathcal{R} \gamma_2$ and $\gamma_1 \rightarrow_{tick} \gamma_1'$, then $\gamma_2 \rightarrow_{tick} \gamma_2'$ and $\gamma_1' \mathcal{R} \gamma_2'$.*
2. *If $\gamma_1 \mathcal{R} \gamma_2$ and $\gamma_1 \Rightarrow_{\vec{\lambda}} \gamma_1'$ for some γ_1' with blocked(γ_1') where $\vec{\lambda}$ does not contain* tick, *then $\gamma_2 \Rightarrow_{\vec{\lambda}} \gamma_2'$ for some γ_2' with blocked(γ_2') and $\gamma_1' \mathcal{R} \gamma_2'$.*

We write $\gamma_1 \preceq_{tick} \gamma_2$ if there exists a tick *simulation $\mathcal{R}$ with $\gamma_1 \mathcal{R} \gamma_2$, and similarly for processes, $P_1 \preceq_{tick} P_2$ if their initial states are in that relation.*

Theorem 6. *If a process P is* tick-*separated, then $[\![P_s]\!]_{wtrace} = [\![P_a]\!]_{wtrace}$.*

Proof. There are two directions to show. $[\![P_s]\!]_{wtrace} \subseteq [\![P_a]\!]_{wtrace}$ is immediate: each communication step of the synchronous process P_s can be mimicked by the buffered P_a with adding an internal τ-step for the communication with the buffer.

For the reverse direction $[\![P_a]\!]_{wtrace} \subseteq [\![P_s]\!]_{wtrace}$ we show that P_a is simulated by P_s according to the definition of *tick*-simulation, which considers as basic steps only *tick*-steps or else the sequence of steps within one time slice.

We define the relation $\mathcal{R} \subseteq \Gamma_a \times \Gamma_s$ as $(\sigma_a, ((c_0, q_0), \ldots, (c_m, q_m)))\mathcal{R}\sigma_s$ iff $\sigma_a = \sigma_s$ and $q_i = \epsilon$ for all queues modelling the channels. To show that $\mathcal{R}$ is indeed a *tick*-simulation, assume $\gamma_a = (\sigma_a, ((c_0, \epsilon), \ldots, (c_m, \epsilon)))$ and $\gamma_s = \sigma_s$ with $\gamma_a \mathcal{R} \gamma_s$. There are two cases to consider.

Case: $\gamma_a \rightarrow_{tick} \gamma'_a$

where $\gamma'_a = \gamma_a[t \mapsto (t-1)]$. By the definition of the *tick*-step, $blocked(\gamma_a)$ must hold, i.e., there are no steps enabled except input from the outside or *tick*-steps. Since immediately $blocked(\gamma_s)$, also $\gamma_s \rightarrow_{tick} \gamma_s[t \mapsto (t-1)]$, which concludes the case.

Case: $\gamma_a \Rightarrow_{\vec{\lambda}} \gamma'_a$

where $blocked(\gamma'_a)$ and $\vec{\lambda}$ does not contain a *tick*-label. The case follows directly from Lemma 4 and the fact that $\gamma'_a \succeq \gamma'_s$ where γ'_a is blocked implies that also γ'_s is blocked.

Since clearly the initial states are in relation $\mathcal{R}$ as defined above, this gives $P_a \preceq_{tick} P_s$. Since $P_a \preceq_{tick} P_s$ and each *tick*-step of P_a can be mimicked by the *tick* step of P_s and each weak step $\Rightarrow_{\vec{\lambda}}$ of P_a can also be mimicked by P_s. That implies $[\![P_a]\!]_{wtrace} \subseteq [\![P_s]\!]_{wtrace}$, as required. $\square$

4   Abstracting Data

Originating from an unknown or underspecified environment, signals from outside can carry *any* value, which renders the system infinite state. Assuming nothing about the data means one can conceptually abstract values from outside into one abstract *"chaotic"* value, which basically means to ignore these data and focus on the control structure. Data not coming from outside is left untouched, though chaotic data from the environment influence internal data of the system. In this section, we present a straightforward dataflow analysis marking variable and timer instances that may be influenced by the environment, namely we establish for each process- and timer-variable in each location whether

1. the variable is guaranteed to be non-chaotic, or
2. the variable is guaranteed to be influenced by the outside, or
3. whether its status depends on the actual run.

The analysis is a combination of the ones from [29] and [17].

4.1   Dataflow Analysis

The analysis works on a simple *flow graph* representation of the system, where each process is represented by a single flow graph, whose nodes $n \in nodes$ are associated with the process' actions and the flow relation captures the intra-process data dependencies. Since the structure of the language we consider is rather simple, the flow-graph can be easily obtained by standard techniques.

We use an abstract representation of the data values, where $\top$ is interpreted as value chaotically influenced by the environment and $\bot$ stands for a non-chaotic value. We write $\eta^\alpha, \eta_1^\alpha, \ldots$ for abstract valuations, i.e., for typical elements from $Val^\alpha = Var \to \{\top, \bot\}$. The abstract values are ordered $\bot \leq \top$, and the order is lifted pointwise to valuations. With this ordering, the set of valuations forms a complete lattice, where we write $\eta_\bot$ for the least element, given as $\eta_\bot(x) = \bot$ for all $x \in Var$, and we denote the least upper bound of $\eta_1^\alpha, \ldots, \eta_n^\alpha$ by $\bigvee_{i=1}^n \eta_i^\alpha$ (or by $\eta_1^\alpha \vee \eta_2^\alpha$ in the binary case). By slight abuse of notation, we will use the same symbol η^α for the valuation per node, i.e., for functions of type $node \to Val^\alpha$. The abstract valuation $[\![e]\!]_{\eta^\alpha}$ for an expression e equals $\bot$ iff all variables in e are evaluated to $\bot$, $[\![e]\!]_{\eta^\alpha}$ is $\top$ iff the abstract valuation of at least one of the variables in e is $\top$.

Depending on whether we are interested in an answer to point (1) or point (2) from above, $\top$ is interpreted as a variable potentially influenced from outside, and, dually for the second case, $\top$ stands for variables guaranteed to be influenced from outside. Here we present *may* and *must* analysis for the first and the second case respectively.

May Analysis. First we consider *may* analysis that marks variables *potentially* influenced by data from outside. Each node n of the flow graph has associated an abstract transfer function $f_n : Val^\alpha \to Val^\alpha$, describing the change of the abstract valuations depending on the kind of action at the node. The functions are given in Table 5. The equations are mostly straightforward; the only case deserving mention is the one for $c?s(x)$, whose equation captures the inter-process data-flow from a sending to a receiving action. It is easy to see that the transfer functions are *monotone*.

Upon start of the analysis, at each node the variables' values are assumed to be defined, i.e., the initial valuation is the least one: $\eta_{init}^\alpha(n) = \eta_\bot$. This choice rests on the assumption that all local variables of each process are properly initialized. We are interested in the least solution to the data-flow problem given by the following constraint set:

$$\eta_{post}^\alpha(n) \geq f_n(\eta_{pre}^\alpha(n))$$
$$\eta_{pre}^\alpha(n) \geq \bigvee \{\eta_{post}^\alpha(n') \mid (n', n) \text{ in flow relation}\} \tag{1}$$

Table 5. May analysis: transfer functions/abstract effect for process P

$$f(c?s(x))\eta^\alpha = \begin{cases} \eta^\alpha[x \mapsto \top] & s \in Sig_{ext} \\ \eta^\alpha[x \mapsto \bigvee\{[\![e]\!]_{\eta^\alpha} \mid n' = g \rhd c!s(e)\}] & s \notin Sig_{ext} \end{cases}$$
$$f(g \rhd c!s(e))\eta^\alpha = \eta^\alpha$$
$$f(g \rhd x := e)\eta^\alpha = \eta^\alpha[x \mapsto [\![e]\!]_{\eta^\alpha}]$$
$$f(g \rhd set\ t := e)\eta^\alpha = \eta^\alpha[t \mapsto on([\![e]\!]_{\eta^\alpha})]$$
$$f(g \rhd reset\ t)\eta^\alpha = \eta^\alpha[t \mapsto off]$$
$$f(g_t \rhd reset\ t)\eta^\alpha = \eta^\alpha[t \mapsto off]$$

For each node n of the flow graph, the data-flow problem is specified by two inequations or constraints. The first one relates the abstract valuation η^α_{pre} before entering the node with the valuation η^α_{post} afterwards via the abstract effects of Table 5. The *least* fixpoint of the constraint set can be found iteratively in a fairly standard way by a *worklist algorithm* (see e.g., [19, 14, 24]), where the worklist steers the iterative loop until the least fixpoint is reached (cf. Figure 1).

---

input : the flow−graph of the program
output : $\eta^\alpha_{pre}, \eta^\alpha_{post}$;

$\eta^\alpha(n) = \eta^\alpha_{init}(n)$;
$WL = \{ n \mid \alpha_n = ?s(x), s \in Sig_{ext} \}$;

repeat
    pick $n \in WL$;
    if $n = g \rhd c!s(e)$ **then**
        let $S' = \{ n' \mid n' = c?s(x) \text{ and } [\![e]\!]_{\eta^\alpha(n)} \not\leq [\![x]\!]_{\eta^\alpha(n')} \}$
        in
            for all $n' \in S' : \eta^\alpha(n') := f_{n'}(\eta^\alpha(n'))$;
    let $S = \{ n'' \in succ(n) \mid f_n(\eta^\alpha(n)) \not\leq \eta^\alpha(n'') \}$
    in
        for all $n'' \in S : \eta^\alpha(n'') := f_n(\eta^\alpha(n))$;
    $WL := WL \backslash \{n\} \cup S \cup S'$;
until $WL = \emptyset$;

$\eta^\alpha_{pre}(n) = \eta^\alpha(n)$;
$\eta^\alpha_{post}(n) = f_n(\eta^\alpha(n))$

Fig. 1. *May* analysis: worklist algorithm

The worklist data-structure WL used in the algorithm is a set of elements, more specifically a set of nodes from the flow-graph, where we denote by $succ(n)$ the set of successor nodes of n in the flow graph in forward direction. It supports as operation to randomly pick one element from the set (without removing it), and we write $WL \backslash \{n\}$ for the worklist without the node n and $\cup$ for set-union on the elements of the worklist. The algorithm starts with the least valuation on all nodes and an initial worklist containing nodes with input from the environment. It enlarges the valuation within the given lattice step by step until it stabilizes, i.e., until the worklist is empty. If adding the abstract effect of one node to the current state enlarges the valuation, i.e., the set S is non-empty, those successor nodes from S are (re-)entered into the list of unfinished one. Since the set of variables in the system is finite, and thus the lattice of abstract valuations, the termination of the algorithm is immediate.

With the worklist as a set-like data structure, the algorithm is free to work off the list in any order. In praxis, more deterministic data-structures and traversal strategies are appropriate, for instance traversing the graph in a breadth-first manner (see [24] for a broader discussion or various traversal strategies).

After termination the algorithm yields two mappings $\eta^\alpha_{pre}, \eta^\alpha_{post} : Node \to Val^\alpha$. On a location l, the result of the analysis is given by $\eta^\alpha(l) = \bigvee\{\eta^\alpha_{post}(\tilde{n}) \mid \tilde{n} = \tilde{l} \longrightarrow_\alpha l\}$, also written as η^α_l.

Lemma 7 (Correctness (may)). *Upon termination, the algorithm gives back the least solution to the constraint set as given by the equations (1), resp. Table 5.*

Must Analysis. The *must* analysis is almost dual to *may* analysis. A transfer function that describes the change of the abstract valuation depending on the action at the node is defined in Table 6. For inputs, $c?s(x)$ in process P assigns $\perp$ to x if the signal is sent to P with reliable data, only. This means the values after reception correspond to the greatest lower bound over all expressions which can occur in a matching send-action.

Table 6. Must analysis: transfer functions/abstract effect for process P

$$f(c?s(x))\eta^\alpha = \begin{cases} \eta^\alpha[x \mapsto \top] & s \notin Sig_{int} \\ \eta^\alpha[x \mapsto \bigwedge\{[\![e]\!]_{\eta^\alpha} \mid n'=g \rhd c!s(e)\}] & s \in Sig_{int} \end{cases}$$

$$f(g \rhd c!s(e))\eta^\alpha = \eta^\alpha$$
$$f(g \rhd x := e)\eta^\alpha = \eta^\alpha[x \mapsto [\![e]\!]_{\eta^\alpha}]$$
$$f(g \rhd set\ t := e)\eta^\alpha = \eta^\alpha[t \mapsto on([\![e]\!]_{\eta^\alpha})]$$
$$f(g \rhd reset\ t)\eta^\alpha = \eta^\alpha[t \mapsto off]$$
$$f(g_t \rhd reset\ t)\eta^\alpha = \eta^\alpha[t \mapsto off]$$

As that is done for may analysis, the data-flow problem is specified for each node n of the flow graph by two inequations (2) (see Table 6). Analogously, the *greatest* fixpoint of the constraint set can be found iteratively by a worklist algorithm (cf. Figure 2). Upon start of the analysis, at each node the variables' values are assumed to be defined, i.e., the initial valuation is the greatest one: $\eta^\alpha_{init}(n) = \eta_\top$.

$$\eta^\alpha_{post}(n) \leq f_n(\eta^\alpha_{pre}(n))$$
$$\eta^\alpha_{pre}(n) \leq \bigwedge\{\eta^\alpha_{post}(n') \mid (n',n) \text{ in flow relation}\} \tag{2}$$

Like the may-analysis case, the termination of the algorithm follows from the finiteness of the set of variables.

Lemma 8 (Correctness ($must$)). *Upon termination, the algorithm from Figure 2 gives back the greatest solution to the constraint set as given by equations (2) resp. Table 6.*

input :   the flow−graph of the program
output : $\eta^{\alpha}_{pre}, \eta^{\alpha}_{post}$;

$\eta^{\alpha}(n) = \eta^{\alpha}_{init}(n)$;
$WL = \{n \mid \alpha_n = g \triangleright x := e\}$;

repeat
    pick $n \in WL$;
    if $n = g \triangleright c!s(e)$ **then**
        let $S' = \{n' \mid n' = c?s(x) \text{ and } [\![e]\!]_{\eta^{\alpha}(n)} \not\geq [\![x]\!]_{\eta^{\alpha}(n')}\}$
        in
            for all $n' \in S' : \eta^{\alpha}(n') := f_{n'}(\eta^{\alpha}(n'))$;
    let $S = \{n'' \in succ(n) \mid f_n(\eta^{\alpha}(n)) \not\geq \eta^{\alpha}(n'')\}$
    in
        for all $n'' \in S : \eta^{\alpha}(n'') := f_n(\eta^{\alpha}(n))$;
    $WL := WL \backslash \{n\} \cup S \cup S'$;
until $WL = \emptyset$;

$\eta^{\alpha}_{pre}(n) = \eta^{\alpha}(n)$;
$\eta^{\alpha}_{post}(n) = f_n(\eta^{\alpha}(n))$

Fig. 2. *Must* analysis: worklist algorithm

4.2   Program Transformation

Based on the result of the analysis, we transform the given system $S = P \parallel \bar{P}$ into an optimized one, denoted by $S^{\sharp}$, where the communication of P with its environment $\bar{P}$ is done synchronously, all the data exchanged is abstracted, and which is in a simulation relation with the original system.

The intention is to use the information collected in the analyses about the influence of the environment to reduce the state space. Depending on whether one relies on the may-analysis alone (which variable occurrences may be influenced from the outside) or takes into account the results of both analyses (additional information which variable occurrences are definitely chaotic) the precision of the abstraction varies. Using only the may-information overapproximates the system (further) but in general leads to a smaller state space.

The second option, on the other hand, gives a more precise abstraction and thus less false negatives. Indeed, it does not, apart from the abstraction caused by introducing chaotic values, abstract the system further as far as the behavior is concerned. It is nevertheless profitable as it allows to remove any unnecessary instances of variables or expressions which are detected to be $\mathbb{T}$ constantly. It furthermore can make further optimizations of the system more effective. For instance, live analysis and the optimization as described in [4] can be effective for more variable instances and thus yield better further reduction when applied after replacing variable instances which are constantly $\mathbb{T}$.

In either case we must ensure that the abstraction of timer values is treated adequately (see below). Here we describe the transformation for the combination of may and must analysis, only, since the alternative is simpler.

Overloading the symbols $\top$ and $\bot$ we mean for the rest of the paper: the value of $\top$ for a variable at a location refers to the result of the must analysis, i.e., the definite knowledge that the data is chaotic for all runs. Dually, $\bot$ stands for the definite knowledge of the may analysis, i.e., for data which is never influenced from outside. Additionally, we write $\mathbb{I}$ in case neither analysis gave a definite answer.

We extend the data domains each by an additional value $\mathbb{T}$, representing unknown, chaotic, data, i.e., we assume now domains such as $\mathbb{N}^{\mathbb{T}} = \mathbb{N} \,\dot\cup\, \{\mathbb{T}\}$, $Bool^{\mathbb{T}} = Bool \,\dot\cup\, \{\mathbb{T}\}, \ldots$, where we do not distinguish notationally the various types of chaotic values. These values $\mathbb{T}$ are considered as the largest values, i.e., we introduce $\leq$ as the smallest reflexive relation with $v \leq \mathbb{T}$ for all elements v (separately for each domain). The strict lifting of a valuation $\eta^{\mathbb{T}}$ to expressions is denoted by $[\![.]\!]_{\eta^{\mathbb{T}}}$.

The transformation is straightforward: guards influenced by the environment are taken non-deterministically, i.e., a guard g at a location l is replaced by *true*, if $[\![g]\!]_{\eta_l^\alpha} = \top$. A guard g whose value at a location l is $\mathbb{I}$ is treated dynamically on the extended data domain. For assignments, we distinguish between the variables that carry the value $\mathbb{I}$ in at least one location and the rest. Assignments of $\top$ to variables that take $\mathbb{I}$ at no location are omitted. Assignments of concrete values are left untouched and the assignments to the variables that are marked by $\mathbb{I}$ in at least one location are performed on the extended data domain.

The interpretation of *timer variables* on the extended domain requires special attention. Chaos can influence timers only via the *set*-operation by setting

Table 7. Transformation

$$\frac{l \longrightarrow_{c?s(x)} \hat{l} \in Edg \qquad x \notin Var_{\mathbb{I}} \qquad [\![x]\!]_{\eta_l^\alpha} = \top}{l \longrightarrow_{c?s(\_)} \hat{l} \in Edg^\sharp} \quad \text{T-INPUT}_{ext}$$

$$\frac{l \longrightarrow_{g \,\triangleright\, c!(s,e)} \hat{l} \in Edg \qquad [\![e]\!]_{\eta_l^\alpha} = \top}{l \longrightarrow_{g^\sharp \,\triangleright\, c!(s,\mathbb{T})} \hat{l} \in Edg^\sharp} \quad \text{T-OUTPUT}$$

$$\frac{l \longrightarrow_{g \,\triangleright\, x:=e} \hat{l} \in Edg \qquad x \notin Var_{\mathbb{I}} \qquad [\![x]\!]_{\eta_l^\alpha} = \top}{l \longrightarrow_{g^\sharp \,\triangleright\, skip} \hat{l} \in Edg^\sharp} \quad \text{T-ASSIGN}_1$$

$$\frac{l \longrightarrow_{g \,\triangleright\, x:=e} \hat{l} \in Edg \qquad x \in Var_{\mathbb{I}} \qquad [\![e]\!]_{\eta_l^\alpha} = \top}{l \longrightarrow_{g^\sharp \,\triangleright\, x:=\mathbb{T}} \hat{l} \in Edg^\sharp} \quad \text{T-ASSIGN}_2$$

$$\frac{l \longrightarrow_{g \,\triangleright\, set\ t:=e} \hat{l} \in Edg \qquad [\![e]\!]_{\eta_l^\alpha} = \top}{l \longrightarrow_{g^\sharp \,\triangleright\, set\ t:=\mathbb{T}} \hat{l} \in Edg^\sharp} \quad \text{T-SET}$$

it to a chaotic value. Therefore, the domain of timer values contains the additional chaotic value $on(\mathbb{T})$. Since we need the transformed system to show at least the behavior of the original one, we must provide proper treatment of the rules involving $on(\mathbb{T})$, i.e., the TIMEOUT-, the TDISCARD-, and the TICK-rule. As $on(\mathbb{T})$ stands for any value of active timers, it must cover the cases where timeouts and timer-discards are enabled (because of the concrete value $on(0)$) as well as *disabled* (because of $on(n)$ with $n \geq 1$). The second one is necessary, since the enabledness of the tick steps depends on the disabledness of timeouts and timer discards via the blocked-condition.

To distinguish the two cases, we introduce a refined abstract value $on(\mathbb{T}^+)$ for chaotic timers, representing all *on*-settings larger than or equal to 1. The order on the domain of timer values is given as smallest reflexive order relation such that $on(0) \leq on(\mathbb{T})$ and $on(n) \leq on(\mathbb{T}^+) \leq on(\mathbb{T})$, for all $n \geq 1$. To treat the case where the abstract timer value $on(\mathbb{T})$ denotes *absence* of immediate timeout, we add edges of the form

$$\frac{}{l \longrightarrow_{t=on(\mathbb{T}) \,\triangleright\, set\ t := \mathbb{T}+} l \in Edg^\sharp} \text{ T-NoTimeout}$$

which set back the timer value to $\mathbb{T}^+$ representing a non-zero delay.

The decreasing operation needed in the TICK-rule is defined in extension to the definition on values from $on(\mathbb{N})$ on $\mathbb{T}^+$ by $on(\mathbb{T}^+) - 1 = on(\mathbb{T})$. Note that the operation is left undefined on $\mathbb{T}$, which is justified by a property analogous to Lemma 1:

Lemma 9. *Let $(l, \eta^\mathbb{T}, q^\mathbb{T})$ be a state of $S^\sharp$. If $(l, \eta^\mathbb{T}, q^\mathbb{T}) \rightarrow_{tick}$, then $[\![t]\!]_{\eta^\mathbb{T}} \notin \{on(\mathbb{T}), on(0)\}$, for all timers t.*

Proof. By definition of the *blocked*-predicate and inspection of the TIMEOUT- and TDISCARD-rule (for $on(0)$ as for Lemma 1) and the behavior of the abstract value $on(\mathbb{T})$ (T-NoTimeout-rule). □

As the transformation only adds non-determinism, the transformed system $S^\sharp$ simulates S (cf. [29]). Together with Theorem 6, this guarantees preservation of LTL-properties as long as variables influenced by $\bar{P}$ are not mentioned. Since we abstracted external data into a single value, not being able to specify properties depending on externally influenced data is not much of an additional loss of precision.

Theorem 10. *Let S_a and S_s be the variant of a system communicating to the environment asynchronously resp. synchronously, and S be given as the parallel composition $S_a \parallel \bar{S}$, where $\bar{S}$ is the environment of the system. Furthermore, let $S^\sharp = S_s^\sharp \parallel \bar{S}$ be defined as before, and φ a next-free LTL-formula mentioning only variables from $\{x \mid \forall l \in Loc.\ [\![x]\!]_{\eta_l^\alpha} = \bot\}$. Then $S^\sharp \models \varphi$ implies $S \models \varphi$.*

5   Example: A Wireless ATM Medium-Access Protocol

The goal of our experiments is to estimate the state space reduction due to re-placing asynchronous communication with the environment by the synchronous one. Primarily interested in the effect of removing queues, we use here the most trivial environment: the *chaotic* one.

We applied the methods in a series of experiments to the industrial protocol Mascara [33]. Located between the ATM-layer and the physical medium, Mascara is a medium-access layer or, in the context of the ISDN reference model, a transmission convergence sub-layer for wireless ATM communication in local area networks. A crucial feature of Mascara is the support of *mobility*. A mobile terminal (MT) located inside the area cell of an access point (AP) is capable of communicating with it. When a mobile terminal moves outside the current cell, it has to perform a so-called *handover* to another access point covering the cell the terminal has moved into. The handover must be managed transparently with respect to the ATM layer, maintaining the agreed quality of service for the current connections. So the protocol has to detect the need for a handover, select a candidate AP to switch to, and redirect the traffic with minimal interruption.

This protocol was the main case study in the Vires project; the results of its verification can be found e.g. in [3, 13, 30]. The SDL-specification of the proto-col was automatically translated into the input language of DTSPIN [2, 11], a discrete-time extension of the well-known SPIN model-checker [16]. For the trans-lation, we used SDL2IF [5] and IF2PML-translators [3]. Our prototype implemen-tation, the PML2PML-translator, post-processes the output from the automatic translation of the SDL-specification into DTPROMELA.

Here, we are not interested in Mascara itself and the verification of its prop-erties, but as real-life example for the comparison of the state spaces of parts of the protocol when closed with the environment as an asynchronous chaotic process and the state space of the same entity closed with embedded chaos. For the comparison we chose a model of the *Mascara control* entity (MCL) at the mobile terminal side In our experiments we used DTSPIN version 0.1.1, an ex-tension of SPIN3.3.10, with the partial-order reduction and compression options on. All the experiments were run on a Silicon Graphics Origin 2000 server on a single R10000/250MHz CPU with 8GB of main memory.

The implementation currently covers the may analysis and the corresponding transformation. We do not model the chaotic environment as a separate process communicating with the system via rendezvous channels but transform an open DTPROMELA model into a closed one by embedding the timed chaotic environ-ment into the system as described in [29], which allows us to use the process fairness mechanism provided by SPIN, which works only for systems with asyn-chronous communication. The translator does not require any user interaction, except that the user is requested to give the list of external signals. The exten-sion is implemented in Java and requires JDK-1.2 or later. The package can be downloaded from http://www.cwi.nl/~ustin/EH.html.

Table 8. Model checking MCL with chaos as a process and embedded chaos

bs	states	transitions	mem.	time	states	transitions	mem.	time
2	9.73e+05	3.64e+06	40.842	15:57	300062	1.06e+06	9.071	1:13
3	5.24e+06	2.02e+07	398.933	22:28	396333	1.85e+06	11.939	1:37
4	2.69e+07	1.05e+08	944.440	1:59:40	467555	2.30e+06	14.499	2:13

Table 8 gives the results for the model checking of MCL with chaos as external process on the left and embedded on the right. The first column gives the buffer size for process queues. The other columns give the number of states, transitions, memory and time consumption, respectively. As one can see, the state space as well as the time and the memory consumption are significantly larger for the model with the environment as a process, and they grow with the buffer size much faster than for the model with embedded chaos. The model with the embedded environment has a relatively stable state-space size.

6   Conclusion

In this paper, we integrated earlier works from [29, 18, 31, 17] into a general framework describing how to close an open, asynchronous system by a timed environment while avoiding the combinatorial state-explosion in the external buffers. The generalization presented here goes a step beyond complete arbitrary environmental behavior, using the timed semantics of the language. We facilitate the model checking of the system by using the information obtained with may and must analyses: We substitute the chaotic value $\mathbb{T}$ for expressions influenced by chaotic data from outside and then optimize the system by removing variables and actions that became redundant.

In the context of software-testing, [9] describes an a dataflow algorithm to close program fragments given in the C-language with the most general environment. The algorithm is incorporated into the *VeriSoft* tool. As in our paper, the assume an asynchronous communicating model and abstract away external data, but do not consider *timed* systems and their abstraction. As for model-checking and analyzing SDL-programs, much work has been done, for instance in the context of the Vires-project, leading to the IF-toolset [5]

A fundamental approach to model checking open systems is known as *module* checking [21][20]. Instead of transforming the system into a closed one, the underlying computational model is generalized to distinguish between transitions under control of the module and those driven by the environment. MOCHA [1] is a model checker for reactive modules, which uses alternating-time temporal logic as specification language.

For practical applications, we are currently extending the larger case study [30] using the chaotic closure to this more general setting. We proceed in the following way: after splitting an SDL system into subsystems following the system structure, properties of the subsystems are verified being closed with an embedded chaotic environment. Afterwards, the verified properties are encoded into an SDL process, for which a tick-separated closure is constructed. This closure is used as environment for other parts of the system. As the closure gives a safe abstraction of the desired environment behavior, the verification results can be transferred to the original system.

References

1. R. Alur, T. A. Henzinger, F. Mang, S. Qadeer, S. K. Rajamani, and S. Tasiran. Mocha: Modularity in model checking. In A. J. Hu and M. Y. Vardi, editors, *Proceedings of CAV '98*, volume 1427 of *Lecture Notes in Computer Science*, pages 521–525. Springer-Verlag, 1998.
2. D. Bošnački and D. Dams. Integrating real time into Spin: A prototype implementation. In S. Budkowski, A. Cavalli, and E. Najm, editors, *Proceedings of Formal Description Techniques and Protocol Specification, Testing, and Verification (FORTE/PSTV'98)*. Kluwer Academic Publishers, 1998.
3. D. Bošnački, D. Dams, L. Holenderski, and N. Sidorova. Verifying SDL in Spin. In S. Graf and M. Schwartzbach, editors, *TACAS 2000*, volume 1785 of *Lecture Notes in Computer Science*. Springer-Verlag, 2000.
4. M. Bozga, J. C. Fernandez, and L. Ghirvu. State space reduction based on Live. In A. Cortesi and G. Filé, editors, *Proceedings of SAS '99*, volume 1694 of *Lecture Notes in Computer Science*. Springer-Verlag, 1999.
5. M. Bozga, J.-C. Fernandez, L. Ghirvu, S. Graf, J.-P. Krimm, and L. Mounier. IF: An intermediate representation and validation environment for timed asynchronous systems. In J. Wing, J. Woodcock, and J. Davies, editors, *Proceedings of Symposium on Formal Methods (FM 99)*, volume 1708 of *Lecture Notes in Computer Science*. Springer-Verlag, Sept. 1999.
6. M. Bozga, S. Graf, A. Kerbrat, L. Mounier, I. Ober, and D. Vincent. SDL for real-time: What is missing? In Y. Lahav, S. Graf, and C. Jard, editors, *Electronic Proceedings of SAM'00*, 2000.
7. J. Brock and W. Ackerman. An anomaly in the specifications of nondeterministic packet systems. Technical Report Computation Structures Group Note CSG-33, MIT Lab. for Computer Science, Nov. 1977.
8. E. Clarke, O. Grumberg, and D. Long. Model checking and abstraction. *ACM Transactions on Programming Languages and Systems*, 16(5):1512–1542, 1994. A preliminary version appeared in the Proceedings of POPL 92.
9. C. Colby, P. Godefroid, and L. J. Jagadeesan. Automatically closing of open reactive systems. In *Proceedings of 1998 ACM SIGPLAN Conference on Programming Language Design and Implementation*. ACM Press, 1998.
10. D. Dams, R. Gerth, and O. Grumberg. Abstract interpretation of reactive systems: Abstraction preserving ∀CTL*,∃CTL*, and CTL*. In E.-R. Olderog, editor, *Proceedings of PROCOMET '94*. IFIP, North-Holland, June 1994.
11. Discrete-time Spin. http://www.win.tue.nl/~dragan/DTSpin.html, 2000.
12. P. Godefroid. Using partial orders to improve automatic verification methods. In E. M. Clarke and R. P. Kurshan, editors, *Computer Aided Verification 1990*, volume 531 of *Lecture Notes in Computer Science*, pages 176–449. Springer-Verlag, 1991. an extended Version appeared in ACM/AMS DIMACS Series, volume 3, pages 321–340, 1991.

13. J. Guoping and S. Graf. Verification experiments on the Mascara protocol. In M. B. Dwyer, editor, *Model Checking Software, Proceedings of the 8th International SPIN Workshop (SPIN 2001), Toronto, Canada*, Lecture Notes in Computer Science, pages 123–142. Springer-Verlag, 2001.

14. M. S. Hecht. *Flow Analysis of Programs*. North-Holland, 1977.

15. G. Holzmann and J. Patti. Validating SDL specifications: an experiment. In E. Brinksma, editor, *International Workshop on Protocol Specification, Testing and Verification IX (Twente, The Netherlands)*, pages 317–326. North-Holland, 1989. IFIP TC-6 International Workshop.

16. G. J. Holzmann. *The Spin Model Checker*. Addison-Wesley, 2003.

17. N. Ioustinova, N. Sidorova, and M. Steffen. Abstraction and flow analysis for model checking open asynchronous systems. In *Proceedings of the 9th Asia-Pacific Software Engineering Conference (APSEC 2002, 4.–6. December 2002, Gold Coast, Queensland, Australia*, pages 227–235. IEEE Computer Society, Dec. 2002.

18. N. Ioustinova, N. Sidorova, and M. Steffen. Closing open SDL-systems for model checking with DT Spin. In L.-H. Eriksson and P. A. Lindsay, editors, *Proceedings of Formal Methods Europe (FME'02)*, volume 2391 of *Lecture Notes in Computer Science*, pages 531–548. Springer-Verlag, 2002.

19. G. Kildall. A unified approach to global program optimization. In *Proceedings of POPL '73*, pages 194–206. ACM, January 1973.

20. O. Kupferman and M. Y. Vardi. Module checking revisited. In O. Grumberg, editor, *CAV '97, Proceedings of the 9th International Conference on Computer-Aided Verification, Haifa. Israel*, volume 1254 of *Lecture Notes in Computer Science*. Springer, June 1997.

21. O. Kupferman, M. Y. Vardi, and P. Wolper. Module checking. In R. Alur, editor, *Proceedings of CAV '96*, volume 1102 of *Lecture Notes in Computer Science*, pages 75–86, 1996.

22. O. Lichtenstein and A. Pnueli. Checking that finite state concurrent programs satisfy their linear specification. In *Twelfth Annual Symposium on Principles of Programming Languages (POPL) (New Orleans, LA)*, pages 97–107. ACM, January 1985.

23. D. Long. *Model Checking, Abstraction and Compositional Verification*. PhD thesis, Carnegie Mellon University, 1993.

24. F. Nielson, H.-R. Nielson, and C. Hankin. *Principles of Program Analysis*. Springer-Verlag, 1999.

25. A. Olsen, O. Færgemand, B. Møller-Pedersen, R. Reed, and J. R. W. Smith. *System Engineering Using SDL-92*. Elsevier Science, 1997.

26. A. Pnueli. The temporal logic of programs. In *Proceeding of the 18th Annual Symposium on Foundations of Computer Science*, pages 45–57, 1977.

27. Specification and Description Language SDL. CCITT, 1993.

28. Specification and Description Language SDL, blue book. CCITT Recommendation Z.100, 1992.

29. N. Sidorova and M. Steffen. Embedding chaos. In P. Cousot, editor, *Proceedings of SAS'01*, volume 2126 of *Lecture Notes in Computer Science*, pages 319–334. Springer-Verlag, 2001.

30. N. Sidorova and M. Steffen. Verifying large SDL-specifications using model checking. In R. Reed and J. Reed, editors, *Proceedings of the 10th International SDL Forum SDL 2001: Meeting UML*, volume 2078 of *Lecture Notes in Computer Science*, pages 403–416. Springer-Verlag, Feb. 2001.

31. N. Sidorova and M. Steffen. Synchronous closing of timed SDL systems for model checking. In A. Cortesi, editor, *Proceedings of the Third International Workshop on Verification, Model Checking, and Abstract Interpretation (VMCAI) 2002*, volume 2294 of *Lecture Notes in Computer Science*, pages 79–93. Springer-Verlag, 2002.

32. A. Valmari. A stubborn attack on state explosion. *Formal Methods in System Design*, 1992. Earlier version in the proceeding of CAV '90 Lecture Notes in Computer Science 531, Springer-Verlag 1991, pp. 156–165 and in Computer-Aided Verification '90, DIMACS Series in Discrete Mathematics and Theoretical Computer Science Vol. 3, AMS & ACM 1991, pp. 25–41.

33. A wireless ATM network demonstrator (WAND), ACTS project AC085. http://www.tik.ee.ethz.ch/~wand/, 1998.

Priority Systems

Gregor Gössler[1] and Joseph Sifakis[2]

[1] INRIA Rhône-Alpes, `goessler@inrialpes.fr`
[2] VERIMAG, `sifakis@imag.fr`

Abstract. We present a framework for the incremental construction of deadlock-free systems meeting given safety properties. The framework borrows concepts and basic results from the controller synthesis paradigm by considering a step in the construction process as a controller synthesis problem.

We show that priorities are expressive enough to represent restrictions induced by deadlock-free controllers preserving safety properties. We define a correspondence between such restrictions and priorities and provide compositionality results about the preservation of this correspondence by operations on safety properties and priorities. Finally, we provide an example illustrating an application of the results.

1 Introduction

A common idea for avoiding a posteriori verification and testing, is to use system design techniques that guarantee correctness by construction. Such techniques should allow to construct progressively from a given system S and a set of requirements $R_1, \ldots, R_n$, a sequence of systems $S_1, \ldots, S_n$, such that system S_i meets all the requirements R_j for $j \leq i$. That is, to allow incremental construction, requirements should be composable [2,6] along the design process. In spite of their increasing importance, there is currently a tremendous lack of theory and methods, especially for requirements including progress properties which are essential for reactive systems. Most of the existing methodologies deal with construction of systems such that a set of state properties always hold. They are founded on the combined use of invariants and refinement relations. Composability is ensured by the fact that refinement relations preserve trace inclusion. We present a framework allowing to consider jointly state property invariance and deadlock-freedom.

Practice for building correct systems is often based on the idea of adding *enforcement* mechanisms to a given system S in order to obtain a system S' meeting a given requirement. These mechanisms can be implemented by instrumenting the code of S or by composing S with systems such as controllers or monitors that modify adequately the overall behavior.

An application of this principle is the enforcement of security policies which are safety properties described by automata [14]. A main requirement for the enforced system is that it safely terminates when it detects a deviation from

F.S. de Boer et al. (Eds.): FMCO 2003, LNCS 3188, pp. 314–329, 2004.

some nominal secure behavior. A more difficult problem is also to ensure system availability and preserve continuity of service [3,10].

Another application of this principle is aspect oriented programming [8] used to build programs meeting (usually simple) requirements. Aspects can be considered as requirements from which code is generated and woven into a program intended to meet the requirements. In aspect oriented programming, aspect composition is identified as a central problem as it may cause unintentional interference and inconsistency [15].

Practice for building correct systems by using enforcement mechanisms raises some hard theoretical problems. For a sufficiently fine granularity of observation, it is relatively easy to enforce safety requirements (as non violations of given state properties) by stopping system progress. It is much harder to devise mechanisms that also guarantee system availability and avoid service interruption. Furthermore, composability of requirements e.g. security policies, aspects, is identified as a main obstacle to rigorous incremental system construction.

We propose a design framework for both safety and deadlock-freedom requirements. The framework consists of a model, *priority systems* and results concerning its basic properties including composability. A priority system is a transition system with a (dynamic) priority relation on its actions. A priority relation $\prec$ is a set of predicates of the form $a_i \prec C_{ij}.a_j$ meaning that action a_i has lower priority than action a_j at all states satisfying C_{ij}. At a given state of the transition system, only enabled actions with maximal priority can be executed. That is, in a priority system, a priority relation restricts the behavior of its transition system exactly as a scheduler restricts the behavior of a set of tasks. The remarkably nice property of priority systems is that they are deadlock-free if they are built from deadlock-free transition systems and from priority relations satisfying some easy-to-check consistency condition.

The proposed framework considers design as a *controller synthesis* [12] problem: from a given system S and requirement R, find a system S' meeting R. S' is the composition of S with a controller which monitors the state of S and restricts its behavior by adequately switching off a subset of *controllable* actions of S. The controller is usually specified as a solution of a fixpoint equation.

The simple case where R means that S' is deadlock-free and does not violate a state predicate U has been studied in various contexts e.g., in [11,1]. The corresponding controller is specified as a *deadlock-free control invariant* which is a state predicate U', $U' \Rightarrow U$, such that

- it is preserved by the non controllable actions of S, that is if U' holds at some state then it remains true forever if only non controllable actions are executed;
- U' is *false* for all deadlock states of S.

Given U', the controlled (designed) system S' is obtained from S by conjuncting the guard of any controllable action a by the weakest precondition of U' under a.

In Section 2, we formalize the relationship between S and S', by introducing *restriction* operators. These are specified as tuples of state predicates in bijection with the set of actions of S. The application of a restriction operator to S is S', obtained from S by conjuncting the guards of its actions by the corresponding state predicates of the restriction. We study properties of deadlock-free control restrictions, that is restrictions corresponding to deadlock-free control invariants.

In Section 3, we show that under some consistency conditions, priorities can be used to represent deadlock-free restrictions. Thus, controlled systems S' can be represented as deadlock-free priority systems. Consistency checking boils down to computing a kind of transitive closure of the priority relation. We show that for static priorities consistency is equivalent to deadlock-freedom.

Composability in our framework means commutativity of application of priorities on a given system. As a rule, the result of the successive restriction of a system S by two priorities $\prec_1$ and $\prec_2$ depends on the order of application and we provide sufficient conditions for commutativity. This difficulty can be overcome by using a symmetric composition operator $\oplus$ for priorities which preserves safety and deadlock-freedom. The restriction of a system S by $\prec_1 \oplus \prec_2$ is a refinement of any other restriction of S obtained by application of $\prec_1$ and $\prec_2$.

An interesting question is whether priorities are expressive enough to represent restrictions induced by deadlock-free control invariants. We bring a positive answer by using a construction associating with a state predicate U a priority relation $\prec_U$. We show that if U is a deadlock-free control invariant then the controlled system S' is equivalent to the system S restricted by $\prec_U$. Furthermore, we provide results relating the controlled systems corresponding to U_1, U_2, $U_1 \wedge U_2$ to restrictions by $\prec_{U_1}$, $\prec_{U_2}$, $\prec_{U_1} \oplus \prec_{U_2}$.

Section 4 illustrates application of the results on an example.

Section 5 presents concluding remarks about the presented framework.

2   Deadlock-Free Control Invariants

2.1   Definitions and Basic Properties

Definition 1 (Transition System). *A transition system B is a tuple $(X, A, \{G^a\}_{a \in A}, \{F^a\}_{a \in A})$, where*

- *X is a finite set of variables;*
- *A is a finite set of actions, union of two disjoint sets A^u and A^c, the sets of the uncontrollable and controllable interactions respectively;*
- *G^a is a guard, predicate on X;*
- *$F^a : \mathbf{X} \to \mathbf{X}$ is a transition function, where $\mathbf{X}$ is the set of valuations of X.*

Definition 2 (Semantics of a Transition System). *A transition system $(X, A, \{G^a\}_{a \in A}, \{F^a\}_{a \in A})$ defines a transition relation $\to: \mathbf{X} \times A \times \mathbf{X}$ such that:*
$$\forall \mathbf{x}, \mathbf{x}' \in \mathbf{X} \ \forall a \in A \ . \ \mathbf{x} \xrightarrow{a} \mathbf{x}' \iff G^a(\mathbf{x}) \wedge \mathbf{x}' = F^a(\mathbf{x}).$$

We introduce the following notations:

- Given two transition systems B_1, B_2 with disjoint action vocabularies such that $B_i = (X_i, A_i, \{G^a\}_{a \in A_i}, \{F^a\}_{a \in A_i})$, for $i = 1, 2$, their *union* is the transition system $B_1 \cup B_2 = (X_1 \cup X_2, A_1 \cup A_2, \{G^a\}_{a \in A_1 \cup A_2}, \{F^a\}_{a \in A_1 \cup A_2})$.
- Given a transition system B, we represent by B^u (respectively B^c) the transition system consisting of the uncontrollable (respectively controllable) actions of B. Clearly $B = B^u \cup B^c$.
- Given a transition system B, we represent by $G(B)$ the disjunction of its guards, that is $G(B) = \bigvee_{a \in A} G^a$ where A is the set of the actions of B.

Definition 3 (Predecessors). *Given* $B = (X, A, \{G^a\}_{a \in A}, \{F^a\}_{a \in A})$ *and a predicate* U *on* X, *the* predecessors *of* U *by action* a *is the predicate* $pre_a(U) = G^a \wedge U([F^a(X)/X])$ *where* $U[F^a(X)/X]$ *is obtained from* U *by uniform substitution of* X *by* $F^a(X)$.

Clearly, $pre_a(U)$ characterizes all the states from which execution of a leads to some state satisfying U.

Definition 4 (Invariants and Control Invariants). *Given a transition system* B *and a predicate* U,

- U *is an* invariant *of* B *if* $U \implies \bigwedge_{a \in A} \neg pre_a(\neg U) = \bigwedge_{a \in A}(\neg G^a \vee U([F^a(X)/X]))$. *An invariant* U, $U \neq$ *false, is called* deadlock-free *if* $U \Rightarrow G(B)$.
- U *is a* control invariant *of* B *if* $U \Rightarrow \bigwedge_{a \in A^u} \neg pre_a(\neg U)$. *A* control invariant U, $U \neq$ *false, is called* deadlock-free *if* $U \Rightarrow \bigvee_{a \in A} pre_a(U)$.

We write $inv[B](U)$ to express the fact that U is an invariant of B. Notice that invariants are control invariants of systems that have only uncontrollable actions.

Proposition 1. *If* U *is a control invariant of* $B = (X, A, \{G^a\}_{a \in A}, \{F^a\}_{a \in A})$ *then* U *is an invariant of* $B' = (X, A, \{(G^a)'\}_{a \in A}, \{F^a\}_{a \in A})$ *where* $(G^a)' = G^a \wedge U[F^a(X)/X]$ *for* $a \in A^c$ *and* $(G^a)' = G^a$ *otherwise. Furthermore, if* U *is a deadlock-free control invariant of* B *then it is a deadlock-free invariant of* B'.

This result allows to build from a given system B and a safety requirement of the form "always U_0" a deadlock-free system B' meeting this requirement, provided there exists a deadlock-free control invariant U of B such that $U \Rightarrow U_0$. The following simple example illustrates this fact.

Example 1. In a Readers/Writers system, we use two counters, non negative integers, r and w to represent respectively, the number of readers and writers using a common resource. The counters are modified by actions of a transition system B specified as a set of guarded commands:

$$a_1 : true \rightarrow r := r + 1 \qquad a_2 : r > 0 \rightarrow r := r - 1$$
$$b_1 : true \rightarrow w := w + 1 \qquad b_2 : w > 0 \rightarrow w := w - 1$$

where a_1 and b_1 are respectively, the actions of granting the resource to a reader and a writer and a_2 and b_2 are respectively, the actions of releasing the resource by a reader and a writer.

We assume that the actions a_1 and b_1 are controllable and we want to enforce the requirement "always U" for $U = (w \leq 1) \wedge (w = 0 \vee r = 0)$. This prevents concurrent access among writers, as well as between readers and writers. It is easy to check that U is a deadlock-free control invariant. In fact, it is easy to check that U is preserved by the uncontrollable actions a_2 and b_2:

$$(r > 0) \wedge U \Rightarrow U[r - 1/r] \text{ and } (w > 0) \wedge U \Rightarrow U[w - 1/w].$$

Furthermore, it is easy to check that $U \Rightarrow pre_{a_1} \vee pre_{a_2} \vee pre_{b_1} \vee pre_{b_2}$.

As $pre_{a_1}(U) \equiv w = 0$ and $pre_{b_1}(U) \equiv (w = 0) \wedge (r = 0)$, we have $inv[B'](U)$ where B' is the controlled transition system:

$$a_1 : w = 0 \rightarrow r := r + 1 \qquad\qquad a_2 : r > 0 \rightarrow r := r - 1$$
$$b_1 : (r = 0) \wedge (w = 0) \rightarrow w := w + 1 \qquad b_2 : w > 0 \rightarrow w := w - 1$$

The notion of *restriction* defined below allows a formalization of the relationship between the initial and the controlled system.

Definition 5 (Restriction). *Given a transition system* $B = (X, A, \{G^a\}_{a \in A}, \{F^a\}_{a \in A})$, *a* restriction *is a tuple of predicates* $V = (U^a)_{a \in A}$. B/V *denotes the transition system* B *restricted by* V, $B/V = (X, A, \{G^a \wedge U^a\}_{a \in A}, \{F^a\}_{a \in A})$.

$V = (U^a)_{a \in A}$ *is a* control restriction *for* B *if* $\bigwedge_{a \in A^u}(\neg G^a \vee U^a) = true$.
$V = (U^a)_{a \in A}$ *is a* deadlock-free restriction *for* B *if* $\bigvee_{a \in A} G^a \wedge U^a = \bigvee_{a \in A} G^a$.

We simply say that V *is a* control restriction *or a* deadlock-free restriction *if the corresponding equation holds for any transition system* B *with vocabulary of actions* $A = A^c \cup A^u$ *(independently of the interpretation of the guards).*

Definition 6 $(U^A, V(U))$. *Given a predicate* U, *we denote by* U^A *the restriction* $U^A = (U)_{a \in A}$, *and by* $V(U)$ *the restriction* $V(U) = (U[F^a(X)/X])_{a \in A}$.
If V_1, V_2 *are two restrictions,* $V_j = (U_j^{a_i})_{a_i \in A}$ *for* $j = 1, 2$, *we write* $V_1 \wedge V_2$ *for the restriction* $(U_1^{a_i} \wedge U_2^{a_i})_{a_i \in A}$.

Proposition 2 (Control Invariants and Restrictions). *Given a transition system* B *and a predicate* U,

a) *If* U *is a control invariant of* B *then* $V(U)$ *is a control restriction of* B;
b) *If* U *is a deadlock-free invariant of* B *then* $V(U)$ *is a deadlock-free restriction of* B;
c) *If* U *is a deadlock-free control invariant of* B *then* $V(U)$ *is a deadlock-free control restriction of* B.

We need the following definitions for the comparison of transition systems.

Definition 7 (Refinement and Equivalence). *Given* $B_i = (X_i, A, \{G_i^a\}_{a \in A}, \{F_i^a\}_{a \in A})$ *for* $i = 1, 2$, *two transition systems and a predicate* U *we say that*

- B_1 *refines* B_2 *under* U, *denoted by* $B_1 \sqsubseteq_U B_2$, *if* $\forall a \in A$. $F_1^a = F_2^a$ *and* $U \wedge G_1^a \Rightarrow U \wedge G_2^a$;
- B_1 *is equivalent to* B_2 *under* U, *denoted by* $B_1 \simeq_U B_2$, *if* $B_1 \sqsubseteq_U B_2$ *and* $B_2 \sqsubseteq_U B_1$.

We write $B_1 \sqsubseteq B_2$ *and* $B_1 \simeq B_2$ *for* $B_1 \sqsubseteq_{true} B_2$ *and* $B_1 \simeq_{true} B_2$, *respectively.*

Property 1. Given transition systems B, B_1, B_2 and restrictions V, V_1, V_2,

1a $B/V \sqsubseteq B$;
1b $(B_1 \cup B_2)/V \simeq B_1/V \cup B_2/V$;
1c $(B/V_1)/V_2 \simeq B/(V_1 \wedge V_2)$;
1d $B_1 \sqsubseteq B_2 \Rightarrow (inv[B_2](U) \Rightarrow inv[B_1](U))$ for any predicate U.

Notice that if the conjunction of control invariants is a control invariant, the conjunction of deadlock-free control invariants is not in general, a deadlock-free control invariant. We investigate conditions for composability.

3   Priority Systems

We define *priority systems* which are transition systems restricted with priorities. Priorities provide a general mechanism for generating deadlock-free restrictions.

3.1   Deadlock-Free Restrictions and Priorities

Priorities

Definition 8 (Priority). *A priority on a transition system B with set of actions A is a set of predicates $\prec = \{C_{ij}\}_{a_i,a_j \in A}$. The restriction defined by $\prec$, $V(B, \prec) = (U^a)_{a \in A}$ is $U^{a_i} = \bigwedge_{a_j \in A} \neg(C_{ij} \wedge G^{a_j})$.*

The predicates C_{ij} specify priority between actions a_i and a_j. If C_{ij} is true at some state, then in the system restricted by $V(B, \prec)$ the action a_i cannot be executed if a_j is enabled. We write $a_i \prec C_{ij}.a_j$ to express the fact that a_i is dominated by a_j when C_{ij} holds. A priority is *irreflexive* if $C_{ij} \Rightarrow \neg C_{ji}$ for all $a_i, a_j \in A$.

Definition 9 (Transitive Closure). *Given a priority $\prec$ we denote by $\prec^+$ the least priority such that $\prec \subseteq \prec^+$, obtained by the rule:*

$a_i \prec^+ C_{ij}.a_j$ *and* $a_j \prec^+ C_{jk}.a_k$ *implies* $a_i \prec^+ (C_{jk} \wedge C_{jk}).a_k$.

Proposition 3 (Activity Preservation for Priorities). *A priority $\prec$ defines a deadlock-free restriction if $\prec^+$ is irreflexive.*

Proof. Suppose that $\prec^+$ is irreflexive. Consider some transition system $B = (X, A, \{G^a\}_{a \in A}, \{F^a\}_{a \in A})$, and let $G = \bigvee_{a \in A} G^a$, and $V(B, \prec) = (U^a)_{a \in A}$. Let $\mathbf{x}$ be a state of B such that $G(\mathbf{x})$, let $A' = \{a \in A \mid G^a(\mathbf{x})\}$, and define a relation

$\prec'$ on A' such that $\forall a_i, a_j \in A' \,.\, a_i \prec' a_j \iff C_{ij}(\mathbf{x})$. As $\prec^+$ is irreflexive, $\prec'$ is a partial order on A', and thus acyclic. If $A' \neq \emptyset$ then $\max A'$ exists and is non-empty. Thus, $\left(\bigvee_{a \in A} G^a \wedge U^a\right)(\mathbf{x}) = \left(\bigvee_{a \in A'} G^a\right)(\mathbf{x}) = \left(\bigvee_{a \in A} G^a\right)(\mathbf{x})$. ∎

The above proposition motivates the definition of priority systems which are transition systems restricted by priorities.

Definition 10 (Priority System). *A priority system is a pair $(B, \prec)$ where B is a transition system and $\prec = \{C_{ij}\}_{a_i, a_j \in A}$ is a priority on B such that $C_{ij} = false$ for all $(a_i, a_j) \in A^u \times A$.*
The priority system $(B, \prec)$ represents the transition system $B / V(B, \prec)$.

The following propositions give properties of priority systems.

Proposition 4. *If $(B, \prec)$ is a priority system, then $V(B, \prec)$ is a control restriction for B.*

Proof. If $V(B, \prec) = (U^{a_i})_{a_i \in A}$ then for all uncontrollable actions a_i, $U^{a_i} = true$ because $C_{ij} = false$. ∎

Corollary 1. *If U is a control invariant of B then U is a control invariant of $(B, \prec)$.*

Proposition 5. *If U is a deadlock-free control invariant of a transition system B then for any priority $\prec$ such that $\prec^+$ is irreflexive, U is a deadlock-free invariant of $(B/V(U), \prec)$.*

Proof. If U is a deadlock-free control invariant of B then $U \Rightarrow G(B/V(U))$ and $inv[B^u](U)$. As $\prec$ defines deadlock-free restrictions, $(B/V(U), \prec)^u = B^u$ and $G(B/V(U)) = G(B/V(U), \prec)$. ∎

Static Priorities

Definition 11 (Static Priority). *A static priority is a priority $\prec = \{C_{ij}\}_{a_i, a_j \in A}$ such that the predicates C_{ij} are positive boolean expressions on guards. We call static restrictions the corresponding restrictions $V(B, \prec) = (U^a)_{a \in A}$, that is restrictions which are tuples of negative boolean expressions on guards.*

It is easy to check that any static restriction defines a static priority. Notice that in a priority system with static priorities, the choice of the action to be executed at some state depends only on the set of the actions enabled at this state. For example, a restriction with $U^{a_1} = \neg G^{a_2} \wedge (\neg G^{a_3} \vee \neg G^{a_4})$ means that in the restricted system the action a_1 can be executed only if a_2 is disabled and a_3 or a_4 is disabled. The corresponding the priority relation is: $a_1 \prec true.a_2, a_1 \prec G^{a_3}.a_4, a_1 \prec G^{a_4}.a_3$

Notation: For a static priorities the notation can be drastically simplified.

If $(U^{a_i})_{a_i \in A}$ is a static restriction then it is of the form, $U^{a_i} = \bigwedge_{k \in K_i} \neg M_i^k$ where M_i^k is a monomial on guards $M_i^k = \bigwedge_{k_w \in W} G^{a_{k_w}}$. Each monomial M_i^k, corresponds to the set of priorities $\{a_i \prec \bigwedge_{k_w \in W \smallsetminus \{j\}} G^{a_{k_w}}.a_j\}_{j \in W}$. This set can be canonically represented by simply writing $a_i \prec \bigwedge_{k_w \in W} a_{k_w}$.

For example if $M_i^k = G^{a_1} \wedge G^{a_2} \wedge G^{a_3}$ instead of writing $a_i \prec (G^{a_1} \wedge G^{a_2}).a_3$, $a_i \prec (G^{a_1} \wedge G^{a_3}).a_2$, $a_i \prec (G^{a_2} \wedge G^{a_3}).a_1$, we write $a_i \prec a_1 a_2 a_3$. We propose the following definition for static priorities.

Definition 12 (Static Priority – Simplified Definition). *A monomial m on a vocabulary of actions A is any term $m = a_{j_1} \ldots a_{j_n}$ obtained by using an associative, commutative and idempotent product operation. Let $\mathbf{1}$ denote its neutral element, and $\mathrm{M}(A)$ the set of the monomials on A.*

A static priority $\prec$ on A is a relation $\prec \subseteq A \times \mathrm{M}(A)$.

Example 2. The static priority $\prec$ corresponding to the static restriction $U^{a_1} = true$, $U^{a_2} = true$, $U^{a_3} = \neg G^{a_1} \vee \neg G^{a_2}$, $U^{a_4} = \neg G^{a_1} \wedge \neg G^{a_2}$, $U^{a_5} = \neg G^{a_1} \wedge \neg G^{a_3} \vee \neg G^{a_2} \wedge \neg G^{a_4} \equiv \neg(G^{a_1} \wedge G^{a_2}) \wedge \neg(G^{a_1} \wedge G^{a_4}) \wedge \neg(G^{a_3} \wedge G^{a_2}) \wedge \neg(G^{a_3} \wedge G^{a_4})$ is: $a_3 \prec a_1 a_2$, $a_4 \prec a_1$, $a_4 \prec a_2$, $a_5 \prec a_1 a_2$, $a_5 \prec a_1 a_4$, $a_5 \prec a_3 a_2$, $a_5 \prec a_3 a_4$.

Definition 13 (Closure). *Let $\prec$ be a static priority. The closure of $\prec$ is the least static priority $\prec^{\mp}$ containing $\prec$ such that*

- *if $a_1 \prec^{\mp} a_2 m_2$ and $a_2 \prec^{\mp} m_3$ then $a_1 \prec^{\mp} m_2 m_3$;*
- *if $a \prec^{\mp} am$, then $a \prec^{\mp} m$ for $m \neq \mathbf{1}$.*

Example 3. For $\prec = \{a \prec bc, b \prec ad\}$, $\prec^{\mp} = \{a \prec^{\mp} bc, b \prec^{\mp} ad, a \prec^{\mp} acd, a \prec^{\mp} cd, b \prec^{\mp} bcd, b \prec^{\mp} cd\}$.

Lemma 1. *If for any $a_i \in A$, $a_i \prec \mathbf{m}_i$ with $\mathbf{m}_i$ a monomial on A, then $a_i \prec^{\mp} a_i$ for some $a_i \in A$.*

Proof. Omitted.

Proposition 6 (Activity Preservation for Static Priorities). *A static priority $\prec$ defines a deadlock-free restriction if and only if $\prec^{\mp}$ is irreflexive.*

Proof. "if": suppose that $\prec^{\mp}$ is irreflexive. By definition, only top elements in $\prec$ can be non-trivial monomials. Thus, $\prec$ is acyclic, and all ascending chains in $\prec$ are finite. Consider some deadlock-free transition system $B = (X, A, \{G^a\}_{a \in A}, \{F^a\}_{a \in A})$, and let $G = \bigvee_{a \in A} G^a$. Let $\mathbf{x}$ be a state of B such that $G(\mathbf{x})$, and let $A' = \{a \in A \mid G^a(\mathbf{x})\}$. As $\prec$ is acyclic, $\max A'$ exists and is non-empty. It remains to show that some element of $\max A'$ is not dominated by any monomial in $2^{A'}$. Suppose that for any $a_i \in A'$ there is some $\mathbf{m}_i \in 2^{A'}$, $a_i \prec \mathbf{m}_i$. In that case, $\prec^{\mp}$ has a circuit by lemma 1, which contradicts the hypothesis. Thus, at least one action in $\max A'$ is maximal in $\prec$.

"only if": suppose that $a \prec^{\mp} a$ for some $a \in A$. By construction of $\prec^{\mp}$, this means that $(A \cup \mathrm{M}(A), \prec)$ contains a tree $(A' \cup \mathrm{M}(A'), \prec')$ with root a such that all leaves are monomials consisting only of the action a. Take $B = (\emptyset, A, \{G^a\}_{a \in A}, \{\emptyset\}_{a \in A})$ with $G^{(a')} = true$ if $a' \in A'$, and $G^{(a')} = false$ otherwise. By definition of $/$, all guards in $B/V(B, \prec)$ are *false*, whereas B is clearly deadlock-free. ∎

Example 4. Consider the static priority $\prec$ on the actions a_1, a_2, a_3, a_4 such that, $a_2 \prec a_3a_4$, $a_3 \prec a_2a_4$, $a_4 \prec a_2a_3$. It is easy to see that $\prec^{\mp}$ is not irreflexive, thus $\prec$ does not define a deadlock-free restriction. By elimination of a_4, as in the proof of Lemma 1, we get: $a_2 \prec^{\mp} a_2a_3$, $a_3 \prec^{\mp} a_2a_3$ which gives by application of the second closure rule, $a_2 \prec^{\mp} a_2$, $a_3 \prec^{\mp} a_3$. Thus $\prec^{\mp}$ is not irreflexive.

Consider the slightly different static priority $\prec_1$ on the actions a_1, a_2, a_3, a_4 such that, $a_2 \prec_1 a_1a_3a_4$, $a_3 \prec_1 a_2a_4$, $a_4 \prec_1 a_2a_3$. It can be checked that $\prec_1^{\mp}$ is irreflexive and thus deadlock-free and contains the chain $a_4 \prec_1^{\mp} a_3 \prec_1^{\mp} a_2 \prec_1^{\mp} a_1$.

Clearly, $\prec_1^{+}$ is not irreflexive as $a_3 \prec_1 G^{a_2}.a_4$, $a_4 \prec_1 G^{a_2}.a_3$. This example shows that for static priorities the use of the specific closure gives finer results than by using Proposition 3.

3.2 Composition of Priorities

Notice that given B and $\prec$, the predicate $V(B, \prec)$ depends on B. The property $((B, \prec^1), \prec^2) = ((B, \prec^2), \prec^1)$ does not hold in general. For instance, consider a system B and priorities $\prec$ and $\prec'$ such that $a_1 \prec a_2$ and $a_2 \prec' a_3$ where a_1, a_2, a_3 are actions of B. If from some state of B the three actions are enabled then in $((B, \prec), \prec')$ only a_3 is enabled while in $((B, \prec'), \prec)$ both a_1 and a_3 are enabled.

We define two composition operations on priorities and study composability results.

Definition 14 (Composition of Priorities). *Given two priorities $\prec^1$ and $\prec^2$ their composition is the operation $\oplus$ such that $\prec^1 \oplus \prec^2 = (\prec^1 \cup \prec^2)^{+}$. Furthermore, if $\prec^1$ and $\prec^2$ are static priorities we define another composition operation, $\bar{\oplus}$ such that $\prec^1 \bar{\oplus} \prec^2 = (\prec^1 \cup \prec^2)^{\mp}$.*

Proposition 7. *The operations $\oplus$ and $\bar{\oplus}$ are associative and commutative.*

Lemma 2. *Let $\prec = \prec^{\mp}$ be an irreflexive closed static priority. Then, any non maximal action a is dominated by some monomial m on maximal actions.*

Proof. Omitted.

Proposition 8 (Composability for Static Priorities). *Given a transition system B and two static priorities $\prec^1$ and $\prec^2$, if $\prec^1 \cup \prec^2 = \prec^1 \bar{\oplus} \prec^2$ then $((B, \prec^1), \prec^2) \simeq (B, \prec^1 \bar{\oplus} \prec^2)$.*

Proof. Let G^a, $(G^a)'$, $(G^a)''$, and $(G^a)'''$ be the guards of action a in B, $B/\prec^1$, $(B/\prec^1)/\prec^2$, and $B/(\prec^1 \bar{\oplus} \prec^2)$, respectively. For some state $\mathbf{x}$, let $A_0 = \{a \in A \mid G^a(\mathbf{x})\}$, $A_1 = \{a \in A \mid (G^a)'(\mathbf{x})\}$, $A_2 = \{a \in A \mid (G^a)''(\mathbf{x})\}$, and $A_3 = \{a \in A \mid (G^a)'''(\mathbf{x})\}$, respectively. Notice that $A_2 \cup A_3 \subseteq A_1 \subseteq A_0$. We show that $A_2 = A_3$.

If $a \in A_2$ then there is no monomial on A_0 dominating a in $\prec^1$, and there is no monomial on A_1 dominating a in $\prec^2$. Thus, either there is no monomial on A_0 dominating a in $\prec^1 \cup \prec^2 = \prec^1 \bar{\oplus} \prec^2$, and $a \in A_3$, or there is a monomial m on A_0 such that $a \prec^2 m$. In the latter case, $m = m'm''$ with m' a non-empty monomial on $A_0 \setminus A_1$, and m'' a monomial on A_1 (i.e., product of actions that are maximal in $\prec^1$). Thus, for any factor a_i of m' there is a monomial m_i on A_0 (and by lemma 2, on A_1) such that $a_i(\prec^1)^+ m_i$. Since $(\prec^1)^+ \subseteq \prec^1 \cup \prec^2 = \prec^1 \bar{\oplus} \prec^2$, we have $a(\prec^1 \cup \prec^2)m_1 \cdots m_k m''$, and $a \notin A_2$, which is in contradiction to the assumption. Thus, $a \in A_3$.

Conversely, if $a \in A_3$, then a is not dominated by any monomial on A_0 in $\prec^1 \cup \prec^2$. Thus, a is maximal among A_0 and A_1 in both priorities, and $a \in A_2$. ∎

Proposition 9 (Composability for Priorities). *Given a transition system B and two priorities $\prec^1$, $\prec^2$, if $\prec^1 \cup \prec^2 = \prec^1 \bar{\oplus} \prec^2$ then $((B, \prec^1), \prec^2) \simeq (B, \prec^1 \bar{\oplus} \prec^2)$.*

Proof. Consider some state $\mathbf{x}$, and let $\prec_{\mathbf{x}}^i$ be the static priority defined by $\prec^i$ at state $\mathbf{x}$: $a_i \prec_{\mathbf{x}}^i a_j \iff C_{ij}^i(\mathbf{x})$, $i = 1, 2$. Notice that $\prec_{\mathbf{x}}^1 \bar{\oplus} \prec_{\mathbf{x}}^2$ is irreflexive whenever $\prec^1 \bar{\oplus} \prec^2$ is irreflexive. The proof follows that of proposition 8 for the static priorities $\prec_{\mathbf{x}}^1$ and $\prec_{\mathbf{x}}^2$ at state $\mathbf{x}$.   ∎

Propositions 8 and 9 provide composability conditions, that is conditions guaranteeing commutativity of two restrictions defined by priorities. The following proposition is easy to prove by using monotonicity properties $\sqsubseteq$ and the definitions of composition operations. It shows that the successive application of priority restrictions can be safely replaced by their composition.

Proposition 10. *For any transition system B and priorities $\prec^1$, $\prec^2$ we have*

- *if $\prec^1 \Rightarrow \prec^2$ then $(B, \prec^2) \sqsubseteq (B, \prec^1)$;*
- *$(B, \prec^1 \bar{\oplus} \prec^2) \sqsubseteq (B, \prec^1 \cup \prec^2) \sqsubseteq ((B, \prec^1), \prec^2)$. Furthermore, for static priorities, $(B, \prec^1 \bar{\oplus} \prec^2) \simeq (B, \prec^1 \oplus \prec^2)$.*

3.3   Safety and Deadlock-Freedom

We present results relating deadlock-free control invariants to priorities. We show that priorities can be used to define any restriction corresponding to a deadlock-free control invariant.

Given a transition system B and a predicate U, the restriction $V(U)$ guarantees the invariance (safety) for U in $B/V(U)$, that is $inv[B/V(U)](U)$. Furthermore, if U is a control invariant then $V(U)$ is a control restriction, that is a restriction that does not affect the guards of uncontrollable actions. As a rule, $V(U)$ is not deadlock-free. We define for a predicate U, a priority $\prec_U$ and study relationships between its restrictions and $V(U)$.

Definition 15. *Given a state predicate U on a transition system, the associated priority $\prec_U$ is defined by $\prec_U = \{pre_a(\neg U) \wedge pre_{a'}(U)\}_{(a,a') \in A^c \times A}$.*

Property 2. The priority $\prec_U$ is transitively closed and irreflexive and thus it defines a deadlock-free restriction.

Proposition 11. *For any transition system B and predicate U, $B/V(U) \sqsubseteq_U (B, \prec_U)$. Furthermore, if U is a deadlock-free invariant of B, $B/V(U) \simeq_U (B, \prec_U)$.*

Proof. As we consider B with initial set of states satisfying U we assume that all the guards G^a of its actions are such that $G^a \Rightarrow U$. Let's verify that if $(G^{a_i})'$ is the restricted guard of action a_i in $(B, \prec_U)$, then $G^{a_i} \wedge pre_{a_i}(U) \Rightarrow (G^{a_i})'$.

We find $(G^{a_i})' = G^{a_i} \wedge \bigwedge_{a_j \in A} \neg (pre_{a_i}(\neg U) \wedge pre_{a_j}(U) \wedge G^{a_j}) = G^{a_i} \wedge \bigwedge_{a_j \in A} (\neg pre_{a_i}(\neg U) \vee \neg pre_{a_j}(U)) = G^{a_i} \wedge \neg pre_{a_i}(\neg U) \vee G^{a_i} \wedge \bigwedge_{a_j \in A} \neg pre_{a_j}(U)$.

Given that $G^{a_i} \wedge \neg pre_{a_i}(\neg U) = G^{a_i} \wedge pre_{a_i}(U)$, we have $(G^{a_i})' = G^{a_i} \wedge pre_{a_i}(U) \vee G^{a_i} \wedge \bigwedge_{a_j \in A} \neg pre_{a_j}(U)$.

From this follows that $B/V(U) \sqsubseteq_U (B, \prec_U)$.

If U is a deadlock-free invariant then for any guard G^{a_i}, $G^{a_i} \Rightarrow U \Rightarrow \bigvee_{a_j \in A} pre_{a_j}(U)$. Thus, we have $G^a \wedge \bigwedge_{a_j \in A} \neg pre_{a_j}(U) = false$. Consequently, $(G^{a_i})' = G^{a_i} \wedge pre_{a_i}(U)$ which completes the proof. ∎

A direct consequence of this proposition is that for any deadlock-free control invariant U, $B/V(U) \simeq_U (B, \prec_U)$. That is the effect of deadlock-free controllers can be modeled by restrictions induced by priorities.

From this proof it also follows that the guards of $B/V(U)$ and $(B, \prec_U)$ agree at deadlock-free states of $B/V(U)$ in U. They may differ at deadlock states of $B/V(U)$ where B is deadlock-free. In other words $(B, \prec_U)$ is a kind of "best deadlock-free abstraction" of $B/V(U)$ under U.

Example 5. We apply the previous proposition for B and U of Example 1. We show that $(B, \prec_U)$ behaves exactly as $B' = B/V(U)$ from any state satisfying the deadlock-free control invariant U.

We have $pre_{a_1}(\neg U) \wedge pre_{b_2}(U) \equiv w > 0$, $pre_{b_1}(\neg U) \wedge pre_{b_2}(U) \equiv w \geq 1$, $pre_{b_1}(\neg U) \wedge pre_{a_2}(U) \equiv r > 0$ and $pre_{a_1}(\neg U) \wedge pre_{b_1}(U) \equiv pre_{b_1}(\neg U) \wedge pre_{a_1}(U) \equiv false$. This gives the priority $\prec_U = \{a_1 \prec_U (w > 0).b_2, b_1 \prec_U (w \geq 1).b_2), b_1 \prec_U (r > 0).a_2)\}$. It can be checked that $(B, \prec_U)$ is indeed equivalent to $(B/V(U))$. The computation of the restricted guards $(G^{a_1})'$ and $(G^{b_1})'$ gives
$(G^{a_1})' = G^{a_1} \wedge (\neg w > 0 \vee \neg G^{b_2}) \equiv w = 0$ and
$(G^{b_1})' = G^{b_1} \wedge (\neg w \geq 1 \vee \neg G^{b_2}) \wedge (\neg r > 0 \vee \neg G^{a_2}) \equiv (w = 0) \wedge (r = 0)$.

The following propositions study relationships between safety and deadlock-free restrictions.

Proposition 12. *If U_1, U_2 are two state predicates and $\prec_{U_1}$, $\prec_{U_2}$ the corresponding priorities, then $B/V(U_1 \wedge U_2) \sqsubseteq_{U_1 \wedge U_2} (B, \prec_{U_1} \oplus \prec_{U_2}) \sqsubseteq_{U_1 \wedge U_2} (B, \prec_{U_1 \wedge U_2})$.*

Furthermore, if $U_1 \wedge U_2$ is a deadlock-free invariant then $B/V(U_1 \wedge U_2) \simeq_{U_1 \wedge U_2} (B, \prec_{U_1} \oplus \prec_{U_2}) \simeq_{U_1 \wedge U_2} (B, \prec_{U_1 \wedge U_2})$.

Proof. Omitted.

This proposition says that $(B, \prec_{U_1} \oplus \prec_{U_2})$ is an upper approximation of $B/V(U_1 \wedge U_2)$. The following proposition shows an even stronger relationship between the two priority systems.

Proposition 13. *If U_1, U_2 are two deadlock-free invariants of B and $\prec_{U_1} \oplus \prec_{U_2}$ is irreflexive then $B/V(U_1 \wedge U_2) \simeq_{U_1 \wedge U_2} (B, \prec_{U_1} \oplus \prec_{U_2})$ is deadlock-free.*

Proof. We have from $B/V(U_1) \simeq_{U_1} (B, \prec_{U_1})$ and $B/V(U_2) \simeq_{U_2} (B, \prec_{U_2})$, $(B, \prec_{U_1} \oplus \prec_{U_2}) \sqsubseteq_{U_1} (B, \prec_{U_1} \cup \prec_{U_2}) \sqsubseteq_{U_1} B/V(U_1)$ and $(B, \prec_{U_1} \oplus \prec_{U_2}) \sqsubseteq_{U_2} (B, \prec_{U_1} \cup \prec_{U_2}) \sqsubseteq_{U_2} B/V(U_2)$. This gives, $(B, \prec_{U_1} \oplus \prec_{U_2}) \sqsubseteq_{U_1 \wedge U_2} B/V(U_1) \wedge V(U_2) \simeq B/V(U_1 \wedge U_2)$. From the previous proposition we get the result. ∎

The following proposition provides for static priorities, a result similar to Proposition 11. It is very useful for establishing safety by using static priorities.

Proposition 14. *Given a state predicate U on a transition system $B = (X, A, \{G^a\}_{a \in A}, \{F^a\}_{a \in A})$, let $\prec_U$ be a static priority such that $\forall a \in A . pre_a(\neg U) \implies \bigvee_{m \, . \, a \prec_U m} \bigwedge_{a_i \in m} G^{a_i}$. Then, $inv[(B, \prec_U)](U)$.*

Proof. By Definition 10 of the semantics of $(B, \prec_U)$. ∎

As shown in the following example, this proposition provides a means to ensure invariance of an arbitrary predicate U by static priorities. The choice of $\prec_U$ is a trade-off between completeness and efficiency. Extreme choices are given by

- $a \prec_U a' \iff pre_a(\neg U) \wedge pre_{a'}(U) \neq false$, which is a priority with singleton monomials only; the closure of this priority may easily be not irreflexive.
- $a \prec_U m \iff \exists \mathbf{x} . (pre_a(\neg U))(\mathbf{x}) \wedge m = \{a' \mid G^{a'}(\mathbf{x})\}$ which is the most fine-grained static priority ensuring invariance of U.

4 Example

We consider a robotic system controlled by the following processes:

- 3 trajectory control processes TC_1, TC_2, TC_man. TC_2 is more precise and needs more resources than TC_1; TC_man is the process for manual operation.
- 2 motion planners, MP_1, MP_2; MP_2 is more precise and needs more resources than MP_1.

We consider for each process P predicates *P.halted* and *P.running* such that *P.halted* $\equiv \neg$*P.running*. Each process P can leave states of *P.halted* (resp. *P.running*) by action *P.start* (resp. *P.stop*), as in figure 1. The robotic system must satisfy forever the following constraints:

1. In order to ensure permanent control of the position and movements of the robot, at least one trajectory control process and at least one motion planner must be running at any time: (TC_1.running $\vee$ TC_2.running $\vee$ TC_man.running) $\wedge$ (MP_1.running $\vee$ MP_2.running).
2. In order to meet the process deadlines, the CPU load must be kept below a threshold, which excludes that both high-precision processes can be simultaneously active: TC_2.halted $\vee$ MP_2.halted.

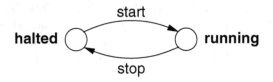

Fig. 1. Transition system of a process

The problem is to find a deadlock-free controller which restricts the behavior of the system so that the above requirement is met. A similar problem has been solved in [13] by using controller synthesis [12]. We propose a solution by finding an appropriate static priority.

We put the global constraint to be satisfied as a predicate U in conjunctive form: $U = (TC_1.\text{running} \vee TC_2.\text{running} \vee TC\_man.\text{running}) \wedge (MP_1.\text{running} \vee MP_2.\text{running}) \wedge (TC_2.\text{halted} \vee MP_2.\text{halted})$.

Invariance of U requires the invariance of each one of the three conjuncts, disjunctions of predicates. We define the static priority $\prec_U$ in the following manner.

For each conjunct D consider the critical configurations where only one literal of the disjunction is *true*. The priority $\prec_U$ prevents critical actions, that is actions that can turn this term to *false*, by keeping them dominated by safe actions enabled in the considered configuration. More formally, for each disjunction D, each critical action a (for which $D \wedge pre_a(\neg D) \neq false$) is dominated by the monomial consisting of the safe actions enabled in D.

For example, take $D = TC_1.\text{running} \vee TC_2.\text{running} \vee TC\_man.\text{running}$. Consider the critical configuration where $TC_1.\text{running} = true$, $TC_2.\text{running} = false$, and $TC\_man.\text{running} = false$. Clearly, $TC_1.stop$ is a critical action for this configuration. Its occurrence can be prevented by the static priority $TC_1.\text{stop} \prec TC_2.\text{start} \cdot TC\_man.\text{start}$. The monomial $TC_2.\text{start} \cdot TC\_man.\text{start}$ is the product of the safe actions enabled at this configuration. In this way, we compute the static priority $\prec_U$ which guarantees invariance of U:

$$TC_1.\text{stop} \prec_U TC_2.\text{start} \cdot TC\_man.\text{start}$$
$$TC_2.\text{stop} \prec_U TC_1.\text{start} \cdot TC\_man.\text{start}$$
$$TC\_man.\text{stop} \prec_U TC_1.\text{start} \cdot TC_2.\text{start}$$
$$MP_1.\text{stop} \prec_U MP_2.\text{start}$$
$$MP_2.\text{stop} \prec_U MP_1.\text{start}$$
$$TC_2.\text{start} \prec_U MP_2.\text{stop}$$
$$MP_2.\text{start} \prec_U TC_2.\text{stop}$$

It is easy to see that $\prec_U^+$ is irreflexive. By Proposition 6, $\prec_U$ is a deadlock-free restriction. By Proposition 14, U is an invariant of $(TC_1 \cup TC_2 \cup TC\_man \cup MP_1 \cup MP_2, \prec_U)$.

This approach can be applied to find deadlock-free control restrictions of arbitrary systems of processes $\{B_1, \ldots, B_n\}$ abstractly modeled as the deadlock-free transition system of figure 1, preserving a predicate U, boolean expression on atomic predicates B_i.running and B_i.halted. For example, U can express requirements on the global system state such as:

- a safety-critical process must not run unless a failure-handling process is running;
- mutual exclusion between concurrently running processes, e.g., between a safety-critical and an untrusted process.

We suppose U to be written as a conjunction of disjunctions

$$U = \bigwedge_{i \in I} (\bigvee_{j \in J_i} B_j.\text{running} \vee \bigvee_{j \in J_i'} B_j.\text{halted})$$

where I, J_i and J_i' are index sets such that any conjunct has at least two atoms that are predicates on two different processes (this is always possible for any predicate U if we have at least two processes).

Invariance of U is equivalent to invariance of all of its conjuncts D_i. Consider the conjunct $\bigvee_{l \in J_i} B_l.\text{running} \vee \bigvee_{l \in J_i'} B_l.\text{halted}$. As in the previous example, consider a critical configuration, that is, a configuration where only one literal is true. We distinguish two cases:

- if that literal is B_j.running (thus $j \in J_i$), then B_j.stop violates U from this configuration characterized by $\bigwedge_{l \in J_i \smallsetminus \{j\}} B_l.\text{halted} \wedge \bigwedge_{l \in J_i' \cup \{j\}} B_l.\text{running}$. This action can be prevented by the static priority

$$B_j.\text{stop} \prec_U \prod_{l \in J_i \smallsetminus \{j\}} B_l.\text{start} \cdot \prod_{l \in J_i'} B_l.\text{stop}$$

In this relation, B_j.stop is dominated by the monomial consisting of the actions of the other processes involved in this configuration.
- if the literal is B_j.halted (thus $j \in J_i'$), then B_j.start violates U, and we apply a similar reasoning and get $B_j.\text{start} \prec_U \prod_{l \in J_i} B_l.\text{start} \cdot \prod_{l \in J_i' \smallsetminus \{j\}} B_l.\text{stop}$.

Let $\prec_U$ be the union of the so defined priorities for all $i \in I$.

By definition of $\prec_U$, for any disjunct D_i of U, any critical action a is dominated by at least one monomial $m(a, D_i) = \prod B_l.\text{start} \cdot \prod B_l.\text{stop}$ consisting of safe actions enabled in D_i. Thus, $pre_a(\neg D_i) \implies \bigwedge_{a_i \in m(a, D_i)} G^{a_i}$, and $pre_a(\neg U) = pre_a(\neg \bigwedge_{i \in I} D_i) = pre_a(\bigvee_{i \in I} \neg D_i) = \bigvee_{i \in I} pre_a(\neg D_i) \implies \bigvee_{i \in I} \bigwedge_{a_i \in m(a, D_i)} G^{a_i}$. By proposition 14, U is an invariant of $(\bigcup_i B_i, \prec_U)$. Notice that $\prec_U$ is minimally restrictive, that is, only transitions violating the invariance of U are inhibited.

Deadlock-freedom of $(\bigcup_i B_i, \prec_U)$ is established by Proposition 14 if $\prec_U^+$ is irreflexive, which depends on the actual predicate U.

5   Discussion

We present a framework for the incremental construction of deadlock-free systems meeting given safety properties. The framework borrows concepts and basic results from the controller synthesis paradigm by considering a step in the construction process as a controller synthesis problem. Nevertheless, it does not directly address controller synthesis and other related computationally hard problems. Instead, it is based on the abstraction that the effect of the controller corresponding to a deadlock-free control invariant can be modeled by deadlock-free control restrictions.

Priorities play a central role in our framework. They can represent any deadlock-free control restriction. They can be naturally used to model mutual exclusion constraints and scheduling policies [4,2]. They are equipped with very simple and natural composition operations and criteria for composability. We provide an equational characterization of priorities and a sufficient condition for representing deadlock-free restrictions. Static priorities are solutions expressed as boolean expressions on guards for which a necessary and sufficient condition for deadlock-freedom is provided.

The use of priority systems instead of simple transition systems is a key idea in our approach. Of course, any priority system is, by its semantics, equivalent to a transition system. Nevertheless, using such layered models offers numerous advantages of composability and compositionality:

- The separation between transition system (behavior) and priorities allows reducing global deadlock-freedom to deadlock-freedom of the transition system and a condition on the composed priorities.

- The use of priorities to model mutual exclusion and scheduling policies instead of using transition systems leads to more readable and compositional descriptions [2].

- In [6,5] priority systems are used to define a general framework for component-based modeling. This framework uses a single associative parallel composition operator for layered components, encompassing heterogeneous interaction. Priorities are used to express *interaction constraints*. For systems of interacting components, we have proposed sufficient conditions for global and individual deadlock-freedom, based on the separation between behavior and priorities.

Our work on priorities found application in generating schedulers for real-time Java applications [9]. This paper uses a scheduler synthesis algorithm that generates directly (dynamic) priorities. Another interesting application is the use of priorities in the IF toolset to implement efficiently run-to-completion semantics of the RT-UML profile [7].

Priority systems combine behavior with priorities, a very simple enforcement mechanism for safety and deadlock-freedom. This mechanism is powerful enough to model the effect of controllers ensuring such properties. They offer both abstraction and analysis for incremental system construction. Our theoretical framework can be a basis for the various approaches and practices using enforcement mechanisms in a more or less ad-hoc manner.

References

1. K. Altisen, G. Gössler, A. Pnueli, J. Sifakis, S. Tripakis, and S. Yovine. A framework for scheduler synthesis. In *Proc. RTSS'99*, pages 154–163. IEEE Computer Society Press, 1999.
2. K. Altisen, G. Gössler, and J. Sifakis. Scheduler modeling based on the controller synthesis paradigm. *Journal of Real-Time Systems, special issue on "control-theoretical approaches to real-time computing"*, 23(1/2):55–84, 2002.
3. L. Bauer, J. Ligatti, and D. Walker. A calculus for composing security policies. Technical Report TR-655-02, Princeton University, 2002.
4. S. Bornot, G. Gössler, and J. Sifakis. On the construction of live timed systems. In S. Graf and M. Schwartzbach, editors, *Proc. TACAS'00*, volume 1785 of *LNCS*, pages 109–126. Springer-Verlag, 2000.
5. G. Gössler and J. Sifakis. Component-based construction of deadlock-free systems (extended abstract). In *proc. FSTTCS'03*, volume 2914 of *LNCS*. Springer-Verlag, 2003.
6. G. Gössler and J. Sifakis. Composition for component-based modeling. In *proc. FMCO'02*, volume 2852 of *LNCS*. Springer-Verlag, 2003.
7. S. Graf, I. Ober, and I. Ober. Model checking of uml models via a mapping to communicating extended timed automata. In S. Graf and L. Mounier, editors, *Proc. SPIN'04*, volume 2989 of *LNCS*. Springer-Verlag, 2004.
8. G. Kiczales, J. Lamping, A. Mendhekar, C. Maeda, C. Videira Lopes, J.-M. Loingtier, and J. Irwin. Aspect-oriented programming. In *Proc. ECOOP '97*, volume 1241 of *LNCS*, page 220ff. Springer-Verlag, 1997.
9. C. Kloukinas, C. Nakhli, and S. Yovine. A methodology and tool support for generating scheduled native code for real-time java applications. In R. Alur and I. Lee, editors, *Proc. EMSOFT'03*, volume 2855 of *LNCS*, pages 274–289, 2003.
10. J. Ligatti, L. Bauer, and D. Walker. Edit automata: Enforcement mechanisms for run-time security policies. Technical Report TR-681-03, Princeton University, 2003.
11. O. Maler, A. Pnueli, and J. Sifakis. On the synthesis of discrete controllers for timed systems. In E.W. Mayr and C. Puech, editors, *STACS'95*, volume 900 of *LNCS*, pages 229–242. Springer-Verlag, 1995.
12. P.J. Ramadge and W.M. Wonham. Supervisory control of a class of discrete event processes. *SIAM J. Control and Optimization*, 25(1), 1987.
13. E. Rutten and H. Marchand. Task-level programming for control systems using discrete control synthesis. Technical Report 4389, INRIA, 2002.
14. F. Schneider. Enforceable security policies. *ACM Transactions on Information and System Security*, 3(1):30–50, 2000.
15. P. Tarr, M. D'Hondt, L. Bergmans, and C. V. Lopes. Workshop on aspects and dimensions of concern: Requirements on, challenge problems for, advanced separation of concerns. In *ECOOP 2000 Workshop Proceedings, Springer Verlag*, 2000.

Preserving Properties Under Change

Heike Wehrheim

Universität Oldenburg, Fachbereich Informatik,
26111 Oldenburg, Germany
wehrheim@informatik.uni-oldenburg.de

Abstract. In this paper we discuss the question which properties of a formally verified component are preserved when the component is changed due to an adaption to a new use. More specifically, we will investigate when a temporal logic property of an Object-Z class is preserved under a modification or extension of the class with new features. To this end, we use the *slicing* technique from program analysis which provides us with a representation of the dependencies within the class in the form of a *program dependence graph*. This graph can be used to determine the effect of a change to the class' behaviour and thus to the holding of a temporal logic formula.

1 Introduction

With the advent of component-based software engineering systems are more and more built from pre-fabricated components which are taken from libraries, adapted to new needs and assembled into a system. Furthermore, for the design of dependable systems formal methods are employed during the construction process to improve the degree of correctness and reliability. The combination of these two techniques — component-based design and formal methods — in system construction poses a large number of new research challenges which are currently very actively taken up.

This paper studies one aspect arising in this area, based on the following scenario of a component-based construction. We assume that we have a library of components which are formally specified and proven correct with respect to certain requirements. During system construction components are taken from the library and (since they might not fully comply to their new use) are modified or even extended with new features. The question is then whether the proven properties are preserved under this specialisation and thus whether we can also get a *re-use* of verification results and not just of components. More specifically, given a component A (which will be a single class here) and its modification or extension C we are interested in knowing whether a property P holding for A still holds for C (see the following figure).

F.S. de Boer et al. (Eds.): FMCO 2003, LNCS 3188, pp. 330–343, 2004.
© Springer-Verlag Berlin Heidelberg 2004

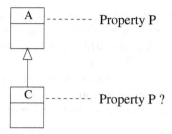

Although the picture might suggest that the relationship between A and C is that of inheritance (since we use the specialisation arrow of UML) we are actually interested in a more general relationship: C may be any class which is constructed out of A, may it be by inheritance or by a simple change of the existing specification.

As a first observation, it can be remarked that even a restriction to inheritance cannot ensure that properties are preserved: a subclass may differ from its superclass in any aspect and thus none of the properties holding for A might be preserved in C. Still, preservation of properties to subclasses is an important and intensively studied topic. Within the area of program verification, especially of Java programs, this question has already been tackled by a number of researchers [6,10,5]. In these approaches correctness properties are mainly formulated in Hoare logic, and the aim is to find proof rules which help to deduce subclass properties from superclass properties. In order to get correctness of these rules it is required that the subclass is a *behavioural subtype* [7] of the superclass. This assumption is also the basis of [14] which studies preservation of properties in an event-based setting with correctness requirements formulated as CSP processes.

In this paper we lift this assumption (although also looking at subtypes as a special case) and consider arbitrary classes constructed out of existing classes. For convenience we will, however, often call the class C the subclass and A its superclass. Instead of employing restrictions on the subclass (in order to preserve properties) we will *compute* whether a property is preserved or not. This computation does not involve re-verification of the property but can be carried out on a special representation of the classes called *program dependence graphs*. Program dependence graphs carry all information about the dependencies within programs (or in our case, specifications) and thus can be used to determine the influence of a change or extension on proven properties. This technique is originally coming from program analysis where *slicing* techniques operating on program dependence graphs are used to reduce a program with respect to certain variables of interest. Slicing techniques (and a similar technique called cone-of-influence reduction) are also being applied in software and hardware model checking for *reducing* programs [4,9,1].

In our framework classes are not written in a programming language but are defined in a state-based object-oriented formal method (Object-Z [11,2]). Correctness requirements on classes are formalised in a temporal logic (LTL [8]). As changes (specialisation) we allow the addition of attributes, the modification of existing methods and the extension with new methods. A comparable study about inheritance of CTL properties is described in [15], however, not employing the program dependence graphs of slicing which allow for a more succinct representation of the dependencies within specifications.

The paper is structured as follows. In the next section we define the necessary background for our study. Section 3 studies property preservation for subtypes and section 4 introduces slicing as a more general technique for computing preserved properties for arbitrary changes. Section 5 concludes.

2   Background

This section describes the background necessary for understanding the results: the definition of classes in Object-Z, the temporal logic LTL and a result showing that LTL-X properties are preserved under stuttering equivalence. Stuttering equivalence will be used to compare super- and subclasses.

2.1   Class Definitions

Classes are described in a formalism very close to Object-Z [11][1]. Object-Z is an object-oriented extension of Z and thus a state-based specification technique.

The following specification of a simple account is the running example for our technique. It specifies the state of an account (with a certain *balance*), its initial value and two methods for depositing and withdrawing money from the account. Methods are specified with enable and effect schemas describing the guard (to the execution of) and the effect of executing the method. For instance, since the account may not be overdrawn, the guard of *Withdraw* specifies that the amount of money to be withdrawn may not exceed the balance. The Δ-list of an effect schema fixes the set of variables which may be changed by an execution of the method.

$Account_0$

$balance : \mathbb{Z}$

Init
$balance = 0$

enable_*Deposit*
$amount? : \mathbb{N}$

true

effect_*Deposit*
$\Delta(balance)$
$amount? : \mathbb{N}$

$balance' = balance + amount?$

---

[1] In fact, it is the Object-Z part of CSP-OZ specifications [3] (a formalism which integrates CSP with Object-Z). We use this formalism since we are ultimately interested in answering the question of property preservation for CSP-OZ.

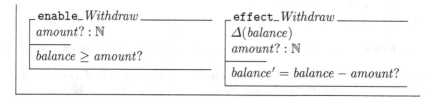

In our definitions we use the following non-graphical formulation of classes. Classes consist of attributes (or variables) and methods to operate on attributes. Methods may have input parameters and may return values, referred to as output parameters. We assume variables and input/output parameters to have values from a global set D. A *valuation* of a set of variables V is a mapping from V to D, we let $R_V = \{\rho : V \to D\}$ stand for the set of all valuations of V; the set of valuations of input parameters Inp and output parameters Out can be similarly defined. We assume that the initialisation schema precisely fixes the values of variables (i.e. is deterministic) in order to have just one initial state[2].

A class is thus characterised by

- A set of *attributes* (or variables) V,
- an *initial valuation* of V to be used upon construction of objects: $I : V \to D$, and
- a set of methods (names) M with input and output parameters from a set of inputs Inp and a set of outputs Out. For simplicity we assume Inp and Out to be global. Each $m \in M$ has a guard $enable_m : R_V \times R_{Inp} \to \mathbb{B}$ ($\mathbb{B}$ are booleans) and an effect $effect_m : R_V \times R_{Inp} \to R_V \times R_{Out}$. The guard specifies the states in which the method is executable and the effect determines the outcome of the method execution.

A class will thus be denoted by $(V, I, (enable_m)_{m \in M}, (effect_m)_{m \in M})$ or (V, I, M) for short. We furthermore need to know the set of variables which are *set* and *referenced* by a schema: $Set(\texttt{enable\_m}) = \varnothing$, $Set(\texttt{effect\_m})$ are the variable appearing in the Δ-list of the effect schema and $Ref(\texttt{enable\_m})$, $Ref(\texttt{effect\_m})$ are those that syntactically appear in the schemas $\texttt{enable\_m}, \texttt{effect\_m}$ respectively.

The semantics of a class is defined in terms of *Kripke structures*.

Definition 1. *Let AP be a nonempty set of atomic propositions. A Kripke structure $K = (S, s_0, \to, L)$ over AP consists of a finite set of states S, an initial state $s_0 \in S$, a transition relation $\to \subseteq S \times S$ and a labelling function $L : S \to 2^{AP}$.*

The set of atomic propositions determines what we may observe about a state. Essentially there are two kinds of properties we like to look at: the values of variables and the availability of methods. Thus the atomic propositions AP_A that we consider for a class $A = (V, I, (enable_m)_{m \in M}, (effect_m)_{m \in M})$ are

---

[2] This assumption is not essential but more convenient.

- $v = d$, $v \in V$, $d \in D$ and
- $enabled(m)$, $m \in M$.

The Kripke structure semantics of a class definition is then defined as follows.

Definition 2. *The semantics of (an object of) a class* $A = (V, I, (enable_m)_{m \in M},$ $(effect_m)_{m \in M})$ *is the Kripke structure* $K = (S, s_0, \rightarrow, L)$ *over* AP_A *with*

- $S = R_V$,
- $s_0 = I$,
- $\rightarrow = \{(s, s') \mid \exists m \in M, \rho_{in} \in R_{Inp}, \rho_{out} \in R_{Out} : enable_m(s, \rho_{in})$
  $\wedge effect_m(s, \rho_{in}) = (s', \rho_{out})\}$,
- $L(s) = \{v = d \mid s(v) = d\} \cup \{enabled(m) \mid \exists \rho_{in} \in R_{Inp} : enable_m(s, \rho_{in})\}$.

Since the atomic propositions do not refer to inputs and outputs of methods, they are not reflected in the semantics. However, inputs and outputs can be embedded in the state and thus can be made part of the atomic propositions (see e.g. [12]).

Figure 1 shows the Kripke structure (without L) of class $Account_0$. The numbers indicate the values of attribute *balance*. All states satisfying *balance* < 0 are unreachable. The upper arrows correspond to executions of *Deposit*, the lower to those of *Withdraw*.

$$\begin{array}{ccccc} \cdots & \bullet & & & \cdots \\ & -1 & 0 & 1 & \end{array}$$

Fig. 1. Kripke structure of class $Account_0$

Furthermore, we have to fix the kind of changes allowed in subclasses. We do not allow to remove methods, but methods can be arbitrarily modified as well as new methods and variables be introduced.

Definition 3. *Let A and C be classes. C is a specialisation of A if $V_A \subseteq V_C$, $M_A \subseteq M_C$ and $I_C \mid_{V_A} = I_A$.*

2.2   LTL Formulae

The temporal logic which we use for describing our properties on classes is linear-time temporal logic (LTL) [8].

Definition 4. *The set of LTL formulae over AP is defined as the smallest set of formulae satisfying the following conditions:*

- $p \in AP$ *is a formula,*
- *if* φ_1, φ_2 *are formulae, so are* $\neg \varphi_1$ *and* $\varphi_1 \vee \varphi_2$,
- *if* φ *is a formula, so are* $X\varphi$ *(Next),* $\Box \varphi$ *(Always),* $\Diamond \varphi$ *(Eventually),*
- *if* φ_1, φ_2 *are formulae, so is* $\varphi_1 \ U \ \varphi_2$ *(Until).*

As usually, other boolean connectives can be derived from $\neg$ and $\vee$. The next-less part of LTL is referred to as LTL-X. LTL formulae are interpreted on *paths* of the Kripke structure, and a formula holds for the Kripke structure if it holds for all of its paths.

Definition 5. *Let $K = (S, s, \rightarrow, L)$ be a Kripke structure. A finite or infinite sequence of states $\pi = s_0 s_1 s_2 \ldots$ is a path of K iff $s = s_0$ and $(s_i, s_{i+1}) \in \rightarrow$ for all $0 \leq i$. For a path $\pi = s_0 s_1 s_2 \ldots$ we write $\pi[i]$ to stand for s_i and π^i to stand for $s_i s_{i+1} s_{i+2} \ldots$. The* length *of a path π, $\#\pi$, is defined to be the number of states (in case of a finite path) or ∞ (in case of an infinite path).*

Usually, paths are assumed to be always infinite (and LTL formulae interpreted on infinite paths). We deviate from that because objects may also exhibit finite behaviour: if no methods are called from the outside anymore, the object just stops. This has, however, consequences on the holding of liveness properties: since for instance s_0 alone is also a path, a liveness property can only hold if it already holds in the initial state. Thus we essentially treat *safety* here. Liveness can be treated if we additionally make some fairness assumptions on the environment of an object (see conclusion for a discussion).

Definition 6. *Let $K = (S, s_0, \rightarrow, L)$ be a Kripke structure and φ an LTL formula, both over AP. K satisfies φ ($K \models \varphi$) iff $\pi \models \varphi$ holds for all paths π of K, where $\pi \models \varphi$ is defined as follows:*

- $\pi \models p$ *iff $p \in L(\pi[0])$,*
- $\pi \models \neg\varphi$ *iff not $\pi \models \varphi$,*
- $\pi \models \varphi_1 \vee \varphi_2$ *iff $\pi \models \varphi_1$ or $\pi \models \varphi_2$,*
- $\pi \models X \varphi$ *iff $\#\pi > 1 \wedge \pi^1 \models \varphi$,*
- $\pi \models \Box\varphi$ *iff $\forall i, 0 \leq i \leq \#\pi : \pi^i \models \varphi$,*
- $\pi \models \Diamond\varphi$ *iff $\exists i, 0 \leq i \leq \#\pi : \pi^i \models \varphi$,*
- $\pi \models \varphi_1 U \varphi_2$ *iff $\exists k, 0 \leq k \leq \#\pi : \pi^k \models \varphi_2$ and $\forall j, 0 \leq j < k : \pi^j \models \varphi_1$.*

For our bank example we for instance have the following properties. The Kripke structure $K_{Account_0}$ of $Account_0$ fulfills

$$K_{Account_0} \models \Box(balance \geq 0) \,,$$
$$K_{Account_0} \models \Box(enabled(Deposit)) \,.$$

2.3   Stuttering Equivalence

For showing that properties are preserved under change, or more particular, that a certain property still holds for a subclass, we will later compare super- and subclasses according to a notion of equivalence called *stuttering equivalence*. Stuttering equivalence is defined with respect to some set of atomic proposition and roughly says that on these proposition of interest two Kripke structures have an equivalent behaviour. All transitions changing propositions outside those of interest are regarded as stuttering steps.

Definition 7. *Two infinite paths* $\pi = s_0 s_1 s_2 \ldots$ *and* $\rho = r_0 r_1 r_2 \ldots$ *are stuttering equivalent wrt. a set of atomic propositions* AP *(*$\pi \approx_{AP} \rho$*) if there are two sequences of indices* $0 = i_0 < i_1 < i_2 < \ldots$ *and* $0 = j_0 < j_1 < j_2 < \ldots$ *such that for every* $k \geq 0$

$$L(s_{i_k}) \cap AP = L(s_{i_k+1}) \cap AP = \cdots = L(s_{i_{k+1}-1}) \cap AP =$$
$$L(r_{j_k}) \cap AP = L(r_{j_k+1}) \cap AP = \cdots = L(r_{j_{k+1}-1}) \cap AP$$

A finite path $\pi = s_0 \ldots s_n$ *is stuttering equivalent to an infinite path* ρ *if its extension with an infinite number of repetitions of the last state, i.e.* $s_0 \ldots s_n s_n s_n \ldots$, *is stuttering equivalent to* σ. *(And similarly for two finite paths.)*

Intuitively, the sequences are equivalent if they can be divided into blocks in which atomic propositions stay stable and the i-th block in π has the same set of propositions from AP as the i-th block in ρ (illustrated in Figure 2).

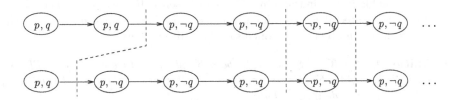

Fig. 2. Stuttering equivalent sequences

Definition 8. *Let* $K_i = (S_i, s_{0,i}, \rightarrow_i, L_i)$, $i = 1, 2$, *be Kripke structures over* AP_1, AP_2, *respectively.* K_1 *and* K_2 *are* stuttering equivalent *with respect to a set of atomic propositions* $AP \subseteq AP_1 \cap AP_2$ *(*$K_1 \approx_{AP} K_2$*) iff*

– *initial states agree on* AP:

$$L_1(s_{0,1}) \cap AP = L_2(s_{0,2}) \cap AP ,$$

– *for each path* π *in* K_1 *starting from* $s_{0,1}$ *there exists a path* π' *starting from* $s_{0,2}$ *such that* $\pi \approx_{AP} \pi'$,
– *and vice versa, for each path* π *in* K_2 *starting from* $s_{0,2}$ *there exists a path* π' *starting from* $s_{0,1}$ *such that* $\pi \approx_{AP} \pi'$.

Stuttering equivalent Kripke structures satisfy the same set of LTL-X properties [1]. The Next operator has to be omitted since stuttering may introduce additional steps in one structure which have no counterpart in the other.

Theorem 1. *Let* φ *be an LTL-X formula over* AP *and* K_1, K_2 *Kripke structures. If* $K_1 \approx_{AP} K_2$ *then*

$$K_1 \models \varphi \quad \text{iff} \quad K_2 \models \varphi .$$

3 Property Preservation

Now that we have set the ground, we have another look at our example and make two changes to the class. The first is an *extension* of the class, we add one new method for balance checking. Here, we use inheritance to avoid having to write the whole specification again.

```
┌─ Account₁ ──────────────────────────────────────────────
│ inherit  Account₀
│
│ ┌─ enable_CheckBalance ─────────────────────────────
│ │
│ │ true
│ └──────────────────────────────────────────────────
│
│ ┌─ effect_CheckBalance ─────────────────────────────
│ │ bal! : ℤ
│ ├───────────────────────
│ │ bal! = balance
│ └──────────────────────────────────────────────────
└─────────────────────────────────────────────────────────
```

The second change is a *modification*, we modify the account such that it allows overdrawing up to a certain amount. Here, we inherit all parts but the definition of *Withdraw* which is overwritten by the new definition.

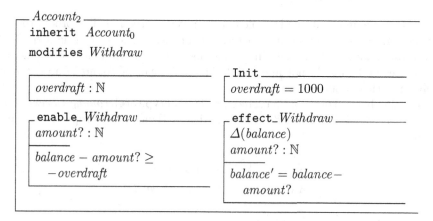

The question is then which of our properties are preserved, i.e. which of the following questions can be answered with yes.

$$K_{Account_1} \models \Box(balance \geq 0)?$$
$$K_{Account_1} \models \Box(enabled(Deposit))?$$
$$K_{Account_2} \models \Box(balance \geq 0)?$$
$$K_{Account_2} \models \Box(enabled(Deposit))?$$

For this simple example, the answers are easy. What we aim at is, however, a general technique which answers such questions. In general, these two changes are of two different types. The changed class can be a *subtype* of the original class (and then all properties are preserved) or it is not (and then a more sophisticated technique has to be applied to find out whether a property is preserved).

In this section, we deal with the first, more simple case. The second case is dealt with in the next section. A subtype can be seen as a conservative extension of a class: new methods may read but may not modify old variables.

Definition 9. *Let $A = (V_A, I_A, M_A)$ and $C = (V_C, I_C, M_C)$ be two classes, C a specialisation of A. C is a subtype of A iff the following conditions hold:*

- *$\forall m \in M_C \setminus M_A: Set_C(\texttt{effect\_}m) \subseteq V_C \setminus V_A$ (m only modifies new variables),*
- *$\forall m \in M_A : enable_m^C = enable_m^A \wedge effect_m^C = effect_m^A$ (old methods not modified).*

Subtypes inherit all properties as long as they are only talking about propositions over the old attributes and methods.

Theorem 2. *Let C, A be classes, C a subtype of A. Let furthermore AP be the set of atomic propositions over V_A and M_A. For all LTL-X formulae φ over AP we then have*

$$A \models \varphi \Longrightarrow C \models \varphi .$$

In fact, the implication also holds in the reverse direction. The proof proceeds by showing that C and A are stuttering equivalent. The stuttering steps in C are those belonging to executions of the new methods: they do not change old attributes and thus do not affect AP. The proof can be found in an extended version of this paper.

Coming back to our example, $Account_1$ is a subtype of $Account_0$: *CheckBalance* only references *balance* but does not modify it. Hence both properties are preserved:

$$K_{Account_1} \models \Box(balance \geq 0)$$
$$K_{Account_1} \models \Box(enabled(Deposit))$$

4   Slicing

In this section we look at the more general case, where the modifications do not lead to subtypes. For this case, we cannot get one general result but have to specifically look at the changes made and the properties under interest.

The technique we use for computing whether a property is preserved under a specific change is the *slicing* technique of program analysis [13]. In program analysis slicing is originally used for debugging and testing, and answers questions like the following: "given a variable v and a program point p, which part of the program may influence the value of v at p?". Here, we like to extract a similar kind of information about our changes: "given some propositions and some change, does it influence the value of these propositions?". Technically, slicing operates on graphs which contain information about the dependencies within a program, so called *program dependence graphs* (PDG). A similar graph is now built for Object-Z classes. It starts from the control flow graph (CFG) of a class (depicted in Figure 3), which contains

- one node n_0 labelled *Init*,
- one node n_{DO} labelled *DO* (nondeterministic choice),
- for every method m two nodes n_{en_m} and n_{eff_m} labelled **enable_m** and **effect_m**.

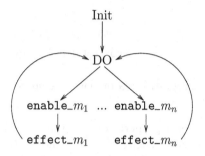

Fig. 3. Control flow graph of a class

The program dependence graph is obtained from this graph by erasing all arrows and adding new ones corresponding to the control and data dependencies of the class. Formally,

Definition 10. *A* program dependence graph *(PDG) of a class specification* (V, I, M) *is a graph* $G = (K, l, \leadsto, \rightarrowtail)$ *with*

- $K = \{n_0, n_{DO}\} \cup \{n_{en\_m} \mid m \in M\} \cup \{n_{eff\_m} \mid m \in M\}$ *a set of* nodes,
- l *a labelling function* with

$$
\begin{aligned}
l : \quad n_0 \quad &\mapsto \textit{Init} \\
n_{DO} \quad &\mapsto DO \\
n_{en\_m} \quad &\mapsto \textbf{enable\_}m \\
n_{eff\_m} \quad &\mapsto \textbf{effect\_}m
\end{aligned}
$$

- $\leadsto \subseteq K \times K$ *the data dependence* edges defined by

$$n \leadsto n' \text{ iff } \exists x \in V : x \in Set(l(n)) \text{ and } x \in Ref(l(n')) \text{ and } n \rightarrow^*_{CFG} n' ,$$

- $\rightarrowtail \subseteq K \times K$ *the control dependence* edges defined by

$$n \rightarrowtail n' \text{ iff } \exists m \in M : l(n) = \textbf{enable\_}m \text{ and } l(n') = \textbf{effect\_}m .$$

Here, we take $Set(DO) = Ref(DO) = \varnothing$. For class $Account_0$ this gives rise to the graph shown in Figure 4.

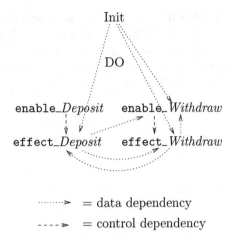

Fig. 4. PDG of class $Account_0$

For computing whether a property of A is preserved in C, we build a PDG including methods and dependencies of *both* A and C. In this $PDG_{A,C}$ we next determine the *forward slice* of all modified or new methods (where we say that *Init* is modified if it assigns new values to variables from A). The forward slice of a set of nodes N is the part of the graph which is forward reachable from nodes in N via data or control dependencies.

Definition 11. *Let C, A be classes, C a specialisation of A. Let furthermore N be the nodes belonging to methods which are changed or new in C, i.e.*

$$N = \{n \mid \big(l(n) \in \{\texttt{enable}[m], \texttt{effect\_m} \mid m \in M_C \setminus M_A\}\big) \vee$$
$$\big(\exists\, m \in M_A : l(n) = \texttt{enable\_m} \wedge enable_m^C \neq enable_m^A\big) \vee$$
$$\big(\exists\, m \in M_A : l(n) = \texttt{effect\_m} \wedge effect_m^C \neq effect_m^A\big)\}$$

The forward slice *of N is the set of nodes in $PDG_{A,C}$ which are forward reachable from N, i.e.*

$$fs(N) = \{n' \in K \mid \exists\, n \in N : n(\leadsto \cup \rightarrowtail)^*_{PDG_{A,C}} n'\}$$

The forward slice of N is the part of the class which is directly or indirectly influenced by the changes. The atomic propositions appearing in this part might be changed. We let AP_N denote the atomic propositions over variables or methods in the forward slice of N.

$$AP_N = \{v = d \mid v \in V_C \setminus V_A \vee \exists\, n \in fs(N) : v \in Set_C(l(n)) \cup Set_A(l(n))\}$$
$$\cup \{enabled(m) \mid \exists\, n \in fs(N) : l(n) = \texttt{enable\_m}\}$$

Since these atomic propositions are potentially affected by the change, a formula talking about them might not hold in the subclass anymore. However, if a formula does not use propositions in AP_N then it is preserved.

Theorem 3. *Let A, C be classes, N the set of methods changed or new in C. If φ is an LTL-X formulae over $AP \setminus AP_N$, then the following holds:*

$$A \models \varphi \Longrightarrow C \models \varphi \; .$$

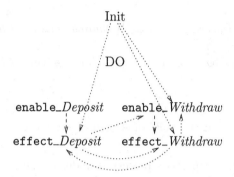

Fig. 5. PDG of $Account_0$, $Account_2$

The proof again proceeds by showing that K_A and K_C are stuttering equivalent wrt. $AP \setminus AP_N$ and is included in an extended version. Since they are stuttering equivalent the implication in the theorem holds in the reverse direction as well.

For our example, the PDG for $Account_0$, $Account_2$ is depicted in Figure 5. The set of changed methods N is $\{Withdraw\}$. Nodes not in the forward slice of $Withdraw$ are $\{Init, DO, \texttt{enable\_Deposit}\}$. The variable *balance* is set by a method in the forward slice, but $\texttt{enable\_Deposit}$ is not in the forward slice. Hence, concerning our properties, we know that one of them is preserved:

$$K_{Account_2} \models \Box(enabled(Deposit))$$

but for the question $K_{Account_2} \models \Box(balance \geq 0)$? we get no answer (and in fact this property does not hold anymore).

The case of changes leading to subtypes can be seen as one particular instance of this more general result: for subtypes we know by definition that the forward slice (of the new methods) will only contain new methods and thus affects only new variables. Hence, the proof of Theorem 3 can be seen as an alternative way of proving Theorem 2.

The PDG of $Account_0$, $Account_1$ is depicted in Figure 6. As can be seen, in the forward slice of *CheckBalance* there is only *CheckBalance*.

5   Conclusion

This work is concerned with the re-use of verification results of classes. Given a verified class the technique presented in this paper can be used to determine

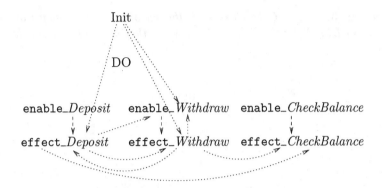

Fig. 6. PDG of $Account_0$, $Account_1$

whether some specific property is preserved under a change made to the class. The technique relies on the representation of the dependencies of a class specification in a program dependence graph. On this graph it is possible to determine the effect of changes on the behaviour of a class. As a special case we looked at changes inducing subtypes in which all properties (talking about the original class) are preserved.

So far, this technique considers a single class only. It could be extended to larger systems either by combining it with compositional verification techniques (e.g. for Object-Z [16]), or by constructing a program dependence graph of the whole system. The latter could be achieved by combining program dependence graphs of the individual objects through a special new dependency arc reflecting the call structure between objects (possibly following approaches for slicing programs with procedures).

Another limitation of the work presented here concerns the treatment of liveness properties. The inclusion of finite paths of a Kripke structure into the interpretation of LTL formulae lead to a restriction to safety properties. There are a number of ways of avoiding this limitation. One way would be to make certain assumptions about the environment of an object in that it infinitely often calls certain methods. These set of methods can be used as a *fairness constraint* on the behaviour of an object. The interpretation of LTL formulae can then be restricted to *fair* paths. If the fairness constraint for the subclass is the same as that for the superclass preservation of properties can be achieved.

As future work, we like to extend the technique presented here to integrated specification formalisms which allow for the modelling of different viewpoints in different formal methods, as for instance CSP-OZ [3].

References

1. E. Clarke, O. Grumberg, and D. Peled. *Model checking.* MIT Press, 1999.
2. R. Duke, G. Rose, and G. Smith. Object-Z: A specification language advocated for the description of standards. *Computer Standards and Interfaces*, 17:511–533, 1995.

3. C. Fischer. CSP-OZ: A combination of Object-Z and CSP. In H. Bowman and J. Derrick, editors, *Formal Methods for Open Object-Based Distributed Systems (FMOODS '97)*, volume 2, pages 423–438. Chapman & Hall, 1997.

4. J. Hatcliff, M. Dwyer, and H. Zheng. Slicing software for model construction. *Higher-order and Symbolic Computation*. To appear.

5. K. Huizing and R. Kuiper. Reinforcing fragile base classes. In A. Poetzsch-Heffter, editor, *Workshop on Formal Techniques for Java Programs, ECOOP 2001*, 2001.

6. G.T. Leavens and W.E. Weihl. Specification and verification of object-oriented programs using supertype abstraction. *Acta Informatica*, 32:705–778, 1995.

7. B. Liskov and J. Wing. A behavioural notion of subtyping. *ACM Transactions on Programming Languages and Systems*, 16(6):1811 – 1841, 1994.

8. Z. Manna and A. Pnueli. *The temporal logic of reactive and concurrent systems (Specification)*. 1991.

9. L. Millett and T. Teitelbaum. Issues in slicing promela and its applications to model checking, protocol understanding, and simulation. *Software Tools for Technology Transfer*, 2(4):343–349, 2000.

10. A. Poetzsch-Heffter and J. Meyer. Interactive verification environments for object-oriented languages. *Journal of Universal Computer Science*, 5(3):208–225, 1999.

11. G. Smith. *The Object-Z Specification Language*. Kluwer Academic Publisher, 2000.

12. G. Smith and K. Winter. Proving Temporal Properties of Z Specifications Using Abstraction. In D. Bert, J.P. Bowen, S. King, and M. Walden, editors, *ZB 2003: Formal Specification and Development in Z and B*, number 2651 in LNCS, pages 260–279. Springer, 2003.

13. F. Tip. A survey of program slicing techniques. *Journal of programming languages*, 3(3), 1995.

14. H. Wehrheim. Behavioural subtyping and property preservation. In S. Smith and C. Talcott, editors, *FMOODS'00: Formal Methods for Open Object-Based Distributed Systems*. Kluwer, 2000.

15. H. Wehrheim. Inheritance of temporal logic properties. In P. Stevens and U. Nestmann, editors, *FMOODS 2003: Formal Methods for Open Object-based Distributed Systems*, volume 2884 of *LNCS*, pages 79–93. Springer, 2003.

16. K. Winter and G. Smith. Compositional Verification for Object-Z. In D. Bert, J.P. Bowen, S. King, and M. Walden, editors, *ZB 2003: Formal Specification and Development in Z and B*, number 2651 in LNCS, pages 280–299. Springer, 2003.

Tools for Generating and Analyzing Attack Graphs

Oleg Sheyner[1] and Jeannette Wing[2]

[1] Carnegie Mellon University, Computer Science Department
5000 Forbes Avenue, Pittsburgh, PA 15213
oleg@cs.cmu.edu
[2] Carnegie Mellon University, Computer Science Department
5000 Forbes Avenue, Pittsburgh, PA 15213
wing@cs.cmu.edu

Abstract. Attack graphs depict ways in which an adversary exploits system vulnerabilities to achieve a desired state. System administrators use attack graphs to determine how vulnerable their systems are and to determine what security measures to deploy to defend their systems. In this paper, we present details of an example to illustrate how we specify and analyze network attack models. We take these models as input to our attack graph tools to generate attack graphs automatically and to analyze system vulnerabilities. While we have published our generation and analysis algorithms in earlier work, the presentation of our example and toolkit is novel to this paper.

1   Introduction

As networks of hosts continue to grow, it becomes increasingly more important to automate the process of evaluating their vulnerability to attack. When evaluating the security of a network, it is rarely enough to consider the presence or absence of isolated vulnerabilities. Large networks typically contain multiple platforms and software packages and employ several modes of connectivity. Inevitably, such networks have security holes that escape notice of even the most diligent system administrator.

1.1   Vulnerability Analysis and Attack Graphs

To evaluate the security of a network of hosts, a security analyst must take into account the effects of interactions of local vulnerabilities and find global security holes introduced by interconnection. A typical process for vulnerability analysis of a network is shown in Figure 1. First, scanning tools determine vulnerabilities of individual hosts. Using this local vulnerability information along with other information about the network, such as connectivity between hosts, the analyst produces an *attack graph*. Each path in an attack graph is a series of exploits, which we call *actions*, that leads to an undesirable state. An example of an undesirable state is a state where the intruder has obtained administrative access to a critical host.

A typical result of such efforts is a floor-to-ceiling, wall-to-wall "white board" attack graph, such as the one produced by a Red Team at Sandia National Labs for DARPA's CC20008 Information battle space preparation experiment and shown in Figure 2. Each

F.S. de Boer et al. (Eds.): FMCO 2003, LNCS 3188, pp. 344–371, 2004.
© Springer-Verlag Berlin Heidelberg 2004

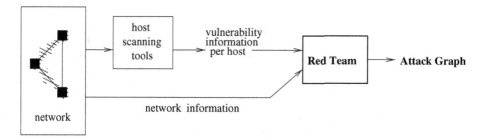

Fig. 1. Vulnerability Analysis of a Network

box in the graph designates a single intruder action. A path from one of the boxes at the top of the graph to one of the boxes at the bottom is a sequence of actions corresponding to an attack scenario. At the end of any such scenario, the intruder has broken the network security in some way. The graph is included here for illustrative purposes only, so we omit the description of specific details.

Attack graphs can serve as a useful tool in several areas of network security, including intrusion detection, defense, and forensic analysis. System administrators use attack graphs for the following reasons:

- To gather information: Attack graphs can answer questions like "What attacks is my system vulnerable to?" and "From an initial configuration, how many different ways can an attacker reach a final state to achieve his goal?"
- To make decisions: Attack graphs can answer questions like "Which set of actions should I prevent to ensure the attacker cannot achieve his goal?" or "Which set of security measures should I deploy to ensure the attacker cannot achieve his goal?"

1.2   Prior Work and Contributions of this Paper

In practice, attack graphs, such as the one shown in Figure 2, are drawn by hand. In earlier work, we show how we can use model checking techniques to generate attack graphs automatically [11, 17]. Our techniques guarantee that attack graphs are sound (each scenario depicted is a true attack), exhaustive (no attack is missed), and succinct (only states and state transitions that participate in an attack are depicted) [16].

In earlier work, we also have presented algorithms for analyzing attack graphs that answer questions such as those posed above [17, 9, 10]. For example, to help system administrators determine how best to defend their system, we cast the decision-making questions in terms of finding a minimum set of actions to remove (or minimum set of measures to deploy) to ensure the attacker cannot achieve his goal. We reduce this NP-complete problem to the Minimum Hitting Set problem [16], which can be reduced to the Minimum Set Cover problem [2], and we then use standard textbook algorithms to yield approximate solutions [3].

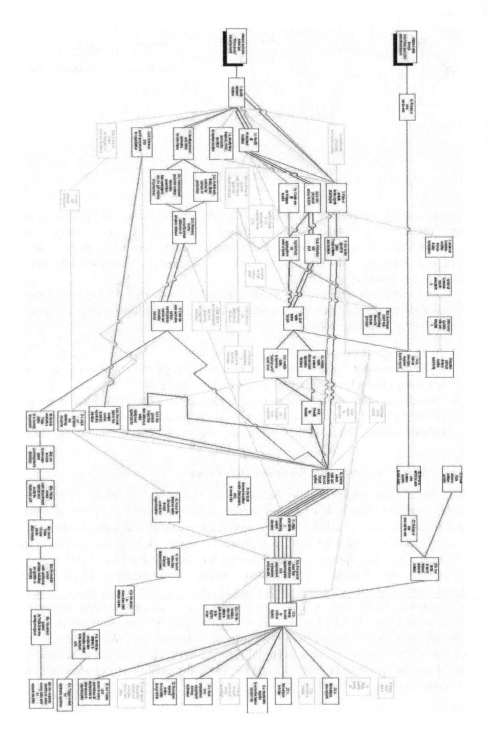

Fig. 2. Sandia Red Team Attack Graph

In this paper, we present the complete details of an example. We use this example to illustrate:

- How we specify network attack models;
- The results of our automatic attack graph generation algorithms;
- The results of our minimization analyses;
- How to use our attack graph toolkit, including how we integrated tools from external sources with ours.

The presentation of this example and our toolkit is novel to this paper.

In Sect. 2 we give general definitions for *attack models* and *attack graphs*. Section 3 narrows the definitions specifically to the domain of network security. Section 4 illustrates the definitions with a small example network. Section 5 focuses on the practical aspects of building a usable attack graph tool. We discuss several approaches to collecting the data necessary to build the network model. Finally, we review related work in Sect. 6.

2   Attack Models and Graphs

Although our primary interest is in multi-stage cyber-attacks against computer networks, we define attack graphs abstractly with respect to models where agents attack and defend a complex system.

Definition 1. *An attack model is a finite automaton $M = (S, \tau, s_0)$, where S is a set of states, $\tau \subseteq S \times S$ is a transition relation, and $s_0 \in S$ is an initial state. The state space S represents a set of three agents $\mathcal{I} = \{E, D, T\}$. Agent E is the attacker, agent D is the defender, and agent N is the system under attack. Each agent $i \in \mathcal{I}$ has its own set of possible states S_i, so that $S = \times_{i \in \mathcal{I}} S_i$.*

Definition 2. *A finite execution of an attack model $M = (S, \tau, s_0)$ is a finite sequence of states $\alpha = s_0 s_1 \ldots s_n$,such that for all $0 \leq i \leq n$, $(s_i, s_{i+1}) \in \tau$. An infinite execution of an attack model $M = (S, \tau, s_0)$ is an infinite sequence of states $\beta = s_0 s_1 \ldots s_n \ldots$, such that for all $i \geq 0$, $(s_i, s_{i+1}) \in \tau$.*

With each agent $i \in \mathcal{I}$ we associate a set of actions A_i, so that the total set of actions in the model is $A = \bigcup_{i \in \mathcal{I}} A_i$. The single root state s_0 represents the initial state of each agent before any action has taken place. In general, the attacker's actions move the system "toward" some undesirable (from the system's point of view) state, and the defender's actions attempt to counteract that effect. For instance, in a computer network the attacker's actions would be the steps taken by the intruder to compomise the network, and the defender's actions would be the steps taken by the system administrator to disrupt the attack.

The specifics of how each agent is represented in an attack model depend on the type of the system that is under attack. In Sect. 3 we specify the agents more precisely for network attack models. Sheyner presents a more formal definition of attack models in his Ph.D. thesis [16].

An attack model is a general formalism suitable for modeling a variety of situations. The system under attack can be virtually anything: a computer network under attack by hackers, a city under siege during war, an electrical grid targeted by terrorists, etc. The attacker is an abstract representation of a group of agents who seek to move the system to a state that is inimical to the system's interests. The defender is an agent whose explicit purpose, in opposition to the attacker, is to prevent this occurrence. The system itself is oblivious to the fact that it is under attack. It goes through its normal routine according to its purpose and goals regardless of the actions of the active agents.

Abstractly, an attack graph is a collection of scenarios showing how a malicious agent can compromise the integrity of a target system. With a suitable model of the system, we can use model checking techniques to generate attack graphs automatically [11, 17, 16]. In this context, correctness properties specify the negation of the attacker's goal: an execution is correct with respect to the property if the attacker does not achieve his goal for that execution. We call such properties *security properties*. An example of a security property in a computer network would be a statement like "the intruder cannot get root access on the web server."

Definition 3. *Given an attack model M, a* security property P *is a subset of the set* $L(M)$ *of executions of M.*

Definition 4. *An execution $\alpha \in L(M)$ is* correct *with respect to a security property P iff $\alpha \in P$. An execution α is* failing *with respect to P (violates P) iff $\alpha \notin P$.*

We say that an attack model M *satisfies* a security property P if it does not have any failing executions (that is, if $L(M) \subset P$). If, however, M does have some failing executions, we say that the set of such executions makes up an attack graph.

Definition 5. *Given an attack model M and a security property P, an* attack graph *of M with respect to P is the set $L(M) \backslash P$ of failing executions of M with respect to P.*

For the remainder of this paper, we restrict the discussion to attack graphs comprised of finite executions only. For a more comprehensive treatment of finite and infinite failing executions we refer the reader to Sheyner [16].

3   Network Attack Graphs

Network attack graphs represent a collection of possible penetration scenarios in a computer network. Each penetration scenario is a sequence of actions taken by the intruder, typically culminating in a particular goal—administrative access on a particular host, access to a database, service disruption, etc. For appropriately constructed network models, attack graphs give a bird's-eye view of every scenario that can lead to a serious security breach.

3.1   Network Attack Model

A *network attack model* is an attack model where the system N is a computer network, the attacker E is a malicious agent trying to circumvent the network's security, and the defender D represents both the system administrator(s) and security software installed on the network. A state transition in a network attack model corresponds to a single action by the intruder, a defensive action by the system administrator, or a routine network action.

Real networks consist of a large variety of hardware and software pieces, most of which are not involved in cyber attacks. We have chosen six network components relevant to constructing network attack models. The components were chosen to include enough information to represent a wide variety of networks and attack scenarios, yet keep the model reasonably simple and small. The following is a list of the components:

1. H, a set of hosts connected to the network
2. C, a connectivity relation expressing the network topology and inter-host reachability
3. T, a relation expressing trust between hosts
4. I, a model of the intruder
5. A, a set of individual actions (exploits) that the intruder can use to construct attack scenarios
6. Ids, a model of the intrusion detection system

We construct an attack model M based on these components. Table 1 defines each agent i's state S_i and action set A_i in terms of the network components. This construction gives the security administrator an entirely passive "detection" role, embodied in the *alarm* action of the intrusion detection system. For simplicity, regular network activity is omitted entirely.

Table 1. Network attack model

Agent $i \in \mathcal{I}$	S_i	A_i
E	I	A
D	Ids	$\{alarm\}$
N	$H \times C \times T$	$\oslash$

It remains to make explicit the transition relation of the attack model M. Each transition $(s_1, s_2) \in \tau$ is either an action by the intruder, or an *alarm* action by the system administrator. An *alarm* action happens whenever the intrusion detection system is able to flag an intruder action. An action $a \in A$ requires that the preconditions of a hold in state s_1 and the effects of a hold in s_2. Action preconditions and effects are explained in Sect. 3.2.

3.2   Network Components

We now give details about each network component.

Hosts. Hosts are the main hubs of activity on a network. They run services, process network requests, and maintain data. With rare exceptions, every action in an attack scenario will target a host in some way. Typically, an action takes advantage of vulnerable or misconfigured software to gain information or access privileges for the attacker. The main goal in modeling hosts is to capture as much information as possible about components that may contribute to creating an exploitable vulnerability.

A host $h \in H$ is a tuple *(id, svcs, sw, vuls)*, where

- *id* is a unique host identifier (typically, name and network address)
- *svcs* is a list of service name/port number pairs describing each service that is active on the host and the port on which the service is listening
- *sw* is a list of other software operating on the host, including the operating system type and version
- *vuls* is a list of host-specific vulnerable components. This list may include installed software with exploitable security flaws (example: a *setuid* program with a buffer overflow problem), or mis-configured environment settings (example: existing user shell for system-only users, such as *ftp*)

Network Connectivity. Following Ritchey and Ammann [15], connectivity is expressed as a ternary relation $C \subseteq H \times H \times P$, where P is a set of integer port numbers. $C(h_1, h_2, p)$ means that host h_2 is reachable from host h_1 on port p. Note that the connectivity relation incorporates firewalls and other elements that restrict the ability of one host to connect to another. Slightly abusing notation, we say $R(h_1, h_2)$ when there is a network route from h_1 to h_2.

Trust. We model trust as a binary relation $T \subseteq H \times H$, where $T(h_1, h_2)$ indicates that a user may log in from host h_2 to host h_1 without authentication (i.e., host h_1 "trusts" host h_2).

Services. The set of services S is a list of unique service names, one for each service that is present on any host on the network. We distinguish services from other software because network services so often serve as a conduit for exploits. Furthermore, services are tied to the connectivity relation via port numbers, and this information must be included in the model of each host. Every service name in each host's list of services comes from the set S.

Intrusion Detection System. We associate a boolean variable with each action, abstractly representing whether or not the IDS can detect that particular action. Actions are classified as being either *detectable* or *stealthy* with respect to the IDS. If an action is detectable, it will trigger an alarm when executed on a host or network segment monitored by the IDS; if an action is *stealthy*, the IDS does not see it.

We specify the IDS as a function *ids*: $H \times H \times A \rightarrow \{d, s, b\}$, where $ids(h_1, h_2, a) = d$ if action a is *detectable* when executed with source host h_1 and target host h_2; $ids(h_1, h_2, a) = s$ if action a is *stealthy* when executed with source host h_1 and target host h_2; and $ids(h_1, h_2, a) = b$ if action a has *both* detectable and stealthy strains, and success in detecting the action depends on which strain is used. When h_1 and h_2 refer to the same host, $ids(h_1, h_2, a)$ specifies the intrusion detection system component (if any) located on that host. When h_1 and h_2 refer to different hosts, $ids(h_1, h_2, a)$ specifies the intrusion detection system component (if any) monitoring the network path between h_1 and h_2.

Actions. Each action is a triple (r, h_s, h_t), where $h_s \in H$ is the host from which the action is launched, $h_t \in H$ is the host targeted by the action, and r is the rule that describes how the intruder can change the network or add to his knowledge about it. A specification of an action rule has four components: *intruder preconditions*, *network preconditions*, *intruder effects*, and *network effects*. The *intruder preconditions* component places conditions on the intruder's store of knowledge and the privilege level required to launch the action. The *network preconditions* specifies conditions on target host state, network connectivity, trust, services, and vulnerabilities that must hold before launching the action. Finally, the *intruder* and *network effects* components list the action's effects on the intruder and on the network, respectively.

Intruder. The intruder has a *store of knowledge* about the target network and its users. The intruder's store of knowledge includes host addresses, known vulnerabilities, user passwords, information gathered with port scans, etc. Also associated with the intruder is the function *plvl: Hosts* $\rightarrow$ *{none, user, root}*, which gives the level of privilege that the intruder has on each host. For simplicity, we model only three privilege levels. There is a strict total order on the privilege levels: *none* $\leq$ *user* $\leq$ *root*.

Omitted Complications. Although we do not model actions taken by user services for the sake of simplicity, doing so in the future would let us ask questions about effects of intrusions on service quality. A more complex model could include services provided by the network to its regular users and other routine network traffic. These details would reflect more realistically the interaction between intruder actions and regular network activity at the expense of additional complexity.

Another activity worth modeling explicitly is administrative steps taken either to hinder an attack in progress or to repair the damage after an attack has occurred. The former corresponds to transitioning to states of the model that offer less opportunity for further penetration; the latter means "undoing" some of the damage caused by successful attacks.

4   Example Network

Figure 3 shows an example network. There are two target hosts, Windows and Linux, on an internal company network, and a Web server on an isolated "demilitarized zone" (DMZ) network. One firewall separates the internal network from the DMZ and another

Fig. 3. Example Network

firewall separates the DMZ from the rest of the Internet. An intrusion detection system (IDS) watches the network traffic between the internal network and the outside world.

The Linux host on the internal network is running several services—Linux "I Seek You" (*LICQ*) chat software, *Squid* web proxy, and a *Database*. The *LICQ* client lets Linux users exchange text messages over the Internet. The *Squid* web proxy is a caching server. It stores requested Internet objects on a system closer to the requesting site than to the source. Web browsers can then use the local *Squid* cache as a proxy, reducing access time as well as bandwidth consumption. The host inside the DMZ is running Microsoft's Internet Information Services (IIS) on a Windows platform.

The intruder launches his attack starting from a single computer, which lies on the outside network. To be concrete, let us assume that his eventual goal is to disrupt the functioning of the database. To achieve this goal, the intruder needs root access on the database host Linux. The five actions at his disposal are summarized in Table 2.

Each of the five actions corresponds to a real-world vulnerability and has an entry in the Common Vulnerabilities and Exposures (CVE) database. CVE [22] is a standard list of names for vulnerabilities and other information security exposures. A CVE identifier is an eight-digit string prefixed with the letters "CVE" (for accepted vulnerabilities) or "CAN" (for candidate vulnerabilities).

Table 2. Intruder actions

Action	Effect	Example CVE ID
IIS buffer overflow	remotely get root	CAN-2002-0364
Squid port scan	port scan	CVE-2001-1030
LICQ gain user	gain user privileges remotely	CVE-2001-0439
scripting exploit	gain user privileges remotely	CAN-2002-0193
local buffer overflow	locally get root	CVE-2002-0004

The IIS buffer overflow action exploits a buffer overflow vulnerability in the Microsoft IIS Web Server to gain administrative privileges remotely.

The *Squid* action lets the attacker scan network ports on machines that would otherwise be inaccessible to him, taking advantage of a misconfigured access control list in the *Squid* web proxy.

The *LICQ* action exploits a problem in the URL parsing function of the *LICQ* software for Unix-flavor systems. An attacker can send a specially-crafted URL to the *LICQ* client to execute arbitrary commands on the client's computer, with the same access privileges as the user of the *LICQ* client.

The scripting action lets the intruder gain user privileges on Windows machines. Microsoft Internet Explorer 5.01 and 6.0 allow remote attackers to execute arbitrary code via malformed Content-Disposition and Content-Type header fields that cause the application for the spoofed file type to pass the file back to the operating system for handling rather than raise an error message. This vulnerability may also be exploited through HTML formatted email. The action requires some social engineering to entice a user to visit a specially-formatted Web page. However, the action can work against firewalled networks, since it requires only that internal users be able to browse the Web through the firewall.

Finally, the local buffer overflow action can exploit a multitude of existing vulnerabilities to let a user without administrative privileges gain them illegitimately. For the CVE number referenced in the table, the action exploits a buffer overflow flaw in the *at* program. The *at* program is a Linux utility for queueing shell commands for later execution.

Some of the actions that we model have multiple instantiations in the CVE database. For example, the local buffer overflow action exploits a common coding error that occurs in many Linux programs. Each program vulnerable to local buffer overflow has a separate CVE entry, and all such entries correspond to the same action rule. The table lists only one example CVE identifier for each rule.

4.1 Example Network Components

Services, Vulnerabilities, and Connectivity. We specify the state of the network to include services running on each host, existing vulnerabilities, and connectivity between hosts. There are five boolean variables for each host, specifying whether any of the three services are running and whether either of two other vulnerabilities are present on that host:

Table 3. Variables specifying a host

variable	meaning
w3svc$_h$	IIS web service running on host h
squid$_h$	*Squid* proxy running on host h
licq$_h$	*LICQ* running on host h
scripting$_h$	HTML scripting is enabled on host h
vul-at$_h$	*at* executable vulnerable to overflow on host h

The model of the target network includes connectivity information among the four hosts. The initial value of the connectivity relation R is shown the following table. An entry in the table corresponds to a pair of hosts (h_1, h_2). IIS and *Squid* listen on port 80 and the *LICQ* client listens on port 5190, and the connectivity relation specifies which of these services can be reached remotely from other hosts. Each entry consists of three boolean values. The first value is 'y' if h_1 and h_2 are connected by a physical link, the second value is 'y' if h_1 can connect to h_2 on port 80, and the third value is 'y' if h_1 can connect to h_2 on port 5190.

We use the connectivity relation to reflect the settings of the firewall as well as the existence of physical links. In the example, the intruder machine initially can reach only the Web server on port 80 due to a strict security policy on the external firewall. The internal firewall is initially used to restrict internal user activity by disallowing most outgoing connections. An important exception is that internal users are permitted to contact the Web server on port 80.

In this example the connectivity relation stays unchanged throughout an attack. In general, the connectivity relation can change as a result of intruder actions. For example,

Table 4. Connectivity relation

Host	Intruder	IIS Web Server	Windows	Linux
Intruder	y,y,y	y,y,n	n,n,n	n,n,n
IIS Web Server	y,n,n	y,y,y	y,y,y	y,y,y
Windows	n,n,n	y,y,n	y,y,y	y,y,y
Linux	n,n,n	y,y,n	y,y,y	y,y,y

an action may enable the intruder to compromise a firewall host and relax the firewall rules.

Intrusion Detection System. A single network-based intrusion detection system protects the internal network. The paths between hosts Intruder and Web and between Windows and Linux are not monitored; the IDS can see the traffic between any other pair of hosts. There are no host-based intrusion detection components. The IDS always detects the *LICQ* action, but cannot see any of the other actions. The IDS is represented with a two-dimensional array of bits, shown in the following table. An entry in the table corresponds to a pair of hosts (h_1, h_2). The value is 'y' if the path between h_1 and h_2 is monitored by the IDS, and 'n' otherwise.

Intruder. The intruder's store of knowledge consists of a single boolean variable 'scan'. The variable indicates whether the intruder has successfully performed a port scan on the target network. For simplicity, we do not keep track of specific information gathered by the scan. It would not be difficult to do so, at the cost of increasing the size of the state space.

Initially, the intruder has root access on his own machine Intruder, but no access to the other hosts. The 'scan' variable is set to *false*.

Actions. There are five action rules corresponding to the five actions in the intruder's arsenal. Throughout the description, S is used to designate the source host and T the target host. $R(S, T, p)$ says that host T is reachable from host S on port p. The abbreviation $plvl(X)$ refers to the intruder's current privilege level on host X.

Recall that a specification of an action rule has four components: *intruder preconditions*, *network preconditions*, *intruder effects*, and *network effects*. The *intruder preconditions* component places conditions on the intruder's store of knowledge and the privilege level required to launch the action. The *network preconditions* component specifies

Table 5. IDS locations

Host	Intruder	IIS Web Server	Windows	Linux
Intruder	n	n	y	y
IIS Web Server	n	n	y	y
Windows	y	y	n	n
Linux	y	y	n	n

conditions on target host state, network connectivity, trust, services, and vulnerabilities that must hold before launching the action. Finally, the *intruder* and *network effects* components list the effects of the action on the intruder's state and on the network, respectively.

Sometimes the intruder has no logical reason to execute a specific action, even if all technical preconditions for the action have been met. For instance, if the intruder's current privileges include root access on the Web Server, the intruder would not need to execute the IIS buffer overflow action against the Web Server host. We have chosen to augment each action's preconditions with a clause that disables the action in instances when the primary purpose of the action has been achieved by other means. This change is not strictly conservative, as it prevents the intruder from using an action for its secondary side effects. However, we feel that this is a reasonable price to pay for removing unnecessary transitions from the attack graphs.

IIS Buffer Overflow. This remote-to-root action immediately gives a remote user a root shell on the target machine.

action IIS-buffer-overflow **is**
    intruder preconditions
        $plvl(S) \geq$ user   *User-level privileges on host S*
        $plvl(T) <$ root   *No root-level privileges on host T*
    network preconditions
        w3svc_T *Host T is running vulnerable IIS server*
        $R(S, T, 80)$ *Host T is reachable from S on port 80*
    intruder effects
        $plvl(T) :=$ root   *Root-level privileges on host T*
    network effects
        $\neg\text{w3svc}_T$ *Host T is not running IIS*
end

Squid Port Scan. The *Squid* port scan action uses a misconfigured *Squid* web proxy to conduct a port scan of neighboring machines and report the results to the intruder.

action squid-port-scan **is**
    intruder preconditions
        $plvl(S) =$ user   *User-level privileges on host S*
        $\neg$scan   *We have not yet performed a port scan*
    network preconditions
        squid_T *Host T is running vulnerable* Squid *proxy*
        $R(S, T, 80)$ *Host T is reachable from S on port 80*
    intruder effects
        scan   *We have performed a port scan on the network*
    network effects
        $\oslash$ *No changes to the network component*
end

LICQ Remote to User. This remote-to-user action immediately gives a remote user a user shell on the target machine. The action rule assumes that a port scan has been performed previously, modeling the fact that such actions typically become apparent to the intruder only after a scan reveals the possibility of exploiting software listening on lesser-known ports.

action LICQ-remote-to-user **is**
    intruder preconditions
        $plvl(S) \geq$ user   *User-level privileges on host S*
        $plvl(T) =$ none   *No user-level privileges on host T*
        scan   *We have performed a port scan on the network*
    network preconditions
        $licq_T$ *Host T is running vulnerable LICQ software*
        $R(S, T, 5190)$ *Host T is reachable from S on port 5190*
    intruder effects
        $plvl(T) :=$ user   *User-level privileges on host T*
    network effects
        $\oslash$ *No changes to the network component*
end

Scripting Action. This remote-to-user action immediately gives a remote user a user shell on the target machine. The action rule does not model the social engineering required to get a user to download a specially-created Web page.

action client-scripting **is**
    intruder preconditions
        $plvl(S) \geq$ user   *User-level privileges on host S*
        $plvl(T) =$ none   *No user-level privileges on host T*
    network preconditions
        $scripting_T$ *HTML scripting is enabled on host T*
        $R(T, S, 80)$ *Host S is reachable from T on port 80*
    intruder effects
        $plvl(T) :=$ user   *User-level privileges on host T*
    network effects
        $\oslash$ *No changes to the network component*
end

Local Buffer Overflow. If the intruder has acquired a user shell on the target machine, this action exploits a buffer overflow vulnerability on a *setuid root* file (in this case, the *at* executable) to gain root access.

action local-setuid-buffer-overflow **is**
    intruder preconditions
        $plvl(T) =$ user   *User-level privileges on host T*

network preconditions
    vul-at$_T$ *There is a vulnerable* at *executable*
intruder effects
    $plvl(T) :=$ root   *Root-level privileges on host* T
network effects
    ⊘   *No changes to the network component*
end

4.2   Sample Attack Graphs

Figure 4 shows a screenshot of the attack graph generated with our attack graph toolkit for the security property

$$\mathbf{G}\ (intruder.privilege[lin] < root)$$

which states that the intruder will never attain root privileges on the `Linux` host. In Figure 4, a sample attack scenario is highlighted with solid square nodes, with each attack step identified by name and CVE number. Since the external firewall restricts most network connections from the outside, the intruder has no choice with respect to the initial step—it must be a buffer overflow action on the IIS Web server. Once the intruder has access to the Web server machine, his options expand. The highlighted scenario is the shortest route to success. The intruder uses the Web server machine to launch a port scan via the vulnerable *Squid* proxy running on the Linux host. The scan discovers that it is possible to obtain user privileges on the Linux host with the *LICQ* exploit. After that, a simple local buffer overflow gives the intruder administrative control over the `Linux` machine. The last transition in the action path is a bookkeeping step, signifying the intruder's success.

Any information explicitly represented in the model is available for inspection and analysis in the attack graph. For instance, with a few clicks we are able to highlight

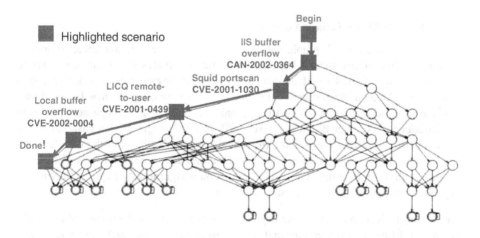

Fig. 4. Example Attack Graph

portions of the graph "covered" by the intrusion detection system. Figure 5 shades the nodes where the IDS alarm has been sounded. These nodes lie on paths that use the *LICQ* action along a network path monitored by the IDS. It is clear that while a substantial portion of the graph is covered by the IDS, the intruder can escape detection and still succeed by taking one of the paths on the right side of the graph. One such attack scenario is highlighted with square nodes in Figure 5. It is very similar to the attack scenario discussed in the previous paragraph, except that the *LICQ* action is launched from the internal Windows machine, where the intrusion detection system does not see it. To prepare for launching the *LICQ* action from the Windows machine, an additional step is needed to obtain user privileges in the machine. For that, the intruder uses the client scripting exploit on the Windows host immediately after taking over the Web machine.

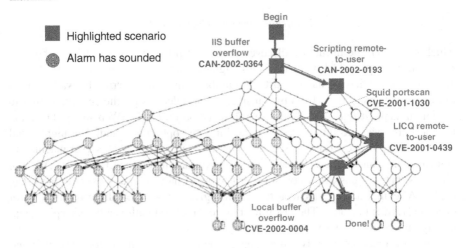

Fig. 5. Alternative Attack Scenario Avoiding the IDS

4.3   Sample Attack Graph Analysis

After generating an attack graph, we can use it to analyze potential effectiveness of various security improvements [16]. To demonstrate the analysis techniques, we expand the example from Sect. 4.1 with an extra host User on the external network and several new actions. An authorized user W of the internal network owns the new host and uses it as a terminal to work remotely on the internal Windows host. The new actions permit the intruder to take over the host User, sniff user W's login credentials, and log in to the internal Windows host using the stolen credentials. We omit the details of the new actions, as they are not essential to understanding the examples. Figure 6(a) shows the full graph for the modified example. The graph is significantly larger, reflecting the expanded number of choices available to the intruder.

Single Action Removal. A simple kind of analysis determines the impact of removing one action from the intruder's arsenal. Recall from Sect. 3 that each action is a triple (r, h_s, h_t), where $h_s \in H$ is the host from which the attack is launched, $h_t \in H$ is the host targeted by the attack, and r is an action rule. The user specifies a set A_{rem} of action triples to be removed from the attack graph. The toolkit deletes the transitions corresponding to each triple in the set A_{rem} from the graph and then removes the nodes that have become unreachable from the initial state.

As demonstrated in Figure 6, this procedure can be repeated several times, reducing the size of the attack graph at each step. The full graph in Figure 6(a) has 362 states. Removing one of two ways the intruder can sniff user W's login credentials produces the graph in Figure 6(b), with 213 states. Removing one of the local buffer overflow actions produces the graph in Figure 6(c), with 66 states. At each step, the user is able to judge visually the impact of removing a single action from the intruder's arsenal.

Critical Action Sets. Once an attack graph is generated, an approximation algorithm can find an approximately-optimal *critical set of actions* that will completely disconnect the initial state from states where the intruder has achieved his goals [16]. A related algorithm can find an approximately-optimal set of security measures that accomplish the same goal. With a single click, the user can invoke both of these exposure minimization algorithms.

The effect of the critical action set algorithm on the modified example attack graph is shown in Figure 7(a). The algorithm finds a critical action set of size 1, containing the port scan action exploiting the *Squid* web proxy. The graph nodes and edges corresponding to actions in the critical set computed by the algorithm are highlighted in the toolkit by shading the relevant nodes. The shaded nodes are seen clearly when we zoom in to inspect a part of the graph on a larger scale (Figure 7(b)).

Since the computed action set is always critical, removing every action triple in the set from the intruder's arsenal is guaranteed to result in an empty attack graph. In the example, we might patch the Linux machine with a new version of the *Squid* proxy, thereby removing every action triple that uses the *Squid* port scan rule on the Linux machine from the intruder's arsenal.

5   Attack Graph Toolkit

We have implemented a toolkit for generating and exploring attack graphs, using network attack models defined in Sect. 3. In this section we describe the toolkit and show several ways to integrate it with external data sources that supply information necessary to build a network attack model. Specifically, it is necessary to know the topology of the target network, configuration of the network hosts, and vulnerabilities present on the network. In addition, we require access to a database of attack rules to build the transition relation of the attack model. We could expect the user to specify all of the necessary information manually, but such a task is tedious, error-prone, and unrealistic for networks of more than a few nodes.

We recommend deploying the attack graph toolkit in conjunction with information-gathering systems that supply some of the data automatically. We integrated the attack graph generator with two such systems, MITRE Corp's Outpost and Lockheed Martin's ANGI. We report on our experience with Outpost and ANGI in Sections 5.4 and 5.5.

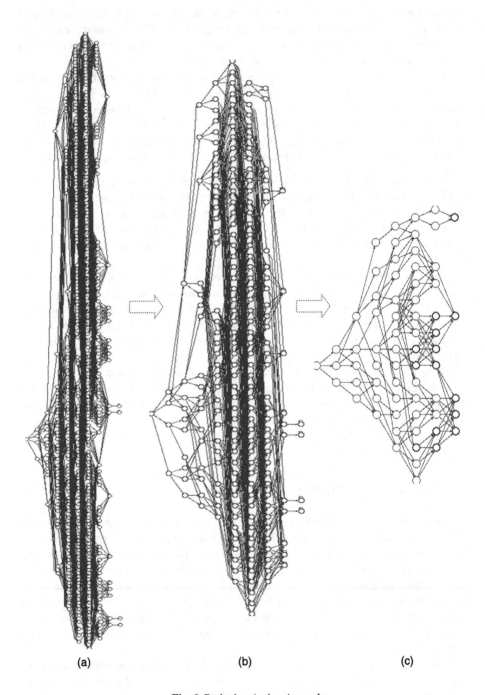

(a)   (b)   (c)

Fig. 6. Reducing Action Arsenal

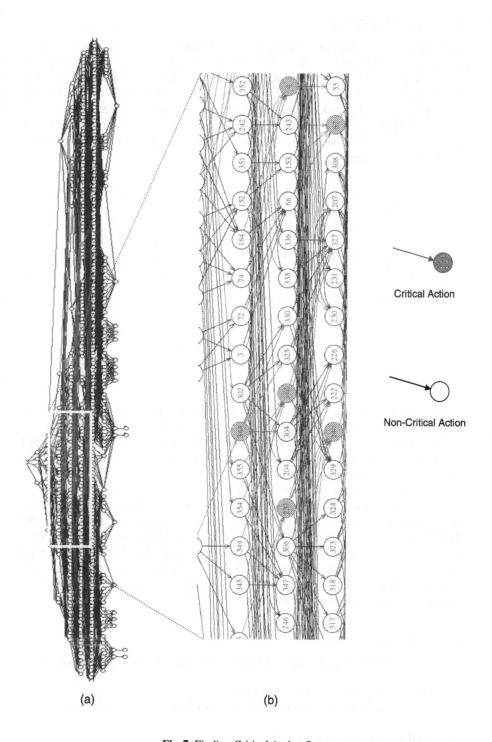

Fig. 7. Finding Critical Action Sets

5.1   Toolkit Architecture

Figure 8 shows the architecture of the attack graph toolkit. There are three main pieces: a *network model builder*, a *scenario graph generator*, and a *graphical user interface* (GUI). The network model builder takes as input information about network topology, configuration data for each networked host, and a library of attack rules. It constructs a finite model of the network suitable for automated analysis. The model is augmented with a security specification, which spells out the security requirements against which the attack graph is to be built. The model and the security specification then go to the second piece, the scenario graph generator.

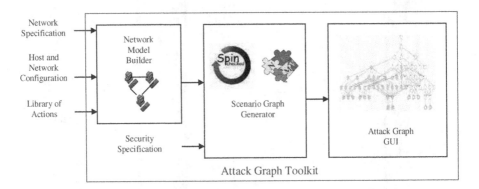

Fig. 8. Toolkit Architecture

The scenario graph generator takes any finite model and correctness specification and produces a graph composed of possible executions of the model that violate the correctness specification. The model builder constructs the input to the graph generator so that the output will be the desired attack graph. The graphical user interface lets the user display and examine the graph.

The model builder's running time is linear in the size of the input specification, typically written in the XML format specified in Sect. 5.2. The algorithm in the scenario graph generator is linear in the size of the output scenario graph [16]. The slowest part of the toolkit is the algorithm that lays out the attack graph on screen. The algorithm uses the network simplex method to find optimal x-coordinates. The simplex method has exponential worst-case performance. The rest of the layout algorithm has cubic complexity. Thus, for large graphs it is sometimes necessary to run analysis algorithms without displaying the full graph on screen.

5.2   The Model Builder

Recall from Sect. 3 that a network attack model consists of six primary components:

1. H, a set of hosts connected to the network
2. C, a connectivity relation expressing the network topology and inter-host reachability
3. T, a relation expressing trust between hosts

4. *I*, a model of the intruder
5. *A*, a set of individual attack actions
6. *Ids*, a model of the intrusion detection system

To construct each of the six components, the model builder needs to collect the following pieces of information. For the entire network, we need:

1. The set of hosts *H*
2. The network topology and firewall rules, which together induce the connectivity relation *C*
3. The initial state of the trust relation *T*: which hosts are trusted by other hosts prior to any intruder action

Several pieces of data are required for each host *h* in the set *H*:

4. A unique host identifier (usually name and network address)
5. Operating system vendor and version
6. Active network services with port numbers
7. Common Vulnerabilities and Exposures IDs of all vulnerabilities present on *h*
8. User-specific configuration parameters

Finally, for each CVE vulnerability present on at least one host in the set *H*, we need:

9. An attack rule with preconditions and effects

We designed an XML-based format covering all of the information that the model builder requires. The XML format lets the user specify each piece of information manually or indicate that the data can be gathered automatically from an external source. A typical description of a host in XML is as follows:

```
1   <host id="typical-machine" ip="192.168.0.1">
2
3     <services>
4       <ftp port="21"/>
5       <W3SVC port="80"/>
6     </services>
7
8     <connectivity>
9       <remote id="machine1" <ftp/> <W3SVC/> </remote>
10      <remote id="machine2"> <sshd/> <W3SVC/> </remote>
11      <remote id="machine3"> <sshd/> </remote>
12    </connectivity>
13
14    <cve>
15      <CAN-2002-0364/>
16      <CAN-2002-0147/>
17    </cve>
18
19  </host>
```

The example description provides the host name and network identification (line 1), a list of active services with port numbers (lines 3-6), the part of the connectivity relation that involves the host (lines 8-12), and names of CVE and CVE-candidate (CAN) vulnerabilities known to be present on the host (lines 14-17). Connectivity is specified as a list of services that the host can reach on each remote machine. Lines 9-11 each specify one remote machine; e.g., `typical-machine` can reach `machine1` on ports assigned to the *ftp* and *W3SVC* (IIS Web Server) services.

It is unrealistic to expect the user to collect and specify all of the data by hand. In Sections 5.3-5.5 we discuss three external data sources that supply some of the information automatically: the Nessus vulnerability scanner, MITRE Corp.'s Outpost, and Lockheed Martin's ANGI. Whenever the model builder can get a specific piece of information from one of these sources, a special tag is placed in the XML file. If Nessus, Outpost and ANGI are all available at the same time as sources of information, the above host description may look as follows:

```
<host id="typical-machine" ip="|Outpost|">

  <services source="|Outpost|"/>
  <connectivity source="|ANGI|"/>
  <cve source="|Nessus|"/>

</host>
```

The model builder gets the host network address and the list of running services from Outpost, connectivity information from ANGI, and a list of existing vulnerabilities from Nessus. Once all of the relevant information is gathered, the model builder creates a finite model and encodes it in the input language of the scenario graph generator. The scenario graph generator then builds the attack graph.

5.3   Attack Graphs with Nessus

A savvy attacker might use one of the many widely available vulnerability scanners [4] to discover facts about the network and construct an attack scenario manually. Similarly, an attack graph generator can use a scanner to construct such scenarios automatically. Our attack graph toolkit works with the freeware vulnerability scanner Nessus [8] to gather information about reachable hosts, services running on those hosts, and any known exploitable vulnerabilities that can be detected remotely.

The scanner has no internal knowledge of the target hosts, and will usually discover only part of the information necessary to construct a graph that includes every possible attack scenario. Using only an external vulnerability scanner to gather information can lead the system administrator to miss important attack scenarios.

Nevertheless, the administrator can run vulnerability scanners against his own network to find out what a real attacker would discover. In the future, sophisticated intruders are likely to use attack graph generators to help them devise attack scenarios. As a part of network security strategy, we recommend running a vulnerability scanner in conjunction with an attack graph generator periodically to discover avenues of attack that are most likely to be exploited in practice.

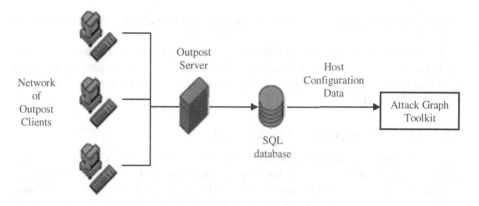

Fig. 9. Outpost Architecture

5.4   Attack Graphs with MITRE Outpost

MITRE Corporation's Outpost is a system for collecting, organizing, and maintaining security-related information on computer networks. It is a suite of inter-related security applications that share a common data model and a common data collection infrastructure. The goal of Outpost is to provide a flexible and open environment for network and system administrators to monitor, control, and protect computer systems.

At the center of the Outpost System is a data collection/probe execution engine that gathers specific configuration information from all of the systems within a network. The collected data is stored in a central database for analysis by the Outpost applications. Outpost collects data about individual hosts only, so it cannot provide information about network topology or attack rules. Since Outpost stores all of the data in a network-accessible SQL database, we retrieve the data directly from the database, without talking to the Outpost server, as shown in Figure 9.

Currently Outpost works with SQL databases supported by Microsoft and Oracle. Both of these packages use a proprietary Application Programming Interface. The model builder includes an interface to each database, as well as a generic module that uses the Open DataBase Connectivity interface (ODBC) and works with any database that supports ODBC. Furthermore, it is easy to add a capability to interface with other types of databases.

An Outpost-populated database contains a list of client hosts monitored by the Outpost server. For the model builder, the Outpost server can provide most of the required information about each individual host h, including:

1. A unique host identifier (usually name and network address)
2. Operating system vendor and version
3. Active network services with port numbers
4. Common Vulnerabilities and Exposures IDs of all vulnerabilities present on h
5. User-specific configuration parameters (e.g., is Javascript enabled for the user's email client?)

Outpost's lists of CVE vulnerabilities are usually incomplete, and it does not keep track of some of the user-specific configuration parameters required by the attack graph toolkit. Until these deficiencies are fixed, the user must provide the missing information manually.

In the future, the Outpost server will inform the attack graph toolkit whenever changes are made to the database. The tighter integration with Outpost will enable attack graph toolkit to re-generate attack graphs automatically every time something changes in the network configuration.

5.5   Attack Graphs with Lockheed's ANGI

Lockheed Martin Advanced Technology Laboratory's (ATL) Next Generation Infrastructure (ANGI) IR&D project is building systems that can be deployed in dynamic, distributed, and open network environments. ANGI collects local sensor information continuously on each network host. The sensor data is shared among the hosts, providing dynamic awareness of the network status to each host. ANGI sensors gather information about host addresses, host programs and services, and network topology. In addition, ANGI supports vulnerability assessment sensors for threat analysis.

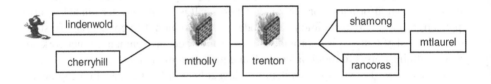

Fig. 10. ANGI Network

Two distinguishing features of ANGI are the ability to discover network topology changes dynamically and focus on technologies for pro-active, automated repair of network problems. ANGI is capable of providing the attack graph model builder with network topology information, which is not available in Outpost and is not gathered by Nessus.

We tested our attack graph toolkit integrated with ANGI on a testbed of five hosts with combinations of the five CVE vulnerabilities specified for the example model in Chapter 4 (p. 352), and one adversary host. Figure 10 is a screenshot of the testbed network schematic. The intruder resides on the host lindenwold. Hosts trenton and mtholly run firewalls, which are initially disabled. We assume that the target of the intruder is the host shamong, which contains some critical resource.

ANGI combines information about each host with data from firewall configuration files into a single XML document. To convert firewall rules into a reachability relation C accepted by the attack graph toolkit, ANGI uses a package developed at MITRE Corp. that computes network reachability from packet filter data [14]. The XML file specifies explicitly five attack rules corresponding to the CVE vulnerabilities present on the hosts. ANGI then calls the model builder with the XML document and a security property as inputs. The security property specifies a guarantee of protection for the critical resource host shamong:

$$\mathbf{G}(intruder.privilege[shamong] < root)$$

The attack graph generator finds several potential attack scenarios. Figure 11 shows the attack graph as it is displayed by the graphical user interface. The graph consists of 19 nodes with 28 edges.

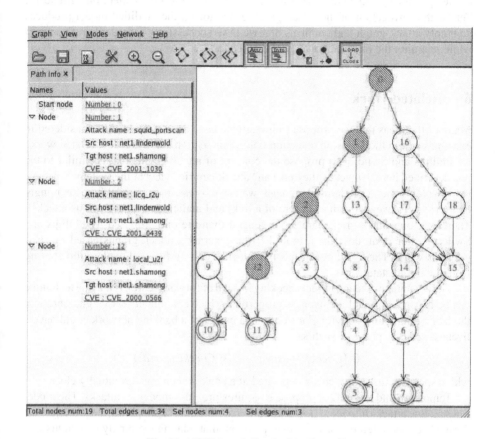

Fig. 11. ANGI Attack Graph - No Firewalls

Exploring the attack graph reveals that several successful attack scenarios exploit the *LICQ* vulnerability on the host shamong. One such attack scenario is highlighted in Figure 11. As indicated in the "Path Info" pane on the left of Figure 11, the second step of the highlighted scenario exploits the *LICQ* vulnerability on shamong. This suggests a possible strategy for reducing the size of the graph. Using the ANGI interface, we enable the firewall on the host trenton, and add a rule that blocks all external traffic at trenton from reaching shamong on the *LICQ* port. ANGI then generates a new XML model file reflecting this change. The new graph demonstrates a significant reduction in network exposure from this relatively small change in network configuration. The modification reduces graph size to 7 nodes and 6 edges with only two possible paths. (Contrast this new graph with the attack graph shown in Figure 11, which has 19 nodes, 28 edges, and 20 paths.)

Looking at the scenarios in this new graph, we discover that the attacker can still reach `shamong` by first compromising the web server on `cherryhill`. Since we do not want to disable the web server, we enable the firewall on `mtholly` and add a rule specifically blocking `cherryhill`'s access to the *LICQ* client on `shamong`. Yet another invocation of the attack graph generator on the modified model produces an empty attack graph and confirms that we have successfully safeguarded `shamong` while retaining the full functionality of the network.

6   Related Work

Many of the ideas that we propose to investigate have been suggested or considered in existing work in the intrusion detection field. This section surveys recent related work.

Phillips and Swiler [13] propose the concept of attack graphs that is similar to the one described here. However, they take an "attack-centric" view of the system. Since we work with a general modeling language, we can express in our model both seemingly benign system events (such as failure of a link) and malicious events (such as attacks). Therefore, our attack graphs are more general than the one proposed by Phillips and Swiler. Swiler et al. describe a tool [19] for generating attack graphs based on their previous work. Their tool constructs the attack graph by forward exploration starting from the initial state.

The advantage of using model checking instead of forward search is that the technique can be expanded to include liveness properties, which can model service guarantees in the face of malicious activity. For example, a model of a banking network could have a liveness security property such as

$$\mathbf{G} \ (CheckDeposited \ \rightarrow \ (\mathbf{F} \ CheckCleared))$$

which specifies that every check deposited at a bank branch must eventually clear.

Templeton and Levitt [20] propose a requires/provides model for attacks. The model links atomic attacks into scenarios, with earlier atomic attacks supplying the prerequisites for the later ones. Templeton and Levitt point out that relating seemingly innocuous system behavior to known attack scenarios can help discover new atomic attacks. However, they do not consider combining their attack scenarios into attack graphs.

Cuppens and Ortalo [6] propose a declarative language (LAMBDA) for specifying attacks in terms of pre- and post-conditions. LAMBDA is a superset of the simple language we used to model attacks in our work. The language is modular and hierarchical; higher-level attacks can be described using lower-level attacks as components. LAMBDA also includes intrusion detection elements. Attack specifications includes information about the steps needed to detect the attack and the steps needed to verify that the attack has already been carried out. Using a database of attacks specified in LAMBDA, Cuppens and Miege [5] propose a method for alert correlation based on matching post-conditions of some attacks with pre-conditions of other attacks that may follow. In effect, they exploit the fact that alerts about attacks are more likely to be related if the corresponding attacks can be a part of the same attack scenario.

Dacier [7] proposes the concept of privilege graphs. Each node in the privilege graph represents a set of privileges owned by the user; edges represent vulnerabilities. Privilege graphs are then explored to construct attack state graphs, which represents different ways in which an intruder can reach a certain goal, such as root access on a host. He also defines a metric, called the *mean effort to failure* or METF, based on the attack state graphs. Orlato *et al.* describe an experimental evaluation of a framework based on these ideas [12]. At the surface, our notion of attack graphs seems similar to the one proposed by Dacier. However, as is the case with Phillips and Swiler, Dacier takes an "attack-centric" view of the world. As pointed out above, our attack graphs are more general. From the experiments conducted by Orlato *et al.* it appears that even for small examples the space required to construct attack state graphs becomes prohibitive. By basing our algorithm on model checking we take advantage of advances in representing large state spaces and can thus hope to represent large attack graphs.

Ritchey and Ammann [15] also use model checking for vulnerability analysis of networks. They use the (unmodified) model checker SMV [18]. They can obtain only one counter-example, i.e., only one attack corresponding to an unsafe state. In contrast, we modified the model checker NuSMV to produce attack graphs, representing all possible attacks. We also described post-facto analyzes that can be performed on these attack graphs. These analysis techniques cannot be meaningfully performed on single attacks.

Graph-based data structures have also been used in network intrusion detection systems, such as *NetSTAT* [21]. There are two major components in NetSTAT, a set of probes placed at different points in the network and an analyzer. The analyzer processes events generated by the probes and generates alarms by consulting a network fact base and a scenario database. The network fact base contains information (such as connectivity) about the network being monitored. The scenario database has a directed graph representation of various atomic attacks. For example, the graph corresponding to an IP spoofing attack shows various steps that an intruder takes to mount that specific attack. The authors state that "in the analysis process the most critical operation is the generation of all possible instances of an attack scenario with respect to a given target network."

Ammann et. al. present a scalable attack graph representation [1]. They encode attack graphs as dependencies among exploits and security conditions, under the assumption of monotonicity. Informally, monotonicity means that no action an intruder can take interferes with the intruder's ability to take any other actions. The authors treat vulnerabilities, intruder access privileges, and network connectivity as atomic boolean attributes. Actions are treated as atomic transformations that, given a set of preconditions on the attributes, establish a set of postconditions. In this model, monotonicity means that (1) once a postcondition is satisfied, it can never become 'unsatisfied', and (2) the negation operator cannot be used in expressing action preconditions.

The authors show that under the monotonicity assumption it is possible to construct an efficient (low-order polynomial) attack graph representation that scales well. They present an efficient algorithm for extracting minimal attack scenarios from the representation, and suggest that a standard graph algorithm can produce a critical set of actions that disconnects the goal state of the intruder from the initial state.

This approach is less general than our treatment of attack graphs. In addition to the monotonicity requirement, it can handle only simple safety properties. Further, the compact attack graph representation is less explicit, and therefore harder for a human to read. The advantage of the approach is that it has a worst-case bound on the size of the graph that is polynomial in the number of atomic attributes in the model, and therefore can scale better than full-fledged model checking to large networks.

7   Summary and Current Status

We have designed, implemented, and tested algorithms for automatically generating attack graphs and for performing different kinds of vulnerability analyses on them. We have built an attack graph toolkit to support our generation and analysis algorithms. The toolkit has an easy-to-use graphical user interface. We integrated our tools with external sources to populate our network attack model with host and vulnerability data automatically.

We are in the process of specifying a library of actions based on a vulnerability database provided to us by SEI/CERT. This database has over 150 actions representing many published CVEs. We have preliminary results in using a subset of 30 of these actions as input to our model builder, allowing us to produce attack graphs with over 300 nodes and 3000 edges in just a few minutes. Most telling, is that once graphs are that large, automated analysis, such as the kind we provide, is essential.

With our current toolkit and our growing library of actions, we are now performing systematic experiments: on different network configurations, with different subsets of actions, and for different attacker goals. The ultimate goal is to help the system administrator—by giving him a fast and completely automatic way to test out different system configurations (e.g., network connectivity, firewall rules, services running on hosts), and by finding new attacks to which his system is vulnerable.

References

1. Paul Ammann, Duminda Wijesekera, and Saket Kaushik. Scalable, graph-based network vulnerability analysis. In *9th ACM Conference on Computer and Communications Security*, pages 217–224, 2002.
2. G. Ausiello, A. D'Atri, and M. Protasi. Structure preserving reductions among convex optimization problems. *Journal of Computational System Sciences*, 21:136–153, 1980.
3. T.H. Cormen, C.E. Leiserson, and R.L. Rivest. *Introduction to Algorithms*. MIT Press, 1985.
4. Cotse.net. Vulnerability Scanners. *http://www.cotse.com/tools/vuln.htm*.
5. Frederic Cuppens and Alexandre Miege. Alert correlation in a cooperative intrusion detection framework. In 23rd *IEEE Symposium on Security and Privacy*, May 2002.
6. Frederic Cuppens and Rodolphe Ortalo. Lambda: A language to model a database for detection of attacks. In *Proceedings of the Third International Workshop on the Recent Advances in Intrusion Detection (RAID)*, number 1907 in LNCS, pages 197–216. Springer-Verlag, 2000.
7. M. Dacier. *Towards Quantitative Evaluation of Computer Security*. PhD thesis, Institut National Polytechnique de Toulouse, December 1994.
8. Renaud Deraison. Nessus Scanner. *http://www.nessus.org*.
9. Somesh Jha, Oleg Sheyner, and Jeannette M. Wing. Minimization and reliability analyses of attack graphs. Technical Report CMU-CS-02-109, Carnegie Mellon University, February 2002.

10. Somesh Jha, Oleg Sheyner, and Jeannette M. Wing. Two formal analyses of attack graphs. In *Proceedings of the 15th IEEE Computer Security Foundations Workshop*, pages 49–63, Nova Scotia, Canada, June 2002.

11. Somesh Jha and Jeannette Wing. Survivability analysis of networked systems. In *Proceedings of the International Conference on Software Engineering*, Toronto, Canada, May 2001.

12. R. Ortalo, Y. Dewarte, and M. Kaaniche. Experimenting with quantitative evaluation tools for monitoring operational security. *IEEE Transactions on Software Engineering*, 25(5):633–650, September/October 1999.

13. C.A. Phillips and L.P. Swiler. A graph-based system for network vulnerability analysis. In *New Security Paradigms Workshop*, pages 71–79, 1998.

14. John Ramsdell. Frame propagation. MITRE Corp., 2001.

15. R.W. Ritchey and P. Ammann. Using model checking to analyze network vulnerabilities. In *Proceedings of the IEEE Symposium on Security and Privacy*, pages 156–165, May 2001.

16. Oleg Sheyner. *Scenario Graphs and Attack Graphs*. PhD thesis, Carnegie Mellon University, 2004.

17. Oleg Sheyner, Joshua Haines, Somesh Jha, Richard Lippmann, and Jeannette Wing. Automated generation and analysis of attack graphs. In *Proceedings of the IEEE Symposium on Security and Privacy*, 2002.

18. SMV. SMV: A Symbolic Model Checker. http://www.cs.cmu.edu/~modelcheck/.

19. L.P. Swiler, C. Phillips, D. Ellis, and S. Chakerian. Computer-attack graph generation tool. In *Proceedings of the DARPA Information Survivability Conference and Exposition*, June 2000.

20. Steven Templeton and Karl Levitt. A requires/provides model for computer attacks. In *Proceedings of the New Security Paradigms Workshop*, Cork, Ireland, 2000.

21. G. Vigna and R.A. Kemmerer. Netstat: A network-based intrusion detection system. *Journal of Computer Security*, 7(1), 1999.

22. Common Vulnerabilities and Exposures. http://www.cve.mitre.org.

Author Index

Benveniste, Albert 1
Bergstra, Jan A. 17
Bhargavan, Karthikeyan 197
Börger, Egon 42

Caillaud, Benoît 1
Carloni, Luca P. 1
Caspi, Paul 1

Damm, Werner 77
de Boer, Frank S. 111
Defour, Olivier 260
Diaconescu, Răzvan 134

Engels, Gregor 157

Fiadeiro, José Luiz 177
Fournet, Cédric 197

Gordon, Andrew D. 197
Gössler, Gregor 314
Groote, Jan Friso 223
Gurevich, Yuri 240

Hungar, Hardi 77

Ioustinova, Natalia 292

Jézéquel, Jean-Marc 260

Küster, Jochen M. 157

Lopes, Antónia 177

Olderog, Ernst-Rüdiger 77

Pierik, Cees 111
Plouzeau, Noël 260
Pucella, Riccardo 197

Rossman, Benjamin 240
Rutten, J.J.M.M. 276

Sangiovanni-Vincentelli, Alberto L. 1
Schulte, Wolfram 240
Sheyner, Oleg 344
Sidorova, Natalia 292
Sifakis, Joseph 314
Stärk, Robert F. 42
Steffen, Martin 292

Wehrheim, Heike 330
Willemse, Tim A.C. 223
Wing, Jeannette 344

Author Index.

Lecture Notes in Computer Science

For information about Vols. 1–3154

please contact your bookseller or Springer

Vol. 3274: R. Guerraoui (Ed.), Distributed Computing. XIII, 465 pages. 2004.

Vol. 3273: T. Baar, A. Strohmeier, A. Moreira, S.J. Mellor (Eds.), <<UML>> 2004 - The Unified Modelling Language. XIII, 449 pages. 2004.

Vol. 3271: J. Vicente, D. Hutchison (Eds.), Management of Multimedia Networks and Services. XIII, 335 pages. 2004.

Vol. 3266: J. Solé-Pareta, M. Smirnov, P.V. Mieghem, J. Domingo-Pascual, E. Monteiro, P. Reichl, B. Stiller, R.J. Gibbens (Eds.), Quality of Service in the Emerging Networking Panorama. XVI, 390 pages. 2004.

Vol. 3263: M. Weske, P. Liggesmeyer (Eds.), Object-Oriented and Internet-Based Technologies. XII, 239 pages. 2004.

Vol. 3260: I. Niemegeers, S.H. de Groot (Eds.), Personal Wireless Communications. XIV, 478 pages. 2004.

Vol. 3258: M. Wallace (Ed.), Principles and Practice of Constraint Programming – CP 2004. XVII, 822 pages. 2004.

Vol. 3256: H. Ehrig, G. Engels, F. Parisi-Presicce (Eds.), Graph Transformations. XII, 451 pages. 2004.

Vol. 3255: A. Benczúr, J. Demetrovics, G. Gottlob (Eds.), Advances in Databases and Information Systems. XI, 423 pages. 2004.

Vol. 3254: E. Macii, V. Paliouras, O. Koufopavlou (Eds.), Integrated Circuit and System Design. XVI, 910 pages. 2004.

Vol. 3253: Y. Lakhnech, S. Yovine (Eds.), Formal Techniques, Modelling and Analysis of Timed and Fault-tolerant Systems. X, 397 pages. 2004.

Vol. 3250: L.-J. (LJ) Zhang, M. Jeckle (Eds.), Web Services. X, 300 pages. 2004.

Vol. 3249: B. Buchberger, J.A. Campbell (Eds.), Artificial Intelligence and Symbolic Computation. X, 285 pages. 2004. (Subseries LNAI).

Vol. 3246: A. Apostolico, M. Melucci (Eds.), String Processing and Information Retrieval. XIV, 332 pages. 2004.

Vol. 3245: E. Suzuki, S. Arikawa (Eds.), Discovery Science. XIV, 430 pages. 2004. (Subseries LNAI).

Vol. 3244: S. Ben-David, J. Case, A. Maruoka (Eds.), Algorithmic Learning Theory. XIV, 505 pages. 2004. (Subseries LNAI).

Vol. 3242: X. Yao, E. Burke, J.A. Lozano, J. Smith, J.J. Merelo-Guervós, J.A. Bullinaria, J. Rowe, P. Tiño, A. Kabán, H.-P. Schwefel (Eds.), Parallel Problem Solving from Nature - PPSN VIII. XX, 1185 pages. 2004.

Vol. 3241: D. Kranzlmüller, P. Kacsuk, J.J. Dongarra (Eds.), Recent Advances in Parallel Virtual Machine and Message Passing Interface. XIII, 452 pages. 2004.

Vol. 3240: I. Jonassen, J. Kim (Eds.), Algorithms in Bioinformatics. IX, 476 pages. 2004. (Subseries LNBI).

Vol. 3239: G. Nicosia, V. Cutello, P.J. Bentley, J. Timmis (Eds.), Artificial Immune Systems. XII, 444 pages. 2004.

Vol. 3238: S. Biundo, T. Frühwirth, G. Palm (Eds.), KI 2004: Advances in Artificial Intelligence. XI, 467 pages. 2004. (Subseries LNAI).

Vol. 3232: R. Heery, L. Lyon (Eds.), Research and Advanced Technology for Digital Libraries. XV, 528 pages. 2004.

Vol. 3229: J.J. Alferes, J. Leite (Eds.), Logics in Artificial Intelligence. XIV, 744 pages. 2004. (Subseries LNAI).

Vol. 3225: K. Zhang, Y. Zheng (Eds.), Information Security. XII, 442 pages. 2004.

Vol. 3224: E. Jonsson, A. Valdes, M. Almgren (Eds.), Recent Advances in Intrusion Detection. XII, 315 pages. 2004.

Vol. 3223: K. Slind, A. Bunker, G. Gopalakrishnan (Eds.), Theorem Proving in Higher Order Logics. VIII, 337 pages. 2004.

Vol. 3221: S. Albers, T. Radzik (Eds.), Algorithms – ESA 2004. XVIII, 836 pages. 2004.

Vol. 3220: J.C. Lester, R.M. Vicari, F. Paraguaçu (Eds.), Intelligent Tutoring Systems. XXI, 920 pages. 2004.

Vol. 3219: M. Heisel, P. Liggesmeyer, S. Wittmann (Eds.), Computer Safety, Reliability, and Security. XI, 339 pages. 2004.

Vol. 3217: C. Barillot, D.R. Haynor, P. Hellier (Eds.), Medical Image Computing and Computer-Assisted Intervention – MICCAI 2004. XXXVIII, 1114 pages. 2004.

Vol. 3216: C. Barillot, D.R. Haynor, P. Hellier (Eds.), Medical Image Computing and Computer-Assisted Intervention – MICCAI 2004. XXXVIII, 930 pages. 2004.

Vol. 3215: M.G. Negoita, R.J. Howlett, L. Jain (Eds.), Knowledge-Based Intelligent Information and Engineering Systems. LVII, 906 pages. 2004. (Subseries LNAI).

Vol. 3214: M.G. Negoita, R.J. Howlett, L. Jain (Eds.), Knowledge-Based Intelligent Information and Engineering Systems. LVIII, 1302 pages. 2004. (Subseries LNAI).

Vol. 3213: M.G. Negoita, R.J. Howlett, L. Jain (Eds.), Knowledge-Based Intelligent Information and Engineering Systems. LVIII, 1280 pages. 2004. (Subseries LNAI).

Vol. 3212: A. Campilho, M. Kamel (Eds.), Image Analysis and Recognition. XXIX, 862 pages. 2004.

Vol. 3211: A. Campilho, M. Kamel (Eds.), Image Analysis and Recognition. XXIX, 880 pages. 2004.

Vol. 3210: J. Marcinkowski, A. Tarlecki (Eds.), Computer Science Logic. XI, 520 pages. 2004.

Vol. 3208: H.J. Ohlbach, S. Schaffert (Eds.), Principles and Practice of Semantic Web Reasoning. VII, 165 pages. 2004.

Vol. 3207: L.T. Yang, M. Guo, G.R. Gao, N.K. Jha (Eds.), Embedded and Ubiquitous Computing. XX, 1116 pages. 2004.

Vol. 3206: P. Sojka, I. Kopecek, K. Pala (Eds.), Text, Speech and Dialogue. XIII, 667 pages. 2004. (Subseries LNAI).

Vol. 3205: N. Davies, E. Mynatt, I. Siio (Eds.), UbiComp 2004: Ubiquitous Computing. XVI, 452 pages. 2004.

Vol. 3203: J. Becker, M. Platzner, S. Vernalde (Eds.), Field Programmable Logic and Application. XXX, 1198 pages. 2004.

Vol. 3202: J.-F. Boulicaut, F. Esposito, F. Giannotti, D. Pedreschi (Eds.), Knowledge Discovery in Databases: PKDD 2004. XIX, 560 pages. 2004. (Subseries LNAI).

Vol. 3201: J.-F. Boulicaut, F. Esposito, F. Giannotti, D. Pedreschi (Eds.), Machine Learning: ECML 2004. XVIII, 580 pages. 2004. (Subseries LNAI).

Vol. 3199: H. Schepers (Ed.), Software and Compilers for Embedded Systems. X, 259 pages. 2004.

Vol. 3198: G.-J. de Vreede, L.A. Guerrero, G. Marín Raventós (Eds.), Groupware: Design, Implementation and Use. XI, 378 pages. 2004.

Vol. 3195: C.G. Puntonet, A. Prieto (Eds.), Independent Component Analysis and Blind Signal Separation. XXIII, 1266 pages. 2004.

Vol. 3194: R. Camacho, R. King, A. Srinivasan (Eds.), Inductive Logic Programming. XI, 361 pages. 2004. (Subseries LNAI).

Vol. 3193: P. Samarati, P. Ryan, D. Gollmann, R. Molva (Eds.), Computer Security – ESORICS 2004. X, 457 pages. 2004.

Vol. 3192: C. Bussler, D. Fensel (Eds.), Artificial Intelligence: Methodology, Systems, and Applications. XIII, 522 pages. 2004. (Subseries LNAI).

Vol. 3191: M. Klusch, S. Ossowski, V. Kashyap, R. Unland (Eds.), Cooperative Information Agents VIII. XI, 303 pages. 2004. (Subseries LNAI).

Vol. 3190: Y. Luo (Ed.), Cooperative Design, Visualization, and Engineering. IX, 248 pages. 2004.

Vol. 3189: P.-C. Yew, J. Xue (Eds.), Advances in Computer Systems Architecture. XVII, 598 pages. 2004.

Vol. 3188: F.S. de Boer, M.M. Bonsangue, S. Graf, W.-P. de Roever (Eds.), Formal Methods for Components and Objects. VIII, 373 pages. 2004.

Vol. 3187: G. Lindemann, J. Denzinger, I.J. Timm, R. Unland (Eds.), Multiagent System Technologies. XIII, 341 pages. 2004. (Subseries LNAI).

Vol. 3186: Z. Bellahsène, T. Milo, M. Rys, D. Suciu, R. Unland (Eds.), Database and XML Technologies. X, 235 pages. 2004.

Vol. 3185: M. Bernardo, F. Corradini (Eds.), Formal Methods for the Design of Real-Time Systems. VII, 295 pages. 2004.

Vol. 3184: S. Katsikas, J. Lopez, G. Pernul (Eds.), Trust and Privacy in Digital Business. XI, 299 pages. 2004.

Vol. 3183: R. Traunmüller (Ed.), Electronic Government. XIX, 583 pages. 2004.

Vol. 3182: K. Bauknecht, M. Bichler, B. Pröll (Eds.), E-Commerce and Web Technologies. XI, 370 pages. 2004.

Vol. 3181: Y. Kambayashi, M. Mohania, W. Wöß (Eds.), Data Warehousing and Knowledge Discovery. XIV, 412 pages. 2004.

Vol. 3180: F. Galindo, M. Takizawa, R. Traunmüller (Eds.), Database and Expert Systems Applications. XXI, 972 pages. 2004.

Vol. 3179: F.J. Perales, B.A. Draper (Eds.), Articulated Motion and Deformable Objects. XI, 270 pages. 2004.

Vol. 3178: W. Jonker, M. Petkovic (Eds.), Secure Data Management. VIII, 219 pages. 2004.

Vol. 3177: Z.R. Yang, H. Yin, R. Everson (Eds.), Intelligent Data Engineering and Automated Learning – IDEAL 2004. XVIII, 852 pages. 2004.

Vol. 3176: O. Bousquet, U. von Luxburg, G. Rätsch (Eds.), Advanced Lectures on Machine Learning. IX, 241 pages. 2004. (Subseries LNAI).

Vol. 3175: C.E. Rasmussen, H.H. Bülthoff, B. Schölkopf, M.A. Giese (Eds.), Pattern Recognition. XVIII, 581 pages. 2004.

Vol. 3174: F. Yin, J. Wang, C. Guo (Eds.), Advances in Neural Networks - ISNN 2004. XXXV, 1021 pages. 2004.

Vol. 3173: F. Yin, J. Wang, C. Guo (Eds.), Advances in Neural Networks – ISNN 2004. XXXV, 1041 pages. 2004.

Vol. 3172: M. Dorigo, M. Birattari, C. Blum, L. M. Gambardella, F. Mondada, T. Stützle (Eds.), Ant Colony, Optimization and Swarm Intelligence. XII, 434 pages. 2004.

Vol. 3171: A.L.C. Bazzan, S. Labidi (Eds.), Advances in Artificial Intelligence – SBIA 2004. XVII, 548 pages. 2004. (Subseries LNAI).

Vol. 3170: P. Gardner, N. Yoshida (Eds.), CONCUR 2004 - Concurrency Theory. XIII, 529 pages. 2004.

Vol. 3166: M. Rauterberg (Ed.), Entertainment Computing – ICEC 2004. XXIII, 617 pages. 2004.

Vol. 3163: S. Marinai, A. Dengel (Eds.), Document Analysis Systems VI. XI, 564 pages. 2004.

Vol. 3162: R. Downey, M. Fellows, F. Dehne (Eds.), Parameterized and Exact Computation. X, 293 pages. 2004.

Vol. 3160: S. Brewster, M. Dunlop (Eds.), Mobile Human-Computer Interaction – MobileHCI 2004. XVII, 541 pages. 2004.

Vol. 3159: U. Visser, Intelligent Information Integration for the Semantic Web. XIV, 150 pages. 2004. (Subseries LNAI).

Vol. 3158: I. Nikolaidis, M. Barbeau, E. Kranakis (Eds.), Ad-Hoc, Mobile, and Wireless Networks. IX, 344 pages. 2004.

Vol. 3157: C. Zhang, H. W. Guesgen, W.K. Yeap (Eds.), PRICAI 2004: Trends in Artificial Intelligence. XX, 1023 pages. 2004. (Subseries LNAI).

Vol. 3156: M. Joye, J.-J. Quisquater (Eds.), Cryptographic Hardware and Embedded Systems - CHES 2004. XIII, 455 pages. 2004.

Vol. 3155: P. Funk, P.A. González Calero (Eds.), Advances in Case-Based Reasoning. XIII, 822 pages. 2004. (Subseries LNAI).